David Yellin

Beverly A. DeVries

ESSENTIALS OF
Integrating the Language Arts

FIFTH EDITION

Holcomb Hathaway, Publishers
Scottsdale, Arizona

Library of Congress Control Number: 2014959903

Copyright © 2015 by Holcomb Hathaway, Publishers, Inc.

Holcomb Hathaway, Publishers, Inc.
8700 E. Via de Ventura Blvd., Suite 265
Scottsdale, Arizona 85258
480-991-7881
www.hh-pub.com

10 9 8 7 6 5 4 3 2 1

Print ISBN: 978-1-62159-030-9
Ebook ISBN: 978-1-62159-031-6

Printed in the United States of America.

Photo Credits:
Front cover, clockwise from upper left: Sergey Novikov/123RF; Anek Suwanna-phoom/123RF; Wavebreak Media Ltd/123RF; Syda Productions/123RF; Mikael Damkier/123RF. *Back cover, top to bottom:* Hongqi Zhang/123RF; Ilka Erika Szasz-Fabian/123RF; Cathy Yeulet/123RF; Franck Boston/123RF. *Page i,* Dmitriy Shironosov/ 123RF; *p. iii,* Graham Oliver/123RF; *p. ix,* Cathy Yeulet/123RF; *p. 1,* Wavebreak Media Ltd/123RF; *p. 20,* Panom Pensawang/ 123RF; *p. 25,* Wavebreak Media Ltd/123RF; *p. 38,* Wavebreak Media Ltd/123RF; *p. 59,* Wavebreak Media Ltd/123RF; *p. 69,* Dmitriy Shironosov/123RF; *p. 79,* Wavebreak Media Ltd/123RF; *p. 81,* Cathy Yeulet Media Ltd/ 123RF; *p. 87,* Ilka Erika Szasz-Fabian/123RF; *p. 92,* Dmitriy Shironosov/123RF; *p. 125,* Tyler Olson/123RF; *p. 161,* Wavebreak Media Ltd/123RF; *p. 169,* Wavebreak Media Ltd/ 123RF; *p. 179,* Cathy Yeulet/123RF; *p. 205,* Cathy Yeulet/123RF; *p. 213,* Dmitriy Shironosov/123RF; *p. 237,* pictrough/123RF; *p. 239,* viewstock/123RF; *p. 270,* tan4ikk/123RF; *p. 277,* Visions of America LLC/123RF; *p. 287,* Cathy Yeulet/123RF; *p. 306,* Panom Pensawang/ 123RF; *p. 315,* Hongqi Zhang/123RF; *p. 321,* Lisa Young/123RF; *p. 349,* Inspirestock International/123RF; *p. 353,* Tyler Olson/123RF; *p. 369,* Cathy Yeulet/123RF; *p. 373,* Inspirestock International/123RF; *p. 405,* Millan/ Dreamstime; *p. 407,* Wavebreak Media Ltd/ 123RF.

Contents

Planning and Delivering Effective Language Arts Instruction   59

Children's and Young Adult Literature
THE CORNERSTONE OF THE LANGUAGE ARTS PROGRAM   79

Listening and Speaking   237

Integrating the Visual and Performing Arts   277

Integrating the Language Arts in the Content Areas   315

APPENDICES

Teacher Resources   349

Children's and Young Adult Literature   353

Self-Diagnostic Instrument   369

Assessment Devices   373

Readers Theater Sample Script   405

Preface

Essentials of Integrating the Language Arts, Fifth Edition, presents a comprehensive view of teaching the language arts. It offers a balanced approach between direct instruction in the communication arts and integrating the language arts with other content areas such as mathematics, social studies, science, music, and art. It explores the important topics of community and parental involvement in education and offers thoughtful coverage of diversity in the schools. Practical teaching ideas are found throughout each chapter.

The fifth edition has been updated to reflect current teaching practices, field knowledge, and research. Significant features and changes in this edition include the following:

- A more streamlined approach to allow readers to move quickly from learning chapter concepts and related theory and research to understanding how they are applied in classroom practices, activities, and strategies.

- Discussion of standards, including the Common Core State Standards (CCSS), with the goal of showing readers how they can apply standards in the classroom to help meet their students' needs.

- New teaching activities that support the chapter topics and that align with the CCSS.

- Additional material to make the book more inclusive of the middle grades.

- To supplement the book's discussions of assessment, inclusion of an appendix offering over 25 classroom assessment tools.

- Discussion of current, quality children's and young adult literature, including informational texts, supported by an appendix offering lists of books by genre.

Essentials of Integrating the Language Arts offers these additional special features:

- "In the Classroom" vignettes, describing real teachers as they implement the book's processes and strategies in the classroom.

- "RRP" (Read Research Practice) boxes offering ideas for activities and projects to enhance and deepen reader understanding.

- In-chapter "Teaching Activities"—evidence-based strategies and activities that future teachers can use in their own classrooms.

- End-of-chapter "Field and Practicum Activities"—brief activities that provide practical application of the chapter concepts your students can use in field and practicum settings.

- Inspirational teaching-related quotations in the book's margins to stimulate class discussions.

- Updated discussions of technology and websites at the end of each chapter to get your students using online resources and creating slide presentations, videos, photo journals, and other multimodal materials as they prepare to integrate technology in their own classrooms.

Whether your students will teach all subjects (self-contained primary/elementary grades) or specialize in the language arts exclusively (departmentalized middle grades), this textbook will help them succeed. Take a moment to review the table of contents to familiarize yourself with the newly organized chapters and their subtopics. The table of contents also lists the helpful resources and tools available in the book's appendices.

We hope readers will use this textbook in an interactive manner, as we have designed it to be used. Encourage your students to discuss each chapter in class and to complete as many of the "RRP" suggestions as possible. Have them access websites and conduct field observations of children and teachers in order to learn from others in the field. Encourage students to keep a journal of reflections about their readings, their observation experiences in classrooms, and other field experiences. Have them share journal reflections with you and with their peers. Each person gets something different out of a textbook and a college course. Teaching is truly a collaborative undertaking—through sharing with others, we all grow in our understanding of how to teach.

ACKNOWLEDGMENTS

We would like to thank the following reviewers, who offered constructive suggestions for improving this book, for this and for earlier editions. The book is better as a result of their efforts.

For this edition: Kathleen Bukowski, Mercyhurst University; Lauren Edmondson, Drury University; Ingrid Frenna, Sierra Nevada College; Sharon Jackson, New Jersey City University; Kimberly Miller, Ohio Dominican University; Natalie Precise, Drury University; Donna Rhinesmith, Truman State University; and Debra Weingarth, Jacksonville State University.

For previous editions: Elizabeth Day, Gail J. Gerlach, Missy Hopper, Rachael Hungerford, Richard Ingram, Linda Kleeman, Sallie J. Launius, Fannye E. Love, Charles E. Matthews, Mark D. McCann, Rolland Menk, M. Priscilla Myers, Martha Olsen, Deborah Pellegrino, Margaret Policastro, Sherron Killingsworth Roberts, Bobbie Smothers-Jones, Pamela A. Solvie, Carol Taylor, Miriam Ward, Gary L. Willhite, and Penelope Wong.

In addition, we would like to offer individual acknowledgments:

David Yellin: I would like to thank my wife, Pamm Yellin, and daughters Lindsay and Aubree for all their support in this project. In addition I would like to thank my colleague and friend Kouider Mokhtari for stimulating professional discussions. Finally, I thank graduate assistants Abdullah Modhesh and Tamara Roman for help in completing this textbook.

Beverly DeVries: I wish to thank my husband for his support in this project and my students, who willingly become partners in action research.

Introduction to the Language Arts

After reading this chapter, you should be able to accomplish the following objectives:

1. Name the six components of language arts.
2. Explain what the acronym IRA represents and its role in guiding the teaching of the language arts.
3. Explain what the acronym NCTE represents and its role in guiding the teaching of the language arts.
4. Discuss the levels of the Learning Experiences Ladder.
5. Discuss characteristics of learning activities that engage students so they develop a love of learning.
6. Discuss the four ways to teach the language arts.
7. Discuss the initiatives that have changed education.

INTRODUCTION

Each semester, to start the first session of my class on teaching language arts, I (author Beverly DeVries) ask my students: "If you were interviewing with a principal for a fourth-grade teaching position, and he told you that his school is departmentalized and you would be teaching language arts, would you know what you had to teach?" Inevitably, I get answers such as, "grammar, spelling, literature, penmanship, reading, and writing." When I tell them there is much more they would need to teach, they ask, "Like what?" They are surprised to hear that they also would be expected to teach speaking, listening, viewing, and visual representing.

In kindergarten through grade 8, the term *language arts* is defined in terms of its six components—reading, writing, speaking, listening, viewing, and visual representing. In this text we share with you learning theories, research, and background information on each component and provide teaching activities related to the six components that are appropriate for primary grades (K–2), intermediate grades (3–5), and middle school (6–8).

If you examine the six language arts components closely, you may realize that three of the components are receptive—reading, listening, and viewing—while the other three are expressive—writing, speaking, and visual representing (see Figure 1.1). When people write, they are expressing their ideas, thoughts, and feelings; others read their stories, poems, letters, or other forms of writing. When people speak, others listen to them; when they visually represent, others view their work. When people read, listen, or view, however, they receive the messages other people have expressed in books, speeches, videos, or other works. In today's society, students read and write in formats beyond traditional print, they listen to and speak beyond simple class reports, and they view and visually represent beyond traditional pictures. We will share with you many different types of activities involving many different formats for each of the components of the language arts. We stress throughout the text that the components of language arts should be integrated in all subject areas. Thus, students read, write, listen, speak, view, and visually represent in literature, math, science, social studies, music, art, and health and physical education classes.

The two major professional organizations concerned with teaching the language arts, the International Reading

> A great teacher makes hard things easy.
>
> **RALPH WALDO EMERSON**

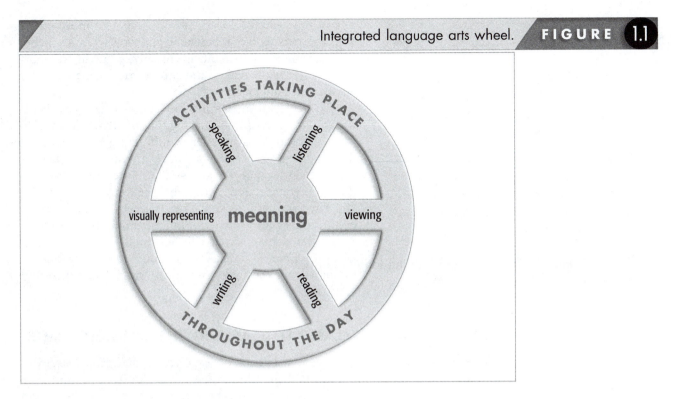

Association (IRA) and the National Council of Teachers of English (NCTE), together created the *Standards for the English Language Arts* (1996). Subsequently, these two organizations with other major educational organizations were active in writing the Common Core State Standards (CCSS) that are discussed later in this chapter.

DEVELOPING A PHILOSOPHY OF EDUCATION

When classroom teachers formulated the *Standards for the English Language Arts,* they were not only pooling their wisdom based on experience, but were also articulating their philosophies regarding child development, their experience with the content and materials of language arts, and their understanding of the teaching/learning process. Successful teachers are also guided by a personal teaching philosophy, a set of beliefs that informs their practices with students.

Throughout this text, you will gradually begin to shape your own philosophy of education, particularly as it relates to how you will teach students about the language arts. You will adopt a philosophy that allows you to make decisions each day—from how you will arrange the furniture in the classroom, to how you will evaluate your students' skills in reading or writing, to which methods and materials you will use to teach spelling and handwriting, to how you will maintain classroom control and discipline. In short, all of the choices regarding how, when, and what you teach will be ultimately dependent on your personal philosophy.

Acquiring such a philosophy is a slow and sometimes arduous process; it requires that you be open to the views of others but strong enough in your own convictions to resist being led by others. In the classic sociological study *The Lonely Crowd* (1961), David Riesman describes two types of individuals: The *other-* or *outer-directed* person conforms, follows, and looks for the approval of others before acting; the *inner-directed* person follows an inner set of beliefs and values that guide his or her decision making. Psychologist Jerome Bruner (1962) saw individual mental growth and development in terms of how people move from a state of outer-directedness to

read RESEARCH practice

Examine the following approaches to viewing the language arts critically. Compare them to your own experiences and observations in the classroom. Your ability to analyze this text, other research literature in the language arts, other learning theories, and your observations in the classroom is part of the process of becoming a reflective teacher with your own personal philosophy of education. As you reflect critically on what you see, hear, and read, you will become a more responsible decision maker in the classroom, which is the hallmark of a professional educator.

one of inner-directedness. As you become a more inner-directed person, your personal philosophy as a teacher will become more evident. Eventually, you will see yourself as a decision maker and others will look to you for advice and guidance.

To help you in this process, the next section of this chapter describes some learning theories that affect teachers and discusses a number of different ways of viewing the language arts. Each language arts approach has its own strengths and weaknesses. Analyze and reflect on them in conjunction with other learning theories that you have studied. Because every student is different and every student also possesses unique strengths and weaknesses, no one approach will be suitable for all students all of the time. For that reason, you will want to choose the best from the many options at your disposal to find your own way.

LEARNING THEORIES RELATED TO TEACHING THE LANGUAGE ARTS

Before examining the various approaches to teaching the language arts, consider four learning theories that greatly affect teaching in general, and thus teaching of the language arts. The research and theories of four psychologists and educators—Lev Vygotsky, Jerome Bruner, Jean Piaget, and Brian Cambourne—have contributed to knowledge about language and thought, which in turn has greatly affected the latest developments in language arts instruction.

Lev Vygotsky (1896–1934)

Lev Vygotsky (1986) observed young children in Russia as they used language in play and other social situations. Based on his observations, Vygotsky concluded that adults greatly influence children's cognitive growth. His observations led him to conclude that children's interactions with adults not only shape their language patterns but also their thought patterns. At first children can understand adult language but cannot reproduce it or generate complex ideas. Later, as speech is internalized, it is used to control thinking. In this sense Vygotsky believed that verbal interactions between children and adults help children "learn how to mean." Meaningful social interactions with adults spur cognitive as well as verbal development in the child. This theory, called the *social interaction theory of development*, has greatly influenced the classroom instruction.

Another key concept of Vygotsky's theory is the notion of the *zone of proximal development*. This refers to the gap between what the child knows and can express on her or his own and what the adult must provide in terms of information and language structures. Children need adults to help them grow linguistically and cognitively. In a sense, the child is always one step behind the adult, straining to keep up. With the proper adult role models, the child's language and thought continue to develop; without them, the child's thought processes are severely limited (Wertsch & Sohmer, 1995).

Jerome Bruner (b. 1915)

Jerome Bruner (1961b, 1962, 1978) was influenced by Vygotsky. According to Bruner, one role of language is to activate thought and concept development. Concept development involves the creation of *schemata*, or models in the brain, which store information necessary for higher-level thinking. The older the child, the greater the role language plays in the creation of these schemata. In one experiment, children were asked to sort pictures into categories. The experimenter noted that children ages 2 to 6 categorize only on the basis of color, shape, or size. Around age 7, children shift from a reliance on perceptual appearances to a reliance on symbolic representation. Consequently, older children can explain their grouping strategy by saying, "They're all tools." The term *tools* permits a form of classification higher than color, shape, or size, all of which are grounded on physical perception.

Bruner also believed in the importance of social interaction for a child's linguistic and cognitive growth. Building on Vygotsky's earlier work, Bruner argued that the child uses the language of adults to move from one stage of language development to another; thus, the child's language builds upon the adult's. Bruner called this process *scaffolding* (1978, 1987). The linguistic scaffold, or structure provided by the adult, allows the child to construct language and internalize the rules of language through experience.

Bruner's theories on thought development and schema formation can be seen in the classroom when teachers use schematic diagrams, semantic maps, and web diagrams. Though these terms are used slightly differently, the processes they represent include similar steps: A verbal brainstorming session leads to a visual representation, which eventually creates a mental picture that the student uses to store information suitable for later problem solving. In the K–8 classroom, students use diagramming, mapping, and webbing to help them comprehend text structures they have read, lectures they will hear, and written work they wish to produce (Pearson & Johnson, 1985; Bruner, 1997).

While researching children, Bruner (1966) also found that they learn best from personal experiences and learn least from verbal explanations. See Figure 1.2 for

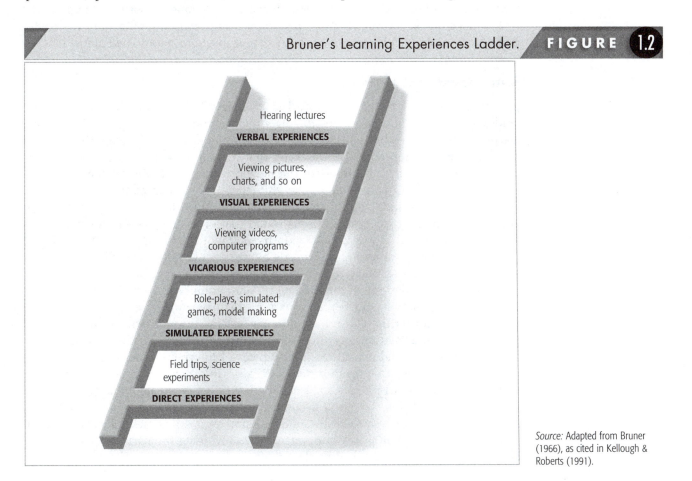

Bruner's Learning Experiences Ladder. **FIGURE 1.2**

Source: Adapted from Bruner (1966), as cited in Kellough & Roberts (1991).

Bruner's Learning Experiences Ladder. Just as the first rung of a ladder is the easiest to climb, the easiest way for students to learn is through direct experiences. Because this is the most effective way a student learns, a teacher should provide as many direct experiences as possible. Obviously, not all teaching takes place through direct experiences; therefore, you should provide many simulated experiences that demand students use more than one sense. These experiences may include playing simulated games, constructing models, or role-playing. If direct or simulated experiences are not available, the next experience, though not as effective because it does not engage as many senses, is the vicarious experience. Many of these experiences, such as computer apps, programs, and videos, are readily available today. Visual experiences are better than a verbal explanation, which is the least effective way to learn. Many textbooks provide pictures, charts, and graphs to explain a concept.

An example of a teacher putting Bruner's theory into practice is Mr. Lopez, a second grade teacher at a large urban school. When preparing to study popular children's author Tomie dePaola with his second graders, Mr. Lopez knew from Bruner's Learning Experiences Ladder that the least effective way for his students to learn about dePaola's life and books would be to lecture them about the author. Therefore, Mr. Lopez decided to read and discuss dePaola's books with his students and view a video of the author working in his studio that explains how he gets his ideas. Mr. Lopez also planned for his students to draw scenes from their favorite dePaola book and act out some of their favorite stories. The last learning experience he planned for his students was for Tomie dePaola to visit the classroom, read some of his books out loud, and draw a picture while the students watched. After the visit, Mr. Lopez encouraged his students to write thank-you notes to dePaola. Mr. Lopez not only put Bruner's theory into practice but also integrated the six components of the language arts with technology. Although not every teacher will be fortunate enough to have well-known authors visit the classroom, they can still arrange a "visit" with an author by browsing his or her website with their class. Many sites now offer webcasts of the authors, and Tomie dePaola and his books are featured in many YouTube videos.

Jean Piaget (1896–1980)

Jean Piaget (1952, 1959, 1964, 1965, 1967) observed children in Geneva, Switzerland, over a period of many years, during which time he formulated his theories on learning and development. Piaget took a developmental view of cognitive growth and language development. He observed that mental growth occurred in tandem with physical growth. It begins with the newborn infant listening to the sounds of the environment and continues as the child imitates sounds of those around her and creates new sounds while exploring language. With increased age also comes vocabulary growth. Joan Tough (1984) found that on average children use about 3 words at 12 months, 20 words at 18 months, 300 words at 24 months, 900 to 1,000 words at 36 months, at least 2,000 words by age 5, and 4,000 words by age 7.

The three terms associated with Piaget's view of language and cognitive development are assimilation, accommodation, and equilibrium. *Assimilation* occurs when new information and perceptions are organized into already existing schemata. Assimilation is therefore a continuous process through which an individual integrates new information into older or established patterns of thought. But what happens when the child encounters a new piece of information or engages in a new experience unrelated to previous ones? Because this new information cannot be structured into an existing pattern, a new pattern must be created. Piaget called this process *accommodation,* which is a continuous process through which new informational patterns are created in the mind to store and utilize new objects, facts, or experiences. *Equilibrium* is a continuous process involving the harmonious interplay between assimilation and accommodation.

Ralph learns about plants by balancing assimilation and accommodation

Ralph, a fifth grader, is studying about plants and flowers. He comes across a new word, *chrysanthemum,* which he cannot pronounce. His teacher helps him with the pronunciation; together they look up the word in the dictionary. Ralph discovers that a chrysanthemum is a type of brightly colored flower. He is already familiar with roses, so he can easily assimilate this new piece of information into his existing concept of flowers. In a later science lesson about the root system of plants, Ralph is confused about how water and minerals travel through a plant. His teacher takes time to briefly explain the concept of plant vessels. Ralph must develop a new schema in his cognitive system to accommodate this information, which he will later use in assimilating higher-level information about the physical properties of matter.

Thus, Ralph maintains a healthy balance between assimilation and accommodation. However, if Ralph had an imbalance in favor of assimilation, he would know only a few broad categories that would be so crammed with facts they would be virtually useless. If he had an imbalance in favor of accommodation, he would know too many narrow categories and never establish a clear relationship among them, which would also inhibit problem solving. The key, in Piaget's terms, is to maintain equilibrium between assimilation and accommodation.

Piaget is most remembered by educators for his work in the area of children's cognitive development; he demonstrated that through assimilation and accommodation, children's mental capacities adapt and grow. In this sense, Piaget is a cognitive constructivist similar to Vygotsky and Bruner. Adaptation to environmental changes leads children through a series of distinct mental stages that correspond to the children's language development (Huitt & Hummel, 2003). Figure 1.3 summarizes Piaget's stages of mental growth.

Piaget's stages of cognitive development. **FIGURE 1.3**

STAGE	CHARACTERISTICS
Sensorimotor (birth to 18 months)	Children act upon real objects to learn about the world. By learning through the five senses, concepts of cause and effect and of object permanence develop.
Preoperational (18 months to 7 years plus)	Children use words as symbols to represent objects and ideas. Learning through play becomes more important; real and imaginary objects are incorporated into activities. As the concept of "word" develops, the power of egocentrism declines. Egocentrism must again be overcome when learning to read and write in school.
Concrete operations (7 to 11 years plus)	Children begin to use logical reasoning and are able to classify and perform simple operations. Concrete, manipulable objects are important for learning abstract concepts. Mental processes, in addition to trial and error, are utilized in problem solving. Learning becomes internalized.
Formal operations (12 years plus)	Children's verbal and logical reasoning is not restricted to physical objects or concrete situations. As language abilities develop, abstract reasoning becomes easier. Wide reading, extensive writing, and small-group oral language activities expand children's cognitive growth.

Sources: Adapted from J. Piaget (1965), *The Language and Thought of the Child;* E. Sarafino & J. Armstrong (1986), *Child and Adolescent Development;* J. Tough (1984), "How Young Children Develop and Use Language"; L. Calkins (1983), *Lessons from a Child.*

Piaget's theory of mental development and its relationship to language can be useful to you if viewed judiciously. Piaget never suggested that the age levels are fixed and absolute. For example, the concrete operations stage of learning persists long into adulthood as the primary way of learning new things. Imagine trying to understand the workings of an automobile engine without having an actual engine to study and greasy parts to handle!

Brian Cambourne

Another theory that emphasizes the importance of students' direct involvement for effective learning is Brian Cambourne's learning theory. Cambourne (1988) posits that eight conditions are necessary for learning to take place: immersion, demonstration, expectation, response, employment, responsibility, approximation, and engagement. Figure 1.4 shows how the eight conditions are interrelated, with student engagement at the center of the learning process.

Immersion, demonstration, expectation, and *response* are led by the teacher. Your goal is to set up a classroom that *immerses* students in worthwhile, authentic learning tasks. This is accomplished by providing (1) numerous opportunities to read about topics that interest the individual student; (2) varied opportunities to learn how to effectively articulate information, stories, poems, and so on, either verbally or in written communication; and (3) many opportunities for students to express themselves through the visual or performing arts. The teacher's job is to *demonstrate* new concepts to the students and model how to use that information in real-life settings. Next, you must set high but realistic standards for all students and *expect* all students to be successful in learning the concept or task. Finally, you need to *respond* to the students with encouraging feedback that praises their approximations and attempts and does not criticize them. Whenever possible, provide this feedback verbally while students are engaged in the task.

FIGURE 1.4 Cambourne's conditions necessary for learning.

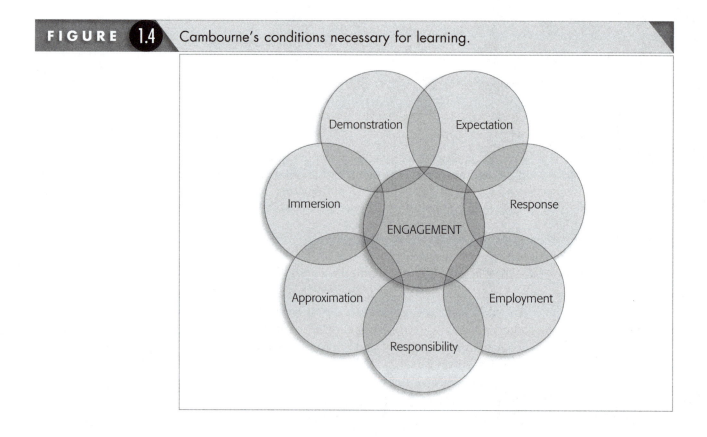

Students bring *employment, responsibility*, and *approximation* to the learning process. Students need to *employ* themselves actively when given opportunities to immerse themselves in reading, writing, and other learning activities; they should not be mere spectators. Students also

must assume *responsibility* for their learning; therefore, they need to be willing to spend more time on tasks that are difficult for them. They also need to assume responsibility for the final results of their learning. Throughout the learning process, there will be times when students may only be able to *approximate* their best work; the learning process does not always result in perfect understanding the first or second time students encounter a new idea or task. However, during this process students should be encouraged to take risks and experiment with new ideas because that is when growth takes place.

After eight years of studies conducted in grades 1 through 5, Cambourne (2001) found that no matter how great the learning activity, if students are not *engaged* deeply in the activity, little learning occurs. He concluded that the following eight characteristics make learning come alive for students:

1. The activity is explicitly linked to other parts of learning. In other words, the activity is not based on an isolated skill.
2. The teacher explains to students the importance of participating in the activity and helps them discover how the material is personally relevant to them.
3. The activity encourages interaction and collaboration.
4. The activity encourages the integration of more than one mode of language (e.g., speaking, reading, writing, listening, viewing, and visually representing).
5. The activity encourages students to use more than one subsystem of language (e.g., semantics [meaning], syntax [sentence grammar], and graphophonic [letter–sound relationship]).
6. The activity encourages students to integrate meaning across different semiotic systems (e.g., oral language, art, music, dance, drama, and pantomime).
7. The activity involves higher-level thinking that allows more than one acceptable response.
8. The activities are developmentally appropriate and do not require a lot of time or money to create.

APPROACHES TO TEACHING THE LANGUAGE ARTS

There are many ways of looking at the entire curriculum area of the language arts. In this section, we present four different approaches to teaching the language arts for you to reflect on and discuss in your class: the separate skills approach, the whole language approach, the integrated approach, and the comprehensive approach. By clarifying some of the similarities and differences among these approaches, we hope to avoid the confusion that arises from using similar terms interchangeably or without clear definitions. As we introduce each of these approaches, we will explain the ideology on which each approach is based.

Separate Skills Approach

The separate skills approach, based on the functional literacy ideology, is one of the approaches observed in the elementary grades due to the way most schools are presently organized. *Functional literacy* encourages students to learn to read and write so they can function in society rather than encouraging them to read critically or to relate reading passages to their lives. In the *separate skills approach,* each language arts subskill area (reading, spelling, handwriting, grammar) is viewed as a unique entity, separate from other subject areas. Often these separate skills are taught during different times of the day. Within these time periods, each subject is further broken down into smaller subskills, such as a lesson on the long vowel sound of /a/ in reading, adding "ing" to words in spelling, and contrasting nouns and pronouns in grammar. Such an approach is based on behaviorist principles of part-to-whole learning (Goodman, 1986). Figure 1.5 shows the separate skills approach in diagram fashion.

In this diagram each language arts subject area and the subskills within each area are isolated from one another. This is a major characteristic of the separate skills approach. Learning is compartmentalized; course content in one area is taught separately from all other areas. Because a pre-determined amount of subject matter must be covered within a specific time block, the class tends to be teacher-dominated, relying on whole-group lecture. Direct, intensive, systematic instruction controlled by the teacher is another characteristic of this approach (Allington, 2002a). As is evident from this discussion, this approach emphasizes covering content by learning separate skills.

Whole Language Approach

The whole language approach stands in contrast to the separate skills approach and is based on the progressive literacy ideology. *Progressive literacy* focuses on a student-centered curriculum that is based on students' interests, needs, and personal backgrounds. This ideology is based on constructivism (the theory based on the premise that students construct knowledge based on what they already know) and on democratic ideals that embrace free interchange of ideas between teachers and students.

Advocates of the *whole language approach,* such as Ken Goodman and Yetta Goodman (1992, 1996), Carol Edelsky (Edelsky, Altwerger, & Flores, 1991), and Constance Weaver (2002), contend, first, that it is a philosophy of language education that looks at the whole student learning language within the natural environment of the home, community, and school. Second, it is a student-centered philosophy that favors giving students choices as to what they will read and write. Third, language arts subjects, such as reading and writing, are not taught separately, but instead are inextricably linked. Finally, whole language advocates argue that

FIGURE 1.5 Separate skills approach charts.

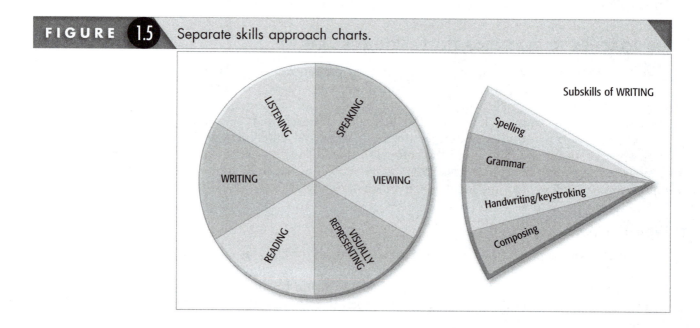

language arts skills are best learned through indirect means by authentic reading, writing, listening, speaking, viewing, and visually representing activities, based on students' interests (Goodman, 1996; Veatch, 1992; Watson, 1989).

Teachers who embrace the whole language approach generally encourage students to choose entire books to read, to write complete stories, and to discuss their reading and writing with the teacher and their peers. Figure 1.6 represents the whole language approach. Note that a slice from the whole language "pie" includes all aspects of the language arts.

In the whole language classroom, students use language to learn about language. This means that the teacher begins at whatever point in learning the student feels comfortable. For most young students, this means starting with listening and speaking activities. Listening to the teacher read books aloud or at the listening center, engaging in discussions about picture books, chatting with one another over their drawings at the art center, and conducting puppet shows give young students confidence in using language they will apply later as they learn to read and write.

Whole language classrooms look different from separate skills classrooms in that much in-class time is devoted to free reading and writing. Whole language teachers believe that only by reading and writing can students become readers and writers. Children's literature books rather than basal readers are at the heart of these classrooms. The students are treated as authors themselves and encouraged to talk about books they have read and share stories they have written.

Integrated Approach

The *integrated curriculum* or *integrated approach* is also based on the progressive literacy ideology. The focus of an integrated approach is on content; it attempts to combine or integrate various subject areas within a single class period. As such, it views all subject matter disciplines (listening, speaking, reading, writing, viewing, and visually representing as well as math, literature, science, social studies, art, music, physical education, etc.) as related in terms of the way students approach learning.

The term *integration* appeared in the 1980s when literacy scholars began linking reading and writing instruction (Tierney & Pearson, 1983). This in turn led to the linking of oral language with reading and writing (Au, Mason, & Scheu,

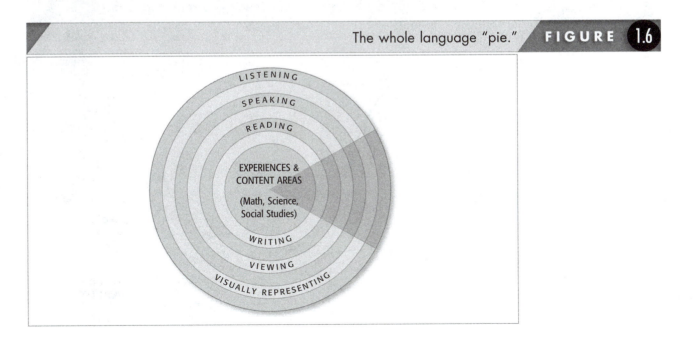

The whole language "pie."   **FIGURE** **1.6**

LISTENING

SPEAKING

READING

EXPERIENCES &
CONTENT AREAS

(Math, Science,
Social Studies)

WRITING

VIEWING

VISUALLY REPRESENTING

1995). This integration of the communication arts reflects the *social constructivist* perspective toward language. This view holds that learners use language as a primary means to construct their knowledge of the world. Learning to read and write involves higher mental processes than mere skill memorization and cuts across all subject content areas. Teachers integrate subject matter content across the various disciplines through the notion of *reading and writing across the curriculum.* This is the use of reading, writing, speaking, listening, viewing, and visual representing activities in subject discipline areas (such as history, math, earth science, art, music, and physical education) to help the student learn the content of that subject. Good teachers realize that the components of language arts are used in every aspect of learning. For example, they expand students' reading beyond the textbook in science by encouraging them to read a biography of Thomas Edison and then write a poem about him using information they learned from the book. Or, they have students in a middle-grade American history class read a book about Meriwether Lewis and then write a diary entry from his point of view. Teachers may also incorporate reading and writing across the curriculum by having students write in their learning logs after a math or science lesson. Figure 1.7 depicts the integrated approach and demonstrates how the six components of the language arts are woven into the study of all subject areas during the study of one theme.

Comprehensive Approach

The *comprehensive approach,* also based on the progressive literacy ideology, is broad and flexible to accommodate the needs of individual learners who benefit from both holistic teaching and the teaching of skills (Callahan & King, 2011; Kaufman, Moss, & Osborn, 2003). Teachers who use the comprehensive approach stress holistic teaching of the language arts and teach skills explicitly when students need them. For example, these teachers use reading and writing workshops, which allow students to read and write authentic texts of their choice. Within each workshop, teachers demonstrate relevant skills to the whole class during the daily minilessons and teach needed skills to individual students during confer-

FIGURE 1.7 In the integrated approach, the six components of the language arts are woven into the study of all subject areas.

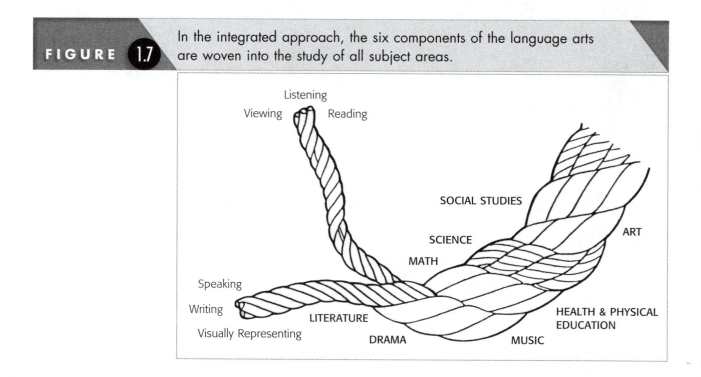

ences. Within each workshop, students also share favorite books as well as their compositions, poems, essays, and other writings with classmates. Figure 1.8 gives an overview of classroom strategies, with a description of their purpose and activities, used by teachers who embrace the comprehensive approach. Figure 1.9 is a graphic depiction of the comprehensive approach.

Classroom strategies used in the comprehensive approach. **FIGURE 1.8**

READING

BUDDY READING
- Older students share love of books with younger students.

INDEPENDENT READING
- All students in school read book of their choice for 15 to 30 minutes.

EBOOKS
- Students follow along as computer reads books.
- Students hear fluent reading.
- Students are introduced to new vocabulary words.

GUIDED READING
- Teachers work with homogeneous groups to teach reading skills.
- Teachers teach phonics, word analysis, vocabulary, etc.
- Students read under teacher's supervision.
- Students read graded books on their instructional level.

LANGUAGE EXPERIENCE APPROACH (LEA)
- Students express themselves while teacher acts as scribe.
- Students recognize words in print they use in their speech.

LITERACY CLUB
- Students who share interest in same book/author read and discuss books.

READING WORKSHOP
- Students choose genre and topics.
- Students share favorite books with peers.

Minilessons
- Teachers share with class information about authors and genres.
- Teachers instruct class on reading skills.

Conferences
- Peers read to each other.
- Teachers give explicit instruction on skills to individuals.

Share time
- Students share favorite sections or passages.
- Students share new vocabulary words.

SHARED READING
- Teachers share good literature that is at higher reading level.
- Students hear advanced vocabulary.
- Teachers and students discuss elements of stories.
- Teachers and students discuss information given in passage.

THINK-ALOUDS
- Teachers model reading strategies.
- Teachers teach metacognition skills.

(continued)

WORD WALLS
- Teachers display words in categories to help students automatically recognize words.
- Students learn patterns within words.
- Students increase their vocabulary.

WRITING

COLLABORATIVE PROJECTS
- Students do authentic research and writing with other students in the classroom, the United States, and the world.

E-PALS
- Students do authentic writing to form new friends around the world.

ONLINE RESEARCH PROJECT
- Students share research projects with other students around the world.

GUIDED WRITING
- Teachers work with homogeneous groups to teach writing skills.
- Teachers teach phonics, word analysis, vocabulary, etc.
- Students practice skills under teacher's supervision.

INTERACTIVE WRITING
- Teachers do majority of writing, and students "share the pen" when they know letters/ words.
- Teachers explicitly teach phonics, word patterns, and other spelling skills.

JOURNAL WRITING
- Students express themselves personally.
- Students write for authentic purposes.

WRITING WORKSHOP
- Students choose genre and topics.
- Students share writing with peers.

Minilessons
- Teachers give explicit instruction on writing skills to class.
- Teachers share types of writing with class.

Conferences
- Peers help with revising and editing.
- Teachers give explicit instruction on writing skills to individuals.

Share Time
- Students share finished product with class.

VISUALLY REPRESENTING AND VIEWING

PUPPET SHOW
- Students work in small groups.
- Students improve expression and fluency.
- Students perform for audience.

READERS THEATER
- Students work in small groups.
- Students improve expression and fluency.
- Students perform for audience.

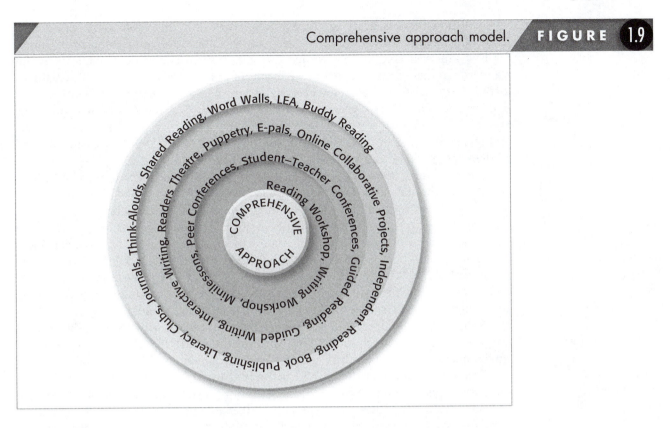

Comprehensive approach model.   **FIGURE** **1.9**

Obviously, the approaches to teaching the language arts have changed over time. If you were to visit classrooms throughout the United States, you would probably encounter every conceivable approach. Some teachers are slow to embrace change and may still use the same method they learned in college. Other teachers embrace new trends quickly, making frequent changes without really understanding the theories behind new approaches. However, all teachers benefit from studying theories and becoming reflective and flexible in their methods. Remember that you are teaching students, not a particular method. One approach to teaching language arts may work with some students; another group may need a different approach. A good teacher always meets the needs of individual students and understands why he or she uses a particular approach.

TEACHERS AND SCHOOLS UNDERGO CHANGE

Schools are always experiencing change. Changes affecting the language arts are the result of ongoing educational research, the growing population of students whose native language is not English, and the increasing diversity in classrooms, which requires inclusive and differentiated teaching practices. Additionally, changing standards have also affected teaching the language arts. The prudent teacher becomes knowledgeable about these changes and adapts her methods to reflect them.

Standards

No matter which approach to teaching language arts teachers embrace, they are challenged to meet the demands of national and/or state standards in an inclusive classroom. *Standards,* also called *benchmarks* or *competencies,* are skills and concepts that students must master by the end of each grade level in each subject area. State standards are written by and issued from each state's Department of Education, and you will find there is great variance among them. For this reason, the Council of Chief State School Officers (CCSSO) and the National Governors Association Center for Best Practices (NGACBP) studied the state standards and developed one set of standards so that when students move from one state to another, they will remain on a similar trajectory as their new classmates and be able to adapt to the curriculum with relative ease. The CCSSO and NGACBP developed the Common Core State Standards for English language arts and literacy in history/social studies, science, and technical subjects. The main purpose of these K–12 CCSS is to ensure that all students are prepared for college or career training by the end of high school.

The IRA and many other professional groups provided feedback to the CCSSO and NGACBP as the standards were being developed (Long, 2010). The CCSS have had an impact on all levels of language arts teaching, especially as teachers have implemented them. If you compare your state standards regarding the language arts to the CCSS, you will likely notice some variations. Some state standards, for example, have specific directions for certain subgroups such as English learners, while the CCSS do not address any specific subgroup. When analyzing and comparing the CCSS with state standards developed prior to the CCSS, you may find that the CCSS emphasize informational reading and writing and higher-level thinking more than some state standards.

As with any change, both veteran and new teachers will need guidance putting the standards into practice. You can find the entire list of the CCSS at www. corestandards.org/assets/CCSSI_ELA%20Standards.pdf.

If you are looking at the CCSS for the first time, notice the beginning of each category (e.g., Reading, Writing, Speak/Listening, Language, Foundational, and so on) includes a page titled "College and Career Readiness Anchor." These anchor standards are the overarching standards for all grades. The standards following the anchor standards define the standards for that subject area by grade levels and are numbered so that they align with the anchor standards. You will also notice that there are two sets of reading standards: one for literature and one for informational texts. Those who wrote the standards understand that reading literature requires skills different from those needed for reading informational text.

Because school principals require teachers to align their lesson objectives with standards, you should become familiar with the formal way to document what standard(s) your lesson is supporting. Imagine that your state has adopted the CCSS, and you are aligning your reading lesson with the first reading anchor standard. Here are a few guidelines about CCSS citations:

- To cite the standard formally, you would write it like this: CCSS.ELA-Literacy. CCRA.R.1. You read this as *Common Core State Standard, English Language Arts, Literacy, College and Career Readiness Anchor, reading, first standard.*
- If you are working with the first reading literature standard for kindergarten, you would write it like this: CCSS.ELA-Literacy.RL.K.1. This reads: *Common Core State Standards, English Language Arts, Literacy, Reading Literature, kindergarten, first standard.*
- If you want to align your sixth-grade objective to the third speaking/listening standard, you would write it like this: CCSS.ELA-Literacy.SL.6.3.
- For less formal citations, you may choose to use a shortened version such as CCRA.W.# (writing) or CCSS W.#.# (writing) that identify whether it is an anchor or grade level standard, the strand, the grade level where appropriate, and the standard number. For readability in this text, we will use the shortened format.

Become familiar with your state standards or the CCSS if your state has adopted them so you know what you will be required to teach. Following is a classroom vignette that shows how one teacher used the CCSS to guide his teaching.

Mr. Wallace uses the CCSS to guide his teaching

Mr. Wallace, a fifth-grade teacher in Michigan, realizes that he needs to engage his students in higher-level thinking activities reflected in the CCSS. One of the fifth-grade Reading Literature standards (CCSS RL.5.9) states: "Compare and contrast stories in the same genre (e.g., mysteries and adventure stories) or their approaches to similar themes and topics" (NGACBP & CCSSO, 2010, p. 12). Mr. Wallace understands that this standard requires his students to be able to identify different themes in stories and then to compare and contrast the different themes, giving evidence for their statements. He constructs a graphic organizer to assist his students in comparing and contrasting two of their favorite novels by Gary Paulsen. Figure 1.10 is the assignment and graphic organizer that he gives to his students after they have read and discussed the two novels as a class. Mr. Wallace first gives time for the students to complete the assignment individually, then they discuss the assignment and graphic organizer as students add or delete any necessary information. Mr. Wallace monitors the students as they work individually. They eagerly search online for information concerning the natural settings of the two novels. At the end of the project, Mr. Wallace realizes that this type of comparison assignment engages the students more than when they merely discuss the literal setting, characters, and plot of a single novel.

Assignment and graphic organizer for comparing and contrasting two texts. **FIGURE 1.10**

We have read and discussed in class *Hatchet* (1999) and *Haymeadow* (1994), two adventure stories by Gary Paulsen. Now compare and contrast the two novels by examining (a) the characters and their personalities, (b) the settings of each novel by searching online to compare the fictional setting of each novel to the actual terrain of each setting, (c) the plots, and (d) the themes. Provide examples of specific ways Paulsen creates suspense, giving direct quotes and references. As a way of brainstorming, first complete the graphic organizer. Be sure to use explicit quotes (with page numbers) to support your stance in each of the four areas.

Hatchet	Haymeadow

SIMILARITIES

Both adventure novels about 14-year-old boys left alone to survive in nature.

DIFFERENCES

Theme

Learns about self as he studies the harmony in nature	His goal is to earn acceptance from his father

Characters

Brian:	John:
"Panic came then. He had been afraid, had been stopped with the terror of what was happening, but now panic came and he began to scream into the microphone, scream over and over. 'Help! Somebody help me! I'm in this plane and don't know . . . don't know . . . don't know . . .' And he started crying with the screams, crying and slamming his hands against the wheel of the plane…his own screams mocking him, coming back into his ears." (p. 18)	"I was fourteen yesterday and nothing changed." (p. 1).
	". . . sometimes the thought came then: The old man (John's father] would have spent more time with his son." (p. 14)
	"He was going to be alone with the sheep for the rest of June, July, and August, until the first week in September. I'll go crazy he thought. Nuts. I don't even know what to do, how to do anything." (p. 24)
At the end of the novel: "It was a strange feeling, holding the rifle. It somehow removed him from everything around him. Without the rifle he had to fit in, to be part of it [nature] all, to understand it and use—the woods, all of it . . . The rifle changed him, the minute he picked it up, and he wasn't sure he liked the change very much . . . ." (p. 190)	"John didn't want his father to leave. There was some new thing between them, from the talk all night, and he didn't want him to leave and he finally said it, 'I don't want you to leave.'" (p. 194)
	"He [John] thought: Ain't it funny what makes a person glad? Just to see that little figure ([his dad] riding back with the packhorse in back of it and you could feel all glad." (p. 195)

(continued)

FIGURE 1.10 Continued.

Roadblocks

As Brian attempts to stay safe from wild animals, he is able to make observations about elements of nature. He observes that animals are only vicious when they feel they are being attacked, and that there is a cycle in nature.

As John attempts to survive the attacks from coyotes, skunks, rattlesnakes, and bears, his main focus is keeping the sheep safe instead of his personal survival.

Settings

Canadian Wilderness

"It is a vast, remote and largely empty land" (www.lawlibrary.unm.edu) sparsely populated. Home to grizzly bears, caribou, and wolverines (www.pc.gc.ca).

Paulsen mentioned moose, but these sources did not mention moose.

"…at the endless green northern wilderness below" (p. 1)

"…the horizon, spread with lakes, swamps, and wandering streams and rivers." (p. 2)

"…ocean of trees and lakes." (p. 5)

Wyoming

Rugged terrain, valleys, large, flat plains. Treeless. Several thousands of ranches of sheep and cattle. 50% of land is used for grazing. Sparsely populated. Because of lack of rain, when it does rain, it CAN result in flashfloods (www.sheppardsoftware.com).

"It was early summer and summers in Wyoming were hot." (p. 1)

The covered wagon that John had to live in for 3 months: "They had to restretch and retie the canvas top to the wagon and clean the stove—a small wood-burning stove in the corner of the trailer . . . It [wagon] was tiny—six feet wide, twelve feet long, with a bunk and wooden boxes nailed sideways to the wooden side to make shelves . . ." (p. 71)

The haymeadow where John spent the 3 months: "It was more than a meadow. More than just hay. It was a wide, shallow valley between two rows of peaks. The haymeadow itself was four sections, but the whole valley was close to four miles across and nearly eight miles long and so beautiful, John thought, that it almost took his breath away." (p. 71)

Sequence of Plot

Brian in plane to visit father

Pilot has heart attack

Plane crashes; Brian survives

Builds shelter

Eats berries and turtle eggs

Porcupine attacks

Rescue plane flies over but he did not have fire signal ready

Attempts to kill self with hatchet

Moose attacks

Tornado comes

Finds survival bag in plane

Uses emergency transmitter to get rescued

Tink is ill so John needs to herd sheep for summer

Skunks, rattlesnake come

His dog is wounded

Stampede comes

Flash flood comes

Pack of coyotes attack, he is injured, and only a few sheep are lost

Discovers labels from food cans were washed away in flood

Attack by bear

After 47 days father and Tink come

John has first real conversation with Father and decides to stay with Tink

CONCLUDING THOUGHTS

Both books are filled with suspense as the two characters need to use their minds and few available items to survive. Both learned a lesson about themselves: Brian learns to live his life in tune with the harmony in nature; John had to earn his father's respect by proving he can do man's work and that he can endure major upsets by himself.

English Learners

According to the National Center for Education Statistics (NCES), "the percentage of public school students in the United States who were English learners was higher in school year 2011–12 (9.1 percent, or an estimated 4.4 million students) than in 2002–03 (8.7 percent, or an estimated 4.1 million students)" (NCES, 2014). Thus, you must be prepared to meet these students' needs.

The World Class Instructional Design and Assessment (WIDA) consortium provides helpful information for teachers needing to identify the levels of language development of English learners. The six levels of development in the areas of speaking, listening, reading, and writing are (1) entering, (2) beginning, (3) developing, (4) expanding, (5) bridging, and (6) reaching. WIDA provides a table of descriptors for what English learners at each level can do. WIDA calls it the "Can Do" list. For example, Kim, a first grader at the beginning level in reading, can be expected to sort words into word families, while Jose, also a first grader, at the bridging level in reading would be able to identify main ideas when reading a passage (see Figure 1.11). You can access the table at WIDA's download library at www.wida.us/downloadLibrary.aspx.

WIDA Can Do descriptors: Grade level cluster 1–2.   **FIGURE 1.11**

For the given level of English language proficiency and with visual, graphic, or interactive support through Level 4, English language learners can process or produce the language needed to:

	Level 1 Entering	Level 2 Beginning	Level 3 Developing	Level 4 Expanding	Level 5 Bridging	
READING	■ Identify symbols, icons, and environmental print ■ Connect print to visuals ■ Match real-life familiar objects to labels ■ Follow directions using diagrams or pictures	■ Search for pictures associated with word patterns ■ Identify and interpret pretaught labeled diagrams ■ Match voice to print by pointing to icons, letters, or illustrated words ■ Sort words into word families	■ Make text-to-self connections with prompting ■ Select titles to match a series of pictures ■ Sort illustrated content words into categories ■ Match phrases and sentences to pictures	■ Put words in order to form sentences ■ Identify basic elements of fictional stories (e.g., title, setting, characters) ■ Follow sentence-level directions ■ Distinguish between general and specific language (e.g., flower v. rose) in context	■ Begin using features of non-fiction text to aid comprehension ■ Use learning strategies (e.g., context clues) ■ Identify main ideas ■ Match figurative language to illustrations (e.g., "as big as a house")	LEVEL 6 – REACHING
WRITING	■ Copy written language ■ Use first language (L1, when L1 is a medium of instruction) to help form words in English ■ Communicate through drawings ■ Label familiar objects or pictures	■ Provide information using graphic organizers ■ Generate lists of words/phrases from banks or walls ■ Complete modeled sentence starters (e.g., "I like ____.") ■ Describe people, places, or objects from illustrated examples and models	■ Engage in prewriting strategies (e.g., use of graphic organizers) ■ Form simple sentences using word/phrase banks ■ Participate in interactive journal writing ■ Give content-based information using visuals or graphics	■ Produce original sentences ■ Create messages for social purposes (e.g., get well cards) ■ Compose journal entries about personal experiences ■ Use classroom resources (e.g., picture dictionaries) to compose sentences	■ Create a related series of sentences in response to prompts ■ Produce content-related sentences ■ Compose stories ■ Explain processes or procedures using connected sentences	

The Can Do descriptors work in conjunction with the WIDA Performance Definitions of the English language proficiency standards. The Performance Definitions use three criteria (1. linguistic complexity; 2. vocabulary usage; and 3. language control) to describe the increasing quality and quantity of students' language processing and use across the levels of language proficiency.

Source: WIDA ELP Standards © 2007, 2012, Board of Regents of the University of Wisconsin System. WIDA is a trademark of the Board of Regents of the University of Wisconsin System. For more information on using the WIDA ELP Standards please visit the WIDA website at *www.wida.us.*

Teachers who use WIDA may need to make connections between the WIDA "Can Do" statements and their state standards or the CCSS if their state has adopted them. In our example, Kim's "Can Do" aligns with CCSS RF.1.3b: "Decode regularly spelled one-syllable words" (p. 16), while Jose's "Can Do" aligns with CCSS RL.1.2: "Retell stories, including key details, and demonstrate understanding of their central message or lesson" (NGACBP & CCSSO, 2010, p. 11). As you work with the WIDA "Can Do" lists and the CCSS or state standards, making connections between them will become easier.

Inclusion

Inclusion is a term that evolved from the Individuals with Disabilities Education Act (IDEA) of 1997. Inclusion is a social and educational practice that supports placing students with disabilities in classes with their same-age peers with proper support and accommodations. When IDEA was signed into law in 1997, it was intended to give a free, appropriate public education in the least restrictive environment for individuals with disabilities identified by the Act. The categories of disabilities include autism, deaf-blindness, deafness, developmental delay, emotional disturbance, hearing impairment, intellectual disability, multiple disabilities, orthopedic impairment, other health impairment, specific learning disability, speech or language impairment, traumatic brain injury, and visual impairment including blindness (National Dissemination Center for Children with Disabilities, 2012). This Act requires all students with disabilities who are eligible for placement within the general education setting to receive an *individualized education program (IEP)*. IEPs must be prepared for any student who is eligible for services as identified by IDEA. The plans are agreed upon by parents, classroom teachers, special education teachers, and administrators who set long-term goals and short-term objectives for the student with a plan of action that will help the student reach state content standards.

The updated IDEA 2004 was signed into law that year. The purposes of this version of IDEA are to ensure that

1. all students with identified disabilities, regardless of severity, receive a free appropriate public education;
2. the identification and evaluation of these students are nondiscriminatory;
3. the rights of students with disabilities and their parents' rights are protected, including due process;
4. students with disabilities are not discriminated against in discipline issues;
5. infants and toddlers with disabilities receive early identification and intervention; and
6. schools and parents receive the tools necessary to assist students with disabilities.

> Who dares to teach must never cease to learn.
>
> **JOHN COTTON DANA**

IDEA 2004 also states that "a learning disability may be present when a student's performance is not adequate to meet grade-level standards when provided with appropriate instruction and research-based interventions" (Mesmer & Mesmer, 2009, p. 281). Eight areas are used as the criteria for determining the existence of a specific learning disability as defined in IDEA. The six areas that focus on the language arts are oral expression, written expression, basic reading skills, fluency, listening comprehension, and reading comprehension.

IDEA 2004 requires schools to have a *Response to Intervention (RTI)* plan, a framework for identifying students with learning disabilities and providing them with instructional services. An RTI plan requires schools to provide appropriate intervention for students who are not performing at grade level in the eight areas. Although the specific approaches vary, the method should involve a cyclical process that begins with assessment, followed by intervention, more assessment, and more intense intervention until students are either performing at grade level or receiving special services for a specific learning disability. Each school district has its own RTI plan, so make sure you understand your district's plan when you begin teaching.

> Teaching means helping a child reach his [or her] potential.
>
> **ERICH FROMM**

Differentiation

As teachers prepare daily lessons, they need to differentiate the learning experience in order to meet the needs of all students. *Differentiation* is the use of a variety of teaching and learning strategies to meet the range of needs evident in a given classroom (Friend & Bursuck, 2009). The content, the process by which the content is taught, and the product that students produce can all be differentiated. Differentiation, however, "is not a recipe for teaching. It is not an instructional strategy. It is not what a teacher does when he or she has time. . . . It is a philosophy" (Tomlinson, 2000, p. 6). According to Tomlinson, teachers who practice differentiation believe that students

- have varying abilities, including the academically gifted.
- have varying interests, including those interested in the visual and performing arts.
- have a variety of learning styles.
- have different background experiences.
- learn at different paces.
- learn best in a community of learners who support them.
- learn best when they can connect school learning to their personal lives.
- need accommodations in order to reach their potential.

Differentiation creates a student-centered classroom because it provides materials and tasks at various levels of difficulty and with varying levels of instructional support. The needs of every student are addressed for each lesson. Some students may have IEPs, whereas others do not. For example, in Mr. Green's classroom, one student needs additional time to complete assignments, while another student needs an adult to sit alongside him so that he remains focused. The student who is blind needs all texts in audio format, large print, or in Braille, and the student with a hearing loss needs to sit close to Mr. Green so that she can hear him and read his lips. The student who is deaf needs someone to sign during instructional times. Mr. Green's students who have been identified as academically gifted need projects that challenge them. Their products may take on different formats than the products of other students. For example, these students may choose to write and produce a play about an assigned novel instead of completing a written book report assigned to other students. All the differentiations are necessary in order for Mr. Green's students to complete lessons successfully.

As you read this text and learn about different activities to use while teaching the language arts, reflect on how you can differentiate your teaching to meet the needs of students who face various challenges, including those who have limited English skills, those who have sensory disabilities, and those who require more challenging, higher-level thinking projects.

TECHNOLOGY IN THE CLASSROOM

Each chapter in this book includes a "Technology in the Classroom" section, and Appendices A.1 and A.2 include lists of additional sites for teachers and students. Fast-paced technology changes over the past two decades have influenced the educational paradigm, making the Internet a useful tool for teachers and students. The following sites offer information about recent research.

www.education-world.com This site offers a wide range of articles for teachers and administrators regarding many education issues.

http://nces.ed.gov/pubsearch The National Center for Education Statistics, part of the U.S. Department of Education, releases the statistical reports for education in the United States. They include such topics as academic achievement and assessment, elementary education, parental involvement, students at risk, and technology.

www.ncte.org This National Council of Teachers of English site includes resources divided into elementary, middle school, high school, and college levels.

www.reading.org The International Reading Association's site includes many free resources in addition to a members-only section.

www.corestandards.org This site lists the Common Core State Standards by subject (Reading: Literature; Reading: Informational Text; Reading: Foundational Skills; Writing; Speaking and Listening; and Language) and grade level.

SUMMARY

Good teaching involves constant and continuous decision making. This is the heart of what it means to be a reflective teacher. To achieve this, you must develop a philosophy of education as it relates to students, teaching, and learning, and you must apply this philosophy specifically to teaching language arts.

There are four main approaches to teaching the language arts. In the *separate skills approach* the language arts curriculum is broken down into many separate subskills, which are taught in isolation from one another. This is more of a managerial system than an instructional approach, with the teacher as the prime manager and students assuming passive roles. The *whole language approach* is more student-centered because, for example, students are given a choice of which books to read and genres to write in. The whole language approach integrates all six of the language arts areas. It focuses on the needs, experiences, and interests of the individual student; it uses authentic texts to develop literacy awareness; and it tries to make learning language a natural extension of using language. The *integrated approach,* as its title suggests, integrates use of the six language arts across the curriculum. The *comprehensive approach* focuses on reading and writing authentic texts and providing a balance of teacher-taught skills as needed by individual students.

The primary focus of this textbook is a comprehensive, integrated approach. We advocate not only the integration of the six communication arts areas but also believe that these areas serve as the foundation for other content areas such as math, social studies, and science. We also stress the accommodation of individual learner needs through both holistic teaching and the teaching of skills explicitly when students need them.

> Teaching is the art of assisting discovery.
>
> **MARK VAN DOREN**

As you embark on your teaching career, you will make many decisions: How will you include all the components of the language arts? What learning theories do you embrace? How do you believe the language arts should be taught? What new policies do you need to consider? What activities will be best for your class? How will you meet the needs of all your students, including those with learning disabilities and those who are academically gifted? This chapter has introduced you to several learning theories, approaches to teaching the language arts, and current policies. The following section includes activities you can use with students in a field placement or tutoring setting. We hope you will evaluate your effectiveness after each lesson. We have also included a Self-Diagnostic Instrument in Appendix C, which you can use to determine your preparedness for teaching various skills of the language arts.

field AND practicum ACTIVITIES

At the end of each chapter, we share integrated activities you can use in your classroom. Some of the ideas are for a specific grade level, but many can be modified to use in a variety of grade levels. We encourage you to keep a collection of these ideas in order to grow your own repertoire.

1. COMPARE APPROACHES TO TEACHING THE LANGUAGE ARTS. This activity gives you an opportunity to experiment with two different approaches to teaching the language arts while working with students. Reflect on which approach you think is more effective for the group of students you taught and why.

For one lesson with one group of students, explicitly teach the rules for using quotation marks in dialogue and follow it with a worksheet of sentences in which the students practice applying the rule. Collect and grade the papers. A week later, give a writing assignment that you know requires the students to use quotation marks in the way you explicitly taught, but do not review the rule with the students. Collect and grade those papers, analyzing in particular how well the students applied the rule.

On another day, share a story with another group of students and talk about how an author uses quotation marks when she wants to show the readers that a person is talking. Give ample time for students to find quotation marks in the story and to discuss how direct quotations make a story come alive. Then invite the students to write their own story, encouraging them to use direct quotations. Collect those stories and analyze whether the students correctly used quotation marks. About a week later, invite the students to write another story using quotations, but do not review the quotation mark rules. Collect and analyze those stories.

Finally, analyze the two lessons to determine whether (1) the students transferred their learning from one lesson to the other, and (2) whether they did better in transferring their learning when you explicitly taught the punctuation rules or when you used the other approach.

FIGURE 1.12 Venn diagram comparing two versions of *The Mitten*.

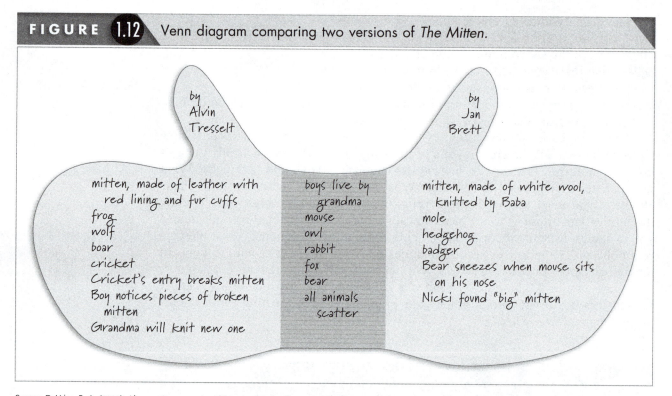

by Alvin Tresselt		by Jan Brett
mitten, made of leather with red lining and fur cuffs	boys live by grandma	mitten, made of white wool, knitted by Baba
frog	mouse	mole
wolf	owl	hedgehog
boar	rabbit	badger
cricket	fox	Bear sneezes when mouse sits on his nose
Cricket's entry breaks mitten	bear	Nicki found "big" mitten
Boy notices pieces of broken mitten	all animals scatter	
Grandma will knit new one		

Source: DeVries, B. A. (2015). *Literacy Assessment and Intervention for Classroom Teachers.* Scottsdale, AZ: Holcomb Hathaway.

2. COMPARE AND CONTRAST TWO VERSIONS OF *THE MITTEN*. CCSS RL.2.9 states that students be able to "compare and contrast two or more versions of the same stories by different authors or from different cultures" (NGACBP & CCSSO, 2010, p. 11). After sharing two versions of *The Mitten*, one by Jan Brett (1999) and the other by Alvin Tresselt (1964), invite a group of second graders to complete the graphic organizer shown in Figure 1.12. *Recommended for primary grades.*

Language Arts Integration
for All Students

OBJECTIVES

After reading this chapter, you will be able to accomplish the following objectives:

1. Explain how parents and other caregivers influence students' oral language.
2. Explain how caregivers can help their student develop reading skills.
3. Explain what caregivers can do to help their student develop writing skills.
4. Explain what teachers can do to better communicate with caregivers.
5. Name some strategies teachers can use to promote multicultural awareness.
6. Name some strategies teachers can use to aid English learners.
7. List some language arts strategies teachers can use to teach students with disabilities.
8. Explain compacting.

INTRODUCTION

In this chapter you will learn about the importance of home and community influences on students' language arts abilities. Teachers need to understand the significance of caregiver–child interaction, the influence of the home, the role of play, and the influence of the community if they are to work with students as individuals. This chapter emphasizes the importance of teachers embracing all diverse learners. The learners highlighted in this chapter are students who are culturally diverse, have various language backgrounds, and have various abilities and disabilities, including giftedness.

Note that throughout this chapter we use the word *caregiver* instead of *parent* in an effort to be more inclusive.

CAREGIVER INFLUENCE ON LITERACY DEVELOPMENT

Long before children enter school they are greatly influenced by their parents, family members, caregivers, and other members of their community. This influence extends to the way children speak (their dialect), their interest in learning to read and write, and their access to books. Language skills that are related to later reading and writing acquisition are heavily influenced by the behaviors of caregivers (Dickinson & McCabe, 2001; Hodge & Downie, 2004). In addition, we know that strong oral language skills lead to strong literacy skills. The reverse is also true: poor oral language skills, both productive and receptive, slow literacy growth. Some early childhood experts now indicate that readiness for school begins in infancy (Lally, 2010). It is in the earliest years that brain structure is shaped, regulating one's urges and developing short- and long-term memory.

As discussed in Chapter 1, Lev Vygotsky (1986) was an early proponent of the importance of social interaction on the cognitive and linguistic development of young children. Vygotsky argued that when infants and very young children interact with adults two things occur: first, children learn that words convey messages and express ideas; second, language helps children to clarify their thinking. For Vygotsky, language and thought are closely linked and allow children to solve real-world problems. As the child grows older he or she requires less direct assistance from the adult, but the social interaction between the two remains a powerful force for intellectual (cognitive) development.

Some teachers, perhaps due to their own negative experiences, may be critical of parents, particularly those whose background, culture, and socioeconomic conditions differ from their own, and they may see parents more as a hindrance than a help. However, research has shown that when teachers listen to parents and caregivers, they form valuable bonds that improve students' literacy skills (Compton-Lilly, 2009).

Caregivers and Language

Oral language learning in the home occurs easily and naturally because it is part of the normal social interaction between caregiver and child. Three main factors explain this (Dickinson & McCabe, 2001):

1. Language in the home is situation specific. The environment consists of concrete objects that make language use part of the real world. The child and caregiver respond to each other in specific situations about real objects. For example, a mother tells her child, "Stop climbing on the sofa now or you won't get a cookie."

2. Language focuses on meaning rather than form. Teachers are often overly concerned with the correct grammatical form of language rather than the student's intended meaning. At home, language is functional and it serves a purpose; the focus is almost always on meaning and not grammar.

3. Language is built on trust; it is one of the primary ways in which caregiver and child are bonded to each other. It is the basis for the expression of one's deepest feelings and emotions. Thus, the home, more so than the classroom, is a safe environment where the child feels most comfortable expressing herself.

Caregivers and Reading

The home is the child's first reading environment. Caregivers and older siblings read to children on a regular basis. Being read to aloud (e.g., bedtime stories) is the fundamental building block for later school experiences with reading. Frank Smith (1997) and Burgess (2003) note that the importance of the reading relationship established between caregiver and child in the earliest years cannot be overemphasized. It is in this relationship that the child learns about the concepts of story, the sounds of language (phonemic awareness), the relationship between sound and symbol (phonics), and books and other texts as sources of information as well

read RESEARCH practice

Take an afternoon to explore the community in which you will teach. What is the nature of the adult–child interaction that you observe in the school? In after-school programs? In parks and recreation areas? In stores? How do these various environments enhance the development of students' oral language?

as enjoyment. Further strengthening this bond is the discussion about books that takes place between caregiver and child. In addition, the young child is exposed to print in the neighborhood, such as street signs and the signs in shop windows; this is known as *environmental print*, another important building block of literacy (MacDonald, 2012). Students whose caregivers read aloud to them on a regular basis are better prepared to succeed with the processes of reading and writing when they arrive in school (Imig, 2014). Figures 2.1 and 2.2 present tips for parents reading to children at home.

Caregivers and Writing

Although not emphasized as much as reading, writing is equally important in the literacy equation. Long before they enter school, young children need opportuni-

---

FIGURE 2.1 Reading to preschool children.

1. From the cover, read the title, author, and illustrator and explain that the author wrote the book and the illustrator drew the pictures.

2. As you read, point to the words. The child understands you are reading words and not the pictures and that one reads from top to bottom and left to right.

3. Stop and discuss the story and pictures.

4. Let the child interrupt and ask questions.

5. Use expression! Make the story come alive.

6. Get the child engaged by asking him or her to predict what will happen next.

7. Let the child chime in on repetitive lines.

8. If the text has rhyme, stop and let the child provide the rhyming word.

9. Ask the child if he or she can find a familiar word in the text.

Source: PBS. (2005). *Literacy tips for the 10-minute parent.* Available online: http://pbskids.org and click on the "Parent" icon.

---

ties, space, and materials for writing. Caregivers can create a small space for the child to write while sitting on the floor or at the kitchen table. Providing thick crayons or chalk and lots of blank paper is necessary for the child to develop the small muscle skills required for writing. The key role of the caregiver is to encourage this activity. Parents and children can write together or exchange simple notes. The key is the activity should be fun and one the child enjoys.

Outside the home the child becomes more aware of the world of print while shopping at stores and noticing street signs (e.g., Maple Street) while riding in

---

FIGURE 2.2 Reading at home with school-age children.

1. When reading to a child, select books that interest the child, but are too difficult for him or her to read.

2. Select chapter books and invite the child to predict what will happen in the next chapter.

3. Talk to the child about the type of books he or she likes and have him or her explain.

4. Talk about favorite authors and what the child likes about their books.

5. Take turns reading with the child.

6. Discuss new words, figurative language, and the author's style of writing.

7. Discuss characters with the child by discussing characters' personalities and motives for their actions.

8. Make reading together a pleasurable time; do not use it as a punishment.

9. Invite the child to listen to all types of reading—newspapers, magazines, recipes, rules to board games.

10. If possible, go to the public library with the child and provide plenty of time to browse to find titles that interest him or her. Read the first page with the child to see if the book captures his or her attention or if it is at the correct reading level.

11. Model reading. Children should see you reading all types of materials.

Source: National Education Association. *Tips for reading to and with children in kindergarten through grade 3.* Available online: http://www.sbschools.org/schools/gb/class_pages/specialists/resource/docs/TipsK3.pdf

| | Suggestions for writing at home. | **FIGURE** **2.3** |

Scribbling on large paper	Labeling family photographs	Writing about vacations
Writing on slate boards	Writing or drawing notes to grandparents	Keeping scrapbooks
Water painting on newsprint		Writing in journals
Drawing with pencils and crayons	Exchanging family notes	Keeping diaries
Finger painting	Posting a home memo board	Labeling trip photographs
Creating collage cutouts and written words	Using sticky notes	Writing to favorite authors online
	Writing holiday cards	

the car. This environmental print helps the young child make the connection between words and the letters he sees (e.g., McDonald's), which he can later use when writing brief notes, labeling drawings, and making grocery lists with a caregiver's help.

Parental and caregiver involvement in aiding the child's writing skills is particularly important now that the Common Core State Standards have introduced standards in most states that are more rigorous than previous state English language arts and reading standards (Beach, 2011). Figure 2.3 offers suggestions for writing activities at home.

The Importance of Play in the Home

Play serves an important role in human development and nurtures cognitive development in many ways. Playing with alphabet blocks, toys, and other objects allows infants and children to explore concepts related to spatial relationships, speed, weight, size, shape, and sequence. Play also establishes the social rules of games and fairness. Young children engaged in play utilize *symbolic representation,* an important ingredient in the development of creativity in which a child pretends an object is something else. For example, a broomstick becomes a horse on the open range. With very young children, there appears to be a progression in the social involvement of early play experiences (see Figure 2.4). Although every type of play is important, associative and cooperative play provide the best opportunities for children to learn through social interaction by using language in purposeful settings.

Two types of play considered valuable for later school learning are dramatic play and language play. In dramatic play students use gestures, words, and symbolic

| | Stages of play. | **FIGURE** **2.4** |

TYPE	DESCRIPTION
Solitary play	Single child and a toy or imaginary playmate
Parallel play	Two or more children engaged in separate activities
Associative play	Two or more children sharing toys but without real interaction
Cooperative play	Joint task pursued; sharing; following rules

props to convey stories to one another. In this highly social environment, students may pretend to plant flowers, bake cookies, or visit the store. The possibilities are endless, and the social, linguistic, and cognitive skills that such play reinforce are invaluable. Similarly, young children engage in language play when they make up songs, riddles, puns, and recite tongue twisters such "Peter Piper picked a peck of pickled peppers." And who doesn't have a favorite knock knock joke? Add to this hundreds of jump rope rhymes such as "A my name is Alice and I come from Alabama and my husband's name is Allan and we sell apples." For a comprehensive collection of these and other songs, chants, jokes, see the classic work *A Rocket in My Pocket,* originally published in 1948 and still relevant today (Withers, 2007).

Teachers and Caregivers: A Team Approach

A central theme of early childhood education is the importance of establishing partnerships among parents, caregivers, community members, and school officials. Particularly for minority children ages 3 to 8, such working partnerships are crucial for the development of readiness skills necessary for school success (Berkley, 2010). Research clearly indicates that when teachers and caregivers work together the student benefits not only academically, but also socially and emotionally (International Reading Association, 2002; Ho 2002; Rasinski & Padak, 2000; Sheldon, 2002; Jordan, Snow, & Porche, 2000; Westat & Policy Associates, 2001). Family involvement in school activities provides students with a positive perception of school.

Parents and caregivers can be involved with the school in two ways: in school and at home. In school they can visit the classrooms to observe their child, volunteer to help in the library, assist with field trips, participate in parent–teacher organizations, and attend parent–teacher conferences and other school events. At home caregivers can discuss the school day, help with homework and special assignments, and, of course, read aloud with their children.

The key is establishing regular communication between the school and home to develop a rapport. At the beginning of the school year, many teachers write a welcoming letter of introduction to inform parents about the class curriculum and goals, school functions, and how to contact the teacher and other school officials. If the student's family speaks a language other than English, translators in the caregiver's language can be found to make communication easier. Figure 2.5 is an example letter of introduction.

You may want to send a monthly newsletter to the home as a way of updating the family about class and school events, special projects, holidays, and testing days. This is in addition to any individual letters, emails, phone calls, and texts (if appropriate) you use to maintain regular communication with caregivers. Make "good news" phone calls or send emails to let caregivers know that their students are making progress in various areas. In upper grades, weekly homework letters can also keep parents abreast of what is due that week or the following week. Generally, the more communication between the school and home, the better. Figures 2.6–2.11 include a variety of ways to maintain that communication.

Unfortunately, some caregivers feel uncomfortable visiting the school. Regardless of the reason for this, your responsibility is to reach out to parents in all ways possible. Figure 2.12 lists a variety of activities caregivers can do at home to aid the literacy development of their student.

> Parents who know their children's teachers and help with the homework and teach their kids right from wrong—these parents make all the difference.
>
> **BILL CLINTON**

Example of a letter of introduction.   **FIGURE** 2.5

Dear Parents and Caregivers:

I am excited to be a new member of this community and to become a partner in your child's learning! This summer I moved to Edmond from Kalamazoo, where I also taught second grade. I already have enjoyed Edmond's new library and Shakespeare in the Park. Besides reading and going to plays, I love country music and long walks.

It is my goal that every one of my students will become a successful reader and that he or she will spend some spare time reading materials that interest him or her. I hope that is also your goal for your child.

Central Elementary is embracing a new reading program this year called "Taking Flight with Books." The school's goal is to have each child read at least 100 pages each week at home. Our school is encouraging caregivers to listen to their child when possible and to discuss the material with him or her. At Open House I will further explain this new program and answer any questions you may have.

Central Elementary Open House is September 4 at 7 P.M. I am eager to meet each one of you and to personally encourage you to become involved at school if you can. At Open House I will have sign-up sheets for different activities—reading with students, playing word activities with students, binding students' books, organizing our classroom library, recording our "Taking Flight with Books" pages, and many other activities. Meanwhile, please save your old candles, scraps of material, and any small broken appliances. Our class will need all these materials for art, science, and social studies projects. I am looking forward to meeting you at Open House on September 4. Please note that if you need to contact me, you can email me at jbarryman@central-elementary.edmond.edu or call me at school between 8:00 and 8:20 any morning.

Sincerely,

Jan Barryman

Estimados padres y principal cuidador/a de los niños,

Mi da mucho gusto ser nuevo miembro de esta comunidad y de hacerme colega en la educación de sus hijos. Este verano me mudé a Edmond de Kalamazoo donde también enseñaba el segundo año de primaria. Ya he disfrutado de la nueva biblioteca y de Shakespeare en el Parque. Además de leer e ir al teatro, me encanta la música country y western (ranchera americana) e ir de paseo y tomar caminatas largas.

Mi meta es que cada estudiante se convierta en un exitoso lector y que cada uno pase su tiempo libre leyendo cosas que le interesen. Espero que esto sea su deseo para sus hijos también. . . .

Example of a reading log.   **FIGURE** 2.6

READING LOG
Taking Flight with Books

Child's Name _____   *Grade* _____

DATE	TITLE/AUTHOR	PAGES	CAREGIVER'S SIGNATURE

FIGURE 2.7 Example of a "Getting to Know Your Child" card.

Getting to Know Your Child

Child's name

Child's best subject

Child's least favorite subject

Child's favorite way to learn

Child's personality

Child's extracurricular activities

Other information you want the teacher to know

Thank you for sharing this information; it will remain confidential.

Caregiver's signature

FIGURE 2.8 Example of a permission request.

Dear _____,

Our class has enjoyed _____ (child's name) poem/story/essay _____ (title of composition). I would like to include it in our next online monthly newsletter, but I need your permission to publish it. Please complete the permission slip at the bottom of this note and return it with _____ (child's name) by _____ (date).

Sincerely,

Jan Barryman

Dear Ms. Barryman,

_____ I give you permission to publish my child's work in the newsletter.

_____ At this time I do not want you to publish my child's work.

Caregiver's signature

Example of part of a monthly newsletter.   **FIGURE** 2.9

Second-Grade Monthly Newsletter

WEEK OF NOVEMBER 3   CENTRAL ELEMENTARY

CONGRATULATIONS!

In the month of October, our class read an average of 116 pages a week! That is 16 pages higher than our goal. We thank you for encouraging us at home, giving us quiet time to read, and for discussing great books with us. We understand that you are turning off the TV and also reading! Keep up the good work!

Activity for the Family

We are learning probability in math. We take two minutes each morning to first predict how many heads and tails we will get when we toss a coin 20 times. Then we see how close we get to our prediction. You can also do this at home as a family activity.

Field Trip

On Friday, November 13, our class is going to see the play *The True Story of the Three Pigs* at 12:00 at the State Fair Ground Theatre. The buses will leave at 11:00 and return at the end of the school day. Our class needs five or six adults who will come with us. Your ticket, like the students' tickets, is free! Please call me if you can help us! When you see one of the Allied Art Council members, thank them for giving us this opportunity! They are providing the free tickets.

Acrostic Poem

Footballs flying through the air,
Apples ripening to bright red,
Leaves turning orange and yellow,
Leaves crunching under feet.

by Juan Garcia

Example of a Happy Gram.   **FIGURE** 2.10

Hear Ye! Hear Ye!

I am happy to inform you that today _____ did the following:

_____

_____

_____

_____

_____

_____

Teacher's signature

FIGURE 2.11 Example of an assignment sheet.

Assignment(s) Not Completed in School or Other Homework

For the Week of _____

DAY	ASSIGNMENTS	CAREGIVER'S COMMENT
Mon.		
Tues.		
Wed.		
Thurs.		

Note: I will not assign homework on Friday; I want to encourage the family to do other activities together.

_____

Teacher's signature

FIGURE 2.12 Activities caregivers can do at home to aid their child's literacy development.

1. Read engaging books that are above their child's reading level so that the child is introduced to an advanced vocabulary.
2. Read in unison with their child.
3. If caregivers cannot read, they can listen with their child to audiobooks or view and discuss wordless books.
4. Model reading in front of their child.
5. Write with their child.
6. Help with spelling by helping their child see patterns within words.
7. Watch and discuss educational TV programs with their child.
8. If caregivers have Internet access at home, they can research a topic together with their child.
9. Make regular visits to the local library with their child.
10. Do word puzzles with their child.

1. Create a class website to inform caregivers of the following:

   ▪ Child's attendance and grades, which only the caregiver can access.

   ▪ Class activities.

   ▪ Community events.

   ▪ Homework assignments.

   ▪ Upcoming school events.

   ▪ Need for volunteers for particular activities.

   ▪ Need for supplies, such as plastic containers, potting soil for science experiments, and shoe boxes to create dioramas.

2. Share websites that caregivers can explore with their child:

   ▪ **http://kids.nationalgeographic.com** gives tips for after-school activities, has links to reinforce reading and writing skills, and has links to information about the world.

   ▪ **www.whitehouse.gov** permits viewers to "tour" the White House and gives historical information about the White House.

   ▪ **Authors' websites.** Appendix B.1 includes a list of children's and young adult literature author websites.

It is easier than ever for educators to communicate with caregivers through today's technology. Many schools and classrooms have their own wikis, blogs, or web pages that convey important information to caregivers. Strive to utilize available technology to enhance communication with your students' parents. Figure 2.13 offers suggestions for ways in which you can do this.

DIVERSITY IN THE CLASSROOM

The demographics of the U.S. population are changing. A majority of the older population is white, while the younger population is more racially and culturally diverse. Between 1980 and 2008, of the total population, the percentage of those who identify as white declined from 80 to 66 percent; the Hispanic population increased from 6 to 15 percent; the Asian/Pacific Islander population increased from 2 to 4 percent, and the African American population remained at about 12 percent (National Center for Education Statistics, 2010). The population of the United States continues to grow; however, the growth is not consistent across the various regions of the United States. Table 2.1 indicates the growth changes by regions.

These national demographic changes are reflected in our public schools. The U.S. Department of Education and the National Institute of Child Health and Development estimate that by the year 2030 English learners will constitute 40 percent of the nation's K–12 students (Hur & Suh, 2012). This diversity is our strength as a nation and should be embraced. Too often our approach is to label or stereotype students who are the least bit different. Our goal as teachers is to remember that every student is unique and deserves special attention in order

TABLE 2.1	U.S. population change by region, 2000 to 2010.			
AREA	**POPULATION IN MILLIONS**		**CHANGE, 2000 TO 2010**	
	April 1, 2000	April 1, 2010	Pop. Gained	Percent
U.S., total	281,421,906	308,745,538	27,323,622	9.7
Northeast	53,594,378	55,317,240	1,722,862	3.2
Midwest	64,392,776	66,927,001	2,534,225	3.9
South	100,236,820	114,755,044	14,318,924	14.3
West	63,197,932	71,945,553	8,747,621	13.8

The Census Bureau groups the states as follows: **Northeast:** Connecticut, Maine, Massachusetts, New Hampshire, New Jersey, New York, Pennsylvania, Rhode Island, and Vermont; **Midwest:** Illinois, Indiana, Iowa, Kansas, Michigan, Minnesota, Missouri, Nebraska, North Dakota, Ohio, South Dakota, and Wisconsin; **South:** Alabama, Arkansas, Delaware, District of Columbia, Florida, Georgia, Kentucky, Louisiana, Maryland, Mississippi, North Carolina, Oklahoma, South Carolina, Tennessee, Texas, Virginia, and West Virginia; **West:** Alaska, Arizona, California, Colorado, Hawaii, Idaho, Montana, Nevada, New Mexico, Oregon, Utah, Washington, and Wyoming.

Source: U.S. Census Bureau, "Population Change and Distribution, 2000 to 2010," Census 2010 Brief, March 2011.

to become a successful learner. In some schools success may be measured by standardized test scores, but equating academic success with test scores does not address the disproportionate percentage of economically disadvantaged minority students who drop out.

Cultural Factors

Because our public schools have such a rich diversity, you must strive to understand how your students' cultural heritage affects how they relate to the school and your teaching style. One model based on Vygotsky's *zone of proximal development* (1986) and James Paul Gee's (1990) concept of *discourse community* can aid teachers as they work with students from diverse cultures. The zone of proximal development, you will recall, refers to the gap between what students can do independently and what they can do with assistance; thus, teachers need to identify those specific tasks with which students require assistance to be successful (see Figure 2.14). A discourse community is the unspoken way a group uses language and the values it holds. A person's family, religious group, and ethnic group are all examples of discourse communities; thus, a person can belong to a number of discourse communities simultaneously. Students who come from discourse communities dissimilar from the school's may be at a disadvantage; this is particularly true of students from different cultures who must adjust to the new discourse community and behavior requirements of the school (Gruenert, 2000).

Expect that students from a variety of cultures will populate your classroom. It is up to you to learn something about these various cultures in order to understand differences in your students' discourse communities. Listed below are some aspects of culture for you to consider (DeVries, 2015).

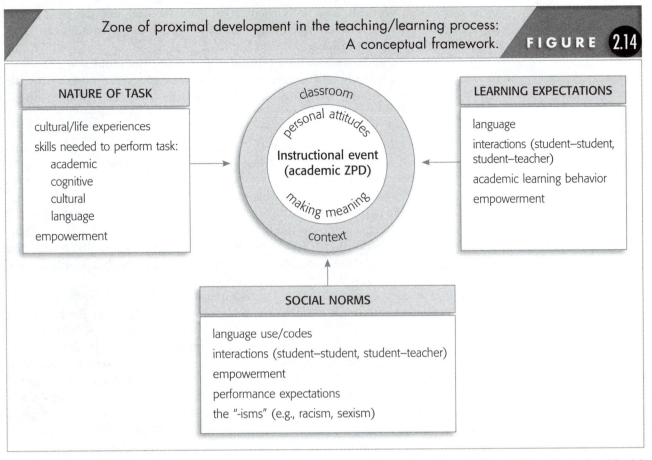

Zone of proximal development in the teaching/learning process: A conceptual framework. **FIGURE 2.14**

NATURE OF TASK

cultural/life experiences

skills needed to perform task:
 academic
 cognitive
 cultural
 language

empowerment

classroom

personal attitudes

Instructional event (academic ZPD)

making meaning

context

LEARNING EXPECTATIONS

language

interactions (student–student, student–teacher)

academic learning behavior

empowerment

SOCIAL NORMS

language use/codes

interactions (student–student, student–teacher)

empowerment

performance expectations

the "-isms" (e.g., racism, sexism)

Source: Figure from Pransky, K. & Bailey, F. (Dec. 2002/Jan. 2003). To meet your students where they are, first you have to find them: Working with culturally and linguistically diverse at-risk students. *The Reading Teacher, 56*(4), 370–383. Reprinted with permission of the International Reading Association via CCC.

- Some families value cooperation over individualization; these students commonly share answers in class.
- Some caregivers instruct children to lower their eyes when being reprimanded; these students may avoid eye contact with you.
- Some caregivers do not ask children questions for which they already know the answer; these students will not respond if they believe you already know the answer.
- In some families, completing a school task incorrectly brings disgrace to the entire family; these students may not volunteer an answer in class unless they are certain they are correct.
- In some families men (or boys) will not accept instruction from a woman.

Each culture is different and presents unique opportunities and challenges; thus, it is incumbent upon you to learn as much as possible about your students' cultural backgrounds. One way many teachers achieve this goal is by adopting aspects of the Reggio Emilia approach, long considered to be the exemplary model of early childhood education (Linn, 2001). American teachers can take study tours to this region of Italy to learn more about the approach to early childhood education that was developed there in the years following World War II. Above all else, the Reggio Emilia method encourages teachers to nurture and value students and emphasize the art and beauty of learning (Chertoff, 2013). Students' dignity is respected, and the classroom's physical environment emphasizes the students' aesthetic development. Students are expected to speak up and teachers are expected to listen; furthermore, the curriculum emerges from the students' interests and is not dictated by teachers or administrators. In short, American educators can learn much from the Reggio Emilia approach.

Traditional U.S. classrooms divide the day into time slots and content areas. In some schools this leads to a "hurry-up" pace or what Donald Graves called the "cha-cha-cha" curriculum, where teachers and students bounce from one subject to another at a rapid pace. Students from other cultures often become lost in such a situation (Harste, 2003).

Effective teachers plan their curriculum with all students in mind, and this can only happen after teachers get to know their students. One popular way to get to know your students is through *interest inventories*. These are questionnaires completed by the students. They are teacher-made and generally utilize a fill-in-the-blank format, a checklist, or a combination of the two. They can be administered early in the school year—even on the first day—to give you some idea of your students' interests in school, particular subjects, sports, television, books, travel, and so on. Appendix D.1 contains an example of one type of inventory suitable for use with upper elementary and intermediate students.

Another way to engage all students is through the *book club approach,* which focuses on reading, writing, and talking about books in class (Kong & Fitch, 2002/3; Barnett & Roberson, 2005). Based on Vygotsky's sociocultural belief that reading and writing should be taught as social functions, book clubs are organized around four elements: small group discussions, whole group discussions, reading, and individual writing. Through collaborative discussion the students learn about the book, the views of other students, and their own views. These discussions support CCRA. SL.1, which requires students to "prepare for and participate effectively in a range of conversations and collaborations with diverse partners, building on others' ideas and expressing their own clearly and persuasively" (NGACBP & CCSSO, 2010, p. 22). Reading the same book establishes a common purpose. Teachers can select books from a variety of cultures that allow students to gain a better understanding of one another. Appendix B.2 lists books from various cultures that work well in book club discussions. Comparing similarities and differences among different cultures enhances students' awareness and acceptance of one another. Overall, the book club approach goes a long way toward slowing things down for the culturally different student, and using authentic texts makes literacy acquisition more likely for them (Kane, 2007).

Just about all educators agree that *multicultural literature* must be used more often in our classroom, not only to help non-native English-speaking students but also to broaden the horizons of other students. Back in 1965 Larrick's seminal study showed that children of color and diversity were not represented in children's literature. Since then, studies have shown that we have made great strides in this area, particularly in the depiction of Hispanic characters in children's books. However, we still have a long way to go (Nilsson, 2005). A book in both English and Spanish that will appeal to younger readers is *The Cazuela that the Farm Maiden Stirred* (Vamos, 2011). Another book for middle-school students that stimulates discussion about social justice issues with a multicultural theme is *Under the Same Sky* (DeFelice, 2005). We encourage all teachers in all grades to include more multicultural literature in their curriculum. Chapter 4 highlights other multicultural titles.

English Learners

As stated earlier, in recent years there has been an exponential growth in the number of students entering our schools whose first language is other than English. These new immigrant students pose unique challenges for our school system (Bauer & Arazi, 2011). Experts estimate that by the year 2050, 40 percent of all U.S. students will come from homes where English is not the native language. Of this group of students, the largest number will come from Spanish-speaking countries. Six states (Texas, California, Arizona, Illinois, New York, and Florida) already have over 100,000 limited English proficiency students. These students are sometimes referred to as second language learners (ESL) or English learners; the terms are often used interchangeably.

> Education takes place in the combination of the home, the community, the school, and the receptive mind.
>
> **HARRY EDWARDS**

The challenge for classroom teachers comes not only from increasing numbers of English learners but also from the many different languages spoken. Today's U.S. school population represents 327 different languages. The most common languages in our schools today are Spanish, Vietnamese, Hmong, Haitian, Creole, Korean, Arabic, Chinese (including Cantonese and Mandarin), Russian, Navajo, Portuguese, and Japanese. As greater numbers of students from Mexico, Latin America, and Asia have entered our schools it has become clear that it takes nearly seven years for them to learn enough English to attain academic parity with native English-speaking students. Seven years is a long time to struggle in the classroom, and many of these students drop out before finishing high school.

Research clearly shows that for these students, learning English cannot be separated from their sociocultural background, which defines their identity (Borrero & Yeh, 2010). Thus, you must be aware of your students' home lives, specific language needs, and cultural differences. Mohr (2004) notes that pull-out programs are not effective and that experts recommend intensive immersion programs in learning to read and write. Many school districts use "scripted literacy programs that focus heavily on fluency and phonics in the primary grades" (Guccione, 2011, p. 568), but one result of emphasizing drills and practice is that English learners in these districts may take part in fewer authentic reading and writing experiences. While no one can deny the importance of explicit instruction for young English learners, such instruction must be balanced by meaningful activities that respect the student's linguistic and cultural heritage (Guccione, 2011). Figure 2.15 lists a few general concepts about other languages and English learners that all teachers should know.

Instructional approaches for English learners

In Chapter 1 we discussed the WIDA table, which lists the levels of English learning with specific "Can Do" tasks for each level. The following section shares ways you can provide English learners access to the core curriculum, keeping in mind their current level of English, while giving them the opportunity to become more proficient. The best learning environment is one that

- permits English learners to use their first language when necessary;
- prepares English learners to learn content in English;
- utilizes individualized or differentiated instruction where possible;
- provides books that are written for different reading levels (e.g., the Ladder series by National Geographic and Scholastic informational books); and
- provides a variety of literacy materials such as newspapers, magazines, pictures, video, online materials, and chapter books (Genesee et al., 2006).

FIGURE 2.15   General concepts about other languages and English learners.

1. Some English learners are literate in their native language; some are literate in their native language and have studied English; some are not literate in their native language and know very little English.

2. Languages differ in phonology, syntax, and orthography.

3. Some languages are alphabetic and all letters are sounded out; others like Chinese use characters with each syllable being one character.

4. Some alphabet languages do not have certain sounds found in English (44 phonemes), while some languages have sounds never uttered in English. For example, Spanish does not contain the short vowel sounds of *a* as in *man,* the short *e* as in *pen,* the short *i* as in *tip,* and the short *u* as in *cup.* Spanish does not have the controlled *r* sound as in the English *arm, fern, girl, for,* and *turtle.*

5. Other languages may share the same letters, but they make different sounds than in English. For example, the long /a/ sound in English is spelled *e* in Spanish.

6. Each language position is sounded differently, which makes some sound combinations possible, others impossible.

7. Some languages have common sounds, but they are placed in different parts of words. For example, Spanish does not have these consonants as final sounds: /b/, /f/, /g/, /p/. Therefore, words like *Bob, sniff, big,* and *pop* are difficult for Spanish-speaking students.

8. English, like French, is a "deep or opaque orthography," meaning that the letter–sound relationships are not consistent. Think about all of the ways the long /a/ can be spelled (e.g., th*ey,* d*ay,* *eig*ht, *ate*).

9. Spanish and Italian are shallow orthographies—the letter–sound relationships in those languages are more consistent than English.

Sources: Bear, D., Helman, L., Templeton, S., Invernizzi, P., & Johnston, F. (2006). *Words Their Way with English Learners.* Upper Saddle River, NJ: Pearson Education, Inc.; Perez-Canado, M. (2005). English-Spanish Spelling: Are They Really Different? *The Reading Teacher, 58*(6), 522–530; Gottardo, A., Chiappe, P., Yan, B., Siegal, L., & Gu, Y. (2006). Relationships Between First and Second Language Phonological Processing Skills and Reading in Chinese–English Speakers Living in English-Speaking Context. *Educational Psychology, 26*(3), 367–393.

With all these linguistic and cultural challenges, where does a teacher begin? First, determine whether a student is literate in his native tongue. Second, find out whether anyone in his home speaks or reads English. Third, read aloud on a daily basis in the classroom so he hears English vocabulary and syntax, which will help develop his comprehension skills. Next, you or an aid should read materials at his WIDA or instructional level to develop his fluency and increase his English vocabulary. Also, don't forget to write along with students as a way of encouraging them to express themselves; writing further develops vocabulary and syntax. Finally, take time to teach specific content vocabulary to English learners by performing word sorts and picture sorts, and using word walls and charts.

When engaging English learners in classroom reading, writing, and speaking activities, you are likely to encounter students *code switching* between two languages— Spanish and English, for example. It is common for emerging bilingual students to insert Spanish words within English sentences when they lack the appropriate English vocabulary; the result may be a sentence like "La consulta era eight dollars" (The office visit was eight dollars). Understand that code switching between languages is a natural part of the learning process. The student who code switches is exhibiting his knowledge of two languages, and this should not be seen as a negative aspect of English language learning.

Sheltered instruction. This model (Echevarria, Vogt, & Short, 2004) is effective for classrooms with English learners. In using *sheltered instruction,* modify your lessons to include the following eight components:

1. *Preparation.* During the preparation stage, identify the lesson's main objective and new vocabulary terms. Gather appropriate trade books for reading along with audio and visual aids and computer programs to clarify difficult concepts.

2. *Building background.* Link the students' background knowledge to the new concepts you are presenting.

3. *Comprehensible input.* Carefully choose words to ensure that the input is comprehensible at the student's level; pictures, graphic organizers, and hand gestures also enhance comprehension.

4. *Multiple strategies.* Use a multiplicity of strategies including KTWL, reciprocal teaching, and mnemonics.

5. *Interaction.* Encourage students to interact with one another using their English skills and to ask you questions.

6. *Practice/application.* Engage students in hands-on activities and encourage them to keep a written journal.

7. *Lesson delivery.* Adjust your speech by speaking slower, enunciating clearly, paraphrasing, giving many examples, providing analogies, and elaborating on students' responses. Write key concepts on the board and continually encourage students to write in their logs, create graphic organizers, and do quick writes.

8. *Review and assessment.* During the review time, informally assess the students' knowledge by asking questions and having students write.

Collaborative reasoning. Middle-school English learners will also benefit from *collaborative reasoning,* or CR (Zhang & Dougherty-Stahl, 2012), which supports CCRA.SL.1: "prepare for and participate effectively in a range of conversations with diverse partners, building on others' ideas and expressing their own clearly and persuasively" (NGACBP & CCSSO, 2010, p. 22). In many classrooms, teachers ask "fast-paced, low-level question–answers" (Zhang and Dougherty-Stahl, 2012, p. 257) that limit the English learner's opportunity to participate. Alternatively, CR is a peer-led, small-group discussion focused on a text with opportunities for various viewpoints. Students come together to discuss a "big question" for each text. For example, in the book *Stone Fox* (Gardiner, 1980), a big question might be: "Should Stone Fox let Willy win the race?" The object of CR is to teach students to work together to find evidence to support their positions, which supports CCRA.R.1: "cite specific textual evidence when writing or speaking to support conclusions drawn from the text" (NGACBP & CCSSO, 2010, p. 10). Also, as a student-led group CR teaches turn-taking and responsibility; the teacher's role is to provide scaffolding from the sidelines as needed to further the group discussion. Collaborative reasoning is similar in many ways to literature study groups used to develop critical thinking among adolescents (Parsons et al., 2011).

For the classroom teacher working with non-English or limited English proficiency students, bilingual books are particularly helpful. As the term implies, these are books written in both English and a second language (often Spanish). Some bilingual books you may want to add to your school or class library are:

Maximilian and the Mystery of the Guardian Angel: A Bilingual Lucha Libre Thriller (2011), by Xavier Garza.

Red Hot Salsa: Bilingual Poems on Being Young and Latino in the United States (2005), edited by Lori Marie Carlson.

The Coyote under the Table; El coyote debajo de la mesa: Folktales Told in Spanish and English (2011), by Joe Hayes.

Dancing with the Devil and Other Tales from Beyond (2012), by Rene Saldana Jr.

The Lemon Tree Caper: A Mickey Rangel Mystery (2011), by Rene Saldana Jr.

My Papa Diego and Me: Memories of My Father and His Art (2009), by Guadalupe Rivera Marin.

Technology. One study examined the effectiveness of three technologies to help students learn English (Hur & Suh, 2012); these were (1) interactive whiteboards, (2) podcasts, and (3) digital storytelling. The use of interactive whiteboards was found to be the most effective. These whiteboards allowed teachers to show pictures or video clips that were relevant to the class discussion. By connecting the pictures to the discussion, students acquired new vocabulary terms more easily. The interactive vocabulary games proved highly motivating to students who were otherwise hesitant to participate in class. The daily podcasts also allowed the students to review the day's lessons; they could hear English spoken fluently, and stop, pause, and replay the podcast to listen at their own pace. Finally, digital storytelling allowed the students to create a digital book report; after reading the book they created a slide presentation to share with the class.

Multimodal texts. English learners may also be motivated through the use of *multimodal texts.* Literacy is no longer defined as solely the ability to read and write; it now includes interacting with a variety of textual forms such as online texts, video games, graphics, videos, and layouts. The relationships among text, pictures, colors, use of space, and typography are rapidly changing. Ajayi (2009) found the integration of multimodal texts employing cell phones, sketching, and advertisements to be particularly appealing to English learners in a junior high school classroom.

One form of multimodal texts, *graphic novels,* capitalizes on both visual images and the written word. The use of graphic novels can help develop English learners' critical literacy skills (Chun, 2009). Here are examples of graphic novels that will appeal to upper elementary and middle-school students and engage them in discussion of diversity and identity:

Maus (1986), by Art Spiegelman

The Complete Persepolis (2007), by Marjane Satrapi

Alia's Mission: Saving the Books of Iraq (2004), by Mark Alan Stamaty

Laika (2007), by Nick Abadzis

The Plain Janes (2004), by Cecil Castellucci

Robot Dreams (2007), by Susan Varon

Anya's Ghost (2011), by Vera Brosgol

Smile (2010), by Raina Telgemeier

Other practices. In addition to the approaches discussed above, many other practices are effective with English learners. Here are a few examples:

- Use the language experience approach (LEA) based on student dictation (see Chapter 7).
- Immerse students in a variety of print experiences.
- Point to the text as you read aloud from trade books.
- Use the process approach, in which students learn to brainstorm, write a rough copy, revise, edit, and share, to encourage writing and sharing.
- Permit students to use their native language at times.
- Encourage working with a partner and in small groups.
- Do dialogue journals between the teacher and student.
- Emphasize comprehension over pronunciation.

- Always connect students' prior knowledge to new concepts.
- Use books that are linked to the cultures of specific students.

For beginning English learners, Bauer and Arazi (2011) recommend the following steps:

- Preview reading texts and new vocabulary through a picture walk.
- Link new vocabulary to the pictures in the book.
- Create bilingual dictionaries.
- Relate new language learning to experiences (e.g., planting a garden).
- Use guided reading instruction in the native language first (utilizing a native speaker from the community) followed by guided reading in English.
- Encourage story retelling focusing on story structure.

One specific challenge for English learners in later grades is dealing with figurative language in reading texts. Commonly used phrases such as "raining cats and dogs" and "go out on a limb" present unique problems for English learners. In fact, figurative language and idioms are common in teacher talk and classroom reading and must be addressed. Palmer and colleagues (2007) recommend the following:

- Teach figurative language through direct explicit instruction.
- Relate each idiomatic expression to the student's real world.
- Explain why figurative language is used in a particular context.
- Model and use figurative language through journaling.
- Create posters of idiomatic expressions to build on visualization learning.

Another strategy recommended for use with English learners is the *think-aloud* (McKeown & Gentilucci, 2007), in which teachers verbalize their thoughts as they solve problems and teach English learners to do the same. The think-aloud strategy is considered part of metacognition related to reading comprehension. It also serves as a pedagogical tool that enhances social interaction within the classroom. The think-aloud strategy allows you to monitor English learners' comprehension by identifying when comprehension of text breaks down and then help them self-correct.

As the percentage of non–English speaking students in our schools increases, you must become more aware of opportunities to encourage oral communication and question asking, develop speaking as well as reading vocabularies, and allow drawing when writing is too difficult. Here is a list of helpful websites for working with English learners:

> **www.cec.sped.org** This is the official website for the Council of Exceptional Children.
>
> **www.epals.com** This site brings students from all over the world together via email and forums.
>
> **www.eslcafe.com** This site for teachers offers discussions forums, quotes, and writing ideas.
>
> **http://iteslj.org** This is the home page for the online *TESL Journal*.
>
> **www.nabe.org** This is the website for the National Association for Bilingual Education.

Assessment and English learners

Many larger school districts have a designated teacher who assesses newly enrolled students and the progress of all English learners. One of the assessments used in this process is the WIDA Measure of Developing English Language (MODEL), a

Mr. Decker creates a language learning experience for himself and his student

The students in Mr. Decker's class are planting seeds and later will write about the experience in their journals. Mr. Decker is having a conversation with Sergio, an emergent bilingual English–Spanish speaker. The teacher is a monolingual English speaker.

Sergio asks, "Mr. Decker, where is my semilla?"

Mr. Decker holds up a seed and says, "Are you asking for your seed?"

"Yes, my seed. I'm going to plantar."

In order to facilitate Sergio's ability to use words in context, Mr. Decker picks up a seed and a cup, and as he hands them to Sergio, he says, "Sergio, here is your seed. You also need dirt and a cup."

Sergio plants his seed in the cup and then goes back to Mr. Decker and says, "Mr. Decker, I'm done. Where's mi diario?" Mr. Decker responds, "I don't understand. What is a diario?"

Sergio points to another student's journal and says, "This."

"Oh, okay, I see," Mr. Decker replies. "*Diario* means 'journal.' Thanks for teaching me a new word. Your journal is on the counter."

Sergio collects his journal, returns to his desk, and happily begins to write about planting seeds. Mr. Decker then assists other students in the class. Both he and Sergio have enjoyed another positive language learning experience together.

series of English language proficiency assessments for kindergarten through grade 12 in the areas of reading, writing, speaking, and listening.

Another standardized assessment that has been used successfully with struggling English learners is the Phonological Awareness Literacy Screening, or PALS. This assessment covers, for grades 1 through 3, word recognition in isolation, developmental spelling, and oral reading in context. Students who do not meet these entry-level standards are further assessed on letter knowledge, phonemic awareness, and concept of word list. The PALS has been most successfully used with Spanish-speaking students (Helman, 2005).

Students at Risk

Despite everyone's best efforts and intentions, some students do not succeed in the elementary and middle school grades. We refer to these students as at risk because they are the group most likely to drop out of high school, fail to acquire the skills necessary to enter the workforce, and possibly become a burden to society. Traditional instructional programs and teaching strategies often do not work with such students (Richardson, 2011; Slavin, 1996). However, some strategies have proven to work with students who are at risk to help them remain in school and eventually graduate. All of these strategies focus on motivating the student to want to succeed.

Many students often find themselves at risk of dropping out of school (Pransky & Bailey, 2002/2003). This is particularly true for students who are African American, Native American, and Hispanic and who have low achievement scores. This *achievement gap* has been the subject of countless debates over the decades but still remains one of the most stubborn problems facing American schools (Evans, 2005; Lewis et al., 2010).

Self-monitoring is an important first-step strategy for students who are at risk. This describes a student's ability to recognize when learning is not taking place, identify the cause of the problem, and make proper adjustments; in this way it is similar to *metacognition*, or the awareness of the learning process. Self-monitoring strategies are most easily taught in the area of reading. Reading is the reconstruction of an author's message through a variety of comprehension skills. When the reader recognizes that comprehension has broken down (e.g., metacognition), she must go back and reread the passage. The rereading strategy is one of the most powerful of self-monitoring tools. Taking notes while reading is another helpful strategy. Teachers need to explain these self-monitoring strategies, model them for students, and then encourage students to use them.

Students who are at risk often are not motivated to learn because they have experienced so much failure in the past. Consequently, they prefer not to risk more failure. There is a high correlation between school achievement and motivation; thus, these students must be encouraged to try. This entails explaining that risk taking is a part of learning and that an occasional failure should not deter the learner. Students who perform well are not afraid to take risks, while other students must be taught that risk taking is part of learning (Gee, 2001).

That success breeds success may seem obvious, but we know that once students experience success in one subject area they are more likely to put forth a greater effort in other academic areas. The students who are weakest and have the greatest risk of dropping out often have experienced years of failure. Their school experiences have taught them not to try and not to take chances on being wrong (Cambourne, 2002).

Working with students who are at risk, therefore, requires creating situations where they can experience success. For example, in-class and homework assignments can be shortened so that the student can complete them successfully. For reading assignments, provide them with a detailed study guide that directs them to the passages containing answers to the questions. Teach the necessary vocabulary terms for each content area; do not assume that students who are at-risk understand the meaning of a word. Make sure they keep vocabulary sheets with definitions handy for easy reference. Finally, these students need tangible evidence of even the smallest successes. Do this with graphs that document progress over time, written comments, and positive letters to caregivers.

Subgoals are important for many reasons. For students who are at risk, typical school assignments often seem impossible. This is because often teachers create long-term assignments with a single end goal, like completing a term paper within four weeks. Such an assignment may seem overwhelming to these students. A better approach would be to design assignments with a series of smaller, attainable subgoals that work toward achieving a main goal. Outlining techniques and graphic organizers also help students focus on smaller goals rather than overreacting to the final goal. For example, in writing a term paper, students should be given credit for the subgoals of taking notes, making an outline, and creating a first rough draft. The final version of the term paper should not determine the student's final grade, but simply serve as one piece of the larger writing project.

Cooperative learning strategies are another way to help students who are at risk, but many schools today are based on competitive or individualistic models (Ediger, 2001). This is a disaster for most students who are at risk. For example, in a classroom set up to emphasize competition through spelling bees, timed exercises, and handwriting awards, students who are weak in these areas invariably experience the most failure. An alternative model is one that emphasizes group cooperation, information sharing, and working toward a single common goal. In the cooperative model, all students can experience success because everyone in the group is concerned with achieving a single goal. This requires a division of labor, interdependence, and cooperation among group members. Although individual accountability is still important, it is reduced in favor of the group effort. Finally, cooperative learning models also further interpersonal and social skills along with content knowledge.

Working with students who are at risk means that your role will change. Typically, teachers are rewarded for controlling behaviors through lectures, rewards, and punishments. For students who are at risk, you will need to encourage, not cajole, your students. Allow students to work in groups, to serve as resources for one another, and to help answer each other's questions. You can move around the room and coach students on a one-to-one basis. Give students the autonomy to work on their own, exhibit independence, and come to believe in their own abilities to succeed (Croninger & Lee, 2001).

One-to-one tutoring has proven to be the single best instructional approach with students who are at risk (Elbaum et al., 2000). However, many educators reject this model because it is both expensive and unrealistic; more money would have to be spent to hire more teachers to allow enough time during the school day for such tutoring to take place. Yet experts in the field, such as Robert Slavin, have concluded that even limited time spent on one-to-one tutoring makes a significant difference for students who are at risk. This means ultimately that schools must make a greater commitment to recruiting volunteers and hiring the paraprofessionals needed for a large-scale tutoring program.

Approximately one thousand school districts in the United States have approached this problem by adopting *Communities in Schools (CIS)* programs. These programs are committed to connecting community resources with schools, families, and individual students who are at risk. CIS programs begin in the elementary grades and continue through high school. One example is Charlotte-Mecklenburg, North Carolina, where CIS serves 6,000 students across 21 schools. Volunteers from community and civic organizations become tutors and mentors for students who are at risk; dentists provide free dental exams; and volunteers from the Junior League teach students about the importance of service projects in the community (Communities in Schools of North Carolina, 2011).

Despite the challenges, research has shown that students who are at risk will benefit from the following best practices (Bell, 2002/2003):

- practicing reading skills in a one-to-one situation
- teaching higher order thinking skills to all students
- reviewing and reteaching at the beginning of each period
- initiating student participation through random selection
- requiring students to speak and write in complete sentences
- fostering an emotional connection to content by allowing students to choose a writing topic or a book that interests them
- demonstrating patience and caring

Students with Disabilities

Students with disabilities were once isolated from the rest of the school population. Today's classrooms include students with a great variety of abilities and disabilities. In Chapter 1, we introduced IDEA, which requires that "a free and appropriate education and related services be provided in the least restrictive environment," and that an IEP be written for each qualifying student. In this section, we discuss some of the disabilities mentioned in the legislation.

Attention deficit hyperactivity disorder

One of the "other health impairments" identified in IDEA is attention deficit hyperactivity disorder (ADHD). There are three types of ADHD: hyperactivity, impulsivity, and inattention. A student who is hyperactive is usually in

read RESEARCH practice

Observe an elementary- or a middle-school classroom that includes students who are identified as differently abled. What specific needs do you note among the students? How does the teacher differentiate instruction to meet the needs of his or her students?

constant motion and has difficulty sitting still and staying on task. Students who are impulsive often act before they think, blurt out answers in class, and sometimes exhibit outbursts of anger. The student who is inattentive often appears to be day-dreaming in class, is unable to focus on a task, or is easily distracted by other voices or movement in the room. Students with ADHD can exhibit one or all of these characteristics. Only a trained psychologist may diagnose ADHD; teachers are not trained to diagnose ADHD and can only report the behaviors they observe.

Segal and Smith (2012) of Harvard Medical School suggest the following tips for teachers working with students with ADHD, augmented with tips on teaching language arts:

1. Use creative hands-on activities in small groups and individually. In language arts, encourage these students to draw or create a 3-D model as a response to a story or informational text.
2. Give directions in small segments and restate them often. In language arts, give students small segments to read and then ask them to retell what they have read.
3. Help students to organize their homework using personal contracts. In language arts, create one folder for writing and another for reading logs.
4. Insist on high levels of participation and call on students. In language arts, ask younger students to hold one side of a big book as you read to the class. Older students can become the discussion leader during small group book conversations.

Autism

Autism is a neurological disorder that affects individuals to varying degrees with varying characteristics. Its primary characteristics include language problems, repetitive behaviors, and difficulty with social interactions. Some students who are autistic do not speak at all, while others speak constantly and in inappropriate situations (Kantrowitz & Scelfo, 2006). Other characteristics may include a failure to relate or bond with people; under- or over-responsiveness to sensory stimulation; a flat affect (speaking without emotion); body rocking or hand tapping; and resistance to environmental change. Although not all students who are autistic exhibit all of these characteristics or to the same degree, autism is nevertheless one of the most severe childhood disabilities. Today, more children are diagnosed with autism than ever before (National Dissemination Center for Children with Disabilities, 2010).

In language arts instruction, techniques and materials usually will have to be modified for students who are autistic. A strict routine is often recommended because a change in environment often agitates these students. Kluth and Dar-mody-Lathan (2003) recommend the following:

- In addition to reading and writing, include listening, drawing, and sign language activities.
- Capitalize on students' interests, allowing long periods of time for a single activity.
- Use a range of visuals, including graphic organizers.
- Read aloud to help with fluency, comprehension, and word recognition.
- Encourage various types of expression and communication (e.g., puppets).

Regardless of the instructional topic or method, strive to create an appropriate educational environment for students who are autistic. Answers to the questions posed in Figure 2.16 should be helpful in establishing a positive learning environment for students with autistic behaviors.

FIGURE 2.16 Questions for assisting students who are autistic.

- Which teaching strategies have been successful with this student in the past?
- Which procedures can be applied in the classroom without extensive support?
- What is the expected effect of any medications prescribed for the child?
- To what degree have the following behaviors been observed in an education setting: unresponsiveness to social stimuli, gaze aversion, overselective response, language disorders, and excessive fantasy and delusions? How disruptive were these behaviors?

Answers to the final question in Figure 2.16, regarding students' behaviors, will be particularly helpful when preparing other students in the classroom to accept their classmate in a positive way. The other students should be prepared for some atypical behaviors and know how to depersonalize their occurrence. Explain that these are not intentional behaviors and the student who is autistic may want to interact with others but not know how. The positive learning environment you create will allow even the student who is autistic to experience success in the classroom.

Deafness

In today's classroom many students who are deaf are being mainstreamed with their hearing peers. This was not the case twenty years ago when these students were excluded from the regular classroom. Thus, it is important for all classroom teachers to have some knowledge of how deaf students learn.

Most children who are deaf learn American Sign Language (ASL) or Signing Exact English (SEE). ASL is an actual language with a vocabulary, sentence structure, regional variations, and unique grammatical rules. For deaf students familiar with ASL, learning to read and write according to English rules is similar to learning a new language. You will need to understand the phonemic, syntactic, and morphological differences between ASL and English in order to help students who are deaf. In English, unknown words can be understood through the use of context clues, whereas ASL uses different words to identify different concepts. For example, the two sentences "The girl is running the race" and "The refrigerator is running cold" represent two different concepts that cannot be understood through context clues alone. Therefore, in ASL the word *running* would be signed in two different ways (Marschark & Hauser, 2012). Unlike ASL, SEE is a sign language system that makes "visible everything that is not heard" (SEE Center, 2014). SEE does not modify the vocabulary or the syntax as ASL does; therefore, deaf students "can see clearly what is said in English" (SEE Center, 2014).

By law, school districts must provide a sign interpreter for the deaf student in your classroom. If you have a sign interpreter in your class, encourage your students to learn some signing so they can communicate with their classmate.

Learning disabilities

Those with learning disabilities constitute the largest group of students with disabilities in the U.S. school system. A *learning disability* is defined as a "disorder in one or more of the basic psychological processes involved in understanding or in using spoken or written language, which may manifest itself in an imperfect ability to listen, think, speak, read, write, spell or to do mathematical calculations" (IDEA, 2004).

These students may also manifest problems in spoken language and exhibit inattention, hyperactivity, impulsivity, and a low tolerance for frustration. Such students are generally part of the regular classroom and consistently achieve below their learning potential (Giangreco, 2007).

The National Information Center for Children and Youth with Disabilities (2000) suggests that teachers who have students with learning disabilities do the following:

- Capitalize on students' strengths; for example, a student who struggles with writing may be able to draw detailed illustrations of learned concepts.
- Provide structure and clear expectations by writing assignments on the board and providing rubrics in advance of assignments.
- Provide opportunities for success; for example, permit a student who struggles with reading to practice a small passage before she reads it to the class.
- Allow for flexibility in classroom procedures; for example, use an audio recorder instead of written notes and texts.
- Use computers/tablets for practice and teach word processing.
- Provide positive reinforcement of appropriate social skills and give appropriate praise for the student's success.
- Allow for the gift of time for the student to grow and mature; accept approximations when learning new concepts and skills.

For students with learning disabilities, learning to read and write is particularly difficult. In some cases, previous negative life experiences as well as literacy learning itself make the acquisition of reading and writing a challenge. Research suggests that early intervention by such programs as Reading Recovery can benefit such students (Jones et al., 2005). Reading Recovery is a one-to-one intervention, conducted by specially trained teachers, intended for first grade students (but sometimes used with second and third graders) who have been identified with serious learning needs. The results are often astounding, with reading achievement accelerated much beyond normal first grade levels.

Students Who Are Academically Gifted

Educators disagree about what constitutes the best learning environment for the student who is gifted: a pull-out program or remaining in the regular classroom. Advocates for the pull-out program argue that the traditional scope and sequence curriculum is too restrictive and does not permit the student to grow. Large class size may hinder the teacher from giving the student who is gifted the attention he needs. To support these students changes need to be made in the curriculum to allow them to (1) reach their potential, (2) engage in in-depth study of a topic, (3) practice divergent thinking, and (4) demonstrate real-life problem solving.

Although there are no national guidelines for working with students who are gifted, most states have legislation that provides funding for gifted programs.

Characteristics of the student who is gifted

The National Association for Gifted Children (2003) classifies students who are gifted as those who (1) have an IQ of 130 or above on the Wechsler Intelligence Scale for Students (WISC III), (2) achieve a score of two standard deviations above the mean, (3) have a score of 97th percentile or higher on standardized achievement

---

FIGURE **2.17** Characteristics of giftedness.

1. Asks lots of questions.
2. Possesses lots of information on specific things.
3. Is very curious; wants to know "Why?" or "How?"
4. Has concern and is sensitive about social, political, and global issues.
5. Has own ideas about how something should be done.
6. Enjoys debating.
7. Has a better reason for not doing something than you have for doing it.
8. Becomes impatient with work that is not perfect.
9. Expects others to be perfect.
10. Finds assignments unchallenging.
11. Thinks deeply and differently about things.
12. Enjoys exploratory levels of learning.
13. Loves abstract ideas.
14. Has a sense of humor.
15. Has a passionate interest in a specific area.
16. Has many interests and hobbies.
17. Can make personal application of concepts.
18. Has a high level of energy.
19. Sees relationships between ideas.
20. Has a good memory.
21. Does not begin a task if there is a possibility of failure.
22. Easily sees subtle cause-and-effect relationships.
23. Prefers to work alone.

Source: Adapted from the Gifted Education Program in Yukon, Oklahoma.

---

tests, or (4) have extraordinary talent in the visual or performing arts. However, experts in the field now contend that other factors besides national and state test scores should be used. For example, it is well known that "low income and minority students continue to be underrepresented in gifted programs" (Renzulli, 2011, p. 61). To change this pattern schools need to look at creative talents and students with high motivation and not merely compare them to national test score norms. See Figure 2.17 for characteristics of giftedness.

The key for the regular classroom teacher working with students who are gifted or students with a disability is collaboration with other specialists in the school and maintaining close contact with caregivers. A team approach is the best approach. Working together the team can create a student profile that addresses student interests, disabilities, and extracurricular activities. A written contract is often helpful and can be drawn up and signed by all participants.

Classroom activities for the student who is gifted

For the student who is academically gifted and spends the majority of her time in the regular classroom, we recommend two models: the enrichment triad and compacting.

Enrichment triad model. This model was designed by Joseph Renzulli and Susan Reis (Reis & Renzulli, 2009) and includes three types of enrichment activities. Type I enrichment activities are designed to expose students to new topics and may involve a Bloom's taxonomy task. (See Figure 2.18 for the taxonomy and Figure 2.19 for an example task.)

Type II enrichment activities focus on the development of higher-level thinking skills. These activities might include research projects in the library, higher-level problem solving, and community service projects. Type III enrichment activities involve real-life problem solving. Usually done in small groups, these activities

Your children need your presence more than your presents.

JESSE JACKSON

Bloom's taxonomy: Type I activity.   **FIGURE 2.18**

Knowledge:	Simple recall of learned facts. *Student will bring to mind what was read, seen, or heard.*
Comprehension:	Translating or interpreting material from one form to another. *Student explains or predicts what did or will happen.*
Application:	Ability to use learned material in personal life. *Student applies rules, concepts, or theories to daily life.*
Analysis:	Ability to break down material into its components. *Student will identify the parts, be able to see the relationships among parts, and recognize the organization of all parts.*
Synthesis:	Ability to put parts together to form a new whole. *Student will research various materials, recognize similarities and differences, and be able to give an oral or written presentation.*
Evaluation:	Ability to judge the value of the material studied. *After studying the material, student will give a value statement with clearly defined criteria.*

Source: Adapted from Bloom, *Taxonomy of Educational Objectives, Handbook I: Cognitive Domain* (1956).

Type I activity: Bloom's taxonomy task on *Color* by Ruth Heller.   **FIGURE 2.19**

1. Explain the four stages used by a printer when applying color to a page in a book.
2. Explain the magic of creating secondary colors.
3. Using the supplies on the table, mix colors to create your own color wheel.
4. Explain which primary or secondary colors create black.
5. Using four transparencies, draw a picture by using each of the transparencies as part of the entire picture; then place the transparencies over each other to show your complete picture.
6. Survey your classmates to find out which color is their favorite and create a bar graph to show the results of the survey.

require finding a solution to a real problem and may involve interviewing city officials, inventing a new product, or creating a written work that is new and original. All three types of enrichment should be implemented in the regular classroom. Some activities are done individually, while others may be better accomplished by working in small groups.

Compacting. Often, students who are gifted become bored in the regular classroom. The pace is too slow or the work not challenging. One successful program for working with these students is known as *curriculum compacting* (Coil, 2008). Simply stated, curriculum compacting allows students who are gifted to skip work they already know and instead substitute more challenging activities. This can be done in any subject, including math, reading, writing, science, and social studies.

Ms. Adams' Quest activity inspires curiosity for her students who are gifted

For five years Ms. Abbie Adams has been teaching sixth-grade students who are gifted in an urban school in Tulsa, Oklahoma. The curriculum she uses emphasizes integrated math and science group projects and advanced textbook assignments in social studies. Her language arts curriculum includes advanced readings in chapter books but does not seem inspiring to her students. This semester she has decided to try something different. Her idea also meets CCSS W.6.2, which requires students to "write informative/explanatory texts to examine a topic and convey ideas, concepts, and information through the selection, organization, and analysis of relevant content" (NGACBP & CCSSO, 2010, p. 42).

"Class, I noticed that you seem to be lacking the energy that normally you bring to your assignments. Therefore, I've decided to try something new to spice things up."

Immediately the students begin whispering among themselves and a few hands go up.

Ms. Adams then states: "I'd like you to wait on questions until I've had a chance to explain the assignment."

"Will we get a choice on what we do?" John in the back calls out.

"Yes, John, you will get a choice," Ms. Adams responds. "Now let me explain what I have in mind. This assignment is called a *quest*. A quest is something you physically do, preferably outside of class, on your own time. Then you will be asked to write it up and present it orally to the class."

More student hands go up and questions begin to fly around the room. Ms. Adams holds her hand up until they are quiet and she can continue.

"There is one big stipulation to the project you choose: it must be something you have never done before."

The students look puzzled. Finally, Ann asks, "What do you mean something we have never done before? I don't understand."

"Well, for example, perhaps you have played softball, basketball, and football. Then playing one of those sports would not be a quest. On the other hand, if you joined a volleyball team for the first time, that would be a quest. Or perhaps you have never gone skiing before—that would be a quest."

"Do we have to try a sport?" asks Roberto.

"No. That was just an example." Ms. Adams continues to give examples, writing ideas on the board. "Maybe you have never baked a cake before. Or seen a foreign film with subtitles. Or tried to play the guitar. Or visited a particular museum. The possibilities are endless. Take some time now to brainstorm among yourselves and make a list of possible ideas. I'll come around and check your lists."

Now the class is caught up in the newness of the idea and begins talking animatedly among themselves. Many interesting possibilities are generated. A time line of two months is set. A deadline for the rough draft paper is due in one month. As a group, the class decides that five minutes will be allowed for each oral presentation and that props can be used.

Curriculum compacting involves three steps. First, the teacher articulates the goals for a particular chapter or unit. Second, the teacher identifies students who have already achieved the goals; standardized test scores can be used here. These students take the post-test to establish exactly which skills they have mastered; the teacher lists in her notebook the skills and concepts not yet mastered. The third step is to establish a contract for the completion of the project, research, or self-directed study. Figure 2.20 shows an example compactor form.

Through the use of both the enrichment triad model and the curriculum compacting model, the needs of the student who is gifted can be met within the typical classroom structure.

Listed below are helpful websites for working with students of all abilities:

www.ascd.org The Association for Supervision and Curriculum Development website provides information on the differentiated classroom.

www.dana.org This organization focuses on brain research and education issues.

Sample compactor form.   **FIGURE** 2.20

The Compactor

Student's name   Age   Teachers

Conference date   Grade   Caregivers

Topics to be covered; tests used to prove competency	Parts of chapter to be completed to ensure competency	Enrichment tasks to be completed

Source: Adapted from J. Renzulli and L. H. Smith (1978), *A Guidebook for Developing Individualized Educational Programs for Gifted and Talented Students.* Copyright © Creative Learning Press, Mansfield Center, CT.

http://eric.org The ERIC Clearinghouse provides information on learning disabilities and students who are gifted.

www.nagc.org This is the site for the National Association for Gifted Children.

www.newhorizons.org/blab.html This site includes online discussions regarding brain research.

www.criticalthinking.com This site offers excellent critical thinking materials for pre-K–12 students.

TEACHING ACTIVITIES ②

TEACHING ALL STUDENTS

1 Home survey

Ask your students to survey their homes. What kinds of books, magazines, newspapers, and electronic sources of information can they find? Have each student make a bar graph of his or her own results. Next, tally all the results in a classwide bar graph poster to be displayed in the room. Discuss the results in class and ways to increase reading for pleasure at home. *Recommended for elementary grades.*

2 Daily schedule

Many young students do not know how to schedule their time. First, discuss the importance of scheduling your time throughout the day and then teach your students how to keep a daily and weekly schedule. Next, ask students to keep an hourly schedule of their time for one week. Finally, ask them to chart the best time for them to schedule their daily homework. *Recommended for elementary grades.*

3   Living languages

Contextual clues are one important way students learn new words. In order to increase students' awareness and appreciation of languages other than English, give students five sentences written in English but with a non–English word embedded in them. Allow students to work in small groups to discover the meaning of the embedded word. Afterward they can illustrate their new word and create a class dictionary. *Recommended for elementary grades.*

4   Community literacy hunt

First teach an in-class lesson on what is meant by *functional literacy:* reading and writing activities in the real world. Next, instruct students as they are out in the community to observe as many examples of community literacy as possible: street signs, store window displays, advertisements, menus, billboards, policemen writing tickets, waitresses taking orders, and so on. Compile a class list and display it as a classroom poster. *Recommended for intermediate grades.*

5   Reading/writing for understanding Native American culture

As a class, have your students read Sherman Alexie's first-person narrative *The Absolutely True Diary of a Part-Time Indian* (2007). After discussing the book, divide students into small groups to research the Native American tribes in your state. For example, Oklahoma has 19 different tribes scattered throughout the state. Nevada, New Mexico, Arizona, South Dakota, and Utah also have many large Indian reservations. What specific challenges do native peoples face? *Recommended for intermediate grades.*

6   Writing in another language

This activity is designed to help your English speaking students understand how difficult it is for students who speak Arabic or Hmong to learn how to write English words. Together with your students, view a YouTube video instructing how to write in Arabic (preview the video beforehand to ensure it is helpful; you may also wish to begin the viewing at a certain point rather than at the beginning). Invite students to practice along with the video. Writing from right to left is much different, as are all the symbols. After some practice, ask students to write the first line as fast as they can without any errors. This is just a brief experience of what it is like for Arabic students to learn our English alphabet.

7   Listening to and interpreting a song in another language

Together with your students watch the YouTube video of Rimi Natsukawa singing "Nada" without English subtitles (https://www.youtube.com/watch?v=J-9fRIyGJJk). Ask students to surmise what they think the song's message is. Then discuss how difficult it is to understand the message of an unknown language even when there is a video to view. After the discussion, watch a video of "Begin" with English subtitles (www.youtube.com/watch?v=dlDX2zUYcVI) and discuss if students correctly interpreted the song the first time around.

8   Walk in another's shoes

This writing activity engages students' imagination, prior knowledge, and creativity while building on cultural awareness. Write the sentence *Never judge a person until you have walked two days in his or her moccasins* on the board. Have the students discuss possible meanings of this sentence. Next, have the students form small groups and give each group a picture of a kind of "moccasin"—a wooden shoe from Holland or a sandal from Guatemala, for example. Ask them to imagine that they are the person who owns the "moccasin" and to write a story about experiences they have had with their "moccasins." Students can share their stories by acting them out, reading them aloud, or placing them in a notebook in the learning center.

9 Pen pals

Contact a special education teacher near your school and ask if his or her class can be pen pals with your students. The two classes can then share letters on a weekly basis. At the end of the semester, invite your pen pals to campus for a pen pal party. You and your students can plan appropriate activities that everyone can enjoy.

10 Understanding the Deaf experience

To help your students experience what it may feel like to be Deaf, view a short educational video with the sound muted. Afterward, ask students to write a paragraph explaining what they learned from the video, even with no sound. Then invite them to share their ideas with classmates.

11 Reading and discussing literature for understanding individuals with special needs

One goal of every teacher should be to have students respect others, including classmates from other cultures, races, and who have special needs. Literature (see the list below) is a great way to engage students in conversations about students who have special needs. *Junkyard Wonders* is a good first choice because the story features more than one character with a special need. After reading the book to the class, divide the students into groups of three and ask them to discuss their thoughts about the name the teacher called the students with special needs. If they think it is a good name, have them explain why and cite specific phrases or pictures that support their stance. If they think it may have offended the characters in the book, have them explain why and provide evidence. If the group thinks it is an offensive name, have them rename the group and explain why theirs is a better choice. This activity aligns with the second grade CCSS SL.2: students must "participate in collaborative conversations with diverse partners about grade 2 topics and texts" (p. 23) and with CCRA.R.1: "cite specific textual evidence when writing or speaking to support conclusions drawn from the text" (NGACBP & CCSSO, 2010, p. 10).

You can engage students in similar conversations using any of the other books mentioned below or listed in Appendix B.3. The goal for such discussions is to get students to think critically about what it means to have a special need and how the person who has no choice in the matter must feel. Never assume, however, that students with disabilities are necessarily interested in reading about other individuals with disabilities.

Books in which the protagonist has some type of special need:

- *Worst Enemies/Best Friends* (2008), by Annie Bryant (dyslexia)
- *Sparky's Excellent Misadventures: My ADD Journal by Me, Sparky* (1999), by Phyllis Carpenter (ADD)
- *Joey Pigza Swallowed the Key* (2011), by Jack Gantos (special education)
- *How Dyslexic Benny Became a Star* (2012), by Joe Griffith (dyslexia)
- *The Gift-Giver* (2005), by Joyce Hansen (dyslexia)

- *How Many Days Until Tomorrow?* (2000), by Caroline Janover (dyslexia)
- *Shelly the Hyperactive Turtle* (2001), by Deborah Moss (ADHD)
- *Thank You, Mr. Falkner* (1998), by Patricia Polacco (learning disability)
- *Junkyard Wonders* (2010), by Patricia Polacco (special learning needs)
- *The Alphabet War: Story about Dyslexia* (2004), by Burton Robb (dyslexia)
- *Niagara Falls, or Does It?* (2003), by Henry Winkler (dyslexia)
- *The Goodenoughs Get in Sync* (2010), by Carol Stock Kranowitz (sensory processing issues)
- *"I Get It! It Get It!" How John Figures It Out* (2011), by Loraine Alderman (auditory processing disorder)

Recommended for elementary grades.

12 Gifted reading/writing activity

Introduce older students to quality chapter books (Newbery Award winners, Newbery honor books, etc.) and have them do a modeled writing following the style of the author. For example, a modern fantasy with powerful writing and beautiful descriptions that will capture the imagination of intermediate grade students is Kathi Appelt's *The Underneath* (2008). Begin by reading the book aloud so the students can hear the beauty of the language. Discuss the story line of love, hate, and revenge among a cat, a dog, a giant alligator, a huge water moccasin, and a man all living in the remote bayou swamplands. Explain the author's use of myth and fantasy. Finally, ask the students to try their hand at their own modern fantasy. *Recommended for intermediate grades.*

TECHNOLOGY IN THE CLASSROOM

The CCSS reading, writing, speaking, and listening standards emphasize the need for students to

- "Integrate and evaluate content presented in diverse media and formats" (CCRA.R.7; NGACBP & CCSSO, 2010, p. 10).
- "Use technology, including the Internet, to produce and publish writing and to interact and collaborate with others" (CCRA.W.6; NGACBP & CCSSO, 2010, p. 18).
- "Integrate and evaluate information presented in diverse media and formats, including visually, quantitatively, and orally" (CCRA.SL.2; NGACBP & CCSSO, 2010, p. 22).
- "Make strategic use of digital media and visual displays of data to express information and enhance understanding of presentations" (CCRA.SL.5; NGACBP & CCSSO, 2010, p. 22).

With so many standards addressing technology, you can be sure you will be using electronic readers, videos, audio devices, and computers in new and interesting ways.

Teachers find that reader response activities for some students are enhanced through various social networking websites such as Facebook and Twitter. These sites can be used within a school district to link students together in collaborative projects and give teachers a chance to interact with other teachers beyond their school (Colwell, Hutchinson, & Reinking, 2012). Integrating digital technology into the language arts program provides great opportunities for expanded learning. Of course, you must carefully supervise such activities.

Taranto and colleagues (2011) also advocate for the use of technology with middle-school students. Because it is such a natural part of their lives, adolescents will naturally gravitate toward technology in the classroom. Technologies such as Blogger.com allow students to transform a read-only online experience to a read and write online experience. In one middle-school language arts class, Wikispace.com is used as a discussion forum for books; students post their comments on a novel, answer critical thinking questions posted by the teacher, and then get to see their peers' responses (Taranto et al., 2011). The teachers involved with this project feel that using the blog and wiki in conjunction with the discussion board enhances the collaborative learning and leads to more peer-to-peer sharing. Online technology utilizing blogs has also been used successfully in collaborative writing projects between university and middle-school students (Witte, 2007).

Similarly, Grisham and Wolsey (2006) found that technology intersected with middle-school students and literacy instruction. To get students engaged in the reading of *The Breadwinner* (Ellis, 2001), a story of a girl living in Afghanistan under the Taliban, the teacher had her students write their comments in electronic threaded discussions with other classes using First Class (her school subscribed to the client software). The teacher found that the use of the technology not only enhanced learning but led to a greater sense of community among the students. They got to choose the groups they would work in, engage in threaded discussion groups, and share information about other books they read, including *The Old Man and the Sea* (Hemingway, 1952), *She Said Yes* (Bernall, 1999), *A Child Called It* (Pelzer, 1995), *Esperanza Rising* (Ryan, 1995), and *The Watsons Go to Birmingham–1963* (Curtis, 1995). The chat room discussions posted in real time made for a heightened literacy discussion.

SUMMARY

As a teacher, you must acquaint yourself with the educational environment of the community in which you work. Working with caregivers, learning about the home environment of students, and discovering the resources in the community are all part of a teacher's job.

Planning a successful language arts program takes time and effort. Understanding your students' varied learning styles, interests, and how multiple intelligences impact learning will guide your preparations. Students at risk of failure also pose particular challenges that also must be addressed.

Effective teachers meet the needs of all their students, including students with learning and physical disabilities as well as students who are gifted. And, of course, teachers across the United States must understand how to work effectively with students whose native language is something other than English.

field AND practicum ACTIVITIES

1. ORAL LANGUAGE DEVELOPMENT REFLECTION. Ask your supervising teacher about the culture of the community in which the school is based. What is the nature of the adult–child interaction that seems predominant? Then, take time to reflect on the oral development of the students in your class. How have their interactions with adults affected their language acquisition? Does the oral development differ between groups in which the adult–child interaction is different? Provide support for your stance. How might the vocabulary development in the two groups differ? Again give evidence for your stance.

2. USING WORDLESS BOOKS TO IMPROVE THE ORAL LANGUAGE OF ENGLISH LEARNERS. Contact a teacher in a local school and ask if he or she has any English learners whose learning disability affects their writing. Ask the teacher if you may work with the student for a couple of weeks on some writing activities. The first time you work with the student, share a wordless book and ask her to write a story on the sticky notes you provide. Afterward, have the student read the story to you and take note of the story's details. Discuss any words that the student attempted to write but either misused or misspelled. Add any word the student wants to remember into her personal dictionary.

3. WORKING WITH STUDENTS WHO ARE GIFTED AND ACADEMICALLY TALENTED. Contact a gifted education teacher in a local public school. Ask the teacher if you may observe and then assist in the classroom throughout the semester. What type of questioning tactics does the teacher use? How do the students interact with one another? What type of questions do the students ask? What are the special needs of these students?

Planning and Delivering Effective Language Arts Instruction

CHAPTER 3

OBJECTIVES

After reading this chapter, you should be able to accomplish the following objectives:

1. Name some of the general principles of learning.
2. Explain the concept of extrinsic motivation.
3. Discuss the four learning domains.
4. Explain the term *kidwatching*.
5. Describe the different learning styles.
6. Explain the theory of multiple intelligences.
7. Describe the teaching strategies presented in the chapter that include all types of learners and learning domains.

INTRODUCTION

Teachers bring many different perspectives to teaching (see Chapter 1 for a review). Some convey specific skills to their students, while others promote a broad-based love of knowledge in their students. Many teachers today use a *balanced* or comprehensive approach in the sense that they teach skills and are concerned about improving their students' test scores, but at the same time, they respect their students' interests and provide them with meaningful learning choices. No matter what their perspective, all good teachers plan for effective instruction.

Effective teaching and student learning does not happen by accident. Good teachers plan their instruction carefully. They spend time creating daily lesson plans for each subject they will teach each hour of the day. They consider their students' special needs and differentiate assignments so all students are motivated and challenged. They also create weekly plans for all student activities and unit plans for long-term projects. They search for all types of narrative and informational texts, print books and e-books, and online sites and resources that support the unit of study. They create projects that encourage independent work as well as small-group cooperative work. Teacher planning also involves finding time to grade students' papers and projects in a timely manner, preparing meaningful homework assignments, evaluating student journals and portfolios, conferencing with individual students, communicating regularly with parents, keeping careful records, and preparing students for standardized tests. Effective teachers also attend conferences and workshops in order to stay current on state standards, new technologies, and effective strategies.

In addition to knowing the learning theories presented in Chapter 1, you will need to consider the general principles about learning and effective instruction we discuss in this chapter. Effective teachers are always learning!

GENERAL PRINCIPLES ABOUT LEARNING

Consider the following general principles about student learning as you plan daily lessons. As you discuss these with your classmates, add to the list principles you have learned through your observations.

- *Positive attitudes toward learning and the learner are essential.* For both teachers and students alike, a positive attitude is crucial for success. The classroom should be a safe, friendly, positive environment for everyone. A teacher's behavior in the classroom, the way he talks to and relates to his students, influences their attitudes toward him, the classroom, and learning in general. Wong and Wong (2009) found that the emotional tone of a classroom is measured by the quality of the positive human interactions.

■ *Learning is constructive and meaningful.* For students to internalize learning, they must construct meaning for themselves and apply that knowledge to their personal lives. That is, understanding comes through personal meaning and identification. The first-grade student in rural North Dakota who is trying to understand her teacher's explanation of a New York City skyscraper must connect it first to something known, a large wheat silo or 36 grocery stores stacked on top of each other. Middle-school students in Washington, DC, preparing for a field trip to the Smithsonian's Holocaust Museum could choose a book from a list provided by the teacher to read before making the trip (see Figure 3.1).

■ *Learning is a habit of the mind.* Students are naturally curious and creative, so strive to create a classroom environment that builds on that curiosity and creativity while

---

Holocaust reading. **FIGURE 3.1**

Anne Frank: Life in Hiding (1988), by Johanna Hurwitz

Anne Frank: The Anne Frank House Authorized: Graphic Biography (2010), by Sid Jacobson and Ernie Colon

Annexed (2010), by Sharon Dogar and Margarita Engle

The Berlin Boxing Club (2011), by Robert Sharenow

Behind the Bedroom Wall (1997), by Laura E. Williams

The Boy in Striped Pajamas: A Fable (2006), by John Boyne

The Boy Who Dared (2008), by Susan Campbell Bartoletti

Darkness over Denmark: The Danish Resistance and the Rescue of the Jews (2002), by Ellen Levine

Emil and Karl (2006), by Yankev Glatshteyn, translated by Jeffrey Shandler

Hitler Youth: Growing Up in Hitler's Shadow (2005), by Susan Campbell Bartoletti

If I Should Die Before I Wake (1994), by Han Nolan

Is It Night or Day? (2010), by Fern Chapman

The Island on Bird Street (1984), by Uri Orlev

Malka (2003), by Mirjam Pressler, translated by Brian Murdoch

Memories of Survival (2005), by Esther Krintz and Bernice Steinhardt

Milkweed (2003), by Jerry Spinelli

Remember WWII: Kids Who Survived Tell Their Stories (2005), by Dorinda Nicholson

The Secret of Priest's Grotto: A Holocaust Survival Story (2007), by Peter Lane Taylor

Tell Them We Remember (1994), by Susan D. Bacharach

Terezin: Voices From the Holocaust (2011), by Ruth Thomson

Then (2010), by Morris Gleitzman

Tunes for Bears to Dance To (1992), by Robert Cormier

What World Is Left? (2008), by Monique Polak

The World Must Know (1993), by Michael Berenbaum

Yellow Star (2006), by Jennifer Roy

also requiring discipline and responsibility. Learners need to be engaged, make a commitment to learning, and be willing to take risks. Risk taking and divergent thinking should be encouraged and rewarded if good learning habits are to be developed.

■ *The curriculum should be developmentally appropriate.* Just as students grow physically from one year to the next, their cognitive and affective skills also develop over time. Your goal is to design activities that are appropriate for your classes and for individual students. Remember that any given classroom includes students with a wide range of cognitive abilities; therefore, you must break down complex concepts for some students and furnish additional resources and challenges to others so they can research a topic in greater depth. Your effectiveness as a teacher will be measured not by how many chapters in the textbook you cover or how many worksheets you assign in a day, but rather by your students' enthusiasm for learning and the individual growth they show over time.

■ *High academic standards should be maintained for all students.* Research in learning achievement shows that when teachers set high expectations for their students, both personally and academically, they get better results (Wong & Wong, 2009). The CCSS adopted by many states focus on preparing all high-school graduates to meet the challenges of college and career. High-school graduates are expected to analyze and synthesize complex informational text, furnish citations to support their stance, and write informational text based on research from multiple sources (NGACBP & CCSO, 2010).

■ *Alternative, authentic assessments should be implemented.* Many schools today are driven by the need to raise their students' standardized test scores (Bartholomew, 2012), and many classrooms are dominated by formative and summative tests. We as teachers must also implement alternative means of evaluating student learning, such as teacher observations and anecdotal record keeping. These and other forms of informal assessment will be discussed in later chapters.

■ *Multimodal learning enhances the learning experience.* Meaningful learning occurs through various modalities. Students need to read bound books and also explore online resources. They should write stories by hand, but also compose on computers and create slide presentations or multimedia presentations to share with others. Students should be encouraged to use the school's tablet computers, digital cameras, or their own smartphones to make their own videos and graphics. Art and music should become integral parts of the math, science, social studies, and literacy curricula (see Chapter 9).

■ *Learning about multiculturalism and diversity widens students' view of the world.* We live in a multicultural world, and helping students learn about and value diversity is not something teachers can leave to chance. Your goal should be to have students read books about people of various economic groups, races, religions, cultures, and viewpoints (see Appendix B.2). Have students do projects on cultures and countries other than their own. Show videos of other lands where people look and live differently than we do. Finally, seek ways for students to communicate with audiences beyond the classroom. In this sense, teaching globally will expand your students' world.

■ *Motivation drives learning and achievement.* Some students may need guidance to discover their interests or learn what the school has to offer. You can use extrinsic rewards (grades, praise, and so forth) to initiate motivation, but ultimately success in learning is its own reward. Paralleling the student's school achievements are growth in self-concept, self-esteem, self-worth, and perceived competence as a learner and as a person.

The new electronic interdependence re-creates the world in the image of a global village.

MARSHALL MCLUHAN

These principles of learning will assist you as you plan learning experiences for each of the four learning domains, which we discuss next.

LEARNING DOMAINS

When planning learning experiences, keep several factors in mind: the abilities and interests of your students, available materials, and the nature of learning. The last of these is probably the most misunderstood, but learning can generally be categorized into four domains: cognitive, affective, psychomotor, and socialization.

Often school curricula—particularly standardized tests—artificially separate these equally important aspects of learning. Even worse, the affective, psychomotor, and socialization aspects of learning may be omitted entirely from the curriculum because they are not frequently a part of standardized tests. The result is a curriculum based exclusively on one type of learning: cognitive. However, studies in child psychology, brain development, and academic achievement have demonstrated that all four learning domains are equally important for young people's complete development (Forehand, 2005; Dettmer, 2006). Because learning domains are studied in other general education courses, we have simply summarized them in Figure 3.2.

The CCSS emphasize the higher levels of cognitive thinking as described by Bloom's taxonomy (Bloom, 1956). Bloom delineated the cognitive domain as a hierarchical arrangement, from low-level memorization to higher-level reasoning abilities. During the 1990s, one of Bloom's former students led a group of cognitive psychologists in updating the taxonomy to reflect 21st-century goals. Two noticeable changes are using verbs rather than nouns to describe the various levels and the transposition of the top two levels. Figure 3.3 indicates the original and revised versions of the taxonomy.

Four learning domains.   **FIGURE 3.2**

	COGNITIVE	**AFFECTIVE**	**PSYCHOMOTOR**	**SOCIALIZATION**
Type	Intellectual	Emotional	Physical	Interactive
Description	The area of learning that stresses the mental or intellectual processes	The area of learning that includes feelings, emotions, attitudes, and appreciation of aesthetics (sense of beauty)	The area of learning involving the use of physical movement to enhance general understanding of school concepts	The area of learning concerned with the physical and verbal communication skills needed to sustain human relations and to function effectively in our society
Activities	Memorizing phonics rules	Observing the class gerbil	Pantomiming Hitting a baseball	Preparing a class newscast
	Defining parts of speech	Listening to poetry	Writing and illustrating poetry	Creating a group social studies mural
	Correcting punctuation errors in workbooks	Displaying *all* children's work in the classroom	Drawing, cutting, pasting, and sewing bookbindings (publishing)	Preparing a readers theater presentation

FIGURE 3.3 The original and new versions of Bloom's taxonomy.

ORIGINAL VERSION		REVISED VERSION
Knowledge	← lowest cognitive level →	Remembering
Comprehension		Understanding
Application		Applying
Analysis		Analyzing
Synthesis		Evaluating
Evaluation	← highest cognitive level →	Creating

Source: Forehand, M. (2005). *Emerging perspectives on learning, teaching and technology.* Online: http://epltt.coe.uga.edu/index. php?title=Bloom%27s_Taxonomy.

Many of the CCSS anchor standards require elementary students to analyze and evaluate (NGACBP & CCSSO, 2010, p. 10):

- "Determine central ideas or themes of a text and analyze their development" (CCRA.R.2).
- "Analyze how and why individuals, events, and ideas develop and interact over the course of a text" (CCRA.R.3).
- "Analyze how specific word choices shape meaning or tone" (CCRA.R.4).
- "Analyze the structure of text" (CCRA.R.5).
- "Delineate and evaluate the arguments and specific claims in a text, including the validity of reasoning as well as the relevance and sufficiency of the evidence" (CCRA.R.8).

Of course, in order for students to analyze and evaluate a text, they must also be able to comprehend it. Understanding the hierarchy of cognitive thought will help you develop students' higher-level thinking.

Read the vignette on the following page, in which Ms. Sparks, a fifth grade teacher, uses a CCSS anchor standard to stretch her students' thinking about how authors' word choices affect the meaning and tone of their writing.

LEARNING STYLES

Research supports the concept that each student has a preferred way to approach a learning situation, called a *learning style* (Carbo, 1997; Dunn, 1996). Additionally, each student also has a preferred environment and mode of learning. For example, some prefer reading an e-book to reading a print book. Some students prefer to work alone, while other students work best when working with groups (Dunn et al., 2010). Some students need some interaction with the teacher in order to stay on task and to learn the concept, while others prefer to work independently (Thomas, 2009). Environmental factors such as lighting; seating; and noise levels from sources such as fans, outside traffic, wind, hall noise, or even tapping of a student's pencil can affect a student's learning (Bernice, 2007).

When a teacher recognizes through *kidwatching*—a term coined by Yetta Goodman (1978) to refer to a teacher's focused observation of students so she can determine what tasks students can and cannot perform—that students have a preferred manner of learning, the teacher should consider that while planning instruction and the classroom environment.

Fling and skim: Ms. Sparks' minilesson exemplifies vivid word choices for students to model

Fifth-grade teacher Ms. Sparks is focusing on CCRA.R.4: "analyze how specific word choices shape meaning or tone" (NGACBP & CCSSO, 2010, p. 10). Her students' writing lacks descriptive words, so she wants them to understand how authors use language. In a minilesson during the language arts block, she shares a piece of literature in which the author uses vivid words that play on the readers' senses. She chooses Hesse's (1999) picture book *Come on, Rain!*

After first reading the entire book, she returns to the phrase describing the mothers' reaction to the rain: "fling off their shoes, / skim off their hose." When Ms. Sparks asks the students to demonstrate what the mothers were doing, one student wonders: "What are hose?" She explains they are similar to girls' tights, so the students begin to fling and skim their shoes and socks. Ms. Sparks asks

students why *fling* and *skim* are good word choices. One student says that if the author had just said that mothers took off their shoes and hose, readers would not envision the exact action. One girl remarks that the word *skim* has an expressive sound that conveys how you peel tights off your legs when they are sweaty. One student notices how *fling* and *skim* both have short "i" sounds and was quite sure Hesse used assonance intentionally to indicate that the action was short and fast.

Ms. Sparks then hands each student a book of poems and asks them to find examples of vivid words and write them down to share with each other. After sharing these words and phrases with each other, Ms. Sparks tells the students that tomorrow they are going to have an opportunity to write with vivid words.

Just as students have preferred ways of learning, every teacher has a preferred method of teaching certain concepts. Some teachers prefer to teach a minilesson to the entire class, while others may prefer to teach new concepts to small groups. Some teachers are physically animated when they teach, while others are calm and soft-spoken. Understand your preferred way of teaching and how to use it most effectively, just as you must understand and teach to each student's strengths.

The following sections briefly discuss common characteristics of various types of learning, using a dichotomous approach (see Figure 3.4). A dichotomous approach contrasts two opposite learning styles, placing each at one end of a continuum. Although some students may appear to fit one of the two extremes, most exhibit some characteristics of both learning styles and thus fall somewhere along the continuum.

Global–Analytic

Two contrasting learning modes are global and analytic. According to Dunn et al. (2010), global learners understand an overall concept before they consider its specific

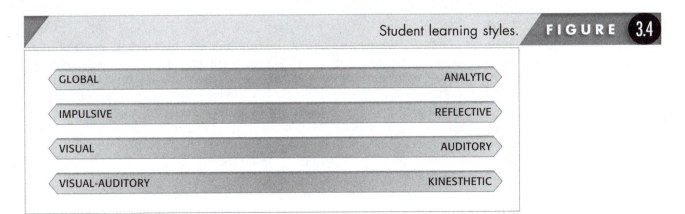

Student learning styles. **FIGURE 3.4**

facts. For example, to create a 3-D model for a project, they first need to see a finished model, before they can concentrate on the specific details of how to construct it. When assigned to read a long passage, global readers usually prefer to skim the material first to get an overview. They learn new vocabulary words in context instead of looking them up before they begin to read or listen to an audio presentation. They appreciate a teacher's brief summary over a lengthy explanation. They appreciate reading materials and lectures that include analogies, stories, or information on how concepts are related. They also appreciate teachers who give them a choice in projects. Global learners are good at multitasking, but teachers often misread this behavior and conclude the student is not paying attention to class activities.

Conversely, Dunn et al. (2010) reported that analytic learners learn best if they are given step-by-step directions and explanations for a project. They appreciate guidelines or a detailed rubric so they understand exactly what is required of them. They analyze a situation and then make a decision based on the analysis. These students recall details of a lecture or reading materials. Unlike the global learners, they cannot multitask; they need to complete one task before they begin another. Analytic learners appreciate concrete questions; they do not like questions that require them to "imagine" or "suppose."

Impulsive–Reflective

Not only will your classroom have global and analytic learners who prefer to work alone or in a group, but you will also have some students who are impulsive and some who are reflective.

The impulsive student is one whose hand always flies up even before you have finished asking a question. These students have little fear of failure and are more concerned with responding than with giving the correct answer. Often they are easily distracted by irrelevant material and miss the main idea or central theme of a book. On any given assignment, they rush to finish but often make many careless errors. Speed rather than accuracy drives the impulsive student.

The reflective student is slow and deliberate. Such students consider all alternatives before responding and approach problem solving in a systematic, critical way. This student may appear to be a daydreamer, lost in thought, or quiet and shy. Often this student is a perfectionist. A favorite of teachers, the reflective student may nonetheless be one who is overly inhibited and anxious about schoolwork. These students may freeze up during test situations. They also respond very negatively when their written assignments are returned with red marks for grammar, punctuation, and spelling errors. In short, these are the students who need to be taught that making mistakes is part of learning and that taking risks is allowed.

Visual–Auditory–Kinesthetic

Teachers who are good kidwatchers determine if their students learn best while listening, viewing, moving around, or doing hands-on activities. *Visual* and *auditory* are the two most common styles relevant in the teaching of reading. Although students utilize both auditory and visual processing while learning to read, it is possible to identify students who have a preference for auditory information presented in a teacher lecture or podcast. Auditory learners learn best when they can focus on listening to the teacher; they are distracted when they are required to take notes. Even in a college classroom, some students can listen to a 50-minute discussion, take no notes, and get a perfect grade on the end-of-the-period quiz.

Visual learners, on the other hand, learn best when material is presented in a format they can see: on the board, on large charts, on overhead transparencies, and in books.

Most approaches to reading today combine aspects of auditory and visual learning; for example, multimedia text combines auditory and visual elements. This eclectic approach is usually appropriate because most students use both auditory and visual styles in learning. However, for some primary-grade students, even this combined approach may not be enough to reinforce new material. Such students may require you to teach reading by using *kinesthetic elements*.

The kinesthetic learning style uses all of the senses, not just sight and hearing. It incorporates tactile manipulation of materials and body movement. This approach implements learning by doing. Research has shown that most young students, as well as underachieving older students, tend to be kinesthetic learners. In the language arts classroom, these students learn best when given opportunities to manipulate letters and words and to engage in language games, pantomime, illustration, and drama.

In addition to understanding students' learning domains and their learning styles, teachers must consider the concept of multiple intelligences.

read RESEARCH practice

Analyze the materials in an elementary classroom and give examples of those that are geared toward the different learning styles. Next, observe some students in this same room. What evidence can you find that these students exhibit a particular learning style preference? Record your observations and share them with your peers.

MULTIPLE INTELLIGENCES THEORY

T hough Howard Gardner's *multiple intelligences theory* (1983) was not written as an educational theory, it has had a great impact on education. While studying stroke victims, Gardner became interested in the various parts of the brain that control different physical functions. He realized, for example, that a person who has lost the ability to speak after a stroke might still be able to sing. In *Frames of Mind*, Gardner (1983) described his theory of seven intelligences. Later, he recognized an eighth intelligence (Checkley, 1997). See Figure 3.5 for a description of the eight intelligences.

Howard Gardner's multiple intelligences theory. **FIGURE 3.5**

INTELLIGENCE	DEFINITION	PERSONALITY TRAITS
Linguistic	Mastery of language	Loves to read, writes well, enjoys jokes, has well-developed vocabulary, speaks well
Musical	Superb musical competence	Sings well, plays instruments well, has ability to compose and hear environmental sounds as music
Logical–Mathematical	Ability to calculate easily and think abstractly	Computes complicated problems in head, enjoys brainteasers, enjoys games such as chess
Spatial	Ability to form spatial images	Is able to create models and sculptures and use maps and compasses
Bodily–Kinesthetic	Ability to use one's body for expressive or athletic goals	Excels in sports and drama, enjoys tactile materials
Intrapersonal	Ability to understand oneself	Is able to express oneself well, possesses high self-esteem
Interpersonal	Ability to understand and "read" others	Loves to socialize, is a natural leader, possesses empathy for others
Naturalist	Ability to classify plants, minerals, and rocks	Loves to study the outdoors, quickly sees things in nature that others do not see

Sources: Adapted from Gardner (1983) and Checkley (1997).

Mr. Furnish is convinced that students should be given choices and also be encouraged to attempt new tasks. During the first part of the year, he observes the many different intelligences that his students display. Throughout the rest of the year, he gives them various types of assignments so they all have the opportunity to develop each intelligence to some degree.

When we join Mr. Furnish in the classroom, his fifth graders are working on CCSS RI.5.9: "Integrate information from several texts on the same topic in order to write or speak about the subject knowledgeably" (NGACBP & CCSSO, 2010, p. 14). During a science unit on earth's natural disasters, students read several trade books about tornadoes, hurricanes, earthquakes, tsunamis, and volcanoes, and Mr. Furnish notices that students have become fascinated by specific aspects of the unit. He knows that some of his students enjoy music, others like to write poems, while others enjoy building 3-D models. Some students prefer working alone, while others are more engaged when working in a small group. Taking all of this into consideration, he has students choose one natural disaster, learn as much as they can about it, and then present their findings to the class.

Mr. Furnish provides his students with many format choices for their report: they can create a multimodal presentation (video or slideshow, for example) with photos and music, write and perform a readers theater, paint a mural, or write a rap song. They can also work alone or work with other classmates who want to explore the same topic in the same manner. Before students begin their projects, they share their ideas with Mr. Furnish so he can be sure they have all the materials they will need.

Mr. Furnish is amazed at his students' projects. One group uses craft sticks and toothpicks to create a 3-D model showing what happens during an earthquake. They use many layers representing the surface under the earth, with small toothpick buildings on the top surface. When they present their project to the class, they give the bottom layer a jolt, and all the toothpick buildings crumble. Another group performs a readers theater script with each character representing a different natural disaster. One boy performs a ballad he wrote about a small town that experienced a tornado. Mr. Furnish and his class learn many new facts as they share their projects.

Gardner proposes that everyone possesses some degree of all eight intelligences, but not everyone has the same strength in each intelligence. Gardner posits that each intelligence must be nurtured in order for it to develop properly and fully. Though many people have a dominant intelligence at birth, a person's culture and environment often promote the development of a specific intelligence, which then develops more fully than the others.

How does this theory relate to the teaching of language arts? Teachers need to recognize that each student's mind is unique and that all subject material can be taught in numerous ways. Figure 3.5 lists personality traits that are associated with each intelligence. Reflect on how these personality traits may affect a student's approach to the reading, writing, listening, speaking, viewing, and visually representing activities that you will do in your classroom.

TEACHING STRATEGIES

You must plan and implement teaching strategies that take all types of learners and learning domains into account. A *teaching strategy* is a specific set of organized teacher behaviors designed to facilitate student learning. Though the goal for the student remains the same—learning new material—the strategy or strategies employed by a teacher to reach that goal vary considerably. The plural term *strategies* is perhaps more appropriate because it reflects the actual classroom practice of teachers who rarely use a single approach for all students in all learning situations. This is as it should be. Good teachers are eclectic strategists: They pick, choose, and adapt various methods to meet specific conditions and students' specific learning needs.

Here we give an overview of five teaching strategies—direct lecture, inquiry-based instruction, learning centers, units, and minilessons—which are general approaches to teaching. More specific teaching strategies and activities related to language arts content are discussed in later chapters.

> The mediocre teacher tells.
> The good teacher explains.
> The superior teacher demonstrates.
> The great teacher inspires.
>
> **WILLIAM ARTHUR WARD**

Direct Lecture

The direct lecture form of instruction is the most traditional, but perhaps the least effective, teaching strategy. Teachers need to cover textbook material and prepare their students for standardized tests; they also recognize their accountability to state politicians and district administrators (Reutzel & Mitchell, 2005). As a result of these demands, some teachers may believe the most efficient way to teach the required curricula is through class lecture.

Direct lecture is also widely used because it allows for a great deal of teacher control. In fact, teachers can control almost all variables of learning in a lecture: the amount of information presented, the manner of presentation, the time allotted for the lesson, and the time allotted for questions and answers. Furthermore, the direct lecture allows a teacher to face the entire class all the time, which at least theoretically ensures a certain amount of classroom control.

The biggest disadvantage of direct lecture is that it tends to make students passive listeners rather than active learners. Because lengthy lectures allow little time for discussion, student understanding is tested almost exclusively by written exams. Finally, the teacher-dominated lecture allows little time in class for students to interact with one another academically; thus, the affective domain and the development of social learning skills are largely ignored.

The classroom vignette on the next page illustrates how a direct lecture can be supplemented with student interaction and engagement.

Inquiry-Based Instruction

In *inquiry-based instruction* (also referred to as *guided discovery*), students learn concepts through some hands-on activity. Instead of lecturing on the major concepts, you create an environment in which students create a project or perform an activity in order to learn the concepts. Although inquiry-based learning is most often observed in the science and social studies areas, it is also applicable to language arts instruction. Consider what students are doing in an inquiry-based lesson: they are reading, writing, and discussing what they are learning. So even if the major concepts you are presenting are related to science or social studies, students are also developing their language skills.

An inquiry-based strategy begins with you presenting a problem or question. Students gather facts, recall past experiences, and foster discussion. Then they organize the data and formulate hypotheses. Students test the hypotheses and either accept,

"Copy this down": Mr. Garrey combats student passivity during a lecture

To begin teaching his students about the parts of speech, Mr. Garrey writes the following definition on the board: *A noun is the name of a person, place, or thing.* Then he says, "Today we are going to learn about nouns. Copy this definition into your notebooks." The class complies.

Mr. Garrey continues. "Here are some examples of nouns," he says. He writes on the board the words *man, New York,* and *apple.* Then he makes three columns on the board: *People, Places,* and *Things.* Next he writes the nouns in the appropriate columns and asks the students to copy the chart into their notebooks.

"Nouns are all around us," Mr. Garrey says. "Can anyone think of a noun you see in this room?" A few hands go up, and he calls on one student.

Bianca: I see pencils, books, and chairs.

Mr. Garrey: Good, Bianca. Let's write those on our list.

As the list grows, he explains, "Some nouns are always written with a capital letter. These are called proper nouns." He writes some proper nouns on the board and directs the students to copy them into their notebooks.

Mr. Garrey then pauses and instructs students to think of three nouns that have not yet been listed, and include those on their own chart. He encourages those students who speak another language to add nouns in that language. After a few minutes, he asks several students to share those added words, and the class briefly discusses them.

reject, or revise them. Finally, they draw conclusions that relate to the original question or problem. Throughout this process, you serve as a guide and resource when needed, but students lead the discussion and investigation; thus, instruction is more indirect.

The primary advantage of inquiry-based teaching is the active involvement of the students. This strategy is characterized by small-group discussion, peer interaction, and cooperative learning and sharing. You can assess the lesson's effectiveness by observing the students: Which students take the lead in discussions? Who are the shy students who do not participate much? Who is having difficulty mastering a new concept? Then create minilessons to address students' specific needs or hold individual conferences. Emily Steffans used a writing workshop with her fifth-grade students to engage them in editorial writing while she observed them working cooperatively using the inquiry-based approach (Ray, 2006).

In terms of the actual content learned in a lesson, research has shown that English learners in particular learn content better through inquiry-based activities. The interaction with classmates and hands-on learning not only help them grasp the content, but also the vocabulary that is connected to the content (Amaral, Garrison, & Klentschy, 2002).

Learning Centers

Unlike a direct lecture or even an inquiry-based strategy, both of which begin with whole-group activities, the learning centers strategy is based on the philosophy that students learn best in small groups working with their peers (Nations, 2006). Many elementary-grade teachers utilize this strategy to some extent.

In an integrated language arts program, students engage in learning center language activities that enhance both language and content learning throughout the day. During project time, students rotate through a variety of centers that the teacher has established. One group might be working at an arts center to get ready for a storytelling production, while others might be at the writing center writing ads for books they have finished. Sometimes students write letters to a favorite author. If the classroom has a listening, language, and literature center, students can listen to audiobooks. Many teachers find that it really helps some of the less capable readers to hear the story as they follow along in the book. Very often, these students will record themselves retelling a story they just completed.

A learning centers strategy has four major components:

1. physical rearrangement of the room
2. control of student movement
3. teacher as resource person
4. evaluation of individual student progress

The physical rearrangement of the room is an important aspect of the learning centers strategy. Chairs and desks can be moved to form separate learning areas. Bookcases and cardboard partitions can also divide the room into special centers. The space arrangement is one that allows students to sit face-to-face rather than in rows. Figure 3.6 shows a sample room arrangement.

Another aspect of the learning centers strategy is movement. Consider the following factors: How will students move from one center to another in an orderly fashion? How long should a group remain at a particular center? Do the students move between centers as groups or individuals? Here are three ways to manage movement in the learning centers approach:

1. Make a bulletin board display showing the various learning centers and their locations. Next, place colored tags on this display to represent your various student groups. When you move the tags from one center to another, the students know that it is time to switch.

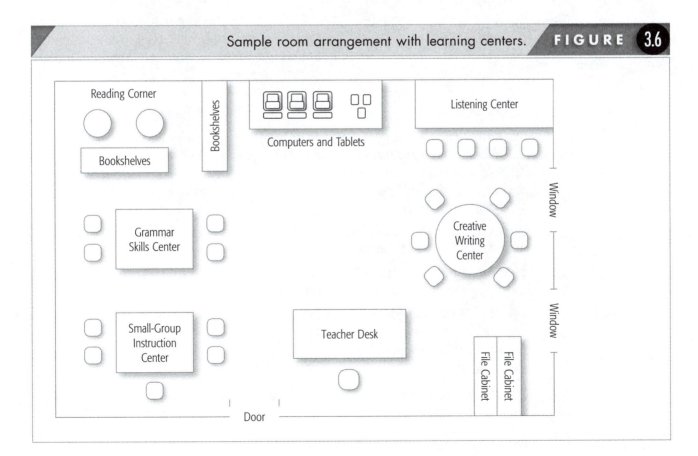

Sample room arrangement with learning centers. **FIGURE 3.6**

Toy vs. toy: Inquiry-based learning helps Ms. Samples' students discover verb/noun recognition

Ms. Samples writes on the chalkboard: *The _____ raced across the street.* She then turns to the class and asks, "Who can read this sentence?" Hands go up. After calling on one student, Ms. Samples asks, "What's wrong with this sentence?"

Camilla: There's a word missing.

Ms. Samples: Okay, who can give us the missing word?

Ryan: Car.

Ms. Samples: Good. Is there another word we could use?

Mateo: Dog.

Chloe: How about camel? (The class laughs, but the teacher writes down all the responses.)

Ms. Samples: Now I want you to work in your groups and see how many more words you can come up with.

The students begin whispering among themselves and writing down their ideas. The brainstorming gets lively. Their lists grow as each group tries to outdo the others. Ms. Samples walks around the room observing the groups.

Ms. Samples: Okay, let's add all your words to our list. Now study the list on the board. What do these words have in common?

Chang-Lin: There are some people. There are some animals.

Aaliyah: Most of the words begin with consonants.

Mateo: They're all one- or two-syllable words.

Ms. Samples: Very good.

Ms. Samples did not anticipate the last two responses; nevertheless, she writes them on the board, even though they are not characteristics of nouns. To get students back on track, she asks, "Can anyone think of a three-syllable word that begins with a vowel but would still fit in our sentence?"

Renata: Elephant.

Teacher: Good. Now let's try some more sentences in our groups.

The students work in their groups, filling in the blanks in the new sentences with nouns. As they brainstorm, more and more of the groups discover that the same word can be either a verb or a noun, depending on how it is used in a sentence. For example: Don't *toy* with your food./My brother brought me a *toy*. The lesson continues in this manner until Ms. Samples thinks that the students are ready to generate their own definition of a noun based on their discoveries.

2. Post a daily learning center schedule and go over it in class. The schedule tells the class groups where they will be throughout the day.
3. Use a consistent written system. Each morning deliver a short letter telling the students what to do during the day and stressing how they will move from center to center. This also reinforces functional reading skills.

In the learning centers strategy, you perform a variety of roles, which may include any or all of the following:

- Conduct minilessons (discussed later) for groups of students.
- Tutor individual students in skill areas.
- Answer questions from individual students at the centers.
- Observe and evaluate individual students at work.
- Direct the movement between centers.
- Serve as a resource for students.

The learning centers strategy can employ many traditional evaluation techniques. These include end-of-the-week tests, unit exams, and standardized tests. In addition, other types of evaluation are associated with the learning centers strategy; two of the most common are observation and work portfolios.

Kidwatching, or careful observation of individual students, is one of the most important forms of evaluation a teacher can perform in the classroom (Goodman & Goodman, 1989). The purpose is to observe a student's learning behavior. How well does the student work in a small group? What kinds of cooperative learning skills does the student exhibit? How well does the student perform a task when left alone? Does the student show initiative? Can the student handle responsibility? Being able to answer these questions allows you to individualize instruction.

> The real voyage of discovery consists not in seeking new landscapes, but in having new eyes.
>
> **MARCEL PROUST**

Teachers often use portfolios to evaluate students' performance during the course of a school year (Benson & Barnett, 2005). Portfolios (or folders for younger students) can also be used in conjunction with the learning centers strategy as a record of the student's work during a period of time. The portfolio or folder contains work samples that the student has completed at each center during the course of a week or longer. Some students' folders will contain more samples than others. But over the course of a few months, every student will accumulate work that is representative of her or his accomplishments during that time, and you can assess the work accordingly. The portfolio or folder, which can be used during family-teacher conferences, should contain evidence of what the student has accomplished and show the areas in which the student has grown.

Learning centers take on many different forms, depending on the physical setup of the classroom and the teacher's preferences. Several types of learning centers and the necessary equipment and materials are as follows:

- *Reading center:* Comfortable chairs; pillows; plenty of magazines, books, newspapers, tablets or other electronic readers, computers.
- *Listening center:* A table with a recording device, CD player, headsets, recorded books. Sites such as Scholastic (http://store.scholastic.com/shop/search/9) and AudioEditions (www.audioeditions.com/?gclid=CNWLiJyd6L4CFaQF7AodNmIAFA) offer recorded books. You can download audiobooks to computers, tablets, and other mobile devices.
- *Creative-writing center:* Table, chairs, extra paper, pencils, a picture file, plus physical props such as an old tennis shoe or candy bar wrapper to stimulate ideas.
- *Publishing center:* Computers with printers, cardboard, stapler, sewing materials for simple bookbinding of finished works, or a simple binding machine.
- *Report-writing center:* Reference materials, note-taking suggestions, computer for online research.
- *Arts/projects center:* Materials for murals, collages, science experiments, and so on.

You may also structure a learning center around a thematic unit you have planned to explore with the class.

Units

According to Jerome Bruner (1961a, 1983), knowledge is structured into large concepts or patterns. A unit is one way of concretely structuring new knowledge and skills for students. Many school districts now have unit plans for each grade. This is to help students remain on the same page as their new classmates as they move from one school to another within a district. Many beginning teachers appreciate this type of planning, which allows them to coordinate with the district's other teachers of the same grade.

IN THE CLASSROOM

Ms. Timberlake livens her lessons with learning centers

Ms. Timberlake, a third-grade teacher, creates a number of interesting learning centers for her students early in the school year. She hopes they will liven up some lessons and also teach the students how to work responsibly without constant supervision. A few weeks into the semester, however, problems arise over how one of the centers should be used. She calls the class together for a reminder about how to work in a learning center.

In this case, Ms. Timberlake uses the listening center as an example and restates the specific instructions for using the listening center by reviewing the procedure: "Class, we are having some difficulties using the listening center properly. I want to review the rules with you again so we won't have to stop in the middle of the lesson. I'll demonstrate this with the Orange Group. Everyone in the Orange Group take your seats at the listening center table and put on your headsets."

She waits until the students are seated and ready. Allowing time for students to get settled is important.

"Everyone ready? Now Brenda will pass out the paper you will need to write your responses. Carlos will be in charge of signaling the group to turn on their devices. Good. Did everyone see how they did it? Now I'll have the Blue Group try." Again she waits while the two groups trade places. Learning how to get organized takes time, particularly with young students.

Then she continues, "Let's see if the Blue Group remembers the rules for using the center. Watch how the helpers do their jobs so no one argues or wastes time. Look how they adjust the headsets, distribute the papers, and turn on their listening devices."

The students are now paying attention as the Blue Group demonstrates the proper procedure. "Does everyone understand how we work at the listening center? Good. Now let's get back to work, and I'll watch to see how you do." The review is over.

Here are 10 questions to keep in mind when planning a unit:

1. What is the major concept I wish to develop?
2. What are the related subsidiary concepts?
3. What background information and experiences should I provide for my students?
4. Where can the students go to find additional information? Websites? School library?
5. Are there sufficient resources within the classroom and school, or must I provide supplementary materials?
6. What resources are available in the community?
7. What specific activities will the students engage in? Individual? Small group?
8. How will I integrate listening, speaking, reading, viewing, visually representing, and writing into this unit?
9. How will I evaluate the unit? A test? A class project? Group or individual reports? Portfolios? Slide presentations? Multimedia presentations?
10. How much time does this unit warrant?

Many teachers answer these questions as a group, because they understand the importance of working together and learning from one another.

As you prepare for the many types of lessons and units, be open to questions that students ask because of their interests. These can become teachable moments. Consider encouraging the student who posed the question to find the answer. Of course, you may have to scaffold the student as she seeks the answer.

An example of a unit that developed from a teachable moment created around a single book is presented in the box. Study the vignette that follows and Figure 3.7 describing how one fifth-grade teacher responded to the needs and interests of her class and created an integrated unit.

One day an impromptu discussion about fear arises among Ms. Whitecloud's fifth-grade students.

"I know someone who won't walk in the woods because he's afraid of snakes," Bobby says.

"Heck, I once saw a water moccasin jump into a boat," Noah says.

"I'd be scared of snakes too if it had been my boat," Liam says.

"Yeah, but you wouldn't be afraid of going out in a boat again, would you?" Alex asks.

"Snakes aren't that scary, but I know someone who's afraid of crowds and small rooms. He won't even ride in an elevator," Abby says.

The talk continues like this, with students sharing about other fears they or people they know have: fear of heights, fear of spiders, fear of the dark.

"What about Superman and Batman?" Lindsay asks. "They aren't afraid of anything."

"How would you like to read a book about a boy who had a fear of the water and discovered his own source of courage?" Ms. Whitecloud asks. She shows them a copy of the book *Call It Courage* by Armstrong Sperry, the story of a young boy in Polynesia who must prove his bravery and overcome his fear of the sea.

The unit stretches from two weeks into a month. The students read the novel in and out of class. They also spend hours making toothpick constructions of traps and huts and balsa wood carvings of canoes as well as doing library and online research and creating multimedia reports. From paper and other art supplies, they make replicas of South Sea islands, huts, and canoes. An entire scene of Polynesia is painted on butcher-block paper and then placed on the classroom wall as a background mural. As the unit comes to an end, the student committees share their reports and posters.

Finally, all of the constructions are combined to make one gigantic scene that the students share with the primary grades. As the younger students are escorted into the room, they marvel at the mural and replicas. Then the fifth-graders begin a dramatic retelling of the entire story. As they speak, they point to the places where specific events have occurred. The primary-grade students are spellbound by the story and also by the 3-D illustrations.

Some of the caregivers wish to see this extravaganza for themselves; they agree to host a Polynesian celebration for the students. They bring in fruit punch, bananas, breadfruit pudding, mangoes, coconut milk, and other exotic foods for the students to sample while Hawaiian music and recordings of the ocean play in the background. What began a month ago as a simple class discussion has become a gala event that the students will remember for years to come.

Figure 3.7 shows the outline Ms. Whitecloud and her students created for the unit on the book *Call It Courage.*

Minilessons

Many teachers use minilessons of 5 to 10 minutes each as an alternative to longer lessons. Calkins (1994, 2001) originally described the minilesson as an alternative to the "maxi-lesson" of 45 minutes. Shorter lessons allow students more time to write during class yet still provide them with new skills and knowledge. Atwell (1998), another well-known process-writing advocate, also uses the minilesson each day to get the writing workshop started with her middle-school students. When carefully planned, the minilesson is a viable alternative to the full-period daily lesson plan. Furthermore, a lesson plan such as one combining a writing workshop with a minilesson reflects the comprehensive approach to teaching. It is authentic and contextually driven yet provides direct instruction on a specific, needed skill. The flow of such a lesson begins with a short minilesson, followed by a longer period for students to work (read/write/practice), and ends with a "coming together" for sharing.

FIGURE 3.7 Sample unit outline: *Call It Courage.*

CONCEPTS TAUGHT

1. Legends
2. Fiction vs. nonfiction
3. Characteristics of the novel
4. How fears develop
5. The nature of courage
6. Survival skills

BACKGROUND INFORMATION

1. Other legends read aloud
2. Map study of Pacific and Polynesia
3. History of Polynesia

MATERIALS

1. 30 copies of the book
2. Other library books by Armstrong Sperry
3. Maps, books, and Internet sites about Polynesia
4. Glue
5. Toothpicks
6. Balsa wood
7. Construction paper

ACTIVITIES

1. In-class reading
2. Home reading
3. Chapter discussion
4. Projects:
   A. Individual paper-and-toothpick construction
   B. Small-group boat and village making
   C. Whole-class wall mural
5. Group multimedia presentation on food, clothing, shelter of Polynesia
6. Dramatization and celebration

The minilesson can be applied to any subject area. It first requires that the teacher understand the immediate needs of the students. Next, the teacher should analyze the skill or behavior to be taught. Finally, the lesson derived from this analysis must be presented without lengthy explanation or theoretical justification, in no more than 10 minutes.

As an observant, reflective, kidwatching teacher, you will soon get a sense of your students' interests, strengths, weaknesses, and needs. Your own minilessons will emerge naturally from this knowledge. Basically, there are three types of minilessons:

1. classroom management (e.g., how to use a listening center, how to choose a book for free reading time);
2. specific skills (e.g., how to write book titles in a report, how to use commas and periods); and
3. techniques or tips (e.g., how to spell *ie* words, how to gear up for writing).

The architecture of minilessons

The Noyce Foundation (2014) suggests the following five steps for planning minilessons, which it refers to as the "architecture" of a minilesson.

1. Connect. State the objective or goal of the lesson, how it connects to previous lessons, and how it will be a part of future lessons. For example, using the CCSS, fourth-grade teacher Mr. Thomas explains how the class has been working on fluent reading and how they have been practicing reading with appropriate rate. Then he says that the part of the standard they will focus on for the day is expression, which is based on the specific part of CCSS RF.4.b on reading with expression, a task the class needs to refine (NGACBP & CCSSO, 2010).

> There is always one moment in childhood when the door opens and lets the future in.
>
> **GRAHAM GREENE**

2. Teach. Teach the concept and demonstrate it when necessary. Continuing with the above example, Mr. Thomas demonstrates the opposite of good expression by reading Bruce Lansky's (2000) four-line poem "My Grandma's Teeth" in a monotone voice without any expression. After that he reads the poem with correct pauses and inflections so that the students understand its humor.

3. Active involvement. Students are asked to quickly practice what they have been taught. In this case, Mr. Thomas asks students to quietly read Lansky's "Good-bye, Goldfish," another four-line poem. After the silent reading, Mr. Thomas asks a few students to read the poem aloud.

4. Link. In this step, the teacher reiterates the minilesson's goal and assigns the task linked to the goal. Mr. Thomas divides his students into two groups to practice reading with expression one of Aaron Shepard's scripts (available on www.aaronshep.com/rt). Mr. Thomas chooses two scripts with many characters so all members of both groups will get a chance to perform. As they get ready to practice their scripts, Mr. Thomas reminds them that at the end of the hour, he will ask them to perform. They are encouraged to help each other with expression.

5. Share. The closing step is used as a time to see if there needs to be further instruction. In Mr. Thomas' room, the students perform their short scripts, and after each performance, he gives them feedback. Teachers should not expect mastery of the skill immediately; that will come later, after considerable practice.

TECHNOLOGY IN THE CLASSROOM

Today's teachers have access to many valuable online resources. Take time to browse the following websites and take advantage of the many ideas they offer.

www.readwritethink.org/ This site, designed by the IRA and the NCTE, has interactive activities on all the areas of literacy. You can navigate by grade level, subject matter, or particular concepts, such as writing acrostic poems. Also useful are the lessons on higher-level thinking strategies for all grades.

http://teachers.net Search for a particular lesson plan by using the search box. Lessons range from writing friendly letters to flip books and storyboards.

www.lessonplanet.com/ This site permits teachers to search for specific lessons for a small fee.

www.criticalthinking.org/pages/remodelled-lessons-k-3/464 This site offers critical thinking lessons for K–3 and may be helpful to teachers who do not feel comfortable with the CCSS higher-level thinking requirements.

SUMMARY

Planning a successful language arts program takes time, but it is time well spent. When planning, consider the four learning domains: cognitive, social, psychomotor, and affective. Knowledge of your students' learning styles and their dominant multiple intelligences will help with the task of individualizing lessons. Instructional strategies include the direct lecture, in which teachers give the information they want students to know; inquiry-based learning, in which students engage in discovery learning; learning centers, in which students work independently to refine skills and complete units in which they learn major concepts about a topic in a structured way; and minilessons, in which teachers provide information in a short lesson, allowing students longer periods of time to practice the concept. Consider the strengths and weaknesses of these various strategies in any given teaching situation.

field AND practicum ACTIVITIES

1. READING WITH EXTENSION. Create a reading comprehension lesson by recording a short story. Have students read the story while they listen to it through headphones. Use kinesthetic activities based on Gardner's multiple intelligences that involve paper, paint, yarn, cardboard, and miscellaneous objects to create a 3-D representation of a scene from the story.

2. MAP MAKING. Teach the whole class the rudiments of map making using the classroom as your subject. After each student has created a map of the classroom, discuss the alternative uses of learning space. Then let students create a map of their ideal classroom. Map making develops visual/spatial skills, one of Gardner's multiple intelligences.

3. CLASS CALENDAR. Show the class a copy of the school calendar and discuss the importance of planning for the school year. Then, together with your students, create your own class calendar. List important class dates, such as students' birthdays, holidays, tests, parties, and field trips.

Children's and Young Adult Literature

THE CORNERSTONE OF THE LANGUAGE ARTS PROGRAM

CHAPTER 4

OBJECTIVES

After reading this chapter, you should be able to accomplish the following objectives:

1. Define the terms children's literature and young adult literature.

2. Explain the various categories of children's and young adult books.

3. Identify five resources for locating information about books.

4. Describe the guidelines for judging children's and young adult books.

5. Describe multiple books that are sensitive to diversity in the classroom.

6. Explain how a teacher can involve students with literature.

7. Explain the roles of teacher as storyteller and student as storyteller.

8. Describe a literature circle. Explain how this activity relates to reader response theory.

9. Explain how to make a character perspective chart with a specific children's or young adult book.

10. Describe how to create a story map.

INTRODUCTION

Literature for children and young adults is often thought of as the cornerstone of language arts programs. In part, this is because children's books are the first literature that young children encounter, typically by hearing stories and books read aloud by parents and caregivers. The classic fairy tales (e.g., *Cinderella*) and folk tales (e.g., *Johnny Appleseed*), along with more modern picture books (e.g., *Owl Moon*), are also the first books that young children learn to read aloud. Finally, quality children's books (e.g., *Brown Bear, Brown Bear, What Do You See?*) serve as literary models when children first attempt their own writing (Anderson, 2010).

For students in later grades, young adult literature continues to support their vocabulary development and their appreciation for a text's use of language. Consider the word choice of Kirby Larson (2013) in *Hattie Ever After*: "She was in the kitchen, kneading bread dough. I was not to be trusted with this particular task. Despite Perilee's expert tutelage, I never managed to bake a loaf of bread any lighter than a flatiron" (p. 3). Some readers may be unfamiliar with the task of *kneading* bread or the weight of a *flatiron*. For many readers, *tutelage* may also be an unfamiliar word. Teachers who take time to discuss these words in small groups help develop their students' vocabulary. While reading Steve Sheinkin's (2010) award-winning *The Notorious Benedict Arnold: A True Story of Adventure, Heroism, & Treachery*, students experience language similar to the way it was written during our country's early years. The book quotes a letter Benedict Arnold wrote to General George Washington: "The severity of the climate, the troops very illy clad, and worse paid . . . . [I]n short, the choice of difficulties I have had to encounter, has rendered it so very perplexing, that I have often been at a loss how to conduct matters" (p. 103). After encountering and discussing this language, students are better prepared should they attempt to write a historical story; they realize that using the language of the period makes the story more believable.

In short, quality children's and young adult literature provides much of the vocabulary for oral language development and builds a foundation for reading and writing.

> There is more treasure in books than in all the pirate's loot on Treasure Island.
>
> **WALT DISNEY**

CHILDREN'S AND YOUNG ADULT LITERATURE DEFINED

C*hildren's literature* can be broadly defined as any material written primarily for children and that they read and enjoy, and *young adult literature* can be defined similarly. Children's and young adult literature comes in many formats, including hardcover books, ebooks, magazines, comics, graphic novels; we may also include audio recordings, films, videos, and online interactive and computer adaptations of popular stories. Peggy Parish, the author of the popular *Amelia Bedelia* series, stated in regard to writing children's literature that "first you have to know what is of interest to children. . . . You have to make every word count. Also, in order to capture and hold a child's attention, there has to be a certain rhythm and flow in a story which complements its essential simplicity" (p. 25). Her point is that writing for children is a specialized form of communication and no easy task.

Christopher Paul Curtis, author of award-winning young adult books, including *Bud, Not Buddy* (1999), has a somewhat different perspective. When asked why he wrote for young adults instead of adults, he explained: "I think that a good story can be read by anybody. If the story is compelling and interesting, it can be read by children and adults. I don't really differentiate that much." When asked what his favorite book was as a child, he replied:

> I didn't have books that I really loved as a child. I read comic books, *MAD Magazine, National Geographic,* and *Sports Illustrated.* I read a lot, but books didn't really touch me, probably because there weren't a lot of books for or about young black children. That's not to say that blacks have to read "black" books, but you do need to read something that really touches you to develop that love for books. (New York Public Library, 2002)

We as teachers can learn from Curtis. It is important to help students of all ages select books with which they can identify. We must also give students access to magazines, comic books, and texts in other formats. It really does not matter what students read, as long as they develop a love of reading!

To select quality, well-liked books, consult the annual Newbery, Caldecott, and Printz award winners each year. In addition, the IRA publishes annual catalogs called *Children's Choices* and *Young Adults' Choices,* summarizing the books young readers have chosen as their favorites.

CCSS RL.2.10 states that "by the end of the year (grade 2) students will read and comprehend literature, including stories and poetry" (NGACBP & CCSSO, 2010, p. 11). This means that teachers can no longer teach only from basal readers and textbooks but must also include quality children's literature. The classroom vignette below shows how one teacher uses appropriate literature in her classroom.

IN THE CLASSROOM

Ms. Carton introduces historical studies through literature

This year Ms. Carton has decided to use the book *Sarah, Plain and Tall* (1986) by Patricia MacLachlan to introduce her fifth graders to aspects of pioneer life on the prairie. She feels that this is a good way to bring the period alive for the students, to help them see that history is not just facts and events but instead is populated with real people who laughed and cried as they lived their everyday lives. When the students finish their first reading of the book, many of them offer initial personal opinions.

Jack: I really like this book because it has a happy ending, and I love happy endings.

Maria: For me the saddest part of the book was the beginning, when the mother dies. I'm glad Sarah came to help them.

LaToya: I really got to know the people in this story. Now I understand a little of what it was like to live then.

Nilda: I liked the father. It was good for him to get another mother for the children.

Ms. Carton continues this line of thought with the following questions:

- Why is it important for Sarah to like Caleb and Anna and Papa?
- How does Sarah improve everyone's life? How does the family improve Sarah's life?
- How did you feel when Sarah finally decides to stay with the family?
- Which person is most like you—Sarah, Anna, Caleb, or Papa?
- What other books have you read about life on the prairie? How do they compare to *Sarah, Plain and Tall?*
- Have you read any other books by Patricia MacLachlan? What did you think about them?

As a conclusion to the project, Ms. Carton asks each student to explore and write about the message of the story in a daily writing journal. In this way, each student is able to give a unique interpretation to the story. Such activities help students to see the value of a piece of literature—its language, sense of story, moral, characters, and particular style.

BOOK CATEGORIES

One of your goals in reading this chapter is to become familiar with the various types of children's and young adult books. If you teach the upper grades, you may hold your students responsible for learning the book categories as a way of enhancing their own appreciation of literature. This section provides brief descriptions of the major children's and young adult book genres along with several good examples of each. Later, when you read these books with students, you can help them understand what is important about each genre and how each story develops. This will improve their comprehension and increase their knowledge of story structure.

Picture Books

Picture books allow readers to comprehend a story through pictures as well as text. The illustrations may be in black and white or color and may comprise paintings, wood cuts, watercolors, collages, or even photographs.

The illustrations of the best picture books complement the text; for example, in Jane Yolen's *Owl Moon* (1987), the soft watercolors by John Schoenherr perfectly capture the winter scene of a father and daughter going owling.

In Andy Rash's *Are You a Horse?* (2009) young students will laugh along with Roy, who receives a saddle for his birthday. Now all he needs to do is find himself a horse. This read-aloud picture book will allow students to chime in "Noooooo" as Roy encounters many different animals, none of which are a horse. Mac Barnett's *Extra Yarn* (2012) tells the story of little Annabelle, who finds a mysterious box of yarn. She begins to knit sweaters for herself, her dog, all of her classmates, and on and on until trouble occurs. The illustrations by Jon Klassen earned him a Caldecott honor award.

> So it is with children who learn to read fluently and well: They begin to take flight into whole new worlds as effortlessly as young birds take to the sky.
>
> **WILLIAMS JAMES**

Additional subcategories of picture books include wordless books and predictable books, which are useful in guiding emerging readers into literacy.

In *wordless books*, the pictures alone tell the story. Even young nonreaders can follow the story through the illustrations; this is a great way to develop oral language skills as well as teach about story structure. Some excellent examples of wordless books are John Goodall's series about a pig, beginning with *The Adventures of Paddy Pork* (1968); Martha Alexander's *Bobo's Dream* (1970), about an adventurous dachshund, Eric Carle's *Do You Want to Be My Friend* (1971); and Mercer Mayer's *A Boy, A Dog, and a Frog* (1967). Older students can enjoy more complex wordless books, such as Aaron Becker's *Journey* (2013) and David Wiesner's *Flotsam* (2006). For a more detailed list of wordless picture books see Jim Trelease's *The Read-aloud Handbook* (2013).

In Chris Raschka's wordless picture book *A Ball for Daisy* (2011), which won the Caldecott Medal for its illustrations, Daisy the dog loses her favorite red ball. Through pictures we follow Daisy's adventures until she finally gets a new ball. Primary-grade teachers can have their students draw and tell their own pet story. Other finely illustrated wordless picture books are Jerry Pinkney's *The Lion and the Mouse* (2009) and David Wiesner's *Mr. Wuffles!* (2013). Pinkney's book retells the classic Aesop's fable with brilliantly colored paintings. After studying and discussing this book, your students may be inspired to check out versions of other Aesop's fables, all of which emphasize a moral to be learned. In *Mr. Wuffles!* Wiesner permits readers to imagine a conversation between aliens and the cat Mr. Wuffles. The cat ignores all his toys in favor of a small spaceship, piloted by real aliens, that has invaded his house.

Predictable pattern books are picture books that contain repetitive language patterns, which allow even very young readers to predict what words are coming next. Classic predictable picture books include Bill Martin's *Brown Bear, Brown Bear, What Do You See?* (1967), Margot Zemach's *Teeny Tiny Woman* (1967), Maurice Sendak's *Chicken Soup with Rice* (1962), and Polly Cameron's *I Can't Said the Ant* (1961). Other predictable pattern books are included in Appendix B.4.

Although picture books are generally associated with young children, many excellent picture books appeal to older students as well. These include Mary Barrett's *Sing to the Stars* (1994), in which young Ephram stops to chat every day with blind Mr. Washington and his dog Shiloh when he walks home from his violin lesson. Only later does he discover that Mr. Washington was once a famous pianist. Both Ephram and Mr. Washington discover that making music is best when it is shared with others. In Calvin Alexander Ramsey's *Ruth and the Green Book* (2010), Ruth's father has just bought a brand new 1952 Buick and the whole family is traveling from Chicago to Alabama. But traveling in the South in the 1950s for an African American family is fraught with danger as the family encounters bigotry and discrimination. Fortunately, they have the *Negro*

read RESEARCH practice

Survey one or two of the teachers in your field experience school. Find out their definitions of the terms *children's literature* and *young adult literature* and how they use this literature in the classroom. Ask them what techniques they use to help students recognize good books; record responses in your notebook. As you read through this chapter, give some thought to your own plans for using literature in the classroom.

Motorist Green Book (a real book), which lists black-owned restaurants, places to stay, and service stations that help make their journey safer. Brian Floca's *Locomotive* (2013) is an informational picture book that details the history of America's early railroads.

Picture books for older readers and even those for young children have grown more complex, demanding more sophisticated reading skills to interpret both the pictures and words. Many picture books incorporate reading cues that extend beyond the letters and words on the page, which requires young readers to interpret and interact with the text beyond decoding the print (Hammerberg, 2001, p. 207). Discussing the relationship between the written text and the illustrations should be a part of every comprehension lesson, even for young students. CCSS RL.1.7 states that the student will be able to "use illustrations and details in a story to describe its characters, setting, or events" (NGACBP & CCSSO, 2010, p. 11). For example, when reading David Macaulay's *Black and White* (1990), students should understand that the author uses various fonts and print sizes to convey different messages. In *Knuffle Bunny* (2004), Mo Willems uses bubble-like comic strips to indicate the speaker's words. In this book, young Trixie becomes upset because Knuffle is left in the laundromat; the size of the letters becomes larger and the text more crooked in the bubbles to indicate the growing problem. In Dennis Fleming's *In the Tall, Tall Grass* (1995), some text runs diagonally and vertically to represent slipping, sliding, pulling, and tugging as the caterpillars eat the leaves. Another example is Fleming's *Barnyard Banter* (1994), with text treatments representing the pigs wallowing in the mud and the frogs jumping. Creative text and pictures in children's books should stimulate class discussions and inspire young writers to be more creative in their own writing.

Other picture books that will appeal to upper elementary and middle grade students are included in Appendix B.5. An excellent resource for teaching students to appreciate picture books is John Stewig's *Looking at Picture Books* (1995). Even if you do not have a background in art, this book will help you analyze picture book illustrations and pass valuable information along to your students to enhance their own comprehension skills.

Traditional Literature (Folklore)

Traditional literature, also known as folklore, is based on the oral storytelling traditions of ancient peoples. These tales have been passed down from generation to generation. Often similar stories emerge from different cultures. For example, Ed Young's *Lon Po Po,* a Chinese version of "Little Red Riding Hood," won the Caldecott Medal in 1990. CCSS RL.4.9 requires students by grade 4 to "compare and contrast the treatment of similar themes and topics (e.g., opposition of good and evil) and patterns of events (e.g., the quest) in stories, myths, and traditional literature from different cultures" (NGACBP & CCSSO, 2010, p. 12). Use different versions of traditional folktales to help students make the comparisons required by this standard.

Types of traditional literature are folktales, fairy tales, myths, epics, and fables. *Folktales* and *fairy tales* often include supernatural beings with magical powers. In both literary genres, central characters engage in a battle of good versus evil, with good usually triumphing. Bruno Bettleheim (1976) argued that children learn positive life lessons from hearing and reading the classic fairy tales: life is filled with difficulties but through courage and perseverance, good triumphs over evil. Characteristics of this literature, also referred to as *traditional fantasy*, include characters that symbolize good and evil, faraway and magical settings, and a fast-paced plot leading to a satisfactory resolution. Classic tales still popular today include "The Story of the Three Bears," "Cinderella," "Hansel and Gretel," "Rumpelstiltskin," "Beauty and the Beast," "Snow White," and "The Frog Prince."

> What is important—what lasts—in another language is not what is said but what is written. For the essence of an age, we look to its poetry and its prose, not its talk shows.
>
> **PETER BRODIE**

Contemporary authors write folktales too. Usually, these modern stories are updated versions of traditional tales. *The Irish Cinderlad* (Climo, 1996) is based on a traditional Irish folktale that is an unusual variation of the Cinderella story. In the Irish version, a young boy grows huge feet. When his mother dies and his father remarries, his three new stepsisters make fun of him and force him to do all the chores. He runs away from home and has many adventures, including losing one of his huge boots to a beautiful princess at a ball. Katherine Patterson is the well-known author of such contemporary realistic fiction as *The Bridge to Terabithia* (1977) and *Jacob Have I Loved* (1980). But she is also the author of *Parzival: The Quest of the Grail Knight* (1998). This is a delightful retelling of the folktale of Parzival, a young boy raised in the wilderness who becomes one of King Arthur's Knights of the Round Table. *Tsunami!* (2009) by Kimiko Kajikawa tells the Japanese tale of the old man sitting on his balcony, high above his little fishing village, who spots the approach of a gigantic killer wave.

Examples of other folktales and collections of folktales that will appeal to upper elementary and middle grade students are included in Appendix B.6.

Legends are tales from long ago with a possible historical basis that is difficult or impossible to verify. In the United States these stories include the tall tales of Paul Bunyan and Pecos Bill, as well as exaggerated tales of real historical characters such as Davy Crocket, Johnny Appleseed, and even George Washington. Find examples of other legends for young students at www.planetozkids.com and www.read-legends-and-myths.com. Native American legends and myths, such as *The Legend of Devil's Tower* (Sioux) and *Grandmother Spider Steals the Sun* (Cherokee), can be found at www.firstpeople.us/. *The Legend of Arthur and Guen: An Original Tale of Young Camelot* (2008), by Jon Koons, will make readers want to read the original stories.

Older students may find urban legends appealing. An *urban legend* is a story that is presumably true although it is typically related as having happened to a "friend of a friend of a friend." Urban legends revolve around incredible, bizarre, or coincidental events that almost never stand up to journalistic scrutiny. For a modern-day urban legend see *The Underground Gators* (2009) by Tina Casey.

Myths are folktales about the supernatural adventures of gods and goddesses. Ancient peoples told these stories to explain the origins of natural phenomena. A collection of myths suitable for young students is *In the Beginning* (1988), compiled by Virginia Hamilton and illustrated by Barry Moser. Many of the classic Greek myths have been retold for youngsters at www.history-for-kids.com. Young readers interested in Greek mythology should also see Eric Kimmel's (2008) *McElderry Book of Greek Myths*. For example, in the myth of *Theseus and the Minotaur*, Theseus battles a giant creature with the head of a bull. In *Perseus and Medusa*, Perseus has to slay Medusa, a monster whose hair writhes with snakes.

Epics are tales of heroism describing the adventures of exemplary individuals. The oldest examples are *The Iliad* and *The Odyssey,* attributed to the Greek poet Homer to celebrate the adventures of the great warrior and king Odysseus as he led his troops in the Trojan War and spent 10 years making his way home. Other familiar epics include the tales of Robin Hood, King Arthur, Beowulf, Roland, Gilgamesh, and Finn McCool.

The *fable* is a brief story with a strong moral; it often includes animal characters that exemplify a single trait, such as the crafty fox or the tortoise and the hare. Although Aesop's collection is best known, fables have also been handed down from many other countries, including India, Persia, and France. One modern fable based on Aesop's original fables is *Contest Between the Sun and the Wind* (2008) by Heather Forest. *Lousy Rotten Stinkin' Grapes* (2009) by Margie Palatini is another modern version of an old fable.

Modern Fantasy/Science Fiction

Fantasy includes literature that is unreal, with magical events and creatures not found in the real world. A subgenre of modern fantasy, *science fiction,* explores possible, though improbable, scenarios that take place in the future. Well-written fantasy and science fiction can ignite students' imaginations and provide them with a solid foundation of literary knowledge.

Modern fantasy includes the magical animal tales of E. B. White and other popular examples such as Michael Bond's *A Bear Called Paddington* (1960), Margery Williams' *The Velveteen Rabbit* (1983), Beatrix Potter's *The Complete Tales of Beatrix Potter* (1987), Rudyard Kipling's *Just So Stories* (1902), and Maurice Sendak's classic *Where the Wild Things Are* (1963). Modern fantasy stories that will appeal to older students include Natalie Babbit's *Tuck Everlasting* (1975), Lloyd Alexander's *Prydain Chronicles* (1973), J. R. R. Tolkien's *The Hobbit* (1937), and the Harry Potter series by J. K. Rowling.

The fantasy genre is tremendously popular among young readers. In 2013, a modern fantasy book won the Newbery Award for best children's literature book. In *The One and Only Ivan,* authors Katherine Applegate and Patricia Castelao tell the story of Ivan the gorilla, his friends Stella the elephant and Bob the stray dog, all of whom live a fairly comfortable life until Ivan's love of art and a new arrival change things. In *Tales of a Sixth-Grade Muppet* (Kirk Scroggs, 2011), sixth grader Danvers Blickensdorfer is struggling with typical middle-school problems. But his life really takes a turn for the worse when he wakes up one morning and discovers he's been turned into a Muppet. Illustrating with simple line drawings, Scroggs combines modern fantasy with humor.

The 39 Clues: The Cahill Files (2013) is an unusual mystery–fantasy series by Clifford Riley. The book begins with the burning of the White House by the British in 1814, then shifts to the great escape artist Harry Houdini, and winds up with the launch of the first nuclear submarines. Young readers of mystery and fantasy will enjoy reading about the convergence of these events.

Super Diaper Baby 2 (2011) is by Dav Pilkey, creator of the silly but very popular Captain Underpants series. With its wacky humor and intentional misspellings, this cannot be considered great literature, but it is important to remember that a teacher's job is to get students hooked on reading, and this book has proven popular with upper elementary students.

Science fiction, including stories published in comic book and graphic novel formats (discussed next), is perhaps more popular today than ever before with middle- and upper-grade readers. Science fiction covers a broad range, from the classics of Madeleine L'Engle and Ray Bradbury to the more recent *Ender's Game Quintet* by Orson Scott Card and the *Jurassic Park* books by Michael Crichton.

Other recent examples of modern fantasy are included in Appendix B.7.

Graphic Novels

Graphic novels combine comic book–style graphic images with detailed stories. Yang (2008) defined graphic novels as long comic books, but this definition does not really capture their enormous popularity among upper elementary and middle-school readers. Perhaps it is the fact that graphic novels often portray young boys and girls with superpowers engaged in fantastic adventures (Callahan, 2009). However, many classic works of literature of all genres have been adapted into graphic novels, and the genre has spawned many well-received original works of non-superhero literature of interest to young adults, such as Marjane Satrapi's *Persepolis* (2000) and Judd Winick's *Pedro and Me: Friendship, Loss, and What I Learned* (2000).

In the United States, one of the first graphic novels to capture the imagination of young people was Art Spiegelman's two-volume nonfiction *Maus: A Survivor's Tale* (1991). This book, which won a Pulitzer Prize in 1992, tells about Spiegelman's parents' experiences as concentration camp survivors in the Holocaust. Sonia Leong's *Romeo and Juliet* (2007) is part of a Japanese manga series on Shakespeare's works. Other favorites among middle-school students are Vera Brosgol's *Anya's Ghost* (2011) and Jeff Smith's *Bone* (2004), a popular fantasy/adventure graphic novel series featuring the three Bone cousins in an epic fantasy that combines comedy with darker elements (Bickers, 2007).

Appendix B.8 lists other graphic novels, and for more information on graphic novel titles, visit Capstone Press (www.capstonepress.com), which specializes in this format.

Contemporary Realistic Fiction

Contemporary realistic fiction portrays life as it is, with people and events that one might encounter in the real world. Often the themes deal with serious issues facing today's children and young adolescents: moving to a new school, the loss of a pet, making friends, divorce, bullying, and alcohol and drug abuse. Popular authors in the genre over the years include Judy Blume, Cynthia Voigt, Betsy Byars, Paula Fox, Richard Peck, and Katherine Paterson. Such authors articulate the hopes, fears, and dreams of young people in a realistic manner, which accounts for their popularity among young readers.

Popular author Gary Paulsen is known for his adventure books, such as *Hatchet* (1987), in which a 13-year-old boy struggles to survive in the wilderness. In *Lawn Boy* (2007), Paulsen takes a humorous approach to a young man's experience with capitalism: a 12-year-old boy receives an old riding lawn mower for his birthday and goes into business for himself mowing the neighbors' lawns. When one of his customers turns out to be a stockbroker, the boy decides to invest his profits. Middle-school teachers can easily use this book to launch an economics unit on how the stock market works.

Walter Dean Myers is another popular author, particularly among adolescent African American males. In *Lockdown* (2003), Myers takes readers inside a juvenile detention center, where 14-year-old Reece is incarcerated for stealing prescription pads and selling them to the local drug dealer. Reece knows his life is headed in the wrong direction, but can he really turn things around? Other books by Myers with similar gritty, hard-nosed themes include *Monster* (2004), *Fallen Angels* (2008), *Bad Boy: A Memoir* (2002), *Slam* (2008), *The Glory Field* (2008), *Scorpions* (1989), *Somewhere in the Darkness* (2008), and *Darius and Twig* (2014).

Realistic fiction may feature adventures and animals. Some classic examples of these tales are *Julie of the Wolves* (1972) by Jean George, *Island of the Blue Dolphins* (1960) by Scott O'Dell, *A Rumor of Otters* (1993) by Deborah Savage, and *The Cay* (1969) by Theodore Taylor. Some of the best animal stories remain favorites over the years including *The Black Stallion* series by Walter Farley, *Where the Red Fern Grows* by Wilson Rawls, and *A Time to Fly Free* by Stephanie Tolan.

Kekla Magoon, recipient of the ALA Coretta Scott King New Talent Award, writes realistic fiction for children and young adults. In *Camo Girl* (2011) she explores the issues of adolescent friendship and racial divides. Ella and Z, two social misfits, have been best friends for years; in sixth grade their friendship is tested when a new boy moves into town.

When students get hooked on a particular author, such as Paulsen, Myers, or Magoon, encourage them to pursue an author study unit. This entails reading a number of books by the author and creating a report comparing and contrasting the titles. The report does not have to be limited to text—it can take many forms, including art, audio, video, slides, and any other form of media the student feels will represent the author.

Other contemporary realistic fiction books for upper elementary and middle-school readers are provided in Appendix B.9.

Mysteries and sports books remain popular subgenres of realistic fiction. Younger readers enjoy solving cases along with boy detective Encyclopedia Brown, a series by Donald J. Sobol, and science sleuth Einstein Anderson, a series by Seymour Simon. Older readers enjoy *The House of Dies Drear* (1968) by Virginia Hamilton and *The Callender Papers* (1983) by Cynthia Voigt. Other mystery books your students will enjoy are included in Appendix B.10.

Elementary and middle school readers also enjoy sports books. For older students, one prolific author is Mike Lupica. Though most of his main characters are in high school, the books will appeal to middle school readers. Other sports books that will appeal to upper elementary and middle-school students are included in Appendix B.11.

Historical Fiction

Historical fiction, a subcategory of fiction, consists of fictional narratives in a historically factual setting. Writers of historical fiction have covered all eras of American history, from pre-Columbian times to the 1960s. Popular historical periods include the colonial era and figures such as Benjamin Franklin and other founding fathers. In most cases the authors of historical fiction strive for authenticity in the settings and the depiction of people's lives during the period they choose. Historical fiction provides a good way for young people to learn about everyday life in other eras, which is often neglected in textbooks. In fact, CCSS RL.7.9 requires students to "compare and contrast a fictional portrayal of a time, place, or character and a historical account of the same period as a means of understanding how authors of fiction use or alter history" (NGACBP & CCSSO, 2010, p. 37).

Teachers who rely on social studies textbooks alone to teach students about history are limiting students' access to the real stories behind notable events. Historical fiction has the ability to capture young peoples' imagination like no textbook can. For example, in *My Brother Sam Is Dead* (1974) by James and Christopher Collier, students read a firsthand, personal account of some of the real violence during the Revolutionary War in America. Tim and his brother Sam are living in rural Connecticut with their parents when the news reaches them that the colonists have defeated the British in nearby Massachusetts. Sixteen-year-old Sam is eager to fight for freedom, but his Connecticut neighbors are either Tories who favor the British or simple farmers who want no part of the war. For older students, Irene Hunt's *Across Five Aprils* (1964) reveals the conflicts of a family divided by the Civil War. The horrors of slavery leading up to the Civil War are vividly depicted in Paula Fox's *The Slave Dancer* (1973). Finally, pioneer life in the Midwest is accurately portrayed in *Sarah, Plain and Tall* (1986) by Patricia MacLachlan (see Figure 4.1).

Even distant historical periods can come alive in historical fiction. For example, 14th-century England is vividly portrayed in Karen Cushman's *The Midwife's Apprentice* (1995), which tells the story of Beetle, a young girl living in a village garbage dump who is taken in by a midwife. The midwife, Jane, teaches the girl the skills that will change her life. Sixteenth-century Japan is the setting for Scott Goto's *The Perfect Sword* (2008), in which young Michio is apprenticed to a master swordsmith and challenged to make the finest sword for a fighting samurai.

In the mid-1800s, thousands of Americans traveled westward on the Oregon Trail, lured by the dream of free land. Gary Paulsen's *Mr. Tucket* (1995) tells the exciting adventure story of 14-year-old Francis Tucket, who, while riding in a wagon train with his family, is captured by Indians and has to prove his manhood or succumb to the perils of nature.

Few U.S. students know much about Russian history or about the brutal discrimination against the Jews during the period of the Czars. In *The Circle Maker* (1996), Maxine Schur tells the story of the young Jewish boy Mendel, who is living in the Ukraine in 1852 and dealing with the harsh punishment of his religious school masters. The worst is yet to come as the Czar's soldiers begin raiding the rural villages of the Ukraine and seizing boys as young as eight to serve in the military.

Even fairly recent U.S. history is not well known by many students. For example, in 1912 the mill workers of Lawrence, Massachusetts, went on strike for better working conditions and decent wages. Throughout New England at that time, mill workers suffered from horrible and sometimes dangerous working conditions. In Katherine Paterson's *Bread and Roses, Too* (2006), two children become unlikely friends as they try to understand their parents' feelings toward the strike.

FIGURE 4.1

Cover illustration from *Sarah, Plain and Tall.*

Source: Jacket art copyright © 1985 by Marcia Sewall. Jacket copyright © 1985 by HarperCollins Publishers, Inc. Used by permission of HarperCollins Publishers.

Another little-known episode in U.S. history took place in 1921 when one of the worst race riots in the country's history erupted between blacks and whites in the city of Tulsa, Oklahoma. After an incident in an elevator between a black man and a white woman, the specifics of which are lost to history but are not believed to be rape, white Tulsans attacked and burned the Greenwood section of Tulsa, the city's thriving and prosperous black district. Anna Myers captures the terror of this time in her book *Tulsa Burning* (2002), about 15-year-old Noble Wayne Chase; his friendship with a black man, Isaac; and the deceitful Sheriff Leonard. Before reading this book your students will want to research the Tulsa race riot online. Chapter 10 offers a detailed multimodal activity based on *Tulsa Burning*.

World War II is often treated in social studies textbooks as a list of places, battles, and dates to remember; the details of the war's major events are often left unexplored. This is when good children's and young adult literature becomes invaluable. For example, in *I Am Rosemarie* (Moskin, 1999), young Rosemarie and her family are Dutch Jews living peacefully in Amsterdam, Holland. In early 1940 there are rumors that the Germans will invade their peaceful nation, but Rosemarie's father ignores them. The Germans do invade, however, and Rosemarie is captured and sent to a concentration camp, testing her will to survive.

Ellen White deals with the U.S. involvement in the Vietnam War (1955–1975) in *Road Home* (1999). Rebecca is a young nurse who is traveling on a helicopter that crashes deep in the Vietnam jungle, and she must learn to survive under the harshest of conditions or die. After reading this book, middle-school students will want to research more about the Vietnam War and compare it with the more recent American wars in Iraq and Afghanistan. In Paul Curtis' *Bud, Not Buddy* (2002), readers travel with 10-year-old Bud Caldwell as he moves from one foster home to another. In the depths of the Great Depression, Bud's quest is to find the father he has never known. Use this book to teach students how telling a story in the first person brings the reader closer to the main character. Another Curtis book that focuses on the Great Depression is *The Mighty Miss Malone* (2012). In a journey to reunite with their father, Deza Malone and her family face many Great Depression–era experiences, such as living in a shanty and riding the rails. Fifth-grade teachers can use these books and others to support student growth in meeting CCSS RL.5.9: "Compare and contrast stories in the same genre on their approaches to similar themes and topics" (NGACBP & CCSSO, 2010, p. 12).

One Crazy Summer (2010) by Rita Williams-Garcia tells the story of three sisters from Brooklyn who travel one summer to Oakland, California, to spend a month with the mother they hardly know. But this is the summer of 1968, when riots break out in Oakland and the sisters get caught up in the Black Panther movement. Few students today are aware of this important part of race relations in U.S. history.

Other examples of historical fiction are included in Appendix B.12.

Biographies and Autobiographies

Biographies are the stories of notable individuals written by other people, and autobiographies are the stories of notable individuals as written by themselves. These books often have much in common with historical fiction, and they can help students become interested in history beyond simply memorizing places and dates. Autobiographies and biographies, if well researched and well written, help bring the stories of famous and influential people alive for readers.

Books are the windows through which the soul looks out.

HENRY WARD BEECHER

The autobiography of young 2014 Nobel Peace Prize winner Malala Yousafzai, who stood up to Taliban repression in Pakistan, is told in *I Am Malala: How One Girl Stood Up for Education and Changed the World* (2014). In *Django: World's Greatest Jazz Guitarist* (2009), Bonnie Christensen tells of the struggles of "Django" Reinhardt, who with a deformed left hand taught himself to play the guitar. *Something Out of Nothing: Marie Curie and Radium* (McClafferty, 2006) encourages young women and scientists to pursue their dreams. In *Boy: Tales of Childhood* (2001) Roald Dahl humorously recounts his childhood that was filled with bullies.

Younger readers will enjoy Cynthia Rylant's picture autobiography *When I Was Young in the Mountains* (1993). Rylant, a well-known children's author, grew up poor in the mountains of West Virginia, living with her grandparents and other relatives in a four-room house. She remembers her grandfather coming home from the coal mines, covered in black dust; she also recalls walking through the woods and cow pastures to the swimming hole where the children bathed. Another author, Jacqueline Woodson, revisits the volatile time of her childhood in *Brown Girl Dreaming* (2014), which is told in moving verse.

In *Who Was Albert Einstein?* (2002), Jess Brallier tells the story of the famous physicist's life in an engaging way that explores how he changed the world. An old but still favorite picture biography for young readers is Clyde Bulla's *Lincoln's Birthday* (1965). Other picture biographies by the prolific author Jean Fritz include the following: *Why Not, Lafayette?* (1999); *Harriet Beecher Stowe* (1994); *Just a Few Words, Mr. Lincoln* (1999); *Who's Saying What in Jamestown, Thomas Savage?* (2007); and *What's the Big Idea, Ben Franklin?* (1993).

An unusual and excellent biography is Russell Freedman's *Lincoln: A Photobiography* (1987), which captures the life of Abraham Lincoln in actual photographs. Another notable biography by Russell Freedman is *Eleanor Roosevelt: A Life of Discovery* (1993).

Other biographies and autobiographies that will appeal to young readers are included in Appendix B.13.

Informational or Nonfiction Books

Nonfiction books, also known as informational books, contain facts and information about a given topic. The intent of the authors of such books is to inform young readers about the real world. As such, they are a great supplement to your school's content area textbooks, which may be dry and include too much information for young readers to handle at once. Informational literature, on the other hand, concentrates on one topic—African lions or the planet Venus, for example—and often includes many appealing photographs and illustrations (Palmer & Stewart, 2003).

Informational writing, also known as *expository text,* uses a structure different from the narrative text used in fiction writing. For example, narrative text is often organized around a setting, character, and plot, whereas informational writing may utilize descriptive, comparison–contrast, question–answer, and chronological structures. These latter structures are often less familiar to young students and therefore must be directly taught by teachers.

Sections of the CCSS standards focus specifically on the reading and writing of informational texts by K–12 students. For example, students by the end of grade 5 will be able to "read and comprehend informational texts, including history/social studies, science and technical texts" (CCSS RI.5.10; NGACBP & CCSSO, 2010, p. 14). You will need to present specific minilessons on informational text structure and give students opportunities to conduct research that requires them to read nonfiction books.

Included in informational texts are some of the first books young readers encounter: alphabet and counting books. Perennial favorites in the former category include Brian Wildsmith's *ABC* (1962), Ed Emberly's *ABC* (1978), and Maurice Sendak's *Alligators All Around* (1962). Favorite books about numbers include *Anno's Counting Book* (1975), and Sendak's *One Was Johnny* (1962). Young readers will also enjoy Peter Spier's *People* (1980). Noted author and illustrator Tomie dePaola has written numerous informational books for young readers, including *The Cloud Book* (1975), *The Kid's Cat Book* (1979), *The Popcorn Book* (1978), and *The Quicksand Book* (1979).

Some of the most prolific writers of informational books for young readers are Gail Gibbons, Jerry Pallota, and Seymour Simon. Gail Gibbons has written over 130 informational books. Her titles include *Coral Reefs* (2010), *Tornadoes* (2010), and *Ladybugs* (2012). Jerry Pallota has written more than 20 alphabet informational books. Some of his titles include *Lion vs. Tiger (Who Would Win?)* (2010), *Tarantula vs. Scorpion (Who Would Win?)* (2012), and *Hammerhead vs. Bull Shark (Who Would Win?)* (2011). *The New York Times* called Seymour Simon the dean of children's science writers. His books include *Bones* (1998), *Muscles* (1998), *Horses* (2006), *Amazing Bats* (2005), *Hurricanes* (2007), *Icebergs and Glaciers* (1987), *Comets, Meteors and Asteroids* (1994), *The Brain* (2006), *Our Solar System* (2007), *Weather* (2006), and many more. For more information, visit his website, www.seymoursimon.com.

Other informational books for young readers include *Tigers* (Marsh, 2014) and *Bats* (Carney, 2010), which use narrative and photographs to show these creatures in their natural settings; *Super Submarines* (Mitton, 2014), which gives a glimpse into the wonder of these underwater vessels; *A Million Dots* (2003) by Andrew Clements, which helps readers visualize very large numbers; *Mama: A True Story in Which a Baby Hippo Loses His Mama During a Tsunami . . .* (2006) by Jeanette Winter; *Fuel the Body: Eating Well* (2008) by Amanda Doering Tourville; *The Human Body (Hidden World)* (2007) by Claude Delafosse and Gallimard Jeunesse; and *The Amazing Circulatory System: How Does My Heart Work?* (2009) by John Burstein.

Older student readers also benefit from informational books, particularly if they are reading below grade level. Remember that science textbooks are written at grade level, which means that in a sixth-grade class, for example, any student reading below the sixth-grade level will have a difficult time comprehending the science content. Supplementing the textbook with informational library books at various reading levels is thus crucial to these students' success. Recommended content area informational books to include in upper elementary and middle school classrooms are the following: *Breaker Boys: How a Photograph Helped End Child Labor* (Burgan, 2012); *Moonbird: A Year on the Wind with the Great Survivor B95* (Hoose, 2012); *Almost Astronauts: 13 Women Who Dared to Dream* (Stone, 2009); *Castle: How It Works* (Macaulay & Keenan, 2012); *Moonshot: The Flight of Apollo 11* (2009) by Brian Floca; *Amazing Whales* (2005) by S. L. Thompson; *The Sea World Book of Whales* (1980) by Eve Bunting; *The Flight of the Pterosaurs* (1986) by Keith Moseley; *The Story of the Statue of Liberty* by Ib Penick; *Black Holes: And Other Bizarre Space Objects* (2006) by David Jefferis; *Inside the Body: A Lift the Flap Book* (1996) by Giuliano Fornari; and *Quest for the Tree Kangaroo: An Expedition to the Cloud Forest of New Guinea* (2006) by Sy Montgomery.

Other informational books that will appeal to students are included in Appendix B.14.

Poetry

Poetry involves expressing feelings and moods in a unique style of language. Poetry can be rhythmical but does not have to rhyme. Poems may follow a specific rhyme scheme, or they may be written in *free verse*. In the upper grades, students analyze the deeper meanings in poems or decipher their rhyme schemes. In the elementary grades your task is to simply get students to enjoy reading poetry, and doing so requires that you expose them to good poetry. Plan to read poetry aloud to your class at least once a week, letting the students listen to and enjoy the language. Strive to select a variety of poems that will interest your class. The many forms of poetry include free verse, acrostic, diamante, haiku, limericks, and visual poems. Introduce your students to all of these types, because what appeals to one student may not appeal to another.

Some favorite poets among young and middle-school students are Shel Silverstein, Jack Prelutsky, and Judith Viorst. Silverstein's *Where the Sidewalk Ends* (1974) is a classic. Prelutsky's *The New Kid on the Block* (1984) is another favorite. Both books emphasize rhyming words and have excellent illustrations. After students have listened to a poem or read a poem on their own, have them use crayons, colored pencils, or even electronic drawing programs to illustrate what the poem means to them.

Collections of humorous poetry that will appeal to young children are Judith Viorst's *If I Were in Charge of the World and Other Worries* (1981) and Eve Merriam's *Jump-on-the-Bed Poems* (1988). Other poets who write for children include Mary O'Neill, Myra Cohn Livingston, and Lee Bennett Hopkins. Two Newbery Medal–winning books of poetry suitable for older students include Nancy Willard's *A Visit to William Blake's Inn* (1982) and Paul Fleischman's *Joyful Noise: Poems for Two Voices* (1988).

Prepare your students for the challenge of analyzing literature and poetry by teaching them about similes and metaphors (see CCSS RL.6.4, 7.4, and 8.4; NGACBP & CCSSO, 2010). Although it is important to emphasize reading and writing poetry for enjoyment when working with students, they should also develop an appreciation for poetry's use of figurative language. To introduce students to figurative language, begin by reading aloud and discussing the examples in Figure 4.2.

Teachers who regularly use poetry in their classroom see an improvement in students' reading and writing skills as well as a positive attitude toward poetry (Stange & Wyant, 2008). See the poetry section later in this chapter and Chapters 6 and 7 on writing for more ideas on using poetry in the classroom. In addition, Appendix B.15 lists anthologies of poetry that will get you started on the enjoyable experience of including poetry in your classroom.

Series Books

Series books such as *The Chronicles of Narnia* by C. S. Lewis have thrilled young readers for generations. Simpler series, such as *Diary of a Wimpy Kid* (2007) by Jeff Kinney, also bring hours of enjoyment and may turn a reluctant reader into a lover of books. Remember, you cannot teach the various skills of reading unless students are first interested in reading. Getting students to enjoy reading is the first and often the hardest step.

FIGURE 4.2   Figurative language: poetry terms.

Simile. A direct comparison using *like* or *as*. Poets use comparisons to explain feelings that cannot be easily explained. "I wandered lonely as a cloud" (from "The Daffodils" by William Wordsworth).

Metaphor. A comparison without using *like* or *as*. When a poet says, "My love is a rose," he is not saying that she has petals and a spiny stem but rather that she is so lovely that images of nature come to mind.

Alliteration. A repetition of initial sounds in a series of words. "Full fathom five thy father lies" (from *The Tempest* by William Shakespeare).

Personification. Giving human characteristics to inanimate objects. "Lightning is angry in the night / Thunder spanks our house" (from "Michael Is Afraid of the Storm" by Gwendolyn Brooks).

Onomatopoeia. Words that represent a literal sound. "A *tap* at the pane, the quick sharp / And blue *spurt* of a lighted match" (from "Meeting at Night" by Robert Browning).

Hyperbole. A gross exaggeration to convey strong emotions or evoke humor. "I'll love you till the ocean / Is folded and hung up to dry" (from "As I Walked Out One Evening" by W. H. Auden).

Oxymoron. A poetic device that creates surprise by placing two opposite or contradictory terms back to back. "Parting is such *sweet sorrow*" (from *Romeo and Juliet* by William Shakespeare).

Assonance. The repetition of a vowel sound within a line or phrase. "Hear the mellow wedding bells / Golden bells" (from *The Bells* by Edgar Allan Poe).

The main characteristic of series books is that they follow a repetitive pattern or story line with familiar characters engaged in various plots. As such they are highly predictable, which provides a good tool for teaching students to make predictions as they read, a basic comprehension skill. For example, mystery series books such as *The Grace Mysteries* by Patricia Finney provide teaching opportunities for identifying specific details and predicting outcomes. Other popular series books include J. K. Rowling's *Harry Potter* books and *The Hunger Games* trilogy (2010) by Suzanne Collins.

Series books remain popular with readers of all ages, and teachers should consider recommending them, particularly to their reluctant readers. See Appendix B.18 for a list of other series books.

Multicultural Books

Given the diverse world we live in and the diversity of our student population, it is more important than ever to introduce your students to literature from other cultures, regions, and religions. The best multicultural literature depicts characters and cultures in a positive but real-to-life manner, free from stereotypes. These books celebrate the uniqueness of peoples throughout the world, yet at the same time emphasize the emotions, feelings, and dreams that all people share (Horning et al., 2012). Multicultural books may be fiction or nonfiction.

Unfortunately, although we now see great diversity in our classrooms, many schools still fail to offer students a wide selection of quality multicultural picture books and chapter books (Temple, 2013). The best multicultural books do not generalize about cultures but reveal specific details that will appeal to students attempting to understand that world. For example, in *Christmas in the Big House* (1994), Patricia McKissack describes the differences between two Christmas celebrations on a Southern plantation in the 1800s—one for the slaves and one for the slave owners.

Allen Say, a Japanese American, writes books based on his family's experiences. They often depict how Japanese Americans had to struggle to adjust to a new culture after immigrating to the United States. Among his best books are *Grandfather's Journey* (1993), *Emma's Ring* (2003), and *Tea with Milk* (1999).

Three books that can stimulate class discussions are *Encounter* by Jane Yolen (1996), *One Green Apple* by Eve Bunting (2006), and *Coolies* by Yin (2003). *Encounter* is told in first person by a Taino Indian boy who lives peacefully in what is now El Salvador until Christopher Columbus arrives on the coast. Bunting's book is about Farah, a Muslim girl who feels alone in her American classroom until she is invited to help make apple cider. *Coolies* exposes the hard, exhausting work of the Chinese laborers, including young boys, as they built the transcontinental railroad. Each of these books can be used to help students "assess how point of view or purpose shapes the content and style of a text" (CCRA.R.6; NGACBP & CCSSO, 2010, p. 10).

As you recall from Chapter 2, Hispanics are the fastest growing ethnic group in the United States. In states such as Florida, New Mexico, Arizona, Texas, and southern California, Hispanics make up a sizeable portion of the school population. But teachers in all 50 states may have Spanish-speaking students in their classrooms, and all teachers should be aware of and include literature from the Hispanic/Latino cultures, including bilingual books. Books written in both Spanish and English will help your non–English speaking students to learn English more quickly and your English speakers to learn some Spanish.

The House on Mango Street (1984) by Sandra Cisneros is an example of a classic Hispanic novel for older students. Through a series of short vignettes, a young Latina girl comes of age in a Spanish-speaking Chicago neighborhood. Isabel Allende, the famous South American adult novelist, is the author of *City of the Beasts* (2002), an adolescent adventure novel about 15-year-old Alex and his grandmother, who must venture into the Amazon jungle. And Julia Alvarez, also known for her adult novels depicting her family's struggle in the Dominican Republic under the dictatorship of Rafael Trujillo, has written the young adult novel *Before We Were Free* (2002). In it, 12-year-old Anita struggles to find her identity while avoiding Trujillo's dreaded secret police.

Classroom teachers wishing to learn more about Hispanic literature for their students should consult the American Library Association's home page for the Pura Belpré Award. This award was established in 1996 and is given annually to a Latino/Latina writer and illustrator who "best portrays, affirms, and celebrates the Latino cultural experience." The 2013 award went to Benjamin Alire Saenz for his book *Aristotle and Dante Discover the Secrets of the Universe* (2012), in which two 15-year-old Mexican American boys growing up in Texas forge a deep friendship, despite their personality differences and complicated family lives, and come to terms

read RESEARCH practice

Be your own judge of children's and young adult literature by reading some of the books mentioned in this section. Keep notes about each book. You may wish to enter them in a database or set up an account with an online book-sharing site such as Goodreads (www.goodreads.com). Record the book's title, author, publisher, and date of publication. You may want to also include a story summary, an estimate of the appropriate reading level, and possible classroom uses. After conferring with your field experience teacher, try reading one of the books to your class.

RRP

with what it means to be a man. Pura Belpré honor books in 2014 included *The Lightning Dreamer: Cuba's Greatest Abolitionist* (2013) by Margarita Engle, which tells the story of 19th-century Cuban abolitionist Gertrudis Gomez. For younger readers, the allegorical picture book *Pancho Rabbit and the Coyote: A Migrant's Tale* (2013), by Duncan Tonatiuh, tells the story of a young rabbit who sets out to find his father, who went north to find work.

Other awards for multicultural books are the Coretta Scott King Award, bestowed annually since 1970 "to outstanding African American authors and illustrators of books for children and young adults that demonstrate an appreciation of African American culture and universal human values" (ALA, 2014); the Asian/Pacific American Awards for Literature, which include young adult and children's picture book categories; and the American Indian Youth Literature Award, given every two years since 2006 to a Native American author by the American Indian Library Association. Lists of these award-winning books can be easily found online. Other multicultural books that would appeal to elementary and middle-school students are included in Appendix B.2.

CHOOSING MATERIALS FOR THE CLASSROOM

ood schools have excellent libraries that are supplemented by individual classroom libraries. Teachers should constantly be on the lookout for new, quality children's and young adult literature. These should include fiction and informational picture as well as chapter books in all genres. Libraries should also reflect today's complex and diverse world, including multicultural literature and literature that combats discrimination of all types.

Resources

Your first best resource is the school librarian. The second best resource is the librarian at your nearest public library. Online research will also reveal a wealth of resources, including literature anthologies, publishers' catalogues, and author websites. The website Where Should I Read Next? (www.whereshouldireadnext.com) allows you to simply click on the country or city on the map to find books that are related to that location. Appendix A.3 of this book will send you to other useful resources, including professional organizations and publications and annual children's and young adult literature awards and booklists.

Guidelines for Evaluating Books

What makes a children's or young adult book a quality work of literature is open to debate. One person's favorite book or author may not appeal to others. There are, however, committees of authors and educators who each year select what they consider to be the best books in particular categories. A good place to start is with the Caldecott Medal winner for picture book illustrations and the Newbery Award winner for chapter fiction books. These awards also include honor awards for runners-up. Savvy teachers also rely on their students to tell them what books they enjoy. Each year the International Reading Association publishes Children's Choices and Young Adults' Choices, lists of favorite books chosen by the young people who read them.

No matter what grade you teach, always provide texts of various reading levels in your classroom for the

read RESEARCH practice

Choose a literature book recommended either in this chapter or by another teacher, and use the guidelines in Figure 4.3 to evaluate it for yourself. Then evaluate an informational book according to the criteria presented in Figure 4.4. Comment in your notebook about the benefits for both teachers and students of evaluating books.

students who need them. For example, a typical fourth-grade class library should include picture books at first- and second-grade reading levels as well as chapter books to challenge students reading at the sixth- and seventh-grade levels.

When evaluating narrative texts, you may find it helpful to think about the guidelines listed in Figure 4.3. For informational texts, use the criteria in Figure 4.4. You should also model the evaluation process for your students so that they have a framework of specific criteria to use in judging books on their own.

In addition to books, good literacy classrooms should include age-appropriate magazines. Here is a short list of quality magazines for young people:

- *Ranger Rick* and *Go Wild* (National Wildlife Federation)
- *Highlights for Children*
- *National Geographic World*
- *Appleseeds, Ask, Spider, Cricket, Dig, Cobblestone, Muse, Faces, Odyssey* (found at www.cricketmag.com).

Books to Reflect Special Needs

Good children's and young adult literature can also sensitize students to the special needs of their classmates. Today's classrooms include students with mental, emotional, and physical disabilities. You can prepare your students for positive interaction with all classmates by reading quality books aloud and making them available to the class, which will help stimulate interesting discussions. A few examples are given following Figures 4.3 and 4.4.

Guidelines for evaluating literature.   **FIGURE 4.3**

1. **Prereading Information**

   What kind of book is this?

   What can my students predict about this story from the cover and title? From the illustrations? From the chapter titles? From the print size?

   How can I use this book in class?

2. **Story Line**

   Does the book tell an interesting story?

   What happens and how does it end?

3. **Setting**

   Where and when does the story take place?

   In view of the story line, does the setting make sense?

4. **Theme**

   What is the underlying idea of the story?

   Is this theme something my students can understand?

5. **Characters**

   Who are the characters?

   Are the characters appealing, consistent in their behavior, and free of stereotypes?

6. **Style and Format**

   What is special about the way the author writes?

   Is it easy to understand what the author is trying to say?

   Do the pictures, colors, and cover fit the story?

   Does the cover reflect what is within?

7. **Reactions**

   How does this story make me feel?

   What does the author do in parts of the story to cause these feelings?

   Is this book as good as other books written by the same author? As good as other books on the same topic?

8. **Evaluation**

   Why did I like or dislike this book?

   What did this book help me to understand?

   Would I recommend this book to my students? Why?

FIGURE 4.4   Textbook and tradebook evaluation checklist.

Rate the statements below, using the following rating system:

5 = EXCELLENT

4 = GOOD

3 = ADEQUATE

2 = POOR

1 = UNACCEPTABLE

NA = NOT APPLICABLE

Further comments may be written in the space provided.

Book Title: _____

Publisher: _____

Copyright date: _____

FORMAT – EYE APPEAL

_____ A. Photographs

_____ B. Photographs that portray diversity in race and gender

_____ C. Colorful charts and diagrams

_____ D. White spaces on page

_____ E. No two side-by-side pages of ALL text

_____ F. Appropriate size of text for grade level

_____ G. Appropriate text font for grade level

FORMAT – STRUCTURE

_____ A. Detailed table of contents

_____ B. Glossary

_____ C. Index

_____ D. Main headings in larger type

_____ E. Subheadings in different font/size

_____ F. New vocabulary in boldface or italics

_____ G. Definitions of new vocabulary in margins

_____ H. Appropriate captions under photographs and illustrations

_____ I. Important facts repeated in illustrations and diagrams

_____ J. Important facts highlighted in separate boxes

_____ K. Pre-chapter questions—literal, inferential, and critical

_____ L. Pre-chapter organizers

_____ M. End-of-chapter questions—literal, inferential, and critical

TEXT

_____ A. Readability appropriate for intended grade

_____ B. New vocabulary explained adequately

_____ C. Appropriate assumption of reader's vocabulary

_____ D. Appropriate assumption of reader's background knowledge

_____ E. Information logically presented

_____ F. Important new information restated through visual aids

_____ G. Clear explanation of new concepts

_____ H. Text is not so oversimplified that relationships among ideas are not clear

_____ I. Appropriate in-depth presentation of information

_____ J. Information presented in a non-encyclopedic manner

_____ K. Sentence structure grammatically correct

_____ L. Appropriate use of conjunctions so relationships among ideas are clear

_____ M. Good pronoun usage

_____ N. Active voice

EXTENSION OF INFORMATION

_____ A. Lists of books where students can get more information

_____ B. Lists of websites where students can get more information

_____ C. Suggestions for outside projects

_____ D. In science texts, good description of appropriate step-by-step experiments

STRENGTHS OF BOOK:

_____

_____

_____

WEAKNESSES OF BOOK:

_____

_____

_____

Recommended for use by _____ (Child's name).

by _____ (Teacher's name).

Source: Literacy Assessment and Intervention for Classroom Teachers (4th ed.), by Beverly DeVries. Copyright © 2015 by Holcomb Hathaway, Publishers, Scottsdale, AZ.

Views from Our Shoes: Growing Up with a Brother or Sister with Special Needs (edited by Donald Meyer, 1997) shares firsthand accounts from young people ages 4 through 18. This frank, easy-to-read book informs readers about many special needs, including seizures, Rett syndrome, autism, cerebral palsy, Down syndrome, attention deficit disorder, blindness, deafness, intellectual disabilities, and others. Patricia Polacco's semiautobiographical *Thank You, Mr. Falker* (1998) tells about young Polacco's own learning difficulties and the many frustrations she encountered at school until she met a great teacher, Mr. Falker. In R. J. Palacio's *Wonder* (2012), August Pullman has a facial deformity that keeps him from attending school until he enters fifth grade. In this funny, inspiring book readers discover how August, or Auggie as he prefers to be called, learns to accept himself. Other books featuring characters with special needs are presented in Appendix B.3.

Books can also help your students deal with special problems in their lives. For example, students may experience the death of a pet, neighbor, friend, classmate, or parent. Marjorie Blain Parker's *Jasper's Day* (2002) is a poignant picture book about the family dog that died. This book should generate thoughtful discussions among your students about the topic of death. *Love Never Stops* (Parga, 2007) helps young readers understand that death does not end the loving memories one has of a family member.

LITERATURE AND LANGUAGE LEARNING

Hearing and reading good children's and young adult literature, both picture and chapter books, enhances students' language, both oral and written. It expands their vocabulary, introduces them to a variety of sentence structures, and allows them to appreciate the beauty of language for storytelling and conveying information. The CCSS Anchor Standards for Reading emphasize the need for students to understand the craft and structure of text. For example, CCRA.R.4 requires students to "interpret words and phrases as they are used in a text, including determining technical, connotative, and figurative meanings, and analyze how specific word choices shape meaning or tone" (NGACBP & CCSSO, 2010, p. 10). Even in the primary grades, teachers can bring attention to the joy of language and how authors use it.

To help your students get a sense of how to use language effectively, frequently read small sections of a text out loud and discuss how the author uses words to add mood or other elements to a poem or story. For example, middle-school teachers may read two pages of rhyme in Dr. Seuss' *Oh, the Places You'll Go!* (1990) and ask students what the author is really attempting to say to readers when he abruptly changes from an exuberant feeling of being the "winning-est winner of all" to the following statement: "I'm afraid that *some* times / You'll play lonely games too. / Games you can't win / 'cause you'll play against you" (unpaged). Since the question has no right answer, give students plenty of time to think about and discuss the games that one cannot win and/or the games that people play against themselves. What is Dr. Seuss trying to get readers to understand?

Books as Language Models

From the wonderful language of books, students become aware of the many ways in which they can use words to express their ideas. For example, students who have heard fairy tales often use the traditional beginning "Once upon a time" in their own made-up tales. These words help students convey the idea of something that happened a long time ago. Without the model of the fairy tale, they may not learn how to convey this idea.

Books also teach students that words express ideas and help them expand their vocabularies as they develop a variety of concepts. For example, a book such as Tana Hoban's *Push–Pull, Empty–Full* (1972) helps youngsters learn about word opposites in a meaningful way. Eric Carle's books *The Very Hungry Caterpillar* (1987), *The Grouchy Ladybug* (1996), and *The Very Busy Spider* (1984) help students acquire proper vocabulary to learn scientific concepts.

As mentioned earlier, books also help students understand figurative language, including similes, metaphors, and alliteration. Mary Ann Hoberman's *A House Is a House for Me* (1978) introduces readers to indirect comparisons or metaphors. For example, a carton is a house for crackers, and a shell is a house for a snail. Other books that treat figurative language in a humorous way are Peggy Parish's *Amelia Bedelia* books, where poor Amelia takes everything too literally; Fred Gwynne's *The King Who Rained* (1970) features words that sound the same but have different meanings, which are called homonyms. Books by Dr. Seuss and Shel Silverstein emphasize playing with language. Recall that the CCSS in the English Language Arts require students beginning in grade 5 to be able to analyze figurative language (NGACBP & CCSSO, 2010). (Refer back to Figure 4.2 for common terms associated with poetry but that are also used in prose writing.)

Text Structure

Reading teachers emphasize comprehension, or understanding, of text. Without comprehension reading becomes mere word calling. To help students improve their comprehension, first help them understand the distinctions between two main types of text: story/fiction writing, called *narrative text,* and informational/nonfiction writing, also called *expository text.*

Narrative text is generally more easily understood by young students because they may already be familiar with the structure from the stories their parents and caregivers read to them. This structure includes a setting (place and time where the story takes place), characters (people or animals), the plot (action or what happens in a story, the events), resolution (the conclusion), and theme (the author's underlying message, often not directly stated). Narrative structure can be taught to students using a visual diagram, called a story grammar (Gonzalez, 2000) (see Figure 4.5).

The structure of expository text differs from that of narrative text. The common organizational patterns found in expository texts are description, chronological sequence of events, comparison–contrast, cause–effect, and problem solution. These patterns will be discussed in more detail in Chapter 10. The following excerpt from *Lincoln: A Photobiography* by Russell Freedman (1987) is an example of description:

> Lincoln was visibly nervous. He was wearing a new black suit and sporting a neatly clipped beard. He held a silk stovepipe hat in one hand, a gold-headed cane in the other. He put the cane in a corner, then looked around, trying to find a place for the hat. Stephen Douglas smiled and took the hat from him. (p. 68)

As is the case with narrative text, a student's knowledge of the structure or pattern of informational text can affect comprehension (McGee & Richgels, 1985; Sinatra, 1991). Because a variety of organizational patterns are utilized, it is not surprising that reading and writing informational texts provides more of a challenge for students than narrative texts. By repeatedly exposing your students to nonfiction books and other

FIGURE 4.5   Story grammar.

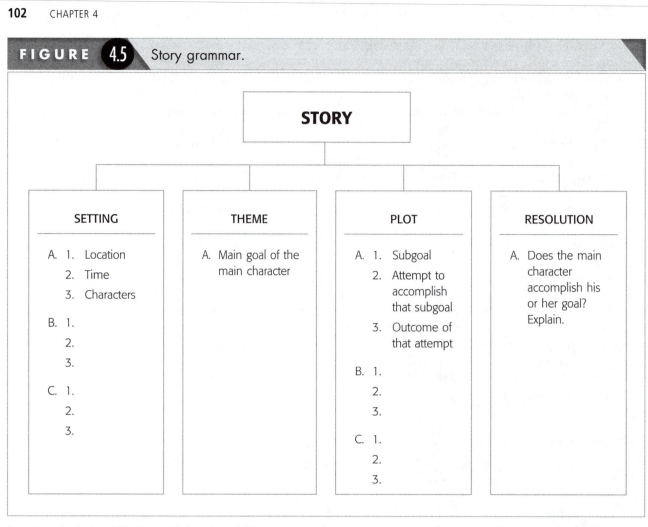

Source: From Cunningham, J. W. & Foster, E. O. (1978, January). The ivory tower connection: A case study. *The Reading Teacher, 31*(4), 365–369. Reprinted with permission of the International Reading Association via CCC. All rights reserved.

expository writing, however, you can help them become more sensitive to the text structures used in such books. Select informational books for read-aloud sessions and include them in your math, science, and social studies units. For example, a unit on Native Americans for students in the middle grades could be enhanced by some of the following informational books:

- Birchfield, D. (2012). *Cherokee History and Culture.*
- Bruchac, J. (1999). *Lasting Echoes: An Oral History of Native American People.*
- Klobuchar, A. (2006). *History and Activities of Native Americans.*
- Phillip, N. (2001). *The Great Mystery: Myths of Native America.*
- Stone, A. (2012). *Creek History and Culture.*

Videos and online resources are also great resources. One possible video for this unit is *Native American Life* (2004), directed by Rhonda Fabian and released by Schlessinger Media.

INVOLVING STUDENTS WITH BOOKS

One of the major goals in every school is to motivate students of all ages to want to read. This is done by teachers reading aloud from good books and allowing time in class for students to read on their own. Nothing excites a student's imagination like a great story or an informational text that motivates her to find another book on the topic. But such motivation does not come easily. You must plan your classroom environment carefully and allow time during the day for listening to and reading from great books and other resources. You can also promote books by engaging in teacher modeling, book talks, reading aloud, the shared book experience, independent reading, and teacher storytelling.

Environment

A stimulating classroom environment goes a long way toward motivating students to want to read. Although there is no one right way to arrange a classroom, the floor plan in Figure 4.6 presents an arrangement that one teacher used successfully to establish a literature-oriented environment. Most importantly, all classrooms should include accessible shelves of books that students are free to browse. Set aside a quiet place for students to read; do this by moving bookshelves to create an enclosed corner and providing large mats for students to relax on. Display colorful book jackets and posters from a variety of genres on classroom walls and bulletin boards to inspire students to read more. Finally, throughout the week devote time to free reading, teacher-led book talks, student-directed literature circles, and student book clubs.

Modeling

Successful literacy-oriented teachers enjoy books and share that enjoyment with their students. They set aside time each day for reading aloud as well as for silent reading. They encourage their students to own and borrow books and make sure that classes have regular trips to the school library and media center. Such teachers also guide students' thinking about books by modeling how to approach a book, read it, and finally evaluate it.

Book Talks

One way for students to share their excitement about books is through book talks, an alternative to the traditional written book report. Book talks can be done in informal, small groups, where students get together and discuss the books they have read. Encourage students to move beyond talking about the plot, setting, and characters of narrative texts, or the main idea of an informational book, and express how the book made them feel. What personal connection, if any, did they have with the book? Book talks can also take place in more formal settings, in which students present their talks to the entire class and ask for comments and feedback. Book talks are an effective way to spread the news about good books to read (Allington, 2002b).

Reading Aloud

As mentioned, teachers at all grade levels should periodically read good books aloud to their class. This is one of the best ways to share great literature, model good reading with intonation, and stimulate discussion. Jim Trelease is one of the leading proponents of reading aloud, and his book *The Read-Aloud Handbook* (2013) is an important reference tool for classroom teachers throughout the country.

FIGURE 4.6   A reading-friendly room arrangement.

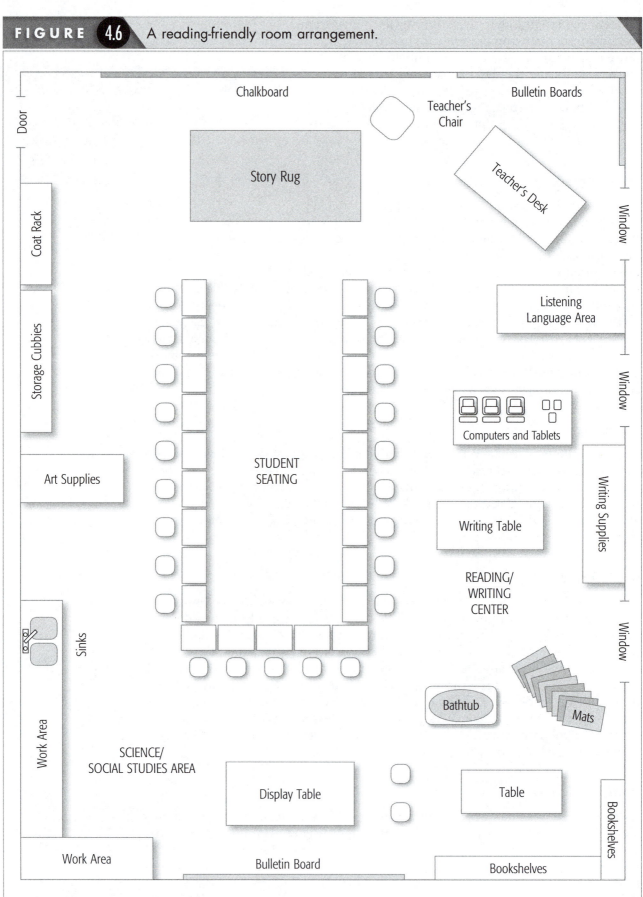

When reading aloud to students, Trelease recommends following these general guidelines:

- Read a variety of appropriate books. Try to appeal to the specific interests of your class.
- Practice reading the book aloud before you try it in front of your students.
- Set aside a specific time during the school day to do a read-aloud.
- When appropriate, enhance book readings with video or audio.
- Make sure students are close enough to see the book's illustrations.
- Settle the students around you first, eliminating any distractions before you read.
- Read with expression and feeling.
- Use props when appropriate; for example, show students cranberries when reading *Cranberry Thanksgiving* (2012) by Wendy Devlin.
- With your class, watch an online video about a particular animal; for example, after reading *Armadillos* (2013) by Sheila Griffin Lianas.
- After reading allow time for student questions and comments.

Shared Book Experiences

Shared book experiences, sometimes known as sharing big books, were first described by Don Holdaway (1991). In its simplest form the teacher reads aloud from a big picture book, while young students gather around in a circle on the rug, close enough so that they can see the pictures clearly. The teacher begins by showing the title and illustrations and asks students to predict what they think this story might be about. The teacher points to each word in the book so students begin making the connection between sounds and letters.

Predictable books with repetitive story lines are good places to begin the shared book experience. For example, in Paul Galdone's *The Three Billy Goats Gruff* (2007), students soon realize that the billy goats chant "trip-trap, trip-trap" when they cross the bridge. Galdone's *The Little Red Hen* (1973) also includes repetitive refrains. Other perennial favorite big books include *A House Is a House for Me* (Hoberman, 1978), *Chicken Soup with Rice* (Sendak, 2004), and *Goodnight Moon* (Brown, 1947).

Big books can also be informational texts. For example, *Full House: An Invitation to Fractions* (2012) and *Each Orange Had 8 Slices* (1994) are big books that introduce students to math concepts.

Independent Reading

Reading aloud to students is important, but equally important is providing time on a regular basis for students to read independently. Beginning in the first grade, the CCSS grade level standards for reading literature require that students be able to read and comprehend stories and poetry at their grade level (NGACBP & CCSSO, 2010), at first with scaffolding and then independently. Therefore, students need plenty of time for independent reading throughout the school day. Depending on where you teach, this practice may be known as USSR (uninterrupted sustained silent reading), SSR (sustained silent reading) or DEAR (drop everything and read) (Garan & DeVoogd, 2008). Implement independent reading by using the following steps:

1. Devote a specified amount of time (for example, 10 minutes to begin with).
2. Instruct each student to bring a book or choose one from the school library to read silently during that time.
3. Everyone reads silently, including the teacher.

4. During independent reading time there can be no interruptions, no talking, no moving about.

5. The independent reading period should be at the same time and follow the same structure each day so that students get in the habit of reading.

Individual free reading time is a crucial aspect of any school's reading program. Most schools, however, leave it up to each teacher to initiate independent reading in her own classroom on her own schedule. A more powerful experience occurs when the entire school, including the principal, all teachers and other staff members, and students stop what they are doing and read silently for 10 or 15 minutes. The positive impact on students is incalculable. If you do not have a school-wide independent reading time, talk to your principal about creating one and share with him or her some of the literature praising the positive effects of such a program (Bryan, Fawson, & Reutzel, 2003).

Teacher Storytelling

Storytelling promotes reading. When you tell a story to students, you are inviting them to read the book, become better acquainted with the characters, and establish their own personal understanding of the events. Through such storytelling efforts, you send a clear message: "I think this is such a great story that I went to the trouble of sharing it so you could enjoy it the way I do."

Storytelling offers a few important benefits that are absent in reading aloud. It allows greater interaction and eye contact between the teller and the audience because the book is no longer a barrier between them. The teller can also improvise with the story and make it a richer experience for the audience. Finally, the teller can use a variety of props, which adds interest and motivates students to use props in their own future storytelling.

Beginning storytellers may find it valuable to read about a storytelling experience of one of the authors in the box on the facing page. Although flannel boards and puppetry are two of the more popular methods for enhancing storytelling, other methods are also effective, especially those using technology.

STUDENTS' RESPONSES TO LITERATURE

Students respond to the literature they read in a great variety of ways. The nature of these responses enhances a child's comprehension of a text, which is your goal. A number of years ago, in the now classic *The Reader, the Text, the Poem: The Transactional Theory of the Literary Work* (1994), Louise Rosenblatt described the importance of the individual reader's interaction with the text and the world around him; this is also known as the *reader response theory*. Reading, Rosenblatt tells us, is a very personal experience; each of us brings unique experiences and emotions to the text we are reading and thus we each experience the same book uniquely.

Readers' previous experiences and knowledge aid them as they read. Effective teachers understand this and help students connect their world knowledge, their previous learning experiences, and their life experiences to new texts they are about to read. These connections are referred to as *text-to-world connections, text-to-text connections,* and *text-to-self connections* (Keene & Zimmerman, 1997; Zygouris-Coe & Glass, 2004).

The text-to-world connections are the connections between the text and the ideas that students have about the world around them. For example, when Mr. Wager introduces Kim Doner's *On a Road in Africa* (2008) to his second graders, he asks them if they have ever seen a television program about animals in Africa.

A story about dachshunds: How storytelling aids language development

When I was trying to convey the importance of storytelling to my undergraduates, I decided that the only thing that would work would be an actual demonstration with a small group of students. I arranged for my students to observe me telling a story to a group of 5-year-olds in the kindergarten class associated with the college.

Because I wanted to ensure a measure of success, I decided to use a story from a book that I had previously read aloud to numerous kindergartners, first graders, and second graders. However, several other reasons also influenced my selection of *Pretzel* (1944) by Margaret Rey. First of all, the story is about two dachshunds—my favorite breed of dog. I also like the overall theme of the story, which is the importance of valuing each individual's unique traits. In addition, the story has a limited number of characters (two main characters) and a series of well-defined events.

Some professional storytellers feel that stories are not enhanced by props and should be told without them. I, an amateur storyteller, do not subscribe to that philosophy. I believe that the right prop can really enhance a story and help to focus the storyteller. Therefore, I began to explore possible props.

Because I wanted to show the contrast between Pretzel's unusual length and the size of other dachshunds, and because the story has a limited number of characters and objects, I decided to use a flannel board. I made that choice based on data from *Storyteller,* in which Ross (1996) recommends using flannel boards to illustrate stories involving a comparison of sizes, folktales, scientific tales explaining phenomena, and accumulative tales such as *I Know an Old Lady Who Swallowed a Fly.*

I made my flannel board by covering a portable cork bulletin board with a large piece of tan felt. For the figures in the story, I used brightly colored pieces of felt and drew enhanced facial features and decorations with magic markers.

Once the props were completed, I began preparing *Pretzel* for the kindergartners. As recommended by many authorities (Ross, 1996), I did not memorize the story. Instead I read it over many times to get a sequence of the events, and I developed a general timeline in my mind of what happened first, what happened second, and so on. I also tried to develop the personality and voice for Pretzel—who was proud, dignified, and helpful—and the traits of Greta, the other dachshund in the story—who was selfish, stuck-up, and spoiled. Once I began telling the story to myself, I began to use particular story phrases such as the following:

> One morning in May five little dachshunds were born.
> Pretzel suddenly started growing—and growing—and growing.
> "I don't care for long dogs," said Greta.

Other than developing the haughty sniff associated with Greta, I didn't add any gestures to the story. However, I did start the story by telling the students a little about my dachshund and allowing them to share some information about their pets. I also decided to let the close of the story be informal by giving the students some time to express their feelings about the story or to handle the felt props. Most of all, I practiced the story in multiple recordings, in the mirror, and in front of friends until they knew it almost as well as I did.

The actual telling went smoothly. With some help from the class's regular teacher, I set the board on a chair and gathered the small group of students around it. As planned, we spent a few minutes talking about my dachshund and the students' experiences with dogs and other pets. Then I launched into my rendition of *Pretzel.* I found that the practice really helped, and I was able to portray Pretzel and Greta in exactly the right light. The students really loved the characters and the story, and we spent several minutes at the end of the story handling the props and saying what we liked best about the tale.

The best part of the experience came after the actual storytelling. Because the students enjoyed handling the props so much, the teacher asked me to leave them in the classroom—a request I was glad to honor. She later told me that the students used the flannel figures frequently in attempts to retell the story and that she was reading the book to them to assist their comprehension of the story.

Also, the experience convinced my students that storytelling is not just a frill—something extra to do on a dreary afternoon. They began to understand that books and storytelling form a core component of a language development program.

Students who have seen many educational programs about African wildlife may readily connect with the text, which is about an animal orphanage in Kenya. The information previously learned from a video or television program will help the students make a connection to the new information in the book.

Text-to-text connections occur when students connect new information in a text to what they have already read on a particular subject. For example, Ms. Tyler, a second-grade teacher, knows that many of her students, when given the opportunity, choose books from the class library about space. One of the leveled readers in the room is *The International Space Station* (Rigby, 2006). Before she passes out a copy to each student in her small reading group, she lets them share the information they know about space from other books they have read so they recall how vast space is. She then introduces *The International Space Station* and tells them they will learn how some people get to live in space in a capsule known as the International Space Station. Activating prior knowledge learned from other texts will not only pique students' curiosity, but it will also allow them to better connect with the text as they read it.

Finally, text-to-self connections occur when students read a novel with a plot that reflects one of their life's experiences, or when they read an informational text about a place they have visited. For example, one student in Mr. Hawk's fifth-grade class, John, lived on a large ranch in Texas, and his father hired Mexican laborers to work his land. John was amazed at how hard the men worked without complaining. When John started reading Cynthia DeFelice's *Under the Same Sky* (2003), he identified with Joe, who also lived on a farm that had Mexican workers. He told Mr. Hawk that it was the best book he had ever read. He said, "DeFelice really nailed it on the head. My father found out that some of our workers were not in the states legally and that some workers were underage. He really felt bad when they were picked up because he saw they were trying to make a better life for their families." It was obvious that John connected his life experiences to the plot in the novel.

Another example of text-to-self connections involves Ben, who visited Mt. Rushmore with his parents over the summer. Ben was excited when Mr. Upchurch, his seventh-grade teacher, suggested that he read *Great White Fathers: The Story of the Obsessive Quest to Create Mount Rushmore* (Talliaferro, 2004). Ben usually chose novels for independent reading, but this time he agreed to an informational book because he wanted to learn more about how the massive sculpture had been carved. He remembered the tour guide talked about the years of work it took to chisel the presidential portraits into the side of the mountain. He told Mr. Upchurch that what he read was really true because he had seen it. Mr. Upchurch understood that one way to get Ben interested in informational text was to suggest books that would connect to Ben's travels.

You can help students make connections to text and to respond to literature through discussions, literature circles, retellings, book publishing, creative drama, art activities, poetry units, and oral and written methods for sharing books.

Discussions

Earlier we described modeling and book talks as ways of enhancing students' interactions with books. The CCSS Speaking and Listening standards require students as early as kindergarten to "participate in collaborative conversations with diverse partners" (CCSS SL.K.1; NGACBP & CCSSO, 2010, p. 23). Book discussions allow students to have collaborative, informal conversations without prior preparation. These are best done in small groups, among friends who wish to talk about what they are reading. Teachers can also lead book discussion groups, and often they follow book retellings or teacher read-alouds. Sometimes, teachers ask groups of students to discuss one aspect of the book they have read, such as the characters, setting, or plot, or the main ideas of informational texts.

For example, the winner of the 2012 Newbery Award, *Dead End in Norvelt* (2011) by Jack Gantos, takes you to the rural community of Norvelt, Pennsylvania, where young Jack is prepared to spend another boring summer. To mentally escape he pretends to be a U.S. Marine fighting the Japanese on Wake Island during World War II or the Spanish conquistador Francisco Pizarro conquering the Incas of Peru. But then his mother sends him to help old Miss Volker with her chores, and he winds up typing the obituaries of Norvelt's deceased citizens. Discussion may focus on how Jack feels working for Miss Volker, or how an adolescent boy livens up a summer in a boring town. Students may also find it interesting that this novel is based on some of the author's childhood experiences.

> Books are friends that never fail.
>
> **THOMAS CARLYLE**

The informational book *Locomotive* (Floca, 2013) is another good choice for a small group discussion. This picture book, winner of the 2014 Caldecott Medal and Robert F. Sibert Award, shares information about the building of the railroad from Nebraska to California. The text and illustrations evoke discussion about the incredible hard work and obstacles that the builders endured. Many students will be interested in how a steam engine works or how workers made tunnels through the mountains.

Literature Circles

Literature circles are student-led collaborative conversations among a group that meets at a regular time each week (Tierney & Readence, 2005). The groups can be structured with a director who keeps the discussion flowing, a literary luminary who decides which parts of the book should be read aloud, and an illustrator who draws pictures relating to the book and shares them with the group. You can also have the group keep a log that records their discussion (Daniels, 2002). Other characteristics of literature circles include the use of multiple texts with multiple copies, whole-group and small-group discussions, and response journals. Your job is to guide and support the group in order to make the process work. Monitor students during the discussion and gather materials from each student's role to determine their progress. This approach takes time, patience, and lots of modeling.

Student Storytelling

The CCSS Speaking and Listening standards emphasize the importance of students telling or recounting a story or experience. For example, CCSS SL.2.4 requires that students retell "with appropriate facts and relevant, descriptive details, speaking audibly in coherent sentences" (NGACBP & CCSSO, 2010, p. 23). Storytelling is a way of stimulating vocabulary growth, improving sentence structure, and building oral language skills. It is also a great way for students to share their reading experiences with others, because students naturally want to tell others about the books they have read. Imagine the delight of the student who hears, imitates, and even dramatizes the giant's refrain in "Jack and the Beanstalk": "Fee. Fie. Foe. Fum. I smell the blood of an Englishman." How wonderful and satisfying it is for students to reach into their storehouse of literature and find just the right words to express ideas and feelings.

Student storytelling can be done extemporaneously or through preparation based on a book read. Very young students can begin telling stories by using wordless picture books; for example, using *Bobo's Dream* (1970), about a dog's dream told entirely in pictures, the student supplies the narrative text. Even older students can enjoy oral storytelling when using more sophisticated wordless picture books, such as John Goodall's *An Edwardian Christmas* (1977) or David Wiesner's *Flotsam* (2006).

Students can use props in their storytelling to enhance the entertainment value for the audience. For example, in telling about Chris Van Allsburg's *The Polar*

Express (1985), one student brought in a small model train and a sleigh bell. The CCSS SL.2.5 requires students to "create audio recordings of informational books, stories or poems; add drawings or other visual displays to stories or recounts of experiences when appropriate to clarify ideas, thoughts, and feelings" (NGACBP & CCSSO, 2010, p. 23).

Appendices D.2–D.4 provide storytelling rubrics for assessing students. Appendix D.2 contains a storytelling rubric, and Appendix D.3 contains a modification of this rubric. Appendix D.4 contains a rubric for voice inflection. Always construct a scoring rubric based on the criteria you give your students. Notice in the modified rubric that the speaking aspect of storytelling is emphasized by assigning more points for it. The modified rubric also emphasizes body movement. Storytelling as an oral language activity will be discussed in Chapter 8.

Story Grammars, Charts, and Maps

After students have experienced an emotional response to a book, go back and help them understand why they enjoyed it by looking at the story's structural elements. As mentioned earlier, a story grammar is a visual picture of a story's structure. Once you have demonstrated a story grammar to the class, have your students use the technique for sharing the stories they have read. Recall that story grammars outline the major elements and events in a story. Figure 4.7 shows a story grammar for "Goldilocks and the Three Bears."

FIGURE 4.7   Sample story grammar: "Goldilocks and the Three Bears."

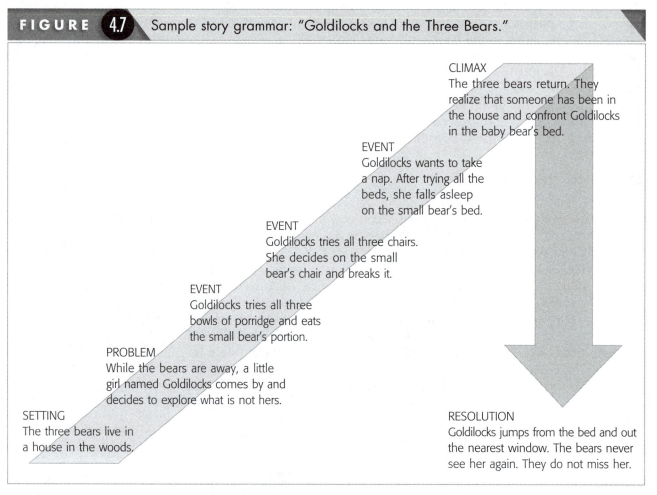

CLIMAX
The three bears return. They realize that someone has been in the house and confront Goldilocks in the baby bear's bed.

EVENT
Goldilocks wants to take a nap. After trying all the beds, she falls asleep on the small bear's bed.

EVENT
Goldilocks tries all three chairs. She decides on the small bear's chair and breaks it.

EVENT
Goldilocks tries all three bowls of porridge and eats the small bear's portion.

PROBLEM
While the bears are away, a little girl named Goldilocks comes by and decides to explore what is not hers.

SETTING
The three bears live in a house in the woods.

RESOLUTION
Goldilocks jumps from the bed and out the nearest window. The bears never see her again. They do not miss her.

Source: Adapted from L. Galda (1987), "Teaching Higher Order Reading Skills with Literature."

Another visual response activity is creating character perspective charts (CPCs). Shanahan and Shanahan (1997) describe CPCs as a way of understanding well-rounded characters, as opposed to flat or minor characters. CPCs help students develop a more complete appreciation for the viewpoints of all the characters in a story. Such charts are especially useful for stories where characters are in conflict. For example, in the illustrated multicultural book *Mufaro's Beautiful Daughters* (Steptoe, 1988), Mufaro has two daughters who are the love of his life. When the king announces that he is seeking a kind and beautiful woman to be his wife, Mufaro sends both daughters to visit him. Along the way one of the daughters proves to be haughty and unkind in her desire to be queen, while the other daughter is humble and generous to others. Figure 4.8 shows a character perspective chart.

Story maps are similar to story grammars in that they create a picture of a story's sequence of events (ReadingRockets, 2012). They also build upon story structure and can be used along with questions to guide youngsters through a re-creation of a story. Some story maps follow a sequential story line, whereas others depict circular plots. Teach the use of story maps by beginning with a simple story, which in turn will require a simple map. After hearing and reading a number of these stories, students begin to internalize a story's structure, including setting, character, plot, and event sequence. Developing this mental schema enables students to better predict what will happen in the stories they read and thus improves their comprehension.

Sample character perspective chart: *Mufaro's Beautiful Daughters.* **FIGURE 4.8**

Main character: Who is the main character?
Nyasha.

Setting: Where does the story take place?
A village and city in Africa.

Problem: What is the main character's problem?
Dealing with her sister's (Manyara's) bad temper.

Goal: What is the main character's goal? What does the character want?
To be good and kind and do the right thing.

Attempt: What does the main character do to solve the problem or get the goal?
Continues to be considerate and kind to every living creature.

Outcome: What happened as a result of the attempt?
The king recognizes her goodness; she becomes queen.

Reaction: How does the main character feel about the outcome?
Happy.

Theme: What point did the author want to make?
Kindness and goodness are rewarded.

Main character: Who is the main character?
Manyara.

Setting: Where does the story take place?
A village and city in Africa.

Problem: What is the main character's problem?
Showing her sister's (Nyasha's) kindness to be a weakness/concealing her bad temper.

Goal: What is the main character's goal? What does the character want?
To marry the king and be queen.

Attempt: What does the main character do to solve the problem or get the goal?
Secretly leaves early for the city to be the first to meet the king.

Outcome: What happened as a result of the attempt?
The king recognizes her faults; she becomes a servant in the king's household.

Reaction: How does the main character feel about the outcome?
Appears to be upset.

Theme: What point did the author want to make?
Selfishness is its own undoing.

Constructing a story map is simply a matter of helping your students illustrate the sequence of events in a story. For example, suppose you have just finished reading Arthur Yorinks's *Hey, Al* (1985) with your students and you say to them, "Tell me what happened in this story." However, instead of simply listing all the events on the board, you draw a circle and instruct the students to put the story events in the correct order around the circle. The completed diagram would look something like the one shown in Figure 4.9. Asking students to draw out their story maps as an art activity further enhances comprehension.

Graphic organizers, discussed and illustrated in Chapter 5, can be used to create an overview of an informational book. Common graphic organizers include the Venn diagrams, timelines, and the cause–effect organizer.

Book Publishing

Students love to become involved in reading by publishing and reading their own books or those of their friends. (We discuss creating bound and digital books in Chapter 6.) One preschool teacher, for example, performed repeated readings of John Langstaff's *Over the Meadow* (1957). Once the students became familiar with the rhyme and rhythm of the story's language, they wanted to compose their own additions to the tale. The students decided they wanted to use pets in a backyard instead of wild animals in a meadow. They broke into small groups and worked on

FIGURE 4.9   Sample story map: *Hey, Al.*

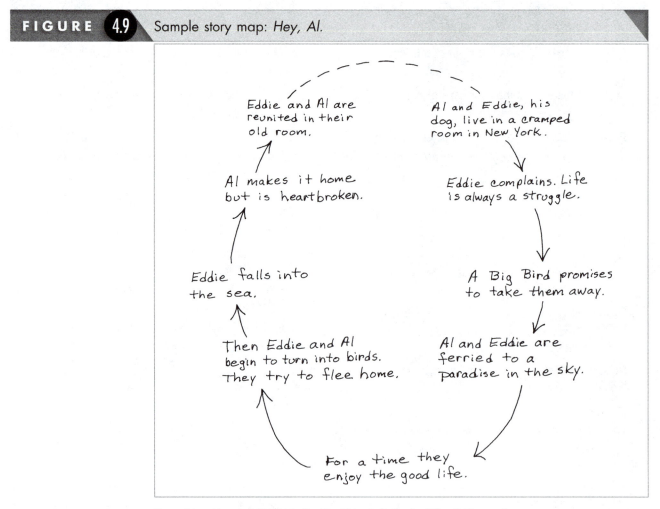

Source: Adapted from L. Galda (1987), "Teaching Higher Order Reading Skills with Literature."

Mr. Funk's fourth-grade class has been listening to and reading various types of stories, including folktales. Today he is going to teach his students how to use story maps to remember the structure of a folktale.

"I've brought another story I think you are going to enjoy," he says. "I want you to listen carefully as I read just the title and opening paragraph. Then I want you to help me draw a kind of map of the story, of what parts you think the story might contain." He begins reading the story "Clever Gretchen."

"Once upon a time there lived a lord who had a daughter named Gretchen, who was as clever as she was good, and pretty besides. Rich merchants and noblemen came from all over the country to ask her hand in marriage, but her father would have none of them. 'The man who marries my daughter,' said he, 'must be the best huntsman in the world.'" Mr. Funk stops reading at this point.

"What kind of a story do you call this?" he asks.

"A folktale," says Ramon.

"How do you know?" asks Mr. Funk.

"Because it begins with 'Once upon a time.'"

"Good for you," says Mr. Funk. "You remember other stories we've heard that begin the same way. Using your previous knowledge of folktales, let's draw a map using some boxes and arrows to show the structure of this story, or at least what we think the structure will be. Afterward we'll read the rest of the story to check our ideas."

Mr. Funk tapes a large piece of butcher paper on the board. "What elements might you expect to encounter in this story just from having heard the first paragraph?" he asks.

"Well, there's a setting and some characters," says Zach. "We already know there's Gretchen and the rich lord."

"There's also a problem," says Lindsay. "They've got to find the best huntsman in the world for Gretchen to marry."

Mr. Funk writes these ideas on the paper in a list and then leads the students in creating a story map outline. They fill the map with their guesses about the story, then listen to Mr. Funk read the rest of the tale. Some of their guesses are correct; others are not and need to be revised. Figure 4.10 shows the revised narrative story map the class produced.

creating their own verses for the story. This is the modeling technique of writing. Here is one student's verse:

> *Over in our backyard in the grass and the sun*
> *Lived an old mother cat and her little kitty one.*
> *"Purr," said the mother;*
> *"I purr," said the one;*
> *So she purred and was glad in the grass and the sun.*
> *Over in the backyard where a big bush grew*
> *Lived an older mother hound dog and her little puppies two.*
> *"Bark," said the mother;*
> *"We bark," said the two;*
> *So they barked and were glad where the big bush grew.*

The class gathered their verses together and put them in a bound book. That gave them the idea to publish all their writings, and eventually they created a class library of their own books.

Poetry Units

As mentioned earlier, the focus of poetry for primary, elementary, and middle-school students should be enjoyment, not the memorization of technical terms

FIGURE 4.10 Sample story map: "Clever Gretchen."

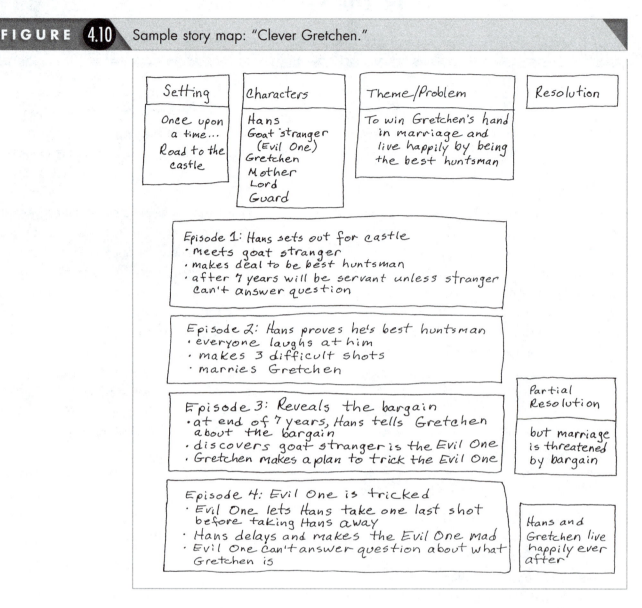

or deep analysis. Poetry has not been a consistent part of the curriculum in all schools; however, the CCSS Reading Literature standards include poetry in addition to stories. The following is a suggested format for a one- to two-week unit on poetry that encourages student response. Remember, a unit is a series of activities all related to the same topic.

Exposure

Begin by exposing students to good poetry by reading aloud to them on a regular basis. As with all oral reading, familiarize yourself with the poem first—practice reading it at home before reading it aloud to your class. Introduce the poem by sharing some insight about it or the poet with the class. A great resource is *Poetspeak: In Their Own Words, About Their Work* by Paul Janeczko (1983), in which poets describe what it means to write a poem, how poetry reflects their lives, and how a poem can have multiple interpretations depending on the reader. This is the listening stage of poetry for students. Appendix B.15 contains a bibliography of poetry sources for school-aged readers.

Sharing

Once you have read a variety of poems aloud to your students over the course of a few days, many of them will want to share their own favorite poems. This can be done as a whole class or in small groups. The latter allows for more students to share their favorite poems in a more intimate setting.

Memorizing

Memorizing a poem is one way for a student to begin to appreciate poetry on a deeper level. However, some students have difficulty with memorization, so this technique should not be overemphasized. Begin by having students choose a short poem to memorize; they will enjoy searching the library for a poem that appeals to them.

If a student wishes to memorize her poem and share it aloud with the rest of the class, suggest a buddy system. One student stands before the class to recite the poem, while the buddy sits up front with a copy of the poem to help with lines if needed.

Copywriting

Have your students select their favorite poem and copy it into their notebooks in their neatest handwriting. Copying not only helps to develop handwriting skills, but also brings the student closer to a better understanding of word choice, rhyme, and rhythm in a poem. Some students may want to create their own poetry books of favorite poems. Having them copy different kinds of poems into their notebooks is among the best forms of preparation for writing original poems. Even professional poets, when faced with writer's block, will copy favorite poems of other poets to get their own creativity flowing.

Illustrating

A companion activity to copying favorite poems is illustrating them. Young students can use crayons and older students can experiment with colored chalk, pen and ink, or programs such as Sketchfu, Sketchpad, or Tux Paint. Many professional poets, such as Shel Silverstein, create their own unique illustrations. Drawing and other art activities should be a regular part of the curriculum, and illustrating poetry provides a great opportunity.

Choral reading

Choral reading involves a whole class or a small group of students reading aloud in unison. Introduce choral reading by first reading a short poem to the class. Then invite students to read it together, using the expression that you modeled. Because your students will imitate your expression, choral reading helps them build fluency, which supports CCSS RF.4 grades K–5. Choral reading also builds self-confidence because it does not require students to read in front of peers.

A good choral reading resource for middle-school teachers is *Joyful Noise: Poems for Two Voices* (1988) by Paul Fleischman. Elementary teachers can choose such poems as "The Happiness Tree" by Andrea Gosline and "What Does a Nose Flattened Against a Window Mean?" by Emily Stew. For more details on choral reading, see Chapter 8.

Writing poetry

Writing poetry should be a part of any poetry unit (see Figure 4.11 for a list of the stages in a poetry unit). First, choose a particular poetry form, such as the diamante, haiku, or limerick. Once your students understand the form, encourage

FIGURE 4.11 Stages in a poetry unit.

1. Exposure
2. Sharing
3. Memorizing
4. Choral reading
5. Copywriting
6. Illustrating
7. Writing poetry

them to try their hand at writing their own example. Students may want to write a poem with a friend or with a group of friends, where each student contributes a line of poetry. If you keep the following guidelines in mind, writing poetry can be one of the most exciting learning experiences your students encounter:

- Poetry does not have to rhyme. In fact, rhyming poetry is quite difficult for young students with limited vocabularies to write.
- Show examples of the various forms of poetry. Students need to see how poetry looks and how it differs visually from prose.
- Be flexible when teaching a fixed poetic form, such as haiku. Not all students will be able to come up with the exact number of syllables per line at first. Proficiency comes with practice.
- Begin by writing a group poem on the board. Students contribute the lines, and you record them. Do not be afraid to change lines; revision is part of the writing process.
- While students are writing their own poems, you should also be writing a poem at your desk to then share with the class. It is important for them to see you engaging with the process as well.

Another fun activity is a poetry relay race. Divide your class into two teams. One student on each team writes a line of poetry and then passes it to the next person to add his line. This continues until the last person in the group contributes a line. When both teams are finished, read the two poems aloud just for fun.

In Chapter 6, the Teaching Activity "Writing Poetry" gives more information about poetry forms and offers additional writing activities.

Sharing Books

We have already mentioned some ways for students to share the books they have read: oral book presentations, bulletin board displays, and book talks. A picture on a bulletin board illustrates what a student thinks about a book, and a book talk enables a student to give her opinion of a story and retell it in a personal way. Some teachers extend this activity by encouraging students to write letters to a classmate who has completed a book talk. Figure 4.12 shows the letters that one teacher and two students wrote in response to a book talk. But there are many other ways for students to share the books they have read with their classmates, including writing journals, letters to authors, bumper stickers, wanted posters, and book ads, or creating mobiles, collages, and models. Many of these activities can be done electronically, if such resources are available and appropriate.

Journals

Journals can be simply a brief record of the books a student has read, the date he finished each one, and a personal comment about them. The length and complexity

Sample letters in response to a book talk. **FIGURE 4.12**

Dear Corey,

I'm glad I finally got to hear your book. You've had it here for a long time and I was curious about it. You did a very nice job reading it. I know everyone has the "gimmies" every now and then just like the bears. Thanks for reading!

Love,
Mrs. Neal

Dear Corey,

I Like your story
I Like the Gimmies.
I think that Bother and Sister
have learnt thier leston.
Mom and Papa have to teach
thier childen a leston.

love,
Tawana

Dear Cory,
I liked your story.
It was funny.
Thank you for reading to us.
You can read good.
Hope you can read agin.
PLEASE read to us agin

Meredith

of comments will reflect the student's age. To introduce your class to journals, share these two books about journal writing: *But I'll Be Back Again: An Album* (1988) by Cynthia Rylant and *Diary of an Early American Boy, Noah Blake, 1805* (1958) by Eric Sloane. Many other children's and young adult books are written in journal format.

Letters

Writing letters, either on paper or via email, to the authors of favorite books gives students a real purpose for writing. Often authors will respond to a student's letter, which is very motivating. Other students may want to write a letter to a character in the book and tell the character what they think of him or her (or it). One book that encourages letter writing is Beverly Cleary's *Dear Mr. Henshaw* (1963), in which a young boy writes to his favorite author.

Bumper stickers

Everyone has his or her favorite bumper stickers. Mine is "One Nuclear Bomb Can Spoil Your Whole Day." Encourage your students to create their own bumper stickers as advertisements for the books they have read. Figure 4.13 shows a bumper sticker created for Sendak's *Where the Wild Things Are* (1963).

Wanted posters

Discuss characterization in the fiction books you read with your class. Distinguish between well-rounded main characters and flat minor characters. Then have your class create wanted posters for their favorite characters, emphasizing their most important traits. Figure 4.14 shows a wanted poster for Winnie the Pooh. Students may wish to use a drawing program on a tablet or computer to create their posters.

FIGURE 4.13   Sample bumper sticker.

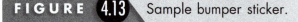

FIGURE 4.14   Sample wanted poster.

Book ads

As a class examine various advertisements in newspapers and magazines. Then have your students create their own advertisements for books they have read. Display the ads around the room and on bulletin boards for other students to read and enjoy.

Mobiles, collages, and models

Mobiles, collages, and models are also ways for students to respond to a book and enhance their reading comprehension skills. Mobiles can be constructed from coat hangers with various cutouts of book characters and settings dangling from strings. Collages are created with small pieces of colored construction paper, colored tissue paper, and pictures from magazines to represent a scene from a book. Students can also create characters out of modeling clay.

TEACHING ACTIVITIES ④

EXPLORING CHILDREN'S AND YOUNG ADULT LITERATURE

1 Creating wordless books

After showing a number of wordless books to your class and discussing how the pictures carry the entire story, hand out construction paper, crayons, and colored pencils. Divide the class into small groups and have them brainstorm ideas for their own story. Once they settle on an idea, let them draw the characters, setting, and establish the various events that make up the plot. Have students share their finished books with other classmates. *Recommended for elementary grades.*

2 Creating fairy tales or folktales

Many fairy tales and folktales express a moral or explain a natural phenomenon. After reading and discussing a variety of fairy tales and folktales, organize your class into small groups. Each group is tasked with coming up with their own original fairy tale or folktale. After writing or typing out their first draft, the group should revise it, proofread it, and correct their errors. Each group's book can then be displayed in the class library for others to read. *Recommended for middle grades.*

3 Creating modern fantasy

Fantasy fiction involves creating an imaginary world with fantastic creatures, superpowers, and other-worldly events. Show your class YouTube videos of interviews with J. K. Rowling in which she discusses how she came to write the Harry Potter series. Then have each of your students create their own modern fantasy story. They may want to refer to other favorite modern fantasy books to get ideas for developing setting, characters, and the rules that govern their imaginary world. *Recommended for middle grades.*

4 Creating historical fiction

After reading a few works of historical fiction, have each of your students select a specific time period in history or a historical figure. Next, have them research the period or person in the library or online. When they have enough information, they can create their own historical novella or short story. During the writing process they may find, as professional authors do, that they need to return to the library or the Internet for more information. *Recommended for intermediate grades.*

5 Creating an informational text

After your class has read a number of informational books, instruct each student to select a topic that interests him or her; for example sharks, hurricanes, or the planet Saturn. Next, have them research their topic in the library or online, take notes, and make an outline. Finally, each student writes his or her own informational book that can later be shared with the rest of the class. Another way for students to share their knowledge is to make a podcast or narrate a slideshow of their report for others to listen to at the listening center. *Recommended for elementary grades.*

6 Creating a multicultural research project

After reading and discussing some quality multicultural literature as a class, have each student select a foreign country to research; this can be done in small groups. The research project that results should include information about the history, geography, language, people, food, and culture of the country. Make sure to give students enough time to revise and proofread the final project. *Recommended for elementary and intermediate grades.*

7 Multicultural reading and presenting activity

Read and discuss some multicultural books, both fictional and informational, in class. Then identify people in your school and community who come from various cultures and countries and have a variety of ethnic and racial backgrounds. Contact these individuals and ask if they would be willing to be interviewed for this class project. If they grant permission, have your students conduct interviews with the individual in groups of two or three. Have them ask the person about their country of origin (if other than the United States), their native language, and unique aspects of their culture. Each group then presents its findings orally to the rest of the class. *Recommended for middle-school grades.*

8 Read-aloud star

The CCSS Reading Foundational Skills standards emphasize fluent reading; for example, CCSS RF.2.4.b states that students "read on-level text orally with accuracy, appropriate rate, and expression on successive readings" (NGACBP & CCSSO, 2010, p. 16). However, asking students to read in front of their peers spontaneously may cause anxiety in some students. Try this instead: After a few weeks of reading aloud to your class on a regular basis, give students the opportunity to be a Read-Aloud Star. Post a list on the bulletin board and have students voluntarily sign up to read a book aloud to the rest of the class. Meet with all student volunteers individually and listen to them read aloud, making helpful suggestions for improving their technique before they read in front of the class. Also recommend that they practice reading the book aloud to their parents the night before they read to the class. *Recommended for primary grades.*

9 Puppet making

Find books and articles on puppetry at your school or public library or online. Decide what type of puppet you will have your students create: a sock puppet, paper bag puppet, papier-mâché puppet, etc. Make a sample puppet and explain how you did it, along with any problems you encountered and how you solved them. Then distribute the necessary materials for the students to create their own puppets. When students have finished, they can use their puppets in future story-telling activities. *Recommended for elementary grades.*

10   Writing haiku

With the help of your school librarian, art teacher, and principal, build into the next school year's budget the purchase of Japanese paintbrushes, ink, and stones. Once acquired, show your students how to use these fine materials to illustrate their Japanese haiku poetry. It will take time for students to become accustomed to these materials. To get your class started on this activity see the following books on haiku:

- *If Not for the Cat: Haiku* (2004), by Jack Prelutsky
- *Yuki and the One Thousand Carriers* (2008), by Gloria Whelan
- *Cool Melons—Turn to Frogs: The Life and Poems of Issa* (1998), trans. by Matthew Golub
- *Henry and Hala Build a Haiku* (2011), by Nadia Higgins

11   Question cubes and fat questions

CCRA.R.8 requires students to "delineate and evaluate the argument and specific claims in a text" (NGACBP & CCSSO, 2010, p. 10). To achieve this goal, elementary students will need to engage in various levels of questioning, from literal and inferential to critical thought. One way to teach them the different kinds of questions is to describe them as *thin* and *fat*. Thin questions require only a "yes" or "no" response without any real thought. Fat questions require thought and cannot be answered with a mere "yes" or "no." Question cubes promote fat questions. To create one, begin with two one-inch wooden cubes and a marker. On one cube write six interrogative words, capitalizing the first letter of each; this becomes the first word in a question (e.g., *Which, What, Why, When, Where, Who, How*). On the other cube, write a verb in lowercase; this signals that it will be the second word in the question (e.g., *did, will, would, should, could, might can, is, are*). Students take turns rolling the cubes; the resulting combination is the beginning of a question about the book they are reading. For example, after sharing *Under the Same Sun* (2014) by Sharon Robinson, daughter of Jackie Robinson, Sam rolls the first cube and gets *Why*; then Jamie rolls *did*. The teacher completes the question by asking the students, "Why did the father take the family to the old slave port in Bagamoyo?" This question will help generate a discussion of the importance of students understanding and appreciating their ancestors. Use this activity with books that have been shared with all students.

read RESEARCH practice

Think of five other ways not mentioned in this chapter in which students can share books. Include them in your notebook with brief descriptions and predictions of how you think they might work in your classroom.

TECHNOLOGY IN THE CLASSROOM

Many websites, CDs, and DVDs deal with children's and young adult literature. For example, Scholastic Book Club produces videos with famous children's authors. Check with your school and local librarians to discover what media related to children's and young adult books are available.

Here are some websites that are useful in exploring literature for young people:

www.ala.org This is the American Library Association's home page.

www.ala.org/alsc/awardsgrants/bookmedia/caldecottmedal/caldecottmedal This site lists the Caldecott Medal and honor books.

www.ala.org/alsc/awardsgrants/bookmedia/newberymedal/newberymedal This site lists the Newbery Medal and honor books.

www.ala.org/emiert/cskbookawards This site lists the Coretta Scott King Award and honor books.

www.apalaweb.org/awards/literature-awards/winners/ This site lists, by year, award-winning picture books, children literature, and young adult books.

www.ailanet.org/activities/american-indian-youth-literature-award/ This site lists the Native American Literary Awards.

www.carolhurst.com This site gives book reviews and activities to use with books.

www.cbcbooks.org This is the Children's Book Council site and has links to book publishers.

www.cyberpg.com/Teachers/folk.html This site lists resources related to folktales.

http://gpn.unl.edu/rainbow This site allows you to purchase DVDs of the *Reading Rainbow* television show.

www.ipl.org/div/askauthor/ This site provides biographical information about several well-known children's book authors.

www.publishersweekly.com/pw/by-topic/childrens/index.html This site offers *Publishers Weekly* news and reviews on children's literature.

www.scholastic.com/teachers This site offers a variety of teaching activities and content, including materials in Spanish.

http://clcd.odyssi.com/index.php/ This is the Children's Literature Comprehensive Database, where you can search for information on the latest in children's books.

SUMMARY

Good books form the foundation of learning in every successful classroom. Sharing a great variety of books with your students is the best way to motivate them to read, which is your primary task as a teacher. To do this you must model good reading, demonstrate how to find books in the library, and encourage your students to share books with each other.

field AND practicum ACTIVITIES

1. AUTHOR EXPERTS. Encourage a group of students to read several books by the same author and note similarities between them. Then help them gather factual information about the author's life and work. Have them construct a bulletin board display highlighting particular books and important facts about the author's life. They can then host a discussion in which they answer other students' questions about the author.

2. BOOKWORMS. Keep track of how many books your students are reading by creating a bookworm. Decorate a face for your worm and attach it to a high spot on a wall. Then cut out the first round segment of the worm and write down the title, author, and illustrator if there is one, of a book you have just read to the class. Write your own name at the bottom of the segment and attach it next to the face. Have plenty of blank segments handy and tell your students to fill one out every time they complete a book. Before you know it, your bookworm will stretch around the room.

3. CHARACTER PARADE. Arrange a time and a day for students to dress up as a favorite literary character. Each student gives three hints about the identity of her or his character, and then classmates have to guess who it is. The student who successfully guesses the identity of the character becomes the next one to present.

4. SHOEBOX STORIES. Each student glues a piece of felt to the inside of a shoebox lid. Then they use different colors of felt to make characters and objects from their favorite stories. Students can store figures from different stories in envelopes they keep in the shoebox. Whenever a student wants to retell or review a story, he uses the shoebox lid as a personal flannel board.

5. CLASS BOOK FILE. Encourage your students to create an index card file of suitable books for the class. Have students complete an index card listing the title, author, and location of the book for each book they read. Also ask the student to include her opinion of the book and her signature. When other students are looking for something to read, they can consult the card file for suggestions. This can then be put in a spreadsheet file for storage and easy retrieval on your computer.

6. THE JOURNAL. Share your journal with your students; perhaps read them an entry or two. Then discuss why people keep journals and what kinds of journals they keep (i.e., a food journal, a travel diary, a dream journal, a reading log, etc). Suggest that they begin to keep a journal for the school year to record their experiences. Try to give students some time each day to write in them.

7. PENNY ARCADE. Once a year have a schoolwide book-sharing event. Each student selects a favorite children's literature character and portrays that character by dressing up in costume and memorizing a brief speech. As parents and other guests come by, they drop a quarter into a jar as the student gives her speech.

Reading

CHAPTER

5

After reading this chapter, you should be able to accomplish the following objectives:

1. Explain the three models of reading.
2. Describe the four pedagogical approaches to reading.
3. Describe the key shifts in reading instruction resulting from the CCSS and newer state standards.
4. Explain how to do a running record.
5. Explain the different kinds of standardized tests.

INTRODUCTION

In May 2013, two horrific tornadoes hit the towns of Moore and El Reno, Oklahoma. Those who made it to the storm shelter safely were aided by reading materials beyond traditional textbooks, trade books, magazines, newspapers, and portable electronic devices. For those in the path of danger, reading materials included radar maps, city maps, charts, and diagrams that people had to follow to stay out of harm's way or get help. Thankfully, such tragedies are rare and reading more commonly involves either entertainment or more practical matters, such as how to prepare a favorite recipe. Reading also helps people connect with others and understand themselves. Literacy is the hallmark of civilization.

Until fairly recently, an individual's reading level was generally gauged by the highest grade she or he had completed in school, but this often presented a distorted picture. In today's workplace, a high reading level allows a person to use complex tools and understand more complex concepts. Thus, the goal of the Common Core State Standards is for all high-school graduates to have the reading skills necessary to read complex texts to be successful in college and their eventual careers.

This chapter looks at the reading process, reading models, comprehension skills, the effect of the CCSS on reading instruction, three pedagogical theories for teaching reading, and finally, reading activities for the primary grades, intermediate grades, and middle-school grades.

READING EXPLORED

"Reading is a complex, cognitive process." —McLaughlin, 2012, p. 436

In the latest edition of *Theoretical Models and Processes of Reading* (Alvermann, Unrau, & Ruddell, 2013), the authors devote more than 1,200 pages to the different viewpoints and models of this complex process. Some researchers have studied reading as a cognitive process, others have studied reading in its sociocultural context, while still others have described reading as a sociocognitive process. The authors of this text believe that reading is a complex, interactive process between reader and author in which readers' world knowledge helps them assimilate new information from the text. We also contend that in our society of multiliteracies, reading and writing cannot be separated from speaking, listening, viewing, and visual representing.

Good readers use their life experience and knowledge about text and language to help construct meaning from the written word. They also monitor themselves as they read to make sure what they are reading actually makes sense. In other words, reading is a very individual process in which what the reader already knows greatly affects what he or she learns from a text. For example, consider what happens when you read the following sentence:

> As the storm approached, the people in the town stored provisions to make sure they would survive.

> *Man's mind, once stretched by a new idea, never regains its original dimensions.*
>
> **OLIVER WENDELL HOLMES**

Depending on what part of the world you are from, the storm might mean a blizzard, a hurricane, a tornado, a monsoon, or a typhoon. Your ideas about provisions might vary from canned tuna and potato chips to dried meat or sacks of rice. Survival might mean "How do we get through a week without electricity?" or "Where can we get brush and wood to make a fire to keep us warm?" Your prior life experiences and the context of the reading situation affect your interpretation of the words in the sentence (Anderson, 2013; McVee, Dunsmore, & Gavelek, 2013).

In reading these words, you are also using your knowledge of both oral and written language. After years of speaking and listening, you easily associate letters with specific sounds in order to figure out a word. You also usually know the right intonation to use as you say the sentence. Your previous experience with writing, grammar, and punctuation enables you to spot the subject and verb of the sentence and know where the sentence begins and ends. In reading the sentence, your mind interacts with the text (writing) to construct meaning. The reading is not done in isolation; it is integrated with your prior knowledge and all the language arts, especially writing.

It is also important to keep in mind the concept of *authentic literacy*. Authentic reading and writing are based on children's literature books and real topics chosen by the students (Duke et al., 2006). By learning and using their literacy skills within an authentic context—that is, by reading books and reading and writing stories, poems, essays, and reports that have meaning to them—students are better prepared for literacy tasks in the real world.

PRACTICAL MODELS OF READING

ur view of reading has been shaped to a great degree by theories and research models of this complex process. Multiple theories are currently used to explain what happens when someone reads. However, none of them perfectly or completely explains the process. New and sometimes conflicting information continually emerges to change our views (Alvermann et al., 2013). Despite this drawback, we present several models that provide practical insights useful to classroom teachers: the bottom-up, top-down, and interactive models.

Bottom-Up Model

The *bottom-up model of reading* has its origins in theories and approaches that emphasize precise identification, or *decoding*, of the individual parts of language. It follows a sequential path that begins with an understanding of the sounds of language and their corresponding letters and moves word by word through sentences, paragraphs, and larger selections of text (Gough, 1972). Through the perception and discrimination of these unique elements, the reader obtains meaning. Essentially, says this model, the language of the text holds the key to its meaning. It is a common-sense approach.

Because decoding, or "cracking the written code of the text," is of prime importance in this model, emphasis is placed on mastering the subskills of reading—those concerned with comprehension (e.g., identifying the main idea and details, following directions, making inferences, and predicting outcomes) as well as those that reflect the rules of language related to letters and sounds (e.g., phonics, structural analysis, spelling patterns, and syllabication). Proponents of the bottom-up approach believe that when readers have learned the various subskills well enough, reading becomes an automatic process of obtaining meaning from the text.

Although research does support the idea that reading contains a hierarchy of subskills, there are some concerns about this approach to teaching reading. First, reading specialists rarely agree on which subskills should be learned by all readers (Roe, Smith, & Burns, 2005). Some emphasize certain skills at the expense of others. Also, many reading educators are convinced that meaning lies not within the text, but within the reader's mind and ability to integrate knowledge with learned strategies for decoding language.

Top-Down Model

The *top-down model of reading* emphasizes the critical role that the reader's mind plays in comprehension, in which understanding, the key objective, takes place through the use of information in the mind rather than through the text itself (Pearson & Stephens, 1992).

Research in psycholinguistics (Goodman, 1967, 1976, 2013) shows that in processing language a person makes use of three cueing systems:

1. *Graphophonic:* the relationship between the sounds of oral language and the letters in the text
2. *Semantic:* the actual meaning of the words and the context in which they are used
3. *Syntactic:* grammar; the rules that govern the organization of the language

According to the top-down model, the reader uses these cueing systems to make predictions or educated guesses about the meaning of what she or he is reading. What the reader expects or anticipates has a profound effect on how he or she actually perceives the textual material.

Suppose you are reading a passage about dolphins and come across a phrase that you read as *the silvery dolphins,* a description that you frequently associate with the mammals. However, further reading shows that the passage is referring to dolphins caught in an oil slick and that your interpretation of the phrase does not really make sense. Upon rereading the phrase, you see that it actually says *the slimy dolphins.* You tested your original hypothesis for the meaning of the phrase and found that it does not work, that there is a mismatch (a *miscue,* in psycholinguistic terminology) between what you perceived and what is actually in the text. You looked for an overall meaning first; when you realized that your first attempt at understanding did not make sense, you then consulted the individual units of language for clarification. This process of attempting to grasp meaning first has caused proponents of the top-down model to view reading as a holistic experience in which a reader's schema influences his or her comprehension (Anderson, 2013).

In accordance with the top-down view, students should be given opportunities to use their minds when reading. They should have experiences with meaningful stories, literature, and big books rather than concentrate on specific language models or rules. However, this emphasis gives some educators cause for concern. They believe that in addition to meaningful experiences, many students truly need to learn specific strategies for processing language.

Interactive Model

The *interactive model of reading* is an attempt to reconcile top-down and bottom-up processing; reading is viewed as a continual interaction between reader and text in which the reader brings meaning to and derives meaning from the page (Ruddell & Unrau, 2013). In this construction of knowledge, the reader attempts to achieve understanding by using prior knowledge stored in mental units of information called *schemata* (Rumelhart, 1980) as well as specific learned strategies for decoding the language of the text.

Reading is thus a highly individualized and personal activity, because each person's schemata and ability to use them are unique. How a person interprets a text depends a great deal on the schemata he or she has developed and how effectively they are used. Therefore, it is possible for two individuals to come to some very different conclusions about the same passage.

Many reading specialists agree with the theory behind the interactive model. However, some have raised questions concerning the specific ways in which the model functions. Are both forms of processing equally important, and do all readers use the processes simultaneously? To date, research has indicated that readers in the stage of emerging literacy may concentrate more on decoding the specific elements in the text than on recalling information in the mind; more mature, efficient readers appear to do the opposite. As more knowledge is gained through research, reading educators may have to modify these views. However, the essential point is that both top-down and bottom-up processing are essential components of reading comprehension. Reading educators need to recognize this when planning instruction for students.

Figure 5.1 offers a visual representation of how these models work. Although each model has its merits, the interactive view provides the most comprehensive and effective description of the reading process, especially when this model is combined with a personal, *transactional relationship* to the world around us (Rosenblatt, 2004). In such a system, each student is part of a dynamic construction of meaning when engaging with text—a process in which cultural, social, and environmental factors influence his or her unique interpretation of the words on the page (Rosenblatt, 2013). In this constructivist view of learning, readers use prior knowledge to make sense of the new ideas shared in the text. Although reading continues to be seen as a holistic construction of knowledge, it also requires specific strategies for understanding textual language (McLaughlin, 2012).

Three models of reading. **FIGURE 5.1**

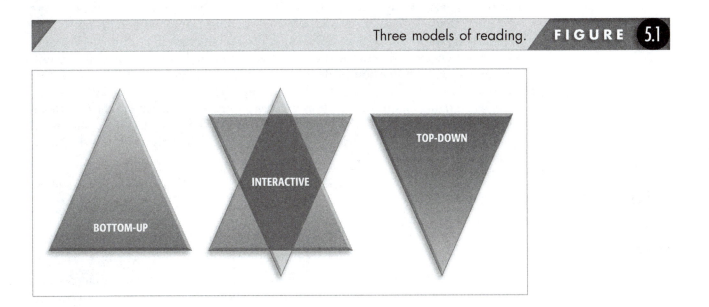

Constructive Approach

In order to construct meaning from the letters and illustrations on the page, readers must use their prior knowledge of words, genre, literary language, and the world to connect with the author. In this constructivist view of learning, readers use prior knowledge to make sense of the new ideas shared in the text.

So what do readers do when they construct meaning? Researchers find that proficient readers set goals, predict, self-monitor, activate prior knowledge, visualize, self question, reread when necessary, socially interact with other readers about text, use context to understand unknown words, change pace when necessary, and summarize, analyze, and evaluate the author's intent (McLaughlin, 2012; Hollenbeck & Saterus, 2013). Constructing meaning from narrative, as opposed to informational, text requires the above skills in addition to others.

To construct meaning from narrative text, readers also need to understand story grammar. They need to know the elements of a story such as characters, setting, plot, theme, and point of view. As they read more complex stories and novels, they need to understand flashbacks. They need to understand that there is a wide range of genres. Historical fiction differs from science fiction, and fantasy fiction differs from realistic fiction. Many students have a preference for a specific type of fiction.

Nonfiction is divided into five categories: informational (e.g., books about science, history, technology, health), concept books (e.g., books about the alphabet, numbers, colors, and shapes), procedural text (how to build or do something), biographies (including autobiographies and memoirs), and reference materials (e.g., atlases, dictionaries) (Duke & Tower, 2004). To comprehend informational text requires a different set of skills. Informational texts are not arranged with a beginning, middle, and end, as stories are arranged. There are no characters with whom the readers can identify. Figurative language is replaced with technical vocabulary that is domain-specific, and each type of content area text differs from one another. Reading story problems in math requires different skills than learning complex science facts. Later in this chapter we discuss informational texts as they relate to the new emphasis found in the CCSS.

We cannot leave this discussion without addressing whether or not digital texts of stories and information aid or hinder comprehension. Most students are mesmerized with e-texts. Tablets are convenient to carry around, and students can interact with them. They enjoy the animation, puzzles, and games that accompany stories, as well as the tablet's ability to pronounce unknown words. These features motivate many students to engage with the text, but some educators are concerned that all these "bells and whistles" detract from comprehension. Figure 5.2 lists some pros and cons of e-texts that researchers have found; however, more research is needed to determine if e-texts are detrimental or supplemental to building students' comprehension skills. At the present time, there is little research that shows a relationship between e-texts and comprehension (Allington, 2013).

After studying Figure 5.2, you may wonder if e-texts have a place in the classroom. Schugar and colleagues (2013) suggest that you ask the following questions when deciding if an e-text will build comprehension skills:

1. Do the extra features distract from the story?
2. Are students able to transfer the reading strategies they have learned from reading traditional text to reading e-text?
3. Does the e-text pass the "quality" test that you use for traditional text?

At the end of this chapter are some e-text resources that do not contain animation.

> Reading helps you think about things, it helps you imagine what it feels like to be somebody else . . . even somebody you don't like!
>
> **PAULA FOX**

The pros and cons of e-texts.   **FIGURE** **5.2**

PROS	SOURCE	CONS	SOURCE
Animation	Roskos, Brueck, & Widman (2009)	Minimal adult–child interaction	Roskos & Brueck, (2009)
Embedded vocabulary	Roskos, Brueck, & Widman (2009)	Minimal number of quality books that aid literacy development	Guernsey (2011)
Video, sound, and music help students draw inferences	Verhallen, Bus, & de Jong (2006)	Videos, sound, and music tax readers' working memory	Bus, Verhallen, & de Jong (2009)
Students' retellings were improved	Pearman (2008)	Readers spend 43% of time with games and puzzles	de Jong & Bus (2003)
Motivators	Schugar, Smith & Schugar (2013)	Animation distracts from comprehension	Schugar, Smith, & Schugar (2013)

READING AND THE COMMON CORE STATE STANDARDS

Recent literature addresses five main shifts from former state reading standards to newer state reading standards and the CCSS for Reading. They are complexity of text, vocabulary building, greater emphasis on informational texts, close reading, and citation of specific textual evidence when drawing conclusions (NGACBP & CCSSO, 2010).

Complexity of Texts

CCRA.R.10 requires students to "read and comprehend complex literacy and informational texts independently and proficiently" (NGCABP & CCSSO, 2010, p. 10). A text's reading difficulty is usually noted in one of several ways. Some books merely state the grade for which the book is intended (e.g., Grade 2). The Accelerated Reading program indicates a book's reading level by listing the specific grade and month the average student can independently read the book (e.g., 3.4 indicates third grade, fourth month). The third way in which books are graded is by the Lexile scale. This scale gives a range of numbers for two grade levels. Because this particular scale is the one used by the CCSS, it was revised "to match the Common Core State Standards' text complexity bands and adjusted upward its trajectory of reading comprehension development through the grades to indicate that all students should be reading at the college and career readiness level by no later than the end of high school" (Finn, 2013, p. 1). This means students will be expected to read more difficult books than under previous systems. Figure 5.3 presents a chart that shows the old Lexile scale with the new one. Based on the changes to the Lexile levels, the other published reading scales, such as the Accelerated Reading scale, will likely also change.

In order for students to comprehend complex texts, they must have a rich vocabulary. Thus, the next section is devoted to vocabulary building.

FIGURE 5.3 Comparison of the original and stretch Lexile bands.

GRADE BAND	ORIGINAL LEXILE BAND	"STRETCH" LEXILE BAND
K–1	N/A	N/A
2–3	450L–725L	450–790
4–5	645L–845L	770–980
6–8	860L–1010L	955–1155
9–10	960L–1115L	1080–1305
11–CCR	1070L–1220L	1215–1355

Sources: http://lexile.com/using-lexile/lexile-measures-and-the-ccssi/textcomplexity-grade-bands-and-lexile-ranges / National Governors Association Center for Best Practices & Council of Chief State School Officers (2010). Common Core State Standards for English, Language Arts, Appendix A (Additional Information). Washington, DC: NGACBP, CCSSO, p. 8.

Vocabulary Building

Vocabulary is an important focus of the CCSS as well as many state standards. CCRA.R.4 states that students are expected to "interpret words and phrases as they are used in a text, including determining technical, connotative, and figurative meanings, and analyze how specific word choices shape meaning or tone" (NGACBP & CCSSO, 2010, p. 10). This standard makes it clear that students are not only expected to have a rich technical vocabulary, but also be able to interpret figurative language and analyze how authors use words to shape the meaning of a text.

Having a rich vocabulary strengthens comprehension (McLaughlin, 2012; Nagy & Scott, 2013; Flanigan, Templeton & Hayes, 2012; Feezel, 2012; Graves & Watts-Taffe, 2008; Guccione, 2011). The Carnegie Council for Advancing Adolescent Literacy (2010) found that one of the challenges to middle-school students' comprehension is the complex vocabulary found in content area texts. Educators have classified words in a number of ways. Stahl and Nagy (2006) identified three tiers of words. Basic words, or tier 1 words, are used in daily conversation (e.g., *studying, spelling*). Tier 2 words are frequently used complex words such as *spiral* or *confidential*. Tier 3 words apply to specific subjects and situations (e.g., *onomatopoeia, hypotenuse*). Other educators use the terms *academic words* and *content-specific words* (Flanigan, Templeton & Hayes, 2012), or *domain-specific words*. Words such as *summarize, analyze, describe, evaluate, compare,* and *contrast* are academic words because they are used in all subject areas, whereas *photosynthesis* and *metamorphosis* are categorized as domain-specific words most frequently encountered in science texts. No matter how words are classified, vocabulary building is important for every student.

How do teachers facilitate students' vocabulary growth? One way is to create a word-rich environment (Graves & Watts-Taffe, 2008). You can create various word walls with different purposes. One wall can focus on synonyms, another on antonyms, still others on onomatopoeia, personification, metaphor, and similes. After sharing Fred Gwynne's *The King Who Rained* (1988), *A Chocolate Moose for Dinner* (1988), *A Little Pigeon Toad* (1998), and any of the Amelia Bedelia series by Peggy Parish, you can create posters in which students write puns that they hear

Reading **133**

or read during independent reading. Teachers can use *Miss Alaineus: A Vocabulary Disaster* (Frasier, 2007) as a springboard to get students competing with one another to find unique words. *Little Mouse's Big Book of Fears* (Gravett, 2007), featuring 23 different types of phobias, is a book you can use to get students to recognize categories of words.

Another way to increase student vocabulary is to teach the common Greek and Latin root words, prefixes, and suffixes (Pacheco & Goodwin, 2013; Flanigan, Templeton, & Hayes, 2012; Goodwin, Lipsky, & Ahn, 2012; McLaughlin, 2012; Guccione, 2011; Blachowicz, Fisher, & Watts-Taffe, 2011). Stahl & Nagy (2006) revealed that high school students' vocabulary consists of approximately 40,000 words and that 70 percent of English words contain Greek or Latin roots, prefixes, or suffixes (Flanigan, Templeton, & Hayes, 2012). Thus, it is prudent for elementary and middle-school teachers to engage students in morphology, a study of the smallest unit of meaning in words.

Goodwin et al. (2012) suggest that when teaching commonly used Greek and Latin units, teachers group prefixes and suffixes into families. For example, the "not" prefix family includes *dis* (disagree), *un* (unhappy), *in* (inactive), *im* (improper), and *a* (amoral); while the "excess" prefix family includes *over* (overtime), *super* (superhero), and *out* (outlandish).

Specific classroom activities that focus on building vocabulary will be explained later in this chapter.

Emphasis on Informational Texts

Recent years have seen an explosion of informational trade books for elementary and middle-school grades. Yopp and Yopp (2012) surveyed 120 classrooms and found that 85 percent of information books were science texts, 12 percent were social studies texts, 2 percent were language books, and only 1 percent consisted of math books. These informational texts are filled with two types of visuals: pictorial and graphical. Pictorial visuals include illustrations and photographs, while graphical visuals include charts and diagrams that augment or support the text. Both pictorial and graphical features appeal to young readers; however, you will need to teach students how to read and learn from these features (Coleman, Bradley, & Donovon, 2012). Coleman and colleagues suggest that teachers use interactive read-alouds to help interpret visual aids. Also requiring students to illustrate what they have learned by labeling their illustrations will solidify their learning of the concepts.

Yopp and Yopp (2012, pp. 480–481) believe that exposing students to informational texts will

- build background knowledge and support content learning;
- expose students to specialized vocabulary;
- offer students experiences with diverse text structures and features;
- familiarize students with language of exposition and the discourse of different disciplines;
- prompt discussions and comprehension activities different from those sparked by stories; and
- serve as a catalyst for literacy for some children.

To comprehend informational text, readers also need to understand the organizational patterns of expository text. The main organizational patterns are enumeration or description, chronological order, sequence, compare/contrast, cause/effect, problem/solution, and persuasion. (Graphic organizers for each of these are given in the Teaching Activities section of this chapter.) Students need an adequate technical vocabulary to understand new concepts. They need to understand relationships between concepts so they understand which are supporting facts and which are main ideas. They need to synthesize information from various sources and connect their existing knowledge of the world with the new information being expressed. They need to be able to analyze the author's purpose and credentials. McLaughlin (2012) also suggests that students be given many different types of text, including traditional print and digital, to read.

Some informal ways teachers can assess students' comprehension are (1) through observation of students as they converse with peers and ask questions about text and authorship, (2) by encouraging students to dramatize the text, (3) by assessing 3-D models that they build, (4) by encouraging students to write poems or songs about the text, and (5) by inviting students to create graphic organizers and story maps of the text.

Finding quality informational texts is an important task for teachers. Figure 5.4 lists associations and agencies that award or identify high-quality children's literature in the content areas. A few of the many authors who write informational texts appropriate for young readers are Gail Gibbons, Seymour Simon, Jerry Pallotta, Paul Showers, and Aliki. The National Geographic Ladder series offers four reading levels for each title at each grade level. These informational books cover a wide area of interests, including bugs, animals, world cultures, and outer space. The National Geographic fiction series *The Quest* ends with a passage that explains what geocaching is and how to participate in it. National Geographic uses photographs, illustrations, charts, and diagrams to help students understand the text. Scholastic TRIO is also a leveled-reading collection that offers books on the same content material on three reading levels: below grade level, on grade level, and above grade level.

FIGURE 5.4 List of associations and agencies that identify high-quality children's and young adult informational literature.

NAME	WEBSITE
American Institute of Physics Science Writing Award for Children	www.aip.org/aip/writing
Association for Library Service to Children Robert F. Sibert Informational Book Award	www.ala.org/ala/mgrps/divs/alsc/awards grants/bookmedia/sibertmedal
Boston Globe–Horn Book Awards for Excellence in Children's Literature	www.hbook.com/bghb
National Council for the Social Studies Notable Trade Books for Young People	www.socialstudies.org/notable
National Council of Teachers of Orbis Pictus Award for Outstanding Nonfiction for Children	www.ncte.org/awards/orbispictus
National Science Teachers Association Outstanding Science Trade Books for Students K–12	www.nsta.org/publications/ostb
Society of Children's Book Writers & Illustrators Golden Kite Award and Magazine Merit Award (both awarded in four categories, one of which is nonfiction)	www.scbwi.org/Pages.aspx/Introduction

Source: Yopp, R. H., & Yopp, H. K. (2012). Young children's limited and narrow exposure to informational text. *The Reading Teacher* 65(7), p. 485.

Close Reading

The CCSS as well as some state standards have brought close reading to the forefront in reading instruction. What is close reading? It "is an instructional routine in which students critically examine a text, especially through repeated readings" (Fisher & Frey, 2012, p. 179). Close reading involves much more than students answering the who, what, when questions. This instructional routine examines

> To acquire the habit of reading is to construct for yourself a refuge from almost all the miseries of life.
>
> **SOMERSET MAUGHAM**

- the organizational structure of the text,
- the "precision of its vocabulary" (Fisher & Frey, 2012, p. 179),
- key details that support the main ideas,
- the purpose of the author through inferential reading, and
- how new information connects with a reader's schemata.

Students must be taught how to engage in close reading during independent reading times. During observations of secondary teachers who engaged students in close reading, Fisher and Frey (2012) identified six actions:

1. Teachers used short passages instead of long passages.
2. The selected texts were above students' independent reading level.
3. Teachers did not engage in preteaching of the material.
4. Teachers engaged students in repeated readings of short passages, each time focusing on a different aspect of the text.
5. They asked questions and required students to cite evidence for their responses.
6. They taught students to underline and make notes in the margins of the short passages.

Even though these were secondary teachers, elementary teachers can use these same techniques when reading narrative and informational texts with students.

McLaughlin (2012) stresses the importance of modeling close reading with elementary students in order to get them to think more critically about a text. For example, you can model close reading of the following short passage from *Owls* (Morgan, 2006):

> Owls are found in many different *habitats.* Most owls prefer woods and forests, where there are plenty of nesting sites. However, the snowy owl is found on the icy *tundra* of the far north, and the tiny elf owl survives in the hot deserts of North America. (Morgan, 2006, p. 9)

After reading these three sentences, you can discuss why woods and forests provide nesting sites. You want students to connect their background knowledge of how branches in trees connect with other branches, making a niche for owls to create secure nests. After the second reading, when students understand the importance of owls finding secure places for their nests, have students consider where snowy owls and tiny elf owls would build nests in their habitats. After a third reading of this text, focus on the bold words and tell students that authors use bold lettering for a reason—to focus on vocabulary words and to point out words that are found in the glossary at the back of the book. When you discuss the meaning of vocabulary words, you are also teaching students a strategy they can use when reading independently.

Read the following classroom vignette, which gives an example of close reading of informational text in a middle-school classroom.

Mr. Banks knew that understanding the meaning of the words *cede, seceded, repealed,* and *dissolve* was crucial for comprehending the text. Using context clues as

Mr. Banks, a middle-school teacher, is studying the Civil War with his students. He is using the following passage from *The Day Fort Sumter Was Fired On* (Haskins, 1995):

> In late 1860, Sumter was not yet finished, and workmen were still completing the interior. But already the government of South Carolina was pressing the Federal government to cede it to the state. In December 1860, following the election of Republican Abraham Lincoln to the presidency, South Carolina had seceded from the Union rather than risk losing its status as a slave state. (Haskins, 1995, p. 4)

After the first reading of this short passage, Mr. Banks prompted the following discussion:

Mr. Banks: What was happening during the late 1860s?

Toby: The Civil War was fought,

Abby: Abe Lincoln was president.

Mr. Banks: What was the Civil War all about?

Jon: The South wanted slaves, but the North did not believe in slavery.

Mr. Banks: From this passage, what can you tell me about Fort Sumter?

Juan: It was still being built because it said the interior wasn't finished.

Toby: It is close to South Carolina and they want it as part of their state.

Mr. Banks: Good information. Can anyone tell me what you think *cede* means?

Juan: I think it means *give* or *sell* because South Carolina wants it.

Mr. Banks: In this case, South Carolina wanted the federal government to give the fort to them. Now who can tell me what *seceded* means?

Aaron: It means *left* the Union. Because it said they wanted to remain being a slave state.

Mr. Banks: Now let's look at the Ordinance, which is a little hard to understand because of the language. Let's start by someone telling me what *repealed* and *dissolve* mean.

Jon: I know in science *dissolve* means that a solid becomes a liquid; I do not think that is what the word means here.

Abby: My parents just got a divorce and I heard the lawyer say something about dissolving the marriage so I think here *dissolve* means *to end.*

Jose: I just looked *repeal* up yesterday as I was reading, and it means something like to resolve or revoke.

Mr. Banks: Great job on using your background knowledge and context clues to figure the meaning of these words. Now that we know the meaning of all these words, does anyone want to summarize what you learned from these two pages?

Aaron: South Carolina wants to no longer be a part of the Union or Northern states because it wants to keep slavery.

Mr. Banks: Great discussion, class! Now you can get into your small groups and read the next two pages together, making sure all of you understand what is happening.

well as their background knowledge about this time in U.S. history, students could conclude what the words mean. A copy of the original Ordinance to dissolve the Union between the state of South Carolina and the other states also added to comprehending this time in U.S. history. After his students read the pages in the Ordinance, Mr. Banks could engage students in the possible differing opinions of South Carolina's citizens. Do students think that all citizens wanted to secede from the other states? What emotions might the citizens have felt when they heard that the Constitution was "repealed; and that the union now subsiding between South Carolina and other States under the name of 'The United States of America,' is hereby dissolved" (Haskins, 1995, p. 5)?

Close reading should also be modeled with narrative texts. For example, teachers of intermediate students can use Sharon Robinson's (2014) *Under the Same Sun*, a personal story of Sharon and her grandmother visiting family in Tanzania and their trip to Bagamoyo, a slave-trading post of the 1860s. Teachers can discuss with students the meaning of *Bagamoyo*—"to let go of one's heart"—and how the African people felt as they were forced to leave their homeland. Teachers can also get students to discuss how the story would have been different if Robinson had used first-person point of view. It may interest students to know that Sharon Robinson is the daughter of baseball legend Jackie Robinson. Motivated students can research Jackie Robinson's struggles as he became the first African American to play Major League Baseball.

Using the concise text of poetry is another means to get students to understand the importance of close reading in order to fully comprehend the passage. In *Red Sings from Treetops: A Year in Color* (Sidman, 2009), we read: "Red squirms on the road after rain" (unpaged). Instead of quickly skipping over this sentence, stop and have students visualize the picture that these words paint in their minds, prompting them with questions such as, What is the red object? What possible red objects/creatures could squirm? What inferences do readers make as they build on prior knowledge?

A poem you can use with middle-school students is Raftery's "Apartment House" (Dunning, Lueders, & Smith, 1974). Without stating the title of the poem, ask students to visualize the first phrase—"A filing-cabinet of human lives"—and ask what they think the poet is describing. Ask students to explain their responses by listening to their inferences (how they connect background knowledge with text) and applaud those who give strong reasons for their responses.

Citing Specific Textual Evidence

Citing specific textual evidence is not new to teachers who routinely ask students questions such as "How do you know?" or "Why do you think that?" When you pose those types of questions, you are encouraging students to engage in higher-level thinking by stating evidence for their responses. Citing evidence is necessary when students gather information from different sources and synthesize what they have learned in written form. However, citing evidence in discussion is also important and should be modeled by you so that when students read independently, they will continue to think about the evidence they are using to draw inferences.

For example, primary-grade teachers can share *Stagestruck* (dePaola, 2005) and then have students discuss how Tommy steals the show in "Peter Rabbit" when he does not get the lead role. Instead, he plays Mopsy and overreacts when he is caught in Mr. McGregor's garden. Thus, the audience laughs at Tommy rather than at Johnny, who plays Peter Rabbit. Afterward, Tommy's mother tells him he must apologize to Johnny and to his teacher. From the illustrations and text, readers may wonder if Tommy's apology was genuine. Ask students their opinion and have them state their reasons. Also have them point to specific text and illustrations to prove their stance.

When studying a unit on slavery, a middle-school teacher can share Polacco's *January's Sparrow* (2009), a picture book about the Crosswhite family, a family of slaves who escape from their heartless master. Well into the story, Francis Troutman, the master's son, barges into the Crosswhites' home in Marshall, Michigan, and tries to force the family back to Kentucky. The townspeople of Marshall come to the Crosswhites' rescue by surrounding Troutman. However, "Francis Troutman straightened his coat and tried to catch his composure" (p. 74). Teachers can ask students what it means to "catch his composure" and then ask them to act it out. After students fully understand the phrase, ask them if Francis really was catching his composure and have them give reasons from the text and/or illustrations to support their view. Different students may have different opinions because they may interpret the illustrations differently. This will give you the opportunity to teach the importance of close reading and citing evidence. Make clear that individuals react differently to the same text (Rosenblatt, 2004) and illustrations, and citing evidence will clarify their stance. Chapter 10 offers specific activities for citing evidence as students write and synthesize information from a number of texts.

Apart from engaging students in different texts so they comprehend complex passages, you should also consider some overall pedagogical approaches that will help them as they learn to read.

PEDAGOGICAL APPROACHES TO READING

There are four pedagogical approaches to reading: cognitive, cultural, linguist, and sociocultural (Fang, 2012). Each of these approaches correlates with the CCSS and CCRA.

Cognitive Approach

First, the *cognitive approach* focuses on building knowledge. Teachers engage students in learning to use comprehension strategies, such as how to predict, infer, monitor, and summarize. See Figure 5.5.

Most readers learn these comprehension strategies through explicit instruction by teachers who also have a passion for reading. McLaughlin and Allen (2009) suggest a five-step process for teaching these strategies:

1. Explain the strategy in detail.
2. Demonstrate the strategy while reading authentic texts.
3. Guide a small group of students through the process as they read a text together.
4. Monitor students as they read independently.
5. Allow time for students to reflect on the strategy.

One strategy should be taught and practiced before introducing other strategies, although be sure to tell students that good readers use multiple strategies simultaneously.

Many teachers in the early grades spend time demonstrating to students how to predict from a story's title what may happen in the story. After reading a few pages, they ask them to affirm or change their predictions. As teachers read, they model how they infer, connecting background knowledge with information that was read, and how they use context to understand unfamiliar words. As they read, teachers also model how they monitor their comprehension by slowing down or

FIGURE 5.5	Before, during, and after reading comprehension strategies.

BEFORE READING	DURING READING	AFTER READING
Predicting	Making inferences	Retelling
Setting a purpose	Self-monitoring	Drawing conclusions
	Visualizing	Elaborating on the author's intent
	Connecting prior knowledge to texts	
	Text-to-text connections	
	Text-to-world connections	
	Text-to-self connections	

rereading passages. Afterward, teachers engage students in summarizing. When reading nonfiction, teachers also model note taking and concept mapping.

Taking notes, engaging in concept mapping, and focusing on vocabulary building are also important aspects of the cognitive approach. This approach correlates with CCRA.R.1, "read closely to determine what the text says explicitly and to make logical inferences from it"; CCRA.R.2, "determine central ideas or themes of a text and analyze their development; summarize the key supporting details and ideas"; and CCRA.R.4, "interpret words and phrases as they are used in a text" (NGACBP & CCSSO, 2010, p. 10).

Cultural Approach

The *cultural approach* to literacy considers more than the cognitive process of literacy; it also considers such factors as the purpose for reading, the reader's interest in the passage or book, and the motivation for reading. Teachers who consider the cultural aspect of reading recognize that students have varying personal and cultural perspectives on issues found in stories and informational texts. Students may identify with a particular cultural group, and this may affect their reading. Some students may not be motivated to read narrative texts because they do not relate to the settings, characters, or plots. Even though no Common Core Anchor standard addresses the cultural aspects of reading, good teachers understand that students' motivation to read greatly influences their ability to comprehend the text.

Linguistic Approach

The *linguistic approach* focuses on decoding, fluency, vocabulary, sentence structure, and the organizational structure of informational texts. Teachers show students how to analyze language patterns found in complex sentences. The linguistic approach is reflected in CCRA.R.4, "interpret words and phrases as they are used in a text, including determining technical, connotative, and figurative meanings, and analyze how specific word choices shape meaning or tone"; and CCRA.R.5, "analyze the structure of texts, including how specific sentences, paragraphs, and larger portions of the text (e.g., a section, chapter, scene, or stanza) relate to each other and the whole" (NGACBP & CCSSO, 2010, p. 10).

Sociocultural Approach

The fourth approach is the *sociocultural approach,* also referred to as the sociopolitical approach, because of the belief in "all texts—written, spoken, linguistic, visual, and multimedia—as inherently ideological and value laden, suggesting that text meaning is neither natural or neutral and must therefore be understood in relation to both intention of the writer/designer and the social-historic and political contexts that govern its production" (Fang, 2012, p. 106). In this approach, students and teachers investigate authorship and discover whose voices are or are not being heard. This approach relates to CCRA.R.4, "interpret words and phrases as they are used in a text, including determining technical, connotative, and figurative meanings, and analyze how specific word choices shape meaning or tone"; CCRA.R.6, "assess how point of view or purpose shapes the content and style of a text"; and CCRA.R.8, "delineate and evaluate the argument and specific claims in a text, including the validity of the reasoning as well as the relevance and sufficiency of the evidence" (NGACBP & CCSSO, 2010, p. 10).

Teaching literacy encompasses all these pedagogical approaches and you will integrate all these approaches eventually as you help students develop their literacy skills.

INSTRUCTIONAL STRATEGIES FOR READING

Although reading lessons can be active and noisy, they are not disorganized. In fact, many teachers find they must take time to carefully structure and sequence the experiences for their classes; however, the students' success and continued enjoyment of reading make it all worthwhile. Below are a number of instructional strategies used by teachers with various approaches to teaching reading.

4-Blocks Literacy Model

The *4-Blocks Literacy Model* developed by Cunningham, Hall, and Defee (1991, 1998) provides a framework for visualizing a comprehensive approach (Sigmon, 1997). The model, at first intended for the primary level and now modified for grades 4 through 8 (Sigmon, 2001), is an outline of what must happen in the two hours devoted to literacy learning each school day. The four blocks are titled Guided Reading, Self-Selected Reading, Working with Words, and Writing. In Guided Reading, the major focus is building comprehension by exposing students to an extensive array of literature and minilessons on skills. Self-Selected Reading helps students attain fluency and confidence by allowing them to work on literature texts that are on their independent reading levels. In the Working with Words block, students read, spell, and use high-frequency words. They also learn word patterns necessary for decoding and spelling. Finally, a major purpose of the Writing block is to help the students build confidence as writers. This is accomplished through using the writing process and applying knowledge of phonics. School districts employing this method provide their teacher with initial training and follow-up support. For more detailed information about this approach, refer to *Implementing the 4-Blocks Literacy Model* (1997) and *Modifying the Four-Blocks for Upper Grades* (2001) by Cheryl Mahaffey Sigmon.

read RESEARCH practice

R R P

Interview teachers from your school district to determine who uses a comprehensive approach to literacy. If possible, observe in their classrooms and make notes on the activities that are in progress. Then compare what you have seen to the information in *Implementing the 4-Blocks Literacy Model* by Cheryl Mahaffey Sigmon (1997). In your journal, describe how these activities support a comprehensive approach to literacy.

Guided Reading

Some type of guided reading is a core element of any literacy program based on the comprehensive approach. The 4-Blocks version of guided reading is primarily a whole-class activity. However, Fountas and Pinnell (1996) advocate for a small-group format in which teachers show students how to read and then support their growth as readers. Generally, in this version of *guided reading,* a teacher works with a small group of students and helps them learn how to use specific reading strategies independently. She also continually observes the students to assess how well they are learning each strategy and its applications. This technique requires that the teacher is aware of the students' specific needs and the processes involved in reading. Fountas and Pinnell (1996, p. 4) identified the essential components of guided reading:

- A teacher works with a small group.
- Students in the group are similar in their reading development and are able to read about the same level of text.
- Teachers introduce the stories and assist students' reading in ways that help to develop independent reading strategies.
- Each student reads the whole text.

- The goal is for students to read independently and silently.
- The emphasis is on reading increasingly challenging books over time.
- Students are grouped and regrouped in a dynamic process that involves ongoing observation and assessment.

> Reading takes us away from home, but more important, it finds homes for us everywhere.
>
> **HAZEL ROCHMAN**

Because literature books, carefully grouped according to developmental difficulty, provide the texts for guided reading lessons, the newly learned strategies can readily be applied to the other balanced literacy reading components: reading aloud, shared reading, and independent reading. In turn, the literature can support as well as be a model and stimulus for the framework's writing components: shared writing, interactive writing, guided writing/writing workshop, and independent writing (Fountas & Pinnell, 1996).

Connecting Reading and Writing Through Reading–Writing Workshops

Writing complements reading by helping students add to and clarify meaning for themselves—to make a book and the language of the book their own (Jensen & Roser, 1990). Both reading and writing are forms of communication; both are active thinking processes that result in meaning. Observations of language development in classes have shown that "in order to write, writers read. In order to learn from reading or respond to reading, readers often write" (Jensen & Roser, 1990, p. 11). Often, students use writing to summarize information or restate in a more concise format what the author has said (Roe, Smith, & Burns, 2005), which helps them understand what they have read. Therefore, it seems natural to make no real distinction between reading and writing in the classroom.

Students who see the connection between reading and writing actually are more perceptive about both processes. Classroom writing opportunities help students to learn reading and writing in meaningful ways. Allowing students to use process writing—to write and read letters and lists, and to keep and share journals—helps them see the complexities of each process from both sides. They see reading as an author would; they see writing from the reader's point of view. In the end, they arrive at a clearer notion of how to make each process work for them. Combining class writing and reading instruction also serves as a meaningful way of helping students acquire the mechanics—grammar, punctuation, spelling—of writing.

Teachers now appreciate that reading is an active, constructive process, as is writing. It is important to implement these research findings and thereby empower students. Perhaps the best way to connect reading and writing is through a *reading–writing workshop*. This strategy organizes reading instruction to promote balanced literacy (Searfoss et al., 2001). In the workshop, students can choose their own materials as they engage in periods of extended reading and writing. Searfoss and colleagues (2001, compiled from pp. 115–119) suggest the following format:

1. *Opening/teacher share time.* This is when the teacher might read a book aloud or promote a particular text through a book talk. For example, a teacher of the second or third grade might read a nonfiction book such as *Fly Traps! Plants That Bite Back* by Martin Jenkins.
2. *Brief lesson.* This is a time period in which skills and various strategies are taught with the whole group. Because there are many cause–effect situations in *Fly Traps!*, this would be an ideal time to teach students how to recognize cause–effect in context. For example, a teacher could ask the students how a bladderwort sets its traps or makes its trapdoor open.

3. *Student-selected reading/writing and response.* This is the major part of the workshop. During this section students must be reading and writing. Options vary from writing in a journal to tape-recording an interesting part of a book to writing a sequel to a book that a student has read. Teachers commonly hold individual reading or writing conferences during this part of the workshop. Students might read other books about plants that eat insects, plan and act out a retelling of the text, or write a response to it in their journal. Teachers monitor students' activities during this time.

4. *Closing/student share time.* This period allows students to share both the texts that they have been reading and their writing responses.

For more information on the workshop approach, see Chapter 10.

Questioning the Author (QtA)

This strategy is based on the idea of students constructing meaning as they proceed through a text (Beck, McKeown, Hamilton, & Kucan, 1997). QtA supports immediate construction of meaning through discussion; students actively formulate their ideas while reading. The approach can be used with either expository, informational texts, or narrative stories and involves the teacher interacting with the students as they try to understand a text they are reading for the first time. The focus of QtA in the classroom is the use of queries that are posed by the teacher. Figure 5.6 is a sample of different types of queries.

FIGURE 5.6 Queries used in QtA.

INITIATING QUERIES

- What is the author trying to say here?
- What is the author's message?
- What is the author talking about?

FOLLOW-UP QUERIES

- What does the author mean here?
- Did the author explain this clearly?
- Does this make sense with what the author told us before?
- How does this connect with what the author told us before?
- Does the author tell us why?
- Why do you think the author tells us this now?

NARRATIVE QUERIES

- How do things look for this character now?
- How has the author let you know that something has changed?
- How has the author settled this for us?
- Given what the author has already told us about this character, what do you think he or she is up to?

Source: Beck, I. L., McKeown, M. G., Hamilton, R. L., & Kucan, L. (1997), *Questioning the Author: An Approach for Enhancing Student Engagement with Text.* Reprinted with permission of Isabel L. Beck and the International Reading Association. All rights reserved.

Book Sharing

This activity provides students with the opportunity to read aloud or orally express their ideas about a particular book they have been reading. They are able to unite speaking and listening with reading and writing. During the *book-sharing* time, the students might retell parts of the stories they have read, explain why they chose certain books, describe what they like or dislike about any book, and even exchange books with one another. If the students are studying about cats, some stories they might mention are *Sam, Bangs, and Moonshine; Millions of Cats; The Owl and the Pussycat; A Cat's Tale; Cat and Canary;* or *Socks and the Tenth Good Thing About Barney*. Book sharing is particularly important because it encourages students to keep exploring new books.

> The elementary school must assume as its sublime and most solemn responsibility the task of teaching every child how to read. Any school that does not accomplish this has failed.
>
> **JACQUES BARZUM**

The activity also helps students see themselves as real readers. Ford (1989/1990) cited a study (Mundi, 1989) in which intermediate students advertised themselves as readers, and primary teachers rented them for oral reading sessions. The program eventually became known as Rent-a-Reader.

Literature Response Charts

In some classrooms, students refine their language competencies through *literature response charts* and bookmaking activities. For example, after reading *Bunnicula* (Zarillo, 1989), the students in Mrs. Jackson's class created the Why We Like Cats chart shown in Figure 5.7, based on the cat character in the book.

Mrs. Jackson noticed that several students in the class enjoyed reading the chart both silently and aloud. She even caught one or two students standing in front of it and repeating the lines to themselves. Mrs. Jackson encourages her students to use charts because she believes they help them appreciate the pattern and structure of language. In this example, she used the chart to help some of the students understand the use of independent and dependent clauses (and cause–effect relationships) in reading and writing.

Literature response chart. **FIGURE 5.7**

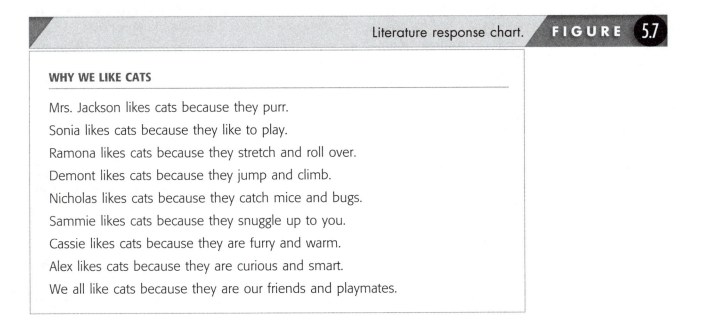

WHY WE LIKE CATS

Mrs. Jackson likes cats because they purr.

Sonia likes cats because they like to play.

Ramona likes cats because they stretch and roll over.

Demont likes cats because they jump and climb.

Nicholas likes cats because they catch mice and bugs.

Sammie likes cats because they snuggle up to you.

Cassie likes cats because they are furry and warm.

Alex likes cats because they are curious and smart.

We all like cats because they are our friends and playmates.

TEACHING ACTIVITIES 5

1 Category word walls

You and your students can create various word wall categories based on what the class is studying or reading. For example, if the class is reading books such as the *A to Z Mysteries* series by Roy and Gurney, the word wall could include words associated with mysteries, such as *bandit, caper, clues,* and *detectives. Recommended for primary grades.*

2 Onomatopoeia sleuths

Display on an electronic board poems like these:

- *Pigs* by Richard Edwards
- *Summertime* by Myra Cohn Liverston
- *From Sing-Song* by Christina Georgina Rossetti
- *Grasshoppers Three* (traditional)

As you and your students read the poems, have them listen for onomatopoeia, words that sound like their meanings, and snap their fingers as they hear the words. Following the reading, discuss the words and have students add the words to their Onomatopoeia Sleuth poster. Later when students write, they will be encouraged to use these words in their writing. *Recommended for primary grades.*

3 Sign-up for reading day

Calling on students to read aloud before they have had time to look over a passage may make them feel anxious. Hurst, Scales, Frecks, and Lewis (2011) suggest that teachers set one or two times a week aside for students to read a favorite, short passage they found during their independent reading time. For this activity, use the following steps and the rubric provided in Figure 5.8.

- Set dates and post them on a sign-up sheet.
- Have students choose a passage and get your approval. The passage should be at the student's reading level, not too lengthy, and school appropriate.
- Have students practice so they can read their selection fluently with good expression, volume, and poise.
- Direct the other students to listen attentively.
- Invite them to applaud and compliment the reader afterward.

Recommended for primary grades.

4 Dramatizing fables

Fables are short stories with a moral. Many of them can be acted out. Begin by reading "The Goose That Laid the Golden Eggs" from Aesop's collection. Have students discuss what the man and wife may be doing each day with the golden egg by considering the following questions:

- Did they go to a bank to trade the golden egg for money? If so, how much money did they get?
- Or did the man and wife secretly hide the golden egg? If so, where did they hide it?

| | | FIGURE 5.8 |

Sign-up reading presentation rubric.

ELEMENT	UNACCEPTABLE 0–1 POINT	ACCEPTABLE 2–3 POINTS	TARGET 4–5 POINTS
Stage Presence	Student did not address the audience and forgot to announce the title and author.	Student did not address the audience, but did announce the title and author.	Student addressed the audience and looked at them, and clearly announced the title and author.
Poise	Student did not stand straight and did not hold the paper so she/he was looking forward.	Student did not stand straight or did not hold paper so her/his face was looking forward.	Student stood straight on both feet and held the paper so head was looking forward.
Volume/ Pronunciation/ Diction	Student mispronounced more than one word and the volume and diction was such that she/he was difficult to hear.	Student pronounced all but one word correctly, and had appropriate volume and diction.	Student correctly pronounced all words at the appropriate volume and had excellent diction.
Rate	Student read either too quickly or too slowly.	Student had appropriate rate, but did not pause for commas and periods.	Student had appropriate rate with good pauses when necessary.
Expression	Student lacked expression; it was evident that she/he did not rehearse the passage.	At times the student had good expression, but the passage did not "come alive" for the audience.	Student had excellent expression that made the passage "come alive" for the audience.

- How did they feel when they realized the goose was like any other goose?
- Did the man blame the woman for killing it or did the woman blame the man?

After the discussion, invite two students to act out the story. Then pair students together and invite them to read other fables from your list. Instruct each group to select one fable and act them out for the class. It does not matter if two groups choose the same fable because their interpretations will differ. *Recommended for primary grades.*

5   Finding clues in mysteries

Gregory and Cahill (2010) found that even young students can learn comprehension strategies. Using the *A to Z Mysteries* series as a shared reading, teach your students to predict, visualize, infer, and ask questions that will help solve the mystery. The books are short and are at the 2.2 reading level. A good selection for the first mystery is *The Empty Envelope* (Roy, 1998).

1. Before reading, share the cover, read the title, and invite students to predict what they think may be the mystery in the book.
2. At the end of the first chapter, invite students to share what pictures they saw in their minds as they first heard the story. Then ask them to name something in the chapter that may be a clue.
3. Write clues down on a flip chart, so near the end of the book they can discuss among themselves which ones they think are most important.
4. Before reading the second and subsequent chapters, review with students what they know so far and have them predict what will happen next.
5. After students have gathered sufficient clues, ask them to predict how the story will end; that is, to solve the mystery.

6. When the book is finished, encourage students to look at the list of clues and discuss which ones helped them solve the mystery.

Recommended for primary grades.

 Describing how characters respond to challenges

CCSS RL.2.3 requires second graders to "describe how characters in a story respond to major events and challenges" (NGACBP & CCSSO, 2010, p. 11). The following activity can be used with any book.

1. Using Kevin Henkes' *Sheila Rae, The Brave* (1987), read the title, author's name, and share the cover with the students, asking if they think Sheila Rae is brave or not and ask them to explain their reason for their stance.
2. Read and discuss the story; make sure students see the illustrations because they augment the text.
3. When finished reading, invite the students to complete the activity found in Figure 5.9.

Recommended for primary grades.

FIGURE 5.9   Activity for describing how a character responds to a major challenge.

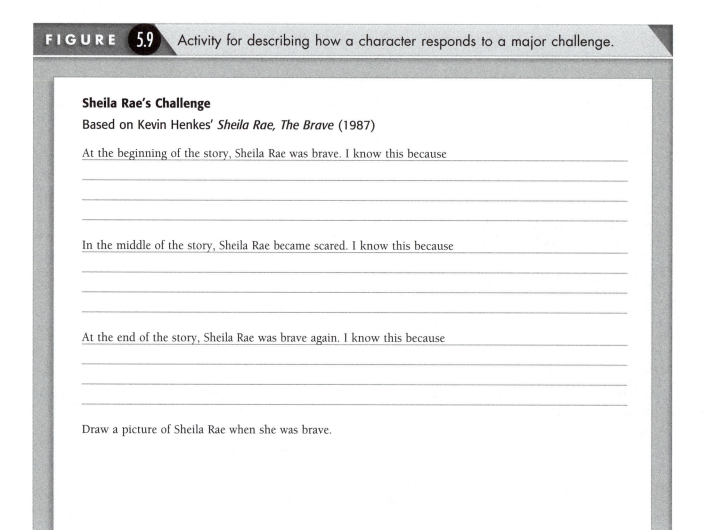

Sheila Rae's Challenge

Based on Kevin Henkes' *Sheila Rae, The Brave* (1987)

At the beginning of the story, Sheila Rae was brave. I know this because

In the middle of the story, Sheila Rae became scared. I know this because

At the end of the story, Sheila Rae was brave again. I know this because

Draw a picture of Sheila Rae when she was brave.

7   Fact versus fiction

CCSS RL.1.5 requires that even first graders be able to "explain major differences between books that tell stories and books that give information, drawing on a wide reading of a range of text types" (NGACBP & CCSSO, 2010, p. 18). After reading the fictional picture books *Armadillo Rodeo* by Jan Brett (2004), *Armadillo's Orange* by Jim Arnosky (2003), and *Armadillo from Amarillo* by Lynn Cherry (1999), lead a discussion with students comparing the traits of the armadillo in these fictional books with the information found in the following nonfiction books— *Let's Look at the Armadillos* by Judith Jango-Cohen (2010), *The Armadillo* (*Wildlife of North America*) by Steve Potts (2006), and *Armadillo* (*Desert Animals*) by Emily Rose Townsend (2006)—and on the websites http://animals.sandiegozoo.org/animals/armadillo, http://animals.national.geographic.com/animals/mammals/armadillo/, and www.animals/mammals/armadillo. Have your students use the graphic organizer in Figure 5.10 to record their information.

After students have completed the graphic organizer, have them synthesize the information from all the sources and make an unstapled book called *Facts vs. Fiction About Armadillos*. (See Figure 5.11 for directions on making such a book.)

A technology alternative to creating an unstapled book would be to have students create slide presentations with audio voice-over based on the information in their graphic organizers. *Recommended for primary grades.*

> Not wanting to reread a good book is like saying, "Paris? I've already been there."
>
> **FAYE MOSKOWITZ**

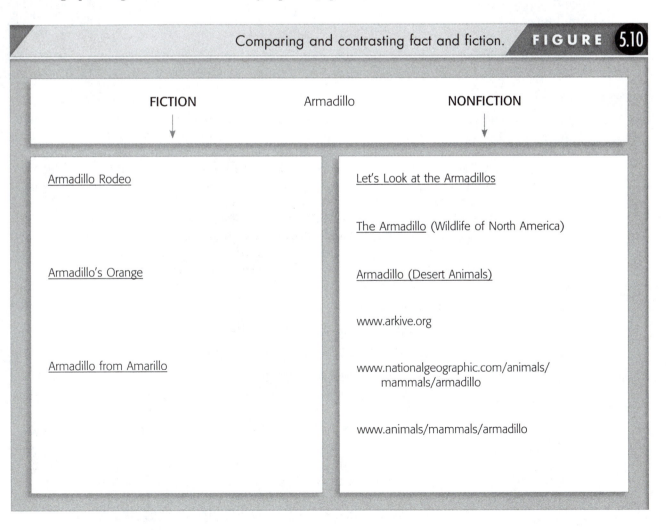

Comparing and contrasting fact and fiction.   **FIGURE 5.10**

FICTION   Armadillo   NONFICTION

FICTION	NONFICTION
Armadillo Rodeo	Let's Look at the Armadillos
	The Armadillo (Wildlife of North America)
Armadillo's Orange	Armadillo (Desert Animals)
	www.arkive.org
	www.nationalgeographic.com/animals/ mammals/armadillo
Armadillo from Amarillo	www.animals/mammals/armadillo

FIGURE 5.11   Directions for an unstapled book.

1. Take two pieces of copy paper.

2. Fold each piece in half by folding the one short edge to the other short edge. On the first piece of paper, starting at the top of the fold, draw a one-inch line down the fold.

3. On the same piece of paper, starting at the bottom of the fold, draw another one-inch line up the fold. Cut on each line.

4. Take the second piece of paper, and draw a line down the fold, beginning one-inch from the top of the paper to one-inch from the bottom of the paper. Cut on the line so you have a slit in the middle of the paper.

5. Lightly roll the first page (the one with the two slits) the long way.

6. Slip the first piece of paper through the slit of the second piece of paper.

7. Fold the booklet in half on the folded crease to complete your book.

8   Vocabulary shoebox

Vocabulary building is an important aspect of comprehension. Feezel (2012) suggests using a shoebox as a way of collecting interesting words that students read during individual reading time as well as words that they have read in their neighborhoods. These are words that interest students or words they want to learn. Students write the word, the sentence in which they found the word, and their name on an index card. Discuss tier 1 and tier 3 with the individual students who submit those words, but choose tier 2 (complex, but frequently encountered words) to introduce to the entire class. Write these words on index cards with definitions that students will understand. On Monday, share the word and the sentence with the class, recognizing the student who submitted the word, and discuss the word with the students. Throughout the week, these words are discussed and become words that are assessed on Friday. *Recommended for intermediate.*

9   Vocabulary spell-off

This is another activity to help students learn new vocabulary words.

1. Share *Miss Alaineus: A Vocabulary Disaster* (Frasier, 2007) with students.
2. Explain that every Friday the class will engage in a Vocabulary Super Bowl.
3. On Monday, give each student a word from a list selected from the topics being studied in science, social studies, health, music, and literature.
4. Give each student a 4 x 6 index card that is divided into squares. (See Figure 5.12.)
5. Ask students to write the word in the upper left-hand square; write the dictionary definition in the upper right-hand square; write one or two synonyms or a definition phrase that classmates will understand in the lower left-hand square; and finally, write a sentence using the word in the lower right-hand square.

Sample card for learning content area vocabulary.   **FIGURE** 5.12

Vocabulary word	Dictionary definition
Miscellaneous	A collection of unrelated objects
Synonym or definition phrase	**Sentence**
Many different kinds	My backpack was filled with miscellaneous items that I no longer needed in school.

6. Each student then becomes the expert on the word and teaches its spelling and definition to the class.

7. Post the words on a bulletin board.

8. On Tuesday through Thursday, have the expert pronounce his or her word and orally challenge a classmate to spell it. Then divide the class into four or five teams.

9. Then you pronounce the word. The group that rings its bell first, spells the word, gives the definition, and uses it in a sentence correctly gets a point.

Recommended for intermediate grades.

10 Collecting puns

A pun is a play on words. Some students need an explanation of a pun in order to understand it. Of course, if students do not get the pun, they often miss the humor in a story. Janet Stevens and Susan Stevens Crummel have created a humorous story with many puns called *Jackalope* (2003). Read this book out loud and invite students to jot down the puns they hear. After the reading, students collect puns from their readings or daily conversation, add them to a bulletin board, and share them with the class. *Recommended for intermediate grades.*

11 Roots and affixes memory

Researchers and educators understand that teaching students the commonly used Greek and Latin root words and affixes helps students build their vocabulary (Flanigan et al., 2012; Goodwin et al., 2012). Using a list of commonly used prefixes and suffixes, make a set of cards with prefixes and suffixes, and another set with the definitions of each. (A good web resource for a detailed list of the common prefixes and suffixes is http://teacher.scholastic.com/reading/bestpractices/vocabulary/pdf/prefixes_suffixes.pdf.) Be sure there is a definition card for every prefix and suffix. Use the cards in the following activity:

1. Take 30 cards, 15 with prefixes and suffixes and 15 with their matching definitions, and place them face down in five rows of six.

2. Students take turns turning over two cards. If they match a prefix or suffix with its definition, they keep the cards; if they do not have a match, they turn the cards over again.

3. The student with the most pairs of cards at the end of the game wins.

4. Use plastic zip bags for each set of cards. You can focus on prefixes or suffixes if you want, or you can use all the cards together for a more challenging game.

Recommended for intermediate grades.

12 Getting the facts correct

At the end of *Jackalope*, the authors explain that a jackrabbit is not really a rabbit but a hare, and their babies are called leverets. They also explain that the antelope of North America is a pronghorn, and that a horned toad is not a toad, but a lizard. After sharing those facts, invite students to look up facts about leverets, hares, pronghorns, or lizards. Based on the creature they choose, divide the students into small groups so they can collaborate on researching their creature. Then invite them to share their information in any creative manner, such as a poem, slide presentation, video, skit, and so forth. *Recommended for intermediate grades.*

13 Graphic organizers

A *graphic organizer* provides a visual structure for new vocabulary and uses charts, timelines, and so forth to organize the vocabulary and concepts of a particular topic (DeVries, 2015). A graphic organizer is really a framework for comprehension. It enables students to visualize the relationships among concepts in a text or passage and then to analyze how those concepts work together. Some of the various formats for graphic organizers include outlines, diagrams, timelines, flowcharts, hierarchic organizers, webs or mapping charts, and causal charts. See Figures 5.13 through 5.16 for examples.

Introduce these graphic organizer formats to students using the following steps:

1. Explain how the different graphic organizers can be used to clarify relationships between concepts and to summarize ideas learned from informational texts.

FIGURE 5.13 Timeline organizer.

	MAGDALENA ESTRADA			
Magdalena was born	She got a virus and her leg went limp	Guatemala doctors could do no more for her	Went to the U.S. for help	She could walk again
1985	1991	1993	1994	1995

FIGURE 5.14 Problem–solution organizer.

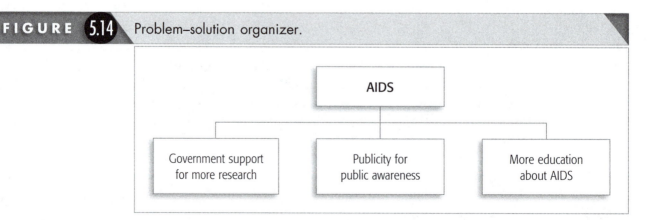

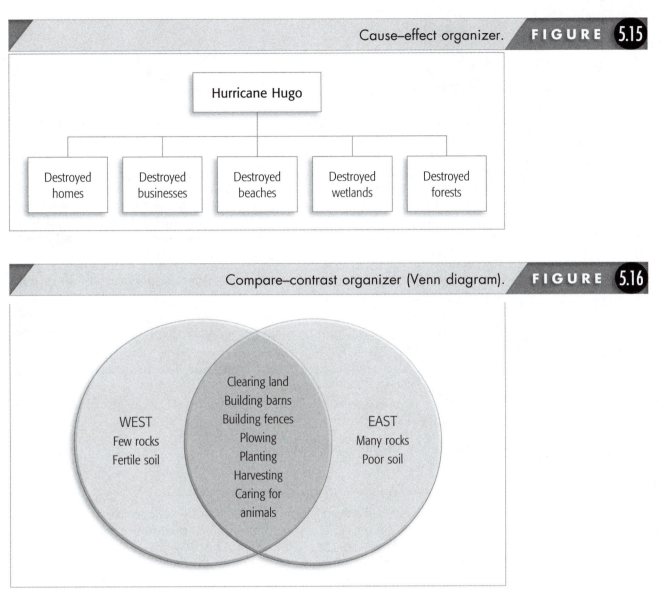

Cause–effect organizer. **FIGURE** 5.15

Compare–contrast organizer (Venn diagram). **FIGURE** 5.16

2. Using a text that has a particular organizational structure, model how to complete a specific type of graphic organizer.

3. With scaffolding, have students read a passage from an informational text and complete a graphic organizer.

4. Ask students to take turns drawing their graphic organizer in front of the class on a posterboard or whiteboard to share what they learned from a passage.

Recommended for intermediate grades.

14 Monologue book report

This activity requires students to understand the point of view of the story and encourages students to step into the shoes of the story's protagonist. Have students wear a piece of clothing that suggests the era in which the story takes place. Instruct them to speak in the first person and have the "character" explain his or her actions and reactions to certain situations in the book, how others misunderstood him or her, and what he or she really thought about the other characters. *Recommended for intermediate grades.*

15   Reciprocal teaching

Reading is a complex process in which a reader merges the information from the text with his or her schema (background knowledge). Teaching students strategies to use before, during, and after reading will facilitate their ability to "read and comprehend complex literary and informational text independently and proficiently" (CCRA.R.10; NGACBP & CCSSO, 2010, p. 10). One activity for developing metacognitive knowledge to help students monitor their own reading is *reciprocal teaching* (Hinson, 2000; Palincsar & Brown, 1986). Palincsar and Brown (1986) recommend that initially the teacher reads a passage and models the four steps of the strategy: preview, predict, summarize, and question. The teacher then gradually transfers the process to the students. Students should read a passage and take turns modeling the four steps as the teacher demonstrated. Reciprocal teaching is interactive and has proven to be an effective and direct way of using teacher modeling to promote student understanding. Stricklin (2011) offers this reading comprehension activity:

1. *Preview:* Model and then invite students to skim the title, main headings, and subheadings to get the main idea of the passage.
2. *Predict:* Model and then invite students to read the captions of photographs, charts, and diagrams. From their skimming, have them write two or three "I wonder" or predicting questions.
3. *Summarize:* After reading the passage, model and then invite students to summarize by writing: "The big idea is . . ."
4. *Question:* Invite students to ask questions they have about the passage. Also ask students to explain whether their "I wonder" questions were answered.

Recommended for intermediate grades.

16   Understanding how authors develop characters

CCSS RL.3.3 requires third-grade students to "describe characters in a story (e.g., their traits, motivations, or feelings) and explain how their actions contribute to the sequence of events" (NGACBP & CCSSO, 2010, p. 12). Because picture book illustrations convey traits, feelings, and motivations, always encourage students to analyze the illustrations as well as the text to determine how the author reveals a character. Kevin Henkes' books are good sources for this. Many students enjoy Henkes' many characters, including Lilly, Owen, Chester, Sheila Rae, and Chrysanthemum. Each of his characters feels real because they have many of the same traits, motivations for their actions, and feelings as third graders. First review Henkes' books and characters as a class. Then invite students to choose a partner and decide which character they wish to describe. They then can use the chart in Figure 5.17 to organize their thoughts. Instruct students to give specific examples from the book that support their ideas. After completing the chart, discuss the various charts as a class. The chart in Figure 5.17 can be modified and used for any text and has a sample entry for you to follow. *Recommended for intermediate grades.*

17   Summarizing through dramatization

Teachers often associate dramatization with narratives; however, for a change of pace and to cater to kinesthetic learners, assign a social studies, math, or science passage to a small group to dramatize. Stress the importance of being accurate so the audience can clearly understand the concept. Making the presentation humorous is acceptable as long as the concepts are demonstrated clearly. For example, students may dramatize subordinating conjunctions in the following way.

Character Chrysanthemum	Title of Book *Chrysanthemum* by K. Henkes	
Feelings	Evidence from Text/page #	Evidence from Illustrations/page #
1. Content with her name before she goes to school.	"C. loved her name." p. 3 "She loved the way it sounded." p. 4	In the picture on page 3, C. has a happy face.
2.		
3.		
Personality traits	Evidence from Text/page #	Evidence from Illustrations/page #
1.		
2.		
3.		
Motivations	Evidence from Text/page #	Evidence from Illustrations/page #
1.		
2.		
3.		

Student 1: I am an independent clause.

Student 2: I am a dependent clause.

Students 1 & 2: And we want to be joined together to make one sentence.

Student 2: I cannot stand alone so I need my friend Independent Clause.

Student 3: I am "Over" and I will connect you two. (He stands between Dependent Clause and Independent Clause and attempts to lock arms together, but it does not work so sadly "Over" walks away.)

Student 4: I am "Because" and I will connect you two. (He stands between Dependent Clause and Independent Clause and attempts to lock arms together, and they can connect!)

Students 1 & 2: Thank you, "Because!"

Student 4: You're welcome.

Of course, students can make the skit longer by including more words. I have found that when students act out concepts they understand them more quickly and remember them longer. *Recommended for middle grades.*

18 Opening spaces for critical literacy

Middle-school teachers should expose students to books that will "lead them to new ways of understanding the world" (Labadie, Mosley-Wetzel, & Roger, 2012). Using picture books with themes of social justice is a good way to begin. Four good book selections are *Roberto Clemente* (Winter, 2005), *Stealing Home: Jackie Robin-*

son: Against the Odds (Burleigh, 2007), *Freedom Summer* (Wiles, 2005), and *White Socks Only* (Coleman, 1996). All four of these books have illustrations that convey as much of the story as the text. Books about athletes are good choices because many middle-school students participate in sports and can identify with injustice on the playing field. Here are a few questions to use to begin such a discussion:

1. Study the character's facial expressions in the illustrations. What do they reveal?
2. Study the setting in the illustrations. What did you learn from them?
3. Explore the point of view. Whose point of view is used to tell the story? Whose voice is *not* heard?
4. How does the illustrator use line, color, shape, and texture to develop the story's mood and influence your emotions?
5. How does the illustrator use space? What/who is in the foreground and what/who is in the background?

This is an opportunity for students to voice their ideas, and your voice should be heard only when conversation breaks down. After the discussion, ask students to consider what they can do in their school to make sure all students are treated fairly in all situations. *Recommended for middle grades.*

19 Read, flip, write

Often when students are asked to summarize their reading, they plagiarize by writing word for word what the textbook states. Matson (2012) taught students to paraphrase by having them read a short passage without taking notes or highlighting text, then flip the page and summarize what they read. Matson suggests teaching this technique by inviting students to talk about a favorite movie or TV show. After they talk about it, invite them to write down what they said. Another method to teach this technique is to have students read a short fable or urban legend, then to flip over the passage and write a summary. The goal is making sure that students do *not* return to the passage as they write. *Recommended for middle grades.*

20 Sticks and stones may break my bones, but words set the tone of a story

The author's choice of words creates the tone of a poem, story, or informational passage. CCRA.R.4 requires students to "interpret words and phrases as they are used in a text, including determining technical, connotative, and figurative meanings, and analyze how specific word choices shape meaning or tone" (NGACBP & CCSSO, 2010, p. 10). You may need to facilitate students' knowledge on how authors use vivid word choice to create tone by reading a passage and then inviting students to discuss in pairs or small groups how words and word phrases create the tone of a passage. *Encounter,* a picture book by Yolen (1992), is a powerful story of a Taino boy who witnessed the arrival of Christopher Columbus. Use the following steps for this activity:

1. Read aloud and discuss the story while showing the illustrations that augment the text.
2. Divide students into groups of three.
3. Give each group the chart found in Figure 5.18.
4. Have the groups discuss the words in each phrase, what they mean in the story, and how the words in the phrase set the tone.
5. Encourage groups to share their ideas with the class.
6. Invite students to find words and phrases that set the tone when reading other texts.

Recommended for middle grades.

| | Sample chart for showing how word choice creates tone in a text. | **FIGURE** 5.18 |

WORD/PHRASE	MEANING	HOW IT CREATES MOOD
"three great-winged birds with voices like thunder . . ."	Great-winged: the birds had a large wing span. Thunder: The bird cries were very deep and loud.	The combined use of the words great-winged and thunder suggests the power and size of the birds. Also the use of thunder suggests danger.
"three great-sailed canoes . . ."		
"The baby canoes spat out many strangers . . ."		
"but the skin was moon to my sun."		
"All along the way I told people . . . I said our blood would cry out in the sand."		
"We took their speech into our mouths, forgetting our own."		

21 Analyzing point of view

CCRA.R.6 states that students should "assess how point of view or purpose shapes the content and style of a text" (NGACBP & CCSSO, 2010, p. 10). To analyze how the objective and first-person points of view shape a story, select some picture books to read to the class. For example, to analyze the objective point of view, read Patricia Polacco's *The Butterfly* (2000), a story of a young French girl and her family who harbored Jews during World War II. Discuss how the author writes what the characters say and what they do, but does not disclose any of the characters' feelings or thoughts. Ask students how the telling of the story from the objective point of view shapes the tone. Then ask them to consider how the story might be different if it were told in first person from Monique's point of view. How would the story change? Would Monique be able to explain the action as well as the author does when told in the objective point of view?

Jacqueline Woodson's *The Other Side* (2001) is a story told from the point of view of an African American girl whose mother told her never to climb over the fence to the "white people's" property. Discuss how this point of view affects the mood of the story. Ask the students to consider how different the story would be if the author used third-person narration or had written it from the white girl's point of view.

After sharing these two picture books, assign the class Walter Dean Myers' *Monster* (1999). As you read a section each day, have students keep a log of the parts of the novel in which the first-person point of view creates tense moods. After reading the entire novel, divide students into small groups of two or three and have them complete the activity sheet found in Figure 5.19. This activity also supports CCRA.R.1, "read closely to determine what the text says explicitly and to make logical inferences from it; cite specific textual evidence when writing or speaking to support conclusions drawn from the text"; and CCRA.R.6, "assess how point of view or purpose shapes the content and style of a text" (NGACBP & CCSSO, 2010, p. 10). *Recommended for middle grades.*

FIGURE 5.19   Activity sheet for analyzing point of view.

Analyzing the Point of View of *Monster* by Walter Dean Myers

In your small group, consider the task and write your reflection in column 2. In the third column, cite the quote and page that supports your reflection. If members in your group have differing opinions, discuss the opinions until you come to a consensus for your group. The following shows the beginning responses of one small group.

TASK	REFLECTION	QUOTE/PAGE NUMBER
1. In the novel, Steve describes the settings in which he finds himself. How does first person aid the reader in understanding how Steve feels about the setting?	Steve was speechless/baffled that he was in a jail cell.	"There is a mirror over the steel sink in my cell . . . When I look into the small rectangle, I see a face looking back at me but I don't recognize it." (p. 1)
	Depression sets in when Steve is ordered to go back to the cell.	"When she left and I had to go back to the cell area, I was more depressed than I have been since I've been here." (pp. 204–205)
2. Find at least 3 settings in which you think Steve describes the setting in such a manner that you can visualize it.		
3. Find three examples in which Steve, while in the courtroom, expresses the feeling of defeat. Explain how first person aids in creating the tone and mood at these times.		
4. The reader learns about the other characters through Steve's eyes. Choose three other characters from the novel and find two specific examples for each in which Steve's description aids the readers in visualizing what type of personalities the other characters have.	Name character #1: Example 1 Osvaldo uses bullying to make himself appear tough	"Osvaldo: 'He don't hang with nobody. He's just a lame looking for a name. Ain't that right, Steve? Ain't that right?'" (p. 81)
	Character #1, Example 1	
	Character #1, Example 2	
	Character #2, Example 1	
	Character #2, Example 2	
	Character #3, Example 1	
	Character #3, Example 2	
5. Did certain scenes in the novel cause you to become upset that Steve was being falsely accused? If so, describe which ones. (Each person's answers may differ for this question.)		
6. As a group, decide on one other area in which you think the novel is enhanced because it is written in first person.		

22 Figurative language in novels

Kirby Larson writes in *Hattie Ever After:* "Opportunity doesn't nibble twice at the same hook. My news was like a heavy stone in a muddy pond, sinking deeper and deeper into my gut" (p. 24). Christopher Paul Curtis, in *The Mighty Miss Malone* (2012), uses many examples of alliteration because Father loves to use them in daily conversation. Father is the one who addresses Deza as the "Mighty Miss Malone." As you read this book with students, stop and ask what specific examples of figurative language mean. By doing this, you draw students' attention to Curtis's art of using figurative language to reveal characters' traits. After reading each chapter, encourage students to fill in the chart found in Figure 5.20, and after reading a number of chapters, have students form small groups and share their examples. This activity supports CCRA.R.4. *Recommended for middle grades.*

23 Determining how details of text develop central idea of novel

CCSS RL.6.2 requires students to "determine a theme or central idea of a text and how it is conveyed through particular details; provide a summary of the text distinct from personal opinions or judgments" (NGACBP & CCSSO, 2010, p. 36). Many students are capable of providing summaries and the central idea of a text, but some students may find it more difficult to find evidence from the text to support their interpretation of it. To help these students, use Cynthia DeFelice's *Under the Same Sky* (2003), a story of a young farmer's son who throughout the novel changes his ideas about illegal migrant farmers. As students read the chapters, they will understand that there is a main theme (friendships develop after understanding each other's culture) with some other central ideas. After reading and discussing the novel, place students into groups of three to complete the chart in Figure 5.21. Working together will give students the opportunity to express their opinions based on evidence found in the text. *Recommended for middle grades.*

24 Figurative language in informational texts

Some students may have the mistaken idea that figurative language is found only in fiction. However, authors of informational text also understand the power of figurative language. One book with many examples is Albert Marrin's *Years of Dust: The Story of the Dust Bowl* (2009). After reviewing types of figurative language such as metaphors, similes, and personification, read this book aloud to students and ask them to listen for figurative phrases. When they hear one, have them raise their

Examples of figurative language in *The Mighty Miss Malone* (Curtis, 2012).			**FIGURE 5.20**
EXAMPLE OF FIGURATIVE LANGUAGE	**TYPE OF FIGURATIVE LANGUAGE**	**INTERPRETATION**	**PAGE #**
"pour cornflakes in his dimple and eat them out with a spoon"	hyperbole	Jimmie has really deep dimples.	p. 5

FIGURE 5.21 Theme or central idea with text evidence using *Under the Same Sky* by DeFelice (2003).

PERSONAL STATEMENT OF CENTRAL IDEA	EVIDENCE OF CENTRAL IDEA FOUND IN TEXT	CITATION/PAGE #
Although many communities need the help of the migrant workers, people hold prejudices against them.	"Some of the neighbors showed up at the town meeting to say that they did not want more housing for the Mexicans."	Page 69

hand, repeat the phrase, and record it on the log sheet such as the one in Figure 5.22. After students have recorded about five examples, stop the reading and have students discuss what the phrases mean and how the figurative language aided them in visualizing the horror of the dust bowl. This activity supports CCRA.R.4. *Recommended for middle grades.*

25   Connecting fiction and nonfiction

Invite students to read either *The Grave Robber's Secret* (Myers, 2011) or *Time of the Witches* (Myers, 2009). After reading and discussing one of the novels, invite students to list the new information they learned about the setting (time and place) and other things they learned through the story. Have students cite specific passages to support their information, which supports CCRA.R.1. For example, after reading *The Grave Robber's Secret*, students can make two columns on a piece of paper. On the left-hand side, they list what they learned about Philadelphia in the 1800s, the nation's first hospital, and medical research during that period. Then, using online and other resources, students can compare what "facts" from the novel

FIGURE 5.22 Log sheet of figurative language with examples from *Years of Dust: The Story of the Dust Bowl* (Marrin, 2009).

PHRASE	TYPE OF FIGURATIVE LANGUAGE	MEANING/REFLECTION	PAGE #
The plains "are wavelike"	Metaphor	Full-grown wheat blows in the Oklahoma wind, and it looks like waves.	6
Farmers had "sown the seeds" of a unique tragedy	Metaphor	Oklahoma farmers were greedy and over-planted the land. When they plowed it and Oklahoma had no rain, it caused dust to blow across Oklahoma and Kansas.	50
Tens of thousands of American men, women, and children, white, black, brown, yellow, who inhabit the "jungle"	Metaphor	The jungle refers to the over-crowded trains that hobos lived in as they attempted to move from one place to another to find work.	76

really happened and what "facts" were augmented to make a thrilling mystery. For example, they might explore whether people really dug up graves to sell body parts for research. This type of activity connects fiction and nonfiction.

To help students develop their oral communication skills, invite them to share their information through multimedia presentations, skits, or readers theater. If you want students to develop their writing skills, assign a paper in which they compare and contrast the facts from the fiction. *Recommended for middle grades.*

26 Interpreting words and phrases in informational text

When reading informational texts, students are often confronted with technical terms that they do not use in daily conversation. This activity is based on the trade book *Oil Spill: Disaster in the Gulf* (Chiang, Crane, Hamalainen, & Jones, 2010).

Often K-T-W-L-E charts are completed using information to be shared by class members. The K-T-W-L-E chart presented in Figure 5.23 is based on vocabulary

A K-T-W-L-E chart for the vocabulary in "The Science of Earthquakes." **FIGURE 5.23**

TERM	K	T	W	L	E
Fault	I'm only familiar with fault meaning a mistake.	Where earthquakes happen.	Want to know if earthquakes can happen any place in the world.	It is the place where the earth's surface shifts.	p. 1 of 2
Epicenter	It must mean the center of something.	A place by the equator.	Why do earthquakes happen by the equator?	It is the center of where the earthquake happens.	p. 1 of 2
Foreshocks		Something that happens before an earthquake.	What are these things?	They are the little shocks that happen before the big quake.	p. 1 of 2
Main shock	This is the big quake.		Where do they all happen?	The main shock is the biggest shock.	p. 1 of 2
After shock	Little shocks that happen after the big one.		How big are they?	They are the little shocks that happen after the big one, and they can occur most of a month or more.	p. 1 of 2
Mantle		?	What does a mantle have to do with earthquakes?	It is one of the layers of the earth; it is part of the earth's skin.	p. 1 of 2
Tectonic plates		?	What are these?	The parts of the earth that keep slowly moving.	p. 1 of 2
Seismographs		Some machine that measures earthquakes.	Where are these machines located?	They are instruments that measure earthquakes that are located at earthquake centers.	p. 1 of 2

Source: Information retrieved from http://earthquake.usgs.gov/learn/kids/eqscience.php.

found in this text associated with drilling oil. In the *K* column students write definitions of the terms they *know;* in the *T* column they write what they *think* the word means. After reading the passage, they write the definition they *learned* from the text in the *L* column; and in the *E* column they write the *evidence* or page number where they found the meaning of the word. *Recommended for middle grades.*

ASSESSING READING

No matter which methods and strategies you choose for your classroom reading instruction, you will want to evaluate and keep track of the progress your students are making. Evaluation is integral to the whole process of instruction. Always remember that the purpose of assessment is to provide you, the teacher, with information that will enable you to do a better job of aligning literacy instruction with performance standards (Akhavan, 2004). Each time you implement a strategy or an activity in your classroom, keep an eye on how it is working and how the students are responding to it.

Informal Reading Inventories

An effective way for teachers to obtain information about students' reading progress is to use an *informal reading inventory (IRI),* an evaluation technique designed to help diagnose a student's reading strengths and weaknesses through the oral reading of a series of graded word lists or sentences and text selections. The word lists or sentences are designed to give you an idea of the student's approximate grade level of reading; the selections of text and accompanying comprehension questions help you to determine which strategies the student uses to decode information and how much of the information the student actually comprehends. IRIs can be bought commercially. Well-known commercially prepared IRIs include the following:

- Bader, L. A. (2012). *Bader Reading and Language Inventory and Graded Word List* (7th ed.). Upper Saddle River, NJ: Prentice Hall.
- Burns, P., & Roe, B. (2010). *Informal Reading Inventory* (12th ed.). Boston: Houghton Mifflin.
- Ekwall, H., & Shanker, J. (2013). *Ekwall–Shanker Reading Inventory* (6th ed.). Boston: Allyn & Bacon.
- Flynt, E., & Cooter, R. (2013). *The Flynt–Cooter Comprehensive Reading Inventory-2: Assessment of K–12 Reading Skills in English & Spanish* (2nd ed.). Upper Saddle River, NJ: Pearson.
- Johns, J. (2010). *Basic Reading Inventory: Pre-Primer Through Grade Twelve and Early Literacy Assessment* (11th ed.). Dubuque, IA: Kendall/Hunt.
- Leslie, L., & Caldwell, J. (2010). *Qualitative Reading Inventory-5* (5th ed.). Upper Saddle River, NJ: Pearson.
- Manzo, A., Manzo, U., & McKenna, M. (1999). *Informal Reading–Thinking Inventory.* New York: Harcourt Brace College Publishers.
- Wheelock, W., & Silvaroli, N. (2011). *Classroom Reading Inventory* (12th ed.). New York: McGraw-Hill.
- Woods, M., & Moe, A. (2010). *Analytic Reading Inventory: Comprehensive Standards-Based Assessment for All Students Including Gifted and Remedial* (9th ed.). Upper Saddle River, NJ: Pearson.

Using an IRI, you can assess each student's independent, instructional, and frustration levels of reading. You can also determine a student's potential for reading by analyzing his ability to comprehend a passage that has been read aloud. The four levels of reading comprehension are as follows (Schulman & Payne, 2000):

1. *Independent level.* Indicates the grade level of materials a student can read on his or her own. Word recognition is 97 to 100 percent and comprehension is 90 to 100 percent.

2. *Instructional level.* Signifies the level of materials that should be used for reading instruction. Word recognition is 92 to 96 percent and comprehension is 70 to 89 percent.

3. *Frustration level.* Occurs when a student begins to encounter great difficulty in reading and does not really comprehend much of what is happening. Word recognition is below 92 percent and comprehension is below 70 percent.

4. *Listening level.* Helps to determine a student's potential for reading. A student's ability to answer 75 percent of the questions about a passage that has been read aloud by the teacher is considered adequate in designating this level.

Running Records

The *running record,* an informal technique similar to an IRI, is gaining in popularity. It is advocated by Clay (1979, 1985, 1991) as a way of indicating how well a student is processing text. In a running record, the student reads a selection from a book with which he or she is quite familiar while the teacher looks at a copy of the same text. As the student reads, the teacher codes the behaviors on a separate piece of paper while maintaining a position of neutrality (Clay, 2000). Checks are recorded for correct words; miscues are noted with as much accuracy as possible. Types of miscues noted are substitutions, multiple attempts at a word, omissions and insertions, and the teacher providing a word for the student. Substitutions are written directly over the text, with multiple attempts noted but not counted. If the teacher tells the student a word, she writes a *T* below the line. With an omission, she writes a dash or line above the word in text. An insertion of a word is noted above the line and a dash is noted below. Repetitions are coded with a check—one for each attempt. Self-corrections, which are a vital component of the record, are not considered errors and are noted by an *SC*. See Fountas and Pinnell (1996) for more variations on completing running records.

In addition to quantitatively analyzing these records, you also need to look at them qualitatively. Note whether or not a student is using letter/sound cues, syntactic cues, or semantic cues when trying to comprehend the meaning of the text. Then you can use the information from the running record to make informed and continuing decisions about future instruction. Running records are an important part of the guided reading component of a comprehensive literacy program (Fountas & Pinnell, 2000). See Figure 5.24 for a visual representation of the coding system in a running record.

Other Informal Assessment Techniques

IRIs and running records provide only a sampling of what a student is capable of in reading, a sampling that can easily be affected by a

FIGURE 5.24   The coding system in a running record.

READING ACTIVITY	TEACHER'S CODE
Correct reading	✓ ✓ ✓ ✓ ✓ for each correct word
Substitution	$\dfrac{attempt}{text}$
Told a word	$\dfrac{—}{text}$ | T
Omission	$\dfrac{—}{text}$
Repetitions	✓ R ✓ R ✓ ✓ Checks indicate correct words ✓ R 2 R indicates repetition ✓ R 3 Number indicates amount
Insertion	$\dfrac{word}{—}$
Self-correction	$\dfrac{attempt}{text}$ | SC

Source: Adapted from Fountas and Pinnell (2000).

student's anxiety or distractions during the test period. These inventories must be supplemented with other types of data, such as your own knowledge of the student's ability and daily progress. Informal assessment, which can be conducted on a daily basis, includes observation; the use of conferences, checklists, and rubrics; and the examination of students' portfolios (their written responses to reading). These techniques embody the ideas of observation, interaction, and analysis put forth by Y. M. Goodman (1989).

Observation

Observation can take place during all types of reading activities. For example, you might note that during silent reading, one student is always pointing to the individual words. This might give you a clue that the student is having some difficulty with word recognition and fluency, something you might want to question the student about later. Your goal is to document language development in a variety of literacy situations.

You can keep track of your observations in several ways. You may simply want to jot your ideas down in a small notebook. However, it may be more efficient to keep more formal anecdotal records, which you can use for sharing information with administrators and caregivers. This type of record allows you to monitor both the entire class and individual students; it helps you to know where progress is occurring and where changes need to be made. A typical format of an anecdotal record is shown in Figure 5.25.

> A person who won't read has no advantage over one who can't read.
>
> **MARK TWAIN**

Anecdotal record form. **FIGURE 5.25**

DATE	STUDENT	ACTIVITY	COMMENTS
4/30	Alice M.	Reading aloud	Alice hesitates frequently—stumbles over words. Possibly book is too difficult. Suggest using a cloze activity to determine independent, instructional, and frustration levels. In the meantime use The Great Kapok Tree (a simpler picture book) as an alternative for reading.

SUMMARY

Conferences and checklists

Check each student's literacy progress daily. You may decide to use center time to conference with individual students and check on the status of their language learning. Conferences are a way of interacting with students that allow you to learn specific information about them and to clarify any confusion you may have about their progress. Conferences can take a variety of forms. Although they may be informal, they have a specific structure. Usually a conference does not last more than seven minutes and generally includes the following five steps:

1. Have the student share and discuss a story.
2. Ask her comprehension questions to help you determine her ability to think about the story.
3. Have her perform an oral reading of a story passage.
4. Give her suggestions for activities to build language competencies, project work, and future book selection.
5. Conduct a conference summary in which you check her log entries to assess how much reading is actually being done and note her specific competencies and needs.

Using these steps, you will know what to look for and will use questions and comments to get that information. You will be equipped to give students direction regarding their upcoming activities. Teachers often use checklists, such as the Reading Conference Checklist in Appendix D.5 to document specific information.

Rubrics

Rubrics provide specific criteria for evaluating student performance at differing proficiency levels. Students receive credit for minimal work, average work, or high-quality work. Some areas have developed statewide standards and train teachers in how to be consistent in their scoring (Garcia & Verville, 1994). Rubrics are helpful in that they give students constructive information about what is expected of them. Appendix D.6 offers a sample reading rubric that you might use.

Portfolio assessment: Analysis of student responses

You may also assess progress by reviewing and analyzing students' written responses to reading, usually kept in writing *portfolios*. The responses your students collect in a portfolio might include such items as a journal, a written summary of a story, several drafts of a poem, a letter to a character in a story, a description of a character accompanied by a portrait, a completely new ending for a story, and completed self-appraisal forms. Many educators advocate using portfolio models or checklists as a means of selecting what should go into each student's folder (Eaton, 2012).

You and your students can work together to create portfolios of selected writing projects. This process provides valuable assessment information for you and also encourages students to engage in self-monitoring, an activity that empowers students by allowing them to assume some responsibility for their own progress (Eaton, 2012). In reviewing your students' various writings, you can begin to make judgments not only about their reading comprehension, but also about the increased sophistication of their written work.

Standardized Tests

In public schools, one aspect of reading evaluation involves *standardized tests,* commercially available tests that measure a student's level of achievement. Some tests give more specific information by diagnosing a student's individual reading strengths and weaknesses.

Achievement tests

Achievement tests provide information about how well a student is functioning in selected aspects of reading. The two basic types of achievement tests are norm-referenced tests and criterion-referenced tests. *Norm-referenced tests* are used to compare a student's achievement level to national *norms,* or standards of performance. These norms are established by giving the tests to large groups of students around the United States and then using the normal distribution of the students' test scores to come up with a standard of achievement. Generally, these tests are used to record and compare the progress of groups of students as well as that of individuals. Comparing an individual student's score with this national standard yields information about how well the student is performing in comparison with his peers. Information from these tests is usually reported in percentiles and stanines.

On the other hand, *criterion-referenced tests* compare the student's achievement level not with that of other students but with a standard established for demonstrating mastery of a specific type of learning. A criterion-referenced test might be used to demonstrate that a student has achieved competency in the ability to comprehend the main idea of a story. Such testing pro-

> We can't solve problems by using the same kind of thinking we used to create them.
>
> **ALBERT EINSTEIN**

Weighing the importance of Mark's struggle with phonemic awareness

At the end of the first semester, it was time for Ms. Brockette, a first-grade teacher, to administer the midyear DIBELS reading assessments. The DIBELS assesses students' phonemic awareness, phonics, fluency, and comprehension. Ms. Brockette was surprised that Mark, who was reading books written at the 2.3 grade level, did not perform well on the phonemic awareness part of the test. He could not tell how many phonemes were in a three-letter word; he could not delete a sound to make a new word (e.g., "Tell me what word you make when you take the /b/ sound off of *beat*"), and could not manipulate sounds within words (e.g., "Say *sand*. Now change the /s/ sound to the /h/ sound. What word do you have?"). Ms. Brockette felt pressure for all her students to perform well on the tests. She told the reading specialist, Mr. Lee, about Mark's situation, and they decided that Mark would meet with Mr. Lee three times a week.

At their first meeting, Mr. Lee asked Mark what he liked to read. Mark said he liked funny stories and books from which he learned something. Mr. Lee had some books at the 1.5 grade level and was pleased that Mark read one with 99 percent accuracy. Mr. Lee then asked Mark to read a book about spiders at the 2.2 grade level, and again Mark read it with 99 percent accuracy and could tell Mr. Lee many details about spiders. Mr. Lee then told Mark they were going to play some word games. Mr. Lee instructed Mark to listen to the words and tell him how many sounds he heard. Mark could not do the task. After some more word games, Mr. Lee found that indeed Ms. Brockette was correct—Mark struggled with all the components of phonemic awareness: hearing sounds within words and deleting sounds and manipulating sounds. Mr. Lee then dictated a sentence—I like to jump rope and ride my bike—and Mark wrote it without any errors.

Because Mark was a good reader and writer, Mr. Lee decided he would work only with phonemic awareness exercises during their time together. However, Mr. Lee realized almost immediately that these tasks made Mark nervous. At their third session, Mark complained that he was not feeling well so Mr. Lee said, "Let's just read today instead of playing those games." Not surprisingly, once Mark started reading a book on snakes his headache went away.

Mr. Lee made a decision—protect Mark's love of reading by forgetting about phonemic awareness! For whatever reason, breaking language down into little pieces was too confusing for Mark, and it was obvious that he could comprehend texts above his grade level and compose texts at his grade level.

vides information only about a particular student's progress in developing needed competencies; it does not compare that student with others.

A *diagnostic test,* also a standardized test, can be used to demonstrate a student's reading strengths and weaknesses by identifying which competencies she does or does not have. Diagnostic tests usually have specific criteria for determining levels of competency. The results of this type of test are often used to plan instruction and remediation.

Although standardized tests provide general information about the success of reading instruction, they do not yield all the information you need to know about students' progress (Anderson et al., 1985). For example, they do not always measure a student's unique reading competencies or weaknesses, how well he understands and differentiates between stories and expository text, or even his attitudes toward reading. Nor do these tests reflect the collaboration and interaction that are so often a part of real-life assessment. *Becoming a Nation of Readers* (Anderson et al., 1985) cautioned that, at best, standardized tests are a partial assessment that should be combined with observation of students' reading proficiency and habits as well as a review of their responses to reading and interactions with others.

BEAR and DIBELS

Some tests assess five reading components: phonic awareness, phonics, vocabulary, fluency, and comprehension. Many school districts like to use these assessments to demonstrate student growth and each school's adequate yearly progress (AYP). Two such assessments are Basic Early Assessment of Reading (BEAR) Scope and Sequence tests and Dynamic Indicators of Basic Early Literacy Skills (DIBELS) tests. The BEAR tests are group tests for kindergarten through third grade, whereas the DIBELS tests are individualized tests for kindergarten through sixth grade. Both tests are given multiple times throughout the year to assess student progress so classroom teachers can provide appropriate instruction to lagging students. DIBELS, for example, enables teachers to work in a preventive rather than remedial mode (Langdon, 2004) and has been shown to be effective with many populations, including urban public school students (Rouse & Fantuzzo, 2006).

TECHNOLOGY IN THE CLASSROOM

As you observe classrooms, you will find many students reading from laptops, tablets, or other mobile devices. Some of the many reasons that digital text has become popular with students is because it permits them to manipulate font size, use text-to-speech features, click on words to receive a definition, and read books for free from various websites. You can project such websites on the classroom whiteboard for large group instruction. For example, if you want to engage the entire class in choral reading, access a poetry website to work on fluent reading. Websites with readers theater scripts can also be used for fluency. Figure 5.26 lists several websites with free reading materials.

FIGURE 5.26 Websites with books, songs, poetry, and readers theater.

www.wegivebooks.com This free site, established by Penguin, offers many titles, and each time the student completes a text, they record it and Penguin gives a free book to one of the organizations listed on their site. This site increases classroom libraries, as long as the classroom has a computer or some other electronic device that can connect to the Internet.

www.gigglepoetry.com/poetrytheater.aspx This site has free readers theatre scripts.

www.aaronshep.com Aaron Shepherd site has readers theater scripts for all grade levels.

www.bussongs.com This site features 2,000 nursery rhymes. Most of them have videos and music.

www.rif.org/books This site has animated stories. Students can read along with the text.

www.nationalgeographickids.com This site features many informational books at various levels. The photographs appeal to many students.

www.nationalgeographiclittlekids.com This site features many informational books written for beginning readers.

"There's an app for that!" Many of us have said those very words, and many of us make use of those apps in our daily lives. So why do teachers tell students to keep their smartphones out of sight in class? Castek and Beach (2013) encourage teachers to permit students to use apps in school because they foster collaboration and provide a way to share learning opportunities. In particular, the concept mapping, note-taking/annotation, and screencasting apps (which capture the action on a computer screen accompanied by a voiceover) allow students to share observations and data that they have collected. Two apps that are particularly geared for science are Leafsnap, which can be used to identify different trees, and Solar Walk, which can be used to observe planetary objects in space. Figure 5.27 lists other apps for concept-mapping and screencasting.

Other apps permit users to type over printed text, record responses, or add pictures from a photo library. Have your students use these apps to personalize texts (Hutchison, Beschorner, & Schmidt-Crawford, 2012). A handy website that offers a long list of iPad apps appropriate for younger students is www.onlineclasses.org/2010/06/16/40-amazingly-educational-ipad-apps-for-kids. This site lists apps for middle-school students: www.appsineducation.blogspot.com/2012/01/english-apps-for-middle-school.html.

> Reading books contains two different delights, both definable as learning. One is the pleasure of apprehending the unexpected: when one meets a new author who has a new vision of the world. The other is the pleasure of deepening one's knowledge of a special field.
>
> **GILBERT HIGHET**

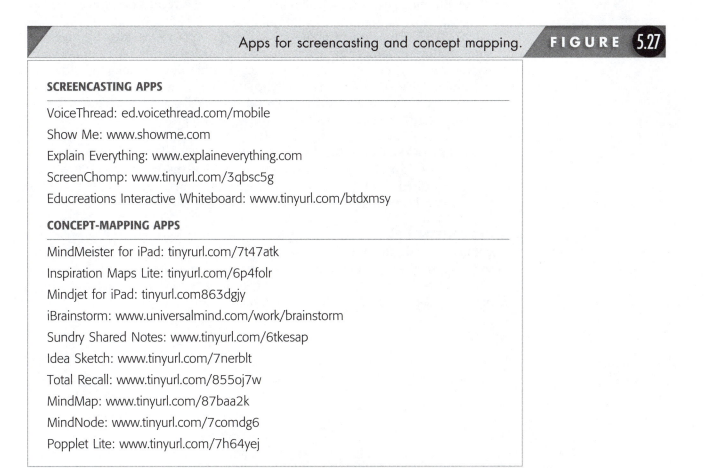

Apps for screencasting and concept mapping. **FIGURE 5.27**

SCREENCASTING APPS

VoiceThread: ed.voicethread.com/mobile

Show Me: www.showme.com

Explain Everything: www.explaineverything.com

ScreenChomp: www.tinyurl.com/3qbsc5g

Educreations Interactive Whiteboard: www.tinyurl.com/btdxmsy

CONCEPT-MAPPING APPS

MindMeister for iPad: tinyrurl.com/7t47atk

Inspiration Maps Lite: tinyurl.com/6p4folr

Mindjet for iPad: tinyurl.com863dgjy

iBrainstorm: www.universalmind.com/work/brainstorm

Sundry Shared Notes: www.tinyurl.com/6tkesap

Idea Sketch: www.tinyurl.com/7nerblt

Total Recall: www.tinyurl.com/855oj7w

MindMap: www.tinyurl.com/87baa2k

MindNode: www.tinyurl.com/7comdg6

Popplet Lite: www.tinyurl.com/7h64yej

Source: Castek, J. & Beach, R. (2013). Using apps to support disciplinary literacy and science. *Journal of Adolescent and Adult Literacy,* *56*(7), pp. 556–557.

SUMMARY

Comprehending fiction and nonfiction, whether in traditional print or digital format, is the goal for all students who complete high school, ensuring they will be ready for the reading required of them in college and career. Comprehension is a complex process in which readers are required to use many different skills. In order for teachers to facilitate readers' growth, they need to understand this complex process. Understanding the theories and research about the reading process aids teachers as they work with students. In order for both beginning and older readers to comprehend text, they need to develop their vocabulary, understand figurative language, recognize the organizational structure of text, and analyze text so they understand its deeper meaning.

In this chapter we have shared some activities that will help you develop your students' skills. We hope you will modify these ideas to fit your classroom.

field AND practicum ACTIVITIES

1. BECOME A CHARACTER. Students sometimes develop a strong feeling for certain characters in a favorite story. You can encourage this affection by having the students compose a short sequel to the story—one in which they actually become the characters in question and behave in ways they deem appropriate. Younger students may want to dictate their ideas to you or into a recording device.

2. CONTEXT CLOZE. Prepare several short reading selections by systematically deleting words not readily recognized by your students. As the students try to understand the text, they will use cues from the words surrounding the deletions to help them fill in the missing words. The purpose of the activity is to highlight the importance of using context to construct meaning. To provide feedback for the students, you may want to include the deleted words on the back of the selections.

3. FLUENCY PARTNERS. Pair a fluent reader in your class with a less fluent student. Have them choose a book they both enjoy and take turns reading aloud to each other. With repeated readings, fluency improves; the more fluent reader serves as a model and coach for the less fluent partner.

4. WORD PATTERNS. By creating word patterns, students learn more about phonics and spelling. Provide students with a set of individual letters (in cardboard, plastic, or wood) that they can manipulate to form words, and assign a particular pattern for them to work on. For example, have students make words that are part of the *ot* family—*cot, dot, got, hot, lot, not, pot, rot, tot,* and *trot.*

The Process of Writing

After reading this chapter, you should be able to accomplish the following:

1. Describe the stages in a process-writing approach.
2. Explain what is meant by a writing workshop.
3. Describe some writing minilessons.
4. Explain several types of journal writing.
5. Describe various types of poetry you will teach and how you will do this.
6. Describe some ways of assessing writing.

INTRODUCTION

Think back to your early years in elementary school. What do you remember about writing? Handwriting drills? Friday spelling tests? An essay on what you did over your summer vacation? Now reflect on your middle-school experience. Do you recall doing much writing? Did you do workbook exercises in sentence diagramming?

Traditionally, writing was not emphasized in the elementary grades in favor of reading instruction. However, middle-school teachers often believed their students already knew how to write; thus, they assigned topics instead of providing real writing instruction. Teachers saw their role as that of the classroom controller, responsible for maintaining discipline and telling students what to do and how to do it. This often resulted in a group of passive students who were unable to take responsibility for their own writing and eventually came to dislike the process.

This chapter introduces you to the *process* that real writers use and the writing workshop approach to classroom organization. You will also learn the many types of writing activities you can use to engage your students, from writing informational text to writing poetry. To get the most out of this chapter you will need to write, write, and write some more. As every writer knows, becoming a better writer takes work—there is no shortcut.

BRIEF HISTORY OF WRITING INSTRUCTION

Prior to the 1970s writing instruction was directed by teachers and focused on skills and drills (Britton, 1986). Depending on the students' grade level, writing usually fell into three categories: assigned topics, the one-shot approach, or practicing a specific skill. Assigned topics were those the teacher determined the entire class would address; individual student choice and motivation were not considered (Hawkins & Razali, 2012).

When given an assigned topic, students completed the writing assignment in a specific time period, usually 30 to 45 minutes. This approach was particularly stressful for many students. Ironically, the No Child Left Behind and Race to the Top programs mandate that standardized tests in writing include a single prompt and time limit.

Throughout the grade levels but particularly in upper grades, writing in previous eras was defined in terms of skills: handwriting, spelling, capitalization, punctuation, and a heavy emphasis on grammar and the parts of speech. Emphasizing these skills in isolation, and thus excluding any real writing in the curriculum, actually hindered students' writing development (Anderson, 2005; Applebee & Langer,

2011). Some classrooms abandoned real writing altogether; students spent their time on isolated workbook activities.

Researchers have long held that writing is a mental process that actually enhances thinking. Lev Vygotsky (1978, 1986), Applebee and Langer (2011), and many others argue that writing is a process of discovery that requires constant rehearsing and revising; it is unique to each individual and cannot be taught as a series of separate rules or skills.

In 1974 the federal government funded a grant to support the Bay Area Writing Project at the University of California Berkeley. Now known as the National Writing Project, the grant continues to give teachers graduate credit to attend summer writing institutes that teach writing as a process and the workshop approach (U.S. Dept. of Education, 2010). The early driving force behind the process approach to writing and the use of writing workshops was James Gray, but writing authorities such as Donald Graves, Nancie Atwell, and Lucy Calkins all subscribe to the process model and workshop organizational approach.

These approaches ushered in a new era in writing instruction, one that focused on letting students engage in a variety of writing activities and express themselves in increasingly sophisticated ways. Writing is about students exploring their world in their own way (DeFord, Mills, & Donnelly, 2012).

THE PROCESS APPROACH MODEL

Writing is a craft and like any other craft, it must be practiced (Fletcher & Portalupi, 1998). Traditionally, an individual learned a craft by working closely with an experienced craftsman or mentor. This is still true in the writing process, with the craftsman being the teacher who models and assists the beginning writer. The process model includes five stages, shown in Figure 6.1, but other models exist, although all are very similar (Atwell, 1998; Calkins, 2001; Fletcher & Portalupi, 2001; Medina, 2006).

Process writing model.   **FIGURE 6.1**

STAGE I PREWRITING	Getting ready, observing, free reading, drawing, storytelling, collection, writing folders, freewriting
STAGE II DRAFTING	Getting ideas down on paper, conferencing with the teacher, comparing papers in small groups, exchanging papers with a buddy, changing content, appearance, length, and so forth
STAGE III REVISING	Rewording the lead or ending, developing a character, eliminating repetitious material, adding details and descriptive words, moving material
STAGE IV EDITING	Proofreading, polishing small details, self-editing, buddy-editing, editing circles
STAGE V PUBLISHING	Reading a work aloud, author's chair or bulletin board, performing the work, placing in the class library, uploading to a website or wiki

Prewriting

In the initial *prewriting* stage, the teacher and students work together to find an idea to write about; writers usually choose their topics rather than have them assigned. This is also known as the *rehearsal stage* of writing, during which the student thinks and plans before putting words to paper. Depending on your students' ages, the prewriting stage can take on different forms. For example, younger students will need help in getting ready to write. They must have a comfortable space, a set time, and a variety of materials available to them, such as computers, paper, pens, pencils, scissors, tape, and paste. Older students should enter class prepared with their writing tools, but the judicious teacher always has tools available just in case.

One of the best things you can do at any grade level in the prewriting stage is to motivate students by reading a great book aloud. See Figure 6.2 for suggestions for middle-school students; for lists of fiction chapter books, informational books, and picture books, see Appendix B and the Association for Library Services for Children, www.ala.org/alsc.

We cannot overemphasize the importance of reading aloud to your students and providing them with uninterrupted time to read in class as part of the prewriting process. Krashen (2005), among many others, has argued that this step not only improves reading comprehension but it is also the foundation for success in writing.

Oral storytelling should go hand-in-hand with teacher read-alouds. Demonstrate storytelling (not memorizing or reading) to your class by using well-known stories with which they are familiar. Use gestures, facial expression, and voice

---

FIGURE 6.2   Authors and books appropriate for and appealing to middle-school readers.

AUTHORS

Lloyd Alexander	Paula Fox	Cynthia Rylant
Katherine Applegate	Jean Craighead George	Laura Schlitz
Avi	Virginia Hamilton	Jerry Spinelli
Judy Blume	Carl Hiaasen	Rebecca Stead
Betsy Byars	Sonia Levitin	Mildred Taylor
James Collier	Lois Lowry	J. R. R. Tolkien
Susan Cooper	Walter Dean Myers	Sheila Turnage
Robert Cormier	Scott O'Dell	Yoshiko Uchida
Sharon Creech	Katherine Paterson	Cynthia Voigt
Chris Crutcher	Gary Paulsen	Laurence Yep
Anne de Graaf	Richard Peck	Jane Yolen
Paul Fleischman	Ann Rinaldi	Paul Zindel

BOOKS TO READ ALOUD

Applegate, Katherine (2013). *The One and Only Ivan.*

De Graaf, Anne (2013). *Son of a Gun.*

Hiaasen, Carl (2002). *Hoot.*

Schlitz, Laura (2013). *Splendors and Glooms.*

Stead, Rebecca (2009). *When You Reach Me.*

Turnage, Sheila (2013). *Three Times Lucky.*

intonation to capture their attention. Once you have modeled storytelling for the class, encourage them to tell their own stories in small groups. You will soon notice how oral storytelling enhances general reading comprehension and stimulates writing ideas (Roskos, Tabor, & Lenhart, 2009).

Dramatic play with young children leads to talking, sharing, and eventually writing. Set up centers to encourage students to role play shopping at the grocery store, going to a pet shop, and other activities. You can include simple props and costumes to enhance the experience. Also include books to stimulate their imagination, such as *Jessica's X-Ray* (Zonta, 2002). You may wish to record the performances to watch later with the students, which will likely enhance their future participation. But first you have to get them speaking to one another and acting out their parts (Kalmar, 2008).

Other activities that help students generate writing ideas include allowing them free time to read books of their own choosing and encouraging them to observe the world around them, not only in the classroom but also on field trips and outside of school. Impart the idea that if they look closely enough, everything has a story to tell. For some students, drawing, painting, and other artistic pursuits provide inspiration for the act of writing, as the young artist rehearses in her mind the story she wants to tell. Also consider storytelling in small groups, oral and written brainstorming to collect ideas, and making lists of favorite books, sports teams, songs, foods, and places to visit to stimulate the writer's imagination (Birckmayer, Kennedy, & Stonehouse, 2010).

Prewriting can also include making an outline or creating a web or cluster diagram. When creating such a diagram, the writer brainstorms to figure out what he knows about a topic as well as what he wants to know about it, which hopefully motivates research online or in the library. The diagram is then created, consisting of lines and circles that show how one word or idea links to another and then another (Tompkins, 2003). Students can also diagram using software programs such as Inspiration (www.inspiration.com). Figures 6.3, 6.4, and 6.5 present examples of graphic organizers.

> Clutter is the disease of American writing. We are a society strangling in unnecessary words, circular constructions, pompous frills, and meaningless jargon.
>
> **WILLIAM ZINSSER**

Outline format. **FIGURE 6.3**

GENERIC	EXAMPLE: TEXAS INDEPENDENCE
I. Main Idea	I. Political Issues
1. Supporting detail	1. Expansion of slavery
2. Supporting detail	2. Independence from Mexico
II. Main Idea	II. Economic Issues
1. Supporting detail	1. Trade with United States
2. Supporting detail	2. Expansion of cotton into Texas
III. Main Idea	III. Two Major Battles
1. Supporting detail	1. The Alamo
2. Supporting detail	2. San Jacinto

FIGURE 6.4   Sample second-grade web: Animals.

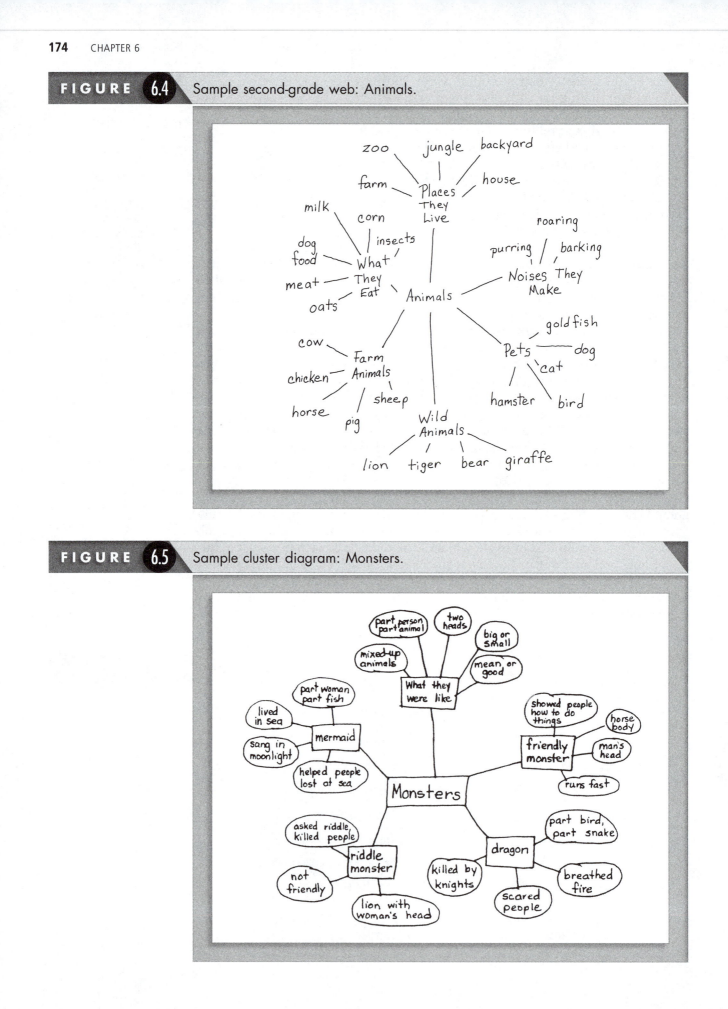

FIGURE 6.5   Sample cluster diagram: Monsters.

Here's how one teacher leads her students to find their own ideas to write about. Mrs. Guen settles into an overstuffed chair in a corner of the room. Her 18 first graders gather around, listening and watching as she reads Eric Carle's *The Very Hungry Caterpillar* (1969). She shows the illustrations of the caterpillar moving from page to page, gobbling up everything in sight and gradually changing into a butterfly. When she is finished reading she asks, "What did this story make you think of?" Hands shoot up. After a number of students respond, she suggests that everyone imagine a favorite insect and move around the room like it.

Soon all of the students are crawling, slithering, walking on all fours, flapping their arms, giggling, and having a great time. Finally, Mrs. Guen settles them down for a brainstorming session of all the words they can think of about their insects. She writes the words on chart paper for all to see.

"Now students," she says, "take out your writing folders. If you want you can draw your story first." Some students go to their desks, others get with a buddy on the rug, still others go to the writing nook made by two bookcases. The writing workshop has begun.

Drafting

In the *drafting* stage, as the term implies, students produce a first draft of their writing. Some teachers call this the "sloppy copy," because nothing about it has to be neat or perfect. The purpose of the rough draft is to get their ideas down on paper; shaping those ideas into a story, report, poem, or pen pal letter comes later. Direct students to focus on the content of the paper, not the mechanics of writing. During the drafting stage students may exchange papers with a buddy, conference with the teacher, or meet in small groups to compare papers (Hawkins & Razali, 2012).

To teach students about the notion of the rough draft, ask a student if you can use his draft as an example to show the class. Discuss the draft in terms of content, appearance, length, and possible changes that may be made later. This discussion will logically lead to the next step—revising.

Revising

Revising is the third step, in which students read their drafts to determine major changes, such as reworking the beginning or ending of a story, developing a character, eliminating repetitious material, adding details or facts to a paragraph or descriptive words to plain sentences, and cutting and pasting to move material around. The term *revision* means to *re-see* a work with new eyes (Rivera, 2012). It is also a time for writers to rethink and reflect on what they are trying to say. Changing, omitting, altering, and rearranging words, sentences, and paragraphs are all part of revision. To do this effectively, students must be willing to reread what they have written and make the necessary changes.

A minilesson at the beginning of a writing workshop to teach revision may involve displaying a sample student draft, perhaps one from a previous class, and identifying by reading aloud the places where the writer could add new information, omit repetitious material, or rearrange sentences or paragraphs. Make the changes on the sample draft yourself so students can see what revision involves.

You can also help your students with the revision stage by holding periodic one-on-one conferences to lead your young writers to want to improve their rough drafts. In *A Fresh Look at Writing* (1994), Donald Graves stressed that teachers should ask the following questions during the conference rather than make suggestions or give advice:

- Does your opening paragraph introduce the main character or describe the setting for your story?
- Have you repeated something that can be omitted?
- How can you make your dialogue sound more realistic?
- If your ending comes too soon, how can you keep the reader in suspense a bit longer?

Although a teacher can always *tell* students how to improve their work, the skill in conferencing is to nudge writers toward discovering how to improve their writing themselves.

Some teachers see revision as an advanced skill suitable only for older students. Not so. Revision can begin early as part of the creative process. In one kindergarten class, for example, the students were engaged in a year-long study of owls. At the beginning of the year the students drew their conception of an owl in very rough, typical kindergarten style, including scribbling to fill in blank spaces. As the year progressed their drawings took on a sophistication that reflected their choices and knowledge; they added, altered, omitted, and rearranged details, just as we do in writing (Chase, 2012). By the end of the school year these kindergarteners could tell you and draw with detail the differences among the rufous owl, the northern saw-whet owl, and the spectacled owl. Revising had become a natural part of their artistic behavior and should carry over into their writings.

Editing

The fourth step is *editing,* which involves proofreading carefully to discover mechanical errors in a piece. These include errors in spelling, capitalization, punctuation, sentence fragments, run-on sentences, tense shifts, and other aspects of grammar. Editing is about polishing the small details in a paper. Students should know how to edit their own papers, but it can also take place through buddy-editing with another student or creating editing circles, where all papers are circulated among small groups of students who focus on only one type of error (e.g., spelling or capitalization). You can place proofreading charts, such as the one shown in Figure 6.6, on desks or on classroom walls for students to refer to during writing time. Finally, of course, you can step in and edit or correct a student's paper, but this should only happen after the student has self-edited or worked with a buddy or editing group. Figure 6.7 is an example of a student's rough draft with editing marks.

read RESEARCH practice

RRP

Select a piece you or someone else has written. Read it with an eye to revising and editing it to be clearer and more concise. Use the proofreading and editing marks as shown in Figures 6.6 and 6.7.

Publishing

The fifth and final stage in the writing process is *publishing.* Traditionally, this involved the students submitting their final papers to the teacher, who then graded and returned them. However, the writing workshop and process approach present many other ways of sharing their students' writing:

- Have students read their work aloud in the author's chair.
- Display students' work on an authors' bulletin board.
- Have students perform the piece in readers theater.

Basic proofreading marks.   **FIGURE 6.6**

Mark	Use	Example
$\wedge$	to insert (add) a letter, word, or sentence	The boys ^are^ hungry.
$\P$	to begin or indent a paragraph	¶ Four horses left the corral. They headed across the fields and toward the mountains. Soon they were gone from sight.
e	to delete (take out) a letter, word, or sentence	We had to ~~the~~ leave the party at 8:00 P.M.
/	to change a capital letter to a lowercase letter	My Friend John left his bike in the street.
$\equiv$	to change a lowercase letter to a capital letter	They flew to charleston, South Carolina.
⬭ SP	to check the spelling of a word	He rode his (bicicle) to school. SP

Sample rough draft with editing marks.   **FIGURE 6.7**

Where the Earth Ends

Where ~~do~~ does ~~the~~ the earth end?

Hi! I'm Amy and this ~~stories~~ story's about a girl ^named Pamela^ who wents to ~~see~~ know wear the earth ends but no one gives her the answer.

One day a girl named Pamela went outside. Her long soft black hair hanging in her face. Her Dad was looking at the sunset. ¶ "Dad where does the earth end? ¶ The earth ends where nobody goes," he said. She ~~Pamela~~ thought she needed a better (anser.)

¶ So she went and found her Mom sitting on the couch. ~~she~~ ~~and~~ asked "Mom where does the earth end? ¶ The earth has no end," her Mom said. ¶ "But it must end," said Pamela. Then her Mom said strangely, "I'll tell you the truth later."

End Part One

FIGURE 6.8   Professional publications for students' writing.

> *Boy's Life,* http://boyslife.org/
>
> *Jack and Jill,* www.uskidsmags.com/magazines/jack-and-jill/
>
> *Scholastic Scope,* http://scope.scholastic.com/
>
> *Cricket,* www.cricketmag.com/
>
> *Highlights for Children,* www.highlights.com/
>
> *Stone Soup,* www.stonesoup.com/
>
> *Anthology of Poetry by Young Americans,* www.anthologyofpoetry.com/

- Place reports or stories in the class or school library for others to read.
- Post the piece on a class website or wiki, or publish in an electronic or printed newsletter, for an audience beyond the classroom.
- Create a bound book that includes pieces from all the students.
- Have students perform a written story or play using puppets.

Some teachers have sought professional venues for publishing their students' writing (see Figure 6.8). One of the earliest practitioners of this was Eliot Wigginton. Beginning in 1966, Wigginton had his high school students conduct interviews of interesting people in their rural Georgia community; then they wrote, revised, and edited articles based on those interviews (Wigginton, 1986). These articles were later published in a magazine called *Foxfire* and eventually published as the well-known Foxfire Books series (Cheek, Hunter Nix, & Foxfire Students, 2006). Continuing this tradition, many elementary and middle-school teachers use publishing as a motivational tool with their students. One site that publishes student writing is KidPub (www.kidpub.com), which describes itself as the "largest writing site for kids" and where your students can post original writings.

To further incorporate technology into the writing process to motivate student writers, encourage them to publish their pieces by creating slide presentations or brief videos using illustrations, text, and sound. Digital storytelling and all its tools may spark students' creativity. Have students share their finished pieces with their classmates.

WRITING WORKSHOP

Although the writing process can take place in a traditional classroom setting, most teachers of writing prefer to convert their classrooms into a *writing workshop*. A writing workshop involves the following: rearranging the furniture in a classroom to create space for writers to work; allotting large chunks of classroom time for actual writing, not just talking about writing; and establishing classroom rules and routines that allow students to work independently and take responsibility for their own work. Depending on the grade level you teach, you will have to modify the rules and routines of the writing workshop. For example, elementary teachers can arrange to have a block of an hour or hour and a half while middle-school teachers in a departmentalized setting may only have a 45-minute block available.

Regardless of your setting—self-contained classroom or departmentalized periods—a writing workshop approach can be implemented by following these principles:

1. Establish a sense of *community* within your classroom by encouraging students to work together as writing buddies or in writing groups. Community means

students support one another in their writing efforts through peer conferences, buddy-editing sessions, group research teams, and other collaborations. A writing workshop is not a competition to see who can finish first.

2. Give students the *choice* of what they write about. You can assist them, but the final choice of what and how to write should be the student's.

3. Make sure students receive feedback or *response* from others during the writing workshop period. This can come in the form of a teacher or peer conference or through an author's chair sharing.

Atwell (1998), Calkins (2001), Fletcher and Portalupi (2001), Applebee and Langer (2011), and many others have described various approaches to the writing workshop. All agree that the physical arrangement of desks, tables, chairs, computers, bookcases, and so forth must create *space* for writers to work comfortably. Each teacher will arrange his or her room in a unique manner that takes into account its physical layout and the materials and equipment available. The important point is to create different kinds of writing spaces to accommodate the different needs of individual students; some may prefer working sprawled out on the rug, while others may prefer their desks, and still others may prefer a round table where they can write alongside their friends.

Writing workshop authorities such as those mentioned above also agree that the teacher must establish the rules for talking and moving within the workshop environment. Rules should be kept simple, established early in the year, and posted on charts around the room so that teachers do not have to repeat themselves. Examples of rules include:

- Speak quietly to your buddy or group.
- When you move around the room for any reason, do not disturb others.
- After using the computers and tablets, please save and close all your files and programs and turn the machine off.

Early organizational minilessons concerning how to talk and move within the writing workshop environment will help avoid problems later on. (More about minilessons and writing workshops below.)

Integrate technology in writing workshops when possible. Use tablets and class computers to enhance students' interest in writing. Some teachers use *blogging* in their writing workshop classroom. Blogging allows students to share ideas for writing with other students. Finally, every writing workshop needs a routine and an *organizational structure* that is clearly communicated to students ahead of time. Although different students will be working on different phases of the writing process at the same time, the writing workshop must be structured. The following is one structure used in many writing workshops.

Status of the Class

Begin the workshop with a quick assessment of where each student is in his or her writing process. Known as *status of the class*, this task is performed by having each student briefly announce what piece they are working on and what stage they are in (prewriting, revising, editing, ready for publishing). This is your opportunity to identify students who need help getting started in their writing project or moving to the next stage.

Minilessons

During a writing workshop, conduct a *minilesson* demonstrating a discrete task or technique. This may be how to organize a writing folder, come up with a writing idea, use capitalization, or develop lead sentences or paragraphs, character descriptions, setting descriptions, dialogue, and so on.

Another type of minilesson is to read aloud from books in which writing is fundamental to the plot or theme. Reading such books is one of the best ways to motivate students to want to write themselves. Examples of books you can use in such a minilesson include *Nikki & Deja: The Newsy News Newsletter* (English, 2010), *Little Miss Matched's the Writer in Me: How to Write Like Nobody Else* (Balch, 2008), and *The Desperate Dog Writes Again* (Christelow, 2010).

Minilessons can also include teacher read-alouds from great picture books that demonstrate a particular lesson, such as how to describe a character or using vivid language to make a setting come alive (Hoffman & Roser, 2012). Each minilesson will depend on the needs of the class as a whole as determined through observation and conferences. One teacher's brief minilesson or writing tip included the following: "In your first rough draft, skip every other line on the page and leave wide margins so you will have enough room to makes additions and other changes." Then she passed around an example of a student paper with plenty of space for changes.

Writing Time

Allowing ample time for writing is a crucial aspect of the writing workshop. The bulk of the workshop period should be given over to students writing on their own. This includes drafting, revising, and editing as appropriate. During this time teachers may model writing by writing themselves or by conducting *miniconferences*. The miniconference can address a specific craft issue in writing, focus on one mechanic of writing, or merely answer specific questions a writer may have. Miniconferences are very brief so they do not take time away from the actual writing.

Good writing takes time and patience and should be done at least three times during the week. With older students who have class periods of 45 minutes, writing workshops can be followed up with homework assignments focusing on additional drafts, revisions, or editing. Regardless, students must know that at least three times during the week in class, they will have uninterrupted time to write.

Sharing

The final element of the workshop is *sharing*. Gather all students into a circle to discuss problems they may have encountered or to listen to students share their work, whether in draft or final form. You may also have students volunteer to read from the author's chair. This sharing time occurs at the end of the period and is brief. Not everyone will get to share every day, so keep careful records of who is ready to share and those who have.

When the writing workshop goes well, students experience what Lucy Calkins (1994) calls "living the writerly life." They think of themselves as real writers who are constantly observing the world around them in new ways to discover new stories to write or topics to write about.

The writing workshop is meant to be an active process, sometimes a bit noisy, sometimes with students moving about (in an orderly fashion); it is not a passive sit-in-your-seat event to listen to the teacher lecture about writing or grammar or spelling. To an outsider

Great writing evolves more from great encouragement than from great criticism.

JOHN MASEFIELD

A minilesson helps solidify Tommy's understanding: Rereading as a revision strategy

Here is one example of how a teacher integrates a brief miniconference into writing time. Ms. Giacobbe notices that Tommy has changed something on his paper by crossing out words and adding new ones. He has also drawn an arrow from one area to another, indicating he will move some things around in his next draft. She asks him about the changes and he replies, "It's easy. When I read it over it didn't sound right. I left out some words by accident so I changed it to make it sound better." Ms. Giacobbe compliments Tommy on his use of this rereading strategy. Not all young writers know enough to reread their writing carefully and make revisions and editing changes accordingly. Later in the semester, as Tommy shares his writing in the author's chair, he knows to add more details to clarify what he wants to say to his audience; his peers' comments have helped him recognize the importance of the audience's perspective. Rereading and writing go hand in hand in the process of completing a final draft.

the workshop approach might seem a bit messy and disorganized, but as we have shown above, it does have structure, it is organized, and it is focused on students learning to take responsibility for their own writing by engaging in inquiry in the true scientific sense of the word (Wolk, 2008).

WRITING AND THE COMMON CORE STATE STANDARDS

The CCSS major headings under writing include Different Text Types and Purposes (e.g., opinion pieces, informative, narrative accounts); Production and Distribution of Writing (e.g., write on a topic and receive feedback from teacher and peers); Writing Process of Revision and Editing (this begins in grade 3); Research to Build and Present Knowledge (e.g., doing research using online and print resources and sharing it with others); Range of Writing (writing and research) completed over an extended period of time, including prewriting, revision, and editing (NGACBP & CCSSO, 2010).

As you move through the CCSS for writing from one grade level to another, you will note that the intent is for students to "demonstrate increasing sophistication in all aspects of language use" (NGACBP & CCSSO, 2010, p. 19). That is, the standards increase in difficulty from grade to grade as would be expected. CCSS W.K.1 includes the following: "Use a combination of drawing, dictating, and writing to compose opinion pieces in which [students] tell a reader the topic or the name of the book they are writing about and state an opinion or preference about the topic or book (e.g., *My favorite book is…*)" (NGACBP & CCSSO, 2010, p. 19). This could include young children's opinions about their favorite sport, hobby, or book. Kindergarten students are expected to "compose informative/explanatory texts," and first graders are encouraged to expand their pieces with a few sequenced sentences: Students will "write opinion pieces in which they introduce the topic or name the book they are writing about, state an opinion, supply a reason for the opinion and provide some sense of closure" (CCSS W.1.1; NGACBP & CCSSO, 2010, p. 19). Second graders are expected to expand on both informative/explanatory texts and narrative texts with more facts and definitions, greater details, and a more elaborate sequence of events: Students will "write opinion pieces in which they introduce the topic or book they are writing about, state an opinion, supply reasons that support the opinion, use linking words (e.g., *because, and, also*) to connect opinion and reasons, and provide a concluding statement or section" (CCSS W.2.1; NGACBP & CCSSO, 2010, p. 19).

Beginning in grade 3, the CCSS expect students to "With guidance and support from peers and adults, develop and strengthen writing as needed by planning, revising, and editing" (CCSS W.3.5) and to use technology: "With guidance and support from adults, use technology to produce and publish writing (using keyboarding skills) as well as to interact and collaborate with others" (CCSS W.3.6; NGACBP & CCSSO, 2010 p. 21).

The CCSS for grades 3, 4, and 5 expect students to conduct research on a specific topic, gather information from a variety of sources (including digital), take notes, categorize information, and summarize or paraphrase information (NGACBP & CCSSO, 2010). The range of writing that students do should reflect their time spent researching, writing, and revising.

The standards for grades 6, 7, and 8 contain the same headings but the expectations become increasingly sophisticated. For example, beginning in grade 6, students are expected to engage in more complex argumentative writing in which they present clear evidence to support their claims as well as the opposing point of view. Their writing should also reflect a more mature understanding of content organization, including clearly stating the topic, using various organizational strategies (such as comparison/contrast or cause and effect), providing concrete details, using precise language and technical terms, and maintaining a more formal style in their writing. In grade 7 under narrative writing, students are expected to use a variety of transition words and phrases. By grade 8 writers should be able to use descriptive details, sensory language, and draw evidence from other texts, both literary and informative. Each grade builds on the previous grade in a sequential fashion, leading to more sophisticated writing (NGACBP & CCSSO, 2010).

The CCSS can be helpful to teachers by suggesting writing assignments and assessment rubrics for grades K through 8. The website www.edutopia.org has an excellent discussion of the CCSS and how technology can be integrated into the classroom.

One way to ensure that you meet the standards set by your district and state is by having your students write in a variety of formats (e.g., informational, poetry, scripts, journals) using a variety of writing activities. The next section offers many writing activities, in some cases coupled with background information, for various grades.

TEACHING ACTIVITIES 6

WRITING

Research on writing shows that for writers to improve they must write a lot (Bromley, 2003; Knipper & Duggan, 2006). The writing workshop allows students to write for large blocks of time, choose what they want to write about, and assume responsibility for their own finished products, but sometimes students also need practice with different types of writing activities. You can post a chart in the classroom that suggests various writing activities such as those discussed in the following sections.

 Alphabet books

Young children can begin their writing experiences by creating their own alphabet books. Representing letters with objects is the key concept to learn at this stage. Begin by reading alphabet books aloud and sharing the illustrations with your class of kindergarteners and first graders, such as *B Is for Bulldozer* (Sobel, 2003). Eventually, students will want to read their own alphabet books to one another, reinforcing that important concept that reading and writing go hand in hand, "like peanut butter and jelly," as one first grader put it.

The art aspect involved in the creation of alphabet books should not be ignored. As Peggy Albers and colleagues argue (Albers et al., 2012), art is not merely a filler activity done at the end of the day but a language in and of itself. It allows for the same creativity and expression as does oral and written language. The visual arts convey themes and messages and enable young children to tell their personal stories, often before they are fully capable writers. At a time when many schools are cutting back on art programs for financial reasons, it is more important than ever that teachers use every opportunity to incorporate art into the curriculum. *Recommended for primary grades.*

> When I began to write, I found this was the best way to make sense of my life.
>
> **JOHN CHEEVER**

2 Interactive writing

Interactive writing is another activity appropriate for beginning writers. It is an event in which teachers and students "share the pen" (Cabell, Tortorelli & Gerde, 2013; Clay, 1993; VanNess, Murnen & Bertelsen, 2013; Williams & Pilonieta, 2012). It is based on Vygotsky's (1978) theory of the zone of proximal development, which states that what students can do with an adult today, they can do independently in the future. Interactive writing teaches a range of foundational literacy skills, including letter formation, letter names, phonemic awareness, spelling, high-frequency words, concepts about print, early reading, and organizing and composing narrative and expository text.

In interactive writing, the teacher asks a student what he would like to write about concerning a shared event (e.g., a story they read together). The student then dictates a sentence with the teacher writing most of it. As she writes she asks the student to listen to the beginning sounds of words, which she stretches so he can distinguish them. She also invites the student to write the letters he knows. While he writes the teacher emphasizes the letter–sound relationships. As the student learns more letter–sound relationships, the teacher gradually turns "the pen" over to him so that he can write more. Eventually, the teacher adds only a few unknown words.

It is important that students generate the ideas for the writing exercise. Young students need to know that writing focuses on composing, not spelling words or filling in blanks. Interactive writing is also an appropriate strategy to use with English learners because the writing task is shared (Wall, 2008). *Recommended for primary grades.*

3 Bound book activity

Teach your students to create their own bound books. Begin by having them describe in detail something they enjoy. Emphasize what comes first, second, and third in the process. Students can write their own stories or work with you or another adult to create a language experience story, in which the student dictates the story and the teacher is the scribe. Next they should illustrate their stories. Finally, invite parents in to assist with binding the stories into books. The finished product can become an integral part of your classroom library for all to enjoy. *Recommended for primary grades.*

4 Collaborating on a short story (fiction)

Probably the most popular genre for young children is the short story, in some cases the very short story. For first graders this could be a few sentences, for older students a few paragraphs all the way up to a few typed pages. Teach students that a story has a beginning, middle, and end, and that its purpose is to entertain.

Teachers reading good picture books aloud and students reading independently are the primary ways that young students learn about the structure and craft of good fiction writing. Older students' narrative writing should include character development, a detailed plot, descriptive settings, and a clear theme.

A key to creating a quality short story is the writer's willingness to revise. Here are some minilesson tips to help students revise their fiction writing:

- Try out three or four new beginnings to your story.
- Add to a character's actions, habits, and dialogue to develop the person more fully.
- Examine the setting; have you described it fully enough?
- Check your transitions. Can the reader follow the flow of the story easily?
- Change the point of view. Retell the story from another character's point of view.
- Try out two or three different endings.
- Add more dialogue to your characters to let them show the action.

For collaborative short story writing, have your class read the short story collection *The House on Mango Street* by Sandra Cisneros (1984), which is about a girl growing up in the Hispanic section of Chicago. As a class analyze what makes a good short story. Next, create writing groups of four to five students who meet periodically to share, discuss, revise, and edit their short stories. Submit the finished short stories to journals or publications such as *Highlights* or post them on a class wiki or website. *Recommended for intermediate grades.*

5 Journal writing

All writers keep journals, sometimes known as *writer's notebooks* (Ballew, 2012; Fletcher, 1996). Have your students keep such a journal as a unique way to record writing ideas, interesting words, snippets of overheard dialogue, character descriptions, strong sentences, interesting language found in texts, or problems the student writer is having with a particular piece. For example, the following young student writes about a poem she is working on about saying goodbye to a best friend who has moved to another town.

> January 14: I'm trying to write about Janey. She was my best friend and I still miss her. I remember how we used to roller skate every day after school round and round in our driveway, while we listened to the Beatles. I don't know if I should try and make every other line rhyme or what.

> January 20: I've finished my poem, I think. It's longer than I imagined. I think I need to go back and take out some stuff. It sounds corny. But the part about skating to the Beatles is good. I can picture it like it was yesterday.

Other types of journals you might want to explore with your students include the following:

A *dialogue journal* is a written conversation between the teacher and student that is passed back and forth between them (De Pass, 2011). It is often initiated by the student having a question for the teacher that cannot be answered during class time, so the student writes it in his journal, hands it to the teacher, who reads and then writes her response to the question; thus begins a sort of dialogue. The dialogue journal can be used to discuss various aspects of writing, such as quotation marks to show dialogue, the meaning of unusual words from content areas such as math or geography, or to discuss a book that the student is reading. Some teachers also use dialogue journals to initiate discussions about nonacademic matters such as problems at home or bullying at school (Regan, 2003). Figure 6.9 is an example of the dialogue journal format.

A *simulated journal* asks the student to pretend to be another person, say a historical figure like George Washington, Marie Curie, Robert E. Lee, Christopher

Dear Kevin,

In class today I noticed that you had trouble keeping your eyes open. You put your head on your desk and dozed off to sleep. I hope it was a good nap, but I'm concerned. Are you still watching the late show on TV? Perhaps you are staying up too late on school nights. Or is something else the matter?

Sincerely,
Mrs. Wanowski

Dear Mrs. Wanowski,

I don't know. I just don't feel well sometimes. I get headaches. So I close my eyes and it feels better. Did you see Monster from the Black Lagoon last night? It was real scary. I'll try not to fall asleep again.

Your Student,
Kevin

Dear Kevin,

No, I didn't see Monster from the Black Lagoon. But, I heard from some other people that it is really good. It started at 11:00 P.M. That means you didn't get to sleep until after 1:00 AM. Maybe that's why you are getting headaches. I also noticed you rubbing your eyes a lot. When I was your age, my mother took me to have my eyes checked. The doctor recommended I wear glasses. At first I didn't like the idea, but then I got used to them. Let's talk about this after class.

Sincerely,
Mrs. Wanowski

Columbus, Rosa Parks, Amelia Earhart, Albert Einstein, or Jackie Robinson. After researching the person's life, the student writes journal entries using the first-person "I" form. Simulated journals work well in social studies as well as studying famous artists (Diego Rivera, Vincent van Gogh) or musicians (Beethoven, Louis Armstrong). This type of writing is great practice for writing first-person fiction narratives.

Journal writing is also a time for students to practice writing in a variety of styles and genres, such as trying out opinion pieces, argumentative writing, or research-based writing.

6   Informational writing

Writing informational text, also known as nonfiction or expository writing, calls for structures and content that differ from narrative or story writing. The main purposes of informational writing include:

- conveying information (a research report).
- describing a procedure (how to do a scientific experiment).
- explaining a natural phenomena (the migration of birds).
- persuading a reader to believe something (a newspaper editorial).
- presenting an argument for or against an issue.

When students write research reports in social studies about famous discoverers and explorers or famous battles of the American Revolution and the Civil War, they are writing informational pieces. This writing usually requires library or online research, interviewing, observing, gathering data, and much rewriting (Hand, Wallace, & Yang, 2004; Boyer, 2006; Elder & Paul, 2005).

Help your students become familiar with the techniques used in informational writing by reading, analyzing, and discussing informational books. Remember, before students can write in a particular genre they must be familiar with that genre through reading. Here are a few examples of appropriate titles for various grade levels:

- For kindergarten students, read aloud *Amazing Whales* (2005) by Sarah L. Thompson.
- For primary grade students, read *How People Learn to Fly* (2007) by Fran Hodgkins and True Kelly, and/or *Moonshot: The Flight of Apollo 11* (2009) by Brian Floca.
- For upper-elementary grade students read *Horses* (2006) by Seymour Simon and *Quest for the Tree Kangaroo: An Expedition to the Cloud Forest of New Guinea* (2006) by Sy Montgomery.

Narrative or fiction writing, which most students are familiar with, is based on plot, setting, and character. In contrast, informational texts use structures such as sequencing information chronologically; comparing and contrasting two people, events, or natural phenomena; or using a cause and effect structure, such as the causes that led up a war. See Chapter 10 for more about organizational text structures.

In addition to reading aloud and encouraging students to read informational texts, Wray and Lewis (1997) suggest that teachers lead students into writing informational text in a variety of ways. First, demonstrate how to conduct library, online, and interview research and take notes accordingly. Second, have students collaborate on a single piece, minimizing the amount of work for any single individual. Third, teach students how to create an overall outline before they begin their research so they know what they are looking for. Informational writing meets the CCSS requirements for having students research and then share that research with peers who can then help with the revision and editing processes. The older the student the more sophisticated the research will be as well as the level of writing (NGACBP & CCSSO, 2010).

Provide support for individual students as they explore beyond their comfort zone; recall Vygotsky's zone of proximal development in which an adult can lead a student into new areas of exploration.

Practicing paraphrasing and citing. The main problem most students have when they find information in a book or online is that they want to copy the exact words and call this their research. Even young children must be taught to put things in their own words (paraphrase) to avoid plagiarism. Recall the Read, Flip, Write activity in Chapter 5, in which students read a short informational passage, flip over the page, and without looking back write what they remember. Another activity you can do with older students is listen to one of the American Rhetoric Top 100 Speeches (www.americanrhetoric.com/top100speechesall.html). After students have listened to a short passage, have them paraphrase what they heard. Students need to practice refining their paraphrasing skills so they do not plagiarize.

Students must also know how to cite a source when they are using someone else's ideas to give them proper credit. They have to learn the mechanics of citing a reference and they must also learn what information to cite. Paraphrasing and source citing are skills that develop only over time. The www.readwritethink.org website offers lessons you can use to help students develop and refine these skills.

> "Write without the paraphernalia of scholarship designed to mystify the lay reader and confound one's colleagues."
>
> **MARGARET MEAD**

I-Search. Another type of writing involving research is the *I-search paper* (Make It Happen, 2000; Zorfass & Copel, 1995). This can be done individually or in small groups. First, students identify a topic they are interested in. Next they formulate a plan for gathering information. For example, three students in a fourth-grade class in Texas wanted to know more about the effects of climate change on our environment. They began by reading newspaper accounts from 2012 about Hurricane Sandy in the Northeast, particularly the damage sustained by communities along the shore in New Jersey and Long Island, New York. Next they researched climate change online and discovered that the ice packs in Greenland and the Arctic Circle are melting at an alarming rate. They contacted and interviewed a meteorologist at their local TV weather station. Finally, they gathered all of their research notes, created an outline, and then composed the rough draft of what would be a final research paper to be shared with the rest of the class.

Quest project. Upper-elementary and middle-school students can conduct research through a *Quest project.* In its simplest version, a Quest project involves a student actually doing something he has never done before and then writing about the experience. The project should be something that is of genuine interest to the student. The teacher helps set the criteria for the project, establishes a reasonable time frame, and assists students as needed. Quest projects at the middle-school level have included constructing a homemade guitar, building a model battleship, riding a unicycle, and fixing a complete meal for their family. Once the experience has been completed, the writing takes place during the regular writing workshop period.

At one school in East Harlem, New York, informational writing has become part of a school-wide experience called the "Mano a Mano" (Hand to Hand) Project. Individually and as a class, the entire school reads scientific works and then creates their own informational texts. This in turn spilled over into all other content areas and culminated in a visual arts project that turned the entire school into a work of art from floor to ceiling. For example, one entire hallway was given over to researching, writing, and then creating murals of the Lenape tribe, who populated East Harlem long before the Europeans arrived. The social interaction and learning that took place in this one school was incredible to see (Bryce, 2012).

Minilessons for informational writing. As with all other types of quality writing, the key to good informational text is revision. Here are some minilesson teaching tips to help students revise their nonfiction/informational writing:

- What message are you trying to get across? What is your purpose in writing?
- Go back and research your topic some more.
- Try a different text structure: chronological vs. comparison–contrast.
- Add additional text features, such as graphs, charts, and diagrams.
- Revise to better reflect your personal writing style. Is your true voice coming through?
- Add creative elements such as similes and vivid words.

7 Film/book comparison contrast

Have your students compare and contrast a story or book with its film adaptation to help them meet CCRA.R.7–9 for the Integration of Knowledge and Ideas (NGACBP & CCSSO, 2010). First read the book as part of a literature circle discussion group. Next watch the film version. Then, as a class analyze the effects of the book's written style with film techniques such as lighting, sound, and camera angles. Finally, have students write an informational paper using a comparison/contrast text structure.

Books for young people that have been made into films include:

- Anderson, L. H. (1999). *Speak*
- Brashears, A. (2001). *Sisterhood of the Traveling Pants*
- Cabot, M. (2000–09). *The Princess Diaries* series
- Chobsky, S. (1999). *The Perks of Being a Wallflower*
- Forman, G. (2009). *If I Say*
- Green, J. (2012). *The Fault in Our Stars*
- Kinney, J. (2007). *Diary of a Wimpy Kid*
- Lowry, L. (1993). *The Giver*
- Meyer, S. (2008). *The Twilight Saga*
- Riordan, R. (2005). *The Lightning Thief*
- Roth, V. (2011). *Divergent*
- Rowling, J. K. (1997–2007). The *Harry Potter* series
- Sachar, L. (1998). *Holes*
- Selznick, B. (2007). *The Invention of Hugo Cabret*
- Snow, A. (2005). *Here Be Monsters*
- Zusak, M. (2005). *The Book Thief*

8 Autobiographies and biographies

Reading aloud from inspirational autobiographies motivates students to write their own autobiographies. Many famous people have written autobiographies intended for younger audiences. For example, the author/illustrator Tomie dePaola told about his early life in *The Art Lesson* (1989). Helen Keller's *The Story of My Life* (1905) and Anne Frank's *The Diary of a Young Girl* (1947) are still popular favorites that are accessible to middle-school students. For very young children, you can introduce autobiographical writing through the *All About Me* format, where children draw first and then write about themselves and their family; later *All About* stories can cover other topics, such as bugs, friends, family members, pets, and so forth. Figure 6.10 gives some examples of one first-grade class's *All About* books. (Note that the teacher chose to correct the children's invented spelling for the final copy, which is sent home to caregivers. This is optional, but not necessary.)

To interest older students in autobiographical writing, begin by sharing a few of the many autobiographies written for upper elementary and middle-school students, such as Jerry Spinelli's *Knots in My Yo-Yo String: The Autobiography of a Kid* (1998); Flip Schulke's *Witness to Our Times: My Life as a Photojournalist* (2002); and Chamique Holdsclaw and Jennifer Frey's *Chamique Holdsclaw: My Story* (2001), the autobiography of the Olympic athlete and six-time WNBA All-Star.

After students have read some of the autobiographies, teach them to use the *positive/negative life events graph* for structuring their autobiography. Demonstrate this approach by drawing a graph on the board with a horizontal line marked 0

All About My Cat

My cat is white and black.
My cat drinks milk.
My cat plays with a yarn ball.
My cat is named Checkers.
I really love my cat.

All About Snakes

I have a pet snake.
Snakes eat mice.
Snakes lose their skin.
Snakes feel smooth.
They are not slimy like
    people think.
Some snakes are poisonous.
Mine is not.

All About My Doll

My doll can speak.
She has a button that you push.
She has blond hair.
The hair is real.
I can dress my doll.
She walks and her arms
    move.

and add ages 1–12 (see Figure 6.11). Next, on the vertical axis, add negative 1–5 below the line and positive 1–5 above the line. Have students think about their life in terms of positive events (e.g., a special birthday, birth of a sibling) and negative events (e.g., having their tonsils taken out, moving to a new school). Instruct students to add dots above and below the line to indicate these events, aligned with the correct age, label them, and then connect the dots for their life graph. Figure 6.11 shows one student's life events graph. As you can see, the positive and negative events in Carrie's life have been fairly equal. Some good events may be followed by a negative event, but the negative is soon followed by a positive event.

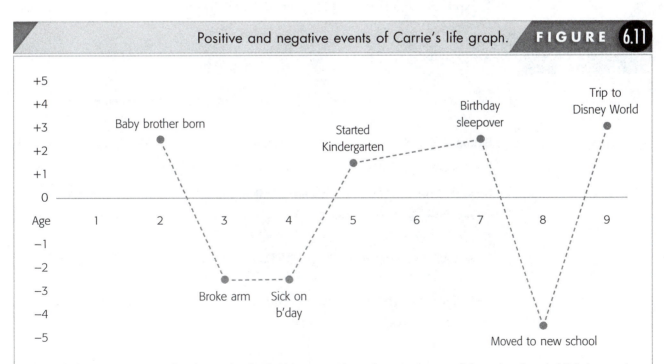

Carrie's low points were the times she broke her arm when she was 3, was sick on her fourth birthday, and moved to a new school when she was 8. Her high points were when her baby brother was born when she was 2, she started kindergarten when she was 5, had a sleepover for her seventh birthday, and went to Disney World when she was 9.

Writing biographies engages students in research, writing, revising, and editing. It allows students to share real experiences and events as described in CCRA.W.3 (NGACBP & CCSSO, 2010). Encourage students to write biographies about their favorite heroes, historical or contemporary. Begin by reading biographies to your class, discussing their characteristics, and then do some research to prepare for writing. Figure 6.12 lists examples of popular biographies for upper-elementary and middle-school students.

9 Writing scripts for plays

Have students write their own plays and then perform them for their own classmates or for other classes. This is one of the most exciting classroom writing activities. The elements of a play are similar to fiction: plot, setting, character, and theme. The main difference you and your students will note is in the extensive use of dialogue in a play. Dialogue is also found in fiction writing, of course, but it is central to playwriting. The story line or plot is literally carried by what the characters say in the play.

Loy (2004) found that playwriting, with its emphasis on dialogue, was particularly useful in teaching her predominantly Spanish-speaking eighth-grade students. Many students who had been reserved suddenly blossomed in her playwriting class.

Begin by reading aloud some published plays for children and young adults. Have students pay particular attention to the dialogue. What rings true? How do the words convey the character's personality? Point out that writing good dialogue means being true to your character. Assign students the task of listening carefully to how people speak, the way they talk, the unusual expressions or idioms people use (e.g., Don't mess with Texas; I'll wop you upside your head). Have them record such expressions in their writer's notebooks for future reference. Everyone speaks

---

FIGURE 6.12 Biographies to read with your class in preparation for writing.

Bernard-Grand, C. T., & Gonzales, T. (2010). *Sonia Sotomayor: Supreme Court Justice.*

Blumenthal, K. (2012). *Steve Jobs: The Man Who Thought Different.*

Denenberg, B. (1990). *Stealing Home: The Story of Jackie Robinson.*

Lasky, K. (2006). *John Muir: America's First Environmentalist.*

Montgomery, S. (2012). *Temple Grandin: How The Girl Who Loved Cows Embraced Autism and Changed the World.*

Nelson, V. M., & Christie, R. G. (2009). *Bad News for Outlaws: The Remarkable Life of Bass Reeves, Deputy U.S. Marshall.*

Reef, C. (2012). *The Bronte Sisters: The Brief Lives of Charlotte, Emily, and Anne.*

Rubin, S. G., Walker, B. G., & Early, D. M. (2011). *Music Was It: Young Leonard Bernstein.*

Say, A. (2011). *Drawing from Memory.*

Viegas, J. (2007). *Pierre Omidyar: The Founder of eBay.*

Winter, J. (2004). *The Librarian of Basra: A True Story from Iraq.*

a dialect; playwriting often draws upon the differing dialects, such as the Southern drawl, to make characters come alive.

> There is no good writing, only rewriting.
>
> **JAMES THURBER**

Once students have written their plays they will want to perform them. Dramatic play acting is one way, but staging a puppet show is another fun activity. Incorporate art into your classroom by teaching students to make finger puppets, sock puppets, and papier-mâché head puppets. Each student can make one character to be used in the puppet theater production of an original play (Crepeau & Richards, 2003). Figure 6.13 lists plays that are appropriate for students in the elementary and middle grades.

The natural cycle for creating plays involves students reading and listening to plays, telling stories to their friends, getting together to write these stories down, transferring the majority of the action to written dialogue, and enjoying the fun of acting in their own play.

A skill benefit of playwriting is that to write dialogue correctly the student will have to learn how to use quotation marks, commas, and other punctuation marks. By studying good dialogue in published plays they will soon be able to exhibit this skill on their own.

Playwriting at all grades levels, whether done individually or collaboratively, places emphasis on writing dialogue. Beginning in the third grade, the CCSS require students to "use dialogue and descriptions of actions, thoughts, and feelings to develop experiences and events or show the response of characters to situations" (CCRA.W.3b; NGACBP & CCSSO, 2010, p. 20). Plays can be interesting as well as informative and use both real and imagined experiences and events, as suggested by CCRA.W.3 (NGACBP & CCSSO, 2010). A good website to consult for playwriting is www.kidsfunwithdrama.com.

10 Writing poetry

Think of your favorite rock, country/western, pop, or rap songs. Listen to the lyrics and think about why you like a particular song. This is poetry. Teaching poetry to young people should be fun. Think of a funny limerick or a commercial jingle that young people will likely know. All of this is poetry. But poetry can also be emotionally powerful, as in the speeches of John F. Kennedy and Martin Luther King, Jr. Poetry is all around us and should be a part of students' lives.

Plays for elementary and middle-school students.   **FIGURE 6.13**

Brosius, P., & Adams, E. (2010). *Fierce and True: Plays for a Teen Audience.*

Fleischman, P. (2007). *ZAP.*

McBride-Smith, B. (2001). *Tell It Together: Foolproof Scripts for Story Theatre.*

Schlitz, L., & Byrd, R. (2007). *Good Masters! Sweet Ladies! Voices from a Medieval Village.*

Shepard, A. (2005). *Stories on Stage: Scripts for Reader's Theatre.*

Soto, G. (2006). *Novio Boy.*

Thomas, A., Batra, T., & Stuyvesant High School. (2002). *With Their Eyes: September 11th: The View from a High School at Ground Zero.*

We live in an age of fast and constant communication. Poetry is a time to slow things down, think, and reflect on life (Cornett & Smithrim, 2001; Heard, 1989). When we read poetry aloud and become aware of the rhythm of language, we are also developing the fluency needed for comprehension to take place. Finally, because most poems are short, writing poetry allows you to teach revision and editing on a manageable scale (Parr & Campbell, 2006).

Getting young students to write poetry can be fun but also challenging. Use the following guidelines for creating a successful poetry unit:

1. Share lots of good poems aloud. Favorite young people's poets include Shel Silverstein, Jack Prelutsky, Kenneth Koch, David McCord, Aileen Fisher, Eve Merriam, John Ciardi, and Lillian Moore. (See also Chapter 4 and Appendix B.15.)

2. Encourage students to bring in their poetry books from home to share with classmates.

3. Practice choral reading poetry as a class, in small groups, in syncopated fashion.

4. Have students illustrate their favorite poems and display the results around the classroom.

5. Begin poetry writing with a small group or class collaboration poem.

6. Show the class the type of poem (e.g., limerick, acrostic, free verse) they are creating so they have a model to follow.

7. Above all, encourage students to enjoy the creative act of making poetry.

The following sections discuss writing activities focused on various forms of poetry. To introduce an activity for one of these forms, first select a representative poem that is appropriate for your grade level and read it aloud to your class. Discuss the poem in terms of rhyme, descriptive language, simile, and metaphor. Next in pairs or individually, have your students write their own poem, modeling the example you have shown. Collect the finished poems and bind them into a book or post them on a class wiki or website.

Free verse. Many poets today write in *free verse,* or non-rhyming poetry. This allows the poet to emphasize other factors, such as the message or story; the description of a person or scene; figurative language such as similes, metaphors, and personification; and stylistic language such as alliteration and onomatopoeia. Provide students with models of these creative language tools. For example, for alliteration, have them listen to or read books such as *Alligator Arrived with Apples* (Dragonwagon, 1986) or *Mammoths on the Move* (Wheeler, 2006).

Figure 6.14 is an example of free verse by a sixth-grade girl from Brooklyn, modeled on the poem "This Is Just to Say" by William Carlos Williams.

Another activity for creating free verse is *magnet poetry.* Use magnetic words and a metal board to create instant poems. Figure 6.15 shows examples of magnet poetry arranged by second- and third-grade students in Jenks, Oklahoma.

Acrostic poem. An *acrostic* is a simple poetry form in which a single word is written vertically on a page. Each letter forms the initial letter of a word for that line of the poem. Some acrostics have only one word per line but others can be much longer. The examples in Figure 6.16 reveal the variety that even a simple form like the acrostic can take. Students may wish to select their own names or a friend's name to begin their first acrostic.

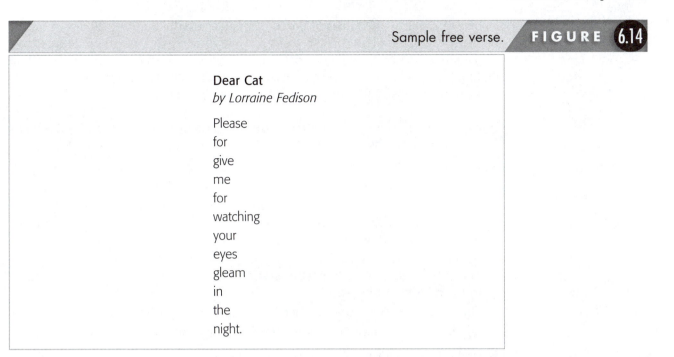

Sample free verse.   **FIGURE 6.14**

Dear Cat
by Lorraine Fedison

Please
for
give
me
for
watching
your
eyes
gleam
in
the
night.

Sample magnet poems.   **FIGURE 6.15**

Beautiful butterfly sparkle
with joy
get up and go
stop in wind.
—2nd grade

The color of dreams
sun, cloud, ocean, stars, moon
live in my heart
They are cool
joy and awesome
—3rd grade

Sample acrostic poems.   **FIGURE 6.16**

Moving
Around
Running
Yelling

When the snow falls
It makes
Nice patterns on
The sidewalk and
Everywhere children are
Running and laughing to be free

Dreaming
About
Visions
Everyday

Aubree has an
Umbrella
Because it is
Raining
Everywhere
Everywhere

Sitting
Always
Mumbling

Couplet. A *couplet* is two lines of poetry. Couplets are the building blocks of longer poems or can stand alone by themselves. They often rhyme but they do not have to. Using the example in Figure 6.17, model your own poem with the first line beginning "Who has . . ." and the second line beginning "But when . . . ." Try various aspects of nature like the sun, the rain, and the clouds.

Diamante. The *diamante* is a seven-line poem written in the shape of a diamond (Tiedt, 1970) that follows strict guidelines:

- First students select two nouns that are opposite (e.g., sun and moon) and place them respectively on lines one and seven of the poem.
- On line two, they write two adjectives that describe the first noun.
- On line three, they write three verbs ending in "ing" (i.e., participles) that describe the first noun.
- On line four, they write two nouns that relate to the first noun and then two nouns that relate to its opposite on line seven. (The focus of the poem shifts in the middle of line four.)
- On line five, they write three participles related to the second noun.
- On line six, they write two adjectives describing the second noun.

Figure 6.18 shows an example of the diamante poetry form.

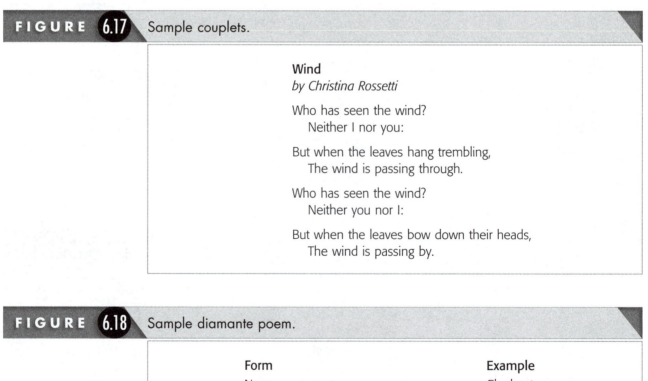

FIGURE 6.17 Sample couplets.

> **Wind**
> *by Christina Rossetti*
>
> Who has seen the wind?
>   Neither I nor you:
>
> But when the leaves hang trembling,
>   The wind is passing through.
>
> Who has seen the wind?
>   Neither you nor I:
>
> But when the leaves bow down their heads,
>   The wind is passing by.

FIGURE 6.18 Sample diamante poem.

Form	Example
Noun	Elephant
Adjective Adjective	Huge, Leathery
Participle Participle Participle	Lumbering, Charging, Snorting
Noun Noun Noun Noun	Jungle, Beast, House, Rodent
Participle Participle Participle	Scampering, Scratching, Squeaking
Adjective Adjective	Timid, Meek
Noun	Mouse

Haiku. The *haiku* is a Japanese form of poetry that has three lines and a total of 17 syllables. The first line contains five syllables, the second line contains seven syllables, and the third line contains five syllables. Traditional haiku offers glimpses of nature and are often organized around the four seasons. Figure 6.19 presents two poems by students modeling famous Japanese haiku. Also see www.GigglePoetry.com for more haiku ideas.

> The only way to teach them to write correctly is to have them write.
>
> **FANNY JACKSON COPPIN**

In the intermediate grades, prepare students to write their own haiku poem by reading *The Greatest of All* (Kimmel, 1991). In this story the emperor writes a haiku in honor of the marriage between his daughter Chuko and Ko Nezumi:

> The very best spouse
>
> For a pretty little mouse
>
> Is another mouse. (Kimmel, 1991, unpaged)

Discuss the format of the haiku and invite students to create another haiku that the sun, cloud, or wind may have written. Encourage students to first brainstorm ideas and then correct the number of syllables per line during the revision process.

Limerick. The *limerick* is a humorous five-line poem that follows a specific rhyming pattern: AABBA. Lines one and two rhyme, lines three and four rhyme, and live five rhymes with lines one and two. Edward Lear popularized the limerick in his *Book of Nonsense* (1828). Figure 6.20 presents one of Edward Lear's own limericks.

"I wish" poem. Kenneth Koch popularized the *"I wish . . ." poem* back in the 1970s, and examples of these poems can be found along with other types of short poems at www.PoetryCraze.com. The whole class can create one poem with each student contributing a line that begins with "I wish . . . ." You can add interest to the poem by including a color, a comic strip character, and a city or country to each line. Students can create endless variations of this poetry form. Koch also gave us the *"I used*

Sample haiku poems. FIGURE 6.19

The first day of spring walking near the water, now, one lovely egret.	In the winter snow a silent mountain waiting quiet but awake.

Sample limerick. FIGURE 6.20

There was a young lady of Norway,

Who casually sat in a doorway;

When the door squeezed her flat,

She exclaimed, "What of that?"

This courageous young lady of Norway.

—Edward Lear

to be . . . But now I am . . ." couplet form of poetry; students can contribute a couplet that can be linked to a larger poem by collaborating with their friends. Figure 6.21 shows student collaboration poems based on patterns developed by Koch.

Concrete or visual poem. Another type of poetry is the *concrete or visual poem.* In this form, individual words or the entire poem are rendered in such a way on the page that they form a shape that represents the meaning of the poem. Concrete shape elements can be incorporated into any poem to add to its visual effect. Figure 6.22 shows an example of concrete poetry.

"Where are you from?" poem. "*Where are you from?*" poetry was developed by classroom teachers at the Oklahoma State University Writing Project's Summer Institute. First, teachers brainstorm with the class about favorite foods, hobbies, family traditions, songs, books, games, and so on in their community. Then the students write down their own ideas in their writer's notebook and use these ideas to answer the question "Where are you from?" A student example follows on p. 197.

FIGURE 6.21 Sample student collaboration poems.

> I wish Superman wore a red cape and lived in Disney Land.
> I wish Beetle Bailey didn't wear a frown in Hollywood.
> I wish Charlie Brown wore a blue suit to Tulsa and
> I wish orange and yellow Garfield lived in Italy eating spaghetti.
>
> I used to be a baby
> But now I am a boy.
> I used to love arithmetic
> But now I play with toys.

FIGURE 6.22 Sample concrete or visual poetry.

> **WHAT AM I?**
> I
> am tall
> but can be
> small. I have limbs,
> but cannot walk. I live
> for centuries, but can be killed
> with powder. I shed, but have no
> hair. I cannot think, have no heart, but
> I
> L
> I
> V
> E

MINILESSONS for REVISING POETRY

Many students who enjoy reading and writing poetry incorrectly assume that poems do not have to be revised. Often young writers of poetry, because the poem is short, fail to revise their work. To help students overcome this misconception, impart these minilesson teaching tips:

- Look for clichés and rewrite them in an original way.
- Rearrange the line breaks.
- Show, don't tell; add details and imagery.
- Take your favorite line, move it to the beginning of the poem, and start over from there.
- Examine your ending. Is it strong and truly conclusive?
- Have you used figurative language? If not, go back and add some.
- Read your poem out loud and revise anything that sounds awkward.

I am from Sunday fried catfish dinner
    And an afternoon nap on the porch
I am from the "Little House" books and
    Ramona Quimby and the Boxcar Children.
I am from swaying wheat fields in the breeze
    And cattle grazing on the prairie
I am also from home-made bread and butter
    And pan-fried chicken dinners.

Things to Do Around poem. Poet Gary Snyder spent many years wandering around the United States, particularly the Northwest, which he writes about in his *Things to Do Around* poems. To create their own Things to Do Around poem, students first choose a city or town they know well. Then they list all the things they like to do there and revise the list adding new items. Finally, they are ready to organize it into a free verse poem like the one written by David Yellin, one of this book's authors, about his hometown.

Things to Do Around Stillwater, Oklahoma

Take a walk down Main Street and check out the Crazy Days Sales.

Share some Cheese Fries with a friend at Eskimo Joe's.

Ride your bike around Boomer Lake but watch out for the joggers.

Read a book by Theta Pond and get chased by the angry geese.

Go two steppin' at Tumbleweeds.

Watch a Bedlam game at the Boone Pickens Stadium.

Poetry allows students to use figurative language such as similes, metaphors, personification, and alliteration to make their writing interesting and lively. Like fiction writing, poetry allows students to experiment with different narrators and utilize precise words and phrases to convey meaning.

For additional poetry activities to use with your students, visit www.poetry teachers.com. Figure 6.23 provides a list of books of poetry for young readers.

11   Publishing student writing

As a class activity, help your young students publish their writing by exploring the many real publishing opportunities for young writers available today. For example, www.noodletools.com/debbie/literacies/basic/yngwrite.html lists dozens of online

FIGURE 6.23 Books of poetry for young readers.

Brown, M. (2012). *Pablo Neruda: Poet of the People.*

Cullinan, B. E., & Wooten, D. (Eds.) (2010). *Another Jar of Tiny Stars: Poems by More NCTE Award Winning Poets.*

Hopkins, L. B. (Ed.) (2010). *Amazing Faces.*

Janeczko, P. (2012). *Requiem: Poems of the Terezin Ghetto.*

Prelutsky, J. (2010). *The Carnival of the Animals.*

Raczka, B. (2012). *Lemonade: And Other Poems Squeezed from a Single Word.*

Salas, L. P. (2012). *Bookspeak: Poems About Books.*

Wardlaw, L. (2012). *Won Ton: A Cat Tale Told in Haiku.*

publishing opportunities for young writers. Each online publishing site has its own list of requirements and directions for submitting work.

The website www.newpages.com/writers-resources/young-authors-guide lists many professional publishing sites geared toward young writers. Your students will need to select an appropriate publication, obtain its guidelines, and then submit their writing accordingly. This site also lists writing contests that your students can enter.

ASSESSMENT/EVALUATION OF WRITING

Assess your students on an ongoing basis to determine what you will teach and when. Assessing student progress and then teaching accordingly is part of the diagnostic-prescriptive approach; it takes much of the guesswork out of instruction.

Today, standardized tests often include a detailed writing evaluation. These tests typically give students a prompt to respond to in a set period of time. Examiners grade the responses according to detailed rubrics and award points for content, style, mechanics, and so on.

Despite the current emphasis on final product and grades, most writing experts believe that alternative forms of assessment should balance out the limitations of standardized tests (Fletcher & Portalupi, 2007; Flower & Hayes, 1981; Seidel, 1998; Young, 1997). The following are other means of assessing your students' writing that reflect effective diagnostic-prescriptive approaches to instruction.

Teacher Observations

When you observe your students at work, you grasp their progress and individual needs. Which students need help with prewriting? Are they brainstorming effectively for ideas? Are they outlining and diagramming their work as needed? Are they seeking information through research and citing sources when appropriate? Are students revising, proofreading, and editing before coming to you for help? These questions are at the heart of assessing student progress in writing.

Some young students do not enjoy writing as much as others. For them, sometimes drawing can take the place of writing. You can evaluate children's drawings just as you evaluate written work. Encourage them to talk about their drawings and to label their pictures. A great read-aloud book for such students is *Patches Lost and Found* (Kroll, 2001), about a girl who does not write but likes to draw. When her pet guinea pig Patches disappears one day, she draws a lost and found poster to which her mother encourages her to add words.

Anecdotal Records

Record your observations on individual students. Assign each student a page in your loose-leaf notebook and their progress for each stage of the writing process. Or you may wish to use an app, such as Confer, for taking anecdotal records. As you document your observations, focus on each student's strengths and weaknesses and avoid merely labeling or grading them.

Teacher–Pupil Conferences

One of the most powerful assessment tools you have is the one-to-one conference. The purpose of the conference is to support the young writer by making suggestions for content, discussing problems she may be having, encouraging revisions, and assisting with editing issues. Mechanical issues should not be the focus of conferences, but they can be constructively discussed toward the end of the writing process when the student has made a real effort to do her own editing.

Student Self-Evaluation

Ultimately, your goal is to have your students evaluate their own work and assess their own progress as writers. Self-evaluation involves recognizing when one is doing something well (e.g., writing a strong lead sentence and paragraph to capture the reader's attention), noting weaknesses (e.g., lacking an ending that ties all elements together), and discovering mechanical errors that need to be edited. A three-column chart with the following headings may help students of all ages: "Skills I learned," "Things I'm working on," and "Things I plan to learn" (Hansen, 1987).

Portfolios

Young writers involved in a writing workshop save their drafts and final copies in a folder or writing portfolio, either in paper or electronic form. By examining the students' portfolios early in the school year, at the midpoint, and at the end of the school year, you and the caregivers can easily identify their progress. For many teachers, the portfolio provides the main alternative to the standardized test (Kirszner & Mandell, 2012; Brookhart, 2008). Some teachers prefer that students include only their final copies in a portfolio, but including drafts along with final copies allows teachers to better assess progress in a piece of writing. Whether you prefer to use a portfolio of final works or of all works, this tool provides a true picture of a student writer's ability. Figures 6.24 through 6.27 represent possible ways of utilizing the portfolio concept to teach skills, maintain records, and evaluate final copies.

Portfolio form for a student's published works.   **FIGURE 6.24**

My Published Works

Name Jackson

DATE	TITLE/AUTHOR	GENRE	AUDIENCE/PLACE OF PUBLICATION
10/14	"My Brother's Bike"	Biography/Informational	Fifth-grade class magazine

FIGURE **6.25** Portfolio form for all of a student's works.

All of My Works

Name Jackson

DATE STARTED	DATE ENDED	TITLE/GENRE	COMMENTS
March 3	March 7	"The Biggest Fish"/ Realistic Fiction	An exaggerated story of a fishing trip I took with my dad.

FIGURE **6.26** Portfolio form for skills a student learned.

Skills I Learned

Name Jackson   Grading Period   1   ②   3   4

DATE	SKILLS	EXAMPLE
4/16	Two different ways to use the apostrophe	"I can't believe you ate my sister's cake."

Find more teacher and student evaluation forms and portfolio rubrics in Appendices D.7, D.8, and D.9.

The 6 + 1 Trait Writing Assessment

With increasing emphasis on standardized tests and writing prompts to evaluate students, some teachers are utilizing the 6 + 1 Trait model, developed by Education Northwest (see http://educationnorthwest.org and Appendix D.10). The 6 + 1 traits listed in Figure 6.28 are similar to the prompts used in many standardized tests and make a handy rubric for students to see how they will be evaluated. Teachers who use this model assess their students' writing on a 1 to 5 scale, with 1 being the lowest score. Though helpful in preparing students for standardized tests, this model is most effective when used in conjunction with a process approach within a workshop setting (Higgins, Miller, & Wegmann, 2006; Spandel, 2008).

You can incorporate the 6 +1 Trait model with prompts as a way of preparing your students for standardized tests. However, no isolated writing test can

Portfolio form for a student's future writing ideas.   **FIGURE** 6.27

Bright Ideas for New Works

Name Jackson

IDEA	GENRE	WHERE I GOT THE IDEA
A scary story about three boys on a camping trip in the desert who get separated from the rest of the group.	Contemporary realistic fiction/ mystery	A camping trip to the Grand Canyon I took with my family last year.

The 6 + 1 Trait® writing model.   **FIGURE** 6.28

1. *Ideas:* Clear development of ideas and information.
2. *Organization:* An identifiable structure to the writing.
3. *Voice:* The distinct style and tone of the writer.
4. *Word choice:* Careful selection of vocabulary terms to support meaning.
5. *Sentence fluency:* How one sentence flows naturally into the next.
6. *Conventions:* The mechanics of writing (spelling, punctuation, capitalization).
+1 *Presentation:* The physical appearance of the writing.

duplicate the thinking process that goes into planning, revising, and editing a written piece in real time. For this reason, many writing experts are critical about statewide and national writing tests that are used to evaluate, measure, and label students as well as the competency of their teachers (Schuster, 2004).

Teacher-Made Rubrics

Most teachers prefer to devise their own rubrics to guide their students in their writing. Rubrics are scoring scales that identify the particular elements to be evaluated; this can be a simple list of two or three items for young children, such as "Capitalize the first word in a sentence," or more complex items for older students, such as "Did you use transition words between paragraphs?" The website http://rubistar.4teachers.org will help you create your own rubric. Appendices D.11–D.14 also provide examples of other writing rubrics.

TECHNOLOGY IN THE CLASSROOM

Many schools have sophisticated technology for student use and, in turn, many students are quite tech savvy. Your students are likely to have grown up with smartphones, tablet computers, and videogame systems, so using online resources and social media is second nature to them. Plan to capitalize on technology skills and tools.

In addition to sites we discussed earlier in the chapter, here are examples of websites that can be incorporated into writing and research projects.

Ask an Expert. Search online for "Ask an Expert"; many organizations, from biology departments to the U.S. Department of Agriculture, offer expert help online. Choose two or three suitable sites and let students submit questions to explore.

www.madsci.org Encourage your students to ask science related research questions and interact with real scientists.

www.kidlink.org This site allows students to interact with and collaborate on writing projects with students in other states and countries.

www.kidpub.com This site lets students to publish their original poems and stories and share them with students around the world.

www.bookadventure.org On this site, students can create their own books and to take quizzes on books that they have read.

SUMMARY

This chapter has focused on two things: the process approach to teaching writing and organizing your class into a writing workshop. The former includes five stages: prewriting, rough draft, revision, editing, and publishing/sharing. The latter concerns the organizational structure of your classroom, which includes the arrangement of chairs, desks, bookcases, and other elements to create comfortable spaces for students to write in. Minilessons are the preferred instructional means to convey skills during the writing workshop.

In addition, a writing workshop assumes that you will provide many different types of writing activities, including journals, short stories, informational reports, and poetry. The Common Core State Standards place particular emphasis on informational writing at all grades.

field AND practicum ACTIVITIES

1. CLASS BULLETIN BOARD. With a group of students, put together a bulletin board featuring their writing. Encourage caregivers and administrators to visit your room and examine it. This is a first step toward getting away from grading every single paper a student writes.

2. YOUNG AUTHORS' FAIR. Ask each student to select his or her best written piece from the semester and bind it into a hardbound book. Then arrange to display the book in a public area, such as the gymnasium or auditorium. Give every student who participates a certificate rather than awarding prizes to the best work.

3. CLASS MAGAZINE. With access to a computer and printer, you can create your own class magazine. It does not have to be fancy, but it should convey to the students the notion of publication in a real journal. Then invite students to submit their best works (fiction, nonfiction, poetry, and so on). Form a student committee to select works for the magazine. Another committee can help with the proofreading, editing, and layout.

Good stories are not written, they are rewritten.

PHYLLIS WHITNEY

4. SONG WRITING. Play some popular rock, country and western, or rap music in class. Discuss the lyrics with your class. Then have students work in small groups to produce their own songs. They should revise and edit them the way they would any other piece of written work.

5. TEACHER WRITING. Keep your own journal for a few weeks; then bring it to class to share with your students. Discuss with them why you keep a journal. When students write stories, letters, or poems in class, you should spend some of that time writing yourself and later share it with them. Save your rough drafts and final copies to show development from one stage to the next.

6. GREETING CARDS. Ask each student to bring in a commercial greeting card. Discuss the cards as a whole class: the artwork, design, message, poetry, humor, and so on. Then instruct each student to select a special occasion or person and design a greeting card with a message, saying, or original poem.

7. WRITING RECIPES. Bring in a few food recipes and discuss them with the entire class. Then discuss other types of "recipes" they could write. For example, one student's "recipe for success" reads: "First, take two cups of laughter and mix in a winning smile. Then sprinkle generously with determination. Next, add a cupful of organization. Spread it all over with intelligence. Bake until beautiful." Create other recipes for love, happiness, or good health.

8. CAREGIVER INTERVIEWS. Have your students find out about their parents' or caregivers' childhoods by interviewing them. Were they shy? Popular? Good at sports? Did they have a favorite toy? TV program? Book? Song? What was their most embarrassing moment? Who were their friends? Where did they live? Have students transcribe this oral interview into an article or fictional short story.

9. DISPLACED CHARACTERS. Have your students select any favorite character from literature. Then ask what the person would think, say, or do if she or he lived in the present. For example, take Huck Finn off the Mississippi River and place him in an inner-city classroom made up of students of various ethnic backgrounds. How would he react to the racial tensions today?

10. SPELLING HUNT. In the whole language and comprehensive approaches, peers help each other with the mechanics of writing. As part of the students' ongoing writing activities, have them pair off and become peer editors for spelling. One of their jobs is to hunt for misspelled words, circle them, and help write them correctly.

The Tools of Writing

OBJECTIVES

After reading this chapter, you should be able to accomplish the following objectives:

1. Describe similarities and differences between the D'Nealian and Zaner-Bloser handwriting methods.

2. Name the characteristics of legible handwriting.

3. Explain methods to teach handwriting effectively.

4. Explain the developmental stages of spelling.

5. Explain methods to teach spelling effectively.

6. Explain the onset–rime and inductive approaches for teaching spelling.

7. Explain the difference between grammar and usage.

8. Name four different types of grammar.

9. Explain the differences among sentence transforming, expanding, and combining.

10. Summarize important rules for capitalizing and punctuating.

INTRODUCTION

In Chapter 6 we described the process approach to writing, which includes prewriting, drafting, revising, editing, and sharing. It is during the editing stage that students need to be aware of the tools of writing, also referred to as the mechanics or skills of writing. These skills begin with legible handwriting and continue with correct spelling, punctuation, capitalization, and grammar. Today, of course, even very young writers use tablets and computers to compose their work and thus need typing and word processing skills in addition to the above. Finally, remember that good writing is about communicating one's thoughts clearly in a well-organized manner (Nauman, Sterling, & Borthwich, 2011).

This chapter deals with teaching those skills through both direct and indirect instruction, while always keeping in mind that they must be taught within the context of real reading and writing, not in isolation. As mentioned in Chapter 5, this process is referred to as *authentic literacy*; authentic reading and writing are based on children's literature books, writing tasks chosen by the students, and tasks they use in daily life (Duke et al., 2006). We develop good readers and writers when we teach skills in context, and not through memorization, worksheets, or repetitious drills. By learning and using these skills within an authentic context, students construct for themselves an understanding of the underlying rules behind the mechanics of language. We refer to this as the *constructivist approach,* in which students in a literate community learn by actually doing—that is, by reading books and reading and writing stories, poems, essays, and reports that have meaning to them (Paugh et al., 2007). Though practice worksheets sometimes have a place within the curriculum, they should be used sparingly and only to reinforce authentic tasks.

REASONS FOR WRITING: THE BEGINNINGS

To understand the importance of writing tools, recall the reasons for writing. Chapter 6 explored the relationship between writing and experience. Students must have experienced something they want to write about, something they want to express in a more permanent form than speech, something they want to share with others. Experience, permanence, sharing—these are the foundation blocks of writing.

Finding out what interests your students is paramount to motivating them to want to write about their experiences. For very young students this presents a dilemma, because they may have limited experiences. This presents preschool and primary grade teachers with their first big challenge: how to provide experiences their students can build upon in their writing.

This means reading aloud to your class on a regular basis from a variety of picture books, engaging in role playing and other dramatics activities, going on regular field trips in and around the school, and showing films and videos of places and things that may be unfamiliar to them. Of course, field trips and hands-on experiences are always best; but when this is not practical, reading books, having discussions, and showing films are excellent substitutes. The key is to provide experiences that some students may lack.

Students also need experience with the world of print. Specifically, they need to see and use the tools of writing. According to Temple, Nathan, Burris, and Temple (1988), young children go about acquiring the tools of writing in the following sequence:

1. Many children begin writing by drawing.
2. At some point, the child calls his or her drawings "writing."
3. Squiggles and scribbles that might be letters appear within the drawing, but only the child can "read" them.
4. By seeing print, children eventually begin to employ the distinctive features of letters and words in their writing, even though they do not yet recognize the relationship between sounds and symbols.

The linguist Noam Chomsky (1974) pointed out that there appears to be an *innate* capacity in children to use language for communication purposes. Research by Ferriero and Teberosky (1983) showed that children also have an inborn need to communicate in a variety of ways, including print. Young children, for example, experiment with paints, chalk, clay, paper, and pencil long before they enter school. This is how they begin to discover and reconstruct for themselves the nature of literacy.

In the preschool years, many children have experiences they wish to share verbally with others. You should encourage this kind of informal talk. To make such events more permanent, encourage students to write or draw a picture of what they saw or did. Picture drawings accompanied by scribbled words build on what the student has already experimented with at home. Drawings and early scribbles at home or at school are thus the student's first acquaintance with the tools of written communication.

Teachers can build on this natural curiosity about reading and writing by using the student's own language to create stories through the *language experience approach (LEA)* (Stauffer, 1970). Although often considered a beginning approach to reading instruction, LEA is also an excellent way to introduce young students to the tools of writing in the classroom. The steps in LEA are as follows:

1. The student dictates a story.
2. The teacher records the story.
3. The teacher reads the story back to the child.
4. The student reads the story back to the teacher.
5. The student traces or copies the story, with teacher assistance.

It is this last step that makes LEA a viable instructional approach in a writing program. Early in her career of researching the acquisition of literacy, New Zealand's Marie Clay (1975) noted that *tracing* and *copying* are strategies commonly used by preschoolers. Clay also noted that children later begin to generate their own writing by employing *invented spellings*, another strategy in the natural acquisition of writing. Tracing, copying, and inventing symbols provide a young student's first encounters with the tools of writing; thus, they are a part of the LEA, which leads young children into the process of writing. Figure 7.1 gives some teaching suggestions for using LEA as a beginning instructional approach to writing.

FIGURE 7.1 Suggestions for using the language experience approach.

- Vary the nature of the experiences used to inspire group charts (class dictates to teacher), keyword vocabulary (individual students' word banks), and individual stories. Use field trips, objects, films, and discussion.

- Try cutting an experience chart story into sentence strips. Later let each child manipulate the strips to reform the story; this is the notion of "composing."

- Type a student's experience story with a basic typeface and make copies for the rest of the class. This is one way to share stories with a wider audience.

- When taking dictation, do not be concerned initially with whether a child's language is grammatically correct. At a later time, when the student is comfortable with the approach, changes in the story form can be made.

- Take dictation from children using a variety of means: chalk, pencil, pen, computer.

- Display experience charts and language-experience stories on bulletin boards around the room and in school hallways for others to read and enjoy.

HANDWRITING: AN INDIVIDUALISTIC TOOL

With prominence of the computer in the classroom, handwriting instruction is viewed by some as no longer as important as it once was. The CCSS, for example, deemphasizes handwriting instruction in the middle and upper grades (Bauerlein, 2013; Hawkins & Razali, 2012). Some states also require that young students be taught keyboarding skills. Be that as it may, developing one's own legible handwriting is still a necessary part of the primary grade curriculum. Although some scholars urge that handwriting be taught as a part of the writing process (Christie, Enz, & Vukelich, 2003), some schools still teach handwriting as a separate skill apart from writing; this is known as *direct instruction*. Teaching handwriting within the normal context of the writing process through revision and editing is known as the *indirect instruction* approach.

Handwriting instruction, particularly the time that it takes in a school week, still remains a controversial topic in the early grades (Hawkins & Razali, 2012). Some schools require that students practice their manuscript writing in grades K through 3 through extensive repetitious practice. These schools may also focus attention on holding the pencil correctly and maintaining an erect body posture during the lesson. Such instructional practices may actually backfire and create a negative attitude toward writing among young students. Instead, we advocate that the goal of handwriting instruction should be *legibility* as achieved through authentic writing activities (Tompkins, 2003).

Legibility refers to handwriting that can be read by someone else; it does not have to be beautiful, it does not have to be perfect, but it does have to be readable (Medwell & Wray, 2008). The teacher's role, of course, in addition to instructing his students how to make the letters of the alphabet should be to model legible handwriting at a board in front of the class. By modeling legible handwriting and praising students for their own legible handwriting, some of the discomfort that may be associated with this skill can be alleviated.

Study Figures 7.2 and 7.3 as examples of two popular handwriting programs found in many schools: the Zaner-Bloser and the D'Nealian methods. Note the similarities and differences among the letters of the two programs. The D'Nealian

Zaner-Bloser handwriting model.   **FIGURE** **7.2**

Source: From *Handwriting: A Way to Self-Expression,* © 1993, Zaner-Bloser, Inc., Columbus, Ohio. Used with permission from Zaner-Bloser, Inc.

D'Nealian handwriting model.   **FIGURE** **7.3**

Source: D'Nealian® Handwriting Model from *D'Nealian® Handwriting Book 2* by Donald Neal Thurber. Copyright © 1999 by Addison-Wesley Educational Publishers, Inc. Reprinted by permission of Pearson Education, Inc.

method was developed (1987) in an attempt to introduce manuscript and cursive strokes early in the instructional period. Note how the manuscript letters are slightly slanted, like cursive letters; in theory this should make the transition from manuscript to cursive easier (Graham, 1999). You will have to decide for yourself if you agree with this assumption.

Handwriting Elements

What, then, constitutes legibility? In addition to being able to be read by someone else, legible handwriting is characterized by four main elements: size, slant, spacing, and distinction.

Size refers to the fact that in the English alphabet we have small (lowercase) and capital or large (uppercase) letters. Students need to be taught the difference and to use both appropriately. Even many adults use capital and small letters inappropriately because handwriting is idiosyncratic, so teaching young students the correct way to form both capital and small letters is important.

Slant is customarily associated with cursive writing, although some students slant their manuscript writing too. It is not necessary to insist that all students slant their letters at the traditional 45-degree angle; as long as their slant is consistent, their handwriting will be legible. Note that left-handed students often slant their letters the reverse of the right-handed student. This is perfectly acceptable.

Two types of *spacing* affect legibility: between letters and between words. A small, consistent space should be left between letters and a slightly larger space should be left between words. The key point is consistency. Inconsistent spacing between letters and words leads to illegible handwriting.

Distinction refers to the fact that certain letters in the English alphabet look alike. For example, in cursive writing an *i* can be mistaken for an *e* if the writer accidentally omits the dot above. Similarly the letters *a, o, u* can easily be mistaken if not carefully written. Letter distinction plays a role in spelling—if you cannot distinguish between certain letters you will not be able to tell if a word is spelled correctly. Figure 7.4 illustrates the characteristics of legibility.

read RESEARCH practice

Visit a preschool or primary-grade classroom. Photocopy samples of students' handwriting. Identify the four main characteristics in determining legibility in handwriting. Also note how handwriting is taught in the classroom. Does the teacher isolate it from real writing or does he or she integrate it into the writing process? At what point does formal handwriting instruction end in this school? As a follow-up, try teaching a calligraphy lesson to a small group of students.

Readiness Skills for Handwriting

Handwriting is both a cognitive as well as a psychomotor skill and is developed over time through practice (Olsen & Knapton, 2012). As stated earlier, we recommend that the practice be authentic, such as labeling objects in the room, or writing pen pal letters, stories, and poems. Repetitious individual letter formation in isolation often discourages rather than motivates young students. A number of prerequisite skills are required before direct instruction in handwriting should begin. *Small muscle development* is necessary for holding a pencil. Assembling jigsaw puzzles and attaching snap beads are helpful in developing these muscles along with activities such as coloring, cutting with scissors, and manipulating small objects in games. *Eye–hand coordination* is necessary and requires cognitive and musculature coordination. Manipulative activities such as typing, sewing, weaving, and hammering develop the eye–hand coordination necessary for writing. Holding any writing tool, such as a crayon, pencil, or pen, requires muscle control of the fingers, which can be developed by manipulating various objects with the hand and fingers or by

Characteristics of legibility.   **FIGURE 7.4**

SIZE: The boy and girl visited New York City.
         THE BOY AND GIRL VISITED NEW YORK CITY.
         the boy and girl visited new york city.

SLANT: I love to eat vanilla ice cream.
         /I/love/to/eat/vanilla/ice/cream./
         \I\love\to\eat\vanilla\ice\cream.\
         I love to eat vanilla ice cream.

SPACING: space   s p a c e
         He left his socks in the room.
         H eleft hi ssoc ks int he r oo m.

DISTINCTION: ∪ l ∪ ∪ l = about

doing simple gardening activities. Beginning writing instruction with thick crayons or markers makes the initial process easier. *Letter and word perception* is also necessary, and is similar to readiness in reading. Immersion in a print-rich environment is the best way for students to distinguish letters and words. Other experiences that contribute to writing readiness include word building with wooden blocks or plastic letters (Zachry, 2011).

Instruction in Handwriting

Despite some debate over the need for direct instruction versus indirect instruction in handwriting, we believe that young students need some overt instruction in letter formation, size, slant, and proper spacing (Hodges, 1991; Olsen & Knapton, 2012). But above all students need real purposes for writing, such as notes to take home to mom and dad or invitations to give to their friends.

Visual-auditory-kinesthetic model

The teaching model for handwriting we suggest is the visual-auditory-kinesthetic (VAK) technique.

Visual. Students need to see the teacher creating letters and words. To construct letters and words themselves students must be able to visualize the letters and words. Teacher modeling and displaying the alphabet and word walls aids in this process.

Auditory. Students are also helped by hearing the specific strokes needed to form each letter. For example, as the teacher demonstrates on the board, he says "To make the capital B, I first put my pencil at the top line and slide it straight down to the bottom line. Next I make two humps." Verbalizing aloud helps the auditory learner to remember how letters are formed.

Kinesthetic. This refers to the sense of touch or bodily movement to enhance learning. Tracing letters in sand or shaving cream, shaping a letter with clay, yarn, or pipe cleaners are examples of kinesthetic techniques.

With legibility as the primary requirement, instruction in handwriting can be confined to minilessons, followed by about 10 minutes per day of practice in grades 1, 2, and 3, including cursive instruction in grade 3. After that, time spent on handwriting instruction should be at the teacher's discretion (Olsen & Knapton, 2012). One way to condense the amount of time spent on handwriting instruction is by teaching a few letters in a single lesson; you can do this easily by introducing letters with similar strokes at the same time. Figure 7.5 suggests a sequence for teaching the letters of the alphabet based on common strokes.

FIGURE 7.5 Possible groupings of letter strokes.

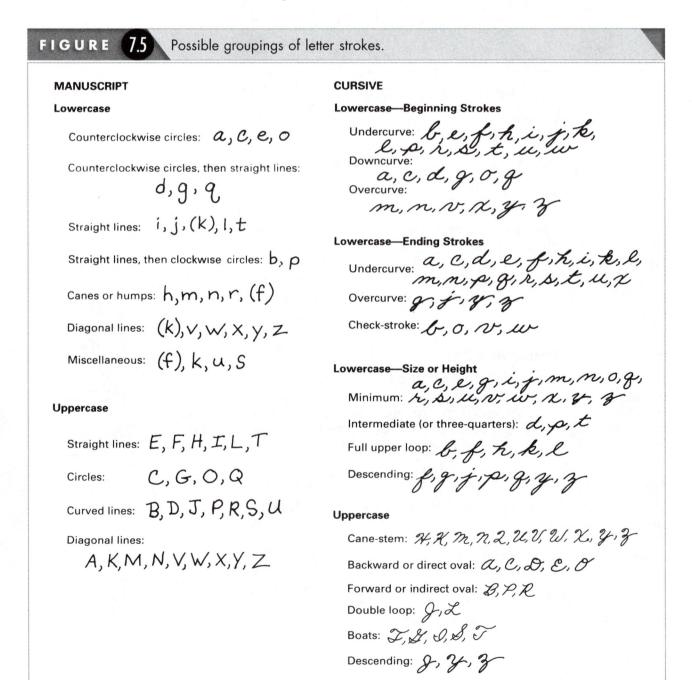

Some issues in handwriting instruction

The major focus of this and the previous chapter is on authentic writing activities performed through a series of drafts, revisions, and edits. However, teachers will confront a few more specific issues surrounding the teaching of handwriting, which this section addresses briefly.

> A teacher is one who brings us tools and enables us to use them.
>
> **JEAN TOOMER**

Tracing vs. copying. Educators are divided over the issue of tracing vs. copying for beginning writers. Both techniques are useful for practicing handwriting, but the goal of writing is to reproduce letters from memory. In addition, copying should not be about just imitating rows of letters. Rather, copying should be related in some way to a real world activity (Zachry, 2011). For example, students may enjoy copying passages from a favorite book. Two books that young students enjoy are Barney Saltzberg's *Beautiful Oops!* (2010) and Lori Ries' *Aggie the Brave* (2010).

Reversals in writing. Young students commonly reverse similar letters (*b* and *d*, for example) as well as reverse words in reading (e.g., *saw* for *was*). This is not unusual and the practice usually disappears as the student gets older (Edwards, 2003). Therefore, do not criticize such errors in young students; calling attention to such minor issues will only frustrate the student and make the learning process that more difficult. Copying letters and words from interesting beginner books such as Paul Thurlby's *Alphabet* (2011) can help correct this problem.

Left-handed writers. There was a time in American education when left-handed students were forced to use their right hand or were given special instruction and generally made to feel inferior (Holder, 2012). By singling out left-handed students and calling attention to the way they slanted their letters, educators created a problem where there wasn't one (Medwell & Wray, 2008). Today we realize there is no need for special instruction for left-handed students; the criterion remains legibility.

Cursive writing. Most students are taught to write in grades 1 and 2 using the manuscript or unjoined stroke. Beginning in grade 3, cursive or continuous joined stroke letter formation is introduced (Edwards, 2003). Because formal handwriting instruction is not taught beyond the elementary grades and many students, particularly boys, revert back to manuscript, the whole need for cursive instruction has been questioned (Edwards, 2003). As stated earlier, the CCSS do not call for cursive writing instruction in the curriculum. Cursive writing instruction is time consuming, and many believe that this time may be better spent instructing students on the use of the keyboard (Braiker, 2011). Others have argued that cursive writing still plays a part in modern society and should be taught (Zezima, 2011).

If you teach cursive handwriting, you may want to introduce it as a fun unit on calligraphy, the art of beautiful or elegant writing (D'Angelo, 1982), but do not emphasize the need to be perfect. Make cursive instruction an enjoyable time for students, and when it is over let them decide if they want to continue with cursive, return to manuscript, or use a combination of the two.

What is most important is providing students interesting ways to practice their handwriting skills. Each day you can present a different activity; this keeps students motivated. For a list of different handwriting activities, see Figure 7.6.

Keep in mind that handwriting is very personal; some students will naturally have beautiful handwriting while others will struggle with legibility. For example, Figure 7.7 shows the different handwriting examples among the same

---

FIGURE 7.6   Functional handwriting activities.

PRIMARY GRADES

- Label lockers, chairs, tables, closets, centers, and so on.
- Make nameplates for books.
- Label paintings and other art projects.
- Write names to check attendance, lunch count, and so on.
- Write stories, poems, and simple plays.
- Write simple invitations and thank-you cards.
- Copy and write letters to caregivers about school events.

INTERMEDIATE GRADES

- Write labels, stories, poems, letters, plays, book reports, reports for social studies, invitations, letters of thanks, announcements, articles for school newspaper, and so on.
- Keep lists or records, diaries, and journals.
- Take notes in class; make outlines.
- Keep attendance reports and weather reports.
- Make plans for classroom activities.

FIGURE 7.7   Second-grade handwriting samples.

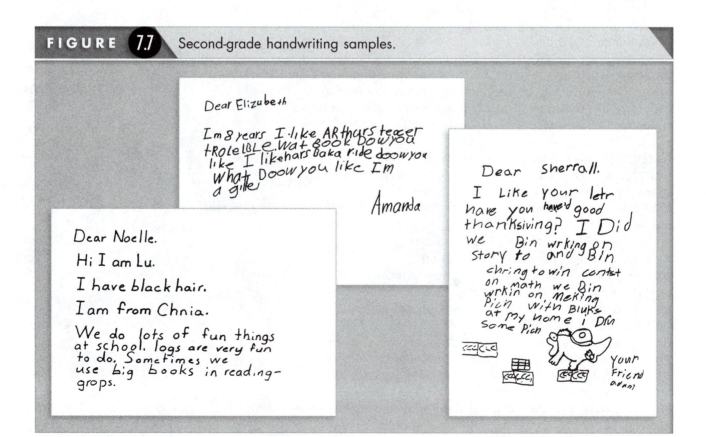

second-grade class. You cannot expect all students to have perfect handwriting. Your attitude will determine whether or not the students feel frustrated or enjoy the task.

> Teaching demands not just desirable personality attributes but specific skills. Skills are not ends in themselves, but they are necessary tools.
>
> **JACOB S. KOUNIN**

SPELLING: A DEVELOPMENTAL PROCESS

Although educators agree that spelling is a crucial part of the curriculum (Tankersley, 2003), some criticize the ubiquitous Friday spelling tests (Dubois, Erickson, & Jacobs, 2007), while others argue that the subject is poorly taught (Darch et al., 2006). Nevertheless, direct spelling instruction is important and it can be taught successfully.

Spelling begins as part of the editing stage in the writing process. Students learn to spell in many diverse ways; thus, there is no one best way to teach spelling (Stothard & Hulme, 2006). As with handwriting, the key is to provide students with a diverse array of practice activities, including games like Scrabble, crossword puzzles, and lessons on synonyms, antonyms, homonyms, and other morphology (word study) activities. Most of all, tie your spelling instruction to authentic reading and writing activities (Edwards, 2003; Medwell & Wray, 2008). Nevertheless, educators agree that motivating students to want to improve their spelling is a difficult task that requires meaningful and challenging activities along with direct explicit teacher instruction (Alderman & Green, 2011).

Very young children who do not yet understand the relationship between sound and symbol will rely on what spelling experts refer to as *invented spelling*. That means the student creates the best approximation he can think of for how a word might look like. Some authorities call this experimental spelling or temporary spelling. The more young students read and write, the more their spelling improves. The point to remember is that spelling develops over time and cannot be rushed, which leads us to the *developmental stages of spelling*.

Developmental Stages of Spelling

Many educators have long recognized that young students develop their spelling skills over time according to distinct patterns (Plumley, 2010; Bear et al., 2007; Leu & Kinzer, 2003). Although different authors use different terms to describe similar stages, we will use the terms *prephonetic, phonetic, orthographic,* and *morphemic/syntactic*.

Prephonetic stage

Preschool and kindergarten children often invent their own spelling for words without understanding the relationship between the sounds of words and the letters that represent them. Their writing may be scribbles or random letters. This stage is also referred to as the precommunicative or emergent stage, where literacy is just beginning.

Phonetic stage

During grades 1 through 3, youngsters become more aware of the sound–symbol relationship of written language in the *phonetic stage*. In their writing, both consonant and vowel sounds are represented by actual letters of the alphabet. Vowels, however, are often still misused or omitted. For example, children may spell house as *hs* and dog as *dg*. This is also sometimes called the letter–name stage of spelling.

Orthographic stage

In this stage use of consonants and vowels becomes more consistent; the student is becoming aware of syllables within words and familiar with consistent word patterns. However, double consonants, the schwa sound, and silent letters still present challenges (Hauerwas & Walker, 2003). Some authors refer to this as the *transitional stage*.

Morphemic/syntactic stage

By fifth grade students have been exposed to words through extensive reading and have been encouraged to write with a process approach for a number of years. They have learned about word meanings and word families, which are related words with similar spelling and meaning. For example, the word groups *manage, manager, managerial* and *family, familiar, familiarity* are related both in meaning and spelling. Understanding of word order or syntax develops. Knowing about root words, prefixes, and suffixes enhances their ability to spell words like *jumped, running,* and *remaking*. This is also known as the derivational or correct stage of spelling and does not occur until all of the reading and writing skills come together.

Figure 7.8 shows examples of the developmental stages.

The following classroom vignette discusses how one young student progressed through the early stages of spelling.

FIGURE 7.8 Examples of the developmental stages of spelling.

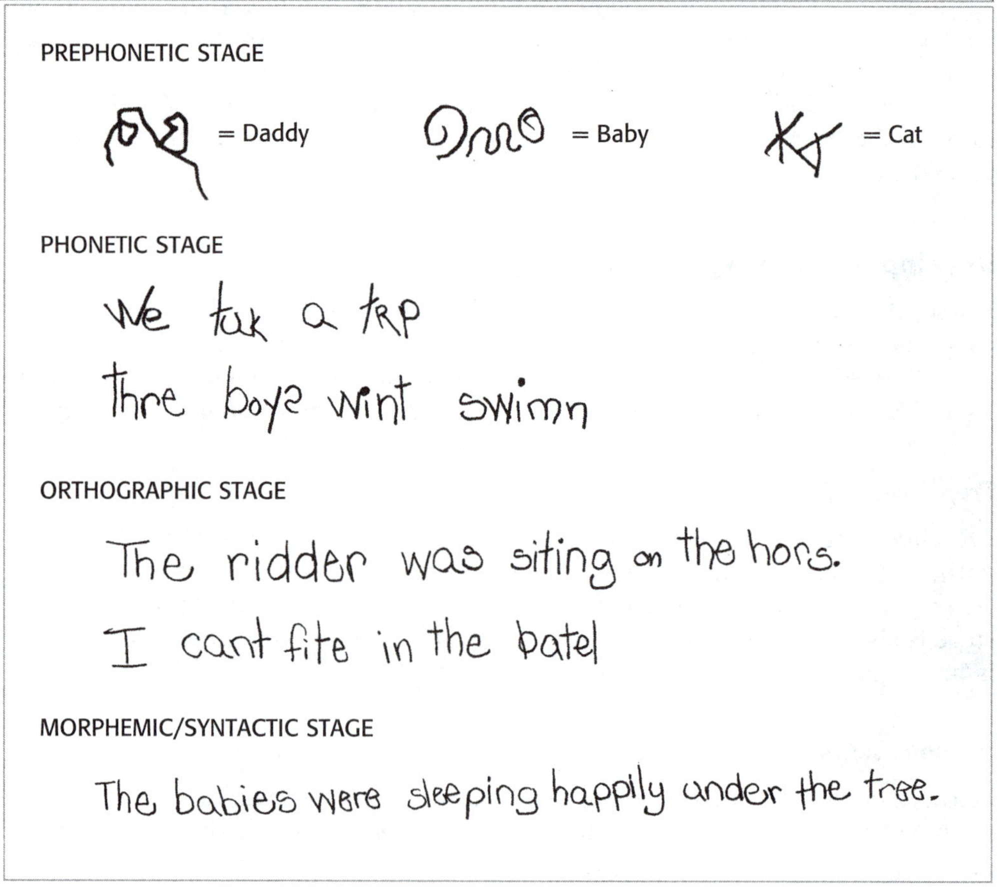

PREPHONETIC STAGE

= Daddy   = Baby   = Cat

PHONETIC STAGE

We tuk a trp
Thre boys wint swimn

ORTHOGRAPHIC STAGE

The ridder was siting on the hors.
I cant fite in the batel

MORPHEMIC/SYNTACTIC STAGE

The babies were sleeping happily under the tree.

Source: Adapted from C. Beers and J. Beers (1981), "Three Assumptions About Learning to Spell"; C. Read (1986), *Children's Creative Spelling;* J. R. Gentry (1987), *Spel . . . Is a Four-Letter Word.*

Brittany has written over 40 books. She is 7 years old. Her mother, a teacher, has been saving all of her drawings, scribbles, and writings since she was an infant. A look at Brittany's progress as a writer exemplifies the developmental stages of spelling. The only difference is that Brittany has moved at a much faster pace than most students, perhaps because she was encouraged by her parents.

Brittany's first interest in print occurred when she was only a few months old. Books were among her favorite playthings, often winning out over toys. Her parents read to her every day. Two of her favorite books were *Animal Sounds* and *My Goodnight Book.* She also enjoyed sitting with books, examining them carefully page by page.

When Brittany was 2 years, 3 months old, her mother purchased some magnetic letters to place on the refrigerator. One day, without being instructed, Brittany took the letters down and began matching them to letters in her picture books. Within a few months, she was playing games with her parents, such as "What does _____ begin with?" Her parents continued reading to her, and her personal library continued to grow.

At age 3½ Brittany began printing the letters of the alphabet in her drawings. Her parents bought her an assortment of crayons, pens, markers, and paper as her interest in writing grew. During this time, her spoken vocabulary also expanded enormously. By age 4, she was continually asking about the words on signs, billboards, cards, junk mail, and the Sunday comic strips. One month after her fifth birthday, she wrote her first word using experimental spelling: BLREA (ballerina).

Early in her writing, Brittany began labeling her drawings and creating little books she could read to her parents. Figure 7.9 shows Brittany's early experimental spellings and some of her drawings; the typed comments are her mother's.

When Brittany entered kindergarten she learned to use the classroom writing center, where the students were encouraged to use experimental spellings. Crayons, pens, pencils, and colored paper were plentiful. Brittany often chose to work at the writing center. Figure 7.10 is one of her earliest examples from school using experimental spellings.

One day Oklahoma storyteller Lynn Moroney visited the class and told the Native American story "Baby Rattlesnake." Brittany was so inspired that she sat down the next day and wrote her own story. As with her previous books, Brittany drew the pictures first and then added the text. The story is fragmented; this is common among young writers, who often assume that their audience knows what they know and thus fail to fill in the missing pieces. Figure 7.11 shows Brittany's version of "Baby Rattlesnake."

Excerpt from *BRITTANYS ANLBOK.* **FIGURE 7.9**

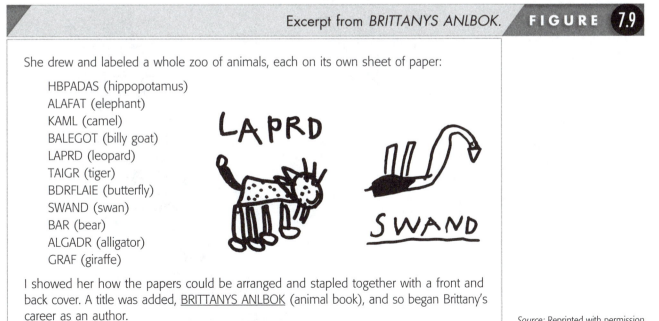

She drew and labeled a whole zoo of animals, each on its own sheet of paper:

HBPADAS (hippopotamus)
ALAFAT (elephant)
KAML (camel)
BALEGOT (billy goat)
LAPRD (leopard)
TAIGR (tiger)
BDRFLAIE (butterfly)
SWAND (swan)
BAR (bear)
ALGADR (alligator)
GRAF (giraffe)

I showed her how the papers could be arranged and stapled together with a front and back cover. A title was added, BRITTANYS ANLBOK (animal book), and so began Brittany's career as an author.

Source: Reprinted with permission of Diane and Brittany Moser.

FIGURE 7.10 Brittany's experimental spellings.

HADDDLKAT	hey diddle diddle cat	THADOGLAF	the dog laughed
ATHAFATL	and the fiddle	TSESSHTAN	to see such fun
KOGAMTOVR	cow jumped over	THDASHRAN	the dish ran
THEMON	the moon	AWAWAAISON	away with a spoon

FIGURE 7.11 Brittany's *THE STORE ABAT BABY RATLSNAK.*

BABY RATL SNAK
WAT AT SPT
AND FADA PRASAT.
WAT WAS ANATS

Baby rattlesnake went outside and found a present. What was in it?

HE WAT BAK
NI THE RAX
WATR HAS MATHR
WAS.

He went back in the rocks where his mother was.

TAN HE WAT
TO FAD THE
CHES DATR.

Then he went to find the chief's daughter.

SE WAS VARE
BUTAFL.

She was very beautiful.

THAN HE WAT
NITHE RAX
AND HD

Then he went in the rocks and hid.

AND SKAPRD OWT
TO GO HCHCHCHCHCHC
CHCHCH

And scampered out to go ch-ch-ch-ch.

ATHAN THE SE
STAPT ONN HAS
TAL.

Then she stepped on his tail.

AND HE SKAPRD
HOUSE ASKWAKL
KD

And he scampered home as quickly [as he] could.

Source: Reprinted with permission of Diane and Brittany Moser.

Implications for spelling instruction

The fact that the developmental stages of spelling correspond to a student's increased chronological age represents the constructivist principle of learning, namely that students in their own way and own time eventually come to understand and recreate the principles of conventional spelling. You can enhance this process by using a variety of instructional practices and activities. For example, help young students recognize rhyming words by reading picture books such as Bill Martin's *Brown Bear, Brown Bear, What Do You See?* (1967), Mem Fox's *Shoes from Grandpa* (1990), Martin Waddell's *Farmer Duck* (1996), Colin McNaughton's *Suddenly* (1994), and Sherrill Cannon's *Peter and the Whimper-Whineys* (2012), all of which have repeated words and phrases that emphasize consistent patterns of English spelling.

> The difference between the right word and the almost right word is the difference between lightning and the lightning bug.
>
> **MARK TWAIN**

These books can serve as springboards for having students write text with rhyming words. For primary grades, you can invite students to write a parody of *Brown Bear, Brown Bear* by suggesting a first line as "Green Snake, Green Snake" or "Black Cat, Black Cat." Students in upper elementary or middle school can take the challenge of writing a parody of *Shoes from Grandpa* about a birthday gift they would like to receive.

Elementary students also benefit from rereading familiar books and poetry with various spelling word patterns. Through wide reading and discussion students discover for themselves the consistency and inconsistency of English spelling (Snowball, 2006). For example, the vowel digraph *ea* has the same visual pattern but varying sounds in *bread, bead,* and *great.* Reading aloud and copying favorite poems is another way to discover familiar patterns in rhyming words; see the work of Shel Silverstein, Jack Prelutsky, Karla Kuskin, and Naomi Shihab Nye.

The middle-school student's spelling program should be fully integrated into authentic reading and writing experiences, not only in the language arts but also in content area subjects such as math, social studies, science, art, and music. As the student's verbal lexicon grows, so too should his spelling vocabulary. Struggling readers particularly have difficulty with subject content vocabulary, so it behooves the content area teacher to reinforce new content area vocabulary terms (e.g., *perpendicular, peninsula, paramecium*) for both reading and writing (Simonsen & Gunter, 2001).

Approaches to Spelling Instruction

Students should be taught to recognize patterns in words instead of memorizing a long list of words that have no similar patterns. Teachers of young students can begin with onset and rime because once they learn the rime and understand how the onset creates a new word, students can learn multiple words instead of one. They can then learn how to analyze the common properties of words, form conclusions about them, and develop for themselves some rules for spelling.

Onset–rime approach for spelling instruction

An *onset* is the initial consonant(s) in a one-syllable word while the *rime* (not to be confused with *rhyme*) is the remaining vowels and consonants. For example, in the word *best* /b/ is the onset and /est/ is the rime. Rimes are also known as *phonograms* or *word families*. By learning many rimes and then changing the onset, students can create many new words such as *rest, test, nest, pest*.

Using onset–rime theory along with rhymes and analogies, Smith (2002) developed a unique approach to teaching students about spelling as well as reading and writing. Here are the steps:

1. Teach students about words that rhyme (e.g., *hat, cat, bat*).

2. Read a book aloud to the class with a rhyming pattern (e.g., *Sheep in a Jeep* by Nance Shaw, 1986); see Appendix B.4 for more rhyming books.

3. Teach some target words and their spelling patterns (rimes) as a way to learn new words by analogy. For example, the target word is *jeep*; the rime is *-eep*; analogies to other words include *keep, sheep, steep,* and *weep*.

4. Together with the students rewrite a predictable book using a structured frame as follows (Walker, 2000):

   ■ Frame taken from *Beast Feast* (Florian, 1994):

   The bat is as batty as can be
   It sleeps all day in a cave or tree
   And when the sun sets in the sky
   It rises from its rest to fly.

   ■ Teacher/student made frame:

   The _____ is _____ as can be.
   It _____ all day in _____ or _____
   And when the sun sets in the sky,
   It rises from its rest to fly.

Inductive approach to spelling instruction

By upper elementary and middle grades spelling should not be about mere memorization but rather about analyzing words, discussing their common properties, and drawing conclusions; this is the constructivist approach to spelling rule formation. For example, you might ask students, "What rules about the sound of /f/ can you discover from the two groups of words below?"

1. fun, foolish, free, stiff, bluff, puff

2. rough, cough, tough, photograph, telephone

   Some spelling rules for /f/ include the following:

1. If the final consonant sound of a one-syllable word is /f/ (or /l/, /s/, or /z/), and the vowel sound is short, the final consonant is doubled (e.g., *puff, hill, grass,* and *buzz*).

2. Words from ancient Greek use the "ph" as a digraph to spell the /f/. For example, *photo, physical, physician,* and *photograph*.

3. The /f/ is never spelled "gh" at the beginning of a word. Sometimes "gh" is silent (bright and thought); and sometimes at the end of a word, it has the /f/ sound (e.g., *rough*).

Teachers can share these "rules," which may help students, but students should always be encouraged to look at a word after they spell it and see if it looks correct. If it does not look correct, they should try spelling the word with other letters that make the sound they hear and/or look it up or ask a friend.

Although spelling rules are too numerous to memorize or use efficiently, Figures 7.12, 7.13, and 7.14 present high-utility generalizations that can be useful to students if placed on wall charts and taught in minilessons.

High-utility spelling rules. **FIGURE 7.12**

RULE 1

When two vowels appear together in the same syllable, a single long vowel sound is often heard.

Examples: seizure, siege, loathsome, feasible, drainage, sleazy, leasable

RULE 2

The long vowel sound /e/ at the end of a word is often spelled -y.

Examples: dropsy, gypsy, stability, hegemony

RULE 3

In spelling the vowel digraphs *ie* and *ei,* the *i* usually comes before the *e* and you hear the long /e/ sound. However, after the letter *c* or when the digraph sounds like long /a/, then the *e* comes before the *i.*

Examples: believe, receive, neighbor, viewpoint, conceive, reign

Exceptions: weird, seize, science

RULE 4

When adding a suffix that begins with a vowel *(-ing)* to words ending in silent *e (bake, dance),* remember to drop the silent *e.* When adding a suffix beginning with a consonant, keep the *e.*

Examples: dance/dancing, value/valuable, fame/famous, elope/elopement, imagine/imaginary

RULE 5

Monosyllabic words ending in a single consonant preceded by a single vowel double the consonant when adding a suffix that begins with a vowel.

Examples: drum/drumming, stop/stopping, big/biggest, snub/snubbed, skim/skimmed

RULE 6

Words ending in -y and preceded by a consonant change the *y* to *i* before adding the suffix unless the suffix begins with i.

Examples: carry/carrier, carrying; study/studious, studying; fly/flies, flying; luxury/luxurious

RULE 7

Add the suffix *-able* to root words that end in silent *e* or to root words that take the prefix *un- (available, advisable).* Keep the *e* with soft *c* and *g* words *(manageable, serviceable).* Add the suffix *-ible* to root words that combine with *-ion (suggest/suggestion/suggestible)* and to words that without the suffix ending are not meaningful *(incredible, visible).*

Examples: admirable, confirmable, indescribable, accessible, perfectible

Source: Reprinted with permission of David Yellin and the *Daily Oklahoman.*

Generalizations about letter sounds. **FIGURE 7.13**

1. The *k* is silent when followed by *n* (know, knob).
2. When *gh* follows the vowel *i,* the *gh* is silent (might).
3. At the beginning of a word, the *w* is silent when followed by *r* (write).
4. At the end of words, the *b* is silent when it follows *m* (comb).
5. *C* sounds like /k/ when followed by *a, o,* or *u* (cat, cot, cut).
6. *C* sounds like /s/ when followed by *i, e,* or *y* (city, center, Cinderella).
7. *G* sounds like /g/ when followed by *o, a,* or *u* (gone, game, gun).
8. *Ph* is /f/ (telephone, photograph).
9. *Q* is always followed by *u* and sounds like /kw/ (quick).

Source: Adapted from *Phonics in Proper Perspective* (10th ed.) by Arthur W. Heilman, © 2005. Reprinted by permission of Prentice Hall, Inc., Upper Saddle River, NJ.

FIGURE 7.14 Generalizations relating to syllabication.

1. Syllables are determined by vowel sounds (road = 2 vowels, but only 1 vowel sound; com-plete = 3 vowels, but only 2 vowel sounds; si-tu-a-tion = 5 vowels, but 4 vowel sounds).

2. When there are double consonants in the middle of words, the word is syllabicated between the two consonants (hid-den, gen-tle).

3. When there is one consonant in the middle of a word, the consonant goes with the second syllable if the preceding vowel is long (stu-dent, be-gan). If the preceding vowel is short, the consonant goes with the first syllable (mod-el, pan-el).

4. Digraphs and consonant blends remain together (teach-er, fa-ther).

5. The affixes form separate syllables (re-peat-ing, grate-ful).

Source: Adapted from *Phonics in Proper Perspective* (10th ed.) by Arthur W. Heilman, © 2005. Reprinted by permission of Prentice Hall, Inc., Upper Saddle River, NJ.

Spelling, Proofreading, and Dictionary Use

Research shows that teaching proofreading skills, especially in middle school, aids students in their spelling (Doyne & Ojalvo, 2010). Although proofreading one's written work should be taught in the early grades as part of the writing process, it should be emphasized even more in the upper grades. Students should learn to proofread their own work and be able to proofread the work of others. If proofreading is reinforced during content area subjects such as math, science, and social studies, it will soon become second nature to many students.

Similarly, students need to be taught how to use the dictionary. In spite of the fact that computers have spell check capabilities, eventually students will need to look up words either in a print dictionary or online. They need to be taught the alphabet, the use of guide words at the top of the page in print dictionaries, how to interpret dictionary entries, and how the same word can be used in different ways depending on the part of speech; for example, "I live in a *house*" but "I *house* my belongings in the attic trunk." Dictionaries also present the etymology or origin of certain words. For example, the word *baloney* comes from the Italian town of Bologna; *frankfurter* comes from Frankfurt, Germany; *tangerine* comes from the port city of Tangiers, Morocco. Young students should use primary grade dictionaries with large print and (usually) a single definition. You may also choose to have pocket dictionaries available that provide the spelling of words but no definitions.

Three Plans for Teaching and Testing Spelling

Although we have established that spelling improves the most when taught as a part of the general writing and editing process, many schools still require that spelling be taught as a separate subject. With that in mind, we present three different approaches to a weekly spelling curriculum.

Plan 1: Pretest/study/retest

This is perhaps the most widely used of the spelling approaches. On Monday the teacher gives a spelling pretest. Then the students correct their own papers while the teacher spells the words correctly. On Tuesday, Wednesday, and Thursday, for about 15 minutes each day, the students practice their spelling words using crossword puzzles, word sort activities, and dictionary skills. The graded retest is given on Friday. Because spelling tests are not a true indicator of how well students spell in their written compositions, time spent on spelling in isolation should be minimized.

Plan 2: Study/test/study

In this approach the teacher introduces words to the students on Monday, and on Monday, Tuesday, and Wednesday they work on activities such as word search puzzles, writing their words in sentences, and finding synonyms and antonyms for their words. Students are tested on Thursday. Only those who do poorly on the Thursday test complete additional study activities on Friday. The main advantage of this approach is that more time is allowed for study and less time is spent on testing.

Plan 3: Self-study

In this approach the teacher gives a test at the beginning of the week and then immediately displays the correct spelling on a wall chart. Classroom spelling time is spent on practice via the cloze procedure, spelling bees, spelling tic-tac-toe, and other games. The next week students receive a new list of words and more practice activities. Every three or four weeks, the teacher selects words from the past weeks' lists and gives a test. This approach emphasizes practice over testing, but it is more challenging for the students and should be used with care. The self-study approach can be combined with authentic writing activities and included in an I Love to Write Day, celebrated nationwide on November 15; see www.ilovetowriteday.org (Micklos, 2011).

In all three cases students are encouraged to display posters and artwork that incorporate their spelling words. Thus, the words are seen on a regular basis and learned through immersion, whereby they become part of the classroom environment. Figure 7.15 gives more suggestions for teaching spelling on a regular basis.

Spelling tips. **FIGURE 7.15**

1. *Use daily free reading.* By encouraging regular reading, students are exposed to thousands of new words. Over time and with use in writing, these words become part of a student's spelling vocabulary.

2. *Use daily freewriting.* Spelling develops through practice: the more practice, the better. Incorporating some freewriting time each day reinforces weekly spelling skills lessons.

3. *Use personal speller dictionaries.* From both their reading and writing, students are encouraged to write down the words they wish to learn in their own speller dictionary. The correct spelling of the word, along with a simple definition, is all that is needed.

4. *Use the dictionary.* Students need to be introduced to the dictionary as a resource tool early in their school years. Begin with simple primary-grade dictionaries and work up to the large unabridged dictionaries. Finding the spelling of an unfamiliar word requires predicting the spelling of the word and then using a trial-and-error approach. Dictionary usage is a habit that takes time to develop.

5. *Maintain a class word wall.* Many teachers cover one section of a class wall with butcher-block paper. Children are encouraged to write their favorite words or new and unusual words they have encountered in their reading on the wall. Throughout the year, the word wall list grows and remains for an easy reference.

6. *Use spelling games.* Practicing spelling is drudgery for some students. Effective teachers try to make this practice more fun by incorporating various spelling games such as word searches, crossword puzzles, spelling jumbles, spelling relay, or big words (also see the activities on the following page).

TEACHING ACTIVITIES 7

SPELLING DEVELOPMENT

The following activities and teaching strategies will enhance spelling development in students.

1 Labeling

Host a "room labeling day" in which students make signs out of strips of construction paper and place them around the room. Have them make labels for *closet, supply cabinet, reading center,* and so on.

2 Language experience charts

Pair an older student, such as a fifth grader, with a first or second grader. The older buddy engages the younger student in an LEA using wordless books such as:

- *Chalk* (Thomson, 2010), in which objects come to life as the characters draw them with magical chalk.
- *The Lion and the Mouse* (Pinkney, 2009), based on Aesop's fable.
- *Deep in the Woods* (Turkle, 1992), a story in which a bear visits a family's home that has three bowls of porridge, three chairs, and three beds.
- *Pancakes for Breakfast* (dePaola, 1978), an easy-to-follow story about an old woman who gathers all the ingredients to make pancakes.
- *Carl's Afternoon in the Park* (Day, 1991), in which Carl the beloved dog is left home to care for his master's baby.

The younger student dictates each page of the story as he interprets it from the illustrations. Using index cards, the older student writes down the story as the younger student explains it, page by page. Next, the younger student copies the story onto another set of index cards. Finally, the younger student reads the story from his own writing. Before the younger student copies the text, you may want to check the spelling of the words.

3 Pocket charts

Students arrange their word cards into sentences using the pocket charts. Later they learn to write the words on a separate sheet of paper, referring to the chart if necessary.

4 Word walls

Every class in grades 1 through 8 should have a word wall, where students can add new words under the letters of the alphabet. You can use these words to determine words for spelling tests. Content area words can also be added to the list. Some teachers require that all words on the wall must be spelled correctly in students' writing.

5 Personal dictionaries

Encourage students to keep their own personal dictionary of words they would like to learn to spell. From their independent reading, they can choose words that they would like to remember.

6 Strategy charts

Have students help create charts with simple suggestions to help them spell difficult words and then display them around the room. For example:

1. Visualize the way you think the word looks.
2. Try alternative spellings and then select one.
3. Think of a word that is similar (e.g, *muscle* and *muscular*).
4. Sound it out or use an analogy (e.g., *night* and *flight*).
5. Ask a friend (Newlands, 2011).

7 Compound word charts

A compound is one word formed from two other words, such as *baseball, classroom,* and *birthday*. Add compound words to your chart each day from books that your students have read.

8 Crossword puzzles

Teach students how to create their own crossword puzzles using their spelling words. They can either create their puzzles by hand or by using one of the many puzzlemaker apps available online. Then have them exchange their puzzle with a classmate.

9 Collective nouns

A Zeal of Zebras: An Alphabet of Collective Nouns (Woop Studios, 2011) is a clever picture book that will enhance students' understanding and spelling of collective nouns while increasing their vocabulary. Its unusual artwork will also entrance them.

10 Text talk

Select target words from a story read in class to teach vocabulary, enhance reading comprehension, and improve spelling by having the students write the words in their notebooks after discussing the words orally (Blamey & Beauchat, 2011).

GRAMMAR: MEANING, NOT MEMORIZING

Grammar instruction has a poor reputation in our schools. It is often associated with memorizing the definitions of the parts of speech (noun, pronoun, verb, adverb, adjective, article, preposition, and conjunction). To learn grammar concepts students complete worksheets, diagram sentences, and label the parts of speech. Yet research shows that many of these activities have little carry-over to the real act of writing and therefore serve no real purpose (Anderson, 2005).

Grammar lessons in general are best taught as a part of authentic reading and writing lessons. Multimedia materials, such as YouTube videos, can also be incorporated into grammar lessons to make them more relevant to students' lives (Schneider, 2005; Morgan, 2002, 2004; Kumaravadivelu, 2003). For example, you can find YouTube clips on each of the parts of speech and various clips that cover all eight parts of speech. Some are cartoon style while others are rap. Both the cartoon and rap videos are catchy and repeat the information so students can sing along and learn the differences between the parts of speech. Teaching a particular part of speech, say adjectives, in a minilesson should be followed up by having the students locate adjectives in their literature books and then using adjectives in short writing assignments. Thus, always follow direct instruction in grammar with activities to allow students to practice what they have just learned within the context of real reading and writing.

Sometimes grammar is confused with usage. The two are not synonymous. Grammar provides the terminology and rules to describe the structure of our language. How words are structured is known as *morphology,* while the way those words are arranged in sentences is called *syntax.* Grammar study involves both words (morphology) and sentences (syntax) in written form. *Usage,* however, is more concerned with the oral choice of words or language used by an individual as part of a specific culture. Unlike grammar, which is rule-controlled, usage is determined by regional and situational factors. When talking about standard and non-standard speech, for example, we are dealing with usage issues. YouTube clips are also available to teach standard English; for example, you can find videos to teach verb tenses or when to use *should* or *could, who* or *whom,* and *to be, to have,* and *to do.*

Finally, grammar instruction should relate to the 10 CCSS ELA Anchor Standards for writing. Grammar lessons that include real writing activities will go a long way toward meeting the CCRA standards for writing without teachers feeling dominated by these requirements (Collier, 2011).

Forms of Grammar and Which Should Be Taught

The CCRA for language include two standards that relate to proper English for both writing and speaking. CCRA.L.1 states that students "demonstrate command of the conventions of standard English grammar and usage when writing and speaking" (NGACBP & CCSSO, 2010, p. 25), and CCRA.L.2 states that students "demonstrate command of the conventions of standard English capitalization, punctuation, and spelling when writing" (NGACBP & CCSSO, 2010, p. 25). With this in mind we turn to teaching grammar in the elementary and middle-school grades. There are various forms of grammar, which makes the issue confusing. Which grammar you teach will depend on your school district and textbook.

Traditional grammar

Traditional grammar is the most widely taught. Its primary focus is on memorizing the definitions for the parts of speech. It utilizes two techniques: parsing and sentence diagramming. *Parsing* means placing the abbreviated letters for the parts of speech (e.g., *n* for *noun, adj* for *adjective,* etc.) above each word in a sentence. *Sentence diagramming* involves creating a diagram of horizontal, vertical, and diagonal lines indicating the various parts of speech and their relationship to one another in a sentence. Figure 7.16 shows sample sentence diagrams. Note that these are among the simplest of sentences to diagram. Diagramming compound and complex sentences is considerably more complicated.

Both parsing and sentence diagramming are difficult to teach, involve much rote memorization, and have not been shown to enhance students' writing abilities. Some argue that parsing prepares students for standardized tests, although there is no evidence of that (Anderson, 2005). The main argument against traditional grammar with all of its memorization and rules is the amount of time it takes, which is time taken away from real writing activities.

I must write, I must write at all costs. For writing is more than living, it is being conscious of living.

ANN MORROW LINDBERGH

Sample sentence diagrams.   **FIGURE** **7.16**

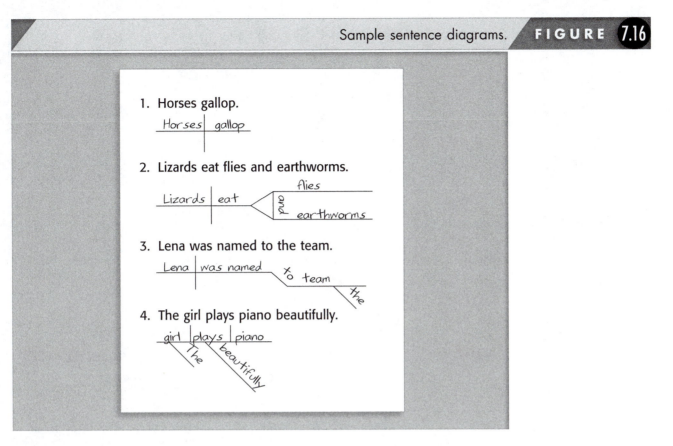

Structural-descriptive grammar

A second kind of grammar is *structural-descriptive grammar*. This name comes from the fact that its purpose is to describe the structure of various English-sentence patterns (see Figure 7.17). In some ways it is similar to traditional grammar in that it still teaches the basic parts of speech; however, it teaches them within the context of actual sentences. Students are taught various sentence patterns and the language (i.e., parts of speech) necessary to describe them. Activities can include finding similar sentence patterns in children's literature and then writing similar sentence patterns in their compositions.

Transformational-generative grammar

Transformational-generative, or TG, grammar is the brainchild of linguist Noam Chomsky. TG grammar differs from traditional and structural grammar in that it focuses on the underlying meaning of sentences, not their superficial physical appearance. It is based on the notion that all native speakers of a language unconsciously possess the rules of that language; this unconscious knowledge allows young students to produce grammatically correct sentences and recognize ungrammatical sentences even at a very young age. Stephen Krashen (1991) was able to demonstrate that these same intuitive principles operate in learning a second language.

TG grammar is not concerned with memorizing the parts of speech but rather with creating meaningful sentences and uncovering the meaning of other sentences. Traditional and structural grammar are concerned with the surface structure of language—the words and word patterns that make up sentences—while TG grammar asks, What does the sentence mean? Meaning is the deep structure of language. The link between surface and deep structure is what TG grammar tries to demonstrate. For example, consider the two sentences: "Felipe hit the ball" and "The ball

FIGURE 7.17   Common sentence patterns and their children's literature sources.

Pattern 1   Noun phrase–Verb

Examples: The two girls danced.

The train started.

[*Ralph Rides Away*, by B. Bishop, 1979.]

Pattern 2   Noun phrase–Being verb–Prepositional phrase

Examples: The ladies were at the circus.

The elephant was on the phone.

[*Wait! Wait! Wait!* by J. Reinach, 1980.]

Pattern 3   Noun phrase–Action verb–Prepositional phrase

Examples: The boy leaped into the pool.

Everyone stared at the goggles.

[*Goggles,* by E. Keats, 1969.]

Pattern 4   Noun phrase–Helping verb with action verb–Prepositional phrase

Examples: The children were reading from their book.

I am calling on the telephone.

[*A Baby Sister for Francis,* by R. Hoban, 1964.]

Pattern 5   Noun phrase–Verb–Object

Examples: The boy kissed the girl.

Paul licked the spoon.

[*Ice Cream for Breakfast,* by M. Brown, 1963.]

Pattern 6   Compound elements

Examples: The boy walked to the store and bought some candy.

She cooked the meals and washed the dishes and made the beds.

[*The Little Red Hen,* by P. Galdone, 1973.]

Pattern 7   Complex sentences and compound-complex sentences

Examples: She walked into the kitchen where she found a large carriage with a large doll lying in it.

The town where he lives is secluded, and I would like to live there, too.

[*The Girl That Would Rather Climb Trees,* by M. Schlein, 1975.]

was hit by Felipe." A non–English speaking person new to the language might assume that from the structure, these are two different sentences because they have different subjects and predicates. However, any native speaker of English recognizes that these two sentences mean basically the same thing; their physical structure and word order have merely been altered. What is important is the meaning of a sentence, not its structure.

Another set of examples demonstrates the fragile and often misleading nature of surface structure. Examine the following sentences carefully:

> Flying planes can be dangerous.
>
> Visiting professors can be a bore.
>
> Jane will marry whom she pleases.

Diagramming or parsing these sentences would be difficult because each has at least two distinctly different meanings. Can you identify them? These are examples of ambiguous sentences, and to fully understand what their authors mean you need more context.

read RESEARCH practice

Observe a traditional grammar lesson in the elementary grades. What specific lesson did you observe? What procedure did the teacher use? How could you tell if the students learned anything? How long did the lesson take? Was any real writing included in the grammar lesson? Suggest alternative ways of teaching the same grammar content.

TEACHING ACTIVITIES 7

GRAMMAR

All of the activities described in this section utilize authentic sentences and require students to create their own sentences. Grammar taught through real applications will have more meaning and transference to students' writing. In contrast, labeling sentences and memorizing the definitions of parts of speech has little in common with the process of real writing.

1 Cloze technique

Although originally designed to test reading comprehension, the cloze technique is an ideal tool for teaching grammar. Simply take a page from a basal reader or children's literature book. Then blank out the particular part of speech you wish to teach—adverbs for example—and photocopy the page. The task for the students is to accurately fill in the blank spaces with the proper adverbs. Afterward, discuss with the class why certain words fit in the blanks and others do not. Figure 7.18 summarizes the steps of this technique. Figure 7.19 is a sample of a cloze test.

Steps of the cloze technique for teaching grammar.   **FIGURE 7.18**

Step 1	Present a sentence or paragraph with all the examples of a single part of speech omitted, such as verbs.
Step 2	Ask the students to brainstorm in small groups all the possible words that fit in the blanks.
Step 3	Ask students, "What do all these terms have in common?" Again the groups can discuss and brainstorm to come up with a generalization. This generalization may or may not fit the definition of a verb.
Step 4	Have the students generate their own sentences with verbs omitted and exchange these with friends.

FIGURE 7.19 A sample cloze test.

Directions: Read the two paragraphs. Fill in the missing blanks with verbs to make the sentences correct.

When Wilma Rudolph _____ four years old, she _____ an attack of double pneumonia and scarlet fever. She was _____ crippled, her left leg paralyzed. The doctors _____ that only with special treatment could she _____ to _____ back the use of her leg.

Every week Wilma's mother _____ her on the long round trip between Clarksville, Tennessee, and the clinic in Nashville. The entire family _____ the proper way to _____ Wilma's leg. By the time she _____ eight years old, Wilma _____ able to walk again with the help of a specially built shoe.

Corrected Version

When Wilma Rudolph _was_ four years old, she _had_ an attack of double pneumonia and scarlet fever. She was _left_ crippled, her left leg paralyzed. The doctors _said_ that only with special treatment could she _hope_ to _get_ back the use of her leg.

Every week Wilma's mother _took_ her on the long round trip between Clarksville, Tennessee, and the clinic in Nashville. The entire family _learned_ the proper way to _massage_ Wilma's leg. By the time she _was_ eight years old, Wilma _was_ able to walk again with the help of a specially built shoe.

2 Editing/proofreading

Teach students to recognize complete sentences and non-sentences or fragments. Also teach them about run-on sentences strung with the conjunction *and.* Then have them go back and proofread their own writing to correct these issues. This should be a regular part of instruction in the writing process.

3 Children's literature

One of the best ways to approach grammar instruction is through children's literature. Parts of speech, capitalization, and punctuation are all best taught through authentic examples from children's literature. Anderson (2005) calls teachers who use this process "sentence stalkers." The approach consists of the following steps:

1. Teach a specific grammatical skill in a minilesson.
2. Select a favorite book students are already familiar with.
3. Find a passage that contains an example of the grammatical skill.
4. Display the passage and discuss the example with your class.

Here are examples from well-known books:

- *Descriptive adjectives (and similes):* "I was as pink as a sunburnt huckleberry, and as lively as a young squirrel in a corn crib." (Wilson Rawls, *Summer of the Monkeys*, 1976, p. 10)
- *Capital letters and use of the comma:* "The next time the water truck came it was driven by Mr. Pendanski, who also brought sack lunches." (Louis Sachar, *Holes*, 1998, p. 35)

- *Active verbs and conjunctions:* "Grandma filled the door, and people looked up in alarm and surprise. She was famous for keeping to herself, but she was every-where at once, if you asked me." (Richard Peck, *A Year Down Under*, 2000, p. 35)

- *Apostrophes to show ownership and the use of commas in compound, complex sentences:* "Miss Hennepin had notified Roy's mother, so he had to repeat the story when he got home from school, and once more when his father returned from work." (Carl Hiassen, *Hoot*, 2002, p. 27)

- *Starting a new paragraph for each new speaker of dialogue:*

  The card says "things you climb." Richard nods and starts giving Mom clues.

  "A jungle gym, a mountain . . ."

  "High things?" Mom guesses.

  Richard shakes his head. "Um . . . stairs . . ."

  (Rebecca Stead, *When You Reach Me,* 2009, p. 41)

Other books you can use to demonstrate and explain grammatical concepts are listed in Figure 7.20.

Books to use to reinforce grammar concepts. **FIGURE 7.20**

A Cache of Jewels: And Other Collective Nouns (1987) by Ruth Heller

A Chocolate Moose for Dinner (1976) by Fred Gwynne (homonyms)

A Mink, a Fink, a Skating Rink: What Is a Noun? (1999) by Brian Cleary

Alfie the Apostrophe (2010) by Moira R. Donohue

Behind the Mask (1995) by Ruth Heller (prepositions)

Brown Bear, Brown Bear, What Do You See? (1967) by Bill Martin (direct address)

Elephants Aloft (1995) by Kathi Appelt (prepositions)

Fantastic! Wow! and Unreal: A Book About Interjections and Conjunctions (1998) by Ruth Heller

–Full and –Less, –Er and –Ness (2014) by Brian Cleary (suffixes)

Hairy, Scary, Ordinary: What Is an Adjective? (2000) by Brian Cleary

If You Were a Contraction (2008) by Trisha S. Shaskan

If You Were an Adjective (2014) by Michael Dahl (This series also includes books on verbs, nouns, antonyms, and homonyms.)

Kites Sail High: A Book About Verbs (1988) by Ruth Heller

Lazily, Crazily, Just a Bit Nasally (2010) by Brian Cleary (adverbs)

Many Luscious Lollipops: A Book About Adjectives (1989) by Ruth Heller

Merry-Go-Round: A Book of Nouns (1990) by Ruth Heller

Mine, All Mine: A Book About Pronouns (1997) by Ruth Heller

Penny and the Punctuation Bee (2010) by Moira R. Donohue

Pitch and Throw, Grasp and Know (2007) by Brian Cleary (synonyms)

Straight and Curvy, Meek and Nervy (2011) By Brian Cleary (antonyms)

Under, Over, by the Clover (2003) by Brain Cleary (prepositions)

Up, Up, and Away: A Book About Adverbs (1993) by Ruth Heller

Word Wizard (1998) by Cathryn Falwell (play with words)

4 Sentence transformations

For simple, active declarative sentences (called *kernel sentences*) transform or change the sentences according to the examples below. Teach a minilesson for each transformation; then have your students complete another example.

- *Kernel sentence.* The man sells bicycles.
- *Negative.* The man does not sell bicycles.
- *Passive.* Bicycles are sold by the man.
- *Negative–passive.* Bicycles are not sold by the man.
- *Question.* Does the man sell bicycles?
- *Negative question.* Doesn't the man sell bicycles?
- *Negative–passive question.* Aren't the bicycles sold by the man?

5 Word substitution

For this minilesson, write a sentence on the board such as "Maria likes to play." Then, examining each of the words in the sentence, ask for substitute words that could be used to make a new sentence, such as "The girls want to practice."

6 Sentence expansions

Young children tend to use simple sentences. Help them develop a more complex sentence structure by having them expand their sentences by adding more and more words. For example, "The boy runs" can become "The little red-haired boy runs quickly to school." "Trees sway" can become "Trees sway lazily and softly in the afternoon breeze." After you have taught this minilesson, encourage the students to use sentence expansions in their writing.

7 Sentence combining

Sentence combining has a long history of proven success (Mellon, 1969; Strong, 1993; Saddler, 2005). To teach this strategy, write two simple sentences on the board. Then combine them into one sentence. You can add words, omit words, or change the sentence around. For older students try combining three, four, or more sentences into one sentence. Here is an example of sentence combining:

> The wind was strong. The leaves fell to the ground.
>
> The leaves fell to the ground because the wind was strong.

For a more complete description of sentence combining and a list of activities, see the work of Richard Nordquist at http://grammar.about.com/od/grammarfaq/f/faqsentcomb.htm.

8 Punctuation and capitalization activities

Both punctuation and capitalization are best taught by posting rules charts on the classroom walls, teaching minilessons, and sharing examples from children's literature. Charts allow students to refer to the rules throughout the year without having to ask for help. Figures 7.21 and 7.22 summarize the uses of common punctuation marks, and Figure 7.23 summarizes capitalization rules. These lists will serve as a reference for students and determine the kinds of minilessons you might teach. Your students' needs will be based on their own writing, not the directives of a textbook. A minilesson might begin with a sentence

Approach writing like life, with a passion—be involved.

JANE YOLEN

Rules for using periods and commas.   **FIGURE** 7.21

PERIOD

Use a period . . .	Examples
1. at the end of a sentence making a statement	1. The men drilled for oil.
2. after abbreviations of titles when the name of the person follows	2. Mrs. Baker, Dr. Jones, Capt. Ahab, Rev. Smith
3. after abbreviations of days of the week and months of the year	3. Mon., Wed., Sun., Jan., Aug., Oct.

COMMA

Use a comma . . .	Examples
1. to separate the day from the year	1. Lindsay was born on May 4, 1982.
2. to separate the names of a city and a state	2. Bethany, OK 73008
3. after the greeting in a friendly letter	3. Dear Pamela,
4. after the closing of a letter	4. Yours truly,
5. to separate items in a list	5. Karen bought milk, bread, and cheese.
6. between long independent clauses connected with *but, and, or, nor*	6. Aubree thought she would swim all day, but the rain changed her plan.
7. to set off parenthetical information	7. Pat Jones, our coach, led the team.
8. to separate the speaker from a quotation	8. John said, "I'm leaving."

Rules for using additional punctuation marks.   **FIGURE** 7.22

Rules	Examples
1. Use a *question mark* after a sentence that asks a question.	1. What is the capital of Virginia?
2. Use an *exclamation point* after a sentence that expresses strong feeling.	2. Help! My desk is on fire!
3. Use an *apostrophe* to . . .	3.
A. indicate a contraction	A. cannot = can't
B. show possession	B. Mary's dress is lovely.
4. Use *quotation marks* . . .	4.
A. to set off a direct quotation	A. Henry said, "Leave here at once!"
B. for titles of articles	B. "The Day I Left Here"
C. for poem titles	C. "Casey at the Bat"
D. for song titles	D. "The Star-Spangled Banner"
5. Use a *colon* . . .	5.
A. to indicate a following explanation or listing	A. They brought the following items to camp: sleeping bag, toothbrushes, and clothes.
B. after the greeting in a business letter	B. To Whom It May Concern:
6. Use a *semicolon* to separate two closely-related independent clauses.	6. Harold made the highest grades in school; he expects to win a scholarship.
7. Use a *hyphen* to divide a word at the end of a line (but only at a syllable junction).	7. Katherine did not believe what the president had said.

FIGURE **7.23**   Rules for capitalization.

Capitalize . . .	Examples
1. the first word in a sentence	1. Our school play is tomorrow.
2. the names of people	2. Margaret and Susan are sisters.
3. the pronoun "I"	3. Do you think I should go to the party?
4. the names of streets, cities, and states	4. We live on Mulberry Road in Sacramento, California.
5. the names of days, months, and holidays	5. On Thursday, December 25, we will celebrate Christmas.
6. the names of rivers, countries, and continents	6. The Amazon River flows through Brazil in South America.
7. the names of languages and nationalities	7. The French, Spanish, and British signed the treaty.
8. the sections of a country	8. They live in the Southwest.

for which punctuation and capitalization have been omitted. Lead the class in correcting the sentence by reviewing the corresponding rules on the wall chart.

Also use examples from age-appropriate books to teach punctuation and capitalization. For example, in the informational picture book *So You Want to Be President* (St. George, 2000), the following passage demonstrates different ways of using capital letters: "Not all Presidents danced, but most had a sport. John Quincy Adams was a first-rate swimmer. Once when he was skinny-dipping in the Potomac River, a woman reporter snatched his clothes and sat on them until he gave her an interview" (p. 30). After writing this passage on the board, first ask the students to find all the capital letters in the passage. Then ask questions such as, "Why are *Not* and *Once* capitalized?" "What about *John Quincy Adams* and *Potomac River*?" The students discuss the passage and you encourage them to practice using capital letters in their writing.

A popular trade book dealing with punctuation in an effective and humorous way is Lynne Truss' (2003) *Eats, Shoots and Leaves: The Zero Tolerance Approach to Punctuation.*

TECHNOLOGY IN THE CLASSROOM

Computers and tablets can be a great help for students learning about the writing process. They can learn to type and use the word processor to produce clean-looking copies of their written work.

Websites that help students and teachers alike with handwriting, spelling, grammar, punctuation, and other writing tools include the following:

http://grammar.ccc.commnet.edu/grammar/ Capital Community College of Hartford, Connecticut, maintains this site, which provides helpful information for grammar and writing.

www.funbrain.com/grammar/ This fun site has beginner and advanced levels and asks students to identify parts of speech.

www.eleaston.com/writing.html This site provides information on citations, grammar, handwriting, punctuation, spelling, and vocabulary.

www.funbrain.com/funbrain/spell This is a good site to improve your spelling and includes many fun spelling games for students of all ages and grades.

www.grammarnow.com This is a great site where you can e-mail questions about grammar problems, composition issues, proofreading, and editing.

www.discoveryeducation.com/free-puzzlemaker/ This site permits you to create mazes, word searches, and crosswords for any type of lesson.

www.readingrockets.org Reading Rockets is a national organization to help launch young readers. The site includes many helpful ideas on teaching spelling and handwriting. It is a service of public television station WETA in Washington, DC.

www.spellitright.talktalk.net/ Spelling It Right helps you to gain confidence in your spelling.

www.spellingbee.com This is the home page for the Scripps Howard National Spelling Bee. You may wish to enroll your school, if it is not already enrolled.

> Most of us speak or write conventionally without being able to specify the rules.
>
> **FRANK SMITH**

SUMMARY

Effective writers communicate clearly with their readers. This requires knowing and using the rules of writing effectively. During the editing phase of the writing process students learn to proofread and correct their errors in spelling, capitalization, punctuation, and grammar.

The mechanics of writing can also be taught through direct instruction. In the early grades specific lessons on handwriting and basic sentence formation are appropriate. Recognizing the developmental stages of spelling means knowing that kindergarten and grade 1, 2, and 3 students use invented spelling and incorrect spelling while they learn about the phonetic, syntactic, and morphological roots of our spelling system. More accurate spelling comes naturally with age for most students.

Tie grammar instruction regarding parts of speech, capitalization, and punctuation to extensive writing activities and reading real literature. Keep isolated workbook exercises to a minimum.

field AND practicum ACTIVITIES

1. SPELLING RELAY. Divide students into small groups and have them collaboratively spell words. One student begins by naming a letter. Each student adds a letter with the goal of spelling a real word. As each student adds a letter, the word that the next student is thinking of may change. Students keep going until one student either is stuck or can only add a letter that will complete the word.

2. SENTENCE RELAY. Play this game in the same way as spelling relay, except have each person in the group add a word. The object is to build as long a sentence as possible. The game ends when a student gives a word that makes a complete sentence.

3. CHAIN SPELLING. This spelling game begins with one student spelling any word. The next person in the group must think of and spell a word that begins with the last letter of the word spelled by the first person. The game continues until someone cannot think of a word beginning with the last letter of the previously mentioned word.

4. JUMBLED SENTENCES. Select headlines or lead sentences from newspaper articles. Cut up the sentences into separate words. Give the separate words to a group of students to unscramble. Depending on which aspect of grammar or punctuation you want to emphasize, the jumbled sentence or headline could contain descriptive adjectives, prepositional phrases, semicolons, and so on.

5. CROSSWORD PUZZLES. Share some crossword puzzle examples with your class. Describe how they work, with words running across and down, using definitions as clues. Have students work in small groups to create their own crossword puzzles using the week's spelling words or words from a book they are reading.

6. TOUCH CENTER. Create a learning center around tactile activities for reinforcing handwriting and spelling. Use sand trays, shaving cream, glue and macaroni, strings, and clay. Young students can create the letters of the alphabet, while older students can practice writing difficult spelling words.

7. PUNCTUATE THIS! Ask students to copy one paragraph from a book they are reading independently but to omit the punctuation marks and capital letters. Have students exchange paragraphs, add the correct punctuation and capital letters, then exchange them again to correct them. They can use the book to check their work.

8. LABELS, LABELS. To help students practice their handwriting skills with a functional purpose, take a class "trip" around your room and identify all the things that need labels. For example, students can label their desks and lockers, various learning centers, supply closets, bulletin boards, and special file cabinets.

9. SPELLING PATTERNS. Teach students some simple English spelling patterns. Then have them look through their reading books for example words to fit the patterns. How many words of the same patterns can they find? Examples: C–V–C (*cat, hat, bad, sad, pig, dog, wig*); C–V–C+E (*save, game, bike, like, tone, dove, bone*); C–V–V–C (*rain, leaf, coat, need*).

10. CIRCUS SPELLING. Pretend that students are attending a circus. For each ride they want to go on, they have to get a ticket. To get a ticket, they have to spell the three words that you read from the ticket. See who can collect the most tickets. Example words: *clown, popcorn, roller coaster.* Some variations on this activity can be county fair, sports events, or travel agents.

11. CLASS NEWSLETTERS. Let students assume responsibility for writing a weekly or monthly newsletter to send home to caregivers or post on your class website. The newsletter can summarize classroom progress in various topics and highlight special events. Students may even want to compose the newsletter on the computer, either in Microsoft Word or by using specialized software such as *The Newsroom*.

Listening and Speaking

After reading this chapter, you should be able to accomplish the following objectives:

1. Discuss the different types of listening.
2. Describe effective strategies to help develop students' listening skills.
3. Explain how teachers can help students develop their speaking skills.
4. Discuss some strategies to help develop students' vocabulary.

INTRODUCTION

Too often teachers assume that students enter the classroom with well-developed listening and speaking skills. Failing to recognize this assumption means they will miss an important opportunity to develop these skills in their students and thus prepare them for college and/or their career. This chapter discusses the importance of good conversation and presentation skills, which involve learning how to listen and speak effectively. The Common Core State Standards referenced in this chapter serve as a benchmark for teaching the listening and speaking skills students need for academic conversation and formal presentations. Vocabulary development, as a natural outgrowth of listening and speaking, is also discussed in this chapter. We provide specific teaching strategies and activities for both listening and speaking, and minilesson ideas for vocabulary building.

DEVELOPING LISTENING SKILLS

We begin with listening because it is the first language skill infants "develop in their thirst to understand their world" (McPherson, 2008, p. 73). The child begins to understand language before he or she can speak it. Thus, listening is really the starting point for all other communication skills, including reading and writing.

Listening Defined

Most people tend to take listening for granted because it is something everyone does unconsciously. Yet despite its universal nature, it is often misunderstood. For example, many teachers assume that a child who hears well is a good listener and therefore does not require instruction in listening. This assumption is false, because hearing and listening are not the same. Hearing is a physical act that involves the reception of sound waves through minute vibrations in the outer, middle, and inner portions of the ear; it is a passive act (Petress, 2000). *Listening*, on the other hand, is a mental process; it is "the awareness of, the tending to, the organization of, and the operationalization of data entering our nervous system via our hearing mechanism" (Petress, 2000, p. 26).

Let us examine the definition of listening in a bit more detail. As a mental process, it depends more on the brain than the ear. Because a listener is a seeker of knowledge, he actively engages his brain to assimilate and accommodate new information and then makes inferences about it (Haroutunian-Gordon, 2011). How many times do students sit through an hour-long lecture without remembering a thing? In such cases, they were likely hearing but not listening.

It is far easier to start something than to finish it.

AMELIA EARHART

Background Information on Listening

Oral language is seldom taught in schools because the emphasis is on developing reading comprehension and writing skills. However, effective communication, which includes listening and speaking, is the number one skill most listed by employers (Zwiers & Crawford, 2011). The Council of Chief State School Officers and the National Governors Association Center for Best Practices recognized the importance of listening and speaking skills when they wrote the CCSS. They understood the demand for strong listening skills for success in college and in the workplace. The CCSS CCRA Anchor standards for speaking and listening include the following (NGACBP & CCSSO, 2010, p. 22):

- "Prepare for and participate effectively in a range of conversations and collaborations with diverse partners, building on others' ideas and expressing their own clearly and persuasively." (CCRA.SL.1)
- "Integrate and evaluate information presented in diverse media and formats, including visually, quantitatively, and orally." (CCRA.SL.2)
- "Evaluate a speaker's point of view, reasoning, and use of evidence and rhetoric." (CCRA.SL.3)

Listening as Process

Many researchers have described the process by which sound is received by the ear and converted into meaningful information by the brain (Jalongo, 2000). Freshour and Bartholomew (1989) reviewed studies on listening and identified the following six steps in the listening process: receiving, attending, understanding, analyzing, evaluating, and reacting/responding.

1. Receiving. The listening process begins when a person receives sounds from the environment. This is the act of hearing. Picture a group of first graders listening to the teacher read Beatrix Potter's classic *The Tale of Peter Rabbit.* In addition to receiving the words of the story, they also receive other sounds from the environment, such as a car horn beeping, a classroom door banging, students laughing in the hallway, and chairs scraping the floor.

2. Attending. As the story of Peter Rabbit continues, the students begin to pick up on certain details, such as the names of the other rabbits and the description of the farmer's garden. The students now choose to attend to their teacher's voice from the many sounds in their environment. But from time to time, they become distracted by other sounds. Attending is an ongoing process that must be evaluated by the teacher periodically. Eventually, however, attending means the students learn to self-monitor and pay careful attention to the task at hand.

3. Understanding. The purpose of listening is to understand the message. The listeners should be forming mental images of the activities of the little rabbits, Mr. McGregor's garden, and Peter's escape in their minds. The words are transformed into thought. Understanding occurs gradually as the brain receives more and more information. As understanding increases, it becomes easier for the listener to focus and block out extraneous noises. But attention does continue to wander, even in older students, which is why people must continually monitor their listening if they want to understand. Understanding requires self-discipline.

4. Analyzing. Meaningful listening requires thinking. Analysis involves raising questions about the validity of the information received. The first graders are familiar with Peter Rabbit; they know what happens next and are already predicting the sequence in their minds. If their teacher changes a scene or misreads a sentence, they will recognize it because the alteration does not fit their analysis and expectations.

5. Evaluating. The teacher is communicating a message; in this case, a particular story. The student listeners either accept or reject that message. If they are interested in the story and focus on it without becoming distracted, they can evaluate the characters' actions and either cheer for Peter's escape or question his actions. Evaluative understanding demands concentrated involvement.

6. Responding. True understanding only comes when the listener reacts or responds to the message in some way. Emotional response, such as clapping at the end of a happy story or booing the entrance of a villain (such as the Big Bad Wolf in *Little Red Riding Hood*), is one type of reaction. Discussing a story after hearing it is another. Engaging in a follow-up activity, such as writing a sequel or drawing a picture of Peter Rabbit, is another way students can respond to what they have heard. Reacting can also include a physical activity, such as role-playing the story. In each of these cases, the students must be able to recall the details of the story; thus, memory becomes a crucial part of the listening process.

Creating a Positive Environment for Listening

Teachers want their students to be active, responsive listeners but are often unsure how to accomplish this objective. You can begin by creating an *emotional environment,* or a positive climate, in which students are comfortable exercising their listening skills and understand the purpose for doing so. The classroom vignette on the facing page illustrates how one teacher changed her approach to listening.

The teacher in this scenario is engaging in reflective teaching and has thought about her performance in the classroom. She has analyzed the issue and even asked a colleague for help. She has formulated a plan to self-monitor her own teaching behavior, and in doing so she has begun to model the practices of a good listener for her students.

Types of Listening

Students use different types of listening for a variety of purposes and situations. Try to identify the different kinds of listening activities that go on during the school day. When you can categorize them, you can better integrate listening instruction within the curriculum. Listening can be categorized as straight-line listening and transactional listening. In *straight-line listening,* the listener receives information from a text, video, lecture, billboard, or any type of media in which the listener is a consumer. The listener makes inferences as a consumer, formulating appropriate responses, and even attempting to formulate reasons for his response (Haroutunian-Gordon, 2011). *Transactional listening* involves a conversation in which two or more people try to attain mutual understanding (Waks, 2011). In transactional

Linda Paul has been teaching in the same school for five years, the last three years in second grade. Her students like her, her colleagues respect her, and she receives favorable ratings from her principal. But Linda is dissatisfied with her performance. Too often she becomes frustrated and disappointed.

"Something is wrong with my teaching," she tells a colleague one day over coffee in the teachers' lounge. "But I can't put my finger on the problem. Maybe I'm just burned out after five years."

"I think you're being too hard on yourself. But if you like, I'll observe in your class this week. I've got a break period on Wednesday afternoon."

Wednesday arrives. Linda is a bit nervous, but she soon forgets about her colleague sitting quietly in the back of the room. The lesson goes well; Linda introduces a story and then reads part of it aloud to the class. The class briefly discusses the story, and then Linda gets the students started on follow-up activities. She feels that the lesson was a success. After school, she catches up with her friend.

"Linda, that was a great lesson," says the colleague, "but I think I know what the problem is that you couldn't quite identify."

"And?"

"Well, it's just that you don't seem to listen to the kids."

"What?"

"You talk to them, you direct them, you guide them, but you rarely listen to what they have to say. Or you listen for a moment and then cut them off because you have to do something else."

"Maybe you're right. What gets me most frustrated is when I'm reading or speaking and the students don't listen to me. Perhaps I haven't set a good example. You've really given me something to think about."

Linda is actually more upset than she appears. She tells her husband what happened, and they talk late into the evening. Later, Linda is unable to sleep so she fixes herself some hot cocoa and ponders the issue of listening. Within an hour she creates a self-checking listening list, shown in Figure 8.1.

Linda's listening list. **FIGURE 8.1**

	Yes	No
Did I listen to my students today?	☐	☐
Did I interrupt student talk?	☐	☐
Did I dominate class discussions?	☐	☐
Do I look at the students when they speak?	☐	☐
Do I listen to all students, those with special needs and others?	☐	☐
Do I remember what they've told me?	☐	☐
Do I think about (reflect on) what the students say?	☐	☐
Do I turn my body to the student who's speaking?	☐	☐
Do I show by my facial expression that I am listening?	☐	☐

read RESEARCH practice

Using Linda's listening list from Figure 8.1, observe a classroom teacher's listening behaviors. Add other listening behaviors as you see them. Does the teacher create a good climate for listening? If so, how? Do the teacher's listening behaviors carry over to the students' listening behaviors?

listening the parties negotiate this understanding as the roles of listener and speaker switch back and forth between them (Zwiers, 2011). The CCSS refer to this type of interaction as "collaborative discussion" in the first Speaking and Listening anchor standard (NGACBP & CCSSO, 2010, p. 23).

These two types of listening can be further broken down into subcategories. Miller (2000) classified listening into five categories. The first three categories are straight-line listening, while the last two are transactional listening or collaborative discussion. See Figure 8.2.

Integrating Listening into the Curriculum

Some educators are divided over whether or not listening should be taught as a separate skills lesson or as part of integrated content lessons. We believe that listening should be an integral part of content area instruction and should always be related to speaking, reading, and writing. This does not exclude direct instruction in listening skills but places such instruction in proper perspective: Listening is always done for a purpose, not just for the sake of listening. A good listening program is integrated throughout the curriculum, and understanding the relationships between listening and reading, listening and speaking, and listening and writing is a good place to start.

Listening and reading

Recall that listening and reading are dual aspects of the receptive process, the way in which people receive information. The brain converts the data received through listening or reading into meaningful information. Thus, both listening and reading are active, cognitive processes because both require thinking to impart meaning to data.

Constructing meaning from sounds (listening) or print (reading) requires that the listener or reader be familiar with language. For example, not knowing the meaning of the term *parallelogram* severely disadvantages a geometry student who needs to solve word problems. An inability to remember larger units of meaning, such as phrases, sentences, and paragraphs (either orally or in writing), further

---

FIGURE 8.2   Types of listening and their subcategories.

STRAIGHT-LINE

1. *Discriminative listening* is listening in order to differentiate sounds in the environment from the sounds of speech.
2. *Creative listening* stimulates the listener's emotions and imagination.
3. *Appreciative listening* is listening for pleasure. It may be listening to music, the rhyme and rhythm in poems, or the humor or suspense in a story.

TRANSACTIONAL/COLLABORATIVE

4. *Purposeful listening* is when the listener attends to information and directions given by the speaker and then responds to the information.
5. *Critical listening* involves the listener's ability to understand the information presented by the speaker, evaluate the information, and formulate opinions about it.

handicaps the student. Consider the following example: A student is confused by the sign *We are in support of striking Afghan hemp workers.* Does the sign's author support a group of people who are refusing to work, or does she favor physically assaulting them? If the confused student reading the sign cannot determine the context of the sentence, he will not be able to respond to it appropriately.

Teachers often remark that poor listening abilities often lead to problems in reading. For example, students who cannot comprehend a sentence that is read aloud to them will likely also fail to comprehend it when they read it themselves. Boodt (1984) even argued that students who are remedial readers are also remedial listeners, and that both issues need to be addressed in tandem.

Listening and speaking

The most obvious way in which listening and speaking are related is that they both share a *common code.* The listener hears the sounds spoken by the speaker and converts the sounds into meaningful units of speech in order to comprehend what the speaker said. Occasionally, students may mishear similar-sounding words, such as *cup* and *cut* or *pen* and *pin.* The latter example may also be a matter of dialect, because some dialects consider *pen* and *pin* to be homonyms. Speakers of nonstandard English who omit the final consonant sounds /t/, /d/, /r/, and /l/ may further confuse the listener by pronouncing the words *fat, fad, far,* and *fall* all like "fa." The ability to hear fine distinctions among similar but not identical words is known as *auditory discrimination* and is often taught as a readiness skill in kindergarten and the primary grades.

Most students develop a listening/speaking vocabulary that exceeds their reading/writing vocabulary. This is natural. Students hear and use words and expressions that they may not recognize easily when they read or be able to recall when they write. The common vocabulary of listening and speaking must later be transferred to the realm of print.

Listening and writing

Listening is part of the receptive process; writing is part of the productive process. Thus, at first glance, it appears that the two are not closely related. But listening and writing are associated and actually support one another. For example, young writers often have difficulty recalling ideas and words they wish to use in writing. They may turn to *internal listening,* a process similar to speaking to themselves, to stimulate thought and memory. Some students even mouth the words they hear inside their heads before putting them down on paper. Even adults often listen to an inner voice, especially when trying to write or read a particularly difficult passage. Finally, professional writers often read their own writing aloud to make sure it sounds how they imagine it.

Teacher Questioning for Listening Development

The primary way to teach listening comprehension skills is through questioning. Asking questions after students listen to a recording or hear a passage read to them is a traditional practice. However, merely asking questions does not mean that listening or learning is taking place. In fact, questioning students often resembles assessment. In order to make questioning part of the instructional process and not just another means of evaluation, you need to know about the different kinds of questions. Questions can be classified in various ways, most of them derived from Bloom's taxonomies, discussed in Chapter 3. But questioning lists, like skill lists, can become lengthy and burdensome. The following hierarchy is intentionally short and simple. It contains four different types of questions: literal, inferential, evaluative, and applied.

Literal question

This type of question calls for a response found directly in the material heard or read. This is also called *on-the-line reading* because the answer is in the book. Taffy Raphael (1982) called this type the *right there question* because the answer is "right there" in the book. Probably because it is the easiest type of question to ask and answer, most teachers tend to overuse it. Basal reader teacher's manuals are heavily weighted with questions regarding information directly stated in the text.

Inferential question

These are questions whose answers must be inferred from the information given in a story or lecture. The answer is not stated directly; instead, it must be discovered by examining the literal information. Raphael (1982) called this *think and search*. Inferential questions are considered more difficult than literal questions because they require the student to analyze information. Often, teachers expect students to respond to questions immediately; Gambrell (1983) found that teachers wait about one second for a student to respond. Giving them an extra few moments to gather their thoughts usually results in a more thoughtful response, especially in the case of inferential questions. This is known as *wait time* or *think time*. Train yourself to give students this extra time and avoid the tendency to call on another student if the first student does not respond quickly enough. Research has also shown that most teachers allow less wait time for students who are remedial than for students who are brighter (Bromley, 1988); being conscious of this effect will hopefully prevent you from succumbing to it.

Evaluative question

This type of question calls for the student to make a judgment about what she heard or read. It is not enough to know what happened in a story or even why it happened. Now the student must also assess the significance of the material in light of her own life experience. Raphael (1982) called this *on my own*. For instance, a character in a story borrows a friend's bicycle in an emergency without asking permission. It is easy to tell what the character did and why he or she did it, but was this action justifiable under the circumstances? Each student must judge this individually by evaluating the information, applying previous knowledge about related situations, and supporting his or her answer.

Applied question

These questions require the student to apply information he heard or read to a totally different situation. In most taxonomies, the applied level is the highest level. Students must first remember facts and then infer additional details and make judgments. Finally, they must recall personal experiences and connect them to what they have heard or read. Raphael called these *writer and me questions*. For example, after a month-long social studies unit on early explorers and discoverers, a fifth-grade teacher asks his students to write an essay exploring the similarities and differences between exploration and discovery in the 15th and 16th centuries and space exploration in the 20th century. This final step, making the cognitive connection between two separate experiences, is what makes the applied question so difficult for many students.

Asking questions at all these levels is a key part of any teacher's repertoire. In addition, encourage students to ask questions to you and their peers. An activity that involves an exchange of questions between teacher and students over common material is known as *reciprocal questioning*.

Teaching Listening

You may find it beneficial to examine the three CCSS for listening as you make your lesson plans. The CCSS Anchor standards for listening focus on (1) students listening to classmates during discussions and conversations (CCRA.SL.1); (2) students listening to diverse media (CCRA.SL.2); and (3) students listening to evaluate a speaker's point of view, reasoning, and evidence (CCRA.SL.3; NGACBP & CCSSO, 2010).

Two strategies that support CCRA.SL.1 and SL.3 and were found to be effective by Swain, Friehe, and Harrington (2004), who developed them into posters, are the Give Me 5 and the TALS strategies. Give Me 5 highlights that listening involves the entire body and all of the senses (see Figure 8.3).

Swain and colleagues suggest that the teacher explain the poster, model the correct listening posture, and refer to it often during the first weeks of school so that the listening posture becomes a part of the classroom procedures. During the year, if any student needs to be reminded to listen, you can merely point to the poster without interrupting the lesson.

The second strategy suggested by Swain et al. focuses on the brain's role in listening. TALS can also be made into an attractive and useful poster (see Figure 8.4). This poster features the outline of a person's face with the acrostic TALS. The T stands for *think*. When listening to a lecture, podcast, or DVD, students are encouraged to listen for the most important ideas. The A stands for *ask*. Students

Sample poster for Give Me Five.   **FIGURE** **8.3**

FIGURE **8.4** Sample poster for TALS.

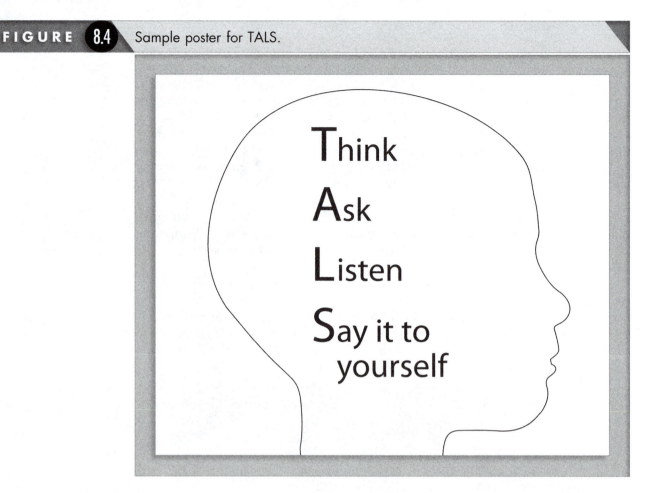

are to ask why the main points are important to remember. The L stands for *listen*. Students are instructed to listen for the interrelatedness and details of the main points. The S stands for *say it to yourself*. Once the students have heard the entire passage, they should repeat the main points to themselves and then whisper them to a neighbor to reinforce them in their minds. These two particular strategies can be used in all grades. Even middle-school students need to be reminded that listening takes effort and that it is a mental activity.

Before considering specific teaching activities related to listening, keep in mind these general guidelines:

1. Model good listening habits yourself: Listen to your students; maintain eye contact with the speaker; nod and use facial expressions to indicate you understand what the student is saying.

2. Get everyone's attention before you start speaking. Stop speaking if students are not attentive.

3. Try not to repeat a student's response in class. Instead, encourage students to listen to each other and to paraphrase what others have said.

4. During lengthy listening periods, encourage students to take notes to help them remember things.

5. Understand how the physical arrangement of your room affects listening comprehension. Are chairs arranged so students can speak face-to-face, or do they have to turn around to see the speaker?

6. Minimize noisy distractions in and around your classroom—from the hallway, from the adjacent rooms, from the heater or air conditioner, from the printer, etc.

7. Analyze your own talking. Do you speak so rapidly that English learners have a difficult time understanding you? Do you speak in a monotone voice that lulls students to sleep? Do you speak so loudly that it hurts students' ears?

8. Be aware of your dialect. Do you speak with an accent that might not be familiar to some students? Do you use slang terms that people from other cultures or parts of the country may not understand?

T E A C H I N G ACTIVITIES (8)

LISTENING

Listening lessons can be taught with a variety of materials and through a variety of activities.

1 Line-up activities

Throughout the day students need to line up quietly to go to music, gym, art, and lunch. Here are a few fun activities to put the time to good use by developing listening skills. Simon Says is a favorite game that helps students to focus and listen. They need to process not only what they are asked to do, but to listen for the words *Simon says*. The Largest and Smallest (Elkeles, 2002) is best for small groups but can be used with large groups. The teacher lists several objects (e.g., coat, pencil, house, palace) and students classify them from smallest to largest (e.g., pencil, coat, house, and palace). *Recommended for primary grades.*

2 Singing songs and finger plays

Listening to songs and inviting students to sing along is one strategy to improve young students' listening skills. To maximize this process listen to the songs without showing the lyrics. Many songs for children feature repetition, so they are easy to learn. Play the song one or two times and then invite students to sing along. One song that is particularly good for developing young people's listening ability is "Little Peter Rabbit Had a Fly upon His Ear" (Beall & Nipp, 1979) because each verse skips a word. Students must listen carefully to follow along. The song goes like this:

> *Verse 1:* "Little Peter Rabbit had a fly upon his ear." (Repeat two times.)
> "And he flicked it 'til it flew away."
>
> *Verse 2:* "Little Peter (rest) had a fly upon his ear." (Repeat two times.)
> "And he flicked it 'til it flew away."
>
> *Verse 3:* "Little Peter (rest) had a (rest) upon his ear." (Repeat two times.)
> "And he flicked it 'til it flew away."
>
> *Verse 4:* "Little Peter (rest) had a (rest) upon his (rest)." (Repeat two times.)
> "And he flicked it 'til it flew away." (Beall & Nipp, 1979, p. 20)

You can find many songs from musicals and movies on YouTube. Good songs to sing with student are those from *Mary Poppins, The Little Mermaid, Beauty and the Beast, The Lion King,* and *Frozen. Recommended for primary grades.*

3 Visualizing the character

With so many forms of multimedia entertainment available these days, not to mention delightful picture books, young students do not have many opportunities to visualize settings, characters, and the action of a story until they begin reading chapter books. You can have students practice visualizing stories by using a read-along audiobook without the print version. After listening to the story, invite students to draw one of the characters. Staple a lined piece of paper to each student's drawing and have them write a description of the character. This activity for kindergarteners supports CCSS SL.K.2, which indicates that students should be able to "confirm understanding of a text read aloud or information presented orally or through other media by asking and answering questions about key details and requesting clarification if something is not understood" (NGACBP & CCSSO, 2010, p. 23). *Recommended for primary grades.*

4 Windsocks

This activity encourages students to visualize a story without having seen any accompanying illustrations. Invite the students to create a windsock (see Figure 8.5) by drawing a scene or character from the story on the top of the windsock and providing the basic elements of the story on the four streamers. On the first streamer students write the title, author, and illustrator; on the second streamer they list the main characters; on the third streamer they give the setting; and on the fourth streamer they provide a short synopsis of the plot or a sequence of events. The American Library Association presents the annual Odyssey Award for the best children's and young adult audiobooks (www.ala.org/alsc/awardsgrants/bookmedia/odysseyaward), which may help you find good titles. This activity supports CCSS SL.2.2: "Recount or describe key ideas or details from a text read aloud or information presented orally or through other media" (NGACBP & CCSSO, 2010, p. 23). *Recommended for primary grades.*

5 Listen and discuss an ending to the story

Record a story, for example, *The Empty Pot* by Demi (1996) or *The Pumpkin Man from Piney Creek* by Darleen Bailey Beard (1995), and stop at the climax. After students have listened to the recording without seeing any pictures, pair students up and ask each pair to discuss a possible conclusion. After they have had time to discuss and agree upon a conclusion, have them share their ending with the class. Later, you can read the ending to the original story. This activity supports CCSS SL.1.1: "Participate in collaborative conversations with diverse partners about grade

---

FIGURE 8.5   Windsock template.

Title/Author	Characters	Setting	Plot

1 topics and texts with peers and adults in small and larger groups" (NGACBP & CCSSO, 2010, p. 23). *Recommended for primary grades.*

6 Listen and sequence the story

Record *The Umbrella* (2004) or *The Mitten* (1999) by Jan Brett. Have students arrange pictures of the story's animals (available on Brett's website) in the order in which they appeared in the story.

7 Pantomime

Pantomime is an effective way to introduce primary grade students to drama. Pantomime requires no speaking but requires students to use their imagination and listening skills, provided you lead them in a directed pantomime. The next classroom vignette demonstrates four different ways to use pantomime to build listening skills. This activity also supports CCSS grade-level speaking and listening standards that expect students to recall details in a text (NGACBP & CCSSO, 2010). *Recommended for primary grades.*

8 Whose voice am I?

For this activity, collect photographs of various school personnel such as the principal, administrative assistants, cafeteria workers, librarian, physical education teacher, music teacher, computer teacher, art teacher, and custodians. Then ask each of these people to record a short poem on an MP3 player, smartphone, or tablet. Encourage each reader to be as expressive as possible. Display the photographs on the chalkboard ledge and write the name of each person over his or her photograph. Have small groups of students listen to the recording and match the photograph with the voice. Encourage students to say why they think the voice is a particular person. Make sure all students to participate in the discussion as they reach their decision. This activity encourages collaborative discussions as required by the speaking and listening standards (NGACBP & CCSSO, 2010). *Recommended for intermediate grades.*

9 Poetry and music

This activity encourages students to listen for the mood of a poem and then create sound effects to augment it. Working in groups, have the students first construct musical instruments from household objects and experiment with the sounds they make. You can make instruments from plastic containers of various sizes or aluminum pie plates and fill them with different materials, such as rice, beans, or cereal. Different materials placed in different-size containers create different sounds. For example, salt in a small plastic container makes a swishing sound; lima beans in a large container makes a castanet sound. Students can also crumple plastic bags, aluminum foil, and wax paper to create different sounds.

As a warm-up activity, instruct each group to experiment with the materials by having them create specific sounds, for example,

thunder	galloping horses
wind	snake
running water	airplane

Allow the class to vote on which group had the best imitation of the sound, and then have those students explain how they created the sound.

After the groups have spent time experimenting with their instruments, give each group a short poem that includes onomatopoeia and instruct them to use

TEACHER 1: MRS. CHANG

As part of a language arts unit on drama, Mrs. Chang has explained and demonstrated the notion of free movement to music. The desks and tables have been moved to create an open space in the center of the room. "When I start the tape," says Mrs. Chang, "I want you to move about the room using your arms, legs, and bodies to show how the music makes you feel." The tape begins with some slow classical music selections, moves into lively folk-dance tunes, and ends with some somber march music.

TEACHER 2: MRS. BIRDSONG

"Good morning, boys and girls," says Mrs. Birdsong. "Let's begin this beautiful day by singing our 'Good Morning Song.'" As they sing together, they move their arms and bodies to imitate the little bird in the song.

Way up in the sky *(stretch way up on your tiptoes)*

The little birds fly *(move your hands like you're flying)*

While down in the nest *(crouch down on the ground)*

The little birds rest. *(fold your head in your arms)*

With a wing on the left *(raise your left elbow)*

And a wing on the right *(raise your right elbow)*

The little birds sleep all through the night. *(rest your head)*

The bright sun comes up *(look up with your eyes wide open)*

The dew falls away *(flutter your fingers)*

"Good morning, good morning," *(raise your arms to the sun)*

The little birds say. *(turn to your partner and shake his or her hand)*

TEACHER 3: MR. JOHNSON

"Let's form a big circle and get real quiet," says Mr. Johnson. "Close your eyes. Listen carefully and you can hear it begin- ning to rain." He rubs his hands together gently and the students imitate him. They rub harder. Then the teacher begins to snap his fingers—first one hand, then the other. The students do the same (it's raining harder now). The teacher slaps his legs. The students slap their legs, faster and faster (the rain is coming down very hard now). They stomp their feet (you can hear the thunder). Then the movements are repeated in reverse order as the rain gradually slows down and finally stops.

TEACHER 4: MS. ALIOTA

"Class, let's go on a bear hunt," says Ms. Aliota (she slaps her legs to imitate a walking sound). The students repeat her actions and chant, "Let's go on a bear hunt." As the teacher leads the hunt, the students repeat what she says and imitate her actions.

"I see a wheat field" (places her hand above her eyes and moves her head back and forth). "Can't go over it. Can't go under it. Let's go through it" (moves her arms through the field).

"I see a fence" (repeats looking gesture). "Can't go around it. Can't go under it. Let's go over it" (hands and arms climbing).

"I see a lake. Can't go over it. Can't go around it. Let's swim across it" (arms swimming).

"I see a tree. Can't go over it. Can't go under it. Let's climb up it" (wraps her arms around the tree and climbs, leg over leg; when she gets to the top of the tree, she looks for bears).

"I see a cave. Can't go over it. Can't go under it. Let's go in" (tiptoes in slowly). "I see two eyes" (touches her eyes). "I see two ears" (touches her ears). "I see a nose" (touches her nose). "I see a mouth" (touches her mouth). *"It's a bear! Run for it!"* (She repeats the actions in reverse order very quickly.)

their instruments to create background music for the poem. Have them perform the poem for the class by reading the poem and playing the background music. Figure 8.6 shows a poem that works well for this activity. Appendix D.15 includes an assessment rubric to use with this activity. Note the assessment covers the pro- cess and product. *Recommended for intermediate grades.*

"Musical" poem.   **FIGURE 8.6**

> "The Small Ghostie"
>
> When it's late and it's dark
> And everyone sleeps . . . shh shh shh,
> Into our kitchen
> A small ghostie creeps . . . shh shh shh.
>
> We hear knocking and raps
> And then rattles and taps,
>
> Then he clatters and clangs
> And he batters and bangs,
>
> And he whistles and yowls
> And he screeches and howls . . .
>
> So we pull up our covers over our heads
> And we block up our ears and WE STAY IN OUR BEDS.
>
> —*Barbara Ireson*

"The Small Ghostie" reprinted with permission of the author.

10   Listening and responding to a video

For this activity, you can use any video of an author or illustrator. Give each student a sheet of paper with the author's or illustrator's name at the top and the letters K, T, W, L, E (Know, Think I know, Want to learn, Learned, Evidence) running across the page (see Figure 8.7). It works best if you choose an author/illustrator who is somewhat unfamiliar to your class. Before you view the video, invite students to fill out the K column with any information they know about the author/illustrator, the T column with information they think they know, and the W column with

Sample K-T-W-L-E chart for viewing an author/illustrator video.   **FIGURE 8.7**

K-T-W-L-E CHART FOR AUTHOR/ILLUSTRATOR

KNOW	THINK I KNOW	WANT TO LEARN	LEARNED	EVIDENCE
He made up Arthur from the show on TV.	He wrote a lot of books about Arthur.	How does he make his drawings?	He makes drawings with watercolors. He puts his kids' names in each book.	The video showed him painting with watercolors. He showed us two books where he had hid his kids' names.

information they want to learn. After they have had ample time to fill out each column, instruct students to put away their papers and enjoy the video. Afterward, invite them to fill out the L column with everything they learned from the video, and write the evidence for these items in the E column. For example, as Figure 8.7 indicates, a video about author Marc Brown (produced by Trumpet Club Books), reveals that he hides his children's names in each book. The evidence is the fact that he showed two books where he hid their names. Students may also have learned that he uses watercolor to add color to his drawings. The evidence is that they saw him using watercolor to paint a picture. This activity supports grade-level speaking and listening standards that require students to recall details from diverse media presentations (NGACBP & CCSSO, 2010). *Recommended for intermediate grades.*

11   Creating a junk box

Students must learn how to follow verbal instructions, and this activity teaches just that. To the extent possible, students should be seated so that they cannot copy off their neighbor—encourage them to work on their own. Give each student one piece of construction paper and tell them to listen carefully because there are no printed instructions. Read aloud the directions on how to make a junk box. Give ample time between steps so students can complete the folds. Figure 8.8 contains the instructions you will read. This is a fun activity to do during those rainy days when the class has indoor recess.

Two books of origami with easy-to-follow instructions are *Origami Magic* by Florence Temko (1993), published by Scholastic, and *50 Nifty Origami Crafts* by Andrea Urton (1992), published by Lowell House Juvenile. *Recommended for intermediate grades.*

FIGURE 8.8   Directions for making a junk box.

Each student needs one piece of 8½″ x 11″ construction paper. Read each direction once and pause long enough for the students to complete the folds:

1. Fold paper in half the long way.

2. Unfold.

3. Fold the two long edges to the crease you just made.

4. Unfold.

5. Fold the paper in half the short way.

6. Unfold.

7. Fold the two short edges to the middle.

8. Do not unfold.

9. Look at your paper and see whether the two raw edges are in the middle. Three creases go across. Fold in each of the four corners, to line up with the first crease that goes across—not all the way to the middle.

10. The strips of paper in the middle of the paper will not be covered by the corners. Fold the two strips of paper back to hold down the four corners.

11. Put your hands behind the strips in the center of the paper. Gently pull your hands away from each other. Your junk box is now complete.

12 Listen and create a cartoon

Read Tomie dePaola's *Days of the Blackbird* (1997) to the class. Afterward, invite the students to create their own cartoon using pictures and dialogue bubbles to depict the main scenes of the story. *Recommended for intermediate grades.*

13 Listen and compare

Read two versions of any fairy tale (e.g., *Pretty Salma: A Little Red Riding Hood Story from Africa* (Daly, 2006) and *Lon Po Po: A Red-Riding Hood Story from China* (Young, 1989) to students without showing them the pictures. After the reading, pair up students and give them the graphic organizer in Figure 8.9, which requires students to compare and contrast the two versions. Have students discuss the two stories and agree upon each of the items they write in the graphic organizer. *Recommended for intermediate grades.*

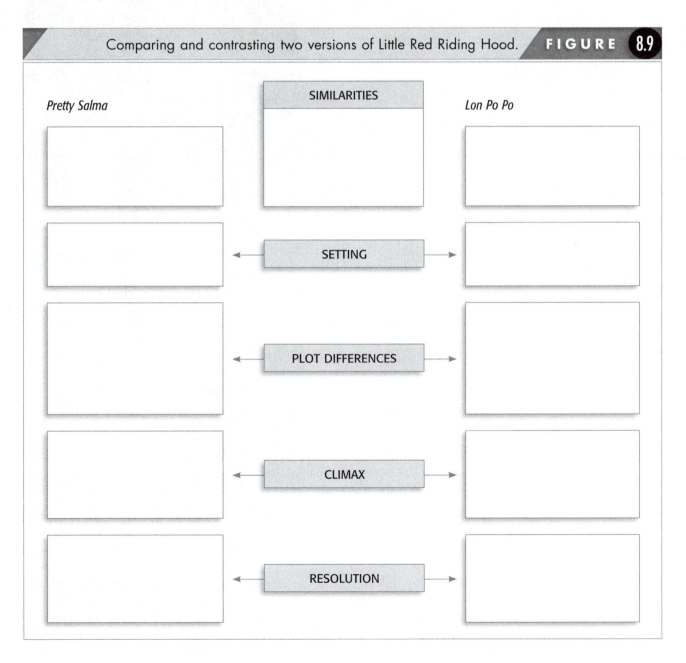

Comparing and contrasting two versions of Little Red Riding Hood. **FIGURE 8.9**

Mrs. Lopez posts a large map of Canada at the front of her room (*concept building*). Over several days her class studies the map and brainstorms what they know about Canada. The students make lists of cities and discover that Canada is divided into provinces instead of states. They also list geographic features such as mountains, rivers, and bays. They watch a film about animal life in Canada. Then Mrs. Lopez reads aloud from E. B. White's *The Trumpet of the Swan* *(reading).* The story begins with young Sam Beaver and his father on a camping trip in the woods of Canada. One day Sam discovers a secret pond hidden beyond the swamp, where a pair of swans has made their nest. The next day Mrs. Lopez picks up the story again (*purpose setting*). "Listen carefully as I read more about Sam Beaver," she says. "You might learn some interesting facts about birds." She reads, "In the spring of the year, nest-building is uppermost in a bird's mind: it is the most important thing there is. If she picks a good place, she stands a good chance of hatching her eggs and rearing her young. If she picks a poor place, she may fail to raise a family. The female swan knew this; she knew the decision she was making was extremely important."

Questioning: Mrs. Lopez periodically pauses to ask the students a question to keep their attention focused: "What season of the year is it?" (literal). "Why do you think birds and other animals give birth in the spring?" (inferential). "Do you think that Sam is doing the right thing by spying on the swans while they build their nest?" (evaluative). "What other things do you think Sam might do on his camping trip? Think of trips you've taken with your family" (applied). "What do you think a *marsh* is?" (vocabulary).

Mrs. Lopez continues reading and the students continue listening. Afterward, the students get into small groups and begin talking about and writing down the facts they have learned. They have dictionaries and other science and social studies reference books at hand. Some groups decide to illustrate what they have heard. Other students consult the map of Canada to find the exact location that E. B. White may have used for this story.

14 Listen and learn from books

This activity is similar to the K-T-W-L-E discussed earlier; however, this is intended for grade 5 because it is more difficult for students to learn from informational text without pictures than it is to learn from a video. This activity supports CCSS SL.5.2: "Summarize a written text read aloud or information presented in diverse media and formats, including visually, quantitatively, and orally" (NGACBP & CCSSO, 2010, p. 24).

Carnival by George Ancona (1999) describes the preparations and unique celebration of the people of Olinda, Brazil. Create a K-T-W-L-E chart and ask the students to put in the K column any information they know about the carnival celebration in Brazil, and in the T column anything they think they know. (They may not know any information, but that is fine.) Then ask to list all the things they want to learn about the carnival celebration in the W column. After students listen to a recording of the book, ask them to list all the things they learned about carnival in the L column and the evidence for each fact in the E column. *Recommended for intermediate grades.*

15 Structured listening activity

The structured listening activity is an example of the direct, systematic approach to listening recommended by Devine (1982), Pearson and Fielding (1982), and others. It includes concept building, purpose setting, reading or telling, questioning, and recitation (Choate & Rakes, 1987). The classroom vignette above exemplifies a structured listening activity. *Recommended for intermediate grades.*

16   Advertising

Students, like all of us, are bombarded by advertisements from all forms of media throughout the day. Advertisers use persuasion and other techniques to change viewers' minds, and readers need to understand these techniques. For this activity, record advertisements shown during children's television programs, those shown during sporting events, and campaign ads run during election season. Explain and give examples to students of the seven propaganda techniques listed in Figure 8.10, and then show them the advertisements you recorded. Have students discuss in small groups of three which techniques were used in each advertisement, which ones were persuasive, and why they were compelling. To assess a student's listening, use the scoring rubric in Appendix D.16. This activity supports CCSS SL.7.3: "Delineate a speaker's argument and specific claims, evaluating the soundness of the reason and the relevance and sufficiency of the evidence" (NGACBP & CCSSO, 2010, p. 49). *Recommended for middle grades.*

Examples of advertising propaganda techniques. FIGURE 8.10	
Name calling	The use of derogatory labels to denounce, put down, or condemn a person or product. The purpose is to make the listener or reader believe the negative image rather than evaluate the merits of the person or product.
Card stacking	Telling one side of the story or presenting only half-truths on an issue. The only information presented paints a favorable picture while omitting unfavorable points. For example, a TV commercial for a popular cereal talks about its vitamins and minerals to give you energy and strong bones. Omitted are the amounts of sugar, preservatives, and food coloring it contains, which weaken muscle tone and rot teeth.
Plain folks	Approach used by many politicians to curry favor and gain approval by portraying themselves as ordinary people; the "good old boy" approach. Such commercials often feature politicians with their shirtsleeves rolled up, wearing hardhats; picking crops; and, of course, kissing babies. One former president portrayed himself as an ordinary peanut farmer from Georgia; another had his picture taken chopping wood for the family fire.
Glittering generalities	The use of vague, general, but attractive expressions to paint a positive picture of a person or product without giving specific details or facts. For example, ficticious politician Joe Smith begins his speech by introducing his lovely wife, Beth (president of the ladies' club), and his handsome son, Tom (captain of the football team); he then proceeds to describe his own activities as a Boy Scout leader, church deacon, and so on. All this is impressive but may have little to do with the office for which he is running.
Testimonial	A direct endorsement by a well-known personality regarding the favorable characteristics of a product or an organization. Movie stars and athletes are used for this tactic because of their appeal to young people. The power of the testimonial lies not in what is being sold but in who is doing the selling; for example, a famous basketball player promoting a particular basketball shoe.
Transfer	Similar to testimonial technique but more subtle. An athlete or actor, usually attractive, is shown using a particular product. The product may have little connection to what the athlete or actor is famous for (e.g., Weird Al Yankovic, a comedian/musician, promoting Radio Shack).
Bandwagon	Approach that emphasizes going along with the crowd or being a part of the group; the herd mentality. The appeal is to sameness and conformity, through such expressions as "Everyone who's anyone . . ."

17   Listen and learn from speeches

Play one of the many famous speeches found on www.americanrhetoric.com. Tell students to listen closely to the main idea and the major sub-points but not to take any notes. Afterward have students identify the main idea and at least three sub-points. Have them write down the ideas first and then discuss them in small groups. This activity supports the CCSS grade-level speaking and listening standards that require students to identify and evaluate the claims in a speaker's argument (NGACBP & CCSSO, 2010). *Recommended for middle grades.*

18   Listen and add to the story (Cooper & Morreale, 2003)

Select a story starter from the ones listed below or create your own and have students sit in a circle. Using a multicolored ball of yarn, students add details to the story while slowly unwinding the yarn until each storyteller reaches a new color of yarn. The student then passes the ball to the student on his left, and that student repeats the process. Remind the students that the story must be logical. Possible story starters include:

■ Once upon a time Jeremy Bull Frog, with a football tucked under his arm, went skipping down to the riverbank, looking for some friends who wanted to play football with him.

■ Long, long ago in a far distant land lived an old man with a generous heart.

■ The subway train rumbled through the long, dark tunnel, while detective George lay asleep in the backseat.

Recommended for middle grades.

read RESEARCH practice

Select one of the propaganda techniques in Figure 8.10 and see how many examples of it you can find in a single day. Use newspapers, magazines, radio, television, lectures, and conversations. How might you teach this technique to elementary or middle-school students? Record your ideas in your journal and try them out in a classroom.

19   Introduce a classmate

This is a good listening activity to use at the beginning of the year when classmates do not know each other. Pair up the students and have them find out the following about each other: (a) full name, (b) birthplace, (c) hobby or favorite sport, (d) favorite song or musical group, and (e) favorite food. Remind them to listen carefully because they will introduce their partner to the rest of the class. After giving ample time for students to glean the necessary information, have the pairs introduce each other, each stating the five pieces of information they learned about the other. *Recommended for middle grades.*

Listening Assessment

You can evaluate students' listening abilities in a number of ways. Many standardized tests, such as the Durrell Listening–Reading Series or the Stanford Achievement Tests, have a listening subtest. Generally, the test requires the teacher or a proctor to read aloud from printed material. The students listen and then answer multiple-choice literal, inferential, and applied comprehension questions related to the material. The tests also include vocabulary questions related to specific terms mentioned in the sentence or paragraph.

As an alternative to standardized tests, some teachers use informal reading inventories (described in Chapter 5). These are administered by one teacher to one student and provide a more accurate assessment. The *Classroom Reading Inventory* (Wheelock & Silvaroli, 2011) is one popular example of an easy-to-use assessment instrument. This inventory is designed to assess independent, instructional, and frustration reading levels of elementary and middle-school students. To determine whether the student's comprehension level is higher by listening than by reading, the *Classroom Reading Inventory* includes graded paragraphs as a listening assessment. The teacher reads the passage aloud and then asks the student questions. If the student answers correctly, the teacher reads the passage at the next level of difficulty. This continues until the student cannot answer the questions correctly, which determines the student's listening capacity level.

Rubrics are effective ways to assess particular listening activities and to show growth in listening skills. (See Appendices D.16 and D.17 for examples.) To create appropriate rubrics, consider the specific criterion for each assignment and consider what weight each item has in comparison to the total score. For example, the rubric for musical poems (Appendix D.15) indicates that a student contributing ideas and listening to classmates' ideas are of equal importance but that both are more important than respecting materials and using indoor voices. If your students have a tendency not to respect materials or talk too loudly when working in small groups, you may need to allot more points in those areas.

read **RESEARCH** practice

Observe a classroom teacher. What examples of indirect and direct listening instruction do you see? Describe a strategy or an activity that relates to listening. What other opportunities exist in the classroom to relate listening skills to reading, writing, and speaking?

Rubrics used to show growth typically use general statements that are based on state or national standards. Use the same rubric from one grading period to the next to illustrate student growth. Appendix D.17 offers a rubric for assessing growth in listening.

DEVELOPING SPEAKING SKILLS

Speaking skills, like listening skills, are often neglected in the classroom or assumed to not require instruction or facilitation. Some teachers believe that because students can talk, they can automatically communicate their thoughts. The CCSS recognize the importance of speaking skills in language arts by including three speaking standards in the Anchor Standards for Speaking and Listening (NGACBP & CCSSO, 2010, p. 22):

1. "Present information, findings, and supporting evidence such that listeners can follow the line of reasoning and the organization, development, and style are appropriate to task, purpose, and audience." (CCRA.SL.4)
2. "Make strategic use of digital media and visual displays to express information and enhance understanding of presentations." (CCRA.SL.5)
3. "Adapt speech to a variety of contexts and communicative tasks, demonstrating command of formal English when indicated or appropriate." (CCRA.SL.6)

Classroom Academic Conversations (Collaborative Discussions)

The CCSS emphasize that in order to communicate effectively through speaking, students must be able to present information so that listeners can follow their line of reasoning, make use of digital media to enhance understanding of presentations, and adapt speech to fit the context or audience. These verbal skills are learned through practice and by observing an effective speaker, such as the teacher.

Two distinctively different types of speaking activities occur in the classroom. One type of speaking is conversation, which is unrehearsed and happens most frequently in small groups and is related to the educational topic at hand. The other type of speaking is the prepared, rehearsed speech given by one person or a small group to a larger group of students. Both types of activities are important to students' literacy growth.

We refer to the first type of speaking as *academic conversations* or *collaborative discussions.* Zwiers and Crawford (2011) list eight benefits of conversation among classmates; it

1. builds academic language.
2. builds vocabulary.
3. increases standard English skills, especially for English learners.
4. builds critical thinking through problem solving, interpreting text, discussing biases, and recognizing different points of view.
5. promotes appreciation for different perspectives.
6. builds creativity.
7. builds content understanding.
8. builds relationships.

Creating a positive environment for academic conversations

The physical arrangement of a classroom most conducive to oral language development, especially academic conversation, is that which is organized around small-group settings. Small groups may sit around a round table, in a circle of chairs, or even on the floor. It is in these small group conversations that "students negotiate meaning, co-construct ideas, clarify thought for each other, or support opinions" (Zwiers & Crawford, 2011, p. 3).

The following student traits and behaviors that enable effective communication to take place are key to creating a positive environment for collaborative discussion (Zwiers & Crawford, 2011):

1. Showing a degree of humility; recognizing that they do not know it all.
2. Respecting opposing points of view by carefully listening to the other's stance and rationale. Encourage students to repeat what another classmate says just to be sure there is no misunderstanding.
3. Showing interest in what others say and realizing they can learn from their classmates.
4. Approaching conversation with a positive attitude and enthusiasm.
5. Exploring the topic to unearth all possible information. Students must be encouraged to be thorough. This means you must give them ample time and a stimulating topic.

Selecting appropriate topics for classroom academic conversations

Once you have organized your small groups, you are ready to select topics that promote useful conversation. The topics should not require students to answer literal questions about a passage that was read. Possible conversation activities can include analyzing the type of propaganda of a magazine advertisement aimed at students, such as soft drinks or athletic shoes. (Teaching Activity 16, p. 255, describes this activity in detail.)

Other topics that stimulate collaborative conversation center around children's and young adult literature. For these and other topics, always encourage students to give a rationale for their stance. One collaborative conversation literature activity is "book bites" (Yopp & Yopp, 2013). Group students into pairs and give each pair a strip of paper with a sentence on it from a picture or chapter book they have not yet read. The pair of students predict the story's main conflict based on that one sentence. Then each pair teams up with another pair, which has a different sentence, and the four students discuss the possible conflict based on both sentences. This process continues, with each pair discussing their sentence with every other pair in the classroom, refining their predictions as they go. See Figure 8.11 for an example of this activity.

A third activity for collaborative conversations is for students to discuss how point of view impacts a story. For example, in *Flying Blind* (Myers, 2003) 13-year-old Ben lives with his adopted father, Professor Elisha Riley, and his pet macaw, Murphy. When traveling in the Florida Everglades, Ben is shocked to learn that thousands

---

Book bites for Patricia Polacco's *Meteor!* (1987). **FIGURE 8.11**

Sentences from text:

"Suddenly, without warning the house started shaking."

"Took the roof, the power lines, and hit a cow!"

"Merchants closed their shops, school was let out before noon, and just about everyone in town headed for the Gaw place."

"As the crowd jostled, trotted, rolled, and bumped through the countryside, bystanders and onlookers joined in and came along."

"They set up all their buzzing testing equipment and put on strange-looking protective suits."

Book Bites Worksheet

Instructions: With your partner, read your sentence. In the first box, write your hypothesis of what the main problem of the story could possibly be. Be sure to explain your reasoning. When you are done, turn to the pair sitting next to you and exchange your sentence with theirs. Decide with your partner if your hypothesis has changed based on this new information. In the second box, write your new hypothesis for what you think the main problem might be. Again, be sure to explain your reasoning. If your hypothesis doesn't change, write the same thing in the second box. Exchange sentences two more times with other pairs so that you have read four different sentences total and formed new hypotheses after reading each one. When you are done, discuss your possible story with the group that had the same four sentences as you did. Explain why you think your version is possible, but listen carefully to the other group to see if you agree with them. If you do not, explain why.

#1 Sentence:	#2 Sentence:
Hypothesis:	Hypothesis:
#3 Sentence:	#4 Sentence:
Hypothesis:	Hypothesis:

In an elementary classroom, gather some students around you in a circle. Explain the guidelines for the collaborative discussion, and then join the circle as a member. To get the group started, suggest topics such as pets, favorite TV programs, weekend or vacation activities, and favorite sports or hobbies. Remember that once the talk starts, the students do not have to stick to the initial topic. Conversations are intentionally free and open-ended.

of egrets are being killed for their feathers, which are sold to adorn ladies' hats. However, when he realizes that his friends kill the birds to make a meager living, Ben struggles with what is right and what is wrong.

Intermediate or middle-school students can discuss if this story would be different if it were not told in first person. Have your students consider the following questions: If the story were told in third person, would the tension be as strong? Explain. If the story were told in third person, would the reader understand Ben's conflict between saving the birds and respecting his friends' livelihood? When you provide students with many opportunities to engage in collaborative conversations, they often ask their own questions about different points of view.

Presentations

The second major type of speaking in the classroom is the presentation. These are speaking activities for which the student prepares. The presentation can take many forms, including a book report, a research project, or a campaign speech. This type of speaking activity requires teachers to create a positive environment.

Creating a positive environment for presentations

A positive oral language environment is one that is risk free, makes students feel relaxed, encourages social interaction with peers, and promotes cognitive growth. To help students prepare for formal presentations, Palmer (2011) suggests that teachers consider the following:

1. Keep in mind the background knowledge and interests of the audience.
2. Make sure the presentation is pertinent to the audience.
3. Make the presentation easy for the audience to follow.
4. Use visual aids that enhance or complement what is being said.
5. Dress for the occasion, even for school presentations.
6. Appear calm and confident.
7. Speak clearly and slowly.
8. Demonstrate passion for the topic.
9. Maintain eye contact with the audience; do not look down or only at the visual aids.
10. Use gestures that complement the speech.
11. Modulate the tone and rate of your voice to convey enthusiasm and avoid speaking in a monotone.

To help your students meet these goals, give ample opportunities for them to present in front of the class and/or larger groups.

Developing your own positive and receptive attitude is key to creating a positive classroom presentation environment. You must demonstrate by your behavior that language use is important, that students should speak in class, and that what they have to say is valuable. In the classroom vignette that follows, identify the many ways the teacher demonstrates a positive and receptive attitude toward language.

It's 8:15 a.m. in Mrs. Majors' second-grade classroom. School does not start for another 15 minutes, and she is at her desk preparing for the day. Already a few students are in the room.

"Hi, Charlie. How was soccer practice yesterday?" she asks.

"It was great, Mrs. Majors. I scored a goal—my first one. And tomorrow we play the Ramblers."

"That's good. I hope your team wins, Charlie."

"Mrs. Majors, look what I brought," says a girl holding up a jar with a spider inside.

"Wow! Where did you get that spider? It's a beauty."

"Me and my brother caught it in the garden with a jar."

More of the students enter the classroom. Many of them stop by Mrs. Majors' desk to chat with her, to share something, or just to say hi. Whenever a student comes to her, Mrs. Majors puts aside her attendance book or whatever she is working on. There will be other times during the day—a few minutes here, a few minutes there—to work on these forms, but when her students speak, Mrs. Majors listens.

Jasmine and her best friend, Aretha, are stapling word cards to the bulletin board under the title "New Words We've Learned." Everyone gets to add a new word each week. The board is already half full, and the students have suggested making it larger because they are learning so many new words.

Later in the day, several students talk about a rocket launch they recently saw on the Internet. Jack says the rocket is called a capsule, but the other students are not sure. "Jack," Mrs. Majors says, "that's a great word. Let's add it to our list." Jack beams as Mrs. Majors prints the word on a card and gives it to him to place on the board. Any time a student uses an unusual word, phrase, or sentence, either orally or in writing, Mrs. Majors calls attention to it and praises the student's originality. Words are valuable in this classroom.

In addition to the bulletin board, Mrs. Majors' classroom features other word displays to encourage students to expand their vocabulary, including hanging mobiles containing spelling words for the students to study. There is also a student-made chart of synonyms, antonyms, and homonyms they have learned. Yet another chart details the history of some common place-names in the community.

TEACHING ACTIVITIES 8

SPEAKING

Once you have formed groups, arranged your room, and acquired some materials, you are ready to begin teaching listening and speaking skills. Most oral language instruction takes place indirectly; that is, you create a positive environment and introduce the activity, and the students do the rest. You create the environment by explaining strategies to your students. Consult the following list of listening and speaking activities. Although we have provided suggested grade levels, any of the activities can be modified to fit different levels. Most of the activities are aligned with the CCSS, because many teachers use them as their state standards.

1 Warming-up activities

Some young students are uncomfortable speaking in front of classmates. By engaging them in some short activities, you can acclimate them to the process. The following three activities are considered warm-ups; they require no student preparation. All of these activities support CCSS SL.K.6: "Speak audibly and express thoughts, feelings, and ideas clearly" (NGACBP & CCSSO, 2010, p. 23). *Recommended for primary grades.*

Explaining one's art. After students have created an art project, invite them to sit in a circle with their projects. Have them stand up one at a time and explain their works. Encourage classmates to ask questions or compliment the artist in an effort to get him or her to elaborate. All comments and questions should be positive so students learn how to compliment and encourage each other.

Sharing a story or poem. Have students write a story or poem and invite them to read their works aloud in front of the class. When they have finished, encourage the class to compliment the author by stating which part of the story or poem they liked the best.

Dialogue improvisation. With your help, students can create new dialogue and act out part of a familiar story. For example, after reading *Annie and the Wild Animals* (Brett, 1985), pass out various animal puppets, such as a crocodile, giraffe, monkey, and raccoon, allowing students to choose which animal they will be. Then, begin the improvisation by assuming the role of Annie, who wants a new pet after losing Taffy, her cat. Put a dish of cornflakes on the floor and wonder aloud about who will come to eat the food. Have the students take turns coming to the plate and responding to Annie's question, "Will you make a good pet?" Have students explain why their animal would not be a good pet.

Pattern the dialogue after Brett's phrase: "I wouldn't be a good pet because. . . ." This type of improvisation gives students an opportunity to repeat something they already know from the story while adding their own creative spin. Other books recommended for dialogue improvisation (Ferguson and Young, 1996) are *The Pigs' Picnic* (Kasza, 1988), *"You Look Ridiculous," Said the Rhinoceros to the Hippopotamus* (Waber, 1966), *A Bag Full of Pups* (Gackenbach, 1981), and *I Wish I Were a Butterfly* (Howe, 1987).

2 Discovering the wonder of figurative language in poetry

CCSS RL.2.4 requires students to "describe how words and phrases (e.g. regular beats, alliteration, rhymes, repeated lines) supply rhythm and meaning in a story, poem, or song" (NGACBP & CCSSO, 2010, p. 11). Jack Prelutsky's poems delight many students because of his rich vocabulary and the figurative language he uses to paint a humorous picture in readers' minds. Many second graders know that goats eat anything. In "A Goat Wandered into a Junkyard" from Prelutsky's *Something Big Has Been Here* (1990), a goat eats many different parts of a car until he finally coughs it up again. This poem is filled with figurative language and rhyme. Before analyzing the way Prelutsky uses figurative language, read the poem aloud to the class simply to enjoy the humor. If you read the poem correctly, students should be able to feel the beat of the poem. As with many of his poems, he uses interesting words that you will want to discuss after you read the poem, and then read the poem again so students get the meaning. Then you can begin to point out how Prelutsky uses different techniques.

> Education is a kind of continuing dialogue, and a dialogue assumes different points of view.
>
> **ROBERT HUTCHINS**

Lines 2, 4, 6, and 8 in the first verse all end in words that have the long /e/ sound: *meal, steel, gears, veneer.* He also uses alliteration within lines: line 6 includes *gobbled, gauges,* and *gears.* Line 4 uses the /s/ sound: *several fragments, steel.* In the last verse Prelutsky repeats the word *cough* for effect: "he coughed and he coughed and he coughed and he coughed / and he coughed up an automobile." After modeling how Prelutsky uses language, invite students to find a poem from your classroom poetry books that features two examples of alliteration or rhyme and have them write three or four sentences explaining how the language creates a vivid picture in their minds. *Recommended for primary grades.*

3 Discovering the wonder of language in picture books

Many authors use language in unique ways to help readers capture the action of the story. Helen Cooper in *Pumpkin Soup* (1998) uses words and formatting to help readers understand the actions of three friends: a duck, a cat, and a squirrel. For this lesson, read the book with students sitting on a rug in front of you so you can show them the placement of words on the page. Cooper weaves the story with onomatopoeia: spoons go *ker-plonk*, Duck and Cat wail, and Squirrel sniffles. After sharing these examples, ask students to find other examples in the text.

Cooper also formats the words on the page into short phrases that indicate specific actions:

"He (duck) drew up a stool,
>   hopped on top,
>   and reached . . .
>   until his beak just touched
>   the tip of the spoon . . ." (unpaged)

Later she writes:

"Then there was trouble,
>   a horrible squabble,
>   a row,
>   a racket,
>   a rumpus,
>   in the old white cabin." (unpaged)

Students may understand *squabble*, but *row*, *racket*, and *rumpus* may be unfamiliar to some second graders, so take this opportunity to explain so they understand the action. The illustrations also help students understand the words. Discuss with students how Cooper uses short lines, each of which represents one step of the action. Then let students find other examples and explain them to the group. Again, this opportunity focuses on speaking skills. *Recommended for primary grades.*

4 Retellings through puppets

Students in the primary grades who find it difficult to speak in front of peers may also shy away from working with other classmates. However, as they progress through school they will be required to speak in front of peers and cooperate as they engage in group activities. CCSS SL.2.4 requires students to "retell stories, or recount an experience with appropriate facts and relevant, descriptive details, speaking audibly in coherent sentences" (NGACBP & CCSSO, 2010, p. 23).

Often puppets can help a student speak in front of peers because of the illusion that the character is speaking instead of them. It is easy to set up a puppet stage curtain by using a tension rod and an old pillowcase. At the closed end of the pillowcase, make one-inch slits on both seams. Put the rod through the slits, and put the rod in the doorway. The performers can stand outside the doorway while the audience stays inside. The curtain is easily stored until the next show. Students can make simple puppets by drawing the character's face on a paper plate and attaching the paper plate to a straw or craft stick with tape.

To get students started with puppet shows, reread some favorite fairy tales such as *The Three Little Pigs, Little Red Riding Hood,* or *Three Billy Goats Gruff.* The text of all of these is repetitive and easy for students to remember. Later, students can create puppet shows with other favorite stories. *Recommended for primary grades.*

5   Wordless books

Wordless books tell stories through pictures alone. Unlike easy-to-read books or picture storybooks, wordless books contain no print at all. While turning the pages slowly, the "reader" adds the narration and dialogue to create a complete story with beginning, middle, and end. Once students see the teacher model the wordless book strategy, they quickly pick up on it and begin telling stories themselves. Students can select a wordless book, study its illustrations, and then "read" their version of the story to the class when they are ready. Figure 8.12 lists some wordless books for use in the classroom. *Recommended for primary grades.*

6   Improvisation with the same item

Divide the class into small groups of three or four students. Give each group an index card with a setting (e.g., a cave, a museum, a pirate ship, a beach). Explain that all groups have different settings, but all groups will be using the same prop—a wooden spoon. Each group must perform a minute-long skit in which they use the spoon and create dialogue to let the other class members know who the performers are. Give students only three to five minutes to plan their skit. Remind students that they must speak loudly and in complete sentences. Once the first group begins to perform, all students become attentive audience members. This activity supports CCSS SL.2.4: "Tell a story or recount an experience with appropriate facts and relevant, descriptive details, speaking audibly in coherent sentences" (NGACBP & CCSSO, 2010, p. 23). *Recommended for primary grades.*

7   Improvisation with various items

This activity also supports CCSS SL.2.4. Divide the class into groups of three or four students. Give each group a different prop (e.g., a black shawl, a string of white beads, a suitcase, a carpenter's apron). Allow three to five minutes for the groups to plan their skits, explaining that all members must talk and that a good skit includes a beginning that sets up the problem, a middle of rising action, and an end with a climax and resolution. *Recommended for primary grades.*

8   Paper-bag puppets

This is another activity that supports CCSS SL.2.4 as well as CCSS SL.2.5: "Create audio recordings of stories or poems; add drawings or other visual displays to stories or recounts of experiences when appropriate to clarify ideas, thoughts, and feelings" (NGACBP & CCSSO, 2010, p. 23).

Paper-bag puppets are another easy and an inexpensive way to introduce students to puppetry. You can create all types of puppets depending on the size of the paper bag. Large paper bags, for example, can be placed over students' heads and worn as full masks, with holes cut out for the eyes, nose, and mouth. The bags can be decorated with crayon, marker, felt, scraps of fabric, and bits of string or yarn. Students can add ears, hair, and even hats made from construction paper with glue, paste, or tape. Smaller paper bags make great hand puppets.

Appendices D.18 and D.19 include two rubrics to use for puppet shows: the rubric found on the http://rubistar.4teachers.org website as well as a modifica-

Wordless books.   **FIGURE** **8.12**

A Ball for Daisy (C. Raschka, 2011)

Amanda and the Mysterious Carpet (F. Krahn, 1985)

Art and Max (D. Wiesner, 2010)

Carl's Afternoon in the Park (A. Day, 1991)

Chalk (B. Thomson, 2010)

Do You Want to Be My Friend? (E. Carle, 1971)

Flotsam (D. Wiesner, 2006)

Follow Me (N. Tafuri, 1990)

Free Fall (D. Wiesner, 1988)

Good Dog, Carl (A. Day, 1985)

Home (J. Baker, 2004)

In the Pond (E. Cristini, 1984)

Journey (A. Becker, 2013)

Junglewalk (N. Tafuri, 1988)

Just in Passing (S. Bonners, 1989)

Mouse Around (P. Schories, 1991)

Mr. Wuffles (D. Wiesner, 2013)

On Top (M. MacGregor, 1988)

Paddy Under Water (J. S. Goodall, 1984)

Paddy's Pay-Day (A. Day, 1989)

ReZoom (I. Banyai, 1995)

Robot Dreams (S. Varon, 2007)

Sector 7 (D. Wiesner, 1999)

Shadow (S. Lee, 2010)

The Adventure of Polo (R. Faller, 2006)

The Arrival (S. Tan, 2007)

The Gift (J. Prater, 1985)

The Grey Lady and the Strawberry Snatcher (M. Bang, 1996)

The Lion and the Mouse (J. Pinkney, 2009)

The Patchwork Farmer (C. Brown, 1989)

The Red Book (B. Lehman, 2004)

The Snowman (R. Briggs, 1978)

The Swan (V. Mayo, 1994)

The Three Pigs (D. Wiesner, 2001)

The Yellow Umbrella (H. Drescher, 1987)

Tuesday (D. Wiesner, 1991)

Where's My Monkey? (D. Schubert, not dated)

Zoom (I. Banyai, 1995)

tion of it, which emphasizes the speaking aspect of the project. Always construct your scoring rubric based on the criteria you give to students. *Recommended for primary grades.*

9 **Record readers theater**

Readers theater is defined by Laughlin and Latrobe (1990) as "a presentation by two or more participants who read from scripts and interpret a literary work in such a way that the audience imaginatively senses characterization, setting and action" (p. 3). Typically, the presentation is enhanced by vocal intonation, facial expressions, and pantomime gestures. A narrator often directs the various reader-actors on and off the stage and communicates scene changes to the audience. Occasionally, simple props and costumes are used to further suggest characters and setting. In this recorded version of readers theater, however, students need to use vocal expression rather than facial expressions, props, or costumes to communicate the story to their audience.

Have a small group of students select a script from your collection. Instruct the students that they are to rehearse the script and work on vocal expression because they will record the story. Because the audience will not be able to see their gestures or facial expressions, their vocal expressions alone must relate the story and setting.

Figure 8.13 lists websites that offer free scripts to use for readers theater, and Figure 8.14 lists books for readers theater. Appendix E contains a short readers the-

FIGURE 8.13 Sources for readers theater scripts.

Dr. Young's Reading Room, www.thebestclass.org/rtscripts.html

ReadWriteThink, www.readwritethink.org/classroom-resources/lesson-plans/readers-theatre-172.html

Reading A-Z, www.readinga-z.com/fluency/readers-theater-scripts/

Busy Teacher's Café, www.busyteacherscafe.com/literacy/readers_theater.html

Fiction Teachers, www.fictionteachers.com/classroomtheater/theater.html

Reading Online, www.readingonline.org/electronic/elec_index.asp?HREF=carrick/index.html

Timeless Teacher Stuff, www.timelessteacherstuff.com

Teaching Heart, www.teachingheart.net/readerstheater.htm

Tim Rasinski, www.timrasinski.com/presentations/readers_theater_1-4.pdf

Aaron Shepard, www.aaronshep.com/rt/index.html

FIGURE 8.14 Cumulative books to use in readers theater.

A Most Unusual Lunch (R. Benders, 1994)

A Perfect Day for a Picnic (T. Finch, 2013)

Good-Night Owl! (P. Hutchins, 1972)

Here Is the Coral Reef (M. Dunphy, 2006)

It's My Birthday (H. Oxenbury, 2010)

Jack's Garden (H. Cole, 1995)

"Not Now!" Said the Cow (J. Oppenheim, 1989)

One-Dog Canoe (M. Casanova, 2009)

One-Dog Sleigh (M. Casanova, 2013)

Shoes from Grandpa (M. Fox, 1989)

"Stop, Stop, You Big Old Bull!" (H. Zieffer, 1995)

The Bag I'm Taking to Grandma's (S. Neitzel, 1995)

The Great Big Enormous Turnip (A. Award, 2013).

The Little Old Lady Who Was Not Afraid of Anything (L. Williams, 1986)

The Napping House (A. Wood, 1984)

The Old Woman Who Lived in a Vinegar Bottle (M. MacDonald, 1995)

Too Much Noise (A. McGovern, 1967)

What Did You Put in Your Pocket? (B. de Regniers, 2003)

Wind Says Good Night (K. Rydell, 1994)

ater about the three little kittens who have grown up to be three cats; and, yes, they lost their hats. This activity supports CCSS SL.2.5. *Recommended for primary grades.*

10 Creating a newscast

A favorite group project to develop students' communication skills is to create a complete newscast. Students should focus on fluency and enunciation so that each speaker is clearly understood. Divide the class into groups and assign each one a segment of the news: local news, state news, national news, global news, advertising, weather, and sports. The groups research and gather information from online articles. Also encourage them to interview caregivers or adults in the school for their segment. Then, each group collaboratively writes the script for its segment and makes sure each student has a speaking part. Next, the groups rehearse their segment so their performance is fluent and intelligible. The teacher then videotapes each segment in the media center or some other quiet spot away from the other students. Later, all the students can view and critique their work. Appendix D.20 has a rubric that can be used for the newscast. This activity supports CCSS SL.5.6: "Adapt speech to a variety of contexts and tasks, using formal English when appropriate to task and situation" (NGACBP & CCSSO, 2010, p. 24). *Recommended for intermediate grades.*

11 Choral reading

When planning to use choral reading with your class, you need to decide which form of the activity is most appropriate. For each type, instruct the students to practice the selection with expression and then record it. The goal is to make the selection come alive for listeners. *Recommended for intermediate grades.*

12 Antiphonal or dialogue

Poems with two parts or a question-and-answer format are appropriate for this type of choral reading activity. Often the deeper voices take one part while the higher voices take the other; this usually translates into a dialogue between a group of boys and a group of girls. Some poems for which this approach is effective are "Who Has Seen the Wind?" by Christina Rossetti and the American folk song "Buffalo Gals."

13 Unison reading

Although unison reading appears simple, it requires practice and skill for the students to keep together. Because everyone reads every line, rhythm and timing have to be perfect. Almost every poem is appropriate for unison reading. Some particularly good poems are "My Name" by Lee Bennett Hopkins, "Dreams" by Langston Hughes, and "Mr. Skinner" by N. M. Bodecker.

14 Cumulative reading

In cumulative reading, one student begins and the others join in one by one. This activity helps those who are nervous in front of classmates gain confidence by joining with others. Stories such as *I Know an Old Lady Who Swallowed a Fly*, retold by Nadine Bernard Westcott, and *Shoes from Grandpa* by Mem Fox can be used for cumulative reading. The following is an example of the first part of *Shoes from Grandpa* to illustrate how cumulative reading works:

Grandpa:	My, Jessie, how you've grown! You'll need a new pair of shoes this winter, and I'll buy them.
Dad:	I'll buy you some socks from the local shops,
Grandpa & Dad:	to go with the shoes from Grandpa.
Mom:	I'll buy you a skirt that won't show the dirt,
Grandpa, Dad, & Mom:	to go with the socks from the local shops, to go with the shoes from Grandpa.

15 Storytelling

Storytelling is one of the oldest forms of entertainment. Encourage students to find a folktale from another country, such as Eric Kimmel's *Anansi and the Talking Melon* (1995), and invite them to tell the folktale to their classmates in an entertaining manner. Remind students that storytelling does not require that they memorize the story. *Recommended for intermediate grades.*

16 Liar's goblet

Most students have heard of the lumberjack Paul Bunyan and his blue ox, Babe. Similarly, many students recognize the name of Pecos Bill, the cowboy. The stories of Paul Bunyan and Pecos Bill are examples of tall tales. Students love to expand on and embellish their own adventures. The liar's goblet activity builds on the idea of the tall tale and on children's enjoyment of exaggeration. It can be taught in the form of a game. First you need a goblet (a cup, glass, or mug will do). One person in the group takes the liar's goblet and makes up a short but exaggerated tall tale. The next person in the group takes the goblet and says, "That's nothing; why I remember . . ." Each student tries to top the previous story; each story, though different, grows more exaggerated. Figure 8.15 lists examples of tall-tale books. This activity supports CCSS SL.4.6: "Differentiate between contexts that call for formal English (e.g., presenting ideas) and situations where informal discourse is appropriate (e.g., small-group discussion); use formal English when appropriate to task and situation" (NGACBP & CCSSO, 2010, p. 24). *Recommended for intermediate grades.*

17 Role-playing a book character

This activity also supports CCSS speaking and listening standards that require students to adapt their speech to differing contexts. The goal of role-playing a book character is to have the students study the characters well enough to understand the traits that make the characters unique. Follow these steps:

1. Read and discuss a story with the class; it can be a picture book appropriate for the grade level or a chapter book.
2. With the class, create a list of the characters' names and their traits.
3. Students must provide evidence of a character's trait by reading the part of the book that demonstrates it.
4. Group students into pairs; one is the character and the other is a reporter.
5. The reporter prepares questions for the character.
6. The character answers the questions, based on his or her identified traits.
7. Each pair performs the interview for the class, with the interviewer using standard English.

This activity builds speaking skills as well as listening and higher-level thinking skills while reading and discussing the story as well as during the interview. The reporter has to develop the questions to ask the character, and the character needs to use imagination to answer the questions. *Recommended for middle grades.*

> I think wisdom is more important than power. I want knowledge, so I read a lot of books and try to write in many different ways.
>
> **MODERN CHINESE WRITER, SHEN CONGWEN**

18 New versions and new endings

Yet another storytelling activity involves changing a story's plot or altering its ending. It works particularly well with folktales and fairy tales. To start this activity, read a number of different versions of the same story to your students. For example, use a few different versions of *The Three Little Pigs*. For a real change, read Jon Scieszka's *The True Story of the Three Little Pigs* (1989). Discuss how a story told from different characters' points of view can vary considerably. Invite students to rewrite a favor-

Tall-tale books.   **FIGURE** 8.15

American Tall Tale Animals (A. Stoutenburg, 1968)

Dona Flor: A Tall Tale About a Giant Woman with a Great Big Heart (P. Mora, 2005)

Fortunately, the Milk (N. Gaiman, 2013)

Heroes in American Folklore (I. Shapiro, 1962)

Holler Loudly (C. Leitich Smith, 2010)

I Was Born Ten Thousand Years Ago (S. Kellogg, 1996)

Jangles: A Big Fish Story (D. Shannon, 2012)

John Henry: An American Legend (E. J. Keats, 1965)

John Tabor's Ride (E. C. Day, 1989)

Johnny Appleseed (S. Kellogg, 1988)

Levi Strauss Gets a Bright Idea: A Fairly Fabricated Story of a Pair of Pants (T. Johnston, 2011)

Meanwhile Back at the Ranch (K. Hawkes, 2014)

Mike Fink (S. Kellogg, 1992)

Miss Sally Ann and the Panther (B. Miller, 2012)

Paul Bunyan (S. Kellogg, 1984)

Pecos Bill (S. Kellogg, 1986)

Prickly Rose (S. Gill, 2014)

Railroad John and the Red Rock Run (T. Crunk, 2006)

Sally and Thunder and Whirlwind (S. Kellogg, 1996)

Tall Tales of America (I. Shapiro, 1958)

The Adventures of Granny Clearwater and Little Critter (K. Willis Holt, 2007)

The Giant of Seville: A Tall Tale Based on a True Story (D. Andreasen, 2007)

The 100-Year-Old Man Who Climbed Out of the Window and Disappeared (J. Jonasson, 2009)

The Legend of Johnny Appleseed (M. Powell, 2010)

The Mostly True Adventures of Homer P. Figg (R. Philbrick, 2009)

The Song of Paul Bunyan and Tony Beaver (E. Rees, 1964)

The True Blue Scouts of Sugar Man Swamp (K. Appelt, 2013)

Windwagon Smith (E. Rees, 1966)

ite fairy tale or story from the antagonist's point of view and create a multimedia slide presentation to present to the class that includes a voiceover, graphics, and background music to accompany the text of the story. This activity supports CCSS SL.6.5: "Include multimedia components (e.g., graphics, images, music, sound) and visual displays in presentations to clarify information" (NGACBP & CCSSO, 2010, p. 49). *Recommended for middle grades.*

19 One-line improvisation

The goal of one-line improvisation is for students to use their imagination and concisely explain in one sentence how to use an object. Show the students an object—a stick, ball, hat, coat, lunchbox, etc. Give the object to any student, whose magical powers allow him to change it into any other object. The student must demonstrate how to use the transformed object and give a one-sentence clue as to what it is. For an example, a student receives a yardstick and decides to turn it into a hockey stick. The student swings the stick and says, "I hope I make this goal!" Classmates must guess what the object is. Of course, the more the game is played, the more creative and brave the students must become. *Recommended for middle grades.*

20 Campaign slogan

Students learn the power of oral persuasion through campaigning for a change within the school. The issue can be for more reading time in the media center, more time in the computer lab, a new school mascot, a new sport during recess, or any other change the students would like to see in their school. After studying the propaganda techniques listed in Figure 8.10, students can divide into teams to write a campaign slogan and create a 30-second advertisement supporting their issue. As with the newscast, the students should rehearse until their delivery is clear and fluent. Then tape each video in the media center and play them all for the class. The class can critique each one, deciding why it is persuasive. Make sure students first name one or two aspects they really like about the ad before they suggest one or two aspects that could make it even better. Appendix D.21 is a rubric teachers can use to assess students' understanding of propaganda techniques. You can train students to perform peer assessments by using the rubric or modifying it to fit the needs of the class. *Recommended for middle grades.*

21 Discussion, solving a problem

Many middle-school students recognize that their building has one or two problems that need attention. The problem may be trash in the hallway, chaos in the lunchroom, no time for physical exercise, bullying, or lack of support at sports events or fine art performances. Listen to the class to determine which problem the students feel needs attention the most. Once they have identified it, divide them into groups small enough to ensure that everyone can participate in a discussion about possible solutions. Encourage them to think of all the details to implement their suggestion. This activity supports CCSS SL.8.1: "Engage effectively in a range of collaborative discussions (one-on-one, in groups, and teacher-led) with diverse partners on grade 8 topics, texts, and issues, building on others' ideas and expressing their own clearly" (NGACBP & CCSSO, 2010, p. 49). *Recommended for middle grades.*

22 Space trip to the moon

This collaborative discussion strategy was developed by NASA as part of its space education program for upper elementary and middle-school students. In this exercise, students receive a list of items and a life-or-death scenario. The students discuss each item on the list and try to rank each according to its usefulness to their survival. As they move down the list of objects, it becomes more difficult to reach a consensus, but the quality of the discussion improves greatly. Figure 8.16 offers a sample situation for this activity. *Recommended for middle grades.*

23 Research presentation

Instruct students to choose a topic from a social studies or science unit that they have studied. Approve their topics before they begin their research to make sure they are neither too narrow nor too broad. Make sure they gather information from at least three sources, and have them produce an oral report augmented with a slide presentation that includes photographs, charts, and diagrams. The presentation should include five to ten slides. Students present their reports to the class, and you assess them on logical sequencing of main ideas, supporting details, the content of the slides, and their oral presentation. This activity supports CCSS SL.8.4: "Present claims and findings, emphasizing salient points in a focused, coherent manner with rel-

Sample NASA survival activity.   **FIGURE** 8.16

SPACE TRIP TO THE MOON

Instructions: You are a member of a space crew originally scheduled to rendezvous with the mother ship on the lighted surface of the moon. Because of mechanical difficulties, however, your ship was forced to land at a spot some 200 miles from the rendezvous point. During the landing, much of the ship and the equipment aboard were damaged; because survival depends on reaching the mother ship, the most critical items still available must be chosen for the 200-mile trip. Below are listed the 15 items intact and undamaged after landing. Your task is to rank them in order of their importance in allowing your crew to reach the rendezvous point. Place the number 1 by the most important item, the number 2 by the second most important, and so on through number 15, the least important.

_____ Box of matches   _____ Five gallons of water

_____ Food concentrate   _____ One case of dehydrated milk

_____ Fifty feet of nylon rope   _____ Two 100-pound tanks of oxygen

_____ Parachute silk   _____ Map of the stars as seen from the moon

_____ Portable heating unit   _____ Signal flares

_____ Two 45-caliber pistols   _____ First-aid kit containing injection needles

_____ Life raft   _____ Solar-powered FM receiver-transmitter

_____ Magnetic compass

evant evidence, sound valid reasoning, and well-chosen details; use appropriate eye contact, adequate volume, and clear pronunciation"; and CCSS SL.8.5: "Integrate multimedia and visual displays into presentations to clarify information, strengthen claims and evidence, and add interest" (NGACBP & CCSSO, 2010, p. 49). *Recommended for middle grades.*

Speaking Assessment

When you wish to assess the students' speaking abilities with a specific assignment, make sure they know from the beginning which areas will be assessed. This allows them to work on those skills while they prepare their assignment. It is then crucial that you follow through by assessing those specific skills during the grading process. At the beginning of the year, you may want to emphasize only adequate coverage of content or volume and eye contact, in which case the rubric should include just those areas. However, toward the end of the year, you may also require visual aids. In this case, it is important that you also assess the speaker's use of the visual aids. Appendix D.22 has an example of a rubric used to assess research presentations given toward the end of the year. Note that on this rubric each aspect of the presentation is of equal importance. However, the rubric used for storytelling is scored differently; the emphasis is on voice inflection, with each aspect given a different value. Appendix D also has rubrics for other speaking activities.

The advantage of using a scoring rubric is that a student can see the strengths and weaknesses of her presentation. To maximize a rubric's usefulness, (1) include encouraging comments to the student and (2) discuss the rubric with her.

VOCABULARY BUILDING

In an integrated approach to the language arts, vocabulary development is a natural by-product of listening and speaking. Concerning vocabulary acquisition, CCRA.L.6 requires students to "acquire and use accurately a range of general academic and domain-specific words and phrases sufficient for reading, writing, speaking, and listening at the college and career readiness level; demonstrate independence in gathering vocabulary knowledge when encountering an unknown term important to comprehension or expression." In addition, CCRA.L.5 calls for

VOCABULARY MINILESSONS

Aspects of vocabulary building that lend themselves to minilessons include:

- *Synonyms:* words that have the same or almost the same meaning, such as *gigantic* and *enormous.*

- *Antonyms:* words that are opposites, such as *hot* and *cold* or *fat* and *slender.*

- *Homonyms:* words that sound alike but are spelled differently and have different meanings, such as *to, too,* and *two; there, their,* and *they're; which* and *witch;* and *wood* and *would.*

- *Words with multiple meaning:* These are common words that sometimes take on new meanings depending on the context. For example, many words can be used as both a noun ("I got a new *bike*") and a verb ("I *bike* to school"). Contextual clues are the most powerful of the reading strategies for determining meanings of such words.

- *Neologisms:* These are new words that have entered the language through extensive usage or as labels for new discoveries, inventions, products, fashions, and so on. Many words associated with computers, scientific discoveries, and popular culture are neologisms. Some examples are *cosplay, blog, selfie, financial meltdown,* and *crowdsourcing.*

- *Portmanteau:* These are new words formed by combining two existing words and omitting some of their letters. Lewis Carroll, the author of *Alice in Wonderland,* originated many early portmanteaus, such as *chortle,* a combination of *chuckle* and *snort. Smog* is a portmanteau of *smoke* and *fog,* and *brunch* refers to a meal that is a combination of *breakfast* and *lunch.* More recent portmanteaus

include *Labradoodle,* a dog that is a cross between a *Labrador retriever* and a *poodle,* and *webisode,* a combination of *World Wide Web* and *episode* and meaning an episode of an online series.

- *Acronyms:* These are words formed from the initials of an organization or phrase that come to stand on their own over time. Many acronyms eventually become actual words. For example, the military says that a soldier who is *absent without leave* is *AWOL;* the *National Aeronautics and Space Administration* is more commonly known as *NASA.*

- *Euphemism:* This is a more pleasant-sounding word used in place of a term with negative connotations. Some euphemisms originate from social pressures of groups offended by certain inaccurate or inadequate terms. For example, the term *sanitation engineer* has replaced *garbage collector* although the job remains the same. In the United States, it is common to ask for the *restroom* instead of the *bathroom.*

- *Regionalisms:* These are expressions associated with particular geographic regions of the country. They are closely related to dialects, the unique pronunciation characteristics of specific areas of a country. For example, in the Northeast, people carry their groceries in a *bag;* in the Midwest, people use a *sack.* In the Deep South, you may hear the term *poke.* All three terms refer to the same object. Similarly, you may hear different terms all referring to the same food: *pancakes, flapjacks, griddle cakes, johnny cakes, a stack.*

students to "demonstrate understanding of figurative language, word relationships, and nuances in word meaning" (NGACBP & CCSSO, 2010, p. 25). Our position is that vocabulary knowledge is important for college and career readiness and that it develops in the normal course of engaging students in listening, speaking, reading, and writing activities. However, you will need to use minilessons to teach vocabulary directly at times. Keep the following guidelines in mind on those occasions:

- Always relate new vocabulary terms to students' prior knowledge and background.
- Focus on elaborating students' use of new terms rather than merely having them memorize definitions.
- Utilize activities that demand active student involvement in vocabulary learning, such as vocabulary games, dramatics, or writing activities, rather than passive fill-in-the-blank exercises.
- Help students develop strategies for acquiring new vocabulary independently, such as constructing concept wheels, semantic word maps, webs, and semantic feature analysis graphs.
- Build a conceptual base for the new vocabulary word.

TECHNOLOGY IN THE CLASSROOM

Devices for recording video are useful to promote speaking and listening skills and to integrate the language arts with the entire curriculum. The website Edtechteacher (http://edtechteacher.org/tools/multimedia/video-classroom/) offers information that will help you and your students produce videos in your classroom.

If you teach in upper elementary or middle school, have your students listen to famous American speeches available online. Use the site American Rhetoric (www.americanrhetoric.com/top100speechesall.html) or search "famous American speeches." Speeches included on the American Rhetoric site include "I've been to the mountaintop" by Martin Luther King, Jr., John F. Kennedy's Inaugural Address, Franklin Delano Roosevelt's First Inaugural Address, and Ronald Reagan's Shuttle *Challenger* Disaster Address. Have sudents listen to and evaluate these speeches.

For younger students, use online search to locate various methods to make simple puppets. Use the search phrase "making puppets YouTube."

One of our favorite sources for free readers theater scripts is Aaron Shephard's site (www.aaronshep.com/rt/RTE.html), which offers scripts for all grade levels. Small groups of students can practice their lines and then perform for the class.

In the video www.youtube.com/watch?v=8wAP_WW8O-I&feature=related, the choral group Asterisk performs "Geographical Fugue" by Ernst Toch. It demonstrates a sophisticated form of choral reading.

SUMMARY

Some teachers mistakenly think that students' listening and speaking skills will develop on their own over the course of the year; they won't. Teachers must provide ample opportunities for students to work on them. Six CCSS standards focus on students developing listening and speaking skills, underscoring their importance for the student's continued success.

Listening is a six-step process that begins with receiving auditory input and ends with responding to that input. You need to help students learn how to analyze and evaluate what they hear so they can respond appropriately. We include many listening activities in this chapter that will aid you throughout your career and help your students meet the CCSS.

Many students of all ages are reluctant to speak or make a presentation in front of the class. To address this, provide multiple and gradated opportunities for students to speak, first informally and later more formally, with the goal of helping them become fluent, confident speakers in front of a group. The speaking activities can begin with a partner or small group and evolve into a five-minute presentation in front of the class.

field AND practicum ACTIVITIES

You can present the following activities as games that are helpful in developing your students' vocabulary, speaking, and listening skills. Work with students in small groups and explain the game. Then let them play it while you observe how they use language and learn new vocabulary terms.

1. GOING ON A PICNIC. Begin by saying, "We are going on a picnic and *Anna* is bringing *apples*." Then have each student think of an object to bring that begins with the same initial sound as his or her own name. Later they can think of objects that begin with the same sound as a friend's name. Once the students understand the pattern, begin the game, with each student repeating all the names and objects mentioned before him. A more challenging version of the game for older students includes the insertion of a descriptive adjective with the same initial sound before the noun. For example, "We are going on a picnic and *Donald* is bringing *delicious doughnuts*."

2. IN YOUR OWN VOICE. First teach students how to give a brief talk on a topic of their choice. Then have them record their talk and analyze their own performance. Do they speak clearly? Too fast? In a monotone? Have students record their talk a second time and see if their delivery improves.

3. CATEGORIES. Name a category (e.g., "vehicles") and have students take turns naming items in the category (car, bus, train, and so on). At any point a student may say "category" and the next person starts over with a new category (e.g., "vegetables"). This game is played to the following rhythm: clap, clap, snap, snap, (category/example). Like this: clap, clap, snap, snap, *vehicles;* clap, clap, snap, snap, *car;* clap, clap, snap, snap, *bus.*

4. ALPHABET GAME. Say what you see inside or outside the classroom beginning with the letter *a.* Have the next person repeat your sentence and add an object beginning with the letter *b.* Then have the third person repeat the two previous sentences and add an object beginning with the letter *c,* and so on. For example, "I see an apple, a box, and a crayon." Encourage the students to use complete sentences.

5. GEOGRAPHY TRAIN. This game combines knowledge of geographic place-names, spelling, vocabulary, listening, and speaking. The first person names a country, a city, a state, or some other place. The next person uses the last letter of the place-name to begin the next term. The game continues until someone cannot think of a name beginning with the last letter of the previous word. For example, "Ethiopia, Alaska, Arkansas, Switzerland, Denver. . . ."

6. NOUN TRAIN. This game is played using the same rules as geography train except that any nouns can be used, for example, "book, kitchen, napkin, noodle . . . ." Another variation on this is a verb train: "sew, walk, knit, talk . . . ."

7. CONTEXT CHALLENGE. This game emphasizes careful listening skills and context clues. Write a challenge word on the board, one the students probably do not know, and then read aloud a passage containing that word. The students can only use the context clues heard in the passage to determine the meaning of the unknown word.

8. ORAL/AURAL MATH. One student dictates a simple addition, subtraction, multiplication, or division problem. The next student solves the problem aloud without using paper or pencil. Later, these oral word problems can combine addition, subtraction, multiplication, and other steps.

9. HOMONYM HOP. First, have students think of as many homonym pairs as possible. Next, have them come up with a silly definition for the word formed by the combination of each pair. See if their classmates can guess the homonyms from their definition, for example: "A naked grizzly is a *bare bear.*" "An unemployed rock star is an *idle idol.*" "An ordinary jet is a *plain plane.*"

10. GROUP EXPERIENCE. This activity allows you to use the language experience approach in the classroom. After returning from a field trip, encourage your students to talk about it. Record their statements on a large language experience chart and have them read the chart. Then encourage them to illustrate some of the sentences or develop their own stories from them. How did the chart help students with their speaking, writing, and spelling?

11. COMMUNITY INTERVIEW. Teach students about interviewing, and then role-play an interview in class. Have each student select a person in the community whom he or she knows well and interview that person about his or her job. Students should try to find out what types of listening, speaking, reading, and writing skills the job requires.

12. PERSONAL CHRONICLES. You can help students understand how simple and fun storytelling is by encouraging them to share the events of their daily lives. You may want to set aside a brief period every day for a few students to share stories of something that happened at home, on the way to school, or at the playground. Some students may even want to record their stories.

13. TONGUE TWISTERS. Tongue twisters are a great way to teach phonemic awareness and phonics. You can start with the familiar "Peter Piper picked a peck of pickled peppers" and have students draw an illustration. Once students understand the concept of alliteration, they can create their own tongue twisters—"two tiny toads touched toes"—and illustrate them.

> True happiness . . . is not attained through self-gratification but through fidelity to a worthy purpose.
>
> **HELEN KELLER**

Integrating the Visual and Performing Arts

OBJECTIVES

After reading this chapter, you should be able to accomplish the following objectives:

1. Integrate the visual arts into the content areas.
2. Integrate drama into the content areas.
3. Integrate dance into the content areas.
4. Integrate music into the content areas.
5. Explain the difference between reading traditional text and electronic text.
6. Identify search engines that are designed for elementary students.
7. Identify ways to assess websites.

INTRODUCTION

As stated in Chapter 1, the six components of language arts are reading, writing, listening, speaking, viewing, and visually representing. Reading, listening, and viewing are the receptive components of the language arts; writing, speaking, and visually representing are the expressive components. With the receptive components, one must be able to decode the message of the sender; with the expressive components, one must be able to clearly communicate to a known and sometimes unknown audience. Before 1996, developing students' reading, writing, speaking, and listening skills was emphasized; however, since the release of the *Standards for the English Language Arts* in 1996 by the National Council of Teachers of English (NCTE) and the International Reading Association (IRA), viewing and visually representing have been added to that list. The *Standards for English Language Arts* stress the importance of interpreting and creating non-print, visual texts:

> Being literate in contemporary society means being active, critical, and creative users not only of print and spoken language but also of the visual language of images, film and television, commercial and political advertising, photography, and more. Teaching students how to interpret and create visual texts such as illustrations, charts, graphs, electronic displays, photographs, film and video is another essential component of the English language arts curriculum. Visual communication is part of the fabric of contemporary life. (International Reading Association & National Council of Teachers of English, 1996, p. 5)

The NCTE and the IRA also understand that the demands of our social, cultural, and economic environments require students to be skilled in all representation modes in order to thrive in today's global society. Literacy no longer refers only to encoding and decoding traditional texts; it also refers to encoding and decoding digital text, the visual arts, music, dance, and drama. Therefore, students must have experience in constructing and translating meaning across the visual and performing arts so they are literate and become lifelong learners in all aspects of the language arts.

The Common Core State Standards emphasize the importance of reading and creating visual as well as print texts. When reading, CCRA.R.7 requires students to "integrate and evaluate content presented in diverse media and formats, including visually and quantitatively, as well as in words." When writing, CCRA.W.7 requires students to "gather relevant information from multiple print and digital sources, assess the credibility and accuracy of each source, and integrate the information while avoiding plagiarism." When speaking, CCRA.SL.5 requires students to "make strategic use of digital media and visual displays of data to express information and enhance understanding of presentations" (NGACBP & CCSSO, 2010, pp. 10, 18, & 22).

This chapter focuses on students becoming proficient in multiple literacies so that they become critical consumers and creators of all sign systems. First, we will review the various components of multimodal communication. Second, we will share ways to effectively integrate the visual arts, drama, music, and dance with the language arts. Then, we will discuss the Internet as a form of multimodal communication, requiring unique literacy skills that teachers need to help students develop.

MULTIMODAL COMMUNICATION

What is *multimodal* communication? It refers to using more than one mode of communication to decode or encode materials. "Multimodal means that ways of signing—images, print, voices, maps and 3-D sculpture—are selected and used to animate social life and social actions" (Enciso et al., 2006, p. 8). The study of multimodal communication is semiotics. *Semiotics* refers to a broad, "interdisciplinary field of studies that examines how meaning is made through signs of all kinds—pictures, gestures, music—not just words" (Siegel, 2006, p. 65). Semiotics does not favor printed text or spoken language over the other sign systems. However, just like printed text and spoken language, other sign systems must hold a common or standard meaning for the creator and the viewer, even though the meaning may be somewhat different because of individual life experiences (Cowan & Albers, 2006).

VISUAL AND PERFORMING ARTS AS SIGN SYSTEMS

Take a moment to consider some of the interdisciplinary fields, including the visual arts, drama, music, dance, animation, digital communication, photography, and music. Consider how an artist carefully selects colors, textures, lines, curves, and hues, and uses space in the artwork of a picture book to convey a message to the viewer. Artists work with forms that are realistic, abstract, or impressionistic. Consider how an actor exaggerates movement, uses facial expressions, gestures, and mime to tell a story to an audience. Consider how composers carefully create melodies, choose chord progressions, and select instruments to communicate a feeling or devise a sonic landscape. When all the elements come together just right, the result can move listeners to tears or elation. Consider how photographers select subjects, direct light, and capture movement to convey a psychological message or present a stunning perspective of nature or life. Consider how sculptors transform common materials into forms that represent an idea or depict something stylistically or realistically. Consider the dancer who conveys emotion and story through kinesthetic movement and physical strength. Consider how filmmakers and animators create fictional worlds and characters that seem utterly real even when they fail to adhere to the laws of physics. Consider how graphic designers combine diagrams, text, video, and photographs to create a heightened version of reality in order to sell things, entertain people, or convey information. In all of these fields, creators use multiple sign systems to communicate or inspire.

In this section, we focus on how viewing, visually representing, and the other sign systems can function as tools for learning, communicating, and expressing emotions. All of these sign systems—visual arts, drama, music, and dance—by their very nature connect students to both their affective and cognitive learning domains, and they become energized in the learning experience (Cowan & Albers, 2006). Students do not need to be gifted in any of these systems to interpret or use them, but they should learn that all sign systems hold common or standard meaning for both the sender and the receiver, even though the exact meaning varies based on individual experience (Short, Kauffman, & Kahn, 2000).

We will explain how you, as a language arts teacher, can help students appreciate the work of artists, dancers, actors, and musicians, and describe classroom activities that will foster students' creativity in each of the areas. For each discipline, we will explain how to integrate the sign system into the language arts.

Visual Art

Visual art is not created solely for decoration; rather, it is also a means to communicate. It "is a window into an artist's experiences in a particular time and culture" (Cornett, 2007), and viewers make meaning by examining a work's details (O'Neil, 2011). This is especially true as students examine illustrations in children's books so they can better comprehend the written text.

In quality picture books, text and illustration interact in four unique ways: by reinforcing, describing, reciprocating, and establishing (O'Neil, 2011).

1. *Reinforcing.* Illustrations reinforce what the text says or suggests. For example, in *Pretty Salma: A Little Red Riding Hood Story from Africa* (Daly, 2006), Granny asks Salma to go to the market. The text tells the reader that "Salma put on her blue scarf, [and] her stripy *ntama*" (Daly, 2006, no page); the illustration depicts the *ntama* as a wrap-around skirt. Without this illustration, readers unfamiliar with West African culture would be puzzled about Salma's outfit.

2. *Describing.* Illustrations also provide information about the characters and setting that enhance readers' understanding of the text. For example, in Marshall's (1988) retelling of *Goldilocks and the Three Bears*, one neighbor considers Goldilocks a sweet child but another neighbor says, "That's what *you* think." The picture provides clues regarding each neighbor's point of view. Goldilocks is shown as a little girl with a big smile, but also as a scamp who jumps off a swing into a large tub of water, thereby drenching three nearby cats who despise getting wet. These illustrated details provide insight into each neighbor's opinion.

3. *Reciprocating.* Illustrations and text are reciprocal, which means that they reinforce the context for each other, resulting in greater comprehension for the reader. For example, in *Hansel and Gretel* (Marshall, 1990), the mother complains to her husband that "Those wretched children of yours are gobbling everything up" (unpaged); and that she, the pretty wife, is going to "waste away" (unpaged). However, the illustration provides the salient detail that the mother is not wasting away; her jowls droop below her chin, and the rest of her body is voluminous.

4. *Establishing.* Finally, illustrations can establish a parallel story. *Green Snake Ceremony* (Watkins, 1995) is a story about the elders of a Shawnee family searching for a green snake for a girl's green snake ceremony. However, the girl is afraid of snakes and does not want to put one in her mouth, even if it means she will gain strength and good luck. Kim Doner, the illustrator, cleverly tells another story through illustrations about the green snake who lives beneath the family's porch. The text tells readers about the family's preparation for

> You have to have confidence in your ability, and then be tough enough to follow through.
>
> **ROSALYNN CARTER**

the ceremony, but at the same time Doner illustrates a humorous story about the snake that is absent from the text. Doner's illustrations about the family's preparations are realistic, while the alternate story of the snake is rendered in cartoon style. Even though the snake's story has no words, readers comprehend it through illustrations.

Research supports the need for visual arts to be a part of the regular school curriculum because of their many benefits to student development. Studying the details in pictures, such as those in picture books, increases students' higher-order thinking skills (Wingert & Brant, 2005) as well as their reasoning skills, because, among other things, it teaches them to examine details and that pictures can express mood (Deasy, 2002). Furthermore, drawing before writing increases students' writing skills (Norris, Richard, & Mokhtari, 1997) and their understanding of the topic about which they are writing. For example, when students draw historical events after reading informational books or historical novels, they increase their understanding of history (Deasy, 2002). Permitting students to study and experiment with art helps them analyze how different colors can be used to convey emotion and mood (Longo, 1999).

read RESEARCH practice

Visit the website of the National Visual Art Education Association (www.arteducators.org/research/naea-standards) to read the national standards for the visual arts and then incorporate them into your language arts program.

When studying art from different cultures, students develop respect for diversity (McDermott, 2003; O'Neil, 2011). McDermott found that when students create art, they learn to focus and concentrate, respect common tools, and share with others. But one of the greatest benefits of students creating works of art is the confidence they gain by being appreciated for their unique viewpoint, which, according to psychologist Abraham Maslow, is a basic human need (McDermott, 2003).

Elements of the visual arts

For students to become critical consumers and creators of the visual arts, they must be familiar with their basic elements. Beginning in kindergarten, teachers can choose famous works of art or pictures from children's literature to show how artists use the elements of line, shape, color, space, texture, and form.

Line. Lines can be thick, thin, short, long, horizontal, vertical, diagonal, jagged, and even dotted. O'Neil (2011) stresses the importance of explicitly teaching students what different lines represent. For example, smooth, soft lines may represent a peaceful and welcoming setting. Horizontal lines may represent stability and calm. Diagonal lines often represent motion and/or tension. Jagged lines may represent a harsh, threatening setting or a devious character. Whether viewing a masterpiece or illustration from a picture book, prompt students to focus on the type of lines they see. Then using higher-level questioning, ask them how the lines contribute to the picture's mood. You can then facilitate a discussion of how the illustrations work together to convey the story's mood. For example, in Paul O. Zelinsky's *Rapunzel* (1997), the lines are primarily straight. All of these straight lines create a feeling of neatness and order to the forest when the prince rides past the tower and hears Rapunzel's voice. However, when the sorceress cuts Rapunzel's hair in a rage, the background depicts slanted, jagged rocks and mountains, representing anger and chaos. In *Smoky Night* (Bunting, 1994), David Diaz uses broad, black outlines to depict the violence of the 1992 Los Angeles riots. Kevin Henkes in *Wemberly* (2000) uses downward, slightly curved lines that resemble a "U" for eyebrows to depict the worried look of Wemberly and her parents when she is about to start school. In contrast, Henkes uses curved lines that resemble a "U" on the students in the classroom to depict their happy, carefree expressions. Pointing out these details to students and encouraging them to examine all illustrations in such a manner will help them comprehend how art can convey mood. Visit the following website to find lessons on how artists use color and line to create mood: www.master worksfineart.com/education/mood/. The explanation includes works by Georges Braque, Joan Miró, and Pablo Picasso.

Shape. The second element of the visual arts is *shape*. Once students know the names of shapes, they can view illustrations in children's books and discuss the types of shapes they see. In Mo Willems' *Edwina* (2006), students can readily find ovals (treetops), rectangles (signs), squares (an ice cream cart), circles (faces), and crescents (birds' bodies). Give students ample time to view the pictures; the longer they look at details, the more shapes they will discover.

Color. Color is the element that often draws a viewer to a picture. Colors can be primary, secondary, or complementary. They can be different tints or saturations. Colors help create mood. Different colors symbolize different emotions and feelings. For example, red often symbolizes a setting that is hot, exciting, or dangerous, or suggests anger. Blue may symbolize a calm, cool, or even an icy setting or character. Dark colors such as brown, gray, or black may symbolize scary, gloomy, or disastrous settings (O'Neil, 2011). If you ask kindergarteners why they think a picture is happy or sad, most will first point out the color and then look at the details of the character's face or posture for clues. Dr. Seuss's *My Many Colored Days* (1996) is a good book to introduce colors and the moods they can create. Of course, give students the opportunity to discuss whether they agree or disagree with an author's use of color and what it represents. In this Seuss title, for example, students may disagree with the "purple day" page. Dr. Seuss found that purple made him feel sad, but some students may associate purple with feelings of royalty because a king's robes are often purple in pictures. The book *Smoky Night* (Bunting, 1994) can also be used effectively to show how color can create mood. In this book, illustrator David Diaz uses dark acrylics to depict despair.

Permitting students to discuss their points of view and reasoning for them develops higher-level thinking skills, which supports CCRA.SL.1: "Prepare for and participate effectively in a range of conversations and collaborations with diverse partners, building on others' ideas and expressing their own clearly and persuasively"; and CCRA.SL.2: "Integrate and evaluate information presented in diverse media and formats, including visually, quantitatively, and orally" (NGACBP & CCSSO, 2010, p. 22).

Space. Space, the fourth element of visual arts, deals with the way the artist positions the main objects (*positive space*), and then what he or she does with the surrounding space (*negative space*). David Wiesner in *The Three Pigs* (2001) uses space differently on each page. On the first page, he uses the full page for the picture. The picture is outlined with a thin dark line. The world, one of the main objects on the page, is in the foreground, and the other objects—the three pigs building a straw house—are in the background. The negative space is filled with a pale blue sky with faint cumulus clouds and a green meadow. Later in the story, there is a completely white double page with a very small picture of the three pigs flying high on a paper airplane in the upper right-hand corner. The use of space in this picture reinforces the feeling that the pigs are flying off to another place and that they are just specks in a much larger world. You can ask students why they think the artist chose to put the object of the picture off to the side rather than in the middle, which will encourage them to think about what the artist was trying to convey by this use of space. When you point out the unique ways artists use space, you encourage students to use space in creative ways when they illustrate their own stories and poems.

Texture. *Texture* refers to how the objects would feel if one could touch them. A few children's books, especially those for pre-verbal children, use actual textured materials such as felt or plastic to create texture, but in most books artists use a variety of techniques to simulate texture. These techniques create the illusion of objects that are rough, smooth, stiff, or silky. Textures can be simulated by using various types of paper, paint, ink, or charcoal; or through a variety of techniques, such as cross-hatching to create rough textures or a single stroke of paint to create a smooth texture. The cross-hatching in Maurice Sendak's *Where the Wild Things Are* (1963) makes the wild creatures appear rough and hairy. In *So You Want to Be President* (St. George, 2000), David Small creates an American flag from smooth strokes on the page where President Taft is speaking. Black hats on the same page are composed of dark, solid strokes to make them appear stiff, suggesting the formality of the occasion.

Form. Form deals with the three-dimensional illusion of the objects. What is the relationship of the height, width, and depth among the main objects? In *Shouting* (Thomas, 2007), illustrator Annie Lee depicts the dancers, drummers, and church-goers as much taller than the onlookers in the apartment building. This makes the viewer feel closer to the dancers and musicians and more removed from the figures in the apartment house. Lee also makes the building's doors, windows, and steps much smaller than the figures in the foreground, helping viewers understand that the apartment is in the background, farther away than the performers. You can also point out how Lee slants the outlines of the steps leading into the apartment house to create the illusion that the top step is farther away than the lower step. Drawing students' attention to these details helps them understand the visual grammar of drawing, which they may in turn incorporate into their own illustrations. Again, give students ample time to study a picture's details and discuss its forms so that they internalize how details create perspective and convey meaning and emotion that add to the story.

LEARNING about ART from BOOKS

Many children's first exposure to the visual arts is through the picture books that caregivers and teachers share with them. A good illustrator makes a story come alive through pictures. Some artists write and illustrate their own stories, while other artists interpret another person's story, and help readers see the story's setting, characters, and plot as they imagine them. When reading picture books and other books with students, learn what you can about the artists' techniques so you can share the information. Teach students the difference between a charcoal drawing and oil painting. Explore how artists use cardboard cutouts, collage, airbrush, cross-hatching, lithography, pen and ink, woodcuts, linoleum cuts, and watercolor to augment the story. Figure 9.1 lists a small sample of the various art techniques used in books.

FIGURE 9.1 Types of artwork in young people's literature.

TYPE OF ART	ILLUSTRATOR	SAMPLE BOOKS
Cardboard Cutouts	David Wisniewski	*The Secret Knowledge of Grown-ups* (2001)
Cartoons	Mo Willems	*The Pigeon Needs a Bath* (2014) *Knuffle Bunny* (2004)
	Hope Larson	*A Wrinkle in Time: The Graphic Novel* (2013)
	John Rocco	*Blackout* (2012)
Collage	Lois Ehlert	*The Scrap Book* (2014)
	Lane Smith	*Kid Sheriff and the Terrible Toads* (2014)
Cross Hatching	Brian Selznick	*The Invention of Hugo Cabret* (2007) *Wonderstruck* (2013)
	Raon Barrett	*Cloudy with a Chance of Meatballs* (1982)
Oils	Jan Brett	*Cinders: A Chicken Cinderella* (2012) *The Animal's Santa* (2014)
	Mike Wimmer	*George: George Washington, Our Founding Father* (2012)
Paper Cut Collage	Christian Robinson	*Rain* (2013)
Sepia Tone	Chris Van Allsburg	*Niagara Falls Barrel Ride* (2011)
Pastels	Lynn Chapman	*Class Three All at Sea* (2008)
Pen and Ink	Kevin Henkes	*Penny and Her Song* (2012) *Lilly's Big Day* (2006)
Graphite Pencil and Watercolor Wash	Jill Barron	*Puss Jekyll and Cat Hyde* (2013)
Photography	J. Patrick Lewis	*Book of Animal Poetry* (2012)
Watercolor	David Wiesner	*Art and Max* (2010) *Mr. Wuffles!* (2013)
	Jerry Pinkney	*A Starlit Snowflake* (2011) *The Lion and the Mouse* (2009)
Woodcuts	John Schirmer	*Have You Seen My Bird?* (2007)
Linoleum Cuts	Leslie Evans	*Winter: An Alphabet Acrostic* (2002)
Colored Pencil	Lynne Cherry	*The Great Kapok Tree* (2000)
Charcoal	Kevin Henkes	*Kitten's First Full Moon* (2004)
Caricature	David Small	*So You Want to Be President?* (2000)
Tissue Paper Collage	Eric Carle	*Eric Carle's ABC* (2007)
Paper Pulp	Denise Fleming	*Go Shapes, Go* (2014)
Digital Art	Don Wood	*Into the Volcano* (2012)
Scratchboard	Brian Pinkney	*Hush Little Baby* (2005) *Duke Ellington* (1998)
	Beth Krommes	*House in the Night* (2012)
Graphic Novels	Aaron Renier	*The Unsinkable Walker Bean* (2010)
	Sid Jacobson & Ernie Colon	*Anne Frank: The Anne Frank House Authorized Graphic Novel* (2010)

Students as critical consumers of the visual arts

Students' exposure to great works of art should extend beyond picture books. Teachers should expose students to many different artists and many different types of art (e.g., cubism, abstract, realism, expressionism, impressionism, surrealism, and pop art). One book that provides information on all these types of art and their creators is *Great Paintings of the Western World* (Gruitrooy, Weisberg, & Gallup, 1997). In addition, use the Internet to access images of masterpieces from museums around the world. Many art museums make at least part of their collections viewable online. You can also find images of most masterpieces by searching on the work's title. You can project the works onto the classroom screen for all students to see. Figure 9.2 lists useful art websites; preview them before using them in class or recommending them to students, caregivers, or other teachers.

When analyzing a work of art, have students describe its various elements—color, form, texture, and shape. Using higher-level questions, guide students to examine details in depth. Students are more likely to include more detail in their own artwork if they understand how famous artists use detail.

Students as creators of the visual arts

Students should not only be viewers of art but also creators. As indicated earlier, creating art helps students with writing, focus and concentration, responsibility, and self-confidence. Encourage students to draw before they write a story. Once they begin to write, encourage them to illustrate their work so the reader can see the characters and scenes. Some students will say, "I can't draw." You can counteract this declaration by reading *The Dot* (Reynolds, 2003). In this story the teacher invites students to "just make a dot and see where it takes you." Vashti makes one dot and at the end of the hour the teacher asks her to sign her picture. The next day Vashti is surprised to see her picture hanging in a frame above the teacher's desk. Vashti decides she can make all sizes and colors of dots, so she creates unique paintings with different types of dots. There is a delightful reading of this book on YouTube.

Students need to understand that art takes discipline and time to refine. Just like writing, it is a process. For example, students can plan their drawing, create a first sketch in pencil, revise it with an eraser, add details and color, and finally display it. Provide ample time for each step and allow students to experiment with all types of materials and genres. Some students may enjoy the variability and happy accidents of watercolors, while others prefer the dependability and predictability of pen and ink. Likewise, some students may want to draw monsters and imaginary realms and others may stick to the realistic world they inhabit. Your job is to demonstrate the basic ways to use different tools and materials. For example, if you want students

Websites of artists and masterpieces.   **FIGURE 9.2**

Artcyclopedia, www.artcyclopedia.com/

FamousPainter.com, www.famouspainter.com/

Kids Art, http://kidsart.com/

Online Art Journey, http://comminfo.rutgers.edu/professional-development/childlit/
    Syllabus/art500.html

Education Index, http://educationindex.com/art/

to experiment with scratchboard after reading one of Brian Pinkney's books, show them how to do it first. Also show students how to apply watercolor, use poster paints, and sketch with pastels. Scaffold students as they practice techniques by giving helpful, clear feedback on specific aspects of their work.

Self-expression is the primary goal of art. Students should understand that art must express their feelings and thoughts—not someone else's. They must understand that being unique is exciting. Showing appreciation for everyone's work permits all students to express themselves in a risk-free environment.

Focus on a different element of art in each lesson. Cornett (2010) suggested several activities to accomplish this:

- *Lines:* Use a flashlight to "draw" different types of lines and have students create similar lines on individual tablets or whiteboards.
- *Shapes:* Ask students to find different shapes in the classroom (e.g., rectangular windows and doors, round light fixtures, square tiles) and draw the basic shape, then add the details. Provide circles, triangles, rectangles, ovals, and other shapes of different sizes and colors and invite students to create pictures that tell a story with these geometric shapes.
- *Texture:* Have students create rubbings of surfaces in the classroom—crayon rubs of the floor, their chairs, their desks, and other textured objects in the room.
- *Color:* Have students focus on the hues and tints of color by using paint samples from the hardware store and have students create names for the colors (for example, sea breeze blue, cookie dough tan). Students can then attempt to make the color by mixing poster paints or acrylics together.
- *Space and composition:* Share a photograph of Mount Rushmore, and then show it as drawn by Chris Van Allsburg in *Ben's Dream* (1982). Van Allsburg focuses on a small section of the massive sculpture and magnifies it to fill the entire space of the page. You can take any picture and have students draw one tiny part of it as if it were under a magnifying glass.
- *Form:* Show students how to draw cubes, cylinders, and spheres and have them practice drawing them on a whiteboard. Encourage them to experiment with the height and width so the form changes.

Students should have many opportunities during their elementary school years to experiment with all different types of art when they illustrate their stories, poems, or informational texts. Cornett (2010) suggested some of the following activities:

- drawing with various tools
- rubbings of many different surfaces with various tools
- chalk drawings
- cross-hatching
- painting at an easel
- printmaking (woodcuts, linoleum cuts)
- collage
- murals
- fiber art
- class quilt
- self-portrait
- papier-mâché
- mobiles
- dioramas
- yarn art
- puppets and masks
- abstract sculptures

Integrating the visual arts

You can easily integrate the visual arts when teaching language arts. Carefully examining the art with young students not only gives them an opportunity to learn about the different techniques that artists use, but it also helps them develop a critical eye as they learn to read and appreciate children's literature. Closely studying the illustrations in Jan Brett's books (www.janbrett.com) will help students comprehend the written material and increase their learning. For example, Brett's illustrations depict the physical features of animals students may have never seen in real life, as well as the environment in which they live. To research her picture books, Brett travels all over the world and observes many cultures to give her drawings authenticity. For example, in *The Umbrella* (2004), students learn about the physical features of a toucan, a kinkajou, a tapir, a quetzal bird, a tree frog, and a hummingbird that live in a rain forest. Students can increase their geography knowledge by consulting a map to see where the rain forests are located. In *The Mitten* (1989), students learn about a mole, a snowshoe rabbit, a hedgehog, an owl, a badger, a fox, and a bear, and they can look up Ukraine on a map. Students then can research for information about the country's people, traditional clothing, and customs.

Students can also learn much from Jerry Pinkney's art found in more than 70 of his picture books. Pinkney, who has been creating art using watercolor and pencil for more than 30 years, has won the Coretta Scott King Award five times. As an artist Pinkney is concerned about rendering details correctly so readers can learn from his illustrations. Because many of his illustrations accompany his works of historical fiction, he makes sure that the characters' clothing and surroundings reflect the story's era. For example, readers of *Goin' Someplace Special* (2001) see what clothing people wore in the 1950s and what cars looked like. Each illustration includes vivid patterns and textures. Pinkney often has people model for him; he takes photographs so he can study details and facial features to draw them as realistically as possible. From his example, students can learn that they too can photograph scenes, objects, or people and then use the photographs as a reference. Some Pinkney books that address the customs of people in different eras are *The Hired Hand* (1997), *Back Home* (1992), *Albidaro and the Mischievous Dream* (2000), and *Black Cowboy* (1999).

Artists also create beautiful illustrations for informational books. These detailed, colorful illustrations often captivate the students' attention and help them comprehend the information. Picture books permit students to observe tiny details of insects and animals that are either hard to see, rare, or dangerous in real life. For example, students get a close-up view of honeybees as they read *The Honey Makers* by Gail Gibbons (2000). Her attention to detail helps students visualize how hives are formed and how bees make honey. As students read *Owls* (2005), they learn about the various owls' physical features and their habitats.

Teachers have a wide selection of quality picture books from which to choose when they integrate art and literature. One wordless book that displays masterpieces found in New York's Metropolitan Museum of Art is *You Can't Take a Balloon into the Metropolitan Museum* (Weitzman & Glasser, 1998). Students can choose one of the works featured in the book and research it online. You can gather all their information and create a class book about art. You can do something similar with *The Man Who Walked Between the Towers* (Gerstein, 2003). Students can research the architecture of the former World Trade Center towers and then compare it to the architecture of the new Freedom Tower or other skyscrapers in Manhattan.

Ms. Furnish's picture-book detectives

After learning about and examining the elements of art, Ms. Furnish invites her fifth-grade class to become picture-book detectives, an idea she got from Claudia Cornett's *Creating Meaning Through Literature and the Arts* (2010). Before reading the book *The Eleventh Hour: Curious Mystery* (Base, 1988), she has her students approach the book like detectives and answer the following questions: What is the setting? Who are the characters? From the pictures, who are the "good" guys and who might be the "bad" guys? What clues in the pictures indicate the sequence of events? What details in the pictures indicate the style or mood of the events? What is the point of view? Ms. Furnish purchased a set of 8 x 10 pictures of *The Eleventh Hour: Curious Mystery* from a teachers' supply store. She did not show the book's cover; she only gave the students its title.

When looking at page one, students think the character bent over the desk might be an overweight man paying bills. Angela then notices he had a tail and decides it must be an animal. Because of its size, Dameon thinks it is an elephant. Jon sees the time on the clock and suggests that the eleventh hour has not arrived yet, but that the action would take place within three hours. Trinity notices the invitation on the floor and says the character is late getting his invitations mailed. Sonja notices the paper on the floor says *G. Base* and the book says "ANI," so she thinks the book is by Graeme Base and the book on the floor is *Animalia*. She also thinks it will be a happy story because the colors are bright and light. However, Juan points out the border with the pencils and the message: "Drawing Conclusions From Sketchy Clues May Lead You Astray. Sharpen Your Eyes and Your Wits. Get the Point," and disagrees with Sonja. He says, "We have a big mystery on our hands; that's what this book is all about. That is why the character's back is turned. We have to find out who he is."

At this point, Ms. Furnish asks the class if they want to see the next picture, but they want to look for more clues in this picture. Ashley sees an airplane, a picture of a car, and the map on the wall and thinks the main character is inviting people from around the world to a party. Ms. Furnish asks if anyone sees clues about what the invitation contains. Nate says maybe the author is inviting readers to a good mystery.

Ms. Furnish planned to go through the entire set of pictures in one class period; however, because students had been practicing looking for details while studying great works of art, they want to make sure they do not miss anything before moving on to the next picture. Thus, it takes them 10 days to play detective with all of the pictures. Many times they ask to go back to different pictures to determine which guest is missing during the games.

Ms. Furnish realizes that studying the details in masterpieces has made her students more critical and observant consumers of picture books.

Drama

Another sign system that should be a part of every language arts curriculum is drama, which includes improvisation, puppet shows, skits, and readers theater (also discussed in Chapter 5). Research indicates that incorporating drama in the classroom offers many benefits; it increases academic achievement (Deasy, 2002; Dupont, 1992; Fiske, 1999), English learners' verbal skills (Vitz, 1983), minority students' reading comprehension and self-concept (Gourgey, Bousseau, & Delgado, 1985), and students' ability to show empathy (Lushington, 2003). Because drama involves teamwork, students learn social skills, how to appreciate others' opinions, compromise, and other aspects of cooperation (Deasy, 2002). Drama also "contributes to aesthetic development" (Cornett, 2007), which is one of people's basic needs according to Maslow.

Elements of drama

The elements of drama are much the same as the elements of literature: characters, conflict, plot, setting, and mood. In a language arts lesson, explain the elements of literature and then relate them to drama. For example, explain that in a play the audience comes to understand the characters through their actions and their relationships with other characters; the audience generally does not know the character's unspoken thoughts, as is often the case in a novel. It is never too early for students to understand that a play is successful when the actors inhabit their characters completely. Actors need to stay in character throughout the play so the audience becomes wrapped up in the story. Focusing on staying in character helps develop students' concentration. To help students develop this ability to stay in character, have them practice being characters, then on the count of three have them freeze for 10 seconds. Ten seconds seem like an eternity for young students!

Setting is also a key element in drama. In some dramatic productions, the setting is merely suggested through simple costumes and minimal stage props, while in other productions elaborate sets create vivid and immersive environments. Mood is created through the lighting, sets, and costumes.

read RESEARCH practice

Go to the AATE site to learn about the national standards for drama, at www.aate.com/?page= NationalStandards. Currently, the National Standards for Theatre Education are grouped into grades K–4, 5–8, and 9–12.

Genres in drama

There are many genres of drama, including tragedy, comedy, historical, and musical. In a language arts lesson, make connections between genres in literature and drama. After reading a story, ask your students what type of literature it is, whether the book would make a great play, and what type of play it could become: comic, tragic, romantic, fantasy, and so on. The main mood of the play usually conveys its genre. In some stories, students realize that some parts will be sad, while other parts will be happy. Students can learn about the importance of comic relief in a tragedy.

Teaching students to become critical consumers of drama

Although it is not necessary for students to experience a play before participating in classroom drama activities, every elementary student should see a play sooner or later. Attending a play often ignites students' creativity and unleashes a desire to act out stories. If your school is located near a university or in a town that has a community theater, investigate taking your class to a matinee for a field trip. Many universities provide free matinees for area schools and give students tours behind stage so they can see how sets are quickly changed while the curtain is down.

Use such an event as a teaching tool by discussing the difference between acts and scenes and how sets can be very elaborate or merely suggestions of a play's setting and time period. Ask the students which characters they identify with and why, and discuss what the actors did to make their characters seem like real people.

Before attending the play, teach the students proper audience etiquette (e.g., no talking or moving around the theater during the performance, turning off all electronic devices, and applauding at the appropriate times).

If the play is based on a work of literature that the students have read, you can discuss how the plot and characters are similar to or different from the book version. Many times, a play will add characters; students can discuss whether this distracted from the story or added to it. In all of these discussions, always ask the "why" questions so students develop higher-thinking skills. Also remember not to judge the students' opinions.

If your class does not have an opportunity to attend a live performance, you can screen a video of a play based on a work of literature. Arrange your room like a theater and teach all of the elements of drama. Again, it is important to give students ample time to critique the video and give their reasoning. Through these types of discussions, students learn to analyze the elements of drama and literature. This will result in better comprehension of an author's works and, ultimately, better writing skills.

Teaching students to become actors and playwrights

When beginning a unit on drama, show students how to stand straight and speak so their voices project to the back row and how to move on stage without turning their backs to the audience or blocking other actors. Such movements are not intuitive and will require much practice. Teach the terms *stage left, stage right, upstage, downstage, cut, exit, on cue,* and *action* and the importance of rehearsing stage directions and cues until the drama is ready for an audience.

Types of drama commonly found in the elementary classroom are improvisation, pantomime, readers theater, storytelling, puppet shows, and theater acting with scripts. The first five types were discussed in Chapter 8. Theater acting involves plays with scripts written by others or by the students themselves. Students memorize their lines, create sets, design costumes, and obtain props. Such plays include all of the oral language activities described in Chapter 8, including movement exercises, pantomime, improvisation, speaking with feeling and expression, discussion and interpretation of scripts, and rehearsing. They also include what for some students is the most difficult aspect of acting: memorization. Because of the pressure this places on younger students, introduce theater acting only after students have experienced other forms of drama. However, even very young students can be taught the rudiments of play acting.

Too often school administrators require teachers to have their class perform a play (the traditional Thanksgiving or Christmas auditorium performance) without any prior preparation in oral communication or acting. This is a mistake. Theater acting should be part of the learning process that leads students to a greater appreciation of literature; builds confidence in oral communication abilities; and enhances social growth, including cooperative learning skills. Children's drama authority Nellie McCaslin (1996) argued that theater acting is a vital part of children's aesthetic education, which too often is missing or minimized in elementary curricula.

To introduce theater acting in the elementary classroom, Dorothy Heathcote (Heathcote & Bolton, 1995) recommended that teachers begin with discussion. Talk about the work to be performed. Encourage the students to make suggestions and decisions about the characters, the setting, the staging, and so on. Then improvise the play or story until everyone has a sense of the action, the characters' movements, and the overall theme of the play or story. Do not be afraid to revise lines, change parts, or recast roles. Depending on the nature of the work selected, older students may wish to conduct additional research about the play's subject matter or time period.

At times, students should be invited to write scripts, either in groups or individually, based on scenes from a book or to write original scripts based on their own stories. Unlike scripts for readers theater, these scripts should not have a narrator—the entire story should be told through dialogue. Appendix B.16 has a list of appropriate books to use for pantomime, improvisation, or script writing. The difference between improvisation and script writing is that students ad lib during improvisation, but plan and write out the script with all the intended action in script writing.

Before students write their first scripts, explain how a script differs from a narrative piece. Teach them how to format a script and how to use parentheses to indicate

Sources of plays for theater acting.   **FIGURE 9.3**

> **www.childrenstheatreplays.com** Free scripts of *Treasure Island, Young Pirates of the Caribbean, A Thousand Cranes, Aladdin, Beauty and the Beast,* plus more.
>
> **www.lazybeescripts.co.uk** Multiple scripts sorted by age and topic.
>
> Shepard, A. (2005). *Stories on Stage: Children's Plays for Readers Theater, with 15 Reader's Theatre Play Scripts From 15 Authors, Including Roald Dahl's The Twits and Louis Sachar's Sideways Stories from Wayside School*
>
> **www.badwolfpress.com/** Scripts, audio recordings, and sheet music organized by topic, grade, and length.

stage directions. Use the formal writing process (prewriting, drafting, revising, editing, and publishing; see Chapter 7) even when writing scripts.

See Figure 9.3 for play suggestions. Additionally, two websites featuring scripts are:

- **www.aaronshep.com/rt** This website offers free scripts for readers theater for grades 1 through high school.
- **http://childrenstheatreplays.com** This website lists scripts that teachers can purchase. Commercial scripts usually require that you pay royalty fees.

Theater acting represents the culmination of a dramatics unit. It integrates listening, speaking, reading, and writing skills like no other single activity. It gives students a heightened awareness of the power of literature to evoke emotions from an audience. It engages them in critical thinking and discussion. However, producing a full-scale play in your class is a huge commitment of time and energy. The sacrifices you make, however, are worth the excitement, enthusiasm, and genuine learning that take place when students discover their talents as actors, playwrights, set designers, and stagehands.

In all senses, drama is a natural fit with language arts because students love to act out stories they enjoy. Doing so helps them develop their listening and speaking skills. Writing scripts helps them develop their reading and writing skills.

Dance

Like other sign systems, dance is a way to communicate, express feelings and emotions, convey a story, and elicit a response from the viewers (Cornett, 2010). Like many teachers, you may shy away from including dance in your curriculum because you do not see yourself as a dancer. However, we hope to build your confidence and convince you that dance belongs in the language arts classroom. Many of the dances appropriate for the classroom fall in the creative dance category—they do not require students to memorize dance steps or a routine. However, you will find that you probably have a number of talented and enthusiastic dancers in your class.

Like visual arts and drama, dance brings many developmental benefits to young people—it increases academic performance (Deasy, 2002; Jay, 1991; Jensen, 2001; MacMahon, Rose, & Parks, 2003); increases pride in one's culture (Hagood, 2006); develops creative problem-solving skills (Fleming, 1990); and develops respect, concentra-

read RESEARCH practice

To learn about the national standards for dance, visit the National Dance Education Organization at www.ndeo.org.

tion, confidence, responsibility, and self-control (Cornett, 2010). Dance is also great exercise that promotes good health (Wright, Hernandez, & Joperd (2014) and fulfills the basic human need for beauty.

Elements of dance

The elements of dance are body, energy, space, and time. Because dance is a means of conveying a message, dancers need to develop all four elements so the audience can interpret the message solely from a dancer's movements. Just like poets who carefully choose words to convey their intended message, dancers must carefully use their bodies, space, time, and physical energy to convey their intended message.

Body. Dancers use all parts of their body, from their head to their toes. Teach students to concentrate on how each part of their bodies move as they stretch, bend, walk, leap, or glide. Where should their hands be when they lean forward? Should their legs be stiff like a robot's or springy like a kangaroo's? All parts need to work together to convey their intended mood and message.

Energy. Dancers must not only be conscious of every part of their body, but they must also apply the appropriate amount of energy in all parts of their body to help convey their message. For example, a dancer's rigid arms or legs may impart a feeling of inner turmoil. However, if a dancer's torso is extended gracefully and she is lightly leaping through the air, she may be conveying a message of inner harmony or happiness. Furthermore, a dancer must learn to modulate his energy so he can crouch down low and jump up high, run quickly to signify fright, or move in slow motion to signify a dreamlike trance. Students can learn to make their dance movements more energetic or less energetic to represent different moods.

Space. Space refers to how each individual dancer moves across a stage and how all the dancers together inhabit the stage. Space also includes the direction of the dancers' movements and the patterns of the routine. Show the students the difference between a dancer who struts from stage right to stage left in a straight line with great energy, arms swinging wide and head held high, and a dancer who shuffles slowly in a small circle, head hung low and arms wrapped around his waist.

Time. Time pertains to all of the timing elements of music—rhythm, tempo, accent, duration, and phrases or patterns. Dancers' movements typically must be in sync with the music to which they are dancing. Ask your students to think about a dancer that they have watched recently, perhaps on a television show. They can comment on how the dancer's movements matched the music's tempo, accent, phrases, and pulse.

Students becoming critical consumers of dance

To help students understand how various dances can communicate various messages, invite a local dancer or dance instructor to come and demonstrate how dancers use their entire bodies and how they use the elements of dance to tell a story or create a mood. You can also show and discuss a DVD of a ballet performance such as *The Sleeping Beauty* by Tchaikovsky to accomplish the same thing. Stress the fact that all dancers are athletes, and that dance takes many forms, from ballet, modern, hip hop, stepping, cheerleading, dance crews, to ice dancing, ballroom dancing, and various kinds of ethnic dancing. You can find many videos online that will

> Education's purpose is to replace an empty mind with an open one.
> **MALCOLM FORBES**

convince both boys and girls of the hard work, athleticism, and talent it takes to become a good dancer.

Students should also have the opportunity to view a live dance performance if possible. Many cities have dance companies that perform different ballets throughout the year, and most perform *The Nutcracker* in December. Matinees are less expensive than evening shows, and many fine arts associations will sponsor schools in low economic areas.

If attending a live performance is not possible, build a library of videos or video clips for the students to use. Shows such as *So You Think You Can Dance* and *Dancing with the Stars* feature many different types of dancing, and YouTube is a good resource for specific types of dances. Figure 9.4 has a short list of other video sources.

read RESEARCH practice

Search online or go to your local public library to find videos, DVDs, books, and other reference materials to learn more about different types of dances and ideas to use in the classroom.

RRP

Students as creators of dance

Students should not only be critical consumers of dance, but they also should learn to enjoy dancing. They can do this by appreciating the concentration and hard work it takes to create a good performance. This means listening closely to the music, following a rhythm, understanding a song's mood, and knowing what they want to convey through their movements.

Most of the dance in the language arts classroom will be creative dance. As a warm-up, play a song that students may recognize from television commercials or cartoons and invite them to write down adjectives that describe how the music makes them feel and list the movements they would use to express that mood. Model for your students how to express a mood through dance. Then have the students perform the movements they wrote down.

Language arts teachers should also make sure students understand the difference between creative dance and pantomime. "Movement becomes dance when there is focus on expressing thoughts and feelings" (Cornett, 2007, p. 284); in contrast, pantomime is moving like the object, animal, or character. For example, in a pantomime, students imitate the walk of a cat; in dance, students express the feelings of a cat being lost in a dark alley.

Dance is often the interpretation of a piece of music, so it is a good idea to have a wide variety of music available so students can listen critically to various beats, tempos, and moods as they are learning this form of interpretation. Discussing a song's beat and rhythm helps students tailor their movements to fit

Dance videos and DVDs.   **FIGURE 9.4**

BrainDance (85 minutes). Available at www.creativedance.org.

Video: *Creative Movement: A Step Toward Intelligence*. Available at www.youtube.com/watch?v=FvX3rKRX7dA. DVD also available.

Dance and Grow (60 minutes). Available from Dance Horizons at www.dancehorizons.com/.

Move 'N Groove Kids (26 minutes). Available at https://movengroovekids.com/.

PBS Video, at www.pbs.org, offers many videos about dance and dancers.

the music. As with visual art, the purpose of creative dance is not for students to imitate you; rather, they need a risk-free environment so they feel free to explore movements. Suggestions for music that includes many moods are listed in Figure 9.5. Many public libraries have these recordings in their music collection, or your district's music teacher may have these recordings. A feature film that shows the various types of ballroom dancing is *Mad Hot Ballroom* (2005).

Integrating dance with the language arts

Many dance forms originate with specific cultures or ethnic groups, so it is easy to enrich a unit on multicultural literature with dance. For example, after reading parts of *Native American Dance Steps* (Evans & Evans, 2003) a class can attend a local event; for example, the Red Earth Festival in Oklahoma features Native Americans from throughout the United States who perform their dances with great passion. At this event, students see the differences in tribal costumes as well as a wide variation of dances. Many other ethnic festivals—Greek, Italian, Polish, and Irish—include dances that can augment your teaching of literature reflecting these cultures. Introduce students to African dances, Irish jigs, Austrian waltzes and minuets, Polish polkas, Native American dances, Dutch street dances, Western square dances, and German folk dances when they are studying the literature of those cultures.

You may wish to have students choose a dance to research and report on. Have them write about the history of the dance, the country in which it originated, and its famous performers. For example, introduce the flamenco dance after reading the chapter "Hispanic Dance and Flamenco" in *Kids Make Music! Clapping and Tapping from Bach to Rock* (Hart & Mantell, 1993). Show students how they can search online to find out the history of flamenco, its well-known performers, and video clips of performances.

Dance is also easily integrated with writing. After viewing a ballet, modern, hip hop, or other dance, students can write poems to describe the feelings the dance evoked, or they can write a narrative that describes the dance. Encourage students to use vivid adjectives and verbs to describe the dance, to increase their vocabulary. Engage students in a writing exercise after they perform a creative dance. How did the music make them feel? What mood did they convey through the dance? What message were they attempting to convey? What movements did they use to convey that meaning? How could the dancers improve their movements in a future performance so they could more clearly convey that message?

Just as you teach your students about authors, you can have students research, read, and report on well-known dancers, past and present. Given the current popu-

---

FIGURE 9.5 Musical compositions appropriate for creative dance.

Bach's *Jesu, Joy of Man's Desiring, Ninth Symphony*	Mozart's *The Magic Flute, A Little Night Music*
Berlioz's *Symphony Fantastique*	Rossini's *William Tell Overture, The Barber of Seville*
Copeland's *Appalachian Spring*	Strauss's *Blue Danube Waltz*
Debussy's *Clouds, Prelude to the Afternoon of a Faun*	Tchaikovsky's *Nutcracker, Swan Lake, The Sleeping Beauty*
Gershwin's *Rhapsody in Blue*	
Handel's *Water Music*	Vivaldi's *Four Seasons*
Haydn's *Clock Symphony, Surprise Symphony*	Any recording of the sounds of nature

larity of television dance competition shows, you may find your students are more interested in dance than ever before. Pique student interest in such a project by choosing one or two dancers, giving a brief outline of their lives, discussing how they became famous, and showing a video of their dancing.

Music

Music is integrated into many elementary classrooms. Kindergarten teachers often use music to teach the days of the week, months of the year, and the alphabet. They use other songs to get students to work off excess energy or come to attention. Elementary teachers often play classical music when students begin individual work. The music is played softly so the students must be quiet to hear it.

Research indicates that music increases academic growth (Deasy, 2002; Kippelen, 2002; Scripp, 2003). In fact, kindergarten students who listened to music scored higher on the DIBELS test than the students who did not listen to music (Register, 2004). Besides academic growth, music promotes physical health (Scripp, 2003), mental health (Jensen, 2000), and cooperation (Hope, 2003).

Many researchers have studied the impact of Wolfgang Mozart's music on people's memory and ability to learn. Scripp (2003) found that listening to music while one studies or reads temporarily affects learning, but he found that being musically literate—able to read, write, and critique music—has a long-term positive effect on learning. Jensen (2000) suggested that if you do listen to music while studying, the best is Baroque music or soft jazz with 65 to 80 beats per minute.

read **RESEARCH** practice

To learn about the National Standards for Music Education, visit http://musiced.nafme.org/musicstandards/

Elements of music

The basic elements of music are tempo, pitch/notation, timbre, dynamics, and texture.

Tempo. Tempo relates to the speed, rhythm, and basic meter of the composition. Songs can be very slow (*largo*), of moderate speed (*moderato*), or very fast (*presto*); note that the terms for tempo are in Italian. Rhythms can be smooth (*cantabile*) or uneven (*syncopated*). The meter is the basic beat of music. The first beat of any meter is accented so it is easy to hear the meter of a composition. The basic meters are a 1-2 beat (2/4 meter), a 1-2-3 beat (3/4 meter as in a waltz), or a 1-2-3-4 beat (4/4 meter as in a march).

Pitch. Pitch is indicated by notes on a staff. The treble clef is for the higher pitches and the bass clef is for the lower pitches. Many elementary students learn how to read the treble clef so they can play in the school band. The duration of a pitch is indicated by whole notes, half notes, quarter notes, and eighth notes. Figure 9.6 has a treble staff with the names of the notes and also a sample of basic meters showing the value of notes. If *legato* is written at the beginning of the piece, the composer intends the musician to move from one pitch to the next in a smooth manner; however, if notes are accompanied by black dots (staccato markings), the composer intends the musician to play one note to the next in a distinct manner.

Timbre. Timbre relates to the unique quality of a voice or musical instrument that distinguishes it from other voices or musical instruments. Two famous singers may both be tenors, but their fans can probably tell them apart due to their timbre. A full orchestra includes four families of instruments—wind, reed, brass, string, and

FIGURE 9.6   Names of notes on treble clef and note values in common time.

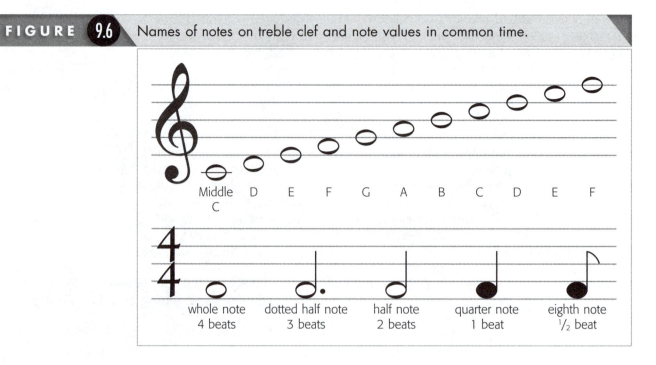

whole note	dotted half note	half note	quarter note	eighth note
4 beats	3 beats	2 beats	1 beat	½ beat

percussion. A violin may play the same notes as a flute, but because their timbres are unique they are easily distinguishable. Use the information in Figure 9.7 to introduce your students to the concept of timbre and how it relates to different musical instruments.

Listeners often have a preference for a particular timbre. Some listeners enjoy the soft sound of a single flute, while others prefer the brassy timbre of the saxophone.

Dynamics. The fourth element of music is dynamics, or its variation in volume. One only has to listen to music for a short period of time to understand that dynamics adds interest to a song. You may become irritated if a singer belts out a song at full volume for its entire duration; conversely, you may find a slow song sung in a breathy voice with just a single guitar very dull. By varying a song's dynamics, perhaps by having slower, softer verses and a louder, more powerful chorus, it becomes more interesting and musically rich. As with tempo, the dynamics of a song are rendered in Italian. Very soft playing is marked *pianissimo; piano* is a little louder, but still soft; *mezzo piano* is half soft; *moderato* is medium loud; *forte* is loud; and *fortissimo* is very loud. If a composer wants the music to become gradually louder, he marks the music *crescendo;* if he wants the music to become gradually softer, he marks the music *decrescendo*.

Texture. The last element of music is texture, which is the layering of different instruments or voices. One voice with no instruments (a capella) creates a different texture than a 50-voice choir and full orchestra. One voice has a thin sound, while the choir and orchestra has a full sound. The former would be considered finely textured and spare (though possibly quite beautiful), and the latter richly textured due to multiple harmonies and the fact that not all instruments play the same notes. One of the differences between a rock band and a single violin playing the same song is the amount of texture each brings to the performance.

Wind instruments. Players produce the sounds of wind instruments by blowing into or over a hole. The flute and piccolo are wind instruments, but most are made of wood.

Reed instruments. Musicians play reed instruments by blowing air through an opening that vibrates a thin piece of wood called a reed; reed instruments are made of either metal or wood. Saxophones, clarinets, and oboes are common reed instruments.

Brass instruments. Players blow into a metal mouthpiece to produce sound on a brass instrument, all of which are made of metal. Common brass instruments are the trumpet, French horn, trombone, and tuba.

String instruments. String instruments make sounds when players pluck, strike, strum, or draw a bow over the strings. Common string instruments are the violin, harp, guitar, and piano.

Percussion instruments. All percussion instruments are struck with a hand, a stick, or a mallet. Drums, chimes, bells, triangles, and tambourines are percussion instruments.

Teaching students to become critical consumers of music

In order for students to appreciate diverse types of music, they need to know music's basic elements, recognize the sound of many instruments, and understand how the elements of music combine to communicate meaning. Most students are familiar with the story of Peter and the wolf, and language arts teachers can find the entire musical production of *Peter and the Wolf* (Prokofiev, 1936) on YouTube to show students how music conveys meaning. The symphony is written so that each character is represented by a different instrument. A narrator usually explains which instrument is being played and how each instrument's theme represents each character. Encourage discussion about how the musical themes and instruments depict the contrast between the characters (e.g., Peter, the wolf, the duck).

Another recording that introduces students to the different instruments in the orchestra is *The Young Person's Guide to the Orchestra* (Britten, 1946). You may

Ms. Chambers expands the curriculum with classical music

Ms. Chambers, a middle-school language arts teacher, thinks she will benefit her students by introducing them to classical music. She was a music major in college and wants to share her passion for such music with her classes. Her school has a band, but no orchestra. The band director usually selects marches or show tunes because the students respond well to that type of music; Ms. Chambers believes that introducing students to classical music in addition to the songs they are learning in band presents an opportunity for them to expand their knowledge base of music.

The faculty is discussing next year's curriculum and the possibility of adding nine-week courses to introduce students to a variety of subjects. Ms. Chambers volunteers to teach a class in classical music appreciation. Many of her colleagues think students will not be interested, but Ms. Chambers persists and is allotted the first nine-week block.

Ms. Chambers knows she will be successful if she chooses the music carefully. Throughout the summer, she listens to TV ads and Saturday-morning children's programs to identify the classical music that may be familiar to her students. She compiles a list of works, creates short biographies of the composers, and develops the course. Of course, being a music major, she accumulates more material than she can use, but this gives her options in case her students do not respond to a certain work the way she hopes.

On the first day of class, Ms. Chambers plays Pachelbel's *Canon in D Major,* a very popular piece that is used in a current light bulb commercial. The students recognize the melody and want to hear the whole work—Ms. Chambers already has the students hooked on classical music! The next day she plays Ravel's *Bolero,* music from a movie she saw advertised on TV. Students enjoy listening to the song's repeated theme played on different instruments. One student exclaims, "This music has passion!"

During the first class, Ms. Chambers learns that three of the students play in the city's youth orchestra, four more take piano lessons, and one girl is rehearsing for the city's annual production of *The Nutcracker.* Ms. Chambers asks them if they would like stage a mini-concert in class on Fridays to play their instruments for each other. Every student who plays an instrument signs up, including the ballerina, and even Roberto, an English learner who plays the drums in his church band.

The students not only enjoy hearing the music Ms. Chambers plays for them, but they also like researching and reading about the composers' lives, different periods of music, and the evolution of various instruments. They are surprised to learn that many famous composers were often poor, not wealthy like today's rock stars. They marvel at the fact that Beethoven was deaf when he wrote his last symphony and that a single moonbeam inspired him to write *Moonlight Sonata.* They are intrigued with Tchaikovsky's life and Haydn's audacity in conducting the premier of *The Farewell Symphony.* Some students are so interested in learning about composers that they choose to write about them for their English class research report. Others write stories to fit a particular musical composition. For example, three students choose the *1812 Overture,* but all three come up with very different plots.

Ms. Chambers' students love the course—some even listen to music in the classroom during their lunch hour. The other teachers are truly amazed that middle-school students can appreciate classical music. Some of the favorite compositions that Ms. Chambers' students enjoy are:

- Pachelbel's *Canon in D Major*
- Bach's *Toccata in D Minor* and *The Passacaglia in C Minor*
- Mussorgsky's *Pictures at an Exhibition*
- Beethoven's *Moonlight Sonata*
- Mozart's *Piano Concerto in C Major*
- Tchaikovsky's *1812 Overture*
- Beethoven's *Fifth Symphony*
- Ravel's *Bolero*
- Debussy's *Clair de Lune*
- Bizet's *Carmen*

want to display pictures of each instrument in class so students can associate its physical attributes with its sound. You can also invite your local high school band director or orchestra director to demonstrate various instruments, because the best way for students to associate an instrument with its sound is to see and hear it being played.

Students as creators of music

Encourage students to create their own music, make notations, and then perform it for the class. A variety of apps are available for this purpose. For example, students with access to a Macbook can create rhythms using GarageBand. They can write creative jingles to sell products, or they can write songs with simple rhyming and melody patterns for language arts lessons. Other apps used to create music can be found on AppCrawlr (http://appcrawlr.com/ios-apps/best-apps-music-production); some apps on this site are free, while others cost as little as $.99. If your school is fortunate enough to have Orff instruments (small percussion instruments used in the Orff approach to teaching music) have students experiment with melody and play their original compositions for the class.

Students should be given the opportunity to sing every day! Singing develops students' oral language skills and it should be a part of every language arts program, especially in the early grades. The best songs for young voices are those that range from middle C to the G above middle C. This range is very small, but as their voices develop, their range expands. Teachers should select from all types of music—patriotic songs, songs from musicals, folk songs, children's songs, and rounds. Ideally, have students read from sheet music or books. If these materials are not available, videos are a fine alternative.

Build cooperation among students by creating a class choir. You can teach students three or four short pieces and then have them perform at a school assembly. Alternately, you can choose a favorite song from a popular musical and have the students create a dance routine and have them perform it at a school function for parents and students. As students get older and some begin taking private music lessons, they should be encouraged to play or sing in front of their peers. Performers learn poise from these experiences, and the audience learns the proper listening skills and etiquette for performances.

Integrating music with the language arts

There are many ways to integrate music with the language arts. As with dance, music enriches the reading of multicultural literature. For example, after reading a book that depicts a different culture or country, students can listen and learn about the types of music popular in those cultures and countries.

Students' vocabulary increases as they learn the Italian musical terms. You can make 8 x 10 posters for each term and its definition. Students should not only be able to read the words and know their definitions, but should also learn the pronunciation. To reinforce these concepts, also use these terms in nonmusical contexts. For example, if a student giving a presentation is not speaking loudly enough, ask her to speak *fortissimo*. Conversely, if the class is rambunctious after lunch, flick the light switch and declare that they are to speak *pianissimo*.

Share with your class some fiction books that feature music prominently, which may inspire students to learn more about a featured instrument, music, or dance. Two trade books for elementary students that are excellent teaching tools to use when introducing the instruments are the hilarious story of *The Remarkable Farkle McBride* (Lithgow, 2000) and the poetic book *Zin! Zin! Zin! A Violin* (Moss, 1995). The latter is featured on an animated *Reading Rainbow* segment (http://

vimeo.com/6366551) narrated by Gregory Hines. The site also has lesson plans to accompany the book.

Have a recording of all the instruments featured in the stories you read so students can hear them as they read about them. After introducing such books, invite your students to write their own stories about an instrument or musical piece. For example, ask students to think about a flute that wishes it had a reed like an oboe or curves like a French horn. Providing some ideas will help spark their imagination. In addition, as you share a storybook, encourage the students to discuss what type of music they hear. Encourage them to find music that fits the mood of a book or a character in a story. Appendix B.17 presents a list of books with music, art, drama, and dance as their themes.

TEACHING ACTIVITIES ❾

INTEGRATING THE VISUAL AND PERFORMING ARTS

The following multimodal activities include suggested grade levels—primary, intermediate and middle school—but feel free to modify them for other grade levels.

1 Understanding how illustrators use color in picture books

Introduce this activity after you have taught students how color "can invoke emotions and conjure atmosphere" (O'Neil, 2011, p. 214). This activity helps students understand the concept of color and emotion as they work with different color swatches.

Because this activity encourages discussion, use small groups. Give each student several swatches (approximately 4" x 5") of various colors, from construction paper, gift wrap, paint chips, tissue paper, or wallpaper. The swatches should contain bright colors, pastel colors, and dark tones.

Ask students to associate each of their swatches with an emotion, season, or mood, such as warmth, peace, spookiness, winter, and sadness. Have them discuss the reasons for their choices. Then, using the same swatches, ask students what color they would choose to represent a particular character or scene from a book that the class has recently read, and why. After the discussion invite students to write a poem that relates the color to the character.

This same activity can be modified for older students by focusing on abstract emotions such as prejudice, despair, or elation. *Recommended for primary grades.*

2 Character descriptions from text and illustrations

To help students understand how text states facts about a character and how illustrations help readers make inferences about characters, O'Neil (2011) suggests students complete a chart that compares what the text tells a reader versus what inferences readers make from the illustrations. Figure 9.8 shows a sample based on one page from *Madeline* (Bemelmans, 1939). *Recommended for primary grades.*

3 Performing for *America's Got Talent*

A good book to use for this activity is Kimmel's *The Greatest of All* (1991), a delightful version of the Japanese folktale "The Wedding Mouse." In the tale, Father Mouse is seeking the Greatest of All as a husband for his daughter because they are important mice who live in the walls of the emperor's palace. He first approaches the emperor, who declines because he is not the Greatest of All; that honor is reserved

Character description in text versus illustrations.   **FIGURE 9.8**

TEXT/PAGE # (FACTUAL INFORMATION)	ILLUSTRATIONS/PAGE # (INFERENCES)
"She was not afraid of mice" (unpaged)	Madeline is not afraid because she is sitting on the floor while attempting to pet some mice. Her hand is out-stretched to one mouse. The other eleven girls stay in the background, with one standing on a chair. Madeline is smiling and the other girls have small circles for their mouths, depicting that they are scared.

for the sun. The father then goes to the sun, who states that he is not the Greatest of All either. The sun sends him to the cloud, who sends him to the wind, who sends him to the wall, who sends him to Ko Nezumi, the humble field mouse who has wanted to marry the daughter all along. The wall considers Ko Nezumi to be the Greatest of All because he can eat a tunnel through the wall and destroy it.

After reading and discussing the theme of the tale, divide students into groups of eight so that each student can become a character. Instruct each group to plan a skit based on the tale. Encourage them to embellish the dialogue between the characters because they are going to perform their skit on *America's Got Talent* (or any other contest your students watch). Give the groups ample time to prepare and then invite the principal and librarian to judge the skits. Afterward, you can show the class the version of the book available on YouTube. *Recommended for intermediate grades.*

4 **Comparing information from illustrations and text in two versions of a fairy tale**

This activity will help students understand the techniques book illustrators use to create their own style. Introduce it after you have had ample time to teach students how illustrators "combine color, line, and shapes to express feelings or describe qualities" (O'Neil, 2011, p. 218).

After reading two versions of a fairy tale from two different cultures, such as Schroeder's (1997) *Smoky Mountain Rose: An Appalachian Cinderella* and Hickox's (1999) *The Golden Sandal: A Middle Eastern Cinderella*, discuss how the illustrators used text and illustrations to depict the culture of each fairy tale. Then invite students to complete a graphic organizer that compares and contrasts the two versions of the story. Figure 9.9 shows a completed example of a graphic organizer. *Recommended for intermediate grades.*

5 **Using art to demonstrate comprehension**

Holdren (2012) explains how teachers can use art to assess students' reading comprehension and their critical thinking. In her study, she used art to encourage "students to become more engaged, to understand text more deeply, and to develop higher level abstract and critical thinking" (p. 693). To conduct a similar activity yourself, use literature circles and invite students to generate questions on a novel that

FIGURE 9.9 Graphic organizer for comparing how illustrators use text and illustrations to depict the same story from different cultures.

Smoky Mountain Rose	*The Golden Sandal*

SIMILARITIES

Both Cinderellas are hated by their stepmother and stepsisters.

Both receive magical help to get to the ball.

Both are kind and loving to the stepsisters.

Both have stepsisters who are jealous and hateful.

Both are turned back into their ragged clothes at a designated time.

Both drop one shoe as they escape the dance.

Both suitors search for the girl who can fit into the shoe.

DIFFERENCES (I = Illustration; T = Text)

Smoky Mountain Rose	*The Golden Sandal*
Rose lives in the Appalachian region. (I)	Maha lives in the Middle East. (I)
Her home is a small shack in the country. (I)	She lives in a Middle Eastern village. (I)
Characters speak in dialect, such as "Y'all watch, some-day, I'm gonna marry me a fine gentleman." (T)	Characters do not use dialect. (T)
A pig brings about the magic. (I,T)	A red fish brings about the magic. (I,T)
A melon and mice become the coach and horses. (I,T)	Maha walks to the wedding. (I,T)
Rose receives a sparklin' glass slipper to wear (I,T)	Maha receives a golden sandal. (I,T)
The clothing and setting depict the rural countryside. (I)	The clothing and setting depict the Middle East. (I)
The stepmother does nothing harmful to Rose.	The stepmother attempts to use a reeking mixture to make Maha's head full of blisters, but instead it makes her hair silky and beautiful. (T)
The suitor finds her feeding the pigs. (I)	The suitor is drawn to the crowing of a rooster above the oven in which her stepmother and sister have hidden her. (I,T)
No sister finds a suitor. (T)	The evil stepsister is to be married to the bride's brother, until he lifts the veil and sees her head without hair and full of blisters. (I,T)
She "fergive and forget" what bad things her step-mother and sisters did to her. (T)	Maha leaves her stepsister living in disgrace with her mother. (I)

the whole class is reading. Then, as a way of assessing their understanding of the novel, invite them to choose any type of visual arts—painting, drawing, sculpture, or photography—to demonstrate their understanding of the novel's theme in either a metaphorical manner or in a synthesized detail manner. For example, after students have read *Hattie Ever After* (Larson, 2013), have them depict just like Hattie did what it means to follow one's dream. Or, have students read two similarly themed books such as *Bird in a Box* (Pinkney, 2011) and *Chains* (Anderson, 2010) and have them express in dance, music, or visual arts what it means to have hope for a better life.

The rubric found in Figure in 9.10 can be used to assess students' (a) ability to fulfill the assignment objectives; (b) art skills and technique; (c) ability to communicate their understanding of the novel in their creation; and (d) understanding of the connection between their artwork and the literature it represents. *Recommended for middle grades.*

Literature circle art project rubric.   **FIGURE 9.10**

Literature Circle Art Project Rubric

Student Name: Period:

Title of Assignment: Date Evaluated:

1. Assignment Objectives	Compelling	Solid	Developing	Minimal	Points	Comments:
▪ Demonstrates consistent work ethic and meets written or oral requirement	4	3	2	1		
▪ Makes important connections with literature	4	3	2	1		
▪ Creates a work of art that demonstrates excellence	4	3	2	1		
2. Skills and Techniques	Compelling	Solid	Developing	Minimal	Points	Comments:
▪ Shows proficiency in use of tools, process, and techniques to communicate ideas	4	3	2	1		
▪ Uses care in creation of work and use of materials	4	3	2	1		
▪ Demonstrates effective use of elements and principles of design to solve art problems	4	3	2	1		
3. Creation and Communication	Compelling	Solid	Developing	Minimal	Points	Comments:
▪ Demonstrates personal interpretation of subject matter in an artistically mature fashion	4	3	2	1		
▪ Demonstrates communication of ideas through artwork	4	3	2	1		
▪ Uses purposeful planning when developing project concepts	4	3	2	1		
4. Literary Connections and Aesthetic Analysis	Compelling	Solid	Developing	Minimal	Points	Comments:
▪ Understands thematic concepts related to the work of literature and the author's purpose	4	3	2	1		Reading Standards:
▪ Critically analyzes & reflects upon artwork making constant connections to the literature	4	3	2	1		
▪ Demonstrates critical thinking, including analysis and evaluation in creative process	4	3	2	1		
48 Possible SEC 1–4 TOTAL						

Assessment Scale: Minimal = 1= Unsatisfactory
Developing = 2 = Average
Solid = 3 = Above average
Compelling = 4 = Exceeds expectations

Note: Adapted with permission from Angeline Parkin-Milambiling, Sarasota County School District, Florida.

Source: T. S. Holdren (2012). Using art to assess reading comprehension and critical thinking in adolescents. *Journal of Adolescent & Adult Literacy, 55*(8), p. 699.

portrait POEM five SENSE poetry

Ask students to write a free verse poem, emphasizing the senses evoked by a piece of music or art: sight, hearing, taste, smell, and touch. Review with them the figures of speech and encourage them to paint vivid visual images in the readers' minds. Each line of the poem may focus on a different sense.

I see . . .

I hear . . .

I taste . . .

I smell . . .

I feel . . .

6 Portrait poem

Encourage students to express themselves in the following activity.

Writing Prompts: Answer the following questions by filling in the blanks. (Sample answers provided.)

1. If I were a color, what color would I be? (red)
2. If I were a shape, what shape would I be? (circle)
3. If I were a texture, what texture would I be? (soft)
4. What does that texture feel like? (sand)
5. If I were a line, what type of line would I be? (curved)
6. If I were a sound, would I be loud, quiet, etc.? (loud)
7. What do I sound like? (thunder)
8. If I were a taste, what would I taste like? (sweet)
9. If I were a mood or an emotion, which mood or emotion would I be? (happy)
10. If I were an element in nature, what element would I be? (warm breeze on a sunny day)

In order to turn your answers into a poem, put each word/phrase into sentences beginning with the words "I am . . ." For example:

I am the color _____. (answer to question 1)

I am a _____. (answer to question 2)

And so on.

In this case, your poem would read as follows:

I am the color red.

I am a circle.

I am soft.

I am sand.

I am curved.

I am loud.

I am thunder.

I am sweet.

I am happy.

I am a warm breeze on a sunny day.

Recommended for middle grades.

Education is what survives after what has been learned has been forgotten.

B. F. SKINNER

7 Connecting culture with art

Adinkra cloth is a hand-painted fabric made in Ghana, which is located in West Africa. The cloth is made by the Ashanti people and tells stories or expresses thoughts through its use of symbols.

1. Invite students to research the Adinkra symbols and their meanings online.
2. Have students draw a decorative border on a piece of watercolor paper.
3. Next, have them draw a vertical and a horizontal line on the paper to create four equal-sized boxes.
4. Then ask them to choose four different symbols and draw them with a black or white crayon. Encourage them to repeat each symbol in the square so each square is filled with the same symbol.
5. Have students use various shades of watercolor to fill the entire paper. The wax from the crayon will resist the watercolors.

This idea is from the site Crayola.com, which offers hundreds of good lesson plans for visual projects. *Recommended for middle grades.*

8 Writing about classical music and/or famous works of art

Many educators lament that the CCSS do not include the fine arts. As teachers, we know that some students like to express themselves through music and visual arts. Thus, we need to be creative and offer a variety of ways for students to integrate music and the other arts into their writing assignments. The following activities support CCRA.W.4, which requires students to "produce clear and coherent writing in which the development, organization, and style are appropriate to task, purpose, and audience" (NGACBP & CCSSO, 2010, p. 18).

- Listen to a piece of classical music and/or view a masterpiece online or in a book. Discuss the elements (tempo, instrumentation, and so on from music; colors, positive and negative space in works of art) in small groups and then as a class.
- Play a portion of a soundtrack from a musical or ballet, such as *Phantom of the Opera* or *Sleeping Beauty,* or play part of a movie soundtrack. After students listen and the class discusses the mood changes, tempo, and dynamics, invite students to write an outline for turning the work into a storyline for a movie. *Recommended for middle school grades.*

9 Multimodal presentation

CCSS RI.6.7 requires students to "integrate information presented in different media or formats; e.g., visually, quantitatively as well as in words to develop a coherent understanding of a topic or issue" (NGACBP & CCSSO, 2010, p. 39). CCSS W.6.6 also calls for students to "use technology, including the Internet, to produce and publish writing as well as to interact and collaborate with others" (p. 43). You may combine these two standards as you engage students in reading books and online passages that address a social issue about which they are passionate, with the end goal of producing a multimodal slide presentation.

Not all students are passionate about the same topics, so brainstorm with your class for ideas. The issues should have both pros and cons. For example, some students may be passionate about eliminating all bottled water because disposable bottles fill landfills and take energy and resources to produce. Other students may feel that bottled water is a healthy drink choice and the real issue is the fact that many people do not recycle. Some students may be passionate about banning offshore drilling, while other students may believe it is necessary to break the United States' dependency on foreign oil. Still other students may think that electric vehicles and hybrid cars are the answer to pollution problems. After gathering ideas, have students who share the same passion form groups of three or four, research the topic, and then share their findings in a multimodal presentation. Be sure to review with students the need to support their opinions using facts and statistics as evidence. In addition, have students research and understand the opposing view of the topic in order to refute it.

Spires, Hervey, Morris, and Stelpflug (2012) suggest the following steps for this type of slide presentation:

1. Ask students compelling questions about social issues that concern them.

2. Narrow each topic to one main question.

3. Explain the differences between websites ending in *.org, .gov.*, and *.com;* copyright laws for quoting texts and copying images from online sources; and the importance of checking the credentials of the site, author, or organization. (We will discuss use of online resources in more detail later in this chapter.)

4. Allow students ample time to gather and analyze information, making sure they carefully cite sources and use quotations and paraphrasing as needed.

5. Ask students to creatively synthesize all the information.

6. Have students create a *storyboard* by drawing or using software, or by selecting images/pictures from online and other sources.

7. Then ask them to finalize their storyboard, choose music to fit content, and then create the slide presentation based on their storyboards.

8. Students may present the finished product in class, publish it on the school website, and/or share it online at www.edublogs.org or www.watchknow.org/default.aspx.

When assessing the presentations, use the following criteria: (1) the authors' purpose is clear; (2) ideas are well synthesized; (3) the sequence is logical; (4) the script uses vivid language; (5) the authors clearly articulate their position; and (6) images are appropriate. Assess the aesthetic and technical quality of the presentation by considering (1) image quality; (2) the natural flow from one image to the next; (3) the quality of audio (music and voiceover); and (4) creativity/originality.

Recommended for middle grades.

two REAL-WORLD EXAMPLES of TRANSMEDIATION

One. Cowan and Albers (2006) shared how they engaged fourth and fifth graders in visual arts, drama, and movement in their language arts class. They first discussed with the students how some visual signs have common cultural meanings. For example, a smiling face or a person performing a cartwheel represents happiness. Any image drawn in a thick circle with two thick diagonal lines drawn over the image represents a negative sign. Artists depict happy scenes by using light colors and curvy lines. Artists depict anger or violence using dark angular lines with dark hues.

Next, Cowan and Albers helped students link their life experiences with positive and negative words. They asked students to focus on one experience and choose an adjective to describe it. Students then were invited to dramatize the emotion represented by the word. After they dramatized the word, they expressed the word by referring to a related color and creating a strong metaphor. For example, one student expressed her feeling when her best friend moved away as "gloomy like black in a dark world."

Finally, Cowan and Albers shared with students the Caldecott Award winner *Shadow* (Centrars, 1983), a poem that personifies a shadow. Centrars uses extended personification, metaphor, and rhythm, all of which help readers to draw vivid pictures in their minds of how and why Shadow does things. The fourth and fifth graders then wrote their own personification poems, using vivid imagery.

Two. Although students learn much from the illustrations in picture books, give them plenty of other opportunities to closely observe and learn about other sign systems. "Keen observation enables the mind to not only see details, but also envision emotional connections, images and metaphors" (Wolf, 2006, p. 11). Roy Smith, an English artist, calls this keen observation "serious seeing." Smith worked with a group of children ages 4 to 7 to teach them that art is all about looking—looking at objects from various angles, and looking at objects close up to see their minute details. He stressed that in visual arts, children "must take what they see and feel and put it to paper, pencil, paint or photograph" (Wolf, 2006, p. 11). Smith trained these young students to first look intently at the intricate shapes and details of an object before they attempt to draw it. When they started drawing, he encouraged them to keep examining the details again and again so the smallest details became large in their eyes. While the students were drawing, Smith and their teacher, Deb Walkling, encouraged them to express what they saw in metaphoric language by responding to such questions as "What is that like?" "What do you think it is saying?" and "How does that make you feel?" Later, these expressions were developed into poems. Smith believed that this passion for seeing the details in objects is the doorway for imagination.

TRANSMEDIATION

In the previous sections, we discussed ways of integrating the different sign systems with the language arts. Transmediation involves a higher form of integration. *Transmediation* is the "process of taking understandings from one system and moving them into another sign system" (Short, Kauffman, & Kahn, 2000, p. 160). Although integration is the study of music, art, dance, and drama as they relate to various subjects, transmediation requires students to engage in higher-level thinking as they take information from a book or any other sign system, process the meaning, and then reproduce the meaning into another form.

Students may use multiple sign systems as they to respond to literature. Students "need to be able to choose the sign systems that are most effective for a particular message or that support their understandings about a particular issue" (Short et al., 2000, p. 170). You may need to coach some of your students how to respond through a variety of sign systems and then choose the one that will be the most effective for them, if they have not had much previous exposure to them.

Sara, a student teacher, put her second graders into small groups and asked them to write skits about fables they had read. After writing the skits, the students suggested several ways to continue learning about and sharing fables. They asked if they could

- make masks out of paper plates for each of the characters,
- listen to musical recordings to find background music to fit the skit's mood, and
- perform their skits for their classmates.

Later, the class wrote invitations to the other second-grade classes and performed the skits for them. Parents heard about the performances and also wanted to see them, so the class wrote invitations to the parents and gave another performance.

In this case, Sara had suggested one response to the fables–writing a skit–and the students expanded the response into other sign systems (art, drama, and music).

Transmediation can be achieved even with very young students—you can help them take the information from picture books, process the information, and reproduce the meaning in another form. For example, children can reproduce the meaning of a 2-D illustration in a 3-D project. After sharing a concept book about numbers, shapes, or the alphabet, have young students create the numbers, shapes, or letters out of modeling clay. Even though their 3-D images may lack the detail and finesse of the professional illustrations, their creations indicate they have gained knowledge. Primary students, after reading *The Honey Makers* (Gibbons, 2000), may want to make beehives out of paper and/or boxes; or after enjoying *The Mitten* (Brett, 1999), students may make papier mâché sculptures of animals featured in the book. These art projects are especially useful for English learners because art is a universal language.

After reading *The Pumpkin Book* (Gibbons, 1999), students may decide to plant their own pumpkin seeds and keep a log to record the seeds' growth. Some students may include photographs in their logs, others may draw illustrations, while still other students may write a poem. Each student's response may be different, but each response indicates what the student has learned from the book and how she chooses to apply it to her own real-world experience. This project is effective for English learners and students with special needs because they can choose a way of responding that matches their interests and skills.

As other examples of transmediation, after students have studied various forms of poetry such as diamante, acrostic, or concrete poems, have them create poems, raps, or jingles based on stories or expository texts. Or, after examining illustrations in picture books, and studying the lines, curves, repetitions, hues, details, colors, and perspectives, students can create music either with rhythm or keyboard instruments that corresponds to the mood of a story or poem. You may also want to demonstrate how to respond to stories and poems through dance and creative movements.

Transmediating music into art is natural. Play many different types of music, discuss the music's mood, and ask students what type of lines, colors, and textures the music suggests. After the discussion, play the music again and permit the students to draw and/or paint a piece that fits the music. Every student, including English learners and students with special needs, will create something unique and each piece should be appreciated.

In all of these activities, students are using higher-level thinking skills to transmediate what they learned in one sign system into another sign system. Begin with short-term activities to help students understand how to reproduce the meaning of text into alternate sign systems. Once students experiment with a variety of sign systems, they begin to understand how they can use them to demonstrate the impact a text had on them. The classroom vignette on page 308 describes how one student teacher worked with her second graders on transmediation.

THE INTERNET AND MULTIMODAL COMMUNICATION

T he Internet can be considered a multimodal form of communication since it comprises images, text, sound, and video. Global economics require today's students to be proficient in using the Internet and to comprehend and respond to information found online. Reading electronic and online text requires higher-level thinking skills such as analyzing, evaluating, and synthesizing (Henry, 2006) as well as technical skills unique to using the Internet.

Skills Unique to Using the Internet

Demonstrate and teach students the following skills that are particular to reading online, including the following:

1. How to use search engines and devise search terms to get results that are as specific as possible. Students need to evaluate the short descriptions found in search-engine results listings to determine which site will most likely answer their questions. If the results seem too broad or unrelated, students need know how to refine their search.

2. How to locate and collect information, take notes from various sources (either electronically or by hand), keep track of their sources, and retrieve them again if needed.

3. How to (a) paraphrase and attribute information, or (b) use direct quotes and cite sources.

4. How to analyze an author's credibility.

5. How to use hyperlinks effectively without becoming distracted.

6. Understanding that graphics (e.g., charts, diagrams, and graphs) are embedded in the text, as opposed to being boxed features, as is sometimes the case in traditional text.

7. How to use a website's audio and video features (e.g., animated graphics, pronunciation guides, etc.) to aid comprehension.

Explain also that search engines use algorithms based on the user's search terms and place websites with the highest number of hits for those search terms at the top of the results lists. Also show students the sponsored results at the top of the results page and suggest that they may want to skip them, because they are basically advertisements.

Using hyperlinks

Students also need to understand how to use hyperlinks that connect them to related texts. This type of reading does not follow the linear organization of traditional texts, and hyperlinks can often distract students from their primary task. One click on a hyperlink may lead students to a topic that may be interesting but unrelated to the issue they are researching. Demonstrate for your students how quickly even an experienced researcher can become sidetracked. Teach students to scan the page, and if the information does not specifically relate to their topic, use the browser's back button to stay on track.

Using other web page features

Web pages offer many features that help students comprehend the information. Digitized pronunciation and pop-up definitions aid comprehension. Similarly, animations may be helpful, but they may also hinder comprehension if students become so distracted by the action that they do not grasp the information the animation explains. Short video clips can also aid or hinder comprehension. Video clips may be so entertaining that students forget to take notes or fully grasp the points they are trying to make. You may need to demonstrate how to view a video, take down the main points, and then view it again to get any information you missed the first time. These steps may need to be repeated a number of times. It is also important for students to cite the video's source and date.

Characteristics of Sites Appropriate for Elementary Students

Many websites are too difficult for elementary students. If you are teaching young students, bookmark appropriate websites and allow them to visit only those sites. Karchmer (2001) found that elementary students need the following:

1. Pages with lots of white space, just like traditional text.
2. Large print.
3. Graphics that explain concepts.
4. Pages that require very little scrolling.
5. Pages that are not overloaded with information. Pages should not have long narrative sections with no graphics.
6. Pages with information that is appropriate for their cognitive level.
7. Pages that are written at students' reading level.

Obviously, the Internet is crucial to every student's success, but you must guide students to use it responsibly and properly so they do not become overwhelmed and so that it becomes a useful tool in their hands.

TEACHING ACTIVITIES 9

USING THE INTERNET

1 Online research project

CCRA.W.6 requires students to "use technology, including the Internet, to produce and publish writing and to interact and collaborate with others" (NGACBP & CCSSO, 2010, p. 18). Using the National Geographic for Kids website, you and your students can find fascinating information about animals, countries, and cultures from around the world. Permit the students to select from one of the site's many research options. Tell them they are to read about the topic on this and two other sites, and then present their findings to the class, using PowerPoint, Live Text, or any other program. Encourage them to add music and graphics so their presentation is interesting to classmates. *Recommended for middle grades.*

2 Connecting research with video production

Middle-school teachers can use their students' fascination with YouTube videos to fuel interest in this group project, which will promote their critical thinking, collaboration skills, aesthetic and technical abilities, and research skills (Spires, Hervey, Morris & Stelpflug, 2012).

> You always pass failure on the way to success.
>
> **MICKEY ROONEY**

For this project, students are likely to use the following tools: tablet, video camera, smartphone, small tripod, flash drive, headphones, music, and online access. They will also need to consult an expert in the field.

1. Have students create groups based on a social issue such as global warming, using social networks in a positive manner, bullying, world hunger, or another topic that interests them.

2. Help them narrow their topic by writing two or three compelling questions to answer.

3. Give students ample time to gather and analyze the information they will need to answer their research questions.

4. Require students to use at least two Internet sites, a book, at least one magazine, and one expert. *Note:* You may need to help students find an expert.

5. Aid students as they seek information from credible sources. If students are not skilled in using search engines, conduct minilessons on finding sources, following links to new sites, checking the credentials of the site's author or organization, and citing sources from the Internet.

6. Have students collaborate as a group to select video clips, images (including photos, items they create themselves, charts, and so on), music and other audio, and the text needed to develop the topic.

7. Once all the materials have been collected, have students collaborate and creatively synthesize the information into a slide-show video. (You are likely to find that some of your students already have experience creating videos, but if needed, elicit help from the school's technology teacher.)

8. After they complete the presentation, have them as a group critically evaluate and revise the video. Give them ample time to produce a polished project.

9. Make sure the result is age-appropriate and then have students publish their project by sharing with classmates or posting it online.

10. Finally, ask each group to suggest possible ways the class can put their findings into action. For example, to alleviate hunger locally, they may choose to collect canned goods and deliver them to a food pantry.

Spires, Hervey, Morris, and Stelpflug (2012) provide a rubric, found in Figure 9.11, that you will want to share with students *before* they begin the project. This rubric focuses on two main areas: intellectual quality and aesthetic and technical quality.

ASSESSMENT OF VISUAL AND PERFORMING ARTS AND MULTIMODAL COMMUNICATION

Assessment is a part of teaching. Because music, drama, dance, and the visual arts are creative expressions, it is difficult to create generalized as opposed to assignment-specific rubrics for these sign systems. Appendices D.23–D.25 offer three brief sample rubrics for use with fifth- and sixth-grade students. These samples are included to encourage you to create rubrics for specific assignments.

FIGURE 9.11 Rubric used in video project evaluation.

	4	3	2	1
Intellectual Quality				
Clear Purpose	Establishes a purpose early on and maintains a clear focus throughout.	Establishes a purpose early on and maintains focus for most of the presentation.	There are a few lapses in focus, but the purpose is fairly clear.	It is difficult to figure out the purpose of the presentation.
Synthesis and Construction of Ideas	Sequential composition; succinct; images create an atmosphere and/or tone, and may communicate symbolism and/or metaphors.	Sequential composition; succinct; images create an atmosphere and/or tone.	Sequential composition; succinct; images are controlled/logical.	Sequential composition; images are acceptable.
Curriculum Connections	Clear and compelling connections to issues of local activism (social studies) and appropriate language use for a general audience (language arts).	Clear connections to issues of local activism (social studies) and appropriate language use for a general audience (language arts).	Clear connections to issues of local activism (social studies) or appropriate language use for a general audience (language arts).	No clear connections to issues of local activism (social studies) and inappropriate language use for a general audience (language arts).
Clear Beginning and Ending	Clear and interesting start and end.	Clear start and end.	Clear start or end.	No clear start or end.
Sources Cited Appropriately	Source information collected for all graphics, facts, and quotes. All documented in MLA format.	Source information collected for all graphics, facts, and quotes. Most documented in MLA format.	Source information collected for graphics, facts, and quotes, but not documented in MLA format.	Very little or no source information was collected.
Aesthetic and Technical Quality				
Image Quality	Video and images are compelling and of high quality. Images clearly support content.	Video and images are of high quality. Images clearly support content.	Some video and images are of high quality. Some images support content.	Video and images are not of high quality. Images do not support content.
Editing/ Transitions	Engaging rhythm; appropriate transitions, enhanced vitality.	Engaging rhythm; some appropriate transitions; evidence of vitality.	Some rhythm; limited transitions; lapses in vitality.	Mechanical rhythm; limited vitality.
Audio (Music and Dialogue)	Consistency in presentation; clearly articulated narration; music stirs a rich emotional response.	Consistency in presentation; clear narration; music stirs an emotional response.	Some consistency in presentation; lapses in clarity of narration; music is evident.	Breaking consistency; monotone style of presentation; inappropriate choice of music.
Creativity/ Originality	Product shows a large amount of original thought. Ideas are creative and inventive.	Product shows some original thought. Work shows new ideas and insights.	Uses other people's ideas (giving them credit), but there is little evidence of original thinking.	Uses other people's ideas, but does not give them credit.

Note:. Rubric elements constructed by students and instructors; level descriptions adapted from rubistar.4teachers.org.

Source: H. A. Spires, L. Hervey, G. Morris, & C. Stelpflug (2012). Energizing project-based inquiry: Middle-grade students read, write, and create videos. *Journal of Adolescent & Adult Literacy, 55*(6), p. 489. Used with permission, via CCC.

TECHNOLOGY IN THE CLASSROOM

Earlier in this chapter we included specific websites that focus on the various topics discussed. Here are a few more:

www.dsokids.com/listen/by-instrument/ This site allows students to click on the name of an instrument, read a short description, and see a picture of it. Students can listen to the instrument play a short phrase, a brief song such as "Twinkle, Twinkle Little Star," and then while it is playing with the entire orchestra. This is a great site for teaching the instruments of the orchestra.

www.youtube.com/watch?v=cIx7khLD2WE Once students are familiar with the instruments of the orchestra, they can sing along with the puppets in this video.

www.youtube.com/watch?v=u2W1Wi2U9sQ This video plays the finale of Pyotr Ilyich Tchaikovsky's *1812 Overture* and shows photographs of the composer.

www.youtube.com/watch?v=_4IRMYuE1hI This video plays the first movement of Beethoven's *Fifth Symphony* and shows photographs of the composer.

www.intermonet.com/colors/ This is a wonderful site to introduce students to impressionist Claude Monet and how he used color. His choices changed a great deal over the course of his career, especially as his eyesight began to fail in his later years.

www.artsoho.net/degas.html This site introduces students to Edgar Degas and his great masterpieces. Students can click on the masterpieces to enlarge the paintings and view them in detail.

www.metmuseum.org/toah/hd/gogh/hd_gogh.htm This site gives students access to Vincent Von Gogh's masterpieces. As you click on each work, it enlarges so you can discuss details of the work with students.

www.teachkidsart.net/category/subject/color-color-mixing/ This site introduces students to the primary and secondary colors and how to mix them to create various hues.

www.pedagonet.com/quickies/triorama.pdf This link offers clear step-by-step directions on how to create a triorama. It also includes a lesson and assessment of using a triorama to present a book report.

www.youtube.com/watch?v=qBDODIWeKbE This site shows ballerinas from the Kirov Ballet dancing Tchaikovsky's "Dance of the Mirlitons" from *The Nutcracker*.

SUMMARY

I f we as educators neglect to teach students how to read and communicate in various visual and performance sign systems—the visual arts, drama, dance, and music—and how to use the Internet effectively, we are not educating them fully. Teachers must introduce students to the basic elements of each sign system and how to communicate using each one. As a teacher, your goal is to integrate the various sign systems into the core subjects. Higher-level thinking is developed when students *transmediate,* or transfer their understanding of a topic from one sign system into another.

We are also responsible for teaching students how to be effective consumers of online information. Students must learn how to choose search words, refine a search, evaluate a site and its author(s) for credibility and reliability, gather information from electronic texts, and record and cite sources.

field AND practicum ACTIVITIES

1. INTEGRATING WRITING AND ART. With a small group of students from the second or third grade, read and discuss Jan Brett's *Umbrella*. Have the students create paper plate puppets, write a puppet script, and perform it for a kindergarten class.

2. HANDWRITING PICTURES. Using individual letters or groups of letters from the alphabet, have students create pictures. They can add eyes, legs, and so on to create stick figures or more advanced figures, or can add other lines and shapes to create houses, trucks, and trains.

3. INTEGRATING WRITING WITH MUSIC. As you share a storybook, encourage the students to discuss what type of music they "hear." Encourage them to find music that fits the mood of a book or a character in a story. Appendix B.17 presents a list of books with music, art, drama, and dance as their themes.

4. INTEGRATING MUSIC AND DANCE. Find a recording of the "Dance of the Flowers" from *The Nutcracker*. Working with a group of elementary school students, listen to the music. Discuss how it makes them feel. Then, invite them to perform creative movements that express the mood of the music.

5. INTEGRATING WRITING AND SCULPTURE. Find the following article: Cowan, K., & Albers, P. (2006). Semiotic representations: Building complex literacy practices through the arts. *The Reading Teacher, 60*(2), 124–137. Working with a group of fifth-grade students, read the book *Shadow* (Brown, 1982) and have them write poems and then create masks that reflect the mood in the poem. *Recommended for intermediate grades.*

6. INTEGRATING MUSIC AND PAINTING. Play a recording of Claude Debussy's *Clair de Lune,* discuss the mood of the music, and then have the students create a watercolor picture that expresses the mood. After students have completed their paintings, have them explain their color choices. *Recommended for intermediate grades.*

7. INTEGRATING LITERATURE AND DRAWING. Share Chris Van Allsburg's *Ben's Dream* with a group of fifth graders. If possible, take them to view a unique tree trunk and have them study it from different views; alternatively, choose an online photograph to share with them. Then, have the students draw a small portion of the trunk, magnifying it as Van Allsburg does. *Recommended for intermediate grades.*

8. BOOK MURALS. Students can respond to books with particularly intriguing illustrations by creating a class mural of a favorite scene on a long piece of butcher paper. This technique also works very well with nonfiction books, especially those about nature. One first-grade class did a terrific job with a prehistoric mural about dinosaurs. *Recommended for intermediate grades.*

9. MICHELANGELO AND SOAP SCULPTURES. Using online resources and books, invite students to research Michelangelo. Encourage students to view his sculptures, pointing out the exquisite expressions revealed in the faces. Afterward, give each student one bar of soap and a plastic knife, and invite them to sculpt any object or creature they desire. (We have found that a white bar of bath soap works the best.) Encourage them to make their work as detailed as possible. *Recommended for middle grades.*

CHAPTER 10

Integrating the Language Arts in the Content Areas

OBJECTIVES

After reading this chapter, you should be able to accomplish the following objectives:

1. Explain why the language arts should be integrated into the content areas.

2. Define content literacy and a literacy event.

3. Describe how students construct content knowledge.

4. Explain the concept of readability and its role in reading and writing.

5. Describe graphic organizers, semantic maps, and semantic features analysis.

6. Indicate the differences between a semantic map and a semantic web.

7. Describe the similarities between the K-T-W-L-E chart and the directed reading–thinking activity (DR–TA).

INTRODUCTION

This chapter introduces you to integrating literacy in the content areas. We place special emphasis on utilizing techniques to help students become strategic readers. These techniques include the directed reading–thinking activity, graphic organizers, semantic feature analysis, and semantic mapping. You will also learn about using social literacy activities in the classroom.

WHY THE LANGUAGE ARTS IN THE CONTENT AREAS?

We authors have always contended that reading, writing, speaking, listening, viewing, and visually representing are integrated components of the language arts. When we read a novel or learn a new fact from an informational text, we want to talk about it with others. When we talk about it, we listen to their reactions or seek additional information. When we write, we get our ideas from reading others' texts, listening to others, or viewing a video or a website. We may also express our ideas through visuals as well as text. Through experiences with all these forms of literacy, students learn how to learn. They become literate and develop into independent self-educators who can acquire all types of content information on their own.

The language arts help people to learn, and they are motivators for learning. When reading, people are trying to find information, locate ideas, and comprehend what the text really says. To accomplish this task, readers use prior knowledge and often make predictions about what they expect to learn. In writing a summary of material or including it in a reading/writing log, readers clarify and even analyze the ideas they have gathered. This analysis may further motivate a person to study the material or seek out additional information to enhance what he or she learned from the text. In other words, reading promotes writing, which in turn encourages further reading (Vacca, Vacca, & Mraz, 2014). In an integrated language arts approach, reading, writing, speaking, listening, viewing, and visually representing become natural ways of making content come alive for students. Through these processes, students can take charge of their learning by interacting with text materials in a variety of ways. To get a better idea of how this happens, read the classroom vignette below, in which content and process learning are integrated.

Mrs. Castleberry's caterpillar unit integrates content and process learning

Mrs. Castleberry's second-grade class is starting a unit on caterpillars and the ways in which they grow and change. The title for the thematic unit is "Caterpillars and Change— What Really Happens?" The basic information for much of the unit comes from science. However, reading, writing, literature, poetry, health, math, art, social studies, and technology all play major roles in the project.

As a way of arousing the students' interest in the topic, Mrs. Castleberry reads *The Very Hungry Caterpillar* by Eric Carle to them. Not only are the students fascinated by Carle's lively and imaginative pictures, but they are also very interested in the variety of foods that the caterpillar eats. When the caterpillar gets a stomachache from overeating, several of the students exclaim, "I'd have one too if I ate all that stuff!" In the end, everyone is delighted that the caterpillar turns into a beautiful butterfly, an event they celebrate by decorating colorful tissue-paper butterflies.

To prepare the students for the information they will be encountering throughout the unit, Mrs. Castleberry also has them fill in the Caterpillar Information Chart (pictured in Figure 10.1). It is an adaptation of an interactive learning chart that is sometimes used in a directed reading–thinking activity (DR–TA) (Monahan & Hinson, 1988).

For the next few weeks, the entire class is involved in a series of caterpillar-related activities. In addition to engaging the school librarian in locating simple passages about caterpillars from the Internet, encyclopedias, and dictionaries, students consult a variety of informational books, including those found in Figure 10.2.

As a way of summarizing its findings, one group of students writes a book of information about caterpillars called *Caterpillars—Everything You Always Wanted to Know and Then Some.*

Many students also undertake firsthand research by observing a variety of caterpillars, cocoons, and chrysalides with a magnifying glass and recording data about their findings on a features chart (pictured in Figure 10.3). The class is a bit surprised to find such a variety of caterpillars and to learn that some turn into moths rather than butterflies.

Mrs. Castleberry finds that most of the class is very interested in learning what caterpillars eat. One group of

students conducts online research on the topic and reports their results to the class. They find that caterpillars are primarily vegetarian, with an emphasis on green, leafy foods. The students feel that this is a very healthy diet and decide to apply this to their own lives by becoming more aware of healthy foods they should be eating. They enjoy this aspect of the unit so much that as a culminating activity for the project the class decides to have a Healthy Caterpillar Snack Party at school. They plan and write a menu and invite the other second-grade class to join them.

Please come to a
HEALTHY CATERPILLAR SNACK PARTY!

Where: Room 213 in
           Longmeadow School

When: April 12, 10:30 A.M.

Given by: Mrs. Castleberry's class

Menu: Carrot sticks
           Pear halves
           Celery sticks with peanut butter
           Lettuce leaves with pineapple
           Radish curls
           Apple juice
           Apple slice

Door prizes: 3-D paper caterpillars made by members of the class!

R.S.V.P. by April 5.

Needless to say, the students in both second-grade classes have a great time and enjoy some very healthy snacks.

FIGURE 10.1 Caterpillar information chart.

Caterpillar Information Chart			
What We Know About Caterpillars	What We Think About Caterpillars	What We'll Learn About Caterpillars	What We Learned About Caterpillars
Caterpillars turn into butterflies. We like them.	Spring might be the best time to see them. Some live in a chrysalis.	We'll be able to find out if a caterpillar lives in a chrysalis or a cocoon.	We learned that there are many kinds of caterpillars. The ones that turn into butterflies live in a chrysalis. The ones that turn into moths live in a cocoon.

FIGURE 10.2 Sample informational books for a thematic unit on caterpillars.

Boring, M., & Garrow, L. (1996). *Caterpillars, Bugs, and Butterflies.*

Earley, C. (2013). *Caterpillars: Find-Identify-Raise Your Own.*

Ehlert, L. (2001). *Waiting for Wings.*

Heiligman, D., & Weisman, B. (1996). *From Caterpillar to Butterfly.*

Nolting, K. & Larimer, J. (2000). *Caterpillars* (Peterson Field Guide: Young Naturalists).

Ryder, J., & Cherry, L. (1996). *Where Butterflies Grow.*

Shapiro, K., & Cassels, J. (2002). *Butterflies.*

Supportive Research

Research has provided a great deal of the rationale for integrating literacy in the content areas. Studies indicate that the most logical place for developing reading, writing, and thinking competencies is in content areas, such as social studies and science (Alvermann, Phelps, & Ridgeway, 2007; Richardson, Morgan, & Fleener, 2011; Vacca et al., 2014). With the adoption of the CCSS and revised state standards, there is an emphasis on students reading, writing, speaking, and listening as they learn about the scientific and social worlds.

Because reading materials in subject areas are much different from the narrative stories that many young readers are accustomed to, they can present a challenge

Caterpillar data collection chart. **FIGURE** **10.3**

			Caterpillar Data				
Name	Moth/ Butterfly	Hair	Spines	Pattern	Body	Horns	Tail
Wooly Bear	Moth	Fine		Light, middle, and dark end	Curls, round	No	Curls, not forked

Caterpillar data collection chart.

to constructing meaning and achieving comprehension (Duke & Roberts, 2010). Instructional approaches that prepare students for complex textual concepts and ideas can go a long way toward helping them comprehend needed information. In other words, literacy instruction in the content areas makes a difference (Vacca et al., 2014).

Reading, writing, speaking, listening, viewing and visually representing allow students to clarify, refine, and apply their knowledge. Because strategies in these areas are so vital to students in comprehending new information, educators use the term *content literacy*—the ability to use reading, writing, speaking, listening, viewing, and visually representing for the acquisition of new content—to describe them (Alvermann et al., 2007; Richardson et al., 2011). The text used to teach content material is usually called informational text. The broad definition that the CCSS use for *informational texts* includes traditional and e-text "biographies; autobiographies; history, social studies, art, and science books; passages that give directions; forms; graphs; diagrams; charts; and maps" (NGACBP & CCSSO, 2010, retrieved from www.corestandards.org/ELA-Literacy/standard-10-range-quality-complexity/range-of-text-types-for-k-5/).

Once students have acquired content literacy, the process of building new knowledge is greatly facilitated. Typical daily instruction allows such students to actively construct content knowledge through the use of reading activities (DR–TA, graphic organizers), writing activities (dialogue journals, reading logs, slide presentations), listening activities (videos, YouTube clips), and speaking activities (multimodal presentations, speeches, debates). Note the integration of viewing and visually representing is in the writing, listening, and speaking example activities.

This approach to learning content gives students the opportunity to make discoveries and to think for themselves. William Bigelow's (1989) students discovered this when they learned their social studies textbook did not convey the whole truth about Christopher Columbus's "discovery" of America. They found out the real reason Columbus came to America had more to do with money than with proving the world was round. They were also amazed by the cruel way he treated the people who were already living here. These students found out that they should not necessarily trust authorities for all their information; they realized the need to become active participants in their learning, to create their own meaning as they progressed (Bigelow, 1989).

A Purpose for Real Reading and Writing

Goodman (1996) stated that students should read "real language"; that is, material really worth reading. According to Goodman and many other educators, a young person's experiences with text should be *literacy events,* in which he or she reads materials that he or she needs and wants to read. These literacy events can involve reading a story, an informational text, or a combination of several different types of texts. The important point is that the student has a self-imposed purpose for reading and writing, such as finding out about caterpillars and their characteristics, their eating habits, and the variety of ways in which they change. When students have such a purpose for acquiring information, they can then become active information seekers and can begin to develop an integrated knowledge base. This type of knowledge resembles the information obtained in the real world rather than the segmented bits of information that are too often learned in classrooms.

Integrating the language arts into the content areas thus establishes a clear purpose for learning. The content of the curriculum provides students with a reason for acquiring information; the actual literacy tasks make learning an active process that involves them with the material. Teachers also need to help students make the connection between school and real-life situations. For example, students can easily see the relationship between reading directions and knowing how to use the Internet.

Through this content literacy process, students are able not only to acquire content information but also to improve their literacy competencies. Students do not learn to read and write in a vacuum; they learn to read and write by reading and writing about something (Tompkins, 2013), and they learn to speak, listen, view, and visually represent in the same way. When the language arts become tools for understanding, creating, and communicating information, students have the opportunity to practice, refine, and extend the literacy skills they already possess by engaging in something meaningful.

Constructing Content Knowledge

Active involvement in reading and writing about a topic leads to the construction of new knowledge that is added to the student's knowledge base. In turn, this growing knowledge base helps students to understand any new information they encounter. Actually, there is a cyclical pattern to the relationship between a student's content knowledge base and the use of literacy activities to acquire further information (Vacca et al., 2014). The more background knowledge a student possesses, the easier it is for that person to implement literacy activities to integrate new content, thus increasing the base of knowledge and facilitating the continued use of literacy strategies. In effect, the more knowledge one has, the more one is able to acquire.

> You can be indifferent to a term paper, a grocery list, but you cannot be indifferent to your writing.
>
> **JANE YOLEN**

In such an approach to learning, both content and process goals are important. The *content goals* relate to the significant information in the text, while the *process goals* focus on what the student needs to do to acquire that knowledge. To attain both sets of goals, the emphasis prior to reading should be on activating each student's prior knowledge. During reading, teacher-modeled strategies should be used to actively involve students in learning. And after reading, students should work to organize and synthesize information for transfer to other learning situations (Tompkins, 2013).

Integrating the language arts in the content areas helps students maximize their acquisition of content knowledge. They will tend to acquire significant chunks of information rather than fragmented, isolated bits. Their learning becomes holistic and meaningful. Also, by building up a wealth of knowledge, students enhance their ability to use the language arts to process information and construct even more new knowledge. They become able to extend their knowledge and to add to their store of information whenever they wish (Tompkins, 2013). This integrated approach puts students in charge of learning, which is really what education is all about.

TEXT CONSIDERATIONS

Because reading and responding to text form a significant part of any content curriculum, one of the first things to consider when you are integrating the language arts in the content areas is the impact different types of text will have on your students. Books in content areas tend to be difficult for students to comprehend. This may be because of the text's organization, the number of concepts it addresses, its readability, its appropriateness for the students and the purpose of the class, and the accuracy of its information (Vacca et al., 2014). Content area textbooks also use specialized vocabulary, and many of these terms are confusing and difficult for students to grasp.

Organizational Patterns

As described in earlier chapters, stories (or narrative text) have certain elements, including a setting, characters, a theme, a plot, and a resolution. Moving into content areas involves a transition from structured narrative stories to informational, or expository, text. This type of text generally has not one but many structures, which can be especially confusing for young readers. Typical informational text can be organized according to cause–effect, comparison–contrast, enumeration, sequence, and problem–solution (Vacca et al., 2014). As with narrative text, you can use minilessons to introduce readers to expository text structures.

Cause–effect

Cause–effect texts show the causal relationship between two sets of ideas and facts. This pattern or relationship points out that one item is unable to exist without the others. The following paragraph is typical of a cause–effect text:

> In 2005, Hurricane Katrina became a catastrophic hurricane when the levees broke and residents did not evacuate when they were warned to leave. As a result, over 1,800 people lost their lives

during the storm and in floods that followed. Damages were estimated in the billions of dollars.

Comparison–contrast

The *comparison–contrast* pattern of text organization focuses on the similarities and differences that are evident in the topics of particular passages. For example (some information adapted from Britton, 2012):

> There are many similarities and differences between crocodiles and alligators. At the first appearance they look alike; however, they have different jaw shapes. Alligators have a "U"-shaped snout, while crocodiles' snouts are more pointed. Crocodiles also have salt glands on their tongues so they can excrete salt so they can live in salt water. Alligators have the salt glands, but they cannot excrete salt water for extended periods of time and typically live in fresh water rather than salt water.

Enumeration

In *enumeration,* or listing, the author describes important information about a particular topic. The author may focus on facts or on particular characteristics and features. The following is a typical listing passage:

> Polar bears live in the Arctic in areas where they hunt seals at openings in sea ice called *leads*. Five nations have polar bear populations: the United States (Alaska), Canada, Russia, Greenland, and Norway. . . .
>
> Polar bears top the food chain in the Arctic, where they prey primarily on ringed seals. They reach these seals from a platform of sea ice. . . .
>
> Adult male polar bears weigh from 775 to 1,200 pounds. A few weigh more than 1,200 pounds, but these individuals would be exceptional. Females normally weigh 330 to 650 pounds. It's not uncommon for female polar bears preparing to enter maternity dens in the fall to weigh over 600 pounds. (Cox, 2014, p. x)

Sequence

Sequence involves putting ideas and topics into a particular order. One way to recognize sequence is through its use of dates and time periods to help organize a passage. Here is an example:

> Benjamin Franklin was born in Boston, Massachusetts, on January 17, 1706. . . . By the age of seven, he had taught himself to read and write. . . . When Ben was about eight years old, his parents sent him to a famous school, the Boston Latin School. (Satterfield, 2005, pp. 4, 5, 6)

Problem–solution

One final expository text organizational pattern is *problem–solution.* Such a pattern shows how a problem develops and then outlines the solutions to the problem. Take a look at the following example:

> In order to effectively address global warming, we must significantly reduce the amount of heat-trapping emissions we are putting into the atmosphere.
>
> As individuals, we can help by taking action to reduce our personal carbon emissions. But to fully address the threat of global warming, we must demand action from our elected leaders to support and implement a comprehensive set of climate solutions.

Tropical deforestation accounts for about 10 percent of the world's heat-trapping emissions—equivalent to the annual tailpipe emissions of 600 million average U.S. cars.

Reducing tropical deforestation can significantly lower global warming emissions and—together with efforts to reduce emissions from fossil fuels—plays an integral role in a comprehensive long-term solution to global warming. (Union of Concerned Scientists, 2014, p. 1 of 1)

Informational materials used in the classroom need to be written clearly and be as organized as possible. They should also be written at a level within the conceptual reach of the students who will be reading them. You will need to take a lead role in deciding whether or not the texts you use have these characteristics. Work toward this goal by testing the readability of the materials that you want to use with students.

> The teacher's task is not to implant facts but to place the subject to be learned in front of the learner and, through sympathy, emotion, imagination and patience, to awaken in the learner the restless drive for answers and insights which enlarge the personal life and give it meaning.
>
> **NATHAN M. PUSEY**

Readability

How readily or easily a text can be read is called *readability* (Monahan & Hinson, 1988). Readability also refers to characteristics of the reader as well as aspects of the written text. The level of difficulty of the textual material quite definitely has an impact upon comprehension. How difficult a text is depends upon the length of the sentences, the complexity of the words and language, the writing style and the author's purpose, the organization of the content, and the layout or appearance of the material. In addition, each reader's prior knowledge of the content, purpose for reading, vocabulary understanding, interests, and attitudes all affect how well he or she is able to understand a text (Manzo, Manzo, & Thomas, 2009).

One way of helping to determine readability is with conventional *readability formulas,* which generally graph the average length of the sentences and the average number of syllables per word (word complexity) in a text. The Fry readability graph (Fry, 1977) is one of the most accepted and widely used formulas. Estimates of textual difficulty can be calculated by hand by following directions and then graphing the results, as illustrated in Figure 10.4. Readability can also be computed using free online readability calculators, such as readability-score.com, which greatly eases the burden of this task for the teacher.

Because readability formulas can be somewhat unreliable, alternatives arose in the 1990s. One of these alternatives is the Lexile system, which rates texts from beginning readers through the college level. Although the developers of the Lexile text analysis (Smith, Stenner, Horabin, & Smith, 1989) claim that it is not a readability formula, it does use the same criteria to compute levels: semantic difficulty (high-frequency words on a list) and syntactic difficulty (sentence length) (Hiebert, 2002). As discussed in Chapter 5 and indicated in Figure 5.3, the Lexile bands were extended in 2012 to ensure that students would be ready for college and career reading as advocated by the CCSS. You can access the Lexile website (www.lexile.com) to find the list of books that are appropriate for that reader's Lexile range.

Like the readability formulas, the Lexile system is not without its issues. For example, the rating for the children's book *Charlotte's Web* is on the same level as the adult novel *The Firm* by John Grisham (Hiebert, 2002).

F I G U R E **10.4** Fry readability graph.

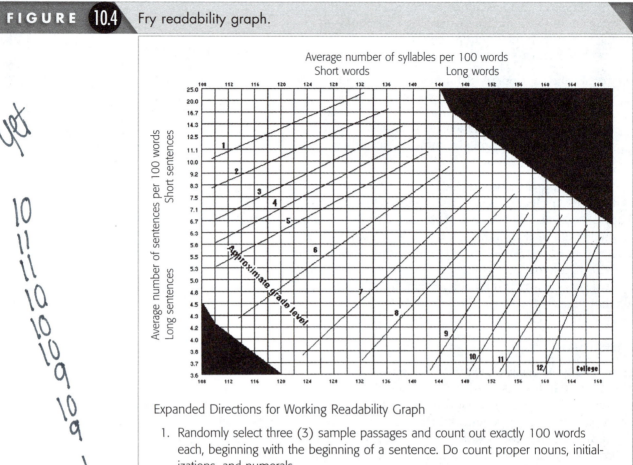

Expanded Directions for Working Readability Graph

1. Randomly select three (3) sample passages and count out exactly 100 words each, beginning with the beginning of a sentence. Do count proper nouns, initializations, and numerals.

2. Count the number of sentences in the hundred words, estimating length of the fraction of the last sentence to the nearest one-tenth.

3. Count the total number of syllables in the 100-word passage. If you don't have a hand counter available, an easy way is to simply put a mark above every syllable over one in each word, then when you get to the end of the passage, count the number of marks and add 100. Small calculators can also be used as counters by pushing numeral 1, then push the + sign for each word or syllable when counting.

4. Enter graph with *average* sentence length and *average* number of syllables; plot dot where the two lines intersect. Area where dot is plotted will give you the approximate grade level.

5. If a great deal of variability is found in syllable count or sentence count, putting more samples into the average is desirable.

6. A word is defined as a group of symbols with a space on either side; thus, *Joe, IRA, 1945,* and *&* are each one word.

7. A syllable is defined as a phonetic syllable. Generally, there are as many syllables as vowel sounds. For example, *stopped* is one syllable and *wanted* is two syllables. When counting syllables for numerals and initializations, count one syllable for each symbol. For example, *1945* is four syllables, *IRA* is three syllables, and *&* is one syllable.

Note: This "extended graph" does not outmode or render the earlier (1968) version inoperative or inaccurate; it is an extension. (Reproduction permitted—no copyright)

Source: Fry's Readability Graph: Clarifications, Validity, and Extension to Level 17. *Journal of Reading, 21* (December, 1977), 249.

particular **CHALLENGES** of **SCIENCE** texts

Many science textbooks pose particular challenges to primary teachers because they present technical terms and abstract concepts in a "dry, uninteresting manner" (Bryce, 2011, p. 474). In recent years publishing companies have added maps, photographs, diagrams, and other visual representations in primary science texts; however, you need to teach students how to read and learn from these visual components by modeling how to interpret them (Coleman, Golson-Bradley, & Donovan, 2012). In order for students to fully understand the concepts in primary science texts, engage the students in the following activities:

1. Introduce textbook features such as the table of contents, glossary, and index.

2. Explain how boldface and italic text denote definitions or other main concepts.

3. Model skimming the material with students, looking at and reading the captions of photographs and illustrations to get a feel for the information in each chapter.

4. Read and discuss the most difficult passages together.

5. Dramatize concepts.

6. Supplement the text with the book's website, online videos, or other information.

7. Conduct a think-aloud as you view the illustrations, charts, and diagrams, explaining how to read them accurately.

8. Guide students as they write and discuss what they have learned (Bryce, 2011; Coleman et al., 2012).

To really determine the suitability of texts for students, it is best to heed the recommendations outlined in *Becoming a Nation of Readers* (Anderson et al., 1985). In the next section we discuss a variety of text–reader factors, all of which are important for successful reading comprehension.

Text and Reader Interaction

To determine how suitable textual material is for particular students, consider the interaction that should occur between the reader and the text. A teacher needs to examine the background knowledge or experience of the reader; the purpose of the material; its relevance, interest, and appropriateness; and the overall predictability of the material for the reader (Manzo et al., 2009).

Some teachers may even wish to make use of an interactive strategy such as the cloze test (Bormuth, 1968) to help determine how well a student can read and comprehend a particular selection. In a cloze test, as discussed in Chapter 5, words are systematically deleted from a text passage, and the student must predict the correct word for each deletion. This technique is effective because it provides some information about the individual's prior knowledge of the material and also indicates how predictable and cohesive the language of the material is for him or her. In essence, a cloze test identifies a student's potential for comprehending selected materials.

Although the cloze procedure may not be something you want to use with every text, it can supplement your knowledge about the literary quality, cohesion, and teachability of particular texts.

TEACHING ACTIVITIES   10

HELPING STUDENTS BUILD INFORMATION

Integrating the language arts in the content areas helps students to build their store of knowledge—a cognitive stockpile of information that can be used to facilitate comprehension of any future text.

Within an integrated curriculum, you need to help students develop the following comprehension and communication competencies:

- understanding and effectively using the specific vocabularies of the various subject areas
- developing strategies to guide and facilitate individual comprehension
- knowing how and when to implement such strategies
- being able to use a variety of resources to reinforce and support comprehension
- developing writing as a learning tool for comprehension and communication

In this section we share activities to develop students' knowledge by connecting reading, writing, speaking, and listening skills. Some of the activities recommended for the middle-school grades suggest that content area teachers work together to build knowledge across the subject areas by coordinating units of study, in which students read novels in literature, nonfiction in social studies and science, and create multimodal presentations with the information in technology class. Many of the activities require collaboration so students have the opportunity to learn from one another.

1   Graphic organizers

Successfully acquiring content information depends on the ability to understand a wide variety of concepts. Understanding these concepts is, in turn, dependent on being familiar with the domain-specific or technical vocabulary of a particular subject area. Therefore, students need to have extensive word knowledge *and* be aware of the strategic links between specialized content vocabularies and their underlying concepts.

You can assist students in their endeavors to obtain, organize, and comprehend information by providing learning experiences that expose them to strategies that help them learn how to develop vocabulary knowledge independently. Then they can continue to gather and use information on their own. As noted in the CCRA standards for reading, students must be able to interpret technical vocabulary and concepts. To introduce new technical vocabulary and concepts, identify the key words in a lesson, arrange them in a diagram, and present it to the students (Vacca et al., 2014; Richardson et al., 2011). Graphic organizers can also be used for a comprehension check or review. In a review lesson, it can be beneficial to give students a diagram that has been partially completed and then let them finish it on their own. The diagram can serve as a catalyst for the students' recollection of concept organization. Figures 10.5 and 10.6 show two approaches to using graphic organizers to build visual as well as verbal structures for specialized vocabulary. *Recommended for primary grades.*

2   Illustrating and writing what I learned

After a shared reading of an informational text, invite students to write and/or illustrate what they learned. (For very young students, their writing may be a drawing.)

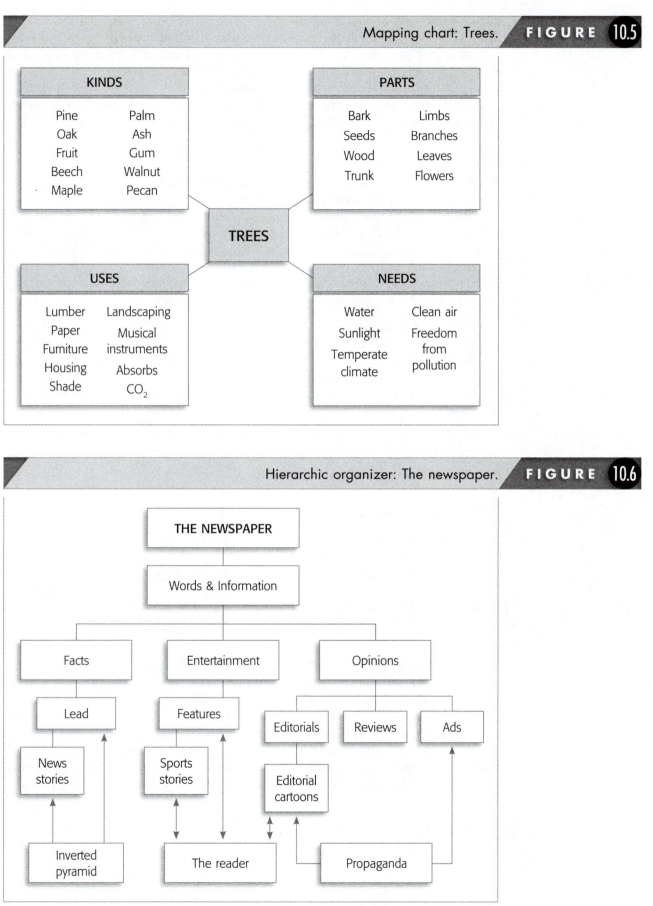

Mapping chart: Trees.   FIGURE 10.5

KINDS

Pine   Palm
Oak   Ash
Fruit   Gum
Beech   Walnut
Maple   Pecan

PARTS

Bark   Limbs
Seeds   Branches
Wood   Leaves
Trunk   Flowers

TREES

USES

Lumber   Landscaping
Paper   Musical
Furniture instruments
Housing   Absorbs
Shade CO_2

NEEDS

Water   Clean air
Sunlight   Freedom
Temperate   from
climate   pollution

Hierarchic organizer: The newspaper.   FIGURE 10.6

THE NEWSPAPER

Words & Information

Facts   Entertainment   Opinions

Lead   Features   Editorials   Reviews   Ads

News   Sports   Editorial
stories   stories   cartoons

Inverted   The reader   Propaganda
pyramid

For example, share with the class the short chapter book *Growl! A Book About Bears* (Berger, 1999). Chapter 1 describes the different types of bears and what they eat; Chapter 2 describes how bears find food; Chapter 3 describes how bears get ready for winter; and Chapter 4 describes when baby bears are born. Share one chapter a day and discuss with the students what they learned. Then invite the students to draw a picture illustrating what they learned, and to write one sentence about their picture. *Recommended for primary grades.*

3 Writing hypotheses

Simple science experiments increase young students' interest in science and help them connect reading, writing, and thinking. One purpose of conducting science experiments is to teach students to read carefully and to accurately record data. Science Bob's website offers many easy experiments for second and third graders. To get started, we suggest you begin with the lava lamp experiment, because the ingredients are inexpensive and students can do the experiment with a partner. This and other experiments can be found at www.sciencebob.com/experiments/lavacup.php. We suggest the following steps for the activity:

1. Divide students into pairs and give each pair the correct materials. Each student receives the hypothesis sheet found in Figure 10.7 so everyone can write their hypotheses and record their findings.

2. Explain what a hypothesis is and tell the students that all scientists write one or two hypotheses before they begin an experiment. Have your students do the same.

3. Have each group read the directions from the hypothesis sheet and do the experiment.

Recommended for primary grades.

4 Paragraph frames

Another primary-grade activity that involves writing is *paragraph frames* (Cudd & Roberts, 1989). These frames use a cloze procedure of sentence starters to help students organize a paragraph they are writing into one of the common organizational patterns of expository text. Frames can be organized according to the concepts of sequence, enumeration, cause and effect, or compare and contrast. A sample paragraph frame is illustrated in Figure 10.8. *Recommended for primary grades.*

5 Comparing and contrasting two creatures

CCRA.R.9 requires that students "analyze how two or more texts address similar themes or topics in order to build knowledge or to compare the approaches the authors take" (NGACBP & CCSSO, 2010, p. 10). The following activity is one that an entire first-grade class can do with the teacher facilitating.

After reading books aloud from Lobel's *Frog and Toad* series and then having students read them independently, invite the class to share attributes about frogs and toads as depicted in these fictional books. The list may include the following:

a. They lived in houses.
b. They could read.
c. They could tell stories.
d. They drank tea.
e. They wore clothes.
f. They flew kites and rode bicycles.

Worksheet for the lava lamp science experiment.   **FIGURE** 10.7

Materials:

    1 clear plastic bottle
    water
    ¼ cup vegetable oil
    1 Alka-Seltzer tablet (salt will also work)
    Food coloring

HYPOTHESIS #1

Write one hypothesis stating what you think will happen when you put the water and oil into the plastic bottle.

_____

_____

Directions:

    Pour water into the plastic bottle until it is nearly full.
    Add the oil and wait approximately two minutes.

DATA FINDINGS #1

Explain what happened to the water and oil.

_____

_____

HYPOTHESIS #2

Write one hypothesis stating what you think will happen when you add the food coloring to the water and oil.

_____

_____

Directions:

    Add around a dozen drops of food coloring to the bottle. Any color will work.
    Observe closely to see what happens.

DATA FINDINGS #2

Explain what happened to the food coloring.

_____

_____

HYPOTHESIS #3

Write a hypothesis stating what you think will happen when you put pieces of Alka-Seltzer into the oil/water solution.

_____

_____

Directions:

    Cut an Alka-Seltzer tablet into about 4 or 5 little pieces and drop them one by one into the bottle.

DATA FINDINGS #3

Explain what happened when you added the Alka-Seltzer to the water/oil solution.

_____

_____

Your teacher explained why each of the steps happened. Write in your own words WHY all the steps happened.

_____

_____

FIGURE 10.8   Sample paragraph frame.

Example 1   (Elena, grade 2)

Before a frog is grown, it goes through many changes. First, the mother frog _____
_____.

Next, _____.

Then, _____.

Finally, _____.

Now they _____

_____

_____

Before a frog is grown,
it goes through many stages. First,
the mother frog lays the eggs. Next,
the eggs hatch and turn into tadpoles.
Then slowly the tadpoles legs begin
to grow. Finally, the tadpole turns
into a frog. Now and then they
have to go into the water to keep
their skin moist.

Stage No. 1.   Stage NO 2.

Stage NO. 3.   Stage NO. 4.
                                    Extraordinary!

Source: From Cudd, E. T., & Roberts, L. L. (1989, February). Using writing to enhance content area learning in the primary grades. *The Reading Teacher, 42*(6), 392–404. Reprinted with permission of the International Reading Association via CCC.

After enjoying Lobel's books, read and share some fact-based books about toads and frogs. Invite students to share what they learned and have them find the page or picture that supports their fact. Using a large flip chart, record their comments, making sure to write down the page number after each fact. Use a different flip chart page for each book, and be sure to write the title, author, and illustrator of each book on top of each page. Possible books to use include those listed in Figure 10.9.

Display the following websites on the whiteboard, and after you have shared each one, ask students to share facts they have learned about frogs and toads.

Suggested books to use in a comparison–contrast activity. **FIGURE** 10.9

Elliot, L., Gerhardt, C., & Davidson, C. (2009). *The Frogs and Toads of North America.*

Shye, M. L. (2013). *Frogs! A Kids' Book about Frogs and Toads: Facts, Figures and High Quality Pictures of Animals in Nature* (a digital book that can be shared on a whiteboard). (Note: Chapter 2 explains the difference between a frog and toad.)

Gibbons, G. (1993). *Frogs.*

Green, E. (2011). *Backyard Wildlife: Frogs.* (An easy read book.)

Cowley, J. (1999). *Red-eyed Tree Frog.* (An easy read book.)

Bishop, N. (2008). *Frogs.*

Guiberson, B. (2013). *Frog Song.* Illus. G Spirin.

- http://allaboutfrogs.org/weird/general/songs.html
- www.kidzone.ws/lw/frogs/facts8.htm
- www.frog-life-cycle.com/frog-toad-difference.html

Using the whiteboard or a big piece of butcher paper, draw a Venn diagram. Explain how a Venn diagram will enable them to compare (how frogs and toads are the same) and contrast (how they are different). Be sure to use the words *compare* and *contrast* so students learn those terms. Ask the students to recall what they learned about toads and frogs. Referring back to the flip charts, write the author and page number of each fact that the students give. Remember: you are modeling how to take notes and how to compare and contrast two creatures. *Recommended for primary grades.*

After you have completed the Venn diagram, invite students to read more books about toads or frogs by engaging them in the following activity.

6   What I learned

When studying a unit about animals, you can share books that are too difficult for most students to read, but students should also be given an opportunity to read a book on the subject that is at their easy or independent reading level so they can learn facts on their own. (Several books about frogs written for lower primary students were listed in Figure 10.9.) To reinforce what students have learned, give them a template of a frog (see Figure 10.10) and have them write the title, author, and illustrator of the book on top, and on the provided lines, write one or two facts in phrase format. *Recommended for primary grades.*

7   Guided reading procedure (GRP)

The guided reading procedure helps students develop the strategies they need to become independent readers. The GRP involves student collaboration, the use of self-questioning and self-correction techniques, and the organization of information. It works best with materials that contain lots of facts the students will need to remember.

GRP is designed to be used as a group strategy. However, at times you may want to modify it so students can use it independently. The *reading guide* consists

FIGURE 10.10 Sample frog template.

of having individual students make decisions about a series of statements at different levels of comprehension; the purpose of the strategy is to guide the student in comprehending a selection by showing him or her the relationship among the ideas. The statements in the guide also serve as initiators for student discussion.

Figure 10.11 presents an example of a guide that a primary teacher used to help her students understand that animals are adapted in special ways to survive in their habitats. She wanted them to organize their ideas about this concept by classifying the animals according to where they live. *Recommended for primary grades.*

8 Semantic mapping

Semantic mapping is a vocabulary strategy (Richardson et al., 2011); as a visual technique, it helps students to expand, organize, and remember new concepts. Although the format of a semantic map is similar to the map version of a graphic organizer, its development is not. Students play an active role in the formation of the map. Their interaction and discussion with the teacher determine its configuration. The key to this strategy is student empowerment: help them use their own knowledge and categorization skills to see new relationships among concepts and vocabulary terms.

Here are the key steps in developing a semantic map (Richardson et al., 2011):

1. Choose a central word from a text that the students are using. If you are doing a unit on different wildlife and their habitats, for example, you might choose the word *owls*.
2. List the word on a large piece of paper or on the chalkboard.

Sample reading guide.   **FIGURE 10.11**

Topic: Animals are adapted to live in different habitats.

Part I   As you read the text, check the statements that are true.

☐   1. *Adapted* means that an animal fits into its habitat.

☐   2. An animal that is adapted cannot get food and water.

☐   3. Deserts are hot and do not have much rain.

☐   4. The polar areas near the North and South Poles are cold most of the year.

☐   5. Polar bears live near the North Pole.

☐   6. Penguins live near the South Pole.

☐   7. Some of the biggest and fastest animals live in the grasslands.

☐   8. Rain forests are hot and wet.

☐   9. Whales live in the ocean.

☐ 10. Whales breathe through fins.

Part II   Classify the animals listed according to where they live. Write each word under the proper heading.

blue whale	kangaroo rat	cattle	ptarmigan	jackrabbit
boa	rattlesnake	buffalo	shark	ermine
zebra	camel	sheep	tree frog	octopus
rhino	penguin	ocelot	seal	arctic tern
musk ox	polar bear	killer whale	walrus	parrot
arctic hare	giraffe	sea urchin	lizard	monkey

Deserts	Polar Areas	Grasslands	Rain Forests	Water

3. Encourage students to think of as many words related to the chosen topic as they can.

4. Have students categorize or group the words.

5. Create the semantic map as the students give you the main topics with related words.

A semantic map developed about owls might look like the one depicted in Figure 10.12. *Recommended for intermediate grades.*

FIGURE 10.12   Sample semantic map: Owls.

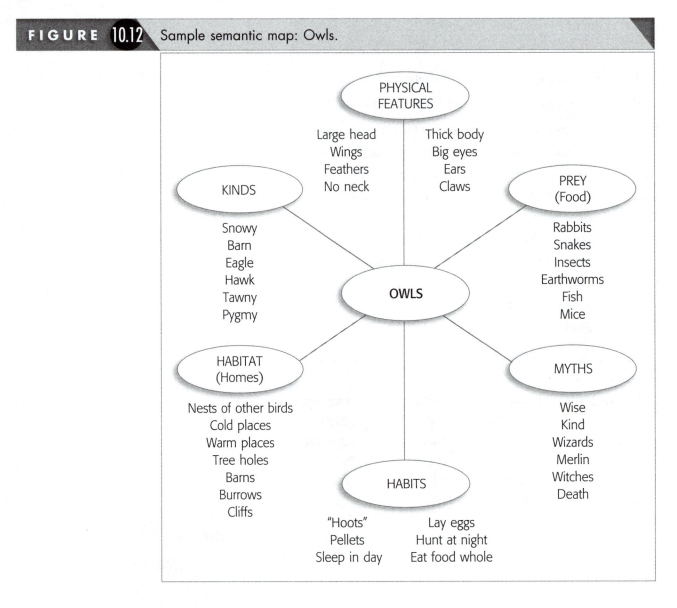

9 Semantic feature analysis

A *semantic feature analysis,* also called features analysis (Readence, Bean & Scott, 2012), is a categorization activity that uses a matrix to illustrate the similarities and differences among related terms. It enables students at all levels to activate their prior knowledge for the purpose of acquiring specific content vocabulary and concepts.

When preparing to use this strategy with your students, use these six steps as a guide (Johnson & Pearson, 1984):

1. Decide upon a category or topic, such as *sea habitats.*
2. List some subcategories of this term (*ocean, salt marsh, coral reef*) in a column on the left side of a page or a board.
3. Help students decide on some characteristics or features shared by the words (salt water, cold water, waves, plants, animals). List these across the top of the page or board.
4. Place a plus sign (+) in the appropriate box to indicate that an item in the category possesses a feature and a minus sign (−) to indicate that the item does not have the feature.

5. Add any new terms or features you come up with.

6. Discuss the matrix and help students note the features shared by the words as well as the uniqueness of each word.

In a science project developed at the elementary school located on Sullivan's Island, South Carolina, students completed the feature analysis illustrated in Figure 10.13. Because of the school's location on the Atlantic Ocean, studying water habitats was an essential educational experience. *Recommended for intermediate grades.*

10 Possible sentences

CCRA.R.4 requires that students "Interpret words and phrases as they are used in a text, including determining technical, connotative, and figurative meanings, and analyze how specific word choices shape meaning or tone" (NGACBP & CCSSO, 2010, p. 10). One effective strategy, called *possible sentences* (Moore & Moore, 1986; Tierney & Readence, 2005), relies primarily on verbal predictions to enhance vocabulary and concept development. Teachers introduce their students to this procedure by presenting new vocabulary in conjunction with familiar words. The students use the words to make up sentences; then they read text to verify the correctness of their sentences. Using possible sentences involves the following five steps:

1. **List important vocabulary terms.** For the passages related to the sea habitat project, you might start by listing and pronouncing the following terms with students: *ocean, rocky intertidal, salt water, tides, seaweed, kelp forest, waves, beach, estuary, sea grasses, mud,* and *brackish water.*

2. **Formulate sentences.** Then ask students to use two or more of the words from the list in a sentence. This sentence should contain information that students think

Sample semantic feature analysis: Sea habitats. FIGURE 10.13

	Salt water	Deep water	Shore or shallow water	Rocks	Sandy or muddy bottom	Cold water	Warm water	Brackish water	Waves	Plants	Animals
Ocean	+	+	+	+	+	+	+	–	+	+	+
Rocky intertidal	+	–	+	+	?	+	+	–	+	+	+
Kelp forest	+	–	+	+	?	+	–	–	+	+	+
Estuary	–	–	+	–	+	+	+	+	–	+	+
Salt marsh	–	–	+	–	?	+	+	+	–	+	+
Sandy beach	+	–	+	–	+	+	+	–	+	+	+
Continental shelf	+	+	+	–	+	+	+	–	+	+	+
Coral reef	+	+	?	+	–	–	+	–	+	+	+
Sea grass bed	+	–	+	–	+	+	+	+	+	+	+
Mangrove swamp	+	–	+	?	+	–	+	+	?	+	+

will actually be in the text. Record this possible sentence, even if it is not correct. This process continues until all of the words have been used at least once. Sentences produced for the sea habitat project might include the following:

- A *kelp forest* has lots of *seaweed* and *salt water.*
- *Tides* and *waves* have an effect on a *rocky intertidal.*
- In an *estuary,* the *mud* and *brackish water* provide a good home for young sea animals.
- *Sea grasses* limit the *ocean's* ability to erode the *beach.*

3. Check sentences. Students read the passages to see if their sentences are correct.

4. Evaluate sentences. After everyone has completed the reading, each sentence is evaluated. Some sentences may need to be omitted; others may need to be restated. For example, students may want to clarify the fourth sentence by stating that sea grasses actually protect the beach from being battered by the ocean's waves.

5. Generate new sentences. The last step is to generate new sentences and to check them for accuracy. Once these are confirmed, students can add them to their reading logs or journals.

This technique is especially good for recalling prior knowledge and encouraging interaction with the text through the use of predictions. It is also a good activity for involving an entire class with a text. *Recommended for intermediate grades.*

11 K-T-W-L-E

In order to fully comprehend content area texts, students must integrate their prior knowledge with new information. The K-T-W-L-E chart introduced in Chapter 8 and presented in Figure 8.7 is a useful activity for activating and integrating students' knowledge about a topic when reading an informational text. Before students begin reading, teachers invite them to write everything they know about a given topic under the K column. Additionally, students may think they know some information about the topic; therefore, they have added the T (think I know) column after the K column. In the W column, students list what they would like to learn about the topic. After they have read and studied the concept, they write in the L column the important facts they have learned about the topic. Since the CCRA.R.1 requires students to "read closely to determine what the texts says explicitly and to make logical inferences from it; cite specific textual evidence when writing or speaking to support conclusions drawn from the text" (NGACBP & CCSSO, 2010, p. 10), the final E column is for students to provide evidence for what they learned by citing page numbers and direct quotes if necessary. *Recommended for intermediate grades.*

12 Guidance strategies

Using guidance strategies with students in the intermediate grades empowers them to become strategic readers; that is, readers who have developed metacognition and are able to motivate and monitor themselves as they comprehend information. By providing assistance based on your students' needs, you can help them to become independent, self-confident learners in all subject areas.

In general, *guidance strategies* are used during the reading process as a way of arousing interest and focusing attention. They help students to activate prior knowledge, monitor the comprehension process, and provide needed follow-up during the post-reading period. The next two activities describe strategies to help guide the reading process from beginning to end: SQ3R and DR–TA.

13 Survey, Question, Read, Retell, Review (SQ3R)

SQ3R requires readers to preview, question, predict, summarize, review, and then clarify information. This approach is very useful with textbooks and difficult printed materials (Cohen & Cowen, 2008). You will want to model this technique by walking students through the following steps:

- *Survey.* Have students review the text by looking at titles, headings, visual aids, questions, and summaries. Encourage them to think about what the material is trying to convey.
- *Question.* Help students to formulate questions based on the preview and then write them down.
- *Read.* Use the questions to guide reading and to gather any other information found in the material.
- *Retell.* Help students to organize a summary to retell what they learned.
- *Review.* For clarification, discuss the answers to the questions from step 2 in class.

14 Directed Reading–Thinking Activity (DR–TA)

DR–TA is another guidance strategy that Stauffer (1969) originally conceptualized as a process to help students understand their purpose for reading. As such, it is particularly suited for selections in the content areas (Readence et al., 2012).

During the DR–TA, you help readers identify purposes for reading, guide them through the reading process, monitor them to determine any difficulties, and help them develop comprehension and skills as appropriate. Activities during the pre-reading, reading, and post-reading stages are as follows:

- *Pre-reading.* Have students activate any prior knowledge by viewing the title, pictures, and headings of the material. Encourage students to make predictions about the selection based on their observations. Write their ideas on the board or a chart.
- *Reading.* Have students read to verify their predictions. Extend their thinking by encouraging them to verify their predictions, summarize what they have read, and predict what might happen next.
- *Post-reading.* Discuss what the students have read and the accuracy of their predictions. Encourage them to point out sections of the material that support or disprove their predictions. Allow the students to discuss the process and summarize what they have learned for themselves.

After the post-reading session, you might want to go back and use this particular material for the development of specific student competencies. Depending on the needs of your students, you may want to use the opportunity to conduct a strategy lesson related to word knowledge, using context clues, summarizing, or monitoring metacognition.

The DR–TA has proved to be a very successful reading strategy and has been the focus of much attention in recent years.

15 Writing songs based on informational text

Developmental psychologist Howard Gardner explained that one of the preferred methods for students to learn is through music. Music is also the way that some students enjoy presenting new information. The following activity encourages both creativity and small group collaboration.

1. After studying a unit or reading one book on a particular subject, have students form groups of three.

2. Instruct them to write down facts that they learned from the reading.

3. Invite them to think of a song for which the entire group knows the tune (e.g., "Row, Row, Row Your Boat" or "Twinkle, Twinkle Little Star").

4. Using the melody and the facts they just wrote down, have students write one or two verses to the song.

5. Give them time to practice their song and then invite them to sing it to the class. Figure 10.14 has two examples of songs written by students.

Recommended for intermediate grades.

FIGURE 10.14 Sample songs based on informational text.

Example 1

Sharks!

To the tune of "Days of the Week" (also the tune to "The Addams Family")

By Ben Siems, Michael Lunn, and Becky Murrow

Five rows of teeth!
Chomp! Chomp!
Five rows of teeth!
Chomp! Chomp!
Five rows of teeth, five rows of teeth,
   five rows of teeth!
Chomp! Chomp!
Long teeth are for catching,
Flat teeth are for grinding,
Serrated teeth for ripping,
And that's the kinds of teeth!
Out on a hunt!
Du-Duh ("Jaws" theme)
Out on a hunt! Du-duh!
Out on a hunt, out on a hunt, out on a hunt!
Du-Duh!
The little shark is hungry
So he goes out hunting
He senses in the water
A fish is getting near!
Life of a shark!
Swim! Swim!
Life of a shark!
Swim! Swim!
Life of a shark, life of a shark, life of a shark!
Swim! Swim!
A shark is always in motion
Swimming throughout the ocean
Even when he's sleeping
And that's the life of a shark!

Example 2

Types of Animals

(To the tune of "Old MacDonald Had a Farm")

By Katie Funk, Sid Childers, and Allison White

Mammals, reptiles, amphibians,
An-a-animals
Fish, and birds and insects too,
An-a-animals
Mammals are warm-blooded,
An-a-animals
They all have hair and live babies.
An-a-animals
With a brown dog here,
And a gray cat there,
Here a girl, there a boy,
Don't forget us humans
Mammals, reptiles, amphibians,
An-a-animals
Reptiles are cold-blooded.
An-a-animals
They all have scales and need sun too.
An-a-animals
With a cranky croc here,
And a slithery snake there,
Here a lizard, there a lizard,
Everywhere a lizard, lizard.
Mammals, reptiles, amphibians,
An-a-animals.
Amphibians can live on land,
An-a-animals
They also live in water too,
An-a-animals
With a tiny turtle here,
And a freaky frog there,
Here a newt, there a newt,
Everywhere a newt, newt.
Mammals, reptiles, amphibians,
An-a-animals.

16 ReQuest

ReQuest is a technique in which teachers use questioning as a means of empowering students by helping them learn how to ask their own questions. The facilitator needs to follow the modeling guidelines set forth by Manzo (1968, 1969), which incorporates reciprocal questioning and critical thinking in a one-on-one teaching situation.

> As you teach, emphasize what interests you.
>
> **WILLIAM GLASSER, M.D.**

Prepare for ReQuest by making sure your material for developing the questions is appropriate for the student and lends itself to making predictions. Select several points at which the student can pause and make some predictions, and initiate the session through the following nine steps (Manzo, 1968; Readence et al., 2012):

1. Each participant receives a copy of the reading selection.
2. Both the teacher and the student read the first sentence(s) silently. Then the teacher closes the book and tells the student to ask the types of questions a teacher would ask in the way a teacher would ask them. The student asks as many questions as he or she sees fit.
3. The teacher responds to the questions, reinforces appropriate questions, and requests rephrasing of questions that are unclear.
4. The student finishes asking questions and closes the book. Then the teacher takes over questioning the student. He or she models appropriate questioning behavior and uses a variety of question types (see Chapter 5).
5. The procedure is repeated with the second sentence. (With older students, a teacher may want to start reading a few sentences at a time rather than just one.)
6. This process continues until enough of the selection has been read (probably the first paragraph or so) for the student to make a prediction about what the rest of the selection is about.
7. The teacher then asks the student to justify the prediction. If the prediction is reasonable, the student continues with silent reading. If not, the exchange of questions continues and the student makes another prediction at a later point.
8. Now the teacher directs the student to read to the end of the selection in order to compare the prediction with what the text conveys.
9. The teacher follows up with a discussion about the merits of the prediction and why it might be possible to have several logical and plausible conclusions to the same selection. Avoid the idea of one right answer. You might even give the student the opportunity to write a new ending for the text.

Recommended for middle grades.

17 Text pattern reading guides

Two specialized types of guides call students' attention to the dominant textual pattern in reading materials. By helping students to recognize and then use a major textual pattern to organize their ideas, you encourage them to develop metacognitive knowledge about relationships in textual information.

Figures 10.15 and 10.16 show two pattern guides that have been used successfully with middle-school students. Both guides were developed to facilitate students' understanding about the Hohokam and the Anasazi Indians as part of a unit on Native Americans. One guide was developed to highlight the interaction of causes and effects on various aspects of tribe members' lives; the other compares the two groups on a variety of factors. *Recommended for middle grades.*

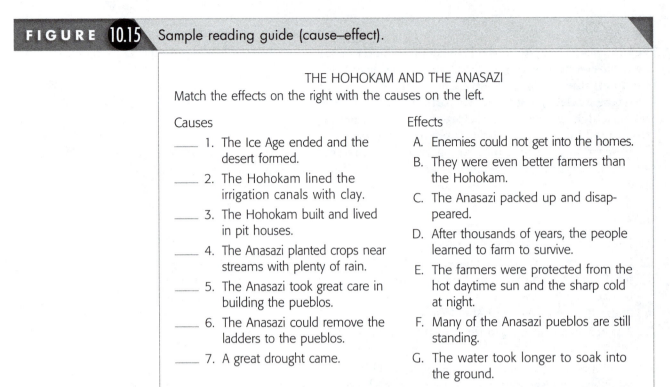

FIGURE 10.15 Sample reading guide (cause–effect).

THE HOHOKAM AND THE ANASAZI

Match the effects on the right with the causes on the left.

Causes

_____ 1. The Ice Age ended and the desert formed.

_____ 2. The Hohokam lined the irrigation canals with clay.

_____ 3. The Hohokam built and lived in pit houses.

_____ 4. The Anasazi planted crops near streams with plenty of rain.

_____ 5. The Anasazi took great care in building the pueblos.

_____ 6. The Anasazi could remove the ladders to the pueblos.

_____ 7. A great drought came.

Effects

A. Enemies could not get into the homes.

B. They were even better farmers than the Hohokam.

C. The Anasazi packed up and disappeared.

D. After thousands of years, the people learned to farm to survive.

E. The farmers were protected from the hot daytime sun and the sharp cold at night.

F. Many of the Anasazi pueblos are still standing.

G. The water took longer to soak into the ground.

FIGURE 10.16 Sample reading guide (comparison–contrast).

The Hohokam	*In* relationship to:	The Anasazi
	Geographic Location	
	Farming Techniques	
	Housing	
	Crafts	
	Fate	

THE HOHOKAM AND THE ANASAZI

18 Social literacy activity

This activity encourages you to introduce social literacies to your students. *Social literacy* means students become aware of social inequities in our country and develop beliefs about how they should be addressed; it is the first step in students becoming full, participating members of society. In this activity, students listen to and discuss the lyrics of a song that highlights the conditions faced by those who are homeless. The songwriter's words and phrases create a tone that conveys the grave inequity of the situation.

Share Bruce Springsteen's song "The Ghost of Tom Joad," a song that highlights the social injustice of homelessness (the song is available online by searching "Ghost of Tom Joad"). Have the students read the words of the first verse, beginning with "Man walks along the railroad track . . ." and ending with "No job, no home, no peace, no rest, no REST!"

Have students discuss the lyrics and what message the songwriter is conveying. Have them consider to what specifically the songwriter is referring with the words "in the Southwest" and "Welcome to the New World Order." Next invite students to research the plight of homelessness and to find statistics regarding the homeless. Have them share their findings with the class by creating a slide presentation using PowerPoint, Prezi, or Soundslides. Then have students discuss what action they can take to draw the public's attention to the inequities they find. Encourage them to take appropriate action that they suggest. *Recommended for middle grades.*

19 Point of view and social literacy

This activity provides a creative manner for students to read informational books about African American men and women who impacted U.S. history. For the activity, use the following steps:

1. Using the books found in Figure 10.17, invite students to choose one of the accomplished African American men and women. In their reading, ask them to focus on the hero's perspective on the African Americans' social standing and other circumstances during his or her life.

2. Discuss students' thoughts about the various influential men and women they have learned about.

3. Invite students to consider those men and women being interviewed by a modern reporter, thus allowing them to express their points of view on various contemporary issues. Have students write the questions and create the responses from the African American hero's point of view. Students should give accurate information, but choose words that will help the audience have empathy for the hero.

4. After they write their rough drafts, have students conference with you and their peers so they can revise their writing to make it better.

5. Collect students' writing and publish a class booklet.

This activity supports CCRA.R.6, which requires students to "assess how point of view or purpose shapes the content and style of a text" (NGACBP & CCSSO, 2010, p. 10). *Recommended for middle grades.*

Suggested book list of African American heroes. **FIGURE 10.17**

Bolden, T. (2005, reprint). *Portraits of African-American Heroes.*

Myers, W. D. (2008). *Ida B. Wells: Let the Truth Be Told.* Illus. B. Christensen.

Pinkney, A. D. (2000). *Let It Shine: Stories of Black Women Freedom Fighters.*

Rappaport, D. (2007, reprint). *Martin's Big Words.* Illus. B. Collier.

Ringgold, F. (2003). *The Bus Ride that Changed History.*

Weatherford, C. B. (2007). *Freedom on the Menu: The Greensboro Sit-ins.*

20   Debate: Drilling in the Gulf

Introduce middle-school students to the idea that many of the conveniences that we enjoy involve a tradeoff. Using *Oil Spill: Disaster in the Gulf* (Chiang, Crane, Hamalainen, & Jones, 2010) as a springboard, have students take a stance regarding whether the United States should drill for oil in the Gulf of Mexico or if the risks are too great. Be mindful that in some geographic areas, students' family members may make their living on oil rigs or elsewhere in the industry. After some discussion, invite students to "write arguments to support [their] claims in an analysis of substantive topics or texts, using valid reasoning and relevant and sufficient evidence" (CCRA.W.1; NGACBP & CCSSO, 2010, p. 18). *Recommended for middle grades.*

21   Multiliteracies presentation

Often when studying U.S. history and science, students ask questions about social issues to which they would like to find answers. Possible topics may include climate change, pollution, civil rights, immigration laws, and so on. Have students brainstorm as a class to come up with topics. Then, students with similar interests can form a group, research the topic, and present their findings to the class in a multimodal format. The following are the possible steps for this activity (Spires, Hervey, Morris, & Stelpflug, 2012), which can be modified for your classroom schedule.

1. Ask a compelling question.
   a. The question should arouse students' curiosity and motivate them to seek an answer.
   b. The question has social importance.
   c. The question aligns with the course of study (e.g., social studies, science, math, fine arts, sports).
2. Gather and analyze information.
   a. Conduct online searches, teaching distinctions between *.org, .gov,* and *.com* sites.
   b. Search subscription and library databases.
   c. Use magazines, books, and other printed sources.
   d. Assess authors and organizations for credibility.
   e. Cite references.
3. Creatively synthesize information.
   a. Decide the most compelling way to present information: compare/contrast, problem/solution, descriptive, or least important to most important argument.
   b. Create a storyboard.
   c. Create videos, photographs, audio, graphs, tables.
   d. Observe copyright laws.
   e. Add music to support the mood of the content.
4. Critically evaluate and revise.
   a. Ensure a natural flow from one image to the next.
   b. Present information clearly and concisely.
   c. Make sure information is compelling
   d. State citations and credits correctly.
   e. Make sure technical and aesthetic aspects are of high quality.
   f. Verify that content is age appropriate.
5. Share by publishing and taking action.

Recommended for middle grades.

22   Connecting fiction with nonfiction

read**RESEARCH**practice

To learn more about how students can put their research into action, visit the following site: www.WKCD.org.

In middle schools, literature and social studies teachers (and teachers in other content areas, as we'll mention below) can integrate students' learning by planning lessons in which students read fiction in their language arts class and nonfiction, including online resources, in their social studies class.

In this activity, students are encouraged to research an event in American history that may not be covered in their history textbook. Our example uses the Tulsa Riots and Black Wall Street. Begin by having all students read Anna Myers' historical novel *Tulsa Burning* (2004). Then have students read newspaper clips from that time period and other articles found online. This activity will also teach students to investigate an author's credentials and cite references. Key elements of this activity include constructing a K-T-W-L-E chart as a prewriting and drafting activity, using a Frayer graphic organizer (described below) for a vocabulary activity, and integrating this unit across the content areas. *Recommended for middle grades.*

K-T-W-L-E prewriting and drafting activity. Have students construct a K-T-W-L-E chart (see Figure 8.7) as a prewriting and rough draft activity. CCRA.R.1 requires students to "cite specific textual evidence when writing or speaking to support conclusions drawn from the text," and CCRA.W.8 requires them to "assess the credibility and accuracy of each source"(NGACBP & CCSSO, 2010, pp. 10, 18). Use an electronic version of the chart in Figure 10.18 to help students stay organized as they focus on meeting the two standards.

Frayer graphic organizer for vocabulary. In order to understand this historical event, it is important that students have a good understanding of relevant vocabulary words. Creating a Frayer graphic organizer (see Figure 10.19) allows students

Extension of the L E of K-T-W-L-E. **FIGURE 10.18**

SOURCE	LEARNED	EVIDENCE	AUTHOR/ ORGANIZATION	CREDIBILITY
http://www1.assumption.edu/ahc/raceriots/default.html				
http://digital.library.okstate.edu/encyclopedia/entries/T/TU013.html				
http://hti.osu.edu/history-lesson-plans/united-states-history/tulsa-riot				
Myers, A. (2004). *Tulsa Burning.* New York: Walker Childrens.				
Madigan, T. (2003). *The Burning: Massacre, Destruction, and the Tulsa Race Riot of 1921.* New York: St. Martin's Griffin.				

FIGURE 10.19 Frayer graphic organizer for the vocabulary of Tulsa riots unit.

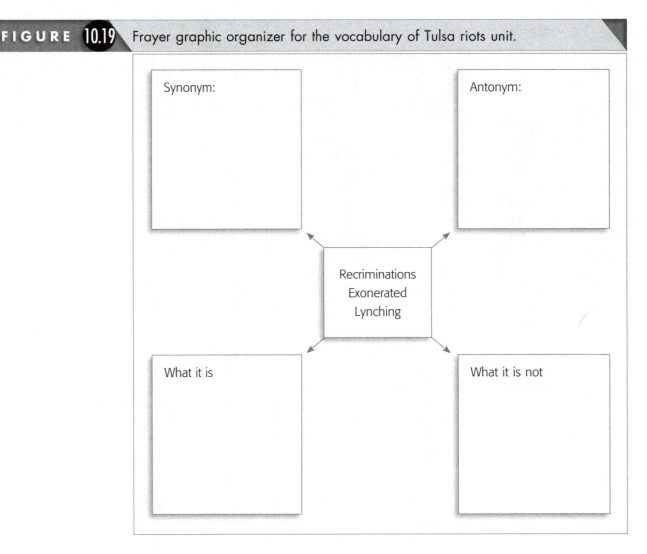

to examine the concepts associated with the Tulsa Riots, along with their synonyms and antonyms. These concepts may include lynching, race riots, the Ku Klux Klan, martial law, legal maneuvering, and exoneration.

Integration of the unit study across the content areas. While the language arts teacher focuses on Myers' novel and the vocabulary words, the social studies teacher engages the students in researching the factual event. The math teacher explains Wall Street and introduces math problems dealing with investments and the rise and fall of the stock market. The art teacher invites students to depict the time period in some art form, while the music teacher leads students in writing a rap song based on the historical event. The technology teacher assists students as they create their final multimodal presentation.

ASSESSMENT OF THE INTEGRATED APPROACH TO LITERACY AND THE CONTENT AREAS

In the integrated approaches using thematic units, you do not assess learning with teacher-made tests and correctly answered worksheets. Assessment must be authentic in nature and "based on what students actually do in a variety of contexts at different points throughout the instructional year" (Seely, 1995, p. 59). Assessment methods may include checklists, anecdotal records, learning logs, dialogue journals, portfolios, teacher conferences, peer assessment, and self-assessment (Manning, Manning, & Long, 1994; Meinbach, Rothlein & Fredricks, 2000). Each student must be assessed each day and assessment must include how cooperatively the student worked in small groups (see Appendix D.26). Appendix D.14 is a rubric for a writing assignment. Each element of the writing assignment is assigned points; these points reflect the importance of that particular element as it pertains to the entire writing project. Other authors who have devised assessment forms and ideas for evaluation include Atwell (1998), Spandel (2012), and Tierney and Readence (2005).

TECHNOLOGY IN THE CLASSROOM

Simulations deserve a place in language arts instruction because they provide motivation for reading, researching, and writing. Computer simulations allow a particular situation or aspect of a content area to come alive for students and also allow them to experience something that would not be possible merely through a text. However, because many simulations do involve text, they provide motivation to read. Furthermore, many simulation programs, such as *Oregon Trail Fifth Edition, Road Adventures USA,* and *Colonization,* require students to make decisions about budgets, relations with other cultures, and time management while playing, thus encouraging higher-level thinking skills.

Computer programs often require users to exercise various problem-solving capabilities and reasoning skills. Examples of such software include *Liberty's Kids, Star Flyers Royal Jewel Rescue, Where in the USA Is Carmen Sandiego? Carmen Sandiego Word Detective,* and *The Reading Trek.* These text-based programs encourage users to make predictions and use evaluation strategies to make decisions and solve problems. In *The Reading Trek* students read excerpts from various literature genres: poetry, fiction, nonfiction, practical reading, and drama. Then they complete five activities for each genre, one each for prereading, reading, comprehension, reflection, and writing about what they have learned. The lessons also involve comprehension and quizzes.

Websites

Here are suggestions of helpful websites, organized by content area.

ARTS

http://memory.loc.gov/ammem/wpaposters/wpahome.html This site contains a collection of over 900 posters produced by the Work Projects Administration during the Great Depression.

http://rmc.library.cornell.edu/ornithology/ This Beautiful Birds site from Cornell University Library traces the development of ornithological illustration in the 18th and 19th centuries and includes biographies of the artists.

GENERAL

www.brainpop.com This site is geared toward various curricular areas. Visitors can watch videos on grammar usage, science, technology, math, and health. A section for educators includes extensive thematic lesson plans and standards correlation.

http://smithsonianeducation.org/ This site informs teachers about Smithsonian educational resources and provides approaches to integrating various subjects.

www.readingrockets.org This literacy site features authors; voting on favorite books; book lists; forums; and resources for national and state organizations, as well as for caregivers and teachers.

www.spaghettibookclub.org This site allows teachers to create a reading program utilizing the site as a place where students can write their own book reviews, create activities, and look for resources for the classroom.

MATH

www.kidskonnect.com/subjectindex/17-educational/math/292-math-sites.html This site lists over 30 sites designed for kids studying math.

http://MathCentral.uregina.ca/index.html A multilingual K–12 math education website, it provides resources for teachers and learners.

SCIENCE

www.billnye.com Bill Nye the Science Guy provides teachers with excellent ideas and suggestions for integrating science activities into all other subject areas including the language arts.

www.envirolink.org This site provides information about all issues related to the environment, including sustainability, wildlife, energy, and climate change.

www.goENC.com This is the site of the Eisenhower National Clearinghouse for Mathematics and Science Education. It has action ideas and lesson plans for all grades.

www.learner.org/exhibits/garbage/global.html This site by the Annenburg Foundation is about garbage and how communities can reduce waste.

www.nasa.gov This is NASA's home page, which has extensive information geared toward both educators and students.

www.ngdc.noaa.gov This is the website of the National Oceanic and Atmospheric Administration and contains many educational resources on geophysics, climatology, and glaciology.

http://starchild.gsfc.nasa.gov/docs/StarChild/StarChild.html This is NASA's site for kids interested in astronomy.

www.solarviews.com This site is a beautiful introduction to the solar system and includes a large library of photographs suitable for multimodal presentations.

www.usgs.gov This site has U.S. maps and earth science data, including an earthquake map that is updated in real time.

www.epa.gov/climatechange/kids/index.html This is the U.S. Environmental Protection Agency's page on climate change for students.

SOCIAL STUDIES

www.americaslibrary.gov/cgi-bin/page.cgi Part of the Library of Congress, this site allows students to explore American history, important Americans, and learn about different places in the United States.

www.castles.org This site has information about specific castles, mostly in Europe, and how they were built.

www.ipl.org/ This site contains numerous newspapers from the United States and around the world.

www.ipl.org/div/potus This site provides information about all the presidents of the United States, and includes text, sound bites, photos, and film clips.

www.jaguar-sun.com/maya.html This site provides information on Mayan history and culture, geared toward upper elementary/middle school students.

www.luminarium.org/lumina.htm This site provides information on English art, culture, and literature of the Medieval, Renaissance, and sixteenth and seventeenth centuries.

www.monticello.org/site/families-and-teachers This website for Thomas Jefferson's home includes resources to introduce students to the president's ideas on government, architecture, agriculture, and his many other pursuits.

http://discoveringegypt.com/ancient-egyptian-kings-queens/ This site offers quick and easy-to-find information on the rulers of Ancient Egypt.

Teaching is the art of assisting discovery.

MARK VAN DOREN

SUMMARY

Using reading, writing, speaking, listening, viewing, and visually representing in the content areas is a natural, commonsense way of allowing students to apply and extend what they know about language. Such an approach gives special meaning to language arts instruction because it encourages students to use these processes in acquiring real and necessary knowledge.

Using the language arts in the content areas is important not only in expanding language competencies but also in developing each student's content literacy—the reinforcing ability both to use one's background knowledge to comprehend new content and incorporate that new content into one's knowledge base.

Remember that the purpose of using the language arts in the content areas is to aid students in their ability to internalize knowledge, and to give students a real and meaningful reason for using the language arts in their daily lives.

field AND practicum ACTIVITIES

1. CLASS CHOICE. Have the class vote on a favorite nonfiction book and build a unit around it. Then brainstorm activities related to the book. Use a diagram with the six branches of reading, writing, listening, speaking, viewing, and visually representing. This diagram should get you started on planning a literature unit.

2. COMMUNITY COMMUNICATION. As part of a social studies unit on community and community service, students can correspond with individuals in a local assisted-living facility or veterans hospital. The exchange of letters will give the students many opportunities for reading and writing. They may want to share events of their daily lives, important happenings, or original writings.

3. MAKE A MAP. After students have had a number of experiences reading, drawing, and labeling maps, they may want to create a map depicting the location of a favorite story. For example, after reading *Owl Moon*, several students might want to draw a map showing the route that the girl and her father took from the farm to the woods and back again.

4. EPALS TRAVELOGUE. Have students use the Internet to find out about another country. *Epals* is the term used to describe electronic pen pals. By going to www.studentsoftheworld.info/, students can choose a group of pen pals in another country with whom to communicate. At first, it might be best to model a class letter with suggested questions students may want to ask. Then, students can correspond individually.

5. KEEP A BOOK BLOG. You and your students can create a blog about a book that the class is reading. Some blogger software is free; for example,

- Movable Type, **www.movabletype.org**
- WordPress, **www.wordpress.org**
- Textpattern, **www.textpattern.com**

Blogging allows you and your students to post your opinions about what you have read for others to see. Family members, authors, and others in the community can join in to post their questions, opinions, and comments on your blog. It adds another dimension to the reading process.

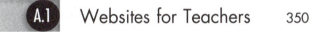

Teacher Resources

A

APPENDIX

APPENDIX A.1 Websites for Teachers.

http://xrds.acm.org/ A student magazine containing book reviews. Available in Spanish.

www.niacc.edu/student-life/technology-services/technology-policy/violation-of-federal-copyright-laws/ This site gives information about copyright issues.

www.ala.org Contains links to the Caldecott and Newbery Award winners. Click on the "Awards and Scholarships" button.

www.americaspromise.org This site gives information on how to become one of Colin Powell's Schools of Promise.

www.carolhurst.com Contains book reviews and activities to use with specific books.

www.ciera.org CIERA is the Center for the Improvement of Early Reading Achievement, and its site has articles and ideas regarding literacy for early childhood and elementary educators.

http://free.ed.gov/ This site has hundreds of free educational resources from federally sponsored programs.

http://smithsonianeducation.org/ This site contains lessons, activities, and nearly 500 educational products.

http://webquest.org/index.php This is the resource page for using the WebQuest model.

http://shopgpn.com/ This site describes books featured on the PBS show *Reading Rainbow,* with recommended activities.

www.grammarly.com/answers/questions/ask/ Grammar hotline for posting questions.

www.grammarnow.com This grammar site will help teachers as they work with students to improve grammar.

www.greenwdassoc.com/ The Greenwood Institute site provides teachers with information regarding mainstreaming, home schooling, and educational research projects.

www.harcourtschool.com This site by Harcourt Inc. has activities designed to be done by individuals or in cooperative groups.

www.ipl.org/ The Internet Public Library provides thousands of links to sites categorized by subject.

www.k12connections.iptv.org Iowa Public Television's (IPTV) website for distance learning.

www.loc.gov/teachers/ This site is a collection of resource materials for teachers. The site links to the American Memory collection, which highlights items important in America's heritage, history, and culture. It offers lesson plans and related activities.

www.learner.org A site of professional development resources.

www.loc.gov/wiseguide This site is part of the Library of Congress, offering several resources for teaching about American history, as well as contemporary figures in American culture. The "Wise Guide" changes monthly and offers links to the best of the library's online materials.

http://oldweb.madison.k12.wi.us/tnl/detectives/ This site provides links to different sites dealing with curricular areas.

http://vptm.ehps.ncsu.edu/ This site provides research about prevention of school violence.

www.ncte.org This is the site for the National Council of Teachers of English.

www.nctm.org This is the home page for National Council of Teachers of Mathematics.

www.ed.gov/esea This is the site for the new Elementary and Secondary Education Act of the federal government.

www.ok.gov/octp/Educator_Preparation/Accreditation_Accountability/index.html The Oklahoma Commission for Teacher Preparation produced this site for teachers interested in the state reading/literacy requirements.

www.reading.org This is the site of the International Reading Association.

http://comminfo.rutgers.edu/professional-development/childlit/ChildrenLit/ Kay Vandergrift's home page. Contains extensive materials on connecting literature across the curriculum as well as lists of multicultural books.

www.sreb.org This is the site for the Southern Regional Education Board, which includes a broad range of information and links to educational sites from early childhood through college.

www.tea.state.tx.us This is the site for the Texas Education Agency. It provides information regarding the legislation in Texas dealing with reading and writing requirements for Texas schools as well as standardized tests.

www.toread.com A study of the reading process and teaching techniques.

http://grammar.ccc.commnet.edu/grammar/ Teaches and reviews grammar.

http://test.dpi.state.wi.us/wilearns/default.asp?ap=1 The Wisconsin Literacy Education and Reading Network Source provides a wealth of articles, activities, and teaching ideas for grades K–12.

www.wolinskyweb.com/word.htm Resource for fun with words.

www.acs.ucalgary.ca/~dkbrown/authors.html An index of authors and illustrators on the Web.

www.carolhurst.com/index.html This site features children's books, ideas for caregivers and teachers, and professional resources.

www.cbcbooks.org This Children's Book Council site contains links to authors.

www.crayola.com This terrific educational activities site for teachers, produced by the Crayola Crayon company, offers many suggestions for classroom activities, projects, and crafts.

www.ctw.org This site has the alphabet according to Sesame Street.

www.cultureforkids.com This site provides information and resources on multicultural activities for the classroom.

www.cyberkids.com This online zine accepts student submissions of poetry and fiction.

www.discoveryschool.com The Discovery School site offers many excellent games and activities in all subject areas.

http://family.disney.com/ This is Disney's family site.

www.ipl.org/div/kidspace Part of the Internet Public Library, offering links to author websites, as well as other literature links.

www.janbrett.com/index.html This is Jan Brett's home page, which offers interactive activities for kids to read and draw, including over 2000 pages of fun activities for use with Jan Brett's books.

www.pbs.org/rogers This site includes activities for children and a list of stories that correlate with the Mr. Rogers' TV program's themes. Lyrics for the songs from the show are also included.

www.discoveryeducation.com/free-puzzlemaker/?CFID=320 8214&CFTOKEN=18370909 This site permits you to create mazes, word searches, crosswords, math squares, etc., for any lesson.

http://school.discoveryeducation.com/students/ This is the DiscoverySchool home page.

APPENDIX A.3   Resources for Finding Magazines and Books for Classroom Use

PROFESSIONAL ORGANIZATIONS/BOOKS

American Library Association (ALA), www.ala.org

International Reading Association (IRA), www.reading. org

National Council of Teachers of English (NCTE), www.ncte.org

The Children's Book Council (CBC), www.cbcbooks. org

Marantz, S. (1995). *The Art of Children's Picture Books: A Selective Reference Guide.* New York: Garland Publishing.

Odean, K. (2002). *Great Books for Girls.* New York: Ballantine.

PROFESSIONAL PUBLICATIONS

Bulletin of the Center for Children's Books, published by the University of Chicago Graduate Library School, http://bccb.lis.uiuc.edu

The Horn Book, published by Horn Book, www.hbook. com

The Lion and the Unicorn, published by Johns Hopkins Press, www.press.jhu.edu/journals, then select *The Lion and the Unicorn*

The New Advocate, published by Christopher Gordon Publishers

ANNUAL CHILDREN'S AND YOUNG ADULT LITERATURE AWARDS AND LISTS

"American Indian Youth Literature Award" presented by the American Indian Library Association, http://ailanet.org/activities/american-indian-youth-literature-award/

"Asian Literary Prize Books" presented by Man Group, www.manasianliteraryprize.org/

"Belpré Award" presented by the Association for Library Service to Children, www.ala.org/alsc/awards-grants/bookmedia/belpremedal/belprepast

"Caldecott Award" presented by the Association for Library Service to Children, www.ala.org/alsc/awardsgrants/bookmedia/caldecottmedal/caldecott honors/caldecottmedal

"Children's Choices" published by the IRA, www.reading.org/resources/booklists/childrenschoices.aspx

"Coretta Scott King–John Steptoe Award for New Talent" presented by the American Library Association,

www.ala.org/awardsgrants/coretta-scott-king-john-steptoe-award-new-talent

"Newberry Medal" presented by the Association for Library Service to Children, www.ala.org/alsc/awardsgrants/bookmedia/newberymedal/newbery honors/newberymedal

"Notable Children's Books in the English Language Arts" compiled by the National Council of Teachers of English, www.childrensliteratureassembly.org/notables.html

"Notable Children's Trade Books in the Field of Social Studies" compiled by the National Council for the Social Studies and the CBC, www.socialstudies.org/resources/notable

"The Odyssey Award" presented by the American Library Association for the best children's and young adult audiobooks (www.ala.org/alsc/awardsgrants/bookmedia/odysseyaward). "Orbis Pictus Award" compiled by the National Council of Teachers of English, www.ncte.org/awards/orbispictus

"Outstanding Science Trade Books for Students K–12" compiled by the National Science Teachers Association, www.nsta.org/publications/ostb

"Printz Award" presented by the Association for Library Service to Children, www.ala.org/yalsa/printz-award#previous

"Pulitzer Prize" presented by Columbia University, www.pulitzer.org/bycat

"Pura Belpré Award" presented by the Association for Library Service to Children, www.ala.org/alsc/awardsgrants/bookmedia/belpremedal

"Teacher's Choices" published in *The Reading Teacher* by the IRA, www.reading.org/resources/booklists/teacherschoices.aspx

"The Coretta Scott King Award" presented by the American Library Association, www.ala.org/emiert/cskbookawards

"The Robert F. Sibert Informational Book Medal" presented by the Association for Library Service to Children, www.ala.org/alsc/awardsgrants/bookmedia/sibertmedal

"Young Adult Choices" published in *The Journal of Adolescent and Adult Literacy* by the IRA and the CBC, www.reading.org/resources/booklists/young adultschoices.aspx

APPENDIX

A P P E N D I X

Children's and
Young Adult Literature

Alexander, Lloyd, www.scholastic.com/teachers/contributor/lloyd-alexander

Allende, Isabel, www.isabelallende.com/

Alvarez, Julia, www.juliaalvarez.com/

Applegate, Katherine, http://theoneandonlyivan.com/

Avi, www.avi-writer.com/

Babbitt, Natalie, www.scholastic.com/teachers/contributor/natalie-babbitt

Barnett, Mac, www.macbarnett.com/

Barrett, Mary, www.marybrigidbarrett.com/

Becker, Aaron, www.storybreathing.com/

Blume, Judy, www.judyblume.com/

Bond, Michael, www.paddington.com/us/home/

Brown, Margaret Wise, http://margaretwisebrown.com/

Bruchac, Joseph, www.josephbruchac.com/

Bulla, Clyde, www.scholastic.com/teachers/contributor/clyde-robert-bulla

Bunting, Eve, www.scholastic.com/teachers/contributor/eve-bunting

Byars, Betsy, www.betsybyars.com/

Carle, Eric, www.eric-carle.com/home.html

Cisneros, Sandra, www.sandracisneros.com/

Cleary, Beverly, http://www.beverlycleary.com/

Climo, Shirley, www.harpercollins.com/cr-100447/shirley-climo

Collier, Christopher, www.scholastic.com/teachers/contributor/christopher-collier-phd

Collier, James, www.scholastic.com/teachers/contributor/james-lincoln-collier

Collins, Suzanne, www.suzannecollinsbooks.com/

Curtis, Christopher Paul, www.nobodybutcurtis.com/

Cushman, Karen, www.karencushman.com/

DeFelice, Cynthia, http://www.scholastic.com/teachers/contributor/cynthia-defelice

dePaola, Tomie, www.tomie.com/

Devlin, Wende, www.harryandwendedevlin.com/

Doner, Kim, http://www.kimdoner.com/

Emberly, Ed, www.edemberley.com/pages/main.aspx

Farley, Walter, www.scholastic.com/teachers/contributor/walter-farley

Fleischman, Paul, www.paulfleischman.net/

Fleming, Denise, www.denisefleming.com/

Floca, Brian, www.brianfloca.com/

Forest, Heather, www.heatherforest.com/

Freedman, Russell, www.scholastic.com/teachers/contributor/russell-freedman

Frey, James, www.bigjimindustries.com/

Fritz, Jean, www.scholastic.com/teachers/contributor/jean-fritz

Galdone, Paul, http://paulgaldone.com/

Gantos, Jack, http://www.jackgantos.com/

George, Jean, www.jeancraigheadgeorge.com/

Gibbons, Gail, www.gailgibbons.com/

Giganti, Paul, Jr., http://paulgigantijr.weebly.com/

Gollub, Matthew, http://matthewgollub.com/

Goto, Scott, www.scottgoto.com/HOME.html

Grisham, John, www.jgrisham.com/

Hahn, Mary, www.hmhbooks.com/features/mdh/

Hamilton, Virginia, www.virginiahamilton.com/

Higgins, Nadia, http://nadiahiggins.wordpress.com/

Hoberman, Mary Ann, www.maryannhoberman.com/

Hopkins, Lee Bennett, www.leebennetthopkins.com/

Hunt, Irene, www.penguin.com/author/irene-hunt/1000040677

Kajikawa, Kimiko, www.author4kids.com/

Kimmel, Eric, http://erickimmel.com/

Kinney, Jeff, www.wimpykid.com/

Koons, Jon, www.jestmaster.com/

L'Engle, Madeleine, www.madeleinelengle.com/

Larson, Kirby, www.kirbylarson.com/

Leong, Sonia, www.fyredrake.net/

Lewis, C. S., https://www.cslewis.com/us

Llanas, Sheila Griffin, www.sheilallanas.com/

Lupica, Mike, www.mikelupicabooks.com/

Macaulay, David, http://hmhbooks.com/davidmacaulay/

MacLachlan, Patricia, www.harpercollins.com/cr-100342/patricia-maclachlan

Magoon, Kekla, http://keklamagoon.com/

Martin, Bill, http://billmartinjr.com/bill_martin

Mayer, Mercer, www.littlecritter.com/

McKissack, Fredrick, www.scholastic.com/teachers/bookwizard/books-by/fredrick-mckissack#cart/cleanup

McKissack, Patricia, www.scholastic.com/teachers/contributor/patricia-c-mckissack-0

Montgomery, Sy, http://symontgomery.com/

Myers, Anna, www.annamyers.info/

Myers, Walter Dean, http://walterdeanmyers.net/

O'Dell, Scott, www.scottodell.com/Pages/home.aspx

Palacio, R. J., http://rjpalacio.com/

Palatini, Margie, www.margiepalatini.com/

Pallota, Jerry, www.jerrypallotta.com/

Parish, Peggy, www.harpercollinschildrens.com/kids/gamesandcontests/features/amelia/peggyparish.aspx

Paterson, Katherine, http://terabithia.com/

Paulsen, Gary, www.randomhouse.com/features/garypaulsen/

Peck, Richard, www.penguin.com/author/richard-peck/1000025091

Phillip, Neil, www.neilphilip.com/Neil%20Philip.html

Pilkey, Dav, www.pilkey.com/

Pinkney, Jerry, www.jerrypinkneystudio.com/

Polacco, Patricia, www.patriciapolacco.com/

Potter, Beatrix, www.peterrabbit.com/en/beatrix_potter/beatrixs_life

Prelutsky, Jack, http://jackprelutsky.com/

Rash, Andy, www.rashworks.com/

Rofes, Eric, www.ericrofes.com/

Rowling, J. K., www.jkrowling.com/

Rylant, Cynthia, www.cynthiarylant.com/

Saenz, Benjamin Alire, http://authors.simonandschuster.com/Benjamin-Alire-Saenz/44544494

Savage, Deborah, www.scholastic.com/teachers/contributor/deborah-savage

Say, Allen, www.houghtonmifflinbooks.com/authors/allensay/

Schur, Maxine, www.maxineroseschur.com/

Scroggs, Kirk, http://kirkscroggs.com/

Sendak, Maurice, www.harpercollins.com/cr-100369/maurice-sendak

Seuss, Dr., www.seussville.com/

Sheinkin, Steve, http://stevesheinkin.com/

Silverstein, Shel, www.shelsilverstein.com/

Simon, Seymour, www.seymoursimon.com/

Sloane, Eric, http://www.ericsloane.com/

Smith, Jeff, www.boneville.com/

Spiegelmann, Art, www.scholastic.com/teachers/contributor/art-spiegelman

Spier, Peter, www.randomhousekids.com/brand/peter-spier/

Steptoe, John, http://www.scholastic.com/teachers/contributor/john-steptoe

Taliaferro, John, http://johntaliaferrobooks.com/

Taylor, Theodore, www.theodoretaylor.com/

Thomson, S. L., www.sarahlthomson.com/

Tolan, Stephanie, www.stephanietolan.com/

Tolkien, J. R., www.tolkiensociety.org/

Van Allsburg, Chris, http://www.chrisvanallsburg.com/flash.html

Viorst, Judith, http://authors.simonandschuster.com/Judith-Viorst/707395

Voigt, Cynthia, www.cynthiavoigt.com/

Whelan, Gloria, http://www.gloriawhelan.com/

White, E. B., www.scholastic.com/teachers/contributor/e-b-white

White, Ellen, www.scholastic.com/teachers/contributor/ellen-emerson-white

Wiesner, David, www.davidwiesner.com/

Wildsmith, Brian, www.brianwildsmith.com/

Willems, Mo, www.mowillems.com/

Williams-Garcia, Rita, www.ritawg.com/

Winter, Jeanette, http://us.macmillan.com/author/jeanettewinter

Yolen, Jane, http://janeyolen.com/

Young, Ed, http://edyoungart.com/

Zemach, Margot, www.scholastic.com/teachers/bookwizard/books-by/margot-zemach#cart/cleanup

Ada, A. (1995). *My Name Is Maria Isabel*. Maria, the new girl in school, is upset when her teacher wants to call her Mary.

Ada, A. (2013). *Dancing Home*. A year of discoveries culminates in a performance full of surprises, as two girls find their own way to belong.

Alter, J. (2003). *Native Americans*. Introduces readers to the Native American culture, customs, religion, foods, and holidays.

Anderson, M. (1994). *The Nez Perce*. Here is an exploration of an Indian tribe that learned to read and write and struggled to coexist with the European settlers, but ultimately lost their way of life.

Birchfield, D. (2012). *Cherokee History and Culture*. Inside this compelling account, the history of the Cherokees is presented in detail, including their devastating journey along the Trail of Tears.

Bruchac, J. (1999). *Lasting Echoes: An Oral History of Native American People*. From Lakota to Apache to Abenaki, from Geronimo to Sitting Bull to lesser-known voices, "Lasting Echoes" is the moving story of the American Indian peoples as seen through their own eyes.

D'Apice, R. (1990). *The Algonquian*. This account reveals another historical perspective on western expansion in the early U.S.

Erdosh, G. (1997). *Food and recipes of the Native Americans*. Chock full of recipes with step-by-step directions for kids to follow, this series is a unique way for kids to eat their way through U.S. history.

Goble, P. (1979). *The Girl Who Loved Horses*. This gorgeously illustrated picture book about a young Native American girl who is charged by her tribe with taking care of the horses has become a classic in children's literature.

Hayden, K. (2002). *Plains Indians*. Crafts, activities, stories, and historical facts give today's children a close look at youngsters of past cultures.

Herrera, J. (2000). *The Upside Down Boy*. This book captures the universal experience of entering a new school and feeling like a stranger in a world that seems upside down.

Herrera, J. (2001). *Calling the Doves*. This bilingual memoir paints a vivid picture of the author's migrant farmworker childhood.

Kamma, A., & Gardner, L. (1999). *If You Lived With the Hopi*. The history of the Hopi (meaning "wise and beautiful people") is explored through a series of questions and answers, such as "Would you live in a teepee?" and "What did girls have to learn?"

Klobuchar, A. (2006). *The History and Activities of Native Americans*. Through recipes, crafts, history, activities, and games this book gives you a chance to experience what life was like for Native Americans.

Lai, T. (2011). *Inside Out and Black Again*. A 10-year old girl and her family flee Vietnam after the fall of Saigon and wind up in Alabama, where she must adjust to many new things.

Landau, E. (1994). *The Hopi*. The Hopis of the Southwest United States were not overtaken by early European settlers; their way of life has survived and is detailed here.

Landowne, Y. (2004). *Selavi, That Is Life: A Haitian Story of Hope*. A young homeless boy living on the streets of Haiti copes with extreme poverty.

Look, L., & Pham, L. (2009). *Alvin Ho*. Second-grader Alvin looks different from his classmates and that's not all that scares him about school.

Morales, Y. (2004). *Just a Minute: A Trickster Tale and Counting Book*. This spirited tribute to the rich traditions of Mexican culture is the perfect introduction to counting in both English and Spanish.

Perez, A. (2011). *My Diary from Here to There*. A young girl describes her feelings when her father decides to leave their home in Mexico to look for work in the United States.

Phillip, N. (2001). *The Great Mystery: Myths of Native America*. This authoritative guide to Native American myth and legend explores the powerful themes and dramatic stories that explain the great mysteries of life, death, how the world was created, and how it will end.

Ringgold, F. (1991). *Tar Beach*. A young black girl in Harlem dreams of leaving her crowded apartment in the city; she imagines her rooftop as a beach far away.

Rohmer, H. (2009). *Heroes of the Environment: True Stories of People Who Are Helping to Protect Our Planet*. The true stories of 12 people from across North America who have done great things for the environment.

Ryan, P. (2002). *Esperanza Rising*. In this chapter book, wealthy 13-year-old Esperanza and her mother must suddenly leave their home and servants in Mexico and flee to California during the height of the Great Depression, when jobs are scarce.

Skarmela, A., & Ruan, A. (2003). *The Composition.* Two soccer loving boys living under the Augusto Pinochet dictatorship in Chile are frightened when their father gets arrested for no reason.

Soto, G. (2007). *A Simple Plan.* A young man's attempt to rid himself of the family dog by leading it so far from home that it becomes lost for good becomes a metaphor for the poet's attempt to rid himself of the pulls of childhood.

Stone, A. (2012). *Creek History and Culture.* In this book, readers see how the Creeks battled to maintain their unique identity—from suffering along the Trail of Tears to taking important roles in the modern Native American activist movement.

Tarpley, N. (2001). *I Love My Hair.* A young African American girl knows her hair looks different than her classmates'.

Books to Meet Special Needs   APPENDIX B.3

Polacco, P. (2010). *The Junkyard Wonders.* This book continues young Patricia's adventures as she endures the name-calling of other students when she enrolls in a new school and is placed in the Special Needs classroom.

Robertson, D. (1992). *Portraying Persons with Disabilities: An Annotated Bibliography of Fiction for Children and Teenagers.* This is an excellent teacher resource for anyone wishing to learn about various special needs in children and adolescents.

Senisi, E. (1998). *Just Kids.* This is an easy to read picture book about various children with different special needs and how they cope with everyday things.

Predictable Pattern Books   APPENDIX B.4

Edwards, D. (2007). *The Pen That Pa Built.* A blanket is made from scratch—from the shearing to the carding, spinning, dyeing, and weaving. And it all starts in the pen that Pa built.

Klassen, J. (2011). *I Want My Hat Back.* A bear almost gives up his search for his missing hat until he remembers something important.

Kuskin, K. (2010). *A Boy Had a Mother Who Bought Him a Hat.* What's a boy to do when his mom buys him everything he wants? Should he take his new toys everywhere?

Martin, B., Jr. (2007). *Baby Bear, Baby Bear, What Do You See?* Young readers will enjoy Baby Bear's quest to find Mama, and they'll revel in identifying each of the native North American animals that appear along the way.

Taback, S. (2002). *This Is the House that Jack Built.* It all started with the cheese that lay in the house. Then came the rat who ate the cheese, and the cat who killed the rat...

Taback, S. (1999). *Joseph Had a Little Coat.* As children turn the pages of this book, they can use the die-cut holes to guess what Joseph will be making next from his amazing overcoat.

Vamos, S. R. (2011). *The Cazuela that the Farm Maiden Stirred.* This is the story of how the farm maiden and all the farm animals worked together to make the rice pudding that they serve at the fiesta.

APPENDIX B.5   Picture Books

Carle, E. (1972). *The Very Hungry Caterpillar*. Carle is well known for his colorful collage illustrations about the eating adventures of the caterpillar.

Cendrars, B. (1982). *Shadow*. (M. Brown, trans. and illus.) This book depicts African culture through collages, woodblock prints, and paintings.

Del Negro, J. (1998). *Lucy Dove*. (L. Gore, illus.) Dark colors set a menacing mood as Lucy struggles with monsters in a graveyard.

DiCamillo, K., & McGee, A. (2010). *Bink & Gollie*. The bright colors by illustrator Tony Fucile enhance the comic adventures of two roller-skating friends.

Fleischman, P. (2009). *The Dunderheads*. A mean teacher gets her just due when a group of six students unite to cause hilarious trouble.

Hodges, M. (1984). *Saint George and the Dragon*. (T.S. Hyman, illus.) With rich detail and romantic paintings this ancient British tale comes to life.

Klassen, J. (2012). *This Is Not My Hat*. A tiny fish steals a tiny hat from a sleeping, but great big fish. Much of the dark humor in this book comes from subtle details in the illustrations and their monochromatic palette.

Novesky, A. (2012). *Georgia in Hawaii*. The illustrations in this book suggest the scale and colorfulness of O'Keefe's paintings while telling the story of her time in Hawaii.

Polacco, P. (1994). *Pink and Say*. This historical fiction picture book traces the meeting of two boys during the Civil War.

Stead, P. (2010). *A Sick Day for Amos McGee*. Zoo characters visit Amos McGee when he is ill because he always cares for them at the zoo.

FOR OLDER STUDENTS

Blumental, D. (2001). *Aunt Claire's Yellow Beehive Hair*. This book shares the joy of families sitting around looking at old family photographs and remembering distant stories.

Fisher, L. (1986). *The Great Wall of China*. The Great Wall of China is one of the finest man-made creations on earth and tells the history of the world's most populated nation.

Fisher, L. (1988). *Pyramid of the Sun, Pyramid of the Moon*. Through illustrations your children will learn about the fascinating and often horrifying story of the Aztec civilization in Teotihuacan, Mexico.

Henson, H. (2008). *That Book Woman*. Young Cal loves to wander the hills, goes to school infrequently, and can't understand why that book lady regularly comes to their holler trying to get him to read books.

Khan, H. (2008). *Night of the Moon*. In this picture book a young girl is excited to experience Ramadan, a Muslim holiday of fasting, but also of celebration and gifts.

Millen, C. M. (2011). *The Ink Garden of Brother Theophane*. During the Middle Ages, at a remote Irish monastery, a young monk is charged with the tedious task of copying by hand the Bible.

Novesky, A. (2010). *Me, Frida*. A newly married Frida Kahlo travels from her home in Mexico to San Francisco along with her famous artist husband, Diego Rivera, but in San Francisco her own artistic talents begin to blossom.

Araujo, F. (1994). *The Perfect Orange: A Tale from Ethiopia.* A young girl travels far to bring her humble gift of an orange to the mighty king of Ethiopia.

Hausman, G., & Hausman, L. (2005). *Horses of Myth.* Explores five different stories about horses from five different countries.

Menchau, R. (2006). *The Honey Jar.* Stories by this Pulitzer Prize winner about the Mayan Indians of Guatemala.

Morris, G. (2008). *The Adventures of Sir Lancelot the Great.* Of all the Knights of the Round Table, there was never one so fearless, so chivalrous, so honorable, so … shiny as the dashing Sir Lancelot, who was quite good at defending the helpless and protecting the weak, just as long as he'd had his afternoon nap.

Oberman, S. (2006). *Solomon and the Ant: And Other Jewish Folktales.* This treasure trove of 43 folktales includes religious, wisdom, riddle, and trickster tales.

Stampler, A. (2010). *Rooster Prince of Breslov.* A silly tale but with some serious overtones about a prince who renounces his life of luxury to go live as a rooster.

Taylor, C. J. (2006). *All the Stars in the Sky: Native Stories from the Heavens.* Mohawk artist and author C. J. Taylor has drawn from First Nations legends from across North America to present a fascinating collection of stories inspired by the night skies.

Tchana, K. (2006). *Changing Woman and Her Sisters: Stories of Goddesses Around the World.* Explores female tales from different cultures.

Tingle, T. (2007). *When Turtle Grew Feathers.* In this story from the Choctaw People, Tim Tingle shows that it was not being slow and steady that won Turtle the big race against Rabbit; it was those feathers!

Zeman-Spaleny, L. (2009). *Lord of the Sky.* Native American tales from the northwestern coast of the United States.

Alexander, W. (2012). *Goblin Secrets.* Desperate to find his brother, Rownie joins up with a troupe of goblins who skirt the law to put on plays.

Hartman, R. (2012). *Seraphina.* Four decades of peace have done little to ease the mistrust between humans and dragons. Folding themselves into human shape, dragons attend court as ambassadors, and lend their rational, mathematical minds to universities as scholars and teachers.

Kirby, M. (2011). *Icefall.* Can Solveig and her siblings survive the long winter months and expose a traitor before he succeeds in destroying a kingdom?

Melroy, C. (2011). *Wildwood.* The first book in the epic middle-grade fantasy series full of magic, wonder, and danger—nothing less than an American Narnia.

Pierce, T. (2011). *Mastiff.* The story about a fierce young woman who fights crime in a world of magic.

Ursu, A. (2011). *Breadcrumbs.* Inspired by Hans Christian Andersen's "The Snow Queen," this is a story of the struggle to hold on, and the things we leave behind.

Amir (2011). *Zahra's Paradise* (Khalil, Illus.). In the aftermath of Iran's fraudulent elections of 2009, young protestor Mehdi disappears, but through the tenacity of his family he is not forgotten.

Crane, S. (2005). *The Red Badge of Courage* (W. Vansant, Illus.). Ordinary farm boy Henry Fleming becomes a soldier and finds his motivation not through patriotism, but instead through cowardice, fear, and egoism.

Eisner, W. (1986). *Will Eisner's The Big City.* Features stories that celebrate life in the Big Apple.

Garza, X. (2011). *Maximilian and the Mystery of the Guardian Angel: A Bilingual Lucha Libre Thriller.* Lucha libre aficionado Margarito accidentally falls over the railing at a match and comes into contact with his greatest hero.

Gonick, L., & Outwater, A. (1996). *The Cartoon Guide to the Environment.* This guide uses fun analogies to introduce topics of environmental science.

Holm, J. (2010). *Babymouse: Burns Rubber.* Babymouse has big dreams of becoming a race car driver, and she and her best pal, Wilson, enter the *Race of the Century.*

Krosoczka, J. (2010). *Lunch Lady and the Summer Camp Shakedown.* Lunch Lady and the Breakfast Bunch kids are looking forward to a relaxing summer vacation with no funny business, but once again, Dee, Hector, and Terrence must help Lunch Lady prevail against a secret enemy!

Martin, M. (2005). *Harriet Tubman and the Underground Railroad.* The true story of Harriet Tubman and how she escaped slavery and then returned 13 times to help guide others to safety.

Robbins, T. (2011). *Lily Renee, Escape Artist: From Holocaust Survivor to Comic Book Pioneer* (A. Timmons & M. Oh, Illus.). Fourteen-year-old Lily escapes danger from the Nazis and teaches herself comic art in order to help support her family when they reunite in New York.

Sartrapi, M. (2003). *Persepolis: The Story of a Childhood.* Wise, funny, and heartbreaking, *Persepolis* is Marjane Satrapi's memoir of growing up in Iran during the Islamic Revolution.

Spiegelman, A. (1997). *Maus: A Survivor's Tale.* A story of a Jewish survivor of Hitler's Europe and his son, a cartoonist who tries to come to terms with his father's story and history itself.

Telgemeier, R. (2012). *Drama.* Callie is the set designer for her school's musical and she is determined to manage the onstage and offstage drama that occurs once the actors are chosen.

Thompson, C. (2006). *Good-bye, Chunky Rice.* Chunky, a young turtle, sets out to sea and leaves his best mouse buddy behind.

Thompson, J. (2008). *Magic Trixie.* Magic Trixie is not allowed to do anything fun, while her baby sister gets away with everything, and she needs to come up with a trick that's really special to impress her friends.

Yezerski, T. F. (2011). *Meadowlands: A Wetlands Survival Story.* New Jersey's wetlands were almost destroyed by settlers; this is the story of how they survived.

Realistic Fiction APPENDIX B.9

Carmichael, C. (2009). *Wild Things*. Eleven-year-old Zoe, an orphan, moves to the country to live with her eccentric uncle.

Cochran, M. (2009). *Girl Who Threw Butterflies*. Eighth-grader Molly Williams is lonely after her father's death and mother's withdrawal. But her father did teach her how to throw a knuckleball and with that she hopes to make the boy's baseball team.

Connor, L. (2008). *Waiting for Normal*. Twelve-year-old Addie has to cope with her mother's strange behavior and life in a trailer park in upstate New York.

Connor, L. (2010). *Crunch*. Dewey is in a crunch when his parents get stranded on a road trip and he is left at home to run the family bike-repair business.

Emerson, K. (2008). *Carlos Is Gonna Get It*. A group of seventh-grade students decide to play a scary prank on Carlos, a student with special needs, but things get dangerously out of hand.

Houtman, J. (2010). *The Reinvention of Edison Thomas*. Middle school student Eddy Thomas loves science and inventing things but has trouble making friends.

John, A. (2010). *Five Flavors of Dumb*. Piper, shy, lonely, and hearing impaired, suddenly finds herself in the awkward position of managing "Dumb," her high school's rock bank.

Korman, G. (2008). *Swindle*. Sixth-grader Griffin Bing gets cheated out of a valuable baseball card by an unscrupulous collector and with his friends, vows revenge.

Mysteries APPENDIX B.10

Butler, D. (2010). *The Buddy Files: The Case of the Lost Boy*. Buddy (aka King) has big problems to solve, but with some help from his friend Mouse (a very large dog) and the mysterious cat with no name, he shows what a smart, brave dog can do.

Cronin, D. (2011). *The Trouble with Chickens*. J.J. Tully is a former search-and-rescue dog who is trying to enjoy his retirement, but must help two chicks track down their missing siblings instead.

Davies, K. (2011). *Great Hamster Massacre*. A bitter-sweet domestic tale about a young girl and her quest for a pet.

Dowd, S. (2008). *The London Eye Mystery*. Ted and his older sister Kat overcome their differences to follow a trail of clues across London in a desperate bid to find their cousin.

Ness, P. (2011). *A Monster Calls*. Conor must face an ancient and wild monster that wants something dangerous from him—the truth.

APPENDIX B.11 — Sports Books

Aksomitis, L. (2009). *Sports Champions.* Sports science, including areas of physiology, psychology, motor control, and biomechanics.

Brignall, R. (2007). *Forever Champions.* True story of the legendary Edmonton (Canada) women's basketball team.

Brown, D. J. (2013). *The Boys in the Boat: Nine Americans and Their Epic Quest for Gold at the 1936 Berlin Olympics.* The true story of the American rowing team from the University of Washington as they competed in the 1936 Olympics in Berlin for a gold medal.

Crossingham, J., & Kalman, B. (2004). *Extreme Sports.* Explosive full-color photos, engaging text, historical trivia, star profiles, and the sports' hot spots energize this exciting series on extreme sports and their cultures.

Fehler, G. (2008). *Beanball.* Star pitcher Luke Wallace suffers a critical injury.

Hamilton, B., Berk, S., & Bundschuh, R. (2006). *Soul Surfer: A True Story of Faith, Family, and Fighting to Get Back on the Board.* The story of surfer Hamilton and her bond with surfing, before and after she lost her arm to a shark.

Hobbs, W. (2008). *Go Big or Go Home.* Fourteen-year-old Brady and his cousin Quinn are into extreme sports until a meteorite strikes their home in the Black Hills of South Dakota.

Macy, S. (Ed.) (2001). *Girls Got Game: Sports Stories and Poems.* This thrilling anthology tells the stories of millions of girls who are not afraid to sweat.

Myers, W. (2008). *Game.* Star Harlem basketball player Drew confronts his own racial feelings when a white boy challenges his position on the team.

Smith, C., Jr. (2007). *Twelve Rounds to Glory: The Story of Muhammad Ali.* A dynamic author-illustrator team follows the three-time heavyweight champ through twelve rounds of a remarkable life.

APPENDIX B.12 — Historical Fiction

Baker, R. (1987). *The First Woman Doctor: The Story of Elizabeth Blackwell, M.D.* The story of Elizabeth Blackwell, America's first woman doctor, who by pursuing her own dream, gave other women the chance to become doctors.

Cline-Ransome, L. (2012). *Words Set Me Free: The Story of Young Frederick Douglass.* Douglass spent his life advocating for the equality of all, and it was through reading that he was able to stand up for himself and others.

Greenberg, J., & Jordan, S. (2002). *Vincent Van Gogh.* A story about one of the 19th century's most brilliant artists and the passion that infused his work.

Lobel, A. (1987). *On the Day Peter Stuyvesant Sailed into Town.* A story about the early founding of New Amsterdam, later to become New York City.

Rappaport, D. (1990). *The Boston Coffee Party.* Two young sisters help the women of Boston during the Revolutionary War to get coffee from a greedy merchant.

Sterling, D. (1987). *Freedom Train: The Story of Harriet Tubman.* Against seemingly impossible odds, Harriet Tubman escaped slavery and then risked her life again and again to help her people make the same journey.

Turkle, B. (1982). *Thy Friend, Obadiah.* A young Quaker boy living in colonial Nantucket is constantly followed by a seagull that he wishes would leave him alone. When it does leave, he wants it back.

Biographies and Autobiographies — APPENDIX B.13

Brallier, J. (2002). *Who Was Albert Einstein?* The story of Einstein's life told in an engaging way that explores the world he lived in and changed.

Lourie, P. (2012). *The Polar Bear Scientists.* The story of the men who spend their lives tracking and studying polar bears in the frozen north.

Smith, C. (2012). *Stars in the Shadows: The Negro League All-Star Game of 1934.* Meet Satchel Paige, Josh Gibson, and other baseball heroes in this unique radio broadcast reenactment of a legendary All-Star Game, marking a pivotal time in sports history.

Solo, H. (2012). *Hope Solo: My Story.* The Olympic gold medal winner and goalie for the American women's soccer team tells her story.

Wadsworth, G. (2012). *First Girl Scout: The Life of Juliette Gordon Low.* A lavishly illustrated account of the fascinating life of the woman who started the Girl Scouts.

Woodson, J. (2014). *Brown Girl Dreaming.* The author's moving perspective on the volatile era in which she grew up, written in powerfully effective verse.

Yousafzai, M. (2014). *I Am Malala: How One Girl Stood Up for Education and Changed the World.* The story of a young woman, who in 2014 won the Nobel Peace Prize, who stood up against repression by the Taliban in Pakistan.

Informational Books — APPENDIX B.14

Aronson, M. (2010). *If Stones Could Speak: Unlocking the Secrets of Stonehenge.* The expert text, stunning photography, and explanatory maps and illustrations will all help young readers see this ancient monument in totally new ways, and inspire future generations of archaeological explorers.

Burleigh, R. (2009). *One Giant Leap.* One small step for man; one giant leap for mankind. This achievement not only brought the moon within reach, but now everything seemed possible. If it could be imagined, it could be done.

DeCristofano, C. (2012). *A Black Hole is NOT a Hole.* Lively and often humorous text explains the role gravity plays in the formation of black holes.

Greenberg, J. (2010). *Ballet for Martha: Making Appalachian Spring.* The story behind the scenes of "Appalachian Spring," from its inception through the score's composition to Martha's intense rehearsal process.

Hopkinson, D. (2014). *Titanic: Voices from the Disaster.* This gripping story follows the *Titanic* and its passengers from the ship's celebrated launch at Belfast to her cataclysmic icy end.

Krull, K., & DiVito, A. (1999). *A Kids' Guide to America's Bill of Rights: Curfews, Censorship, and the 100-Pound Giant.* Use this book to help students appreciate how the Bill of Rights has influenced our history and continues to operate in our country.

Markle, S. (2011). *The Case of the Vanishing Golden Frogs: A Scientific Mystery.* Follow a team of scientists working to save these frogs and protect frog populations worldwide in this real-life science mystery.

Roth, S., & Trumbore, C. (2013). *Parrots Over Puerto Rico.* The story of the rescue and return of the Puerto Rican parrot.

Ruelle, K., & DeSaix, D. (2010). *The Grand Mosque of Paris: A Story of How Muslims Rescued Jews during the Holocaust.* Not just a place of worship, this hive of activity was an ideal temporary hiding place for escaped prisoners of war and Jews of all ages during the Holocaust, especially children.

Rusch, E. (2013). *Eruption! Volcanoes and the Science of Saving Lives.* An account of the perilous, adrenaline-fueled, life-saving work of an international volcano crisis team (VDAP) and the sleeping giants they study, from Colombia to the Philippines, from Chile to Indonesia.

Sheinkin, S. (2012). *Bomb: The Race to Build—and Steal—the World's Most Dangerous Weapon.* This is the story of the plotting, the risk-taking, the deceit, and genius that created the world's most formidable weapon.

Brooks, G. (2007). *Bronzeville Boys and Girls*. A celebration of the lives of African American children, illustrated by Faith Ringgold.

Cullinan, B., & Wooten, D. (Eds.) (2009). *Another Jar of Tiny Stars*. Children select their favorite poems.

Engle, M. (2008). *The Surrender Tree: Poems of Cuba's Struggle for Freedom*. Serious poems for middle school students.

Hopkins, L. B. (Ed.) (2008). *America at War*. Covering all of America's wars.

Kennedy, C. (2005). *A Family of Poems*. Caroline Kennedy selects her favorite children's poems.

Panzer, N. (1994). *Celebrate America in Poetry and Art*. Paintings, drawings, sculpture and photographs from the National Museum of Art and the Smithsonian Institute complement this great collection of poetry.

Florian, D. (2001). *In the Swim*. For ages 4–8, this is a whimsical collection of intelligent and funny rhymes.

Florian, D. (2001). *Lizards, Frogs, and Polliwogs*. For ages 4–8, this is a great collection of wordplay poetry.

Prelutsky, J. (2000). *It's Raining Pigs and Noodles*. For ages 4-8, this book presents lively poetry with skillful line-drawn illustrations.

Prelutsky, J. (2002). *Scranimals*. For ages 4-8, this work includes outlandish wordplay with ink and watercolor illustrations.

Young, J. (2006). *R Is for Rhyme: A Poetry Alphabet*. For ages 6-10, a poetry book with a funny twist on factual information.

Brett, J. (1989). *The Mitten*. Woodland animals find a lost mitten and crawl inside, each one bigger than the last. Finally, a big brown bear is followed in by a tiny brown mouse and what happens next makes for a wonderfully funny climax.

Brett, J. (1991). *Berlioz the Bear*. A strange buzzing sound coming from inside Berlioz's double bass causes him to steer his mule-driven bandwagon of musicians into a hole in the road. Who will rescue the wagon?

Brett, J. (1997). *The Hat*. Hedgie the hedgehog discovers the wisdom of the adage "Don't go poking your nose where it doesn't belong" only after curiosity gets this prickly fellow in a pickle.

Brett, J. (2004). *The Umbrella*. When Carlos drops his umbrella to climb a tree for a better view of the animals, they all cram into the banana-leaf umbrella as it floats by.

Bunting, E. (1994). *Smoky Night*. In a night of rioting, Daniel and his mother are forced to leave their apartment for the safety of a shelter.

Carle, E. (1981). *The Very Hungry Caterpillar*. This classic tale teaches children about numbers, days of the week, and time.

Carle, E. (1982). *The Very Grouchy Ladybug*. The Grouchy Ladybug is a bad-tempered braggart that meets its match and becomes a better-behaved bug.

dePaola, T. (1975). *Strega Nona*. When Strega Nona leaves him alone with her magic pasta pot, Big Anthony is determined to show the townspeople how it works.

dePaola, T. (1983). *Legend of the Bluebonnet*. When a killing drought threatens the existence of the tribe, a courageous little Comanche girl sacrifices her most beloved possession for much needed rain and a very special gift in return.

Ernst, L. (1995). *Little Red Riding Hood: A Newfangled Prairie Tale*. A hungry wolf discovers that broad-shouldered, sharp-eyed, tractor-driving Grandma has no patience for pesky predators.

Galdone, P. (1968). *The Bremen Town Musicians*. A cacophonous quartet encounters and outwits a band of robbers, and in the process discovers just what they've been looking for.

Giovanni, N. (2005). *Rosa*. This picture-book tribute to Rosa Parks is a celebration of her courageous action to give up her seat on the Montgomery, Alabama, city bus and the events that followed.

Karlin, B. (1989). *James Marshall's Cinderella.* A retelling of the well-known story of the girl with the wicked stepsisters.

McGovern, A. (1967). *Too Much Noise.* Peter goes off to the village wise man to find out what he can do about his noisy house.

Salley, C. (2002). *Epossumondas.* Three main characters with many other animal characters that Epossumondas encounters at his auntie's home.

Sauer, T. (2009). *Chicken Dance.* Chickens learning to do four different dance steps. Fun and humorous.

Scieszka, J. (1987). *The True Story of the Three Little Pigs.* A spoof on the three little pigs story, this time told from the wolf's point of view.

Stead, P. (2010). *A Sick Day for Amos McGee.* Zoo characters visit Amos McGee when he is ill because he always cares for them at the zoo.

Wheeler, L. (2004). *Farmer Dale's Red Pickup Truck.* Farm animals are on their way to town and get stuck in the mud.

Wood, A. (1984). *The Napping House.* A new take on cumulative rhyme, the napping house menagerie includes a dozing dog, a snoozing cat, a slumbering mouse, and a wakeful flea who ends up toppling the whole sleep heap with one chomp!

Woodson, J. (2001). *The Other Side.* A fence segregates the African American side of town from the white side, but two girls strike up a friendship, and get around the grown-ups' rules by sitting on top of the fence together.

Young, E. (1989). *Lon Po Po: A Red-Riding Hood Story from China.* Vibrant pastels and watercolors add drama to the ancient Chinese version of the favorite fairy tale "Little Red Riding Hood."

Young, E. (1992). *Seven Blind Mice.* Seven blind mice investigate the strange Something by the pond, but it's only when the seventh mouse goes out and explores the whole Something that the mice see the whole truth.

For older students, teachers can read various versions of different fairy tales and invite students to act out the different versions so they can see how very different a tale can become. Following are three versions of Cinderella.

Hickox, R. (1998). *The Golden Sandal.* This version of Cinderella is set in the Middle East.

Hughes, S. (2003). *Ella's Big Chance.* This version of Cinderella is set during the Jazz Age.

Schroeder, A. (1997). *Smoky Mountain Rose.* This humorous version of Cinderella is set in the Appalachian Mountains.

Upper elementary students can be challenged with taking a wordless book and adding dialogue as they present it to the class. Following are suggested texts for this type of improvisation.

Fleischman, P., & Hawkes, D. (2004). *Sidewalk Circus.* The Garibaldi Circus is coming soon, but for those with clear eyes, the performers may already be in the ring.

Pinkney, J. (2009). *The Lion and the Mouse.* After a ferocious lion spares a cowering mouse that he'd planned to eat, the mouse later comes to his rescue, freeing him from a poacher's trap.

Rohmann, E. (2002). *My Friend Rabbit.* When Mouse lets his best friend, Rabbit, play with his brand-new airplane, trouble isn't far behind.

Wiesner, D. (1991). *Tuesday.* The whimsical account of a Tuesday when frogs were airborne on their lily pads.

APPENDIX B.17 Books with Music, Art, Drama, or Dance Themes

MUSIC

Aliki. (2003). *Ah, Music!* About composers and instruments, artists and performers, history, and diversity.

Brett, J. (1991). *Berlioz the Bear.* A strange buzzing sound coming from inside Berlioz's double bass causes him to steer his mule-driven bandwagon of musicians into a hole in the road. Who will rescue the wagon?

Celenza, A. (2002). *The Farewell Symphony.* An engaging fictionalized telling of the story behind Franz Joseph Haydn's famous symphony, this is a perfect introduction to classical music and its power.

Celenza, A. (2003). *Picture at an Exhibition.* When his friend Victor suddenly dies, composer Mussorgsky is deeply saddened. But, with the help of his friends, and through his own music, Modest finds a way to keep Victor's spirit alive.

Ganeri, A., & Kingsley, B. (1996). *The Young Person's Guide to the Orchestra.* Introduces the sights and sounds of the orchestra.

Gray, M. (1972). *Song and Dance Man: The Art of Bob Dylan.* A comprehensive and insightful interpretation of Bob Dylan's lyrics and how they coincide with the events taking place in his life.

Isadora, R. (1979). *Ben's Trumpet.* The story of a jazz musician who grew up in the twenties.

Keats, E. (1964). *Whistle for Willie.* Peter longs to learn how to whistle so he can call for his dog and his dog will come running.

Lithgow, J. (2000). *The Remarkable Farkle McBride.* Young Farkle McBride is a musical genius: He plays the violin, the flute, the trombone, and the drums with incredible skill. But he's never satisfied: Something is missing.

Marsalis, W. (2005). *Jazz ABZ: A Collection of Jazz Portraits.* A celebration of the spirit of 26 stellar jazz performers, from Armstrong to Dizzy.

McMillan, B. (1977). *The Alphabet Symphony: An ABC Book.* Photographs of an orchestra reveal different letters of the alphabet.

Moss, L. (1995). *Zin! Zin! Zin! A Violin.* Instruments are introduced one by one until an entire orchestra is assembled onstage.

Munoz-Ryan, P. (2002). *When Marian Sang.* A harmonious introduction to one of our country's most important singers, who is best known for her historic concert at the Lincoln Memorial in 1939, which drew an integrated crowd of 75,000 people in pre–Civil Rights America.

Prokofiev, S. (1961). *Peter and the Wolf.* Introduces children to the instruments of the orchestra.

Thomas, J. C. (2007). *Shouting!* Propelled by gospel music, "shouting" is when people in church get so happy and filled with spirit that they break out in song, stomp their feet, clap their hands, and raise them high.

Williams, V. B. (1984). *Music, Music for Everyone.* Rosa organizes her friends into the Oak Street Band in order to earn money her family needs because of her Grandma's illness.

ART

Allsburg, C.V. (1982). *Ben's Dream.* On a terrifically rainy day, Ben has a dream in which he and his house float by the monuments of the world, half submerged in floodwater.

Beaumont, K. (2005). *I Ain't Gonna Paint No More.* To the tune of "It Ain't Gonna Rain No More," one creative kid floods his world with color, painting first the walls, then the ceiling, then *Himself!*

Ehlert, L. (1994). *Color Zoo.* Encourages children to imagine new animals for the zoo using familiar shapes and colors.

Gerstein, M. (2003). *The Man Who Walked Between the Towers.* A lyrical evocation of Philippe Petit's 1974 tightrope walk between the World Trade Center towers.

Gruitrooy, G., Gallup, A., & Weisberg, E. (2005) *Great Paintings of the Western World.* Features 300 of the most splendid works of Western art of all time.

Heller, R. (1995). *Color.* Young readers and artists will enjoy peeling away the transparent overlays to discover how primary colors are mixed, and how a full-color painting breaks down into its primary colors.

Jonas, A. (1989). *Color Dance.* The girl in red, the girl in yellow, the girl in blue, and the boy in black and white create a living kaleidoscope, step by step by step.

Reynolds, P. (2003). *The Dot.* This story entices even the stubbornly uncreative among us to make a mark—and follow where it takes us.

Shalom, V. (1995). *The Color of Things.* In this rhyming book, Jill saves the town from two evil villains who drained all the colors away.

Walsh, E. (1995). *Mouse Paint*. Three white mice discover three jars of paint—red, blue, and yellow—and present to children a lighthearted lesson in color.

Weitzman, J. P. (1998). *You Can't Take a Balloon into the Metropolitan Museum*. A lost balloon soars past eighteen famous paintings and sculptures through New York City.

Yolen, J. (1988). *Owl Moon*. A poetic story that lovingly depicts the special companionship of a young child and her father as well as humankind's close relationship to the natural world.

DRAMA

Aliki. (1999). *William Shakespeare and the Globe*. Using her characteristically thorough and animated words and pictures, and quotations from Shakespeare's plays, Aliki has created a five-act masterpiece that is the definitive introduction to the playwright and his word.

dePaola, T. (2005). *Stagestruck*. Tommy gets a part with no lines in his first-grade class play, but he finds a way to improvise.

DANCE

Ackerman, K. (1988). *Song and Dance Man*. Three children follow their grandfather up to the attic, where he pulls out his old bowler hat, gold-tipped cane, and his tap shoes, and shows them that you're only as old as you feel.

Archambault, J., Martin, B., & Rand, T. (1986). *Barn Dance*. Beckoned by the sweet sound of a country fiddler and the rhythmic thumping of dancing feet a young boy wonders who could possibly be having a barn dance in the middle of the night.

dePaola, T. (1979). *Oliver Button is a Sissy*. A little boy must come to terms with being teased and ostracized because he'd rather read books, paint pictures, and tap-dance than participate in sports.

Gerstein, M. (2003). *The Man Who Walked Between the Towers*. A lyrical evocation of Philippe Petit's 1974 tightrope walk between the World Trade Center towers.

Glassman, B. (2001). *Giants of Art & Culture: Mikhail Baryshnikov, Dance Genius*. A readable and balanced portrait of Baryshnikov that provides unique insights into the world of dance.

Glover, S., & Weber, B. (2000). *Savion! My Life in Tap*. This exciting biography treats readers to an inside look at Savion Glover's work while also providing a brief yet compelling history of tap dancing.

Gray, L. (1999). *My Mama Had a Dancing Heart*. A ballet dancer recalls how she and her mother would welcome each season with a dance outdoors.

Gray, M. (1972). *Song and Dance Man: The Art of Bob Dylan*. A comprehensive and insightful interpretation of Bob Dylan's lyrics and how they coincide with the events taking place in his life.

Hart, A., & Mantell, P. (1993). *Kids Make Music!: Clapping & Tapping from Bach to Rock*. Those hands will soon be clapping, those feet will be tapping, those faces will be grinning and they will be humming anything from Bach to rock.

Hesse, K. (1999). *Come on, Rain!* A lyrically written, soul-renewing experience of a summer downpour after a sweltering city heat wave.

Jonas, A. (1989). *Color Dance*. The girl in red, the girl in yellow, the girl in blue, and the boy in black and white create a living kaleidoscope, step by step by step.

McKissack, P. (1988). *Mirandy and Brother Wind*. Mirandy is sure she'll win the cake walk if she can catch Brother Wind for her partner, but he eludes all the tricks her friends advise.

Patrick, D., & Ransome, J. (1993). *Red Dancing Shoes*. A little girl's feet feel magical in her new, red dancing shoes, until she falls in the mud.

Walters, K., & Cooper, M. (1990). *Lion Dancer: Ernie Wan's Chinese New Year*. This Chinese New Year, 6-year-old Ernie will perform his first Lion Dance on the streets of New York City.

Walton, R. (2001). *How Can You Dance?* This energetic celebration of movement will encourage kids to boogie through any mood.

Angleberger, T. (2010). *Origami Yoda*. Origami Yoda can predict the future and suggest the best way to deal with a tricky situation. His advice actually works, and soon most of the sixth grade is lining up with questions.

Clare, C. (2007). *The Mortal Instruments*. When 15-year-old Clary Fray heads out to the Pandemonium Club in New York City, she hardly expects to witness a murder. Then the body disappears into thin air.

Collins, S. (2010). *The Hunger Games*. Twelve boys and 12 girls are forced to appear in a live event called The Hunger Games. There is only one rule: kill or be killed.

Dashner, J. (2013). *The Maze Runner*. Thomas wakes up in an ever-changing maze, remembering nothing but his name.

Kinney, J. (2007). *Diary of a Wimpy Kid*. The hazards of growing up before you're ready are uniquely revealed through words and drawings as Greg records them in his diary.

Lowry, L. (2006). *Giver Quartet*. Set in a future society that is at first presented as a utopia and gradually appears more and more dystopic, the novel follows a boy named Jonas as he receives the memories from his predecessor and discovers how shallow his community's life has become.

Patterson, J. (2012). *Middle School*. Anything Rafe has never done before, he's going to do it, from learning to play poker to going to a modern art museum.

Raskin, E. (2004). *The Westing Game*. No one knows why an eccentric, game-loving millionaire has chosen a virtual stranger—and a possible murderer—to inherit his vast fortune; One things' for sure: Sam Westing may be dead... but that won't stop him from playing one last game!

Riordan, R. (2008). *39 Clues*. Minutes before she died Grace Cahill changed her will, leaving her descendants an impossible decision: You have a choice—one million dollars or a clue.

Riordan, R. (2010). *Heroes of Olympus*. Jason, Piper, and Leo wake up on a bus full of kids to discover they are going to Camp Half-Blood, a school for demigods.

Riordan, R. (2008). *Percy Jackson & The Olympians*. Percy discovers he's the son of Poseidon and must team up with his best friend, a satyr, and the demi-god daughter of Athena to prevent a catastrophic war between the gods.

Russell, R. (2011). *Dork Diaries*. Follow Nikki's life through sketches, doodles and diary entries as she starts her new school; battles with her mum for an iPhone; and meets her arch-nemisis, the school's queen bee, Mackenzie.

Sobol, D. (1985). *Encyclopedia Brown*. Encyclopedia Brown must solve brain-twisting mysteries by using his famous computer-like brain.

Warner, G. (1989). *The Boxcar Children*. The Aldens begin their adventure by making a home in a boxcar. Their goal is to stay together, and in the process they find a grandfather.

Self-Diagnostic Instrument

This short (38-item) test is designed to help you determine the basic skill areas in the language arts in which you are weak. Any errors that you make here should be seen as areas that require your review.

Write your responses on the indicated lines. When you have finished, check your answers against the correct choices listed at the end of this appendix.

Structural Analysis and Phonetics

1. A morpheme placed at the beginning of a word to alter the meaning of that word is called a _____.

2. A _____ comes at the end of a word and alters its meaning.

3. The root word in *redevelopment* is _____.

4. The underlined portion of the word <u>pr</u>aying is called a _____.

5. The common phonetic element in *chop, ship, moth,* and *when* is called a _____.

6. The common phonetic element in *hoist, round, gown,* and *boy* is called a _____.

7. The correct syllabication and accent for *coconut* and *cogitate* are _____.

8. Which of the following words contains a prefix?
   a. record   c. recruit
   b. realize   d. recover

1. _____   5. _____

2. _____   6. _____

3. _____   7. _____

4. _____   8. _____

Spelling and Vocabulary

Select the *synonym* of the underlined word in each sentence.

9. Jake is the most <u>ingenious</u> person in our family.
   a. sincere   c. sociable
   b. modest   d. clever

10. Examination determined that the tumor was <u>benign.</u>
    a. noncancerous   c. malignant
    b. kind   d. bestial

11. She reportedly suffered from <u>chronic</u> head colds.
    a. constant   c. painful
    b. bellicose   d. perceptible

12. The <u>mendicant</u> approached them on the street.
    a. merchant   c. beggar
    b. police officer   d. salesperson

Select the *antonym* of the underlined word in each sentence.

13. His <u>nefarious</u> character was well known to all.
    a. clever   c. wicked
    b. kindly   d. generous

14. He made a <u>lucrative</u> investment last year.
    a. fortunate   c. unprofitable
    b. rewarding   d. fraudulent

15. The boy was called a <u>dolt</u> by his teachers.
    a. clever fellow   c. prankster
    b. delinquent   d. doll

9. _____   13. _____

10. _____   14. _____

11. _____   15. _____

12. _____

Choose the word in each pair that is spelled correctly and write it on the line below.

16. Sarah (recieved, received) a sweater for her birthday.

17. The boys found (their, there) books where they had left them.

18. Today the natural (environment, enviroment) is threatened by industrial pollution.

19. Try to use correct (grammar, grammer) in your composition.

20. The stars were (shining, shinning) brightly in the sky.

21. We will (definately, definitely) meet you at eight o'clock.

22. The city was (fourty, forty) miles from the airport.

16. _____   20. _____

17. _____   21. _____

18. _____   22. _____

19. _____

Proofreading

One word in each line is spelled or used incorrectly. Write the correct word on the line below.

23. There are too main points to

24. be considired. First, the cost

25. of the entire operation must be less then

26. the transpertation of the various materials.

27. Second, the sight of the building

28. should depend on the advise of an expert.

23. _____   26. _____

24. _____   27. _____

25. _____   28. _____

Punctuation, Capitalization, and Parts of Speech

29. Which of the following sentences is punctuated correctly?
    a. The lake which is calm, is not deep
    b. She ran down the steps, and across the street.
    c. The road stretched forever, we drove on until midnight.
    d. "I'll never see you again," she said.

29. _____

Indicate on the lines below which word (or words) in each line should be capitalized.

30. They lived on hester street for

31. 10 years before moving to michigan,

32. where her husband taught english at the college.

30. _____ 32. _____

31. _____

Write the name of the part of speech for the underlined word in each line.

33. There were 70 <u>large</u> elephants

34. in the parade. They walked, <u>slowly</u>

35. swinging their heavy <u>trunks.</u>

36. <u>Around</u> the square they trudged

37. for hours. <u>However,</u> their pace never changed.

38. Which of the following sentences is punctuated correctly?

    a. They gathered up their coats, hats scarves and left.

    b. Where have all the flowers gone!

    c. Today, unlike previous days, the weather is clear.

    d. I will leave now: but tomorrow I shall return.

33. _____ 36. _____

34. _____ 37. _____

35. _____ 38. _____

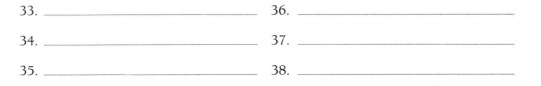

Answers

1. prefix
2. suffix
3. develop
4. blend
5. digraph
6. diphthong
7. có co nut, coǵ i tate
8. d (recover)
9. d (clever)
10. a (noncancerous)
11. a (constant)
12. c (beggar)
13. b (kindly)
14. c (unprofitable)
15. a (clever fellow)
16. received
17. their
18. environment
19. grammar
20. shining
21. definitely
22. forty
23. two, *not* too
24. considered, *not* considired
25. than, *not* then
26. transportation, *not* transpertation
27. site, *not* sight
28. advice, *not* advise
29. d
30. Hester Street
31. Michigan
32. English
33. adjective
34. adverb
35. noun
36. preposition
37. conjunction
38. c

Assessment Devices

NAME _____   DATE _____

SCHOOL _____   AGE _____

1. How much do you like to read? (Check one answer.)

   ☐ A little   ☐ A lot   ☐ Not at all

2. What newspapers do you read?

   _____

3. What are your favorite comic strips in the newspaper?

   _____

4. What magazines do you read?

   _____

5. What three living women do you admire most?

   A. _____   B. _____   C. _____

6. What three living men do you admire most?

   A. _____   B. _____   C. _____

7. Who are your heroes (men or women)?

   _____

8. What hobbies do you have?

   _____

9. What are your favorite television programs?

   _____

10. How many television programs do you watch each day?

   _____

11. How many hours each day do you usually spend watching television?

   _____

12. How many hours a day do you spend on the computer?
    Do you use the computer to play games or to search websites?

   _____

13. What are your favorite movies?

   _____

14. Who are your favorite movie, television, and music stars?

_____

15. What are the three best fiction books you have ever read?

    A. _____   B. _____   C. _____

16. What are the three best nonfiction books you have ever read?

    A. _____   B. _____   C. _____

17. What men or boys from fiction or nonfiction do you remember best?

_____

18. What women or girls from fiction or nonfiction do you remember best?

_____

19. What books have you read that you disliked very much? Why?

_____

20. Check the kinds of things you like to see, read, or hear about. (You may check as many as you wish.)

    ☐ Love stories   ☐ Criminals   ☐ Horses

    ☐ Baseball   ☐ Murder mysteries   ☐ Basketball

    ☐ War stories   ☐ Jokes   ☐ Space travel

    ☐ Mathematics   ☐ Famous people   ☐ Cowboy stories

    ☐ Historical tales   ☐ How to make things   ☐ Travel articles

    ☐ Mythology   ☐ Football   ☐ Encyclopedias

    ☐ Real-life adventures   ☐ Teenagers' problems   ☐ Politics

    ☐ Poetry   ☐ Nature stories   ☐ Health

    ☐ Movie stars   ☐ Scientific experiments

21. What is your favorite subject in school?

_____

22. What subject do you like least?

_____

APPENDIX D.2 Rubistar Storytelling Rubric

STUDENT'S NAME _____ DATE _____

CATEGORY	4	3	2	1
Knows the Story	The storyteller knows the story well and has obviously practiced telling the story several times. There is no need for notes and the speaker speaks with confidence.	The storyteller knows the story pretty well and has practiced telling the story once or twice. May need notes once or twice, but the speaker is relatively confident.	The storyteller knows some of the story, but did not appear to have practiced. May need notes 3–4 times, and the speaker ill-at-ease.	The storyteller could not tell the story without using notes.
Speaks Clearly	Speaks clearly and distinctly all (100–95%) the time, and mispronounces no words.	Speaks clearly and distinctly all (100–95%) the time, and mispronounces one word.	Speaks clearly and distinctly most (94–85%) of the time, and mispronounces no more than one word.	Often mumbles or cannot be understood *or* mispronounces more than one word.
Setting	Lots of vivid, descriptive words are used to tell the audience when and where the story takes place.	Some vivid, descriptive words are used to tell the audience when and where the story takes place.	The audience can figure out when and where the story took place, but there isn't much detail (e.g., once upon a time in a land far, far away).	The audience has trouble telling when and where the story takes place.
Characters	The main characters are named and clearly described (through words and/or actions). The audience knows and can describe what the characters look like and how they typically behave.	The main characters are named and described (through words and/or actions). The audience has a fairly good idea of what the characters look like.	The main characters are named. The audience knows very little about the main characters.	It is hard to tell who the main characters are.
Audience Contact	Storyteller looks at and tells the story to all members of the audience.	Storyteller looks at and tells the story to a few people in the audience.	Storyteller looks at and tells the story to 1–2 people in the audience.	Storyteller does not look at or try to involve the audience.
Voice	Always speaks loudly, slowly, and clearly. Is easily understood by all audience members all the time.	Usually speaks loudly, slowly, and clearly. Is easily understood by all audience members almost all the time.	Usually speaks loudly and clearly. Speaks so fast sometimes that audience has trouble understanding.	Speaks too softly or mumbles. The audience often has trouble understanding.

CATEGORY	4	3	2	1
Pacing	The story is told slowly where the storyteller wants to create suspense and told quickly when there is a lot of action.	The storyteller usually paces the story well, but one or two parts seem to drag or be rushed.	The storyteller tries to pace the story, but the story seems to drag or be rushed in several places.	The storyteller tells everything at one pace. Does not change the pace to match the story.
Acting/Dialogue	The student uses consistent voices, facial expressions, and movements to make the characters more believable and the story more easily understood.	The student often uses voices, facial expressions, and movements to make the characters more believable and the story more easily understood.	The student tries to use voices, facial expressions, and movements to make the characters more believable and the story more easily understood.	The student tells the story but does not use voices, facial expressions, or movement to make the story-telling more interesting or clear.
Connections/ Transitions	Connections among events, ideas, and feelings in the story are creative, clearly expressed, and appropriate.	Connections among events, ideas, and feelings in the story are clearly expressed and appropriate.	Connections among events, ideas, and feelings in the story are sometimes hard to figure out. More detail or better transitions are needed.	The story seems very disconnected and it is very difficult to figure out the story.
Duration	The storytelling lasts 5–7 minutes.	The storytelling lasts 4 or 8 minutes.	The storytelling lasts 9 minutes.	The storytelling lasts less than 3 minutes or more than 9 minutes.
Listens to Others	Always listens attentively to other storytellers. Is polite and does not appear bored or make distracting gestures or sounds.	Usually listens attentively to other storytellers. Rarely appears bored and never makes distracting gestures or sounds.	Usually listens to other storytellers, but sometimes appears bored. Might once or twice accidentally make a gesture or sound that is distracting.	Does not listen attentively. Tries to distract the storytellers, makes fun of them, or does other things instead of listening.

APPENDIX D.3   Modified Rubric for Storytelling

STUDENT'S NAME _____   DATE _____

TITLE/AUTHOR OF STORY _____

Category	SCORE
Category	**SCORE**
Knows the story (5 points)	_____
Story in correct sequence (5 points)	_____
Speaks clearly/projects (20 points)	_____
Audience contact (10 points)	_____
Intonation (15 points)	_____
Pacing (10 points)	_____
Use of dialogue (15 points)	_____
Facial expressions (10 points)	_____
Gestures (10 points)	_____
Use of props (5 points)	_____
Appropriate body movements (5 points)	_____
Duration (5 points)	_____
Listens to others (5 points)	_____
Total	_____

Comments:

Storytelling Rubric Emphasizing Voice Inflection **APPENDIX** **D.4**

STUDENT'S NAME

STORY

Appropriate Material (15 points)   **SCORE**

    Length (2 of 15)

    Engaging (5 of 15)

    Age appropriate (3 of 15)

    Interesting (5 of 15)

Facial Expression (13 points)

Voice Inflection (50 points)

    Pleasing tone (5 of 50)

    Variety of pitch (10 of 50)

    Clear diction (10 of 50)

    Change for dialogue (10 of 50)

    Appropriate dialect (5 of 50)

    Variety of rate (10 of 50)

Appropriate Body Movement (12 points)

Special Effects/Props (10 points)

Total

Comments:

APPENDIX **D.5** **Reading Conference Checklist**

STUDENT'S NAME _____ DATE _____

TITLE _____

TYPE OF MATERIAL _____

Word Recognition	EXCELLENT	GOOD	OK	NEEDS HELP
Decoding				
Use of context clues				
Use of structural clues				
Use of dictionary				
Conceptual connections				

Comprehension	EXCELLENT	GOOD	OK	NEEDS HELP
Main idea				
Supporting details				
Relationships				
(Cause–effect)				
(Compare–contrast)				
Description of characters				
Sequence of events				

Literary Connections

Retelling summary: _____

Child's opinion of the material: _____

Further responses: _____

Suggestions for future reading: _____

Summary of the conference: _____

STUDENT'S NAME _____   DATE _____

Activity	CONSISTENT	INCONSISTENT
Reads and understands all independent books.	_____	_____
Completes daily and monthly reading.	_____	_____
Completes literature response log on time.	_____	_____
Has log that contains high-quality entries.	_____	_____
Contributes thoughtful comments to literature circles.	_____	_____
Listens and responds to peer comments in literature circles.	_____	_____
Completes all assignments on time.	_____	_____
Has work that shows effort and attempts to achieve quality.	_____	_____

Point Credit System

A—consistent for all areas (7 of 8)

B—consistent for most areas (6 of 8)

C—consistent for many areas (5 of 8)

D—consistent for some areas (4 of 8)

F—consistent for a few areas (3 of 8)

Source: Slightly adapted by permission of Regie Routman: *Invitations: Changing as Teachers and Learners K–12* (Heinemann, a division of Reed Elsevier, Inc., Portsmouth, NH, 1994).

APPENDIX **D.7** **Portfolio Form for Student's Self-Assessment of Writing**

NAME _____   DATE _____

NAME OF WORK _____

1. I got my idea from _____

    _____

    _____

2. I got the background information from _____

    _____

    _____

3. The part that was hard to write was _____

    _____

    because _____

    _____

    _____

4. I especially liked the part _____

    _____

    because _____

    _____

    _____

5. I could improve it by _____

    _____

    _____

6. New vocabulary words I used _____

    _____

    _____

Teacher's Comments _____

_____

_____

_____

Teacher's Quarterly Evaluation Form of Student's Writing | **APPENDIX** | **D.8**

NAME _____

DATE _____ QUARTER 1 2 3 4

1. What was your favorite piece of work this quarter? Explain why.

   _____
   _____
   _____

2. What piece did you like the least? Explain why.

   _____
   _____
   _____

3. Did you make good use of your time? Explain.

   _____
   _____
   _____

4. What things did you learn about yourself as you were writing?

   _____
   _____
   _____

5. Which type of new genre will you attempt next quarter? Why do you want to try it?

   _____
   _____
   _____

6. What one aspect of writing would you like most to learn next quarter?

   _____
   _____
   _____

Student's Signature _____

Teacher's Signature _____

APPENDIX   D.9   Teacher's Portfolio Assessment Rubric

STUDENT'S NAME _____   DATE _____

		EXCELLENT				POOR
GOALS		5	4	3	2	1

Writing Process	uses various prewriting strategies (brainstorming, webbing, illustrating, etc.)					
	writes a rough draft (ability to put thoughts on paper)					
	revises rough draft (checks details, sequence, clarity, etc.)					
	edits/proofreads (alone, with peers, or with teacher)					
	publishes or shares (final copy or oral reading to classmates or teacher)					
Writing Skills	writes complete sentences					
	uses descriptive words in writing					
	uses correct format when writing paragraphs					
	uses correct format when writing letters					
Usage	makes subjects and verbs agree					
Mechanics	punctuates at the end of sentences					
	capitalizes the beginning of sentences					
	uses commas correctly					
	uses quotation marks correctly					
	capitalizes proper nouns in writing					

Teacher Comments:

Source: Reprinted with permission of the Mid-Del School District, Oklahoma.

6 + 1 Trait® Writing Assessment   **APPENDIX D.10**

SCORING CONTINUUM

WOW!

Exceeds expectations

5 *Strong*

Shows control and skill in this trait; many strengths present

4 *Effective*

On balance, the strengths outweigh the weaknesses; a small amount of revision is needed

3 *Developing*

Strengths and need for revision are about equal; about half-way home

2 *Emerging*

Need for revision outweighs strengths; isolated moments hint at what the writer has in mind

1 *Not Yet*

a bare beginning; writer not yet showing any control

IDEAS

⑤ This paper is clear and focused. It holds the reader's attention. Relevant anecdotes and details enrich the central theme.

③ The writer is beginning to define the topic, even though development is still basic or general.

① As yet, the paper has no clear sense of purpose or central theme. To extract meaning from the text, the reader must make inferences based on sketchy or missing details. The writing reflects more than one of the problems [identified in full version].

ORGANIZATION

⑤ The organization enhances and showcases the central idea or theme. The order, structure, or presentation of information is compelling and moves the reader through the text.

③ The organizational structure is strong enough to move the reader through the text without too much confusion.

① The writing lacks a clear sense of direction. Ideas, details, or events seem strung together in a loose or random fashion; there is no identifiable internal structure. The writing reflects more than one of the problems [identified in full version].

VOICE

⑤ The writer speaks directly to the reader in a way that is individual, compelling, and engaging. The writer crafts the writing with an awareness and respect for the audience and the purpose for writing.

③ The writer seems sincere, but not fully engaged or involved. The writing has discernable purpose, but is not compelling.

① The writer seems indifferent to the topic and the content. The writing lacks purpose and audience engagement.

WORD CHOICE

⑤ Words convey the intended message in a precise, interesting, and natural way. The words are powerful and engaging.

③ The language is functional, even if it lacks much energy. It is easy to figure out the writer's meaning on a general level.

① The writer demonstrates a limited vocabulary or has not searched for words to convey specific meaning.

SENTENCE FLUENCY

⑤ The writing has an easy flow, rhythm, and cadence. Sentences are well built, with strong and varied structure that invites expressive oral reading.

③ The text hums along with a steady beat, but tends to be more pleasant or businesslike than musical, more mechanical than fluid.

① The reader has to practice quite a bit in order to give this paper a fair interpretive reading. The writing reflects more than one of the problems [identified in full version].

CONVENTIONS

⑤ The writer demonstrates a good grasp of standard writing conventions (e.g., spelling, punctuation, capitalization, grammar, usage, paragraphing) and uses conventions effectively to enhance readability. Errors tend to be so few that just minor touch-ups would get this piece ready to publish.

GRADES 7 AND UP ONLY: The writing is sufficiently complex to allow the writer to show skill in using a wide range of conventions. For writers at younger ages, the writing shows control over those conventions that are grade/age appropriate.

③ The writer shows reasonable control over a limited range of standard writing conventions. Conventions are sometimes handled well and enhance readability; at other times, errors are distracting and impair readability.

① Errors in spelling, punctuation, capitalization, usage, and grammar and/or paragraphing repeatedly distract the reader and make the text difficult to read. The writing reflects more than one of the problems [identified in full version].

PRESENTATION (OPTIONAL)

⑤ The form and presentation of the text enhances the ability for the reader to understand and connect with the message. It is pleasing to the eye.

③ The writer's message is understandable in this format.

① The reader receives a garbled message due to problems relating to the presentation of the text.

Writing Rubric: Holistic Scoring and Student Self-Evaluation **APPENDIX** **D.11**

Holistic Scoring

In holistic scoring, written papers are given a quick, general reading for overall content, clarity, organization, flow, and development of thoughts. For teachers who have many papers to grade, this is a time-saving yet effective device to evaluate students' writing. Before using the four-point scale, you must be clear in your own mind what constitutes a 4, 3, 2, 1 grade.

Holistic Scoring for Student Self-Evaluation

Although holistic scoring was originally developed for teachers, it can be modified to be used by students who have been taught to self-evaluate their own work. It can also be used in a buddy system where peers evaluate one another.

Holistic Scoring Rubric Using a Four-Point Scale

1 = Ineffective Piece: Many problems; not going anywhere.

2 = Ineffective Piece but Salvageable: Has problems but I know how to solve them.

3 = Effective Piece: This works; is well organized, clearly written, and has no mechanical errors.

4 = Most Effective Piece: Includes all components of #3 plus it says something; exemplifies strong writing; moves the reader.

After you have rated your pieces 1, 2, 3, 4, write three reasons for each of the scores. Cite specific examples from the pieces to support your reasons.

_____

_____

_____

_____

_____

_____

_____

_____

_____

_____

_____

_____

_____

_____

_____

_____

APPENDIX D.12 Rubric for Story Writing

TITLE:

NAME: DATE:

3 POINTS	2 POINTS	1 POINT	0 POINTS	SCORE
Title is creative, relates to action, and sparks interest in readers.	Title is related to action.	Title does not relate to action.	No title was given.	
Evidence of prewriting with descriptive setting and characters, with sequence of plot.	Evidence of some prewriting with names of characters and some events of plot.	Little evidence of prewriting with only names of characters.	No evidence of prewriting.	
Many vivid descriptive words to paint a picture of time and place of action.	Some descriptive words to explain time and place of action.	Few descriptive words to explain time and place of action.	No descriptive words to explain time and place of action.	
Many vivid, descriptive words to paint a picture of characters' physical appearance and actions.	Some descriptive words to explain characters' physical appearance and actions.	Characters are named, but reader knows little about their physical appearance.	Most characters do not have names; they are identified as "the boy" or "the girl."	
Characters come to life through appropriate amount of dialogue.	There is dialogue, but characters do not come to life.	There is very little dialogue and it is difficult to distinguish who is speaking.	There is no dialogue.	
The story comes to life through vivid action verbs (active voice). The story's action creates mood.	The story has active voice, but the verbs are not vivid.	The story shifts from active to passive voice.	The story is told in passive voice.	
The main character's problem is revealed at the beginning of the story with many roadblocks to make the plot exciting.	It is clear what the main character's problem is, but the plot lacks an appropriate number of roadblocks.	It is not clear what is the main character's problem, and there are only two insignificant roadblocks.	There is no clear problem because there are no roadblocks.	
The plot has a clear climax with an appropriate resolution.	The plot has a clear climax, but the resolution is too long.	The plot has somewhat of a clear climax, but there is no resolution.	There is no climax; thus no resolution.	
Original illustrations are detailed, colorful, attractive, and relate to the text on the page.	Original illustrations are somewhat detailed and colorful, but do not always relate to the text.	Original illustrations somewhat relate to the text. They lack color and details.	Illustrations are not present, or they are merely stick figures.	
All of the written requirements (number of pages, font size, font style, amount of text on pages) are present.	The required font size and style and the number of pages are present.	The required font size and font style are present.	The required font size is present.	
Uses many transition words from one event to the next.	Uses transition words for main roadblocks or setting changes.	Uses transition words, but some are inappropriate.	Transitions are missing.	
The story contains many creative details, figures of speech, and other vivid words that contribute to the readers' enjoyment. Author's imagination is unique.	The story contains a few creative details and vivid words that contribute to the readers' enjoyment. Author has good imagination.	The details and word choice distract from the story.	There are no creative details or vivid word choice. The story lacks imagination.	
The story contains no spelling, punctuation, capitalization, or grammar errors.	The story contains no more than two of the following errors: spelling, punctuation, capitalization, or grammar.	The story contains no more than three of the following errors: spelling, punctuation, capitalization, or grammar.	The story contains four or more of the following errors: spelling, punctuation, capitalization, or grammar.	

TOTAL SCORE: ____ /39
(Acceptable score is 31 or 80%).

Rubric for Middle Grades Writing Portfolio Assignment   **APPENDIX** **D.13**

STUDENT'S NAME _____   DATE _____

TITLE OF PROJECT _____

POSSIBLE POINTS   **POINTS YOU EARNED**

1. Portfolio in separate binder with cover
   sheet, name, date, title   **10**   _____

2. Separate table of contents, dividers, drafts,
   and final copies   **10**   _____

3. Typed, double-spaced, neat appearance   **10**   _____

4. Content: Written in clear and interesting
   manner   **10**   _____

5. Content: Work attempts to say something
   important   **60**   _____

6. Mechanics: Proofread and edited for errors   **50**   _____

TOTAL   **150**   _____

APPENDIX D.14 **Research Report Rubric for Grades 5–6**

TITLE

NAME   DATE

3 POINTS	2 POINTS	1 POINT	0 POINTS	SCORE
All sources (text and graphics) are accurately cited in the required format.	All sources are documented, but not in the required format.	At least one source is not documented, but others are in required format.	Two or more sources are not documented or some sources are not in required format.	
Notes are organized in a neat, orderly fashion.	Notes are recorded legibly and are somewhat organized.	Notes are recorded.	There are no notes.	
Graphic organizer or outline has been completed and shows clear, logical relationships between all topics and subtopics.	Graphic organizer or outline has been completed and shows all main topics with a few subtopics.	Graphic organizer or outline has been completed, showing only main topics.	Graphic organizer or outline has not been completed.	
At least three articles or books and at least three Internet sources were used.	At least two articles or books and at least three Internet sources were used.	At least two articles or books and at least two Internet sources were used.	Only one article or book and only one Internet source were used.	
In the introductory paragraph, the main concept and subtopics are clearly stated.	Introduces main concept, but does not let readers know subtopics at the beginning of the paper.	Readers need to infer the main concept.	An introductory paragraph is missing.	
Report is logically organized, using headings, illustrations, and/or multimedia where appropriate.	Report is logically organized, using a few headings and illustrations.	Report is logically organized, but includes no heading or illustrations.	Report is not logically organized.	
In an engaging manner, the report presents facts, definitions, details, and quotations to support subtopics.	The report includes facts, definitions, details, and quotations to support subtopics.	Report includes facts and details, but does not include necessary definitions or quotations.	Report is lacking necessary facts and details; topic is not well developed.	
Uses transition and connecting words in paragraphs and between paragraphs so that ideas are easy to follow.	Uses transition and connecting words within paragraphs.	Transition and connecting words are missing in paragraphs and between paragraphs.	Sentences are simple with no connecting words.	
Uses a variety of domain-specific words that are associated with the topic, and defines them when appropriate.	Uses some domain-specific words associated with the topic.	Uses only one or two domain-specific words.	No domain-specific words are used throughout the paper.	
Student had three peers and teacher read report for content. Student accepted suggestions readily.	Student had two peers and teacher read report for content. Student accepted most suggestions.	Student had one peer and teacher read report for content. Student did not readily accept suggestions.	Student had no peer read report for content.	
Student had three peers edit the report. Student accepted suggestions readily.	Students had two peers edit the report. Student accepted only some of the suggestions.	Student had one peer edit the report. Student accepted few suggestions.	Student had no peer edit the report.	
Finished product was neatly prepared and shared and posted on the bulletin board or online.	Finished product was neatly prepared and shared orally OR posted on the bulletin board or online.	Finished product was somewhat neat. Student posted it on the bulletin board.	Student did not share his/her report in any manner.	

3 POINTS	2 POINTS	1 POINT	0 POINTS	SCORE
Finished product had title page, page numbers, table of contents, and reference page.	Finished product was missing one of the following: title page, page numbers, table of contents, or reference page.	Finished product was missing two of the following: title page, page numbers, table of contents, or reference page.	Finished product was missing three or more of the following: title page, page numbers, table of contents, or reference page.	
The report contained no spelling, punctuation, capitalization, or grammar errors.	The report contained no more than one of the following errors: punctuation, spelling, capitalization, or grammar.	The report contained no more than two of the following errors: spelling, punctuation, capitalization, or grammar.	The report contained more than three of the following errors: spelling, punctuation, capitalization, or grammar.	
The report was well organized with all paragraphs correctly constructed.	The report was well organized with only one paragraph not correctly constructed.	The report was organized with only two paragraphs not correctly constructed.	There was no clear organization to the report. It lacked well-constructed paragraphs.	
The topic was age appropriate and interesting.	The topic was age appropriate and somewhat interesting.	The topic was age appropriate with only a few new pieces of information.	The topic was age appropriate, but contained no new information.	

TOTAL SCORE: _____ /45

(Acceptable score is 36 or 80%).

APPENDIX D.15 Rubric for a "Musical Poem"

STUDENT'S NAME _____ DATE _____

TITLE OF POEM _____

TRAIT   **SCORE**

Contribution While Working with Small Group

    Gave suggestions (10 points)   _____

    Listened to classmates' ideas (10 points)   _____

    Respected materials (5 points)   _____

    Used indoor voice (5 points)   _____

Performance

    "Music" fit the poem's mood (10 points)   _____

    Appropriate expression (10 points)   _____

    Poise (5 points)   _____

    Volume (5 points)   _____

    Rate (5 points)   _____

Good Audience Member

    Listened to other groups (5 points)   _____

    Gave appropriate response to other groups (5 points)   _____

Total   _____

Comments:

Rubric for Listening to an Advertisement   **APPENDIX**   **D.16**

STUDENT'S NAME _____   DATE _____

PRODUCT _____

TRAIT   **SCORE**

Contribution While Working with Small Group

     Gave suggestions (10 points)   _____

     Listened to classmates' ideas (10 points)   _____

     Cooperated while listening (5 points)   _____

     Used indoor voice (5 points)   _____

     Accurately identified each technique (10 points)   _____

Total   _____

Comments:

APPENDIX **D.17** Rubric for Indicating Growth in Listening Skills

STUDENT'S NAME _____ DATE _____

Minus sign (−) = never
Plus sign (+) = sometimes
Exclamation sign (!) = most of the time

	GRADING PERIOD			
Competency	1ST QUARTER	2ND QUARTER	3RD QUARTER	4TH QUARTER
Listens attentively to teacher				
Listens attentively to classmates' presentations				
Can follow simple two-step directions				
Can restate two-step directions				
Shows respect for others in small groups				
Makes contributions in group discussions				

Comments:

STUDENT'S NAME _____   DATE _____

CATEGORY	4	3	2	1
Puppet Construction	Puppets were original, had creative details, and were constructed well. No pieces fell off during the performance.	Puppets were original and constructed well. No pieces fell off during the performance.	Puppets were constructed fairly well. No pieces fell off during the performance.	Puppets were not constructed well. Pieces fell off during the performance.
Puppet Manipulation	Puppeteers always manipulated puppets so audience could see them.	Puppeteers usually manipulated puppets so audience could see them.	Puppeteers sometimes manipulated puppets so audience could see them.	Puppeteers rarely manipulated puppets so audience could see them.
Playwriting	Play was creative and really held the audience's interest.	Play was creative and usually held the audience's interest.	Play had several creative elements, but often did not hold the audience's interest.	Play needed more creative elements.
Voice Projection	Voices of puppeteers were always audible to people sitting in the back row.	Voices of puppeteers were usually audible to people sitting in the back row.	Voices of puppeteers were sometimes audible to people sitting in the back row.	Voices of puppeteers were rarely audible to people sitting in the back row.
Accuracy of Story	All important parts of story were included and were accurate.	Almost all important parts of story were included and were accurate.	Quite a few important parts of story were included and were accurate.	Much of the story was left out or was inaccurate.
Expression	Puppeteers' voices showed a lot of expression and emotion.	Puppeteers' voices showed some expression and emotion.	Puppeteers' voices showed a little expression and emotion.	Puppeteers' voices were monotone and not expressive.
Staying in Character	Puppeteers stayed in character throughout the performance.	Puppeteers stayed in character through almost all of the performance.	Puppeteers tried to stay in character through some of the performance.	Puppeteers acted silly or showed off.
Scenery	Scenery was creative, added interest to the play, and did not get in the way of the puppets.	Scenery was creative and did not get in the way of the puppets.	Scenery did not get in the way of the puppets.	Scenery got in the way of the puppets *or* distracted the audience.

Source: RubiStar, http://rubistar.4teachers.org. Used with permission.

APPENDIX D.19   Modified Rubric for a Puppet Show

STUDENT'S NAME _____   DATE _____

STORY _____

CATEGORY   **SCORE**

Process

  Puppet construction (5 points)   _____

  Cooperated with group (10 points)   _____

Product

  Puppet manipulation (5 points)   _____

  Voice projection (10 points)   _____

  Expression (10 points)   _____

  Staying in character (10 points)   _____

Total   _____

Comments:

STUDENT'S NAME _____   DATE _____

PIECE OF NEWSCAST _____

TRAIT   **SCORE**

Contribution While Working with Small Group

    Gave suggestions (10 points)   _____

    Listened to classmates' ideas (10 points)   _____

    Researched information (10 points)   _____

    Cooperated during taping (5 points)   _____

    Used indoor voice (5 points)   _____

    Contributed creative ideas (5 points)   _____

Performance

    Organization (10 points)   _____

    Articulation (10 points)   _____

    Volume (5 points)   _____

    Rate (5 points)   _____

    Poise (5 points)   _____

Good Audience Member

    Listened to other groups (5 points)   _____

    Gave appropriate response to other groups (5 points)   _____

Total   _____

Comments:

APPENDIX D.21 Rubric for a Propaganda Activity

STUDENT'S NAME _____ DATE _____

PRODUCT _____

TRAIT	SCORE
Contribution While Working with Small Group	
Gave suggestions (10 points)	_____
Listened to classmates' ideas (10 points)	_____
Cooperated while listening (5 points)	_____
Used indoor voice (5 points)	_____
Performance	
Clear use of propaganda technique (10 points)	_____
Well articulated (10 points)	_____
Creative advertisement (10 points)	_____
Volume (5 points)	_____
Rate (5 points)	_____
Poise (5 points)	_____
Good Audience Member	
Listened to other groups (5 points)	_____
Gave appropriate response to other groups (5 points)	_____
Total	_____

Comments:

Rubric for Assessment of Presentation Skills   APPENDIX D.22

STUDENT'S NAME _____   TOPIC _____

TOTAL SCORE _____   GRADING PERIOD   1   2   3   4

Superior = 5   Excellent = 4   Fair = 3   Adequate = 2   Weak = 1

Content

_____ Clarity of purpose   _____ Supporting details

_____ Introduction   _____ Conclusion

_____ Main points   _____ Interesting

Presentation

_____ Rate   _____ Standard English

_____ Volume   _____ Eye contact

Visual Aids

_____ Neatly prepared   _____ Manipulation

_____ Appropriate size   _____ Support topic

Comments:

APPENDIX D.23 Rubric for Assessing Visual Arts: Fifth–Sixth Grade

CATEGORY	TARGET	ACCEPTABLE	UNACCEPTABLE
Technique	Student accurately identifies all artists' techniques used in all picture books.	Student accurately identifies 8 artists' techniques used in picture books.	Student accurately identifies 7 or fewer artists' techniques used in picture books.
Artist	Student can name 10 artists and can identify their country, era, and type of art. Student can name 2 works done by each artist.	Student can name 6–9 artists and can identify their country, era, and type of art. Student can name 2 works done by each artist.	Student can name 3–5 artists and can identify their country, era, and type of art. Student can name 2 works done by each artist.
Eras	Student can identify the eras of art and give at least 5 major characteristics of the eras.	Student can identify 3 eras of art and give at least 5 major characteristics of the eras.	Student can identify 2 eras of art and give at least 5 major characteristics of the eras.
Elements	Student can name and explain all of the elements of art and can explain the elements while viewing a masterpiece.	Student can name and explain all of the elements of art.	Student cannot name and explain all of the elements of art.
Types	Student can name the following and give 4 main characteristics of each: cubism, expressionism, surrealism, realism, pop art, abstract expressionism, impressionism.	Student can name 4–6 of the following and give 4 main characteristics of each: cubism, expressionism, surrealism, realism, pop art, abstract expressionism, impressionism.	Student can name 3 of the following and give 4 main characteristics of each: cubism, expressionism, surrealism, realism, pop art, abstract expressionism, impressionism.
Creations	Student explores how to use the elements to create a unique expression.	Student tends to use the same techniques to create a unique expression.	Student tends to copy others' ideas and does not explore different ways to create moods.

Rubric for Assessing Drama: Fifth–Sixth Grade   **APPENDIX**   **D.24**

CATEGORY	TARGET	ACCEPTABLE	UNACCEPTABLE
Script Writing	Student correctly formats and writes creative scripts for readers theater, puppet shows, and skits.	Student correctly formats and writes scripts for readers theater, puppet shows, and skits, but they are not original.	Student does not correctly format or write original scripts for readers theater, puppet shows, and skits.
Acting/RT	Student uses creative expressions when performing readers theater and stays in character throughout the performance.	Student uses some expression when performing readers theater and stays in character throughout the performance.	Student does not use expression when performing readers theater and does not stay in character throughout the performance.
Acting/ Improvisations	Student uses creative expressions when performing improvisations and stays in character throughout the performance.	Student uses some expression when performing improvisation and stays in character throughout the performance.	Student does not use expression when performing improvisation and does not stay in character throughout the performance.
Acting/Plays	Student easily memorizes lines, creates believable characters, and stays in character when performing a play.	Student can memorize lines, create believable characters, and most of the time stays in character when performing plays.	Student struggles to memorize lines, cannot create believable characters, and cannot stay in character when performing plays.
Elements	Student can name and describe all of the elements of theater.	Student can name and describe two of the elements of theater.	Student can name and describe only one of the elements of theater.

APPENDIX **D.25** **Rubric for Assessing Music: Fifth–Sixth Grade**

CATEGORY	TARGET	ACCEPTABLE	UNACCEPTABLE
Notation	Student can name all of the notes on the treble clef and bass clef.	Student can name all of the notes on the treble clef.	Student cannot name all of the notes on the treble clef.
Intervals	Student can accurately sight read and sing simple melodies that he/she creates and melodies others create.	Student can accurately sight read and sing simple melodies that he/she creates.	Student cannot accurately sight read and sing simple melodies that he/she creates.
Rhythms	Student can accurately clap rhythms in any meter, using whole, half, quarter, and eighth notes that he/she creates and that others create.	Student can accurately clap rhythms in any meter, using whole, half, quarter, and eighth notes that he/she creates.	Student cannot accurately clap rhythms in any meter, using whole, half, quarter, and eighth notes that he/she creates.
Listening/ Instruments	Student can identify all of the instruments in the orchestra by category and by specific instrument when listening to a composition.	Student can identify all of the instruments in the orchestra by category when listening to a composition.	Student cannot identify all of the instruments in the orchestra by category when listening to a composition.
Listening/Eras	Student can identify the periods of music—baroque, classical, romantic, and 20th century—when listening to compositions.	Student can identify only two periods of music— baroque, classical, romantic and 20th century—when listening to compositions.	Student cannot identify any periods of music when listening to compositions.
Listening/Genre	Student can identify the following genres while listening to compositions: marches, waltzes, concertos, jazz, soul.	Student can identify three of the following genres while listening to composi- tions: marches, waltzes, concertos, jazz, soul.	Student can identify two of the following genres while listening to compositions: marches, waltzes, concertos, jazz, soul.
Composers	Student can name 10 composers and can identify their country, era, and type of music. Student can name two compositions done by each composer.	Student can name 6–9 composers and can identify their country, era, and type of music. Student can name two compositions done by each composer.	Student can name 3–5 composers and can identify their country, era, and type of music. Student can name two compositions done by each composer.

Cooperative Learning Self-Assessment Form **APPENDIX** **D.26**

TODAY'S DATE _____

I WORKED WITH (names of group members) _____

NAME OF ACTIVITY/PROJECT _____

Check if the statement fits you

- ☐ I talked quietly.
- ☐ I shared materials.
- ☐ I listened well to others.
- ☐ I did not demand my own way.
- ☐ I did my share of the work.
- ☐ I cleaned up the area.

Today I learned from (name of classmate) _____ the following:

_____

_____

_____

_____

_____

_____

_____

_____

_____

Today I taught (name of classmate) _____ the following:

_____

_____

_____

_____

_____

_____

_____

_____

_____

Signature _____

APPENDIX **D.27** **Teacher's Evaluation Form**

STUDENT _____   DATE _____

PROJECT _____

	SUPERIOR	GOOD	ADEQUATE	NEEDS WORK
Creative	_____	_____	_____	_____
Accurate information	_____	_____	_____	_____
Well organized/attractive	_____	_____	_____	_____
Indicates research	_____	_____	_____	_____
Bibliography (appropriate number of references)	_____	_____	_____	_____
Bibliography format correct	_____	_____	_____	_____
Clearly presented	_____	_____	_____	_____
Participation in the group	_____	_____	_____	_____

Additional comments

_____

_____

_____

_____

_____

_____

_____

_____

Discussed with student on this date _____

Student's Signature _____

Readers Theater Sample Script

THE STORY OF THE THREE CATS WHO LOST THEIR HATS

Narrator 1: You have all heard the story of the three kittens who lost their mittens, well . . .

Narrator 2: Those sweet little kittens grew up to be quite the adventuresome cats.

Narrator 1: This is the story of those three cats who lost their hats.

Flat Cat, Fat Cat, Pat Cat: Oh Mother, dear, see here! See here! Our hats we have lost!

Mother: Oh no, not again! How did this happen?

Flat Cat: Well, you see, I was touring down Route 66 in my BMW convertible and all was going well until I turned the curve and the Oklahoma wind came swooping down the plain and ripped my hat right off my head!

Narrator 1: And that's the truth! I saw it with my own two eyes!

Mother: (*glaring at Fat Cat*) And I suppose you were riding with him.

Fat Cat: Oh no, not at all!

Mother: Well, then, how did you lose your hat?

Fat Cat: Well, I too was cruising Route 66 on my Harley.

Mother: Your what?

Fat Cat: My Harley.

Mother: Who is Harley?

Narrator 2: *(addressing audience)* You must understand that Mother does not believe any cat should get from point A to point B any way other than prowling on all four paws.

Fat Cat: Like I was saying, I was cruising down Route 66 on my Harley, you know Mom, a motorcycle, and I too turned the curve and the Oklahoma wind came rushing down the plain and ripped my hat off my head!

Narrator 1: And that is the truth! I saw it happen with my own two eyes! That wind just swooped down and lifted Fat Cat's hat right off his head!

Mother: Oh dear, oh dear! What can we do?

Narrator 2: The third cat, Pat Cat, is standing with a smirk on her face.

Mother: *(looking at Pat Cat)* Now tell me, how did you lose your hat? Which one of your brothers were you riding with?

Pat Cat: Neither! I was flying my biplane over Route 66 when I spotted two hats! I recognized them as Flat Cat's and Fat Cat's hats! I slowed my engine, swooped down low, and snatched hat 1 and hat 2. Here they are!

Fat Cat and Flat Cat: Our hats we have found!

Mother: Pat Cat, but you still did not tell me how you lost your hat!

Narrator 1: Pat Cat puts her paw to her head.

Pat Cat: Oh no! I must have been so excited about seeing and catching their hats, I did not realize that mine must have blown off!

Narrator 1: Just then . . .

Narrator 2: Pat Cat's hat came fluttering down right on top of Pat Cat's head!

Narrator 1: And Flat Cat, Fat Cat and Pat Cat

Narrator 2: And don't forget Mother

Narrator 1 and Narrator 2: Were happy once again!

Source: From *Literacy Assessment and Intervention for Classroom Teachers* (4th ed.), by Beverly DeVries. Copyright ©2015 by Holcomb Hathaway, Publishers, Scottsdale, AZ.

References

Ajayi, L. (2009, April). English as a second language learners' exploration of multimodal texts in a junior high school. *Journal of Adolescent & Adult Literacy, 52*(7), 585–595.

Akhavan, N. (2004). *How to align literacy instruction, assessment, and standards.* Portsmouth, NH: Heinemann.

ALA. 2014. The Coretta Scott King Book Awards. Retrieved from www.ala.org/emiert/cskbookawards.

Albers, P., Dooley, C., Flint, A., Holbrook, P., & May, L. (2012, Jan.). Writing the image, writing the world. *Language Arts, 89*(3), 163–165.

Alderman, G., & Green, S. (2011). Fostering lifelong spellers through meaningful experiences. *The Reading Teacher, 64*(8), 599–605.

Allington, R. (2002a). *Big brother and the national reading curriculum: How ideology trumped evidence.* Portsmouth, NH: Heinemann.

Allington, R. (2002b, June). What I've learned about effective reading instruction. *Phi Delta Kappan.*

Allington, R. (2013). What really matters when working with struggling readers. *The Reading Teacher, 66*(7), 520–230.

Alvermann, D., Phelps, S.,& Ridgeway, V. (2007). *Content area reading and literacy: Succeeding in today's diverse classrooms.* Boston: Pearson.

Alvermann, D., Unrau, N., & Ruddell, R. (Eds.). (2013). *Theoretical models and processes of reading.* Newark, DE: International Reading Association.

Amaral, O. M., Garrison, L., & Klentschy, M. (2002, Summer). Helping English learners increase achievement through inquiry-based science instruction. *Bilingual Research Journal, 26*(2), 213–239.

Ancona, G. (1999). *Carnival.* Illus. G. Ancona. Orlando, FL: Harcourt.

Anderson, J. (2005). *Mechanically inclined: Building grammar, usage and style into writer's workshop.* Portland, ME: Stenhouse.

Anderson, L. H. (2010). *Chains.* New York: Atheneum.

Anderson, N. A. (2010). The value of children's literature. Retrieved from www.education.com/reference/article/value-childrens-literature/.

Anderson, R. C. (2013). Role of the reader's schema in comprehension, learning, and memory. In D. Alvermann, N. Unrau, & R. Ruddell (Eds.), *Theoretical models and processes of reading* (pp. 476–488). Newark, DE: International Reading Association.

Anderson, R. C., Hiebert, E. H., Scott, J. A., & Wilkinson, I. (1985). *Becoming a nation of readers: The report of the Commission on Reading.* Washington, DC: National Institute of Education, the National Academy of Education.

Applebee, A., & Langer, J. (2011, July). A snapshot of writing instruction in middle school and high school. *English Journal, 100*(6), 14–27.

Atwell, N. (1998). *In the middle: New understandings about writing, reading and learning* (2nd ed.). Portsmouth, NH: Boynton/Cook.

Au, K. H., Mason, J. M., & Scheu, J. A. (1995). *Literacy instruction today.* New York: HarperCollins.

Balch, B. (2008). *Little Miss Matched's the writer in me: How to write like nobody else.* New York: Workman Publishing.

Ballew, J. (2012). *A literate life: The writer's notebook.* New York: Teacher's College, National Writing Project.

Barnett, C. G., & Roberson, S. (2005, Oct. 6–9). *Teacher book clubs: A tool for collaboration.* Paper presented at the annual meeting of the American Association of School Librarians Conference, Pittsburgh.

Bartholomew, B. (2012). Where's literature in the Common Core? *Educational Leadership, 69*(7), 82–85.

Bauer, E., and Arazi, J. (2011). Promoting literacy development for beginning English learners. *The Reading Teacher, 64*(5), 383–386.

Bauerlein, V. (2013, Jan. 30). The new script for teaching handwriting is no script. *Wall Street Journal.*

Beach, R. (2011, May). Issues in analyzing alignment of Language Arts Common Core Standards with State Standards. *Education Researcher, 40*(4), 179–182.

Beall, P. C., & Nipp, S. H. (1979). *Wee sing: Children's songs and fingerplays.* New York: Price Stern Sloan.

Bear, D., Invernizzi, M., Templeton, S., & Johnston, F. (2007). *Words their way: Word study for phonics, vocabulary, and spelling instruction* (4th ed.). Upper Saddle River, NJ: Prentice Hall/Merrill.

Beck, I. L., McKeown, M. G., Hamilton, R. L., & Kucan, L. (1997). *Questioning the author: An approach for enhancing student engagement with text.* Newark, DE: International Reading Association.

Becker, A. (2013). *Journey,* Illus. A. Becker. New York: Candlewick.

Bell, L. I. (2002/2003). Strategies that close the gap. *Educational Leadership, 60*(4), 32–34.

Bemelmans, L. (1939). *Madeline.* Illus. L. Bemelmans. Penguin Group.

Benson, B., & Barnett, S. (2005). *Student-led conferencing, using showcase portfolios* (2nd ed.). Thousand Oaks, CA: Corwin Press.

Berger, M. (1999). *Growl! A book about bears.* New York: Scholastic.

Berkley, T. (2010, Nov.). Sparking innovation in U.S. communities and school districts. *Phi Delta Kappan, 92*(3), 29–31.

Bernice, N. (2007). Extreme makeover: Classroom edition: Changing the environment to match students' learning styles. Alexandria, VA: Association for Supervision & Curriculum Development. Retrieved from www.ascd.org/ascd-express/vol1/118-bernice.aspx.

Bettelheim, B. (1976). *The uses of enchantment: The meaning and importance of fairy tales.* New York: Random House.

Bickers, J. (2007). The young and graphic novels. *Publishers Weekly.* Retrieved from www.publishersweekly.com.

Bigelow, B. (1989). Discovering Columbus: Rereading the past. *Language Arts, 66*(6), 635–643.

Birckmayer, J., Kennedy, A., & Stonehouse, A. (2010). Sharing spoken language: Sounds, conversations, and told stories. *Young Children, 65*(1), 34–39.

Blachowicz, C. L., Fisher, P. J., & Watts-Taffe, S. (2011). Teaching vocabulary: Leading edge research and practice. In T. Rasinski (Ed.), *Rebuilding the foundation: Effective reading instruction for 21ˢᵗ century literacy* (pp. 203–222). Bloomington, IN: Solution Tree.

Blamey, K., & Beauchat, K. (2011). Word walk: vocabulary instruction for young children. *The Reading Teacher, 65*(1), 71–75.

Bloom, B. S. (1956). *Taxonomy of educational objectives: The classification of educational goals. Handbook 1: Cognitive domain.* New York: David McKay.

Boodt, G. (1984). Critical listening. *The Reading Teacher, 37*(4), 390–394.

Borelli, F. (2001). The school–home connection. *Media & Methods, 37*(5), 34–37.

Bormuth, J.R. (1968). Cloze test readability: Criterion referenced scores. *Journal of Educational Measurement, 5*(3), 189–196.

Borrero, N., and Yeh, C. (2010, Nov.). Ecological English language learning among ethnic-minority youth. *Education Researcher, 39*(8), 571–581.

Boyer, T. A. (2006, July/August). Writing to learn in social studies. *The Social Studies,* 158–160.

Braiker, B. (2011, Jan. 24). Tossing the script: The end of the line for cursive? *ABC News.* Retrieved from http://abcnews.go.com/US/end-cursive/story?id=12749517.

Brett, J. (1988). *The mitten.* Illus. J.Brett. New York: G.P. Putnam's Sons.

Brett, J. (2004). *The umbrella.* Illus. J.Brett. New York: G.P. Putnam's Sons.

Britton, A. (2012). Crocodilian Biology database. Online: http://crocodilian.com/cnhc/cbd-faq-q1.htm

Britton, J. (1986). *Language and learning.* New York: Penguin.

Bromley, K. (1988). *Language arts: Exploring connections.* Boston: Allyn & Bacon.

Bromley, K. (2003). Building a sound writing program. In L. M. Morrow, L. B. Gambrell, & M. Pressley (Eds.), *Best practices in literacy instruction* (pp. 143–165). New York: Guilford Press.

Brookhart, S. M. (2008). Portfolio assessment. In T. L. Good (Ed.), *21st century education: A reference handbook.* Tucson, AZ: Sage.

Bruner, J. S. (1961a). *The process of education.* Cambridge, MA: Harvard University Press.

Bruner, J. S. (1961b). *A study of thinking.* New York: Wiley & Sons.

Bruner, J. S. (1962). *On knowing.* Cambridge, MA: Harvard University Press.

Bruner, J. S. (1966). *Toward a theory of instruction.* Cambridge, MA: Harvard University Press.

Bruner, J. S. (1978). The role of dialogue in language acquisition. In A. Sinclair, R. J. Jarvella, & W. M. Levelt (Eds.), *The child's conception of language.* New York: Springer-Verlag.

Bruner, J. S. (1983). *Child's talk: Learning to use language.* New York: W. W. Norton.

Bruner, J. S. (1987). *Making sense: The child's construction of the world.* London: Metheun Publishing Company.

Bruner, J. S. (1997). *The culture of education.* Cambridge, MA: Harvard University Press.

Bryan, G., Fawson, P., & Reutzel, D. R. (2003). Sustained silent reading: Exploring the value of literature discussion with three non-engaged readers. *Reading Research and Instruction,43*(1), 47–73.

Bryce, N. (2011). Meeting the reading challenges of science textbooks in the primary grades. *The Reading Teacher, 64*(7), 474–485.

Bryce, N. (2012). Mano a mano: Arts based non-fiction literacy and content area learning. *Language Arts, 89*(3), 179–193.

Burgess, S. (2003). Shared reading correlates of early reading skills. *Reading Online.* Retrieved from ww.readingonline.org/articles/burgess/index.html

Burleigh, R. (2007). *Stealing home: Jackie Robinson: Against the odds.* Illus. M. Wimmer. New York: Simon & Schuster.

Bus, A. G., Verhallen, M. J. A. J., & de Jong, M. T. (2009). How onscreen storybooks contribute to early literacy. In A. G. Bus & S. B. Neuman (Eds.), *Multimedia and Literacy Development: Improving Achievement for Young Learners* (pp. 153–167). New York: Routledge.

Cabell, S. Q., Tortorelli, L. S., & Gerde, H. K. (2013) How do I write . . . ? Scaffolding preschoolers' early writing skills. *The Reading Teacher, 66*(8), 650–659.

Calkins, L. (1983). *Lessons from a child: On the teaching and learning of writing.* Portsmouth, NH: Heinemann.

Calkins, L. (1994). *The art of teaching writing* (2nd ed.). Portsmouth, NH: Heinemann.

Calkins, L. (2001). *The art of teaching reading.* New York: Longman.

Callahan, M., & King, J. (2011). Classroom remix: Patterns of pedagogy in a techno-literacies poetry unit. *Journal of Adolescent & Adult Literacy, 55*(2), 134–144.

Callahan, R. B. (2009). Perceptions and use of graphic novels in the classroom. Unpublished Master's Thesis. Ohio University.

Cambourne, B. (1988). *The whole story: Natural learning and the acquisition of literacy in the classroom.* Jefferson City, MO: Scholastic.

Cambourne, B. (2001). What do I do with the rest of the class? The nature of teaching-learning activities. *Language Arts, 79*(2), 124–135.

Cambourne, B. (2002). Holistic, integrated approaches to reading and language arts instruction: The constructivist framework of an instructional theory. In A. E. Farstrup & S. J. Samuels (Eds.), *What research has to say about reading instruction* (pp. 25–47). Newark, DE: International Reading Association.

Carbo, M. (1997). Reading styles times twenty. *Educational Leadership, 54*(6), 38–42.

Carnegie Council for Advancing Adolescent Literacy (2010). *Time to act: An agenda for advancing adolescent literacy for college and career success.* New York: Author.

Castek, J., & Beach, R. (2013). Using apps to support disciplinary literacy and science. *Journal of Adolescent and Adult Literacy 56*(7), 554–564.

Cecil, N. L. (2015). *Striking a balance: A comprehensive approach to early literacy* (5th ed.). Scottsdale, AZ: Holcomb Hathaway.

Center for Public Education (2010). Face of our changing nation. Retrieved from www.centerforpubliceducation.org.

Chase, M. (2012). Revision process ad practice: A kindergarten experience. *Language Arts, 89*(3), 166–178.

Checkley, K. (1997). The seventh . . . and eighth. *Educational Leadership, 55*(1), 8–13.

Cheek, A., Hunter Nix, L., & Foxfire Students (Eds.) (2006). *The Foxfire 40th anniversary book: Faith, family and the land.* New York: Anchor.

Chertoff, E. (2013, January 17). Reggio Emilia: From postwar Italy to NYC's toniest preschools. *The Atlantic.*

Chiang, M., Crane, C., Hamalainen, K., & Jones, L. (2010). *Oil spill: Disaster in the gulf.* New York: Scholastic.

Choate, J., & Rakes, T. (1987). The structured listening activity: A model for improving listening comprehension. *The Reading Teacher, 41*(2), 194–200.

Chomsky, N. (1974). *Aspects of the theory of syntax.* Cambridge, MA: Harvard University Press.

Christelow, E. (2010). *The desperate dog writes again.* New York: Clarion Press.

Christie, J., Enz, B., & Vukelich, C. (2003). *Teaching language and literacy* (2nd ed.). Boston: Allyn & Bacon.

Chun, C. (2009, Oct.). Critical literacies and graphic novels for English-language learners: Teaching *Maus. Journal of Adolescent and Adult Literacy, 53*(2), 144–153.

Clay, M. (1975). *What did I write?* Portsmouth, NH: Heinemann.

Clay, M. (1979). *Reading: The patterning of complex behavior* (2nd ed.). Auckland, New Zealand: Heinemann.

Clay, M. (1985). *The early detection of reading difficulties* (3rd ed.). Portsmouth, NH: Heinemann.

Clay, M. (1991). *Becoming literate: The construction of inner control.* Portsmouth, NH: Heinemann.

Clay, M. (1993). *Reading Recovery.* Portsmouth, NH: Heinemann.

Clay, M. (2000). *Running records for classroom teachers.* Portsmouth, NH: Heinemann.

Cohen, V. L., & Cowen, J. E. (2008). *Literacy for children in an information age.* Belmont, CA: Thompson Wadsworth.

Coil, Carolyn. (2008). Keys to successful differentiation: Training, time practice and sharing. *E-zine, 2*(3). Retrieved from www.carolyncoil.com/ezine23.htm.

Coleman, E. (1996). *White sock only.* Illus. by T. Geter. New York: Albert Whiteman.

Coleman, J., Golson-Bradley, L., & Donovan, C. (2012). Visual representation in second graders' informational book composition. *The Reading Teacher, 66*(1), 31–46.

Collier, L. (Sept. 2011). Keeping students at the center of the Common Core classroom. *NCTE Council Chronicle, 21*(1), 6–9.

Colwell, J., Hutchinson, A., and Reinking, D. (2012, March). Using blogs to promote literary response during professional development. *Language Arts, 89*(4), 232–243.

Communities in Schools of North Carolina (2011). CISNC website. Retrieved from www.cisnc.org.

Compton-Lilly, C. (2009, July). Listening to families over time: Seven lessons learned about literacy in families. *Language Arts, 86*(6), 449–457.

Cooper, P., & Morreale, S. (2003). *Creating competent communicators*. Scottsdale, AZ: Holcomb Hathaway.

Cornett, C. (2010). *Creating meaning through literature and the arts: An integration resource for classroom teachers* (4th ed.). Upper Saddle River, NJ: Pearson/Merrill/Prentice Hall.

Cornett, C. E. (2007). *Creating meaning through literature and the arts: An integration resource for classroom teachers* (3rd ed.). Upper Saddle River, NJ: Pearson/Merrill/Prentice Hall.

Cornett, C. E., & Smithrim, K. L. (2001). *The arts as meaning makers: Integrating literature and the arts throughout the curriculum*. Toronto, ONT: Pearson Education Canada.

Cowan, K., & Albers, P. (2006). Semiotic representations: Building complex literacy practices through the arts. *The Reading Teacher, 60*(2), 124–137.

Cox, D. J. (2014) What are Polar Bears? Online: www.polarbearsinternational.org/about-polar-bears/essentials/what-are-polar-bears.

Crepeau, J., & Richards, M. (2003) *A show of hands: Using puppets with children*. St. Paul, MN: Redleaf Press.

Croninger, R., & Lee, V. (2001). Social capital and dropping out of high school: Benefits to at-risk students of teachers' support and guidance. *Teachers College Record, 86*(4), 548–581.

Cudd, E. T.,& Roberts, L. (1989). Using writing to enhance content area learning in the primary grades. *The Reading Teacher, 42*(6), 392–404.

Cullinan, B., & Wooten, D. (Eds.). (2010). *Another jar of tiny stars: Poems by more NCTE award-winning poets*. New York: Wordsong.

Cunningham, P., Hall, D., & Defee, M. (1991). Nonability-grouped, multilevel instruction: A year in a first grade classroom. *The Reading Teacher, 44,* 566–571.

D'Angelo, K. (1982). Developing legibility and uniqueness in handwriting with calligraphy. *Language Arts Journal, 59*(1), 23–27.

Daly, N. (2006). *Pretty Salma: A Little Red Riding Hood story from Africa*. New York: Clarion Books.

Daniels, H. (2002). Recent research on literature circles. *In literature circles: Voices and choices in book clubs and reading groups.* Portland, ME: Stenhouse.

Darch, C., Eaves, R., Crowe, D., Simmons, K., & Conniff, A. (2006). Teaching spelling to students with learning disabilities: A comparison of rule–based

strategies versus traditional instruction. *Journal of Direct Instruction, 6*(1), 1–16.

Day, A. (1991). *Carl's afternoon in the park*. New York: Farrar, Straus & Giroux.

de Jong, M. T., & Bus A. G. (2003). How well suited are electronic books to supporting literacy? *Journal of Early Childhood Literacy, 3*(2), 147–164.

De Pass, R. (2011). *Dialogue journals in the classroom*. Education Planet. Retrieved from www.lessonplanet.com/article/writing/dialogue-journals-in-the-classroom.

Deasy, R. (Ed.). (2002). *Critical link: Learning in the arts and student academic and social development*. Washington, DC: Arts Education Partnership.

DeFelice, C. (2003). *Under the same sky*. New York: Farrar, Straus, & Giroux.

DeFord, D., Mills, H., & Donnelly, A. (2012). Toward a different kind of writing instruction. *Language Arts, 89*(3), 194–203.

dePaola, T. (1978). *Pancakes for breakfast*. New York: HMH Books.

dePaola, T. (2005). *Stagestruck*. New York: G. P. Putnam's Sons.

Dettmer, P. (2006, Winter). New Blooms in established fields: Four domains of learning and doing. *Roeper Review, 28*(2), 70–78.

Devine, T. (1982). *Listening skills schoolwide: Activities and progress*. Urbana, IL: National Council of Teachers of English.

DeVries, B. A. (2015). *Literacy assessment & intervention for classroom teachers* (4th ed.). Scottsdale, AZ: Holcomb Hathaway.

Dickinson, D., & McCabe, A. (2001). Bringing it all together: The multiple origins, skills, and environmental supports of early literacy. *Disabilities Research and Practice, 16*(4), 186–202.

Doner, K. (2008). *On a road in Africa*. Illus. K. Diner. Tricycle Press.

Doyne, S., & Ojalvo, H. E. (2010, Nov.). Going into detail: Developing proofreading skills. *New York Times*. Retrieved from http://learning.blogs.nytimes.com/2010/11/08/going-into-detail-developing-proofreading-skills/.

Dragonwagon, L. (1986). *Alligator arrived with apples: A potluck alphabet book*. New York: MacMillan.

Dubois, K., Erickson, K., & Jacobs, M. (2007). Improving spelling of high frequency words for transfer to written work. Unpublished master's thesis, Saint Xavier University, Chicago, IL.

Duke, N. K., Purcell-Gates, V., Hall, L., & Tower, C. (2006). Authentic literacy activities for developing comprehension and writing. *The Reading Teacher, 60*(4), 344–355.

Duke, N. K., & Tower, C. (2004). Nonfiction texts for young readers. In J. V. Hoffman & D. L. Schallert

(Eds.). *The texts in elementary classrooms* (pp. 125–144). Mahwah, NJ: Erlbaum.

Duke, N., Purcell-Gates, V., Hall, L., & Tower, C. (2006, December). Authentic literacy activities for developing comprehension and writing. *The Reading Teacher, 60*(4), 344–355.

Duke, N., & Roberts, K. L. (2010). The genre-specific nature of reading comprehension and the case of informational text. In D. Wase, R. Andrews, & J.Hoffman (Eds.), *The international handbook of English language and literacy teaching* (pp. 74–86). London, UK: Routledge.

Dunn, R. (1996). *How to implement and supervise a learning styles program.* Alexandria, VA: Association of Supervision and Curriculum Development.

Dunn, R., Craig, M., Fevre, L., Markus, D., Pedota, P., Sookdeo, G., Stock, J., & Terry, B. (2010). No light at the end of the tunnel vision: Steps for improving lesson plans. *The Clearing House, 85,* 194-206. Online DOI: 101080/00098650903507 460.

Dunning, S., Lueders, E., & Smith, H. (1974). *Reflections on a gift of watermelon pickle . . . And other modern verse.* New York: Scholastic.

Dupont, S. (1992). The effectiveness of creative drama as an instructional strategy to enhance reading comprehension skills. *Reading Research and Instruction, 31*(3), 41–52.

Eaton, S. E. (2012). 27 great resources on using portfolio for language learning and literacy. Online: http://drsaraheaton.wordpress.com/2011/06/10/resources-on-using-portfolios-for-language-learning/

Echevarria, J., Vogt, M. E., & Short, D. (2004). *Making content comprehensible to English learners: The SIOP model.* Boston: Allyn & Bacon.

Edelsky, C., Altwerger, B., & Flores, B. (1991). Whole language: What's new. In C. Edelsky (Ed.), *Literacy: Justice for all.* London: Falnon.

Ediger, M. (2001). Cooperative learning versus competition: Which is better? Arlington, VA. (ERIC Document Reproduction No. ED 461894).

Edwards, L. (2003). Writing instruction in kindergarten: Examining an emerging area of research for children with writing and reading difficulties. *Journal of Learning Disabilities, 36*(2), 136–148.

Elbaum, B.,Vaughn, S., Hughes, M. T., & Moody, S. W. (2000). How effective are one-to-one tutoring programs in reading for elementary students at risk for reading failure? A Meta-analysis of the Intervention Research. *Journal of Educational Psychology, 92*(4), 605–619.

Elder, L., & Paul, R. (2005). Critical thinking . . . and the art of substantive writing. *Journal of Developmental Education, 29*(1), 40–1.

Elkeles, C. (2002). Listening skills. *Articles for Educators.* Retrieved from www.articlesforeducators.com/member.asp?aid=4.

Enciso, P., Katz, L., Kiefer, B., Price-Dennis, D., & Wilson, M. (2006). Words, signs, and social relations. *Language Arts, 84*(1), 8–9.

English, K. (2010). *Nikki & Deja: The newsy news newsletter.* New York: Clarion Press.

Evans, R. (2005). Reframing the achievement gap. *Phi Delta Kappan, 86*(8), 582–589.

Fang, Z. (2012). Approaches to developing content area literacies: A synthesis and a critique. *Journal of Adolescent and Adult Literacy, 56*(2), 103–108.

Feezel, G. (2012) Robust vocabulary instruction in a readers' workshop. *The Reading Teacher, 66*(3), 233–237.

Ferriero, E., & Teberosky, A. (1983). *Writing before schooling.* Portsmouth, NH: Heinemann.

Finn, C. E. (2013). The Common Core State Standards initiative: Using Lexile measures to access college and career readiness. Retrieved from http://www.lexile.com/using-lexile/lexile-measures-and-the-ccssi/text-complexity-grade-bands-and-lexile-ranges.

Fisher, D., & Frey, N. (2012). Close reading in the elementary schools. *The Reading Teacher, 66*(3), 179–188.

Fiske, E. (Ed.). (1999). *Champions of change: The impact of the arts on learning.* Washington, DC: The Arts Education Partnership and The President's Committee on the Arts.

Flanigan, K., Templeton, S., & Hayes, L. (2012). What's in a word? Using content vocabulary to generate growth in general academic vocabulary. *Journal of Adolescent & Adult Literacy, 56*(2), 132–140.

Fleming, G. A. (Ed.). (1990). *Children's dance.* Reston, VA: American Alliance for Health, Physical Education, Recreation and Dance.

Fletcher, R. (1996). *A writer's notebook.* New York: Harper Collins.

Fletcher, R., & Portalupi, J. (2001). *Writing workshop: The essential guide.* Portsmouth, NH: Heinemann.

Fletcher, R., & Portalupi, J. (2007). *Craft lessons: Teaching writing K–8* (2nd ed.). Portland, ME: Stenhouse.

Floca, B. (2013). *Locomotive.* Illus. B. Floca. New York: Atheneun/Richard Jackson.

Flower, L., & Hayes, J. R. (1981). A cognitive process theory of writing. *College composition and communication, 32,* 365–387.

Ford, M. P. (1989/1990). Maximizing literacy opportunities through cross-age groupings. *Reading Today, 7*(3), 14.

Forehand, M. (2005). *From emerging perspective on learning, teaching and technology.* Online: http://epltt.coe.uga.edu/index.php?title=Bloom%27s_Taxonomy.

Fountas, I. C., & Pinnell, G. S. (1996). *Guided Reading.* Portsmouth, NH: Heinemann.

Fountas, I. C. & Pinnell, G. S. (2000). *Guiding Readers and writers (Grades 3–6): Teaching comprehension, genres, and content literacy.* Portsmouth, NH: Heinemann.

Frasier, D. (2007). *Miss Alaineus: A vocabulary disaster*. New York: Sandpiper.

Freshour, F., & Bartholomew, P. (1989). Let's start improving our own listening. *Florida Reading Quarterly, 25*(4), 28–30.

Friend, M., & Bursuck, W. (2009). *Including students with special needs: A practical guide for classroom teachers* (6th ed.). New York: Pearson.

Fry, E. (1977). Fry's readability graph: Clarifications, validity, and extensions to level 17. *Journal of Reading, 21*(93), 242–252.

Galda, L., & Cullinan, B. E. (2002). *Literature and the child* (5th ed.). Belmont, CA: Wadsworth/Thompson Learning.

Gambrell, L. (1983). The occurrence of think-time during reading comprehension instruction. *Journal of Educational Research, 77*(3), 77–80.

Garan, E., & DeVoogd, D. (2008). The benefits of sustained silent reading: Scientific research and common sense converge. *The Reading Teacher, 62*(4), 336–344.

Garcia, M., & Verville, K. (1994). Redesigning teaching and learning: The Arizona student assessment program. In S. Valencia, E. Hiebert, & P. Afflerbach (Eds.), *Authentic reading assessment: Practices and possibilities*. Newark, DE: International Reading Association.

Gardiner, J. (1980). *Stone Fox*. New York: Crowell Junior.

Gardner, H. (1983). *Frames of mind: The theory of multiple intelligences*. London: Paladin Books.

Gee, J. (1990). *Social linguistics and literacies: Ideology in discourses*. London: Falmer.

Gee, J. (2001). Seminar presented at the Centre for Expansion of Language and Thinking (CELT): Rejuvenation Conference. Chicago, IL. In B. Cambourne (2002), The conditions of learning: Is learning natural? *The Reading Teacher, 55*(8), 758–762.

Genesee, F., Lindholm-Leary, K., Saunders, B., & Christian, D. (2006). *Educating English language learners.* Cambridge, MA: Cambridge University Press.

Giangreco, M. (2007). Extending inclusive opportunities. *Educational Leadership, 64*(5), 34–38.

Gibbons, G. (1993). *Frog*. Illus. by G. Gibbons. New York: Holiday House.

Gonzalez, D. (2000). Story grammar and oral fluency. *Journal of the Imagination in Language Learning and Teaching, 5*. Retrieved from www.njcu.edu/cill/vol5/gonzalez.html.

Goodman, K. S. (1967). *On reading*. Portsmouth, NH: Heinemann.

Goodman, K. S. (1976). Behind the eye: What happens in reading. In H. Singer & R. Ruddell (Eds.), *Theoretical models and processes of reading* (2nd ed.). Newark, DE: International Reading Association.

Goodman, K. S. (1986b). *What's whole in whole language?* Portsmouth, NH: Heinemann.

Goodman, K. S. (1996). *Ken Goodman on reading: A common-sense look at the nature of language and the science of reading*. Portsmouth, NH: Heinemann.

Goodman, K. S., Bird, L. B., & Goodman, Y. M. (Eds.). (1992). *The whole language catalog: Supplement on authentic assessment*. Santa Rosa, CA: American School Publisher.

Goodman, K. S., & Goodman, Y. (1989). A kidwatcher's guide to spelling. In K. Goodman, Y. Goodman, & W. Hood (Eds.), *The whole language evaluation book*. Portsmouth, NH: Heinemann.

Goodman, Y. M. (1978). Kidwatching: An alternative to testing. *The National Elementary Principal, 57*(2), 41–45.

Goodman, Y. M. (1989). Roots of the whole-language movement. *The Elementary School Journal, 90*(2), 113–127.

Goodwin, A., Lipsky, M., & Ahn, S. (2012). Word detectives: Using units of meaning to support literacy. *The Reading Teacher 65*(7), 461–470.

Gough, P. B. (1972). One second of reading. In J. F. Kavanagh & I. G. Mattingly (Eds.), *Language by ear and by eye: The relationships between speech and reading* (pp. 331–358). Cambridge, MA: MIT Press.

Gourgey, A., Bousseau, J., & Delgado, J. (1985). The impact of an improvisational dramatics program on student attitudes and achievement. *Children's Theater Review, 34*(3), 9–14.

Graham, S. (1999). Handwriting and spelling instruction for students with learning disabilities: A review. *Learning Disabilities Quarterly, 22*, 78–98.

Graves, D. (1994). *A fresh look at writing*. Portsmouth, NH: Heinemann.

Graves, M. F. & Watts-Taffe, S. (2008). For the love of words: Fostering word consciousness in young readers. *The Reading Teacher, 62*(3), 184–193.

Gravett, E. (2007). *Little mouse's big book of fears*. Illus E. Gravett. New York: Simon & Schuster Books for Young Readers.

Gregory, A., & Cahill, M. A. (2010). Kindergartners can do it too! Comprehension strategies for early readers. *The Reading Teacher, 63*(6), 515–520.

Grisham, D., and Wolsey, T. (2006, May). Recentering the middle school classroom as a vibrant learning community: Students, literacy and technology intersect. *Journal of Adolescent and Adult Literacy, 49*(8), 648–660.

Gruenert, S. (2000). Shaping a new school culture. *Contemporary Education, 71*(2), 14–18.

Guccione, L. (2011). Integrating literacy and inquiry for English Learners. *The Reading Teacher, 64*(8), 567–577.

Guccione, L. (2011, May). Integrating literacy and inquiry for English learners. *The Reading Teacher, 64*(8), 567–577.

Guernsey, L. (2011, June 1). Are e-books any good? Retrieved from www.slj.com/2011/06/books-media/ebooks/are-ebooks-any-good/.

Gwynne, F. (1988a) *A chocolate moose for dinner*. Illus. F. Gwynne. New York: Aladdin.

Gwynne, F. (1988b) *The king who rained*. Illus. F. Gwynne. New York: Aladdin.

Gwynne, F. (1998) *A little pigeon toad*. Illus. F. Gwynne. New York: Aladdin.

Hagood, T. (2006). Values and voice in dance education: The merit of fostering tradition, experiment, diversity, and change in our pedagogy. *Art Education Policy Review, 108*(2), 33-37.

Hammerberg, D. (2001). Reading and writing "hypertextually": Children's literature, technology and early writing instruction. *Language Arts, 78*(3), 207–216.

Hand, B., Wallace, C. W., & Yang, E. (2004). Using a science writing heuristic to enhance learning outcomes from laboratory activities in seventh-grade science: Quantitative and qualitative aspects. *International Journal of Science Education, 26*, 131–149.

Haroutunian-Gordon, S. (2011). Plato's philosophy of listening. *Educational Theory, 61*(2), 125–139.

Harste, J. (2003). What do we mean by literacy? *Voices in the Middle, 10*(3), 8–12.

Haskins, J. (1995). *The day Fort Sumter was fired on: A photo history of the Civil War*. New York: Scholastic.

Hauerwas, L. B., & Walker, J. (2003). Spelling of inflected verb morphology in children with spelling deficits. *Learning Disabilities Research and Practice, 18*, 25–35.

Hawkins, L., & Razali, A. B. (2012, May). A tale of 3 Ps—Penmanship, product and process: 100 years of elementary writing instruction. *Language Arts, 89*(5), 305–317.

Heard, G. (1989). *For the good of the earth and sun: Teaching poetry*. Portsmouth, NH: Heinemann.

Heathcote, D., & Bolton, G. (1995). *Drama for learning: Dorothy Heathcote's mantle of the expert approach to education*. Portsmouth, NH: Heinemann.

Helman, L. (2005, April). Using literacy assessment results to improve teaching for English language learners. *The Reading Teacher, 58*(7), 668–677.

Henkes, K. (1987). *Sheila Rae, the brave*. Illus. K. Henkes. New York: Puffin Books.

Henry, L. (2006, April). Searching for an answer: The critical role of new literacies while reading on the Internet. *The Reading Teacher, 59*(7) 614–627.

Hesse, K. (1997). *Out of the dust*. New York: Scholastic.

Hesse, K. (1999). *Come on, Rain!* Illus. J. J. Murth. New York: Scholastic.

Hickox, R. (1999). *The golden sandal: A Middle Eastern Cinderella*. Illus. W. Hillenbrand. New York: Holiday House.

Hiebert, E. (2002). Standards, assessment an text difficulty. In A.E. Farstrup & S. J. Samuels (Eds.), *What research says about reading instruction* (pp. 337–369). Newark, DE: International Reading Association.

Higgins, B., Miller, M., & Wegmann, S. (2006). Teaching to the test . . . not! Balancing best practices and testing requirements in writing. *The Reading Teacher, 60*, 310–319.

Hinson, B. (Ed.) (2000). *New directions in reading instruction revised*. Newark, DE: International Reading Association.

Ho, B. (2002). Application of participatory action research to family school intervention. *School Psychology Review, 31*(1), 106–122.

Hodge, T., & Downie, J. (2004). Together we are heard: Effectiveness of daily language groups in a community of preschool. *Nursing and Health Science, 6*, 101–107.

Hodges, R. (1991). The conventions of writing. In J. Flood, J. M. Jensen, D. Lapp, & J. R. Squire (Eds.), *Handbook of research on teaching the English language arts*. New York: Macmillan.

Hoffman, J., & Roser, N. (2012, May). Reading and writing the world using beautiful books: Language experience re-envisioned. *Language Arts, 89*(5), 293–304.

Holdaway, D. (1991). Shared book experience: Teaching reading using favorite books. In C. Kamii, E. Ferreiro, F. Siegrist, H. Sinclair, B. Cuttings, J. Milligan, et al. (Eds.), *Early literacy: A constructivist foundation for whole language*. Washington, DC: National Education Association.

Holder, M. K. (2012). Teaching left-handers to write. Handedness Research Institute. Retrieved from http://handedness.org/action/leftwrite.html.

Holdren, T. S. (2012). Using art to assess reading comprehension and critical thinking in adolescents. *Journal of Adolescent and Adult Literacy, 55*(8), 692–703.

Hollenbeck, A., & Saterus, K. (2013). Mind the comprehension iceberg and avoiding *Titanic* mistakes with the Common Core State Standards. *The Reading Teacher, 66*(7), 558–568.

Hoose, P. (2012). *Moonbird: A year on the wind with the great survivor B95*. New York: Farrar.

Hope, S. (2003, Summer). Questions and challenges concerning music's role in education. *Journal for Learning Through Music, 2*.

Hopkins, L. B. (Ed.). (2010). *Amazing faces*. Illus. C. Soentpiet. New York: Lee & Low.

Horning, K., Febri, C., Lindgren, M., & Schliesman, M. (2012). 50 multicultural books every child should know. Retrieved from http://ccbc.education.wisc.edu/books/detailListBooks.asp?idBookLists=42.

Hughes, C. (2012). *Tigers*. National Geographic.

Huitt, W., & Hummel, J. (2003). *Piaget's theory of cognitive development*. Valdosta, GA: Valdosta State University.

Hur, J. W., & Suh, S. (2012). Making learning active with interactive. *Computers in the Schools, 29*(4), 320–338.

Hurst, B., Scales, K., Frecks, E., & Lewis, K. (2011). Sign up for reading: Students read aloud to class. *The Reading Teacher, 64*(6), 439–443.

Hutchison, A., Beschorner, B., & Schmidt-Crawford, D. (2012). Exploring the use of the iPad for literacy learning. *The Reading Teacher, 66*(1), 15–23.

IDEA (2004). U.S. Department of Education. Retrieved from http://idea.ed.gov/explore/home.

Imig, D. (2014, May 7). More books at home linked to higher reading scores. Retrieved from www.urbanchildinstitute.org/articles/updates/.

International Reading Association & National Council of Teachers of English (1996). *Standards for the English language arts.* Newark, DE, and Urbana, IL: Authors.

International Reading Association (2002). *Family–school partnerships: Essential elements of literacy instruction in the United States.* Newark, DE: Author.

Jalongo, M. R. (2000). *Early childhood language arts* (2nd ed.). Boston: Allyn & Bacon.

Jay, D. (1991). Effects of a dance program on the creativity of preschool handicapped children. *Adapted Physical Activity Quarterly, 8,* 305–316.

Jensen, E. (2000). *Music with the brain in mind.* San Diego, CA: Brain Store.

Jensen, E. (2001). *Arts with the brain in mind.* Alexandria, VA: Association for Supervision and Curriculum.

Jensen, J. M., & Roser, N. L. (1990). Are there really 3 R's? *Educational Leadership, 47*(6), 7–12.

Johnson, D. D., & Pearson, P. D. (1984). *Teaching reading vocabulary* (2nd ed.). New York: Holt, Rinehart & Winston.

Jones, N., Johnson, C., Schwartz, R., and Zalud, G. (2005, Spring). Two positive outcomes of Reading Recovery: Exploring the interface between Reading Recovery and Special Education. *The Journal of Reading Recovery, 4*(3), 19–34.

Jordan, G. E., Snow, C. E., & Porche, M. V. (2000). The effects of a family literacy project on kindergarten students' early literacy skills. *Reading Research Quarterly, 35*(4), 524–546.

Kalmar, K. (2008). Let's give children something to talk about. *Young Children, 63*(1), 88–92.

Kane, S. (2007, Sept.). Does the Imposter Strategy pass the authenticity test? *Journal of Adolescent & Adult Literacy, 51*(1), 58–64.

Kantrowitz, B., & Scelfo, J. (2006, November 27). What happens when they grow up. *Newsweek,* 47–53.

Karchmer, R. (2001). The journey ahead: Thirteen teachers report how the Internet influences literacy and literacy instruction in their K–12 classrooms. *Reading Research Quarterly, 36*(4), 442–466.

Kaufman, D., Moss, D. M., & Osborn, T. A. (Eds.) (2003). *Beyond the boundaries: A transdisciplinary approach to learning and teaching.* Westport, CT: Praeger.

Keene, E. & Zimmerman, S. (1997). *Mosaic of thought.* Portsmouth, NH: Heinemann.

Kimmel, E. (1995). *Anansi and the talking melon.* Illus. J. Stevens. New York: Holiday House.

Kippelen, V. (2002, March). *The halls are alive.* Retrieved from http://connectforkids.org.

Kirszner, L., & Mandell, S. (2012). *The brief Wadsworth handbook* (7th ed.). Farmington Hills, MI: Wadsworth.

Kluth, P., & Darmody-Lathan, J. (2003). Beyond sight words: Literacy opportunities for students with autism. *The Reading Teacher, 56*(6), 532–534.

Knipper, K., & Duggan, T. (2006). Writing to learn across the curriculum: Tools for comprehension in content area classrooms. *The Reading Teacher, 59,* 462–470.

Kong, A., & Fitch, E. (2002/2003). Using book club to engage culturally and linguistically diverse learners in reading, writing, and talking. *The Reading Teacher, 56*(4), 352–362.

Krashen, S. (1991). Bilingual education: A focus on current research. In *National Clearinghouse for Bilingual Education,* Vol. 3. Washington, DC.

Krashen, S. (2005). Is in-school free reading for children? Why the National Reading Panel Report is (still) wrong. *Phi Delta Kappan, 86*(6), 444–451.

Kroll, S. (2001). *Patches lost and found.* New York: Winslow Press.

Kumaravadivelu, B. (2003). *Beyond methods: Macrostrategies for language learning.* New Haven, CT: Yale University Press.

Labadie, M., Mosley-Wetzel, M., & Roger, R. (2012). Opening spaces for critical literacy. *The Reading Teacher, 66*(2), 117–127.

Lally, J. R. (2010, Nov.). School readiness begins in infancy. *Phi Delta Kappan, 92*(3), 17–21.

Langdon, T. (2004). DIBELS: A teacher-friendly basic literacy accountability tool for the primary classroom. *Teaching Exceptional Children, 37*(2), 54–58.

Lansky, B. (2000). *If pigs could fly . . . and other deep thoughts.* Illus. by S. Carpenter. New York: Meadowbrook.

Larrick, N. (1965, Sept. 11). The all-white world of children's books. *Saturday Review, 48,* 63–65, 84–85.

Larson, K. (2013). Hattie ever after. New York: Delacorte Press.

Laughlin, M., & Latrobe, K. (1990). *Reader's theatre for children: Scripts and script development.* Englewood, CO: Litran's Unlimited.

Leu, D. J., & Kinzer, C. (2003). *Effective literacy instruction: Implementing best practice* (5th ed.). Upper Saddle River, NJ: Merrill/Prentice Hall.

Lewis, S., Simon, C., Uzzell, R., Horowitz, A., and Casserly, M. (2010). A call for change: The social and educational factors contributing to the outcomes of black males in urban schools. Washington, DC: Council of the Great City Schools.

Linn, M. (2001, Dec.). An American educator reflects on the meaning of the Reggio experience. *Phi Delta Kappan, 83*(4), 332–340.

Long, R. (2010). Common Core Standards released. *Reading Today, 27*(6), 26.

Longo, P. (1999, November 8). *Distributed knowledge in the brain: Using visual thinking networking to improve students' learning.* Boston: Learning and the Brain Conference.

Loy, D. (2004). English language learners, classroom drama. *The Quarterly, 26*(1).

Lushington, K. (2003, December). Lighting the fire of imagination through theatre and drama in Ontario schools. Retrieved from www.code.on/pages/dramaarticle.html.

Macaulay, D. & Keenan, S. (2012). Castle: How it works. New York: Roaring Books.

MacDonald, S. (2012). *Environmental Print.* Retrieved from http://sharonmacdonald.com/environmental-print.aspx.

MacMahon, S., Rose, D., & Parks, M. (2003). Basic reading through dance programs: The impact on first-grade students' basic reading skills. *Education Review, 27*, 104–125.

Make It Happen (2000). The I-Search Unit. Education Development Center. Retrieved from www2.edc.org/fsc/mih/i-search.html.

Manning, M., Manning, G., & Long, R. (1994). *Theme immersion inquiry-based curriculum in elementary and middle schools.* Portsmouth, NH: Heinemann.

Manzo, A. V. (1968). *Improving reading comprehension through reciprocal questioning.* Unpublished doctoral dissertation, Syracuse University, NY.

Manzo, A. V. (1969). The ReQuest procedure. *Journal of Reading, 13*(3), 123–126.

Manzo, U. C., Manzo, A. V., & Thomas, M. M. (2009). *Content area literacy: A framework for reading-based instruction* (5th ed.). New York: John Wiley & Sons.

Marrin, A. (2009). *Years of Dust: The story of the Dust Bowl.* New York: Scholastic.

Marschark, M., & Hauser, P. C. (2012). *How Deaf children learn.* New York: Oxford University Press.

Marshall, J. (1988). *Goldilocks and the Three Bears.* Illus. J. Marshall. Dial Books for Young Readers.

Marshall, J. (1990). *Hansel and Gretel.* Illus. J. Marshall Puffin Books.

Matson, S. (2012). Read, flip, write. *Journal of Adolescent and Adult Literacy, 56*(2), 109.

McCaslin, N. (1996). *Creative drama in the classroom* (6th ed.). New York: Longman.

McDermott, P. (2003). *Using the visual arts for learning: The case of one urban charter school.* Paper presented at the 15th Annual Ethnographic and Qualitative Research in Education Conference. Pittsburgh, PA: Duquesne University.

McGee, L., & Richgels, D. J. (1985). Teaching expository text structure to elementary students. *The Reading Teacher, 38*(8), 739–748.

McKeown, R., and Gentilucci, J. (2007, Oct.). Think-aloud strategy: Metacognitive development and monitoring comprehension in the middle school second-language classroom. *Journal of Adolescent & Adult Literacy, 51*(2), 136–147.

McLaughlin, M. (2012). Reading comprehension and what every teacher needs to know. *The Reading Teacher, 65*(7), 432–440.

McLaughlin, M., & Allen, M. B. (2009). *Guided reading in grades 3–8* (2nd ed.). Newark, DE: International Reading Association.

McPherson, K. (2008). Listening carefully. *Teacher Librarian, 35*(4), 73–75.

McVee, M. A., Dunsmore, K., & Gavelek, J. (2013). Schema theory revisited. In D. Alvermann, N. Unrau, & R. B. Ruddell (Eds.), *Theoretical models and processes of reading* (pp. 489–524). Newark, DE: International Reading Association.

Medina, A. (2006). The parallel bar: Writing assessment and instruction. In J. S. Schumm (Ed.), *Reading Assessment and Instruction.* New York: Guilford Press.

Medwell, J. & Wray, P. (2008). Handwriting—A forgotten language skill. *Language and Education, 22*(1), 34–47.

Meinbach, A. M., Rothlein, L., & Fredricks, A. (2000). *The complete guide to thematic units: Creating the integrated curriculum* (2nd ed.). Norwood, MA: Christopher-Gordon.

Mellon, J. (1969). *Transformational sentence combining: Method of enhancing the development of syntactic fluency in English composition* (Research Report No. 10). Urbana, IL: National Council of Teachers of English.

Mesmer, E., & Mesmer, H. A. (2009). Response to intervention (RTI): What teachers of reading need to know. *The Reading Teacher, 62*(4), 280–290.

Micklos, J. (2011 Oct./Nov.). Celebrate I Love to Write Day. *Reading Today, 29*(2), 14–15.

Miller, W. H. (2000). *Strategies for developing emergent literacy.* Boston: McGraw-Hill.

Mitton, T. (2014). *Super Submarines: Amazing Machines.* New York: Kingfisher.

Mohr, K. (2004). English as an accelerated language: A call to action for reading teachers. *The Reading Teacher, 58*(1), 18–26.

Monahan, J., & Hinson, B. (Eds.). (1988). *New directions in reading instruction.* Newark, DE: International Reading Association.

Moore, D. W., & Moore, S. A. (1986). Possible sentences. In E. K. Dishner, T. W. Bean, J. E. Readence, & D. W. Moore (Eds.), *Reading in the content areas* (2nd ed.).Dubuque, IA: Kendall/Hunt.

Morgan, B. (2002). Critical practice in community-based ESL programs. *Journal of Language, Identity and Education, 1*, 141–162.

Morgan, B. (2004). Modals and memories: A grammar lesson on the Quebec referendum on sovereignty. In B. Norton & K. Toohey (Eds.), *Critical ESL Pedagogies.* Cambridge, MA: Cambridge University Press.

Morgan, S. (2006). *Owls.* Laguna Hills, CA: QEB Publishing.

Mundi, S. (1989). Rent-a-reader. *Learning, 17*(5), 70.

Myers, A. (2003). *Flying blind.* New York: Walker & Company.

Myers, A. (2004). *Tulsa burning.* New York: Walker Childrens.

Myers, W. D. (1999). *Monster.* New York: HarperCollins Publishers.

Myers, W. D. (2014). *Darius and Twig.* New York: Amistad.

Nagy, W. E., & Scott, J. A. (2013). Vocabulary processes. In D. Alvermann, N. Unrau, & R. Ruddell (Eds.), *Theoretical models and processes of reading* (pp. 458–475). Newark, DE: International Reading Association.

National Association of Gifted Children (2003) found at their website under nagc.org/index.

National Center for Education Statistics (2014). The condition of education 2014. Online: http://nces.ed.gov/pubsearch/pubsinfo.asp?pubid=2014083

National Center for Education Statistics (2010, July). Status and trends in the education of racial and ethnic groups: Highlights. Retrieved from http://nces.ed.gov/pubs2010/2010015/.

National Dissemination Center for Children with Disabilities (2012). Categories of disability under IDEA. Retrieved from http://NICHCY.org.

National Dissemination Center for Children with Disabilities (2010). Autism. Retrieved from http://www.ldonline.org/article/Autism.

National Governors Association Center for Best Practices, & Council of Chief State School Officers (2010). Common Core State Standards for English Language Arts and Literacy in History/Social Studies, Science, and Technical Subjects. Washington, DC: Author. Retrieved from http://www.corestandards.org/the-standards.

National Information Center for Children and Youth with Disabilities (2000). *General information about learning disabilities.* Retrieved from www.kidsource.com/NICHCY/learning_disabilities.html.

Nations, S. (2006). *More primary literacy centers: Making reading and writing stick.* Maupin House.

Nauman, A., Sterling, T., & Borthwich, A. (2011, Feb.). What makes writing good? An essential question for teachers. *The Reading Teacher, 64*(5), 318–328.

New York Public Library (2002, August). Author chat with Christopher Paul Curtis. Retrieved from http://www.nypl.org/author-chat-christopher-paul-curtis.

Newlands, M. (2011, April). Intentional spelling: Seven steps to eliminate guessing. *The Reading Teacher, 64*(7), 531–534.

Nilsson, N. (2005, March). How does Hispanic portrayal in children's books measure up after 40 years? *The Reading Teacher, 58*(6), 534–548.

Norris, E., Richard, C., & Mokhtari, K. (1997). The influence of drawing on third graders' writing performance. *Reading Horizons 38*(1), 13–30.

Northwest Regional Education Laboratory (1998/1999). 6 + 1 Traits Writing Assessment and Instruction. Retrieved fromhttp://educationnorthwest.org.

Noyce Foundation (2014). Planning for mini-lessons. Retrieved from http://www.noycefdn.org/documents/ecrw/profdev/InductionDay1/I1-05_Arch-Mini-lesson.pdf.

O'Neil K. E. (2011). Reading pictures: Developing visual literacy for greater comprehension. *The Reading Teacher, 65*(3), 214–223.

Olsen, J., & Knapton, E. (2012). *Stepping into handwriting.* Gaithersburg, MD: Handwriting without Tears.

Pacheco, M. B., & Goodwin, A. (2013). Putting two and two together: Middles school students' morphological problem-solving strategies for unknown words. *Journal of Adolescent and Adult Literacy 56*(7), 541–553.

Palincsar, A. S., & Brown, A. L. (1986). Interactive teaching to promote independent learning from text. *The Reading Teacher, 39*(8), 771–777.

Palmer, B., Shackelford, V., Miller, S., and Leclere, J. (2007, Jan.). *Journal of Adolescent & Adult Literacy, 50*(4), 258–267.

Palmer, E. (2011). *Well spoken: Teaching speaking to all students.* Portland, ME: Stenhouse.

Palmer, R. G., & Stewart, R. (2003). Non-fiction trade book use in the primary grades. *The Reading Teacher, 57*(1), 38-48.

Park, K. & Amen, H. (2012). Bats. National Geographic.

Parr, M., & Campbell, T. (2006). Poets in practice. *The Reading Teacher, 60,* 38–46.

Parsons, S., Mokhtari, K., Yellin, D., and Orwig, R. (2011, May). Literature study groups: Literacy learning "with legs." *Middle School Journal, 42*(5), 22–30.

Paugh, P., Carey, J., King-Jackson, V., & Russell, S. (2007, Sept.). Negotiating the literacy block: Constructing spaces for critical literacy in a high stakes setting. *Language Arts, 85*(1), 31–41.

Paulsen, G. (1994). *Haymeadow.* New York: Yearling.

Paulsen, G. (1999). *Hatchet.* New York: Delacote Books.

Pearman, C. J. (2008). Independent reading of CD-ROM storybooks. Measuring comprehension with oral retellings. *The Reading Teacher, 61*(8) 594–602.

Pearson, P. D., & Fielding, L. (1982). Research update: Listening comprehension. *Language Arts, 59*(6), 617–629.

Pearson, P. D., & Johnson, D. D. (1985). *Teaching reading comprehension.* New York: Holt, Rinehart & Winston.

Petress, K. (2000). Listening: A vital skill. *Journal of Instructional Psychology, 26*(4), 261–262.

Piaget, J. (1952). *The origin of intelligence in children.* New York: International Universities Press.

Piaget, J. (1959). *The language and thought of the child* (A. Gabain, Trans.). London: Routledge & Kegan Paul.

Piaget, J. (1964). *The psychology of intelligence.* Boston: Routledge and Kegan Paul.

Piaget, J. (1965). *The language and thought of the child.* New York: Meridian Books.

Piaget, J. (1967). Language and thought from the genetic point of view. In D. Elkind (Ed.), *Six psychological studies* (A. Tenzer, Trans.). New York: Random House.

Pinkney, A. D. (2011). *Bird in a box.* New York: Little, Brown and Co.

Pinkney, J. (2009). *The lion and the mouse.* New York: Little, Brown.

Plumley, K. (2010). How to improve spelling skills. Retrieved from www.connectionsacademy.com/Oklahoma.

Polacco, P. (1987). *Meteor!* Illus. P. Polacco. New York: Philomel.

Polacco, P. (2000). *The Butterfly.* Illus. P. Polacco. New York: Philomel Books.

Polacco, P. (2009). *January's Sparrow.* New York: Philomel Books.

Pransky, K., & Bailey, F. (2002/2003). To meet your students where they are, first you have to find them: Working with culturally and linguistically diverse at-risk students. *The Reading Teacher, 56*(4), 370–383.

Prelutsky, J. (2010). *The carnival of the animals.* Illus. M. GrandPre. New York: Knopf.

Raphael, T. (1982). Teaching questioning–answer strategies for children. *The Reading Teacher, 36*(2), 186–191.

Rasinski, T., & Padak, N. (2000). *Effective reading strategies: Teaching children who find reading difficult.* Upper Saddle River, NJ: Merrill.

Ray, K. (2006). Exploring inquiry as teaching stance in the writing workshop. *Language Arts, 83,* 238–247.

Readence, J., Bean, T. & Scott, B. (2012).*Content area literacy: An integrated approach* (10th ed.). Dubuque, IA: Kendall Hunt.

Reading Rockets (2012). Story maps. Retrieved from http://www.readingrockets.org/strategies/story_maps.

Regan, K. S. (2003, Nov.–Dec.). Using dialogue journals in the classroom. *Teaching Exceptional Children, 36*(2), 36–41.

Register, D. (2004, Spring). The effects of live music, groups versus an educational children's television program on the emergent literacy of young children. *Journal of Music Therapy, 41*(1), 2–27.

Reis, S., & Renzulli, J. (2009). Myth 1: The gifted and talented constitute a single homogeneous group. *Gifted Child Quarterly, 53,* 233–239.

Renzulli, J. (2011, May). More changes needed to expand gifted identification and support. *Phi Delta Kappan, 92*(8), 61.

Reutzel, D. R., & Mitchell, J. (2005). High stakes accountability themed issue: How did we get here from there? *The Reading Teacher, 58*(7), 606–608.

Reynolds, P. (2003) *The dot.* New York: Candlewick.

Richardson, J. (2011, Feb.). Hunting for a drop-out solution. *Phi Delta Kappan, 92*(5), 4.

Richardson, J., Morgan, R., & Fleener, C. (2011). *Reading to learn in the content areas* (8th ed.).Belmont, CA: Wadsworth Cengage Learning.

Ries, L. (2010). *Aggie the brave.* Illus. F. W. Dormer. New York: Charlesbridge.

Riesman, D. (1961). *The lonely crowd.* New Haven, CT: Yale University Press.

Rigby Publishing (2006). *The International Space Station.* Boston: Author.

Rivera, D. (2012). Revising (or re-seeing) your essay. *Tutoring the Whole Writer.* Retrieved from http://tutoringthewholewriter.com/2012/11/14/revising/.

Robinson, S. (2014). Illus. A. Ford. *Under the same sun.* New York: Scholastic.

Roe, B., Smith, S., & Burns, P. (2005). *Teaching reading in today's elementary school* (9th ed.). Boston: Houghton Mifflin.

Rosenblatt, L. M. (1994). *The reader, the text, the poem: The transactional theory of the literary work.* Carbondale: Southern Illinois University Press.

Rosenblatt, L. M. (2004). The transactional theory of reading and writing. In R. B. Ruddell & N. J. Unrau (Eds.), *Theoretical models and processes of reading* (5th ed.). Newark, DE: International Reading Association.

Rosenblatt, L. M. (2013). The transactional theory of reading and writing. In D. E. Alvermann, N. J. Unrau, & R. B. Ruddell (Eds.), *Theoretical models and processes of reading* (6th ed., pp. 923–956). Newark, DE: The International Reading Association.

Roskos, K., & Brueck, J. (2009). The e-book as a learning object. In A. G. Bus & S. B. Neuman (Eds.), *Multimedia and literacy development: Improving achievement for young learners* (pp. 77–88). New York: Routledge.

Roskos, K., Brueck, J., & Widman, S. (2009). Investigating analytic tools for e-book design in early literacy learning. *Journal of Interactive Online Learning, 8*(3), 218–240.

Roskos, K., Tabors, P., & Lenhart, L. (2009). *Oral language and early literacy in preschool: Talking, reading, and writing* (2nd ed.). Newark, DE: International Reading Association.

Ross, R. (1996). *Storyteller.* Little Rock, AR: August House Publishers.

Rouse, H. L., & Fantuzzo, J. W. (2006). Validity of the dynamic indicators of basic early literacy skills as an indicator of early literacy for kindergarten children. *The School Psychology Review, 35*(3), 341–355.

Roy, R. (1998). *A to Z mysteries: The empty envelope.* New York: Random House.

Ruddell, R. B., & Unrau, N. J. (2013). Reading as a motivated meaning-construction process: The reader, the text, and the teacher. In D. E. Albermann, N. J. Unrau, & R. B. Ruddell (Eds.), *Theoretical models and processes of reading* (pp. 957–977). Newark, DE: International Reading Association.

Rumelhart, D. L. (1980). Schemata: The building blocks of cognition. In R. Spiro, B. Bruce, & W. Brewer (Eds.), *Theoretical issues in reading comprehension.* Hillsdale, NJ: Erlbaum.

Saddler, B. (2005). Sentence combining: A sentence-level writing intervention. *The Reading Teacher, 58,* 468–471.

Salley, C. (2002). *Epossumondas.* Illus. J.Stevens. Orlando, FL: Harcourt.

Salley, C. (2004). *Why Epossumondas has no hair on his tail.* Illus. by J. Stevens. Orlando, FL: Harcourt.

Salley, C. (2006). *Epossumondas saves the day.* Illus. by J. Stevens. Orlando, FL: Harcourt.

Salley, C. (2009). *Epossumondas plays possum.* Illus. by J. Stevens. Orlando, FL: Harcourt.

Saltzberg, B. (2010) *Beautiful oops!* New York: Workman.

Sarafino, E., & Armstrong, J. (1986). *Child and adolescent development* (2nd ed.). St. Paul, MN: West Publishing Co.

Satrapi, M. (2007). *The complete Persepolis.* New York: Knopf.

Satterfield, K. H. (2005). Benjamin Franklin: A man of many talents. New York: HarperCollins.

Schneider, J. (2005, October). Teaching grammar through community issues. *ELT Journal, 59*(4), 298–305.

Schroeder, A. (1997). *Smokey Mountain Rose: An Appalachian Cinderella.* Illus. B. Sneed. Dial Books for Young Readers.

Schugar, H. R., Smith, C., & Schugar, J. T. (2013). Teaching with interactive picture e-books in grades K–6. *The Reading Teacher, 66*(8), 615–624.

Schulman, M. B. & Payne, C.D. (2000). *Guided reading: Making it work.* New York: Scholastic.

Schuster, E. (2004). National and state writing tests: The writing process betrayed. *Phi Delta Kappan, 85*(5), 375–378.

Scripp, L. (2003). Critical link, next steps: An evolving conception of music and learning in public school education. *Journal of Learning Through Music, 2,* 119–140.

Searfoss, L., Readence, J., & Mallette, M. (2001). *Helping children learn to read* (4th ed.). Boston: Allyn & Bacon.

SEE Center (2014). Retrieved from http://seecenter.org.

Seely, A. (1995). *Integrated thematic units.* Westminster, CA: Teacher Created Materials.

Segal, J., & Smith, M. (2012). ADD/ADHD and School. *Harvard Health Publications.* Harvard Medical School. Online: http://www.helpguide.org/articles/add-adhd/adult-adhd-attention-deficit-disorder-treatment.htm.

Seidel, S. (1998). Wondering to be done: The collaborative assessment and conference. In D. Allen (Ed.), *Assessing student learning: From grading to understanding* (pp. 21–39). New York: Teachers College Press.

Shanahan, T. (2011, August). Common Core Standards: Are we going to lower the fences or teach kids to climb? *Reading Today, 29*(1), 20–21.

Shanahan, T., & Shanahan, S. (1997). Character perspective charting: Helping children to develop a more complete conception of story. *The Reading Teacher, 50*(8), 668–677.

Sheldon, S. (2002). Parents' social networks and beliefs as predictors of parent involvement. *The Elementary School Journal, 102*(4), 301–316.

Short, K., Kauffman, G., & Kahn, L. (2000). "I just need to draw": Responding to literature across multiple sign systems. *The Reading Teacher, 54*(2), 160–173.

Sidman, J. (2009). *Red sings from treetops: A year in color.* Illus. by P. Zagarenski. Boston: Houghton Mifflin Harcourt.

Siegel, M. (2006). Rereading the signs: Multimodal transformations in the field of literacy education. *Language Arts, 84*(1), 65–77.

Sigmon, C. M. (1997). *Implementing the 4-Blocks Literacy Model.* Greensboro, NC: Carson-Dellosa.

Sigmon, C. M. (2001). *Modifying the Four-Blocks for upper grades: Matching strategies to students' needs.* Greensboro, NC: Carson-Dellosa.

Simonsen, F., & Gunter, L. (2001). Best practices in spelling instruction: A research summary. *Journal of Direct Instruction, 1*(2), 97–105.

Sinatra, R. (1991). Integrating whole language with the learning of text structure. *Journal of Reading, 34*(6), 424–433.

Slavin, R. (1996). Neverstreaming: Preventing learning disabilities. *Educational Leadership, 53*(5), 4–7.

Smith, D., Stenner, A.J., Horabin, J., & Smith, M. (1989). *The Lexile scale in theory and practice: Final report.* Washington, DC: Metametrics. (ERIC Document Reproduction Service No. ED 307577.)

Smith, F. (1997). *Reading without nonsense* (3rd ed.). New York: Teacher's College Press.

Smith, M. (2002). *The effects of rhyme–rime connection training on second grade reading performance.* Unpublished doctoral dissertation. Stillwater: Oklahoma State University.

Smith, S. (2003, April 2) Why not dance? *Chicago Tribune,* p. 2.

Snowball, D. (2006). Spelling strategies make smart use of sounds and spelling patterns. *Instructor Magazine, 24*(7), 12–14.

Spandel, V. (2008). *Creating young writers: Using the six traits to enrich writing process in primary classrooms* (2nd ed.). Boston: Pearson, Allyn & Bacon.

Spandel, V. (2012). *Creating Writers: 6 Traits, Process, Workshop, and Literature* (6th ed.). New York: Pearson.

Spiegelman, A. (1986). *Maus: A survivor's tale.* New York: Pantheon.

Spires, H., Hervey, L., Morris, G., & Stelpflug, C. (2012). Energizing project-based inquiry: Middle-grade students read, write, and create videos. *Journal of Adolescent and Adult Literacy, 55*(6), 483–493.

Stahl, S., & Nagy, W. (2006) *Teaching word meanings.* New York: Lawrence Erlbaum.

Stamaty, A. (2004). *Alia's mission: Saving the books of Iraq.* New York: Knopf.

Stange, T., and Wyant, S. (2008). Poetry proves to be positive in the primary classroom. *Reading Horizons, 48*(1).

Stauffer, R. G. (1970). *The language experience approach to the teaching of reading.* New York: Harper & Row.

Stauffer, R. G. (1969). *Directing reading maturity as a cognitive process.* New York: Harper & Row.

Stevens, J., & Stevens Crummel, S. (2003). *Jackalope.* Illus. by J. Stevens. San Diego, CA: Harcourt.

Stone, T. L. (2009). Almost astronauts: 13 women who dared to dream. New York: Candlewick.

Stothard, S., & Hulme, C. (2006). A comparison of phonological skills in children with reading comprehension difficulties and children with decoding difficulties. *Journal of Child Psychology and Psychiatry, 36*(3), 399–408.

Stricklin, K. (2011). Hands-on reciprocal teaching: A comprehension technique. *The Reading Teacher, 64*(8), 620–625.

Strong, W. (1993). *Sentence combining: A composing book* (3rd ed.). New York: McGraw-Hill.

Swain, K., Friehe, M., & Harrington, J. (2004). Teaching listening strategies in the inclusive classroom. *Intervention in School and Clinic, 40*(1), 48–54.

Talliaferro, J. (2004). *Great white fathers: The story of the obsessive quest to create Mount Rushmore.* New York: Public Affairs.

Tankersley, K. (2003). *The threads of reading: Strategies for literacy development.* Alexandria, VA: ASCD.

Temple, C., Nathan, R., Burris, N., & Temple, F. (1988). *The beginnings of writing* (2nd ed.). Boston: Allyn & Bacon.

Temple, E. (2013). 10 great multicultural books. Retrieved from http://flavorwire.com/400364/10-great-multicultural-childrens-books.

Thomas, E. (2009). Analysis of the learning styles of highly- versus poorly-achieving seventh-, ninth-, and eleventh-grade students by age, attitude, and gender. (Doctoral dissertation, St. John's University.)

Thomson, B. (2010). *Chalk.* New York: Two Lions.

Tierney, R. J., & Pearson, P. D. (1983). Toward a composing model of reading. *Language Arts, 60*(5), 568–580.

Tierney, R. J., & Readence, J. E. (2005). *Reading strategies and practices: A compendium* (6th ed.). Boston: Allyn & Bacon.

Tomlinson, C. A. (2000). Reconcilable differences? Standards-based teaching and differentiation. *Educational Leadership, 58*(1), 6–11.

Tompkins, G. (2003). *Literacy for the 21st century: Teaching reading and writing in pre-kindergarten through grade 4* (3rd ed.). Upper Saddle River, NJ: Merrill/Prentice Hall.

Tompkins, G. (2013). *Literacy for the 21st century: A balanced approach* (6th ed.) Boston: Pearson.

Tough, J. (1984). How young children develop and use language. In D. Fontana (Ed.), *The education of the young child.* Oxford: Basil Blackwell Publishers.

Trelease, J. (2013). *The read-aloud handbook* (7th ed.). New York: Penguin.

Truss, L. (2003). *Eats, Shoots & Leaves: The Zero Tolerance Approach to Punctuation.* London: Profile Books.

Turkle, B. (1992). *Deep in the woods.* New York: Puffin.

U.S. Department of Education (2010). National Writing Project: Online: http://www.nwp.org/cs/public/print/doc/about/annual_reports.csp.

Union of Concerned Scientists (2014). *Solutions to Global Warming. Online:* ww.ucsusa.org/global_warming/solutions.

Vacca, R. T., Vacca, J. A., & Mraz, M. (2014). *Content area reading: Literacy and learning across the curriculum.* Boston: Pearson.

Vamos, S. (2011). *The Cazuela that the farm maiden stirred.* New York: Charlesbridge.

VanNess, A. R., Murnen, T., & Bertelsen, C. (2013). Let me tell you a secret: Kindergarteners can write! *Reading Teacher, 66*(7), 574–585.

Veatch, J. (1992). Whole language and its predecessors. *Journal of Reading Education, 18,* 69–77.

Verhallen, M. J. A. J., Bus, A. G., & de Jong, M. T. (2006). The promise of multimedia stories for kindergarten children at risk. *Journal of Educational Psychology, 98*(2), 410–419.

Vitz, K. (1983). A review of empirical research in drama and language. *Children's Theater Review, 32*(40), 17–25.

Vygotsky, L. (1978). *Mind in society: The development of higher psychological processes* (M. Cole et al., Eds.). Cambridge, MA: Harvard University Press.

Vygotsky, L. (1986). *Thought and language* (A. Kozulin, Ed.). Cambridge, MA: MIT Press.

Waks, L. (2011). John Dewey on listening and friendship in school and society. *Educational Theory, 61*(2), 191–206.

Walker, B. (2000). *Diagnostic teaching of reading* (4th ed.). Upper Saddle River, NJ: Merrill/Prentice Hall.

Wall, S. (2008), Easier said than done: Writing an autoethnography. *International Journal of Qualitative Methods, 7*(1), 38–53.

Watkins, S. (1995). *Green snake ceremony.* Illus. K. Doner. Tulsa, OK: Council Oak Books.

Watson, D. J. (1989). Defining and describing whole language. *The Elementary School Journal, 90*(2), 129–141.

Weaver, C. (2002). *Reading process and practice* (3rd ed.). Portsmouth, NH: Heinemann.

Wertsch, J., & Sohmer, R. (1995). Vygotsky on learning and development. *Journal of Human Development, 38,* 332–337.

Westat & Policy Studies Associates (2001). *The longitudinal evaluation of school change and performance in Title I schools.* Washington, DC: U.S. Department of Education.

Wheeler, L. (2006). *Mammoths on the move.* Orlando, FL: Harcourt.

Wheelock, W., & Silvaroli, N. (2011). *Classroom reading inventory* (12th ed.). New York: McGraw-Hill.

Wiesner, D. (2013). *Mr. Wuffles!* Illus. D. Wiesner. New York: Clarion.

Wigginton, E. (1986). *Sometimes a shining moment: The Foxfire experience.* Garden City, NY: Doubleday.

Wiles, D. (2005). *Freedom summer.* Illus. by J. Lagarrigue. New York: Aladdin.

Williams, C., & Pilonieta, P. (2012). Using interactive writing instruction in the kindergarten and first-grade English language learners. *Early Childhood Education Journal, 40*(2), 145–150.

Wingert, P., & Brant, M. (2005, August 15). Reaching your baby's mind. Retrieved from www.msnbc.msn.com/id/3032542/site/newsweek/.

Winter, J. (2005) *Roberto Clemente: Pride of the Pittsburgh Pirates.* Illus. R. Colon. New York: Aladdin Paperback.

Withers, Carl (2007). *A rocket in my pocket.* New York: Holt, Rinehart & Winston.

Witte, S. (2007, Oct.). That's online writing, not boring school writing: Writing with blogs and the Talkback Project. *Journal of Adolescent & Adult Literacy, 51*(2), 92–96.

Wolf, S. (2006). The mermaid's purse: Looking closely at young children's art and poetry. *Language Arts, 84*(1), 10–20.

Wolk, S. (2008). School as inquiry. *Phi Delta Kappan, 90*(2), 115–122.

Wong, H. K., & Wong, R. (2009). *The first days of school: How to be an effective teacher* (4th ed.). Mountain View, CA: Harry K. Wong.

Wood, A. (1984). *The napping house.* Illus. D. Wood. San Diego, CA: Harcourt Brace, Jovanovich.

Woodson, J. (2001). *The other side.* Illus. E. B. Lewis. New York: G.P. Putnam's and Sons.

Woop Studios (2011). *A zeal of zebras: An alphabet of collective nouns.* San Francisco: Chronicle.

World Class Instructional Design & Assessment (2014). Can do descriptors. Retrieved from www.wida.us/downloadlibrary.aspx.

Wray, D., & Lewis, M. (1997). *Extending literacy: Children reading and writing non-fiction.* New York: Routledge.

Wright, G., Hernandez, B., & Joperd, M. (2014). Collaborating dance with artists, technical directories, health education physical educators, and other professionals. *The Journal of Physical Recreation & Dance, 85*(8), 9–12.

Yang, G. (2008). Graphic novels in the classroom. *Language Arts, 85,* 185–192.

Yolen, J. (1992). *Encounter.* Illus. D. Shannon. Orlando, FL: Voyager Press.

Yopp, H. K. & Yopp, R. H. (2013). *Literature-based reading activities: Engaging students with literary and informational text* (6th ed.). New York: Pearson.

Yopp, R. H., & Yopp, H. K. (2012). Young children's limited and narrow exposure to informational text. *The Reading Teacher, 65*(7), 480–490.

Young, A. (1997). Mentoring, modeling, monitoring, motivating. *New Directions for Teaching and Learning, 69,* 27–39.

Young, E. (1989). *Lon PoPo: A Red Riding Hood Story from China.* Illus. E. Young. New York: Philomel Books.

Zachry, A. (2011, Jan. 30). Handwriting readiness. *Pediatric Occupational Therapy Tips.* Retrieved from http://drzachryspedsottips.blogspot.com/search?q=handwriting+readiness.

Zezima, K. (2011, April 17). The case for cursive. *New York Times.* Retrieved from www.nytimes.com/2011/04/28/us/28cursive.html.

Zhang, J., & Dougherty-Stahl, K. (2012). Collaborative reasoning: Language-rich discussions for English learners. *The Reading Teacher, 65*(4), 257–260.

Zonta, P. (2002). *Jessica's X-ray.* New York: Firefly Books.

Zorfass, J., & Copel, H. (1995). The I-search: Guiding students toward relevant research. *Educational Leadership, 53*(1), 48–51.

Zwiers, J., & Crawford, M. (2011). *Academic conversations: Classroom talk that fosters critical thinking and content understandings.* Portland, ME: Stenhouse.

Zygouris-Coe, V. & Glass, C. (2004). Making connections: Text to self, text to text, and text to world. Retrieved from http://forpd.ucf.edu/strategies/strattext.html.

Author Index

Title Index

Subject Index